——— Blackwell Philosophy Guides ———

Series Editor: Steven M. Cahn, City University of New York Graduate School

Written by an international assembly of distinguished philosophers, the *Blackwell Philosophy Guides* create a groundbreaking student resource – a complete critical survey of the central themes and issues of philosophy today. Focusing and advancing key arguments throughout, each essay incorporates essential background material serving to clarify the history and logic of the relevant topic. Accordingly, these volumes will be a valuable resource for a broad range of students and readers, including professional philosophers.

The Blackwell Guide to
the Philosophy of
Education

Edited by

Nigel Blake, Paul Smeyers,
Richard Smith, and Paul Standish

Blackwell
Publishing

© 2003 by Blackwell Publishers Ltd
a Blackwell Publishing company

350 Main Street, Malden, MA 02148-5018, USA
108 Cowley Road, Oxford OX4 1JF, UK
550 Swanston Street, Carlton South, Melbourne, Victoria 3053, Australia
Kurfürstendamm 57, 10707 Berlin, Germany

First published 2003 by Blackwell Publishers Ltd

Library of Congress Cataloging-in-Publication Data

The Blackwell guide to the philosophy of education / edited by Nigel Blake . . . [et al.].
p. cm. — (Blackwell philosophy guides ; 9)
Includes bibliographical references and index.
ISBN 0-631-22118-2 (alk. paper) — ISBN 0-631-22119-0 (pbk. : alk. paper)
1. Education—Philosophy. I. Blake, Nigel. II. Series.

LB14.7 .B57 2002
370′.1—dc21
2002066430

A catalogue record for this title is available from the British Library.

Set in 10/12.5pt Galliard
by Graphicraft Limited, Hong Kong
Printed and bound in the United Kingdom
by TJ International, Padstow, Cornwall

For further information on
Blackwell Publishing, visit our website:
http://www.blackwellpublishing.com

Contents

Notes on Contributors

The Editors

Nigel Blake works at the Open University, UK, and is Chair of the Philosophy of Education Society of Great Britain. **Paul Smeyers** is Professor of Education at the Catholic University, Leuven, Belgium, where he teaches philosophy of education. **Richard Smith** is Professor of Education and Director of Combined Social Sciences at the University of Durham, UK. **Paul Standish** is Senior Lecturer at the University of Dundee, UK, and Editor of the *Journal of Philosophy of Education*. Their recent collaborations include *Thinking Again: Education after Postmodernism* (1998), and *Education in an Age of Nihilism* (2000).

The Contributors

Hanan Alexander heads the Center for Jewish Education and the Ethics and Education Project at the University of Haifa, Israel, where he also teaches philosophy of education and curriculum studies. He served previously as Editor-in-Chief of *Religious Education: An Interfaith Journal of Spirituality, Growth, and Transformation*, Vice President for Academic Affairs at the University of Judaism, and Lecturer in Education at UCLA. He is the author of *Reclaiming Goodness: Education and the Spiritual Quest* (2001).

Sharon Bailin is a Professor in the Faculty of Education, Simon Fraser University, Canada. Her research involves philosophical investigations in the areas of critical thinking and creativity. Recent publications include *Achieving Extraordinary Ends: An Essay on Creativity* (1992), articles on critical thinking and science education, on epistemology, understanding, and critical thinking, on common misconceptions of critical thinking, and on conceptualizing critical thinking (with R. Case, J. R. Coombs, and L. B. Daniels).

Ronald Barnett is Professor of Higher Education and Dean of Professional Development at the Institute of Education, University of London, UK. As well as being a world authority on the conceptual and theoretical understanding of higher education and universities, he is a member of the Institute's senior management team. Two of his books, *The Idea of Higher Education* and *The Limits of Competence*, have won national prizes in the UK. His latest book is *Realizing the University in an Age of Supercomplexity*. The University of London has conferred on him the rare distinction of a higher doctorate in education.

David Blacker is Associate Professor in the School of Education at the University of Delaware, USA. He is the author of *Dying To Teach: The Educator's Search For Immortality* (1997). His scholarly work in the philosophy of education has appeared in several journals, including, most recently, the *American Journal of Education*, *Educational Theory*, and the *Journal of Philosophy of Education*. He is currently working on a book about theories of justice and democratic education.

Michael Bonnett is a Senior Lecturer in philosophy of education at Cambridge University, UK. He is the author of numerous articles in academic journals and edited collections and he is also author of the book *Children's Thinking* (1994). He is currently working on a book on the philosophy of environmental education.

David Bridges is Professorial Fellow in the Centre for Applied Research in Education at the University of East Anglia, UK, and Executive Director of the Association of Universities in the East of England. His books include *Education and the Market Place* (1994) (edited with T. H. McLaughlin), *Consorting and Collaborating in the Education Market Place* (1996) (edited with C. Husbands), *Education, Autonomy and Democratic Citizenship* (ed.) (1998) and *Ethics in Educational Research* (edited with M. McNamee) (2001).

Eamonn Callan is Professor of Education and Associate Dean at Stanford University School of Education, USA. He taught for many years at the University of Alberta in Canada before moving to Stanford in 1999. He is the author of *Creating Citizens* (1997).

Stefaan Cuypers is Associate Professor of philosophy at the Catholic University of Leuven in Belgium. He is responsible for teacher training in philosophy and is associate editor of *Philosophical Explorations: An International Journal for the Philosophy of Mind and Action*. He has recently published *Self-Identity and Personal Autonomy: An Analytic Anthropology* (2001).

John Darling was, until his recent untimely death, Codirector of the Centre for Educational Research at the University of Aberdeen, UK. His research interests were particularly focused on the philosophy and history of progressive education. His publications include *Child-Centred Education and its Critics* (1994).

Andrew Davis is a Senior Lecturer in Education at Durham University, UK. Before moving into higher education he taught the 4–11 age range for many years. He is committed to applying analytical philosophy to current policy issues in education. He is the author of *The Limits of Educational Assessment* (1998) and coauthor of *Mathematical Knowledge for Primary Teachers* (1998). He is currently researching the extent to which external agencies can coherently impose teaching methods.

Pradeep A. Dhillon is Assistant Professor of Philosophy of Education at the University of Illinois, USA. She is the author of *Multiple Identities: A Phenomenology of Multicultural Communication* (1994) and coeditor of *Lyotard: Just Education* (2001). She has published several essays on aesthetics, language, and philosopy of education, and is now engaged in a book project on Kant and international education.

Joseph Dunne is Senior Lecturer in Philosophy of Education at St. Patrick's College, Dublin, Ireland. His book *Back to the Rough Ground: "Phronesis" and "Techne" in Modern Philosophy and in Aristotle* was published in 1993.

Penny Enslin is Professor of Education at the University of the Witwatersrand, Johannesburg, South Africa. Her research and teaching interests are in the field of democracy and civic education, with particular reference to liberal democracies. She has published locally and internationally on civic education in South Africa, nation-building and citizenship, political liberalism, and gender and citizenship.

Jim Garrison is Professor of Philosophy of Education at Virginia Polytechnic Institute, USA. His recent books include *The New Scholarship on Dewey* (1995), *Dewey and Eros* (1997), and *William James and Education* (forthcoming) (coedited with Ronald L. Podeschi and Eric Bredo). He wrote the chapter on education for the companion volume to *The Collected Works of John Dewey*, edited by Larry Hickman, and was an invited participant at the World Congress of Philosophy in 1998. He is a past president of the Philosophy of Education Society.

Maxine Greene is Professor of Philosophy and Education and William F. Russell Professor in the Foundations of Education (Emerita), Teachers College, Columbia University, USA, where she is also founder of the Center for the Arts, Social Imagination, and Education. She is Philosopher-in-Residence at Lincoln Center Institute for the Arts in Education and is past president of the American Educational Research Association, the American Educational Studies Association, and the Philosophy of Education Society. Her many books include *Releasing the Imagination: Essays on Education, the Arts, and Social Change* (1995).

Morwenna Griffiths is Professor of Educational Research at Nottingham Trent University, UK. She is working on a continuing project focusing on social justice, gender, and partnership in education. Her books include: *Educational Research for Social Justice: Getting off the Fence* (1998), *Feminisms and the Self: The Web of Identity* (1995), and *In Fairness to Children: Working for Social Justice in the Primary*

School (1995) (with Carol Davies) She and Margaret Whitford edited *Feminist Perspectives in Philosophy* (1988).

Paul Hager is Professor of Education at the University of Technology, Sydney, Australia. His research interests include Bertrand Russell's philosophy, philosophy of education, and workplace learning. His book *Continuity and Change in the Development of Russell's Philosophy* (1994) won the 1996 Bertrand Russell Society Book Award. His recent (2001) book is *Life, Work and Learning: Practice in Postmodernity*, coauthored with David Beckett.

J. Mark Halstead is Reader in Moral Education and Director of the RIMSCUE Centre at the University of Plymouth, UK. He is the author of *Education, Justice and Cultural Diversity* (1988), coeditor with T. H. McLaughlin of *Education in Morality* (1999), and coauthor with Monica Taylor of *The Development of Values, Attitudes and Personal Qualities: A Review of Recent Research* (2000).

Pádraig Hogan is a Senior Lecturer in Education at the National University of Ireland, Maynooth. He is author of *The Custody and Courtship of Experience – Western Education in Philosophical Perspective* (1995), editor or coeditor of a number of other books, and author of over 60 articles. A former President of the Educational Studies Association of Ireland and a former General Editor of that association's journal, *Irish Educational Studies*, he is currently an Assistant Editor of the *Journal of Philosophy of Education*.

Terry Hyland qualified as a teacher in 1971 and has taught in schools and in further, adult, and higher education. He was Lecturer in Continuing Education at Warwick University from 1991–2000 and was appointed Professor in Post-Compulsory Education and Training at the Bolton Institute in September 2000. His book *Competence, Education and NVQs: Dissenting Perspectives* was published in 1994 and *Vocational Studies, Lifelong Learning and Social Values* was published in 1999.

Ruth Jonathan is Professor of Education and Social Policy at the University of Edinburgh, UK. She has written extensively on liberalism, education, and issues in social justice and equity. Her book *Illusory Freedoms: Liberalism, Education and the Market* was published in 1997. She was recently Reviews Editor of the *Journal of Philosophy of Education* and is a past Chair of the Philosophy of Education Society of Great Britain.

Terence H. McLaughlin is University Senior Lecturer in Education in the University of Cambridge and Fellow of St. Edmund's College, Cambridge, UK. He is also Director of Studies in Philosophy at St. Edmund's College and Visiting Professor in the Institute of Educational Studies, Kaunas University of Technology, Lithuania. He has written widely in the field of philosophy of education and has recently published *The Contemporary Catholic School. Context, Identity and Diversity* (coedited with Joseph O'Keefe and Bernadette O'Keeffe) (1996) and *Education in Morality* (coedited with J. Mark Halstead) (1999).

Jane McKie is a Lecturer in Continuing Education at the University of Warwick, UK. She teaches courses in equal opportunities, study skills, theories of adult learning and teaching, and aspects of religious studies and mythology, and contributes to the administration of the Open Studies program. With a background in psychology, social anthropology, and religion and philosophy, her research is interdisciplinary. She is a member of the Philosophy of Education Society of Great Britain.

Jan Masschelein is Professor of Philosophy of Education in the Department of Educational Sciences at the Catholic University, Leuven, Belgium. His primary areas of scholarship are educational theory, critical theory, critical pedagogy, and philosophy of dialogue. He is the author of many articles and contributions in this field and of two books: *Pädagogisches Handeln und Kommunikatives Handeln* (1991) and *Alterität, Pluralität, Gerechtigkeit. Randgänge der Pädagogik* (1996) (coauthored with M. Wimmer). Work in progress includes a book on the "logic" of the learning society.

Al Neiman received his Ph.D. from the University of Notre Dame, USA, with a dissertation on skepticism in the philosophy of St. Augustine. From 1982 until 1998, he served as assistant dean in Notre Dame's College of Arts and Letters, and as Director of the university's required humanities core program. Since 1998, he has taught in the department of philosophy as well as Notre Dame's "Great Books" Program of Liberal Studies.

Nel Noddings is Lee Jacks Professor of Education Emerita, Stanford University, USA. Her latest books are *Starting at Home: Caring and Social Policy* (2001) and *A Sympathetic Alternative to Character Education* (2001).

Sven Erik Nordenbo is Associate Professor of Education at the University of Copenhagen Department of Education, Philosophy, and Rhetoric, Denmark. He is the author of six books, most recently *Subject Didactics. An Educational Discussion of Teaching Philosophy* (in Danish) (1997), and many articles in Danish and international journals on philosophy of education, history of education, and educational theory and practice. He is former vice-president of the Danish Society for Philosophy and Psychology, currently national editor of *Scandinavian Journal of Educational Research*, and coeditor of the *Danish Yearbook of Philosophy*.

Shirley Pendlebury is Professor of Education and Head of the School of Education at the University of the Witwatersrand, Johannesburg, South Africa. Her main areas of publication and research are practical wisdom in teaching, democratic theory and education, and issues in educational policy and justice.

Michael Peters is Professor of Education at the University of Glasgow (UK) and the University of Auckland (New Zealand). He has research interests in educational theory and policy, and in contemporary philosophy. He has published over 20 books and edited or coedited collections in these fields, including *Education and the Postmodern Condition* (1995), *Poststructuralism, Politics and Education* (1996), *Curriculum in the Postmodern Condition* (2000), *Poststructuralism: Politics and Theory* (2001), and *Nietzsche's Legacy for Education: Past and Present Values* (2001). His recent authored books include (with James Marshall) *Wittgenstein: Philosophy, Postmodernism, Pedagogy* (1999).

Harvey Siegel is Professor of Philosophy, University of Miami, USA. He is the editor of *Reason and Education: Essays in Honor of Israel Scheffler* (1997), and the author of *Relativism Refuted: A Critique of Contemporary Epistemological Relativism* (1987), *Educating Reason: Rationality, Critical Thinking and Education* (1988), *Rationality Redeemed? Further Reflections on an Educational Ideal* (1997), and many papers in epistemology, philosophy of science, and philosophy of education.

Michael Slote is Professor of Philosophy at the University of Maryland, USA. He is the author of *From Morality to Virtue* (1992) and, most recently, of *Morals from Motives* (2001). A former Tanner lecturer and a member of the Royal Irish Academy, he is now engaged in a large book project on "moral sentimentalism."

Kenneth Wain is a Professor in Education at the University of Malta where he teaches philosophy of education and moral and political philosophy. He is also very active in the world of practice, recently chairing two important national commissions on the National Curriculum in Malta. He has published in a wide range of international journals, and the following books: *Lifelong Education and Participation* (ed.) (1984), *Philosophy of Lifelong Education* (1987), *The Maltese National Curriculum: A Critical Evaluation* (1991), *Theories of Teaching* (1992), and *The Value Crisis: An Introduction to Ethics* (1995).

John White is Professor of Philosophy of Education at the Institute of Education, University of London, UK. His interests are in interrelationships among educational aims and applications to school curricula. His recent books include *Education and the Good Life: Beyond the National Curriculum* (1990), *Education and the End of Work* (1997), *Do Howard Gardner's Multiple Intelligences Add Up?* (1998), and *Will the New National Curriculum Live up to its Aims?* (2000) (with Steve Bramall).

Patricia White is Research Fellow in Philosophy of Education at the Institute of Education, University of London, UK. Her recent publications include *Civic Virtues and Public Schooling: Educating Citizens for a Democratic Society* (1996) and a four-volume international collection of work in philosophy of education, *Philosophy of Education: Themes in the Analytic Tradition* (1998) (coedited with Paul Hirst). Her research interests lie in ethics and political philosophy in their bearing on issues in the policy and practice of education.

Kevin Williams is Head of Education at Mater Dei Institute, Dublin City University, Ireland. He is author/editor of several books on the school curriculum, the most recent of which is the coedited collection *Words Alone: The Teaching and Usage of English in Contemporary Ireland* (2000).

Colin Wringe has taught in schools and in further education and is at present a Reader in Education at Keele University, UK. He has written a number of books on classroom teaching and philosophy of education, including *Children's Rights: A Philosophical Study* (1981), *Democracy, Schooling and Political Education* (1984), and *Understanding Educational Aims* (1988). His current research interests are in the fields of spiritual, moral, and citizenship education. He is treasurer of the Philosophy of Education Society of Great Britain, of which he is a foundation member.

Foreword

In a sense philosophy of education is as old as philosophy. Enquiries into the nature of knowledge, or of the good life, or of the just society, all involve, either explicitly or implicitly, questions about learning – about the practices people should be initiated into and the values they should come to espouse. Perhaps because of this pervasive presence, the history of the subject is a complex one. While in some countries systematic philosophical enquiry into educational questions has been well established over a long period (one thinks of the USA, Scandinavia, and Germany as prominent examples), in the United Kingdom sustained, self-critical academic study in this area is only some 40 years old. Starting at the height of the British Analytical Philosophy movement and deeply influenced by the work of a number of leading thinkers of the time, a small group of philosophers began to focus on educational questions, quickly produced a series of now classic writings, and initiated a new era of disciplined philosophical reflection on educational aims and processes. While drawing at times on thinkers across the history of philosophy it was nevertheless primarily a concerted attempt to elucidate and critically examine the conceptual relations, logical structures, and justificatory patterns within current educational ideals. Its distinctive impact on educational theory and practice was above all in the new rigor it brought to the discussion of important issues rather than any distinctively new educational beliefs or practical policies that it espoused. The significance of this new philosophical approach to education was however far-reaching and not only in the United Kingdom, since parallel developments were emerging around the world, not least in North America. Philosophy of education had in a new sense "arrived."

In keeping with the spirit of the times, however, certain substantive philosophical doctrines embedded in this new approach remained unexamined, presupposed not only in the prevailing traditions of educational thought that this pioneering work sought to elucidate but also in the philosophical methods it powerfully employed. It was to be some 15 or 20 years before critical attention was firmly focused on these topics and the emergent discipline moved into new, exciting, and more wide-ranging areas. Provoked by new demands on public education, due to widespread economic and social changes in Britain and elsewhere, and by major developments in academic philosophy arising not only in Britain but in the USA and Continental Europe, philosophy of education progressively emerged as a much enriched and exploratory activity. Education came to be much more broadly conceived as ranging across all concerns to do with the personal development of human beings both individually and within all types of personal, social, and institutional relationships. The major philosophical doctrines of the Enlightenment, particularly those concerning human nature, reason, values, and social relationships, which figured so forcefully in the pioneering work in philosophy of education, came to be seen much more clearly within the evolving context of contemporary Western philosophy in general. In these circumstances the discipline itself matured into the dynamic domain it now is, contributing ever more significantly to our understanding of the most fundamental problems of educational theory and practice.

This *Blackwell Guide to Philosophy of Education* brings together a team of the most distinguished contemporary contributors to the subject. Internationally known as specialists working on the issues they here tackle, they are indeed fitting guides to current thinking on the crucial questions now central to the discipline. This volume thus celebrates what philosophy of education has become and what it has achieved. But it does so in a fashion that starkly reveals the deep importance of serious philosophical work if we are ever really to understand what education is all about and how best it can be undertaken in practice. This is undoubtedly a landmark volume, one much needed to inform current debates and one that should be much used by all those genuinely seeking to find solutions to the many pressing educational dilemmas that confront contemporary societies.

Paul H. Hirst
Emeritus Professor of Education
University of Cambridge

Introduction

Nigel Blake, Paul Smeyers, Richard Smith, and Paul Standish

This collection is born of the belief that important and creative work is currently being done in philosophy of education. It seemed therefore worthwhile to bring together some of the themes and topics currently being addressed, and some of the writers addressing them. In this Introduction we set out to show how what appears in this book marks both changes from and continuities with the past. There are three parts: one focusing on the English-speaking heritage, one on the Continental European,[1] and one on the institutional constraints and possibilities of philosophy of education. We have set things out in this way because it is the conjunction of these three dimensions, we believe, that has in large part brought about the present fruitful condition of our subject.

I

There have always been philosophers interested in education, but for some education has occupied a central position in their social and political philosophy. Among the clear examples are Plato, Aquinas, Locke, and Rousseau, while Dewey went so far as to claim that education is philosophy "in its most general phase." Kant and Hegel also paid attention to the universities, and Nietzsche's writings are particularly rich with educational insights. Nor must it be forgotten that around the world there have been writers on education whose significance in their own time and within their own culture was immense, but whom modern philosophy of education has largely consigned to oblivion: we might instance Maimonides, Confucius, and Lao-Tzu. Philosophy of education is sometimes, and justly, accused of proceeding as if it had little or no past. Yet philosophy of education as a distinct subdiscipline, with its own literature, traditions, and problematics, did not develop until the nineteenth century. And to say even this is to refer to it as a discipline only in a much looser sense than we normally do today. It established its presence – as evidenced by publications, conferences, and academic appointments – slowly in the first half of the twentieth century (see Kaminsky, 1993, for a detailed account). Two particularly significant milestones were the founding of the American Philosophy of Education Society in 1941 and the launching of *Educational Theory* 10 years later. In the mid to late 1960s what had been a toehold in the academy, in the English-speaking countries at any rate, became a firm footing. New journals were founded, including the *Journal of Philosophy of Education, Studies in Philosophy and Education*, and *Educational Philosophy and Theory*. A distinctive body of work began to appear, notably Israel Scheffler's *The Language of Education* (1960) in the USA and Richard Peters' *Ethics and Education* (1966) in the UK, followed by work by Paul Hirst and Robert Dearden and their colleagues at the Institute of Education in London. These writers and their pupils spread the influence of philosophy of education into the colleges and university departments of education throughout the English-speaking world.

The style of philosophy of education that became thus influential was, as is well-known, predominantly analytical. Following developments in "ordinary-language philosophy" in the English-speaking countries after World War II, analytical philosophy of education sought to bring a new rigor to its subject. Where students had been exposed to a rather woolly version of educational theory in which the various theoretical disciplines could barely be distinguished, and perhaps had acquired a nodding acquaintance with some ideas of the Great Educators (Plato, Rousseau, and so on), the new philosophy of education aimed for something more systematic. It saw its task as dispelling the confusions and mystification engendered by careless thinking: a conception that would have been familiar to philosophers as diverse in other respects as John Locke and Ludwig Wittgenstein. Being heavily rationalist and cognitive in its emphasis it tended to demarcate education sharply from enterprises such as socialization and therapy, and was generally critical of the "progressivism" of the time for blurring the crucial boundaries and losing sight of the content and purposes of education. Philosophers of education trained in this somewhat austere and uncompromising style learned to identify and expose fallacies in reasoning, to do battle against fundamental errors such as ethical relativism and the epistemological reductivism inspired by work in the sociology of knowledge. Among the highlights of analytical philosophy of education were two major collections: the significantly titled *Education and the Development of Reason*, edited by Dearden, Hirst, and Peters (1972), and Richard Peters' *Philosophy of Education* in the Oxford Readings in Philosophy series (1973).

Those inspiring this phase of philosophy of education's development saw themselves as aiming for a coherent and systematic rationalization of educational beliefs and practices. And this was to be achieved by importing the rigor and the supposed ideological neutrality of linguistic and analytic methods in philosophy proper. So ironically, just when the new student movements were launching critiques of the ideology of the era of "the end of ideology," and drawing on radical Continental philosophy to do so, the philosophy of education was applying to itself the methodological stringencies required of any discipline of the "postideological" dispensation, by appeal to recent developments in Anglo-Saxon analytical philosophy.

R. F. Dearden, who was himself a prominent figure in the (British) revolution, offers this characterization of the period of reform:

Throughout the 1950's, and in direct response to developments in general philosophy, a new conception of philosophy of education was slowly forming and finding sporadic expression. But all of this was very far from a state of affairs in which it would become natural to think of educational studies as divided into various disciplines, of which philosophy of education would be one. Yet by 1977, Mary Warnock could uncontroversially open her book *Schools of Thought* by saying that "it cannot any longer be seriously doubted that there is such a thing as the philosophy of education". (Dearden, 1982, p. 57)

Dearden indicates the process of transition of philosophy of education from a loose and ill-defined area of discourse into a legitimate academic discipline: a transition accomplished by bringing the specialism into line with linguistic and analytic developments. Thus philosophy of education came to be seen not as ideologically fundamental to education but rather as epistemologically *foundational*: as the judge of matters of value and meaning, and the arbiter of appropriate theory for explaining human behavior in the educational sphere.

Much has changed in the quarter of a century since then. But if we have put together this volume partly in order to record those changes, it is not in order to celebrate the demise of the analytical movement. Analytical philosophy of education brought a refreshing impatience with jargon, cant, received opinion, and sloganizing of all kinds. Its insistence on the autonomy of education as a field of human endeavor is a legacy much needed in recent years. Its relentless pursuit of clarity and truth and its eye for the misleading metaphor still command respect, even if the metaphor of clarity might itself be, in the jargon of those days, "unpacked," and even if truth has now come to seem a little less innocent. These are qualities we need no less 25 years on, particularly where the increasing commercialization of education and the growing *dirigisme* of governments add their voices to the confusion.

Certainly there are criticisms that can be made, however, of analytical philosophy more generally. Analytical philosophy of education relied too much on the notion that the distinctions made in ordinary language, once recovered and clarified, have the power to sweep away the obscurities introduced by tendentious ways of thinking and writing. Its aspiration to map the logical geography of educational concepts was naïve in its supposition that there is such a geography, unitary and two-dimensional, to be definitively mapped. The analysis of such concepts, seen as a matter of clarifying the rules or conditions under which such concepts are used or applied, borrowed from the later Wittgenstein the notion of language as a rule-governed activity; but it was blind to the fact that the notion cannot disclose the necessary and sufficient conditions, or indeed foundations, which philosophers of education were looking for.

In the realm of ethics analytical philosophy of education was particularly ill-served by the tradition on which it attempted to draw. From Hume's devastation of religious faith, through to Ayer's derogation of moral and aesthetic talk as just persuasion (or a power game, as we would put it less politely today), pure analysis was always unfriendly to norms and values. The hard-headed, again supposedly anti-relativistic, positivism of this tradition brought with it, as its shadow, a pervasive scepticism about norms, notoriously marginalized as "nonsense" by the application of any form of the verifiability principle. Yet educators need to see normative talk as reasonable if they are to avoid either limp agnosticism about values on the one hand or dogma on the other. It is true, moreover, that the analytic approach took from empiricism various ideas on whose solidity subsequent work has cast doubt. Such ideas often had the effect of limiting the scope which philosophy of education took for itself. In the case of the "is–ought gap" or "naturalistic fallacy," for example, the effect was to reduce the rich field of ethics to a matter of making "value judge-ments." Recent re-examination of empiricist epistemology has shown up its own inherent subjectivist and relativist tendencies: tendencies making it unfit for the antirelativist role which some still seek to enlist it for.

As it emerged as a discipline of education, philosophy of education found itself as much in competition as in partnership with the other disciplines, especially sociology. In particular, issues concerning objectivity and relativism were bones of contention between the disciplines, and easily moved to the center of philosophical concern. It sometimes treated philosophizing as *merely* a matter of exercising techniques, as if they could be brought to bear irrespective of the material or topic under analysis, and without any great knowledge of matters of substance. It was therefore largely insouciant about the history of philosophy, and about work being done in cognate areas of philosophy (such as political philosophy or aesthetics). Lastly, it almost wholly ignored work being done outside the English-speaking countries.

The Wittgensteinian equation of objectivity with intersubjectivity provided pointers to worthwhile new directions. With this intersubjective turn came a new philosophical interest in the social and in social practices, so necessary for any serious consideration of education. And this in turn disclosed anew the hitherto overlooked rationality of those practices associated with the normative sphere – of moral delib-eration and political debate, of the arts, or of the religious way of life, or even of the worlds of work or sport. Indeed, it brought with it a real doubt that any rational practice can be conceived without internal norms, over and above the norms of epistemic coherence. But not even a post-Wittgensteinian form of linguistic analysis would suffice to secure the depth of insight into the rationality of the ethical, the aesthetic, or other normative spheres which philosophers of education needed. The analyses of the language of morals by R. M. Hare, for instance, went not much beyond identifying the purely formal requirement of universalizability as a criterion of moral claims, and seemed actually incapable of justifying any substantive moral commitments. (And of course, this approach left aesthetics without even this formal support.) So even in its renovated form analysis remained inadequate. For analytic philosophers of education, particularly needing some way to conceptualize freedom, equality, respect for persons, democracy, and justice, the deontological tradition in ethics required closer attention, and necessarily this involved recourse to Kant and Kantian universalism (see in particular Peters, 1966).

In what has become a classic paper, Abraham Edel (1972) argued that analytic philosophy of education was at a crossroads: it had not fulfilled its promise. Further criticisms came increasingly, and especially, from younger scholars concerned with the problems of teaching in periods of intense social transformation, and who could not see guidance coming from an analytic philosophy of education which they saw as just irrelevant. A balanced overview here must involve a critical appreciation both of the strengths of the Kantian influence on philosophy of education at this juncture in its development and of its limitations.

By the mid-1970s in the UK the seminal work of Richard Peters and Paul Hirst established as paradigmatic a constellation of interests and arguments which in retrospect appear, if anything, yet more tightly interknit even than they seemed at the time. An education for the citizens of a liberal democracy was necessarily a politically unbiased education, rather than indoctrination. Thus the curriculum would be grounded in the recognition that certain activities were intrinsically worthwhile, rather than instrumentally opportune – politically, economically, or in terms of social control. And of these worthwhile activities, a special educational importance attached to those informed by intelligent understanding of forms of knowledge, because a diverse group of discrete forms of knowledge in turn underlay, conjointly, the rationality constitutive of personal autonomy; and such was the legitimate personal autonomy that precluded indoctrination in a liberal democratic state, while properly guiding the thoughts and actions of mutually respectful and responsible democratic citizens. Thus autonomy was both a primary educational aim (some went so far as to say the uniquely overriding educational aim), and respect for the autonomy of pupil or student was a major requirement in teaching.

The depth of the Kantian influence here can be appreciated by noting the pervasiveness of various conceptions and instantiations of autonomy, over and above those explicitly mentioned. To identify any activity as *intrinsically* worthwhile is to secure an *autonomy of values* from social, political, or cultural demands. To differentiate forms of knowledge is to demonstrate their *mutual autonomy* – the independence of truth and rationality in, say, the sciences from truth and rationality in politics or philosophy. In both these respects, while the actual arguments of Peters and of Hirst, in particular, seem proximately inspired by Wittgenstein's notions of language games and forms of life, the earlier authority for these ideas is clearly found in the trinity of the Kantian Critiques, of Pure Reason, Practical Reason, and of Judgement: critiques which secure the mutual autonomy of scientific, ethical, and aesthetic rationalities, and particularly the autonomy of ethics.

We have here a further indication of why philosophy and sociology at that time sat so badly together, and also a clue to later developments. Where the philosophers so strongly emphasized differentiation, mutual independence, the illegitimacy of non-rational forms of influence between people, disciplines, institutions, and forms of life, sociology tended to do exactly the opposite, preferring to locate education within totalizing syntheses – that, for instance, of Talcott Parsons if not that of Marx. (Many philosophers, in contrast, are more at home with the post-Kantian Weber.) Typically, the sociological emphasis was precisely on the heteronomy of both the individual and his or her ideologically determined thinking. But ironically, it is precisely since social and cultural theory have themselves begun to embrace the skepticism toward totalizing theory that Lyotard (1984) announced, and that philosophy of education always evinced, that philosophy itself has begun to display, to bend a phrase from Lyotard, "incredulity towards autonomy." And with this increasing incredulity has come a drift away from analyticity.

As the agenda of education changed through the 1970s and 1980s (we heard less, for instance, of tradition as conservative educational policies took increasingly instrumentalist and vocational forms), and as internal problems with the deontological perspective became clearer, other influences began to make themselves felt. Aristotelian emphases in ethics re-emerged, drawing partly on the new Oxford naturalism of Foot, Anscombe, and the Warnocks, but more strongly on the post-Marxist social philosophy of Alasdair MacIntyre and, later, the work of Charles Taylor and of other critics of liberalism, such as Michael Sandel. Martha Nussbaum's literary reception of Aristotle was also an important influence. But these later developments, some of which were characterized as communitarian, were themselves, of course, sometimes reactions to that modern monument of the deontological tradition which is the theory of justice of John Rawls – work whose influence in English-speaking philosophy of education cannot be exaggerated, and which underpins a small academic industry in political theory of education in the USA. In the USA too Scheffler's legacy, rooted in the philosophy of science, bore rich fruit.

There were at the time distinctive problems and issues that began to turn attention away from an analytical and Kantian approach. First, problems with liberalism itself grew sharper as, in many parts of the English-speaking world, particularly the UK, USA, and New Zealand, government by the New Right threw into relief the ambiguity of liberalism between political and economic forms, an ambiguity not widely regarded as compatible. While economic liberalism brought with it its own set of internal problems in relation to educational provision, choice, segregation, and privilege (see Part II), it often also brought with it social (and educational) authoritarianism, vividly so in the UK and USA. This in turn heightened and exacerbated the already brewing dissent of those social groups who felt themselves, and typically were indeed, marginalized by the social mainstream. Multiculturalism in education was the first index of such problems (ill-distinguished from issues of race), while identity issues revolving around gender, sexuality, ethnicity, and religion were soon manifest as well. If these problems were most dramatic in the USA (where fundamentalism emerged as an important issue) they were nonetheless salient across the whole developed, and indeed the developing, world. (South Africa's special problems need particular acknowledgement in this context.)

Thus issues about identity and community became important at the same time that liberalism was increasingly questioned in its own right. The supposed formal neutrality of liberalism was first doubted, then increasingly, under communitarian scrutiny, impugned as inadequate to explain the imperative character of the moral, or to legitimize substantive moral beliefs. Since the authority of liberal neutrality depended significantly on its suprasocial appeal to the universal Good Will of a transcendental and purely formal post-Kantian ego, and since the doctrine of the ego had so little to say to the new concerns with identity and community, a neo-Kantian perspective finally seemed an irrelevance to many in the field. Ethical universalism has come to seem no longer compelling but problematic.

When we turn to the Continental European scene below, we note that a perceived crisis of modernity manifested itself there as a crisis of legitimacy for educational theory and fostered a re-examination of the theory–practice question. The perceived crisis of liberalism in the English-speaking educational world constitutes a crisis of modern legitimation in its own right. Since none, after the political impact of the New Right, can disregard the nonphilosophical aspects and roots of this crisis, it is not so surprising that the social concepts of modernity and modernism have also achieved salience in the English-speaking tradition of educational studies. And if the pre-eminent theorist of postmodernity, Jean-François Lyotard, characterizes the postmodern by the demise of Grand Narrative and the rise of small narratives or *petits récits* (Lyotard, 1984), it is no surprise that theories of postmodernism have spoken loudly to many educationists now concerned with issues of identity and pluralism, including many philosophers. So it is that in the English-speaking world as well as in Continental Europe debates about modernity, legitimacy, and practice have sprung into new life in philosophy of education, along with renewed scepticism about universalism, both in ethics and epistemology.

Thus many philosophers of education today face anew two fundamental questions for their own orientation: if, with the demise of universalism, theory can no longer claim universal validity, then how are we to characterize *practice*, both in education and philosophy of education; and where might theory come from, if there is still any need for theory at all? Aristotle and the hermeneutic tradition have proved helpful resources to those who wish to argue for the autonomy of educational practice: a response which solves the theory–practice problem by dissolving it. Increasingly it has been claimed that education is itself a practice with its own internal rationality, mediated by tradition, which does not need to be informed by external theory from the "disciplines of education," including philosophical value theory, and that practical action in education should not be conceived on a technicist model of the application of high-level generalizations to particular cases. It is in this context in particular that there has been a revival of interest in Deweyan pragmatism as a form of resistance to the idea of philosophy as foundational for educational theory and practice.

If a new scepticism about universality weakened any familiar felt need for theoretical foundations for practice, this was just as well, given that philosophy generally was, it seemed, abandoning any pretence to offer foundations. To search for foundations is to try to discriminate truth claims by relating them, typically by analysis, to more fundamental claims whose truth can be certainly known, and thus universally acknowledged. There are those who fear – and those, particularly of a sociological cast of mind, who hope – that to abandon a search for foundations is to abandon any idea of truths that can transcend particular circumstances, contexts, languages, discourses, or theories. But these are further questions. To give up the project of discriminating truth by reference to foundations is not to give up any faith in truth at all. It does not translate directly into a new relativism, though some will no doubt wish to lead it in that direction. It does, on the other hand, encourage deep reconsideration of the ways in which language relates to practices and realities, from social institutions to personal experiences, from literature to philosophy and on to the sciences, from self and discourse to teaching and learning.

Accordingly, it was not just in pragmatism, newly vivified by Quine, Sellars, and especially Richard Rorty, that the search for foundations was repudiated as a profound philosophical mistake. Postanalytic developments in philosophy of science in the English-speaking world pointed the same way, and slowly it became better appreciated that the same lessons had always been there in the later work of Wittgenstein (and of post-Wittgensteinians such as Ryle and Strawson) for those who looked deeply enough to see them. And it is no coincidence that, by the 1990s, English-speaking philosophers were more ready than they had been for a long time to read and take seriously continental philosophers: Critical Theorists, post-structuralists, deconstructionists, hermeneuticists, and phenomenologists (speaking very roughly) such as Heidegger, Foucault, Lyotard, Derrida, Habermas, Gadamer, and Levinas. For all these theorists, in some way or other, also reject the search for foundations as mistaken. And once the battle over foundations is given up, a deeper conversation as to what philosophy really can do and how it should properly be written takes on a new international resonance. So it is also no coincidence that the institutional field of philosophy of education has enjoyed extensive internationaliza-tion in the last decade, much helped and encouraged, as in any other academic sphere, by the new opportunities for communication and research afforded by the Internet – an internationalization reflected significantly by the range of contributors to this book.

If educational practice, then, does not need theory in quite the way it was once thought to, why does theory flourish and its forms proliferate? Theory thrives in part because educational practice itself has come under extreme pressure from a new managerialism, whose aim, in Lyotard's famous analysis, is to maximize the "per-formativity" of the economic system. This new educational pragmatism, impelled by globalization, seems to be draining practice of normative interest and validity. The traditions that have long mediated teaching and learning are currently under radical assault from managerialist reformers, operating within a taken-for-granted worldview of economic crisis. Globalization, it is claimed, exacts competitive supremacy in vocational achievement from populations, reductively conceived as workforces. The cost of failure is steep economic decline, and the rights and interests of individuals as citizens, and as autonomous subjects of action and experience, necessarily dwindle, if not vanish, in interest and importance. (The personal delight of Lifelong Learning is often proposed as the solvent for such embarrassing dichotomies.)

The theories informing this new managerialism are of course fiercely unphilo-sophical. They theorize themselves either as common sense or as positivism, innocent as they are of the profound problems that beset positivism and that have long invalidated it in its original home in philosophy. The new theoretical emphases are on statistics and the countable, on observation and testing, on the useful and on "what works." Its new watchwords are skills, competences and techniques, flexibility, independence, targets and performance indicators, qualifications and credentials, learning outcomes. Profound objections, from both theoretical and practical per-spectives, to these shibboleths are angrily dismissed as idle or self-indulgent diver-sions from brute educational necessities, and often regarded as complicit with the failures, some real and some confected, of a 1960s educational progressivism. The standard under which this movement marches is itself that of "raising standards."

Those in philosophy who deplore and resist, in part or in whole, this suborning of the educational tradition need a new recourse to theory. The autonomy of educa-tion as a practice itself needs protection: a protection whose aims and understandings in turn need theorizing. Theory is required, in this instance, not as legitimation for principles and actions but as a form of deeper reflection on the nature and implica-tions of the very educational enterprise. Conceived like this, the role of theory begins to look like interpretation rather than explanation (and we remember at this point that Wittgenstein described the role of philosophy itself in very much the same way). The new managerialism is characterized as much as anything by its vocabulary, style, and use of documentation, in its discourse and its archives. So a philosophical interest in discourse and dialogue and ways of theorizing them begin to seem as important in resistance to managerialism as it is for theorists of practice. The Continental tradition seems particularly fruitful in these respects. A close reading of texts, canons, and discourses can be profoundly revealing, holding perhaps the power to commend anew the educational tradition before managerialism. The post-structuralist movement has also taught us ways to "read" the human subject: it discloses a new appreciation of the splintered and beleaguered subjects of experience and action themselves. Deconstructionism in particular has heightened awareness of the interpretive depths and subtleties of education as a play of texts, discourses, and readers. If the subject is ineluctably caught in the play of knowledge and power, it is still well worth asking, "what knowledge and which powers?"

II

In Continental Europe, philosophy of education developed out of the educational thought of Kant and Herbart.[2] Here the approach to philosophy of education was always academically more securely rooted in the philosophical canon. Because they did not face the same needs of professionalization, Continental writers have displayed a general lack of interest, to date, in English-speaking linguistic and analytic philosophy – though with some notable exceptions – and a greater interest in social and anthropological theory and social philosophy. In contrast to the postwar English-speaking world, where philosophy of education concerned itself primarily, though not exclusively, with analysis and accounts of schooling, the Continental counterpart was mainly concerned with problems in the wider field of child-rearing. Its central theme was the transition between childhood and maturity, and the induction of the child into cultural tradition, while it conceived this enculturated maturation as a form of emancipation (*Bildung*). This program, along with its critiques, both unequivocally entrenched in the Enlightenment tradition, has dominated the development of the discipline in Continental Europe. From this philosophical position, education can appear to be the "means" to becoming properly human, that is to say *rational*. In escaping the tutelage of one's inclinations and passions, by putting oneself under the guidance of reason, one realizes – makes real – one's true nature. But the conception of education as a "means" to this "realization" was not interpreted in a narrowly instrumental means–end fashion, as is sometimes alleged. Nor was it intended as any form of individualism, for the condition of rationality was potentially universal for humanity and, being prospectively the same for everyone, precluded false consciousness and alienation.

The *Bildung* paradigm is now being seriously challenged. Radical social demands, reflecting a heightened sense of cultural pluralism, have caused crises in education, in Europe no less than in the English-speaking world, and these have naturally induced a parallel crisis, concerning what schooling still has to offer, in Continental philosophy of education. Some, however, would go further and locate these problems as aspects of a wider crisis of rationality itself. The questions at the heart of it are whether reason, and reason alone, can ever be a valid guide to action, and even whether rational thinking is ever the objective and universal guide it claims to be – questions that have pressed themselves from Nietzsche onwards. (For the British heirs of empiricism, of course, much of this anxiety goes back as far as Hume.) Phenomenology, existentialism, neo-Marxism, the Frankfurt School, and other traditions have all attempted a rational critique of the overambitious Enlightenment project of rationality, in the spirit of "the critique of reason by reason" which is itself part of the tradition of the Enlightenment. In particular, criticisms have been made of a technicist or means–end rationality which some claim to find implicit in Kant's philosophy, and of problems involved in a Kantian notion of "becoming human."

Another widespread perception, shared in the English-speaking world and Continental Europe, and of course far beyond, is that we have reached a turning point or even the terminus of "modernity." Whether our new condition is conceived as advanced modern, late modern, or postmodern, any such predicament necessitates the re-evaluation of the educational program outlined above, the reconsideration of what might be preserved and what might be discarded. Not surprisingly, the traditional approach or framework of education has been criticized by twentieth-century philosophers of education themselves, drawing on the critical insights of movements such as those mentioned above.

As we hinted earlier, changing notions of philosophy of education accompany shifting concepts of education no less than new developments in philosophy. In Northern Europe, the principal concern in education for radical critics is typically the child-centered movement, or "reform-pedagogy." For them, legitimate child-rearing can no longer be characterized simply as an activity pursued by adults in order to bring children to adulthood, since this seems to entail a kind of instrumental manipulation of the child. The validity of a post-Kantian idea of *Bildung* is thus now in question. But not all take this radical route. Across different centers of philosophy of education, a varied landscape emerges. Some philosophers of education continue to follow the traditional paths as if nothing has really changed. After all, within the traditional North European approach several paradigms could always be found: phenomenology, existentialism, transcendental (Kantian) pedagogy, critical rationality, *geisteswissenschaftlich*-hermeneutic, and critical-emancipatory.

A leading traditional approach to the theory–practice problem is the insistence on *Allgemeinbildung* (see Klafki in Tillmann, 1987; Pleines, 1987), which could be translated as "general development." One of the aims of *Allgemeinbildung* is self-determination. Its general character can be justified by reference to Kant's practical philosophy and the recognition of human freedom as an aim in itself. Education is necessary because, in practice, Kantian self-determination is not given but achieved and requires cultivation by a teacher. The curricular content most suited to self-determination has to be specified and justified, and this raises problems concerning the epistemologically general and the morally universal, and questions of the relations between self-determination and communal solidarity. In response, Oser (1986) draws upon Kohlberg's investigations of the laws of the development of moral reasoning in the individual. And of course this traditional approach has been echoed in the English-speaking tradition.

Nonetheless, in general, the scene is dominated mainly by those who have put these positions in question (see for instance *Zeitschrift für Pädagogik*, 1990, vol. 36, no. 1). Some of these writers, particularly in the German literature, see the late modern crisis of educational theory as one of legitimation or justification, and so discussion of the relationship between theory and practice is widespread. As in conservative circles in the English-speaking world, some see theory and practice as straightforwardly reconciled by an appeal to "common sense" (see Herrmann et al., 1987). But what exactly is common sense, and just how "common" is it? Post-Marxists speak rather of *praxis*, of a critical practice, in education as elsewhere, itself suffused by defeasible theory, while a basic claim in the anti-Marxist *system-theory* of Luhmann and Schorr (1982) is that theory cannot formulate any rules for the legitimation of actions. Instead, educational practice must be characterized by the self-sufficiency of the system. Indeed human agents themselves have to be understood as a self-referential system, and this too, it is argued, is incompatible with any technicist kind of approach. But systems theory does not legitimate practice. Rather, it problematizes the very demand for legitimacy, as itself nothing more than an internal function of a given and ineluctable system.

However, just as Habermas, in his later work, resists the cynical pessimism of Luhmannian systems theory, the radical *critical-emancipatory* tradition, which draws importantly on the Frankfurt School, also shares many of the interests in autonomy of *Allgemeinbildung*. Thus, the critical-emancipatory tradition survives in the Continental tradition, though it has never flourished widely in the English-speaking world. For the latter, it is the pessimism of Horkheimer and Adorno's *Dialectic of Enlightenment* (1947) that seems most characteristic of Frankfurt before Habermas. But even in Continental Europe this particular phase of Critical Theory had nothing to say to education. If reason entails distantiation from a prereflective bond with nature, and thus the possibility of transforming nature into an object to be dominated, then the consequent fear of being dominated, as part of nature oneself, induces a will of domination over others. So if education is the cultivation of reason, it is also a key to domination – a "scandalous" belief, repudiated in the English-speaking world in reaction against the student revolts of the late 1960s. By contrast, the critical-emancipatory tradition proper to Continental Europe has been able to draw on both the earlier and later work of the first Frankfurt School and the constructive work of Habermas and his circle. This remains relatively poorly known in the English-speaking world, though it is possible to trace a line of descent through to interest in discourse ethics in North America.

More recently, a different radical reaction to the blind alley in which education allegedly finds itself has been *antipedagogy* (see Giesecke, 1987). An education that depends upon preparation for the future for its "justification" cannot be justified if established knowledge can no longer be relied on as a guide to a rapidly changing future. In such circumstances, education is but a form of socialization, inducing a loss of personal responsibility, and the manipulation of relationships and of communication. For some philosophers of education in Northern Europe, this suspicion has evolved into a full condemnation of all pedagogy. It was this position, at the end of the 1980s, that evolved into a full-blown postmodernism, a repudiation and decon-struction of foundational conceptual frameworks and of the kind of rationality that has come to dominate the Western world.

III

The nature and development of philosophy of education has been strongly affected by its relationship to two institutional issues with which, particularly in the English-speaking countries, it has always been closely connected: professional teacher educa-tion, and educational research. In many countries teacher education has changed radically over the past 40 years, and this change is directly related to an altered conception of the relevance of theory to practice. The discipline-based study of education in initial teacher education has been displaced in many countries by what is presumed to be a more practical approach – one that often involves a kind of deskilling of teachers, notwithstanding its espousal of the vocabulary of skills and competences. Whereas in the past educational research fed directly into initial teacher education, the tendency now is for there to be a greater separation: on the one hand, there is the training in skills and competences that will equip teachers to deliver the curriculum effectively, while on the other hand research is expected to orientate itself more and more to providing the evidence that may influence or inform policy. It goes without saying that the increased prominence of external funding in the support of research accelerates this trend.

These changes have occurred against a backdrop of uncertainty about education at two levels at least. In the first place there has been a tendency to doubt the success of teachers in preparing young people to live in an increasingly complex world; in some countries teachers are routinely blamed for failure in this respect. Secondly, the credentials of educational research have been called into question: while some have castigated it as "barmy theory," the more common response within the academy, if not among the wider public also, is to see it as lacking in scientific credentials, and as loaded with ill-founded ideas and spurious jargon. These factors have led to interference and change in the study of education in the university, and have engendered an unsteadiness and self-consciousness within the academic com-munity about its role and about the rationale for its research.

In the light of this, the currently burgeoning literature on the methodology of educational research is no surprise. Questions about the relation between quantit-ative and qualitative research are legion, dominated at one extreme by an anxiety to live up to the highest standards of empirical science and at the other by a desire to align research with the insights and approaches of postmodernism. As for social scientific rigor, there are two factors that militate against achieving it. The first is the sheer complexity of educational practice and the consequent difficulty and ques-tionable justifiability of isolating factors for study. This is a problem not only of coping with the number of variables that impinge on any educational practice but of acknowledging and dealing adequately with the essentially contestable terms that characterize such practice. Thus, in connection with the problem of multiple variables, one of the leading figures in British educational research has recently argued that research in education should seek to provide "fuzzy generalization" rather than the clearer and more certain results that its parent sciences seek (Bassey, 2001). The second is the seeming obligation on researchers not merely to describe but to provide evidence as to what might "work better," as contemporary parlance is inclined to phrase this. What works better depends on a range of normative assumptions that extend beyond the kind of thing that empirical studies in the social sciences typically undertake. Hence there is often an unsteady mix of descriptive and prescriptive elements in the research that ensues. Sometimes this problem is exacerbated by a seeming reluctance to acknowledge the substantive educational values that researchers espouse, a reluctance that stems either from the self-conscious adoption of a "scientific" stance of objectivity or from a more knee-jerk and ultimately relativistic refusal to be "judgemental." There are also problems with the adoption of postmodernist ideas insofar as these are sometimes received without the kind of disciplinary background in post-structuralist thought that would give them greater cogency. Hence "postmodernist" theory of education tends to be dogged by subjectivism, relativism, and scepticism, often seeming closer to a rerun of the 1970s sociology of knowledge than to ideas emanating from the likes of Derrida, Foucault, and Lyotard.

As has been explained, in many countries, and especially in the English-speaking world, the institutional place of philosophy of education – as of the history and sociology of education – and its leverage on policy and practice within the academy have in many respects been weakened during the period in question in favor of such growth industries as school effectiveness and school improvement. It goes without saying that we regret this trend and that we are pleased that it is not replicated in all countries. But this must lead us to pose the question: what has philosophy to say about educational research?

In his recent book *Philosophy of Educational Research* Richard Pring makes a strong case for philosophy's place in educational research, not least in making clear the nature of that into which research is being conducted. Pring effectively exposes the fallacies that lie behind the sometimes doctrinaire positions that have been adopted in the dichotomization of quantitative and qualitative research. The role of philosophy is not confined here, however, to conceptual clarification. There are deep divisions between educational researchers based upon philosophical positions and these are rarely made explicit. There is a need for greater attention to the kind of language we use when we explain our social and educational practices. Research must avoid becoming entrenched in a variety of "-isms," Pring argues, but must instead relate back to the ordinary language in which those practices come to take shape. Careful attention to the meaning and significance of educational practices – the careful drawing of distinctions concerning such matters as learning, teaching, personal and social development, culture – can be a frustration to those whose social science aspirations are toward large-scale generalization: "Failure to recognize these distinctions has led in the past to overblown theories of learning which simply do not apply in practice and are now leading us to an oversimplified science of teaching" (Pring, 2000, p. 158). And such matters as learning and teaching can only be conceptualized in the thinnest way if they are not contextualized in traditions of enquiry and the values to which they are committed.

There are vigorous debates about the nature and function of educational research, as we have noted above. Yet often these have a kind of sterility about them, and Pring's arguments are helpful in showing why this is so. The earnestness of such debates has tended to lead to a kind of piety about the nature of good research practice in education, motivated in part, no doubt, by anxiety about securing its academic credentials as a fully fledged, independent discipline (with the institutional muscle this tends to bring with it). At one level, such a concern is wholly legitimate, but there is reason to be sceptical about this, especially where there are claims to a kind of rigor that the circumstances of educational practice do not admit. Over the past decade the so-called disciplines of school effectiveness and school improvement have been prominent on the scene, and in many respects they have seemed to fulfill the requirement of providing policy makers with evidence on which to base their policies. But it is very difficult to see how these can be regarded as disciplines in their own right. Indeed education itself must surely be seen as a field of study that involves a variety of approaches from a number of disciplines. One consequence of weakening the influence on education of disciplines such as history, psychology, sociology, and philosophy has been the growth of pseudo-disciplines, approaches that lack the critical traditions of enquiry that are the source of coherence and rigor. They lack the body of literature with its community of academics, developed over a period of time, upon which any discipline must depend. Another consequence is the rise of instant "experts."

A more coherent approach to the study of education involves a return to the disciplines of psychology, sociology, history, and philosophy of education, a return with a number of qualifications added. Just as one of the great values of studying history is that it can present us with pictures of how things might be done differently, so too across these disciplines there is an important role for comparative studies. Similarly the value to be gained from the gathering and analysis of data regarding current practice in the light of theory drawn from psychology and sociology especially, perhaps also from economics, is not to be doubted.

Philosophical approaches to education can take a number of forms, and they can blend with other means of achieving understanding, drawn perhaps from literature, the social sciences, psychotherapy, linguistics, and so on. First, philosophical analysis should continue to concern itself with problems rooted in the use of language in educational discourse. In an earlier conception, in what we have above described as the analytical tradition, the role of the philosopher was the familiar one of conceptual underlaborer, aiming for greater clarity both in theory and practice in psychology, sociology, and other social sciences of education (for example, regarding concepts such as intelligence, skills, and development), and in current policy and practice (for example, lifelong learning and citizenship). Analytic techniques remain useful. But the concept of clarity used here is a narrow one (clarity as perspicuity), and perhaps clarity is not *always* our primary aim. Philosophy of education can no longer disregard a wide variety of other philosophical approaches to language: speech act theory, discourse theory, post-structuralism and deconstruction, hermeneutics, generative grammar, a variety of forms of literary analysis, and Wittgensteinian semantics revisited. What these offer is not always (even if it is sometimes) clarity, but insight into things unclear and sometimes a different kind of mastery with which to resist what Wittgenstein called the bewitchment of the intelligence by language. Educational thought and writing still needs these forms of insight.

Secondly, philosophy of education can still address the assumptions and values embedded in other disciplinary approaches in the study of education, whether these are explicitly promoted or tacitly assumed in policy and practice. What it can no longer do, however, is stand itself on a different level of analysis, and hence of authority, prescribing and proscribing *de haut en bas* – a stance in which the underlaborer suddenly turns out to be a king in disguise. Other disciplines have, in recent decades, sharpened their own higher-level understanding of their own projects. They expect to speak to philosophers at the same level of abstraction (if they speak to them at all), and often even by reference to the same literatures. Furthermore, at least some schools of philosophy have achieved a greater self-consciousness about the extraphilosophical pressures that constrain and mold their own practices. Perhaps most significantly of all, the conception of philosophy as sovereign can only rest on precisely that faith in foundations which, as we have seen, is now generally lost. Arguably, debate between philosophy and other disciplines needs now to be an engagement on equal terms, and with less concern for territory.

Thirdly, and more ambitiously, philosophy of education can engage in explorations of what education might be or might become: a task which grows more compelling as the "politics of the obvious" grow more oppressive. This is the kind of thing that Plato, Rousseau, and Dewey are engaged in on a grand scale. It can revisit but also problematize its canonical questions about such matters as the aims of education, the nature of knowledge, and the point of particular curriculum subjects, about human nature and human practices. For it may now be that some of these questions themselves will come to be seen as misleading. In particular, they seem to favor essentialist answers that can no longer command plausibility in the wake of any loss of foundations. And it is worth noting that some of the key texts that have shaped modern conceptions of education are literary or hybrid in form (e.g., *The Republic, Emile*). They are clearly amenable to some of the new kinds of linguistic analysis mentioned above.

Of course, a number of distinctions can be drawn between the kinds of approach that are manifested by different philosophical traditions of enquiry: for example, by feminism, pragmatism, phenomenology, post-structuralism, postpositivism. Too much concern about such distinctions, however, is likely only to distract from the practical problems to which education must be addressed. What needs to be remembered is the fact that education is broad and complex. If enquiry into educational practices is followed through, questions are raised of the most deep kind, and these touch on all the major areas of philosophy (epistemology, ethics, metaphysics, politics, aesthetics, and so on, as well as philosophy of science, philosophy of history, etc.). Hence, philosophy of education is not a subdiscipline of philosophy but rather, it might reasonably be claimed, something more like a field of "applied" philosophy. Yet this also seems not to get things quite right, suggesting as it does that philosophy can sort out the problems and then hand over the solutions to educational practice. A recurrent concern in this book is with the exercise of practical reason and with philosophy *in* practice (see Part III). Hence philosophy of education generally requires not narrow concentration but a flexible and imaginative drawing from different aspects of the "parent" discipline in relation to specific but typically highly complex problems of practice. And this undertaking, threatening as it is to safe havens of narrow specialism and expertise, can be disconcerting.

The return to the disciplines that is advocated here is not to be seen as a rejection of interdisciplinarity. Disciplines evolve through the historical development of traditions of enquiry, each incorporating its own self-criticism and dissent, and all of them fragmenting from time to time in rival paradigms and approaches. The boundaries of disciplines are characteristically fuzzy, and border disputes are rarely of great value. But none of this undermines the value of such disciplines. Without them research is in danger of kicking in mid-air and of being susceptible to posturing, faddishness, and whim. Above all we would emphasize that a return to the disciplines does not preclude, and needs to be accompanied by, a hospitable re-examination of quite what constitutes each discipline. Certain chapters in this book would not have looked much like philosophy of education to those practicing it 40 years ago. This is part of the evolution of philosophy of education.

It has become a familiar demand that work in education should be *accessible* to the "users" of that research: the policy makers, administrators, and teachers. There is every reason for those writing in philosophy of education to attempt to reach a broad audience. But it is a mistake to suppose that research must always be styled in this way. Sometimes complex philosophical enquiry is needed to expose and unravel the conceptual knots in which the discourse of educational theory and practice has become caught up. Sometimes the approach to questions of value requires a changing of the prevailing discourse in ways that fly in the face of common and professional understanding, precisely because it has become steeped in that discourse. Sometimes there are lines of thought developed by major philosophers, ancient and modern, that are worthy of exploration and interpretation, where attempts at simple exegesis can only end in a travesty of such views. Sometimes it is desirable to take risks in what is thought and said.

The influence of such work may be indirect, and the kind of influence it is allowed to have will in part be a function of political decisions. Are administrators and policy makers to be encouraged to become cognisant of such research? If initial teacher training may not be the place to explore such matters in depth, will the continuing professional development of teachers enable them to reflect on what they are doing by introducing them to the kind of questioning that is philosophy's stock-in-trade? Here too we must note a development likely to have a long-lasting influence on the direction of philosophy of education. In recent years in the UK and elsewhere many universities have begun degrees in Education which are not intended for prospective teachers. Here the long-standing and constraining connection between Education and schooling is sundered, with potentially liberating effects both for philosophy of education and for our thinking about education in its broadest sense. Ultimately schooling itself stands to benefit from this broadening of focus.

It will be evident from the headings of our Parts how different this *Guide* is from most previous collections or anthologies. We have throughout foregrounded the way in which philosophy of education has moved away from introspection to draw on, and to influence in turn, a wider world of ideas and practice. Thus the authors of Part I, *Social and Cultural Theories*, examine – and in the case of feminism, exemplify – the connections between philosophy of education and some of the most important theoretical movements of the twentieth century. In Part II, *Politics and Education*, the issues discussed are ones familiar around the world, as is the range of literature drawn on to illuminate them. Part III, *Philosophy as Education*, deals with dimensions of the way that the practice of philosophy itself may be educative, and education fail to the extent that it is not philosophical, rather than philosophy being a separate business from education, relevant to it only as it helps us to analyze and understand it. Part IV, *Teaching and Curriculum*, brings together writers who have done much in recent years to sharpen our philosophical understanding of post-16 education and lifelong learning, information and communications technology, assessment, skills and competences, and the enduring signficance of that frequently debased ideal, progressivism. Lastly, Part V, *Ethics and Upbringing*, provides informed insights into questions which are both as old as philosophy itself and given fresh interest by changing notions of the self and its moral relations with others

We asked our authors to write in pairs because we hoped that in this way a livelier sense would emerge of the contrasts and different approaches possible to each topic. We left it entirely to our authors how they handled this. Some have merged their separate identities in a seamless chapter, some have written separately, some have dovetailed their contributions, some have argued with each other and some have developed their chapter as a kind of conversation. There is a sense here of the different *styles* of philosophy of education that are possible, as well as of the different traditions and backgrounds from which the various writers come. We believe that they are all still speaking to each other (and, more remarkably, to us), and it may be that out of this collaboration further interesting work in philosophy of education will emerge.

Notes

1 Of course there are many important distinctions to be made here: there is no one "Continental European tradition." But to deal at all adequately with this would require a much longer and more complex essay.
2 Here a distinction must be made: it was Northern Europe that particularly felt the influence of Kant and Herbart.

Part I

Social and
Cultural Theories

Chapter 1

Pragmatism and Education

Jim Garrison and Alven Neiman

I

We begin with what Richard Bernstein calls "the pragmatic *ethos*" (Bernstein, 1992, p. 323). We may understand pragmatism as emerging out of the theory of meaning. Peirce introduces pragmatism in 1878 with the famous pragmatic maxim: "Consider what effects, which might conceivably have practical bearings, we conceive the object of our conception to have. Then our conception of these effects is the whole of our conception of the object" (Peirce, [1878] 1992, p. 132). There is no difference of meaning so fine that we cannot detect it in terms of a difference of possible consequences. If the consequences of two conceptions are identical, their meaning is identical. This emphasis upon consequences provides the starting point for almost any pragmatic analysis.

It might seem that the emphasis on consequences provides the foundation of pragmatism, but antifoundationalism is the first ingredient that Bernstein insists is part of the pragmatic ethos. Curiously, he does not mention consequences, probably because almost every pragmatist already assumes their importance. Nonetheless, antifoundationalism when conjoined with the crucial role of consequences sets up an internal paradox that leads to many ironies. We call it "the pragmatic paradox." The coauthors of this paper think the pragmatic paradox one of the chief glories of pragmatism. The *ethos* of pragmatism is extremely open, tolerant, and accommodating; it evades attempts to totalize it into a single dogmatic vision. The hope is that our paper will illustrate this pragmatic paradox.

Other ingredients of the pragmatic ethos, according to Bernstein, include fallibilism (presumably, pragmatism itself is fallible). Next comes "the social character of the self and the need to nurture a critical community of inquirers" (Bernstein, 1992, p. 328). Pragmatism rejects the atomistic individual born with innate free will and

Section I written by Jim Garrison; Section II by Alven Neiman. Both parts, however, were the results of mutual exploration of what we call "paradoxical pragmatism."

rationality championed by much of modern philosophy. Instead, minds and selves *emerge* socially in critical and creative dialogue with the rest of the community. Third, "For the pragmatists, contingency and chance are not merely signs of human ignorance, they are ineradicable and pervasive features of the universe" (ibid., p. 329). Fourth is pluralism. This pluralism is not only interdisciplinary; it is often anti-disciplinary when the disciplines suppress plurality of thought, feeling, and action. Bernstein advocates an "*engaged fallibilistic pluralism*" that requires "resolving that however much we are committed to our own styles of thinking, we are willing to listen to others without denying or suppressing the otherness of the others" (ibid., p. 336). Fallibilistic pluralism listens quite well; consequently, pragmatism offers hospitality to other philosophies and other ways of knowing. This makes it an ideal philosophy for a *field* of theory and practice such as education. The coauthors of this paper hope to illustrate this hospitality by engaging in a dialogue regarding their differences about how to explore the richness of pragmatism in the field of education. We will conclude by inviting the reader into the conversation opened up by the pragmatic ethos.

Peirce, unlike James and Dewey, does not address education at length in any of his work. Let us, however, consider three ideas crucial to pragmatism having immediate educational application.[1] All three greatly influence subsequent pragmatists. First, there is the pragmatic maxim itself. Working out the meanings of educational ideas, proposals, and so forth through their consequences by using creative imagination, reflective thought, and actual experimentation would clear away a great deal of educational rubbish.

Second, Peirce thinks that a belief is an embodied habit of action evincing emotion. Peirce observes, "Our beliefs guide our desires and shape our actions . . . The feeling of believing is a more or less sure indication of there being established in our nature some habit which will determine our actions" (Peirce, [1887] 1992, p. 114). Peirce concludes:

> The genuine synthetic consciousness, or the sense of the process of learning, which is the preeminent ingredient and quintessence of reason has its physiological basis quite evidently in the most characteristic property of the nervous system, the power of taking habits. (Ibid., p. 264)

The pedagogical implication is clear: learning must have a firm biological basis and mind is not separate from the body, its feelings, desires, and interests. Furthermore, learning, believing, and knowing are an intimate part of doing and feeling. Educators ignore these intimate relationships at their peril.

The goal of inquiry is to investigate the consequences of our hypotheses and habits of belief in order to determine the validity of their meaning and the soundness of their claims to truth. The ideally educated person would hold their habits of belief with full consciousness, complete self-control, and in accordance with the results of the finest inquiries thus far carried out by the largest, longest lasting community possible.

Third, Peirce gives the community of inquiry a large role to play in determining the ultimate meaning of reality itself. He writes:

The real, then, is that which, sooner or later, information and reasoning would finally result in, and which is therefore independent of the vagaries of me and you. Thus, the very origin of the conception of reality shows that this conception essentially involves the notion of a COMMUNITY –, without definite limits, and capable of an indefinite increase of knowledge. (Peirce, [1868] 1992, p. 52)

Peirce has a particularly strong understanding of the individual as subordinate to the community. James has a much stronger sense of "subjectivity" while Dewey lies somewhere in between. For all three, though, the social nature of the self is important, and the self becomes temporally extended due to its participation in the community and its emergent, evolving meanings. All three fully recognized the role of the community in educating the individual.

Peirce's close friend, William James, dramatically altered the character and direction of pragmatism. In Dewey's assessment, "Peirce was above all a logician; whereas James was an educator and humanist and wished to force the general public to realize that certain . . . philosophical debates have a real importance for mankind, because the beliefs which they bring into play lead to very different modes of conduct" (Dewey, [1925] 1984, p. 8). With James, pragmatism descends from the Olympian heights and becomes more concerned with everyday practical affairs. Furthermore, James directly addresses education in his famous *Talks To Teachers on Psychology* (James, [1899] 1958). With James the possible topics of educational interest become so vast that one hardly knows where to begin. For the sake of continuity, we begin with habit.

James makes practical use of Peirce's understanding of the relation between learning and habit when he derives the following pedagogical principle:

The great thing, then, in all education, is to make our nervous system our ally instead of our enemy . . . For this we must make automatic and habitual, as early as possible as many useful actions as we can . . . The more of the details of our daily life we can hand over to the effortless custody of automatism, the more our higher powers of mind will be set free for their own proper work. (James, 1890/1950, Vol. I, p. 122)

Purely cognitive psychologists who separate mind from body and thought from feeling can never arrive at such a powerful conclusion. One only has to look at the almost exclusively cognitive curriculum in our schools to realize James's immensely powerful, though simple, principle, is still underappreciated. Usually we confine the body to gym class; elsewhere emotions are viewed as the sources of disciplinary problems that destroy the desire to learn.

From his reflections on habit, James affirms the following connection between the individual and society: "Habit is thus the enormous fly-wheel of society, its most precious conservative agent" (ibid., p. 122). We acquire our habits from our habitat, especially the customs of our social habitat, our community. James, like Peirce, thought it important that habits come under our control; that is why reflective learning is so important. At a deeper level, it is why cultural critique is so important. Culture has us before we have it; if we are ever to possess ourselves and realize our unique potential, we must critique and reconstruct the culture that has us first.

James's pragmatism makes human needs, interests, and purposes pre-eminent in thought and action. He insists, "My thinking is first and last and always for the sake of my doing, and I can only do one thing at a time" (James, [1890] 1950, vol. II, p. 333). This stance leads James to reject one of the most cherished dogmas of Western thought, the ideal of eternal, immutable essences. James boldly proclaims: "*[T]he only meaning of essence is teleological and that classification and conception are purely teleological weapons of the mind.* The essence of a thing is that one of its properties which is so *important for my interests* that in comparison with it I may neglect the rest" (ibid., p. 335). This is a specific instance of James's teleological orientation, but an especially astounding one. It subordinates logical essences to human purposes and interests. It is a realization that essence is not a question of metaphysical existence, but of practical inquiry, and, for James, all inquiry is practical inquiry. On such a view, ontology (essences) is not a matter of metaphysics. A chemist might insist H_2O is the essence of water, but, according to James, that is only "for his purpose of deduction and compendious definition" (ibid., p. 335). Such a view, though, is not some reality-denying subjectivism.

To someone who insists that some aspect of some existent is the only "real" essence, James responds that such a person is, "Merely insisting on an aspect of the thing which suits his own petty purpose, that of naming the thing; or else on an aspect which suits the manufacturer's purposes, that of producing an article for which there is a vulgar demand. Meanwhile the reality overflows these purposes at every pore" (ibid., p. 334). The reference to "overflow" is important. This alludes to James's "Stream of Consciousness" found in Chapter IX of Volume I of his *Psychology*. The notion that reality and the experience of reality is a continuous stream directly challenges the atomism of the British Empiricists, John Locke, George Berkeley, and David Hume. For James, experience is continuous and holistic; selective attention driven by selective interests discriminates objects from the infinite flux of existence according to our finite needs, desires, interests, and purposes.

The educational consequences are immense. First, if essences are but teleological weapons of the mind, then what of the essence of human beings? The answer is obvious; we do not have an antecedently existing essence. Instead, each individual must work out the essence of their existence within the culture they happen to find themselves. In particular this means that the essence of humanity is not "rational being." This means that there are no fixed aims of education. The consequence for curriculum is equally obvious: there is no predetermined body of knowledge that is of most worth. Further, it makes no sense to confine the curriculum to the cognitive when the body and its emotions, especially selective interests, are so important. The world we attend to is the world toward which we respond. If we attend to our world poorly, we become fools regardless of how perfect our ratiocination. Educators influenced by James would return to the classical Greek concern with the body and with educating *eros* (passionate desire) to desire the good.

James replaces the notion that human beings are a substance with the notion of transactional functional coordination as the fundamental unit of activity. James's psychology rejects the notion of the mind as a metaphysical (thinking) substance in favor of a thoroughgoing teleological functionalism that eventually came to dominate psychology in North America. It also influenced other prominent schools of psychology. For instance, James V. Wertsch remarks that "much of Vygotsky's admiration of William James stemmed from the fact that the latter had rejected substantialism" (Wertsch, 1985, p. 200). James is always thinking about the living functional organism in its environment as constantly striving to maintain its dynamic equilibrium while growing. Educators should think of living functional children in their classroom environment constantly striving to maintain dynamic equilibrium while growing, and not as computers processing information. The metaphors we choose influence how we think about education. The living organism, though, is no metaphor.

In the Preface of *Talks To Teachers*, James remarks that one of the talks connects to his "philosophic essays" and deals with "the pluralistic or individualistic philosophy" (James, [1899] 1958, p. 19). James thinks, "There is no point of view absolutely public and universal. Private and incommunicable perceptions always remain over, and the worst of it is that those who look for them from the outside never know *where*" (ibid., p. 19). James connects the fact that each individual has a "passionate inner meaning" to pluralistic democracy. The implication for education in a pluralistic democracy is clear; educators must respect the uniqueness of each individual and cultivate it that each may make their unique social contribution.

Although a pioneer of scientific psychology, James warned:

[Y]ou make a great, a very great mistake, if you think that psychology, being the science of the mind's laws, is something from which you can deduce definite programmes and schemes and methods of instruction for immediate schoolroom use. Psychology is a science and teaching is an art; and sciences never generate arts directly out of themselves. An intermediary inventive mind must make the application by using its originality. (ibid., p. 24)

In the twentieth century, educational researchers, policy analysts, and educational technocrats largely ignored James's wisdom. Instead, researchers have sought for what James's student, E. L. Thorndike, calls "the laws of learning." Thorndike derived his laws from a version of associationism that he calls "connectionism." Unlike the laws of association of the British Empiricists, these laws hold between situations and responses rather than ideas. Other psychologists pursued laws between stimulus and response. Nonetheless, some kind of psychological atomism dominates.

Once we have these scientific laws, they may dictate educational policy and teaching practice in detail. All that remains is for technocrats to design expert systems, such as teacher-proof curricula, and administer them properly. Proper administration relies on another Thorndikian principle. In her biography of Thorndike, titled *The Sane Positivist*, Geraldine Joncich begins a chapter with a passage from Thorndike's *Educational Psychology*: "We conquer the facts of nature when we observe and experiment upon them. When we measure them we have made them our servants" (Joncich, 1968, p. 282). The famous Thorndike principle is a statement of his metaphysical commitment to measurement: "Whatever exists, exists in some amount. To measure it is simply to know its varying amounts" (cited in Joncich, 1968, p. 282). In the field of education those in charge seem to assume we make the facts our servants when we design multiple choice, pencil and paper, machine-graded, and norm-referenced tests. These tests provide a number allowing us to measure student learning and teacher "productivity." Norm-referenced testing is anathema to the pluralistic democrat precisely because it ignores the "passionate inner meaning" that makes democratic individuals unique. "Norms" have little value to pluralistic democrats.

While positivism is dead philosophically, it remains dominant practically. Thorndike's victory internationally is one of the major reasons most educators completely ignore pragmatism. The fate that befell James in twentieth-century education followed James's disciple, John Dewey. In many nations throughout the world, the talk is Dewey, but the practice is Thorndike.

In his autobiographical essay, "From Absolutism to Experimentalism," Dewey acknowledges the great influence of this "biological conception of the *psyche*" as found in the *Psychology* of William James (Dewey, [1930] 1984, p. 157).[2] Combined with Dewey's neo-Darwinianism, James confirmed Dewey's naturalism while appealing to his desire for organic unity. Dewey observes, "Many philosophers have had much to say about the idea of organism; but they have taken it structurally and hence statically. It was reserved for James to think of life in terms of life in action" (ibid., p. 158). The etymology of pragmatism flows from the ancient Greek *pragma*, meaning act, deed, affair, although pragmatists are most interested in intelligent action. The crucial idea connecting biological functioning with mental functioning, for James, is habit. Habit plays a major role in Dewey's educational philosophy. We may recover a great deal of Dewey's educational philosophy from James's pedagogical principles, biological orientation, and emphasis on habit.

Due to space constraints, we call attention to those aspects of Dewey's adaptation of Peirce and James's emphasis on habit that are usually overlooked. His understanding of the functioning of habit is not mechanical and rationalistic. Dewey writes, "Rationality . . . is not a force to evoke against impulse and habit. It is the attainment of a working harmony among diverse desires. 'Reason' as a noun signifies the happy co-operation of a multitude of dispositions" (Dewey, [1922] 1983a, p. 136). Habits, for Dewey, as for his mentors, are dispositions to act evincing emotions. For Dewey, "'Reason' is not an antecedent force which serves as a panacea. It is a laborious achievement of habit needing to be continually worked over" (ibid.). The laborious achievement of a working harmony among diverse desires is an aesthetic as well as cognitive comprehension of rationality. It is also moral.

Dewey also notes, "The objective biological approach of the Jamesian psychology led straight to the perception of the importance of distinctive social categories, especially communication and participation" (Dewey, [1930] 1984, p. 159). Significantly, Dewey's *Human Nature and Conduct* is subtitled "An Introduction to Social Psychology." Equally significantly, the title of the first chapter reads "Habits as Social Functions" (Dewey, [1922] 1983a, p. 15). The customs of a culture inscribe themselves upon the biological body as habits.[3] The social nature of the self truly is part of the pragmatic ethos.

Dewey explicitly rejected "Social Darwinism" with its self-serving and antidemocratic rhetoric about the survival of the fittest. The question is always, fit for what? Dewey learned from Huxley that even *laissez faire* economists must weed their garden if they want lovely flowers. As reflective creatures, we can come to know the environmental contingencies that determine conduct. Through creative inquiry, we can transform the world according to our desires. We can create a world where everyone is fit to survive and thrive, not just those who excel at crude capitalism. Human beings often determine the conditions of selection, and there need not be any single scale of success.

The community needs individuals to perform a large array of vital functions if it is to thrive. That a given community elects to reward only a small number of those functions, say, entrepreneurial success, is a condemnation of that society. As a neo-Darwinian, Dewey knows the key to survival is diversity not homogeneity; the racist is simply scientifically wrong. He acknowledged individual differences and inequality in the physical and cognitive performance of various tasks, but a democratic community is primarily concerned with moral equality. Dewey remarks, "moral equality means incommensurability, the inapplicability of common and quantitative standards" (Dewey, [1922] 1983, p. 299). For Dewey, every individual has a unique potential, regardless of any given physical or psychological inequality. The goal of education is to aid every individual to achieve their unique potential that they may make their unique contribution to society. The result is an aristocracy of everyone:

> Democracy in this sense denotes, one may say, aristocracy carried to its limit. It is a claim that every human being as an individual may be the best for some particular purpose and hence the most fitted to rule, to lead, in that specific respect. The habit of fixed and numerically limited classifications is the enemy alike of true aristocracy and true democracy. (Ibid., pp. 297–8)

The only way Social Darwinism can gain a foothold is by convincing the community that there are only a very few hierarchies. Social Darwinism has remained influential in the political lives of almost all capitalistic nations. It fails to understand the community as a functionally complex organism in a complex, diverse, and ever-changing environment.

For Dewey, education is a social function. Until we know what sort of society is best, we do not know what sort of education is best. Dewey develops two criteria for evaluating any society; they are, "How numerous and varied are the interests which are consciously shared? How full and free is the interplay with other forms of association?" (Dewey, [1916] 1980, p. 89). Oppressive societies, such as those devoted to Social Darwinism, eliminate diverse interests in favor of the special interests of the powerful few. Such societies are maladaptive because they are unable to respond agilely to environmental change. Diversity provides alternatives, thereby funding freedom. The danger in a society having narrow interests is that instead of attending to the interests of others and the possibilities they express, the prevailing purpose becomes, as Dewey puts it, "the protection of what it has got, instead of reorganization and progress through wider relationships" (ibid., p. 91). Isolationism reduces freedom because it reduces our capacity to imagine the alternative possibilities that aid free choice and action. Isolationism is self-oppression. Dewey concludes:

> The two elements in our criterion both point to democracy. The first signifies not only more numerous and more varied points of shared common interest, but greater reliance

upon the recognition of mutual interests as a factor in social control. The second means not only freer interaction between social groups . . . but change in social habit – its continuous readjustment through meeting the new situations produced by varied intercourse (ibid., p. 92)

By the standards of freedom, creativity, and dialogue, pluralistic democracy is, for Dewey, the best possible society we know of for sustaining growth.

Dewey understood democracy as moral, economic, and educational, not just political. His pluralistic conception of democracy leads Dewey to the following definition of democracy:

A democracy is more than a form of government; it is primarily a mode of associated living, of conjoint communicated experience. The extension in space of the number of individuals who participate in an interest so that each has to refer his own action to that of others, and to consider the action of others to give point and direction to his own, is equivalent to breaking down barriers of class, race, and national territory which kept men from perceiving the full import of their activity. (ibid., p. 93)

The governmental structure assumed by a democracy is of secondary concern. It does not matter as long as it promotes communication. Conversation for Dewey is about creating and sharing meaning; it is about growth. We may secure and continue the conversation in many diverse ways, and diversity is the key to creative conversation; it is also the key to good classrooms.

For Dewey, democracy is the most logical form of government. Further, he asserts that democracy is the best way to pursue logic. Dewey affirms that for logic, "The final actuality is accomplished in face-to-face relationships by means of direct give and take. Logic in its fulfillment recurs to the primitive sense of the word: *dialogue*. Ideas which are not communicated, shared, and reborn in expression are but [monological] soliloquy, and soliloquy is but broken and imperfect thought" (Dewey, [1927] 1984, pp. 371). Dewey's etymology here is correct, *Logos* derives from the ancient Greek for speech, word, or discourse. By adding different voices to a conversation, we may alter the conditions of rational inquiry; we may also reconstruct social conditions. So, also, with the canons of rationality. Dewey holds a communicative theory of rationality and democratic social action.

The goal of Dewey's philosophy of education is to release the human potential for growth. Growth through freedom, creativity, and dialogue is, for him, the all-inclusive ideal, the greatest good. Dewey asserts, "Since growth is the characteristic of life, education is all one with growing; it has no end beyond itself" (Dewey [1916] 1980, p. 58). For him, the capacity to cultivate growth is the criterion for evaluating the quality of all social institutions.

Dewey believes that democracy is the social structure that contributes most to freeing intelligence to grow, and, therefore, education should be democratic. He writes:

The aim of education is to enable individuals to continue their education . . . the object and reward of learning is continued capacity for growth. Now this idea cannot be applied to all the members of a society except where intercourse of man with man is mutual, and except where there is adequate provision for the reconstruction of social habits and institutions by means of wide stimulation arising from equitably distributed interests. And this means a democratic society. (ibid., p. 107)

Dewey favors a dynamic planning over a static planned society. He thought an education that emphasizes community, communication, intelligent inquiry, and a reconstructive attitude can best serve the citizens of an ever-evolving world. For him, it is clear that a democratic society is the best choice in the long haul. For Dewey, we do not have a democratic society unless all institutions, business, industry, union, and government are democratic. At the very least, if citizens are to become participatory democrats then the schools they attend must become democratic in the participatory sense he describes.

We do not have time to go into the detail of Dewey's pedagogical method, but we must at least note and correct one common error. Dewey did not believe in "student-centered teaching" if that means, "let the child do what it wants." Indeed, Dewey wrote *Experience and Education* to correct the excess of "progressivism"'s misinterpretations of his work. Dewey's position of method may help clear up the mess.

Dewey is clear that method is not separable from subject matter. For Dewey, method, or structure, is structure for a purpose: "Method means that arrangement *of* subject matter which makes it most effective in use. Never is method something outside of the material" (Dewey, [1916] 1980, p. 172). When the use is pedagogical, we should arrange the subject matter to make it most effective for teaching others. Dewey clearly states, "The subject matter of the learner is not . . . identical with the formulated, the crystallized, and systematized subject matter of the adult" (ibid., p. 190). The same holds for any pedagogical situation. That is, "the teacher should be occupied not with subject matter in itself but in its interaction with the pupil's present needs and capacities. Hence simple scholarship is not enough"(ibid., p. 191).

Subject matter knowledge alone does not make a good teacher. Teachers teach subject matter to students. It is a triangle enclosing a pedagogical space. Just teaching the subject matter does not mean one is teaching well. To teach well, the teacher must connect the subject matter to the needs, desires, interests, stage of cognitive development, and so forth of the student, within the physical, social, and political context that the students and teachers find themselves. Good teaching requires moral and aesthetic, not just cognitive, perception of the needs and abilities of the student. It also requires a complete and confident command of the subject matter to reconfigure it to meet the needs of every individual student.

In acknowledging the influence of James, Dewey makes an important reservation:

> To say that it proceeded from his *Psychology* rather than from his essays collected in the volume called *Will to Believe*, his *Pluralistic Universe*, or *Pragmatism*, is to say something that needs explanation. For there are, I think, two unreconciled strains in the *Psychology*. One is found in the adoption of the subjective tenor of prior psychological tradition. . . . The other strain is objective, having its roots in a return to the earlier biological conception of the *psyche*. (Dewey, 1930/1984, p. 157)

It is easy to identify the influence of the works other than the psychology in Dewey's work. Still, Dewey shied away from what he saw as residuals of subjectivism, dualism, and the philosophy of consciousness in James's philosophy.

II

Pragmatism's Other Face: The Varieties of William James's Experience

The first part of our paper stressed the open, pluralistic, even paradoxical quality of pragmatism. It is always possible to avoid paradoxes, often by artificial means, but we would rather embrace and explore them. This is especially true when doing so allows one to indicate and elaborate significant implications of pragmatism in a perhaps unexpected area. In this case, the area we have in mind is that of spirituality and education. More specifically, this part will develop aspects of the pragmatic paradox which arise as one comes to a better understanding of that too often misunderstood pragmatist classic, William James's *The Varieties of Religious Experience*.

It should not surprise us that William James, ardent evangelist for pluralism, would have presented the world with more than one philosophical vision, more than one stance toward the universe. Yet there are still those who would arrive too easily at James's "central vision," or "the" philosophy of William James. James himself vigilantly warns us against giving in too easily to this tendency, not only as it applies to his own work, but to "reality as a whole." Consider, for example, the following remarks from the introduction to James's *Talks to Teachers*:

> According to that (pluralistic) philosophy, the truth is too great for any one actual mind, even though that mind be dubbed "the absolute," to know the whole of it. The facts and worths of life need many cognizers to take them in. There is no point of view absolutely public and universal. Private and non-communicable perceptions always remain over, and the worst of it is that those who look for them from the outside never know where. (James, 1992, p. 708)

Even the tendency to refer to James as a pluralist is dangerous. For what can this amount to, in the end, besides another act of hubris, yet another attempt get to the bottom of this very, very complex, "bottomless" man?

Richard Poirier's recent attempt to propose another, less canonical, William James may be helpful in dealing with such a question. (Poirier, 1992).[4] To begin with, Poirier rightfully insists upon James's weariness of any description that might serve to "use him up," which might suggest a means by which James could be fully understood, explained totally. According to Poirier, James's espousal of various personas (for example, medical doctor, physiologist, scientific psychologist, pragmatist, radical empiricist, or pluralist) serves him at various times merely with temporary resting-places. It provides James with a deep scepticism about the ability of language to "grab hold of reality," with various "selves" he can try on for this purpose or that.

Poirier constructively argues that we can profitably imagine James as a "poetic," rather than a "scientific," pragmatist. As such, he becomes more closely aligned with creative spirits such as Emerson, Frost, and Stein and more distanced from theorists including Peirce, Dewey, and Mead. For the poetic (and paradoxical) pragmatist, understanding is embodied in a profound but healthy irony, an irony that enables skillful authors to produce texts that exhibit multiple and changing meanings. Selves are constantly suggested, while earlier suggestions are constantly "written off" (Poirier, 1987). In "writing off the self," the poetic pragmatist avoids the ignominy of "postmodern metaphysics" (there is no self!). It is an urgent imperative not to take any "self-representation" too literally. Attention to the nuances within ever-evolving meanings allows authors to remain present, all the while, embodied in the form and structure of their work, of their life.

Utilizing Poirier's own metanarrative of pragmatism, I shall here try to locate yet "another William James," a James explicitly in tension with Jim Garrison's more canonical version described above. In doing so, I recognize the dangers of relying on anything even slightly resembling a "skeleton key" to James's thought. However, there is no way to avoid the paradox of James's pragmatism completely.

I begin with recent suggestions made by Richard Gale (Gale, 1999) in order to highlight a picture of James as multiple not only in philosophy but also personally, as a "divided self" from whom educationalist wayfarers in the desert of postmodernism can learn integrity in the midst of fragmentation. According to Gale, the best way to begin this search for "another William James" is to take seriously the idea that James, as much artist as scientist, can be understood (in contrast to John Dewey) as a great "singer of the blues." (According to Gale, Dewey was tone deaf to the blues!) I want to suggest that once we take this metaphor seriously, we can begin to think more easily of James as a great spiritual teacher, as addressing the realm of the spirit in the spirit of the blues. In other words, we will be better able to find in *The Varieties of Religious Experience* (hereafter VRE) a redemptive philosophy of education for tragedy, an education by which fragmented postmodern selves can begin a transformation into postmodern saints.

Early on in VRE, James quite explicitly suggests that he is searching for a viable "science of religion." This science, it may seem, would complement other works of the author, especially his great *Principles of Psychology*. Yet, I have doubts that such a reading exhausts such materials. In fact, if VRE were merely an attempt at "psychological science" we would have to approve of the many criticisms of James as hopelessly subjective in presenting his materials. We would have to agree with Peirce's suggestion that he was just too emotional, too autobiographical, too feminine, too chronically disposed to autobiography, to do productive science. Here I provide a reading in which such criticisms miss the larger point of James's projects in psychology.

Let us imagine VRE, then, as an enactment of life's tragedy performed by the author whose book VRE is. If we understand the point of tragic performance, we will not "attend" with the goal of distancing ourselves from a subject matter in order to obtain objective "knowledge that," for example, some claim or another about the human condition that we can study and debate. The point of tragedy is not simply to give us theory. Instead, tragedy aims at evoking a more visceral reaction and response in the audience. My suggestion implies that VRE is to be read, in part, as an acting out of a state of affairs that evokes fear and pity, that provides the means by which these emotions can be "worked through," powerfully experienced and integrated into the mature and transformed personality of the viewer-participant. We cannot understand the educational value of VRE unless we see it as something more, perhaps even something other, than a statement of theory or doctrine. Echoing a distinction provided us by the great philosophical historian Pierre Hadot, we must read VRE as an enactment of spiritual exercise *through* tragedy and beyond, as a "philosophy as a way of life," rather than merely "philosophy as theory" (Hadot, 1995). On this reading, the most important "science" of religion in the book is actually *theoria*, that is, contemplative discipline.

This thesis in no way denies the value of the nontragic or (as Gale puts it) the "Promethean" William James. Certainly there is enough evidence in texts and life for us to productively understand him, following Garrison's suggestion, as a great debunker of a tradition of metaphysics that separated the (pure) thinking self from the world in such a way as to make liberating action impossible. On this account James, freed from Descartes by Darwin, is a pioneer of pragmatism, the author of key elements of a powerful educational scheme that is primarily motivated by the desire to empower the embodied self so it may enact adaptive and productive social transformation. In an exaggerated form recently espoused by Richard Rorty, pragmatism allows us to imagine a postmetaphysical culture in which democracy as a way of life, rather than the Platonic escape from the embodied world of chance and contingency, exists as the greatest good and the greatest adventure (Rorty, 1989).

According to at least one well-known metanarrative of pragmatism, metaphysics of this Platonic, world-weary, type need flourish only where rationality of a truly practical as well as theoretical kind is impossible. The great contribution of James, in formulating this doctrine, is as a John the Baptist to John Dewey. On this account, a much more sophisticated Dewey shapes hints taken from his insightful but muddle-headed teacher into a perfected, post-Darwinian vision of practical reasoning. Within this vision, ever-evolving means of technical mastery are finally yoked to embodied intelligence. In Rorty's cheerful development of this vision, the final triumph of pragmatic Prometheanism will arrive on the day in which all need for metaphysics as blues medicine will have disappeared, an era in which properly educated human beings will understand the endlessly liberating possibilities of human action. Freed from the need to answer to someone or something beyond or outside ourselves (perhaps "God" or "Truth"), human beings can finally develop their full potential as members of a truly democratic society.

For the Promethean such as Dewey, tragedy is out of the question (see Boisvert, 1999). Perhaps the ultimate Promethean was Plato, who both imagined a world in which suffering was unnecessary and a way of life in which such a world could be realized. According to the catechism discussed above pragmatism outlaws this kind of Platonic escapism. For Sidney Hook, pragmatism can contend with the tragedy inherent in human interactions without going beyond the merely human (Hook, 1974). It does this by honestly and realistically employing the method of human intelligence in order to make the best we can out of a situation in which there are no goods without attendant evils. But how does James differ from Hook, how might he suggest that tragedy should be met?

It is worth wondering what James has to say about "the tragic sense of life." Now more than ever,

> unmeaning, incomprehensibility . . . is always around us on every side . . . Nor is this obscurity only in the world around us. It indwells us. We do not make much sense to ourselves, and much of the sense that we do make is fragile and illusory (nor is this only a consequence of our infinite capacity for self-deception). (Lash, 1988, p. 221)

VRE is not simply a valuable attempt at a psychology of religious conversion. It is an enduring document of a great, far-sighted man struggling with the deepest problem of our age.

There is a famous passage in *The Varieties Of Religious Experience*, in which William James, in the midst of describing various dimensions of what he calls "the sick soul," refers to an account of "panic-fear" by a French sufferer. Here is a part of that account:

> There arose in my mind the image of an epileptic patient whom I had seen in the asylum, a black-haired youth with greenish skin, entirely idiotic . . . He used to sit there like a sort of sculptured Egyptian cat or Peruvian mummy, moving nothing but his black eyes and looking absolutely non-human. This image and my fear entered into a species of combination with each other. *That shape am I*, I felt, potentially. Nothing that I possess can defend me against that fate, if the hour for it should strike for me as it struck for him. (James, 1985, p. 160)

The passage is famous precisely because we now know that this panic-fear is James's own, taken from the years of his own first major breakdown. According to a now discredited, overly Promethean, picture of his development, James was saved, once and for all, from morbid-mindedness through reading the work of the great volitionist Charles Renouvier. The account highlights Promethean aspects of a supposedly "once and for all" recovery:

> I think that yesterday was a crisis in my life. I finished the first part of Renouvier's 2nd essay, and saw no reason why his definition of free will (sustaining of a thought because I choose to when I might have other thoughts) need be the definition of an illusion. . . . I shall assume for the present . . . that it is no illusion. My first act of free will shall be to believe in free will. (Quoted in Simon, 1999, p. 127)

Thanks to the work of a new generation of biographers and exegetes, we are now much less inclined to believe that this journal entry from 1870 marks the end of James's problems with morbid-mindedness. We are more aware than ever before of the ways in which James never entirely vanquished his melancholia, that, in fact, during the very years in which the Gifford lectures that became VRE were conceived James was subject to numerous, debilitating attacks (Simon, 1999, pp. 290 ff.). VRE shows us a would-be Promethean self heroically struggling with the dark night of the soul. Moreover, it presents a means by which the Promethean can honorably sur-render to darkness, only in order to be born again. *Varieties of Religious Experience* is, according to his recent biographer, Linda Simon, at least in part the result of James's struggles to fend off the fear of incipient madness, of loss of control, of death. Yet it begins in relative calm, with analytic chapters devoted to medical materialism, a delineation of James's topic qua scientist, and a description of healthy-mindedness as a state of personality and a way of religious conversion. After several lectures praising healthy-mindedness, James writes the following:

> There are people for whom evil means only a mal-adjustment with *things*, a wrong correspondence of one's life, with the environment . . . But there are others for whom evil is no mere relation of the subject to particular outer things, but something more radical and general, a wrongness or vice in his essential nature, which no alteration of the environment, or any superficial rearrangement of the inner self, can cure. (James, 1985, p. 134)

According to the persons described by James as morbidly minded, life cannot help but appear to be inherently confusing, fragmentary, full of conflict, always threatened by chaos. Once one recognizes the nature of evil, darkness remains a part of a perpetual vision. Here is the stuff of tragedy: "The normal process of life contains moments as bad as any of those which insane melancholy is filled with, moments in which radical evil gets its innings and takes its solid turn. The lunatic's visions of horror are all drawn from the material of daily fact . . ." (ibid., p. 163). The Darwinian vision that enables pragmatism to liberate humanity from escapist Platonism also reveals a living world in which there is no life without death, no good without evil:

> Here on our very hearths and in our gardens the infernal cat plays with the panting mouse, or holds the hot bird fluttering in her jaws. Crocodiles and rattlesnakes and pythons are at this moment vessels of life as real as we are . . . And whenever they or other wild beasts clutch their living prey, the deadly horror which an agitated melancholic feels is the literally right reaction on the situation. (ibid., p. 164)

The sick soul, according to James, can only view the universe as a kind of double-storied mystery:

> Peace cannot be reached by the simple addition of pluses and elimination of minuses from life. Natural good is not simply insufficient in amount and transient, there lurks a falsity in its very being. Cancelled as it all is by death if not by earlier enemies, it gives no final balance and can never be intended for our lasting worship. (ibid., p. 166)

If this is right, if the healthy minded, "single-storied," vision is inadequate, Hook's pragmatic response to tragedy will not do. But how are we to know if James is right, if the latter view is more complete, and thus, more true, than that of the Promethean pragmatist and his healthy-minded friends?

We are, to be sure, given arguments; but mostly we are given stories, stories of famous people such as Tolstoy and John Bunyan, less famous folk such as Henry Alline and Billy Bray, but most of all, albeit indirectly, William James. This is not accident. In tragic performance, it is the story, and not the argument, that is the key. Tragic recognition, like recognition in education, is something more, at times perhaps something wholly other, than recognition of validity or soundness of argument. In James and his story, discerning readers will recognize a sufferer in need of salvation. Engrossed in a chilling performance, they will hang on the edge, waiting to see how the story comes out. They, most of all, will recognize, in their pity and terror, that the story is theirs also.

How does James, having taken us into tragedy, take us out, or through? Again, stories are the key, even though argument is employed. These stories highlight aspects of saintliness. But what is saintliness? James's elucidation is not new:

> The metaphysical mystery . . . that he who feeds on death that feeds on men possesses life supereminently and excellently, and meets best the secret demands of the universe, is the truth of which asceticism (i.e. the twice born philosophy) has been the faithful champion. The folly of the cross, so inexplicable by the intellect, has yet its indestructible vital meaning. (Ibid., pp. 362, 364)

Saintliness, as James presents it, involves a resolute process of knowledge and transformation. First of all, it requires an examination of the self that provides an authentic recognition of our ultimate powerlessness in the face of death. Secondly, it requires a decision, hard fought for and not easily followed through, to turn one's will and life over to something greater than oneself, within the community, toward God. These steps, in turn, illicit a new-found ability to exhibit compassion based on a recognition of one's true self in the other, and the other in one's true self, a regathering of virtues found nowadays more in soldiers than in spiritual sufferers snacking on "chicken soup for the soul" in comfortable bookstores. It is as if we reach a two-storied Prometheanism, which is no longer Prometheanism at all, "the moral equivalent of war." And thus it is saintly understanding that truly knows that it is through suffering, through self-sacrifice, that one is reborn. It is only within the saint that one finds a redemptive gratitude expressed in the recognition that no one owes us anything, yet we are all responsible for everyone else.

Applied directly to our roles as educational theorists and practitioners, James's performance is highly instructive. For it allows us to question all too common enlightenment visions of education as infinitely perfectible, as well as nihilistic, postmodern views which mistake less than perfection for nothing at all. If. James's criticisms of Platonic antitragedy apply to "the normal processes of life," then surely they apply to something as common as education. After reading VRE, it should no longer be that difficult to take seriously the idea of education as inherently tragic.

A fairly recent exchange between Nicholas Burbules and Rene Arcilla on "the tragic sense of education" brings this Jamesian idea beautifully into focus. Burbules, commenting on Sidney Hook's response to tragedy, recognizes that a sense of hope merely concerned with better outcomes is not enough for educational researchers or practitioners (Burbules, 1990). Such a hope would not, to use James's terminology, recognize the need, in the midst of tragedy, for a multistoried view of the situation. What is needed, more specifically, is perhaps a sense of education worth practicing for its own sake, or as Arcilla ultimately describes it, a sense of the self and its duties deeper than the mere addition of pluses and subtraction of minuses can account for (Arcilla, 1992).

Thus, Burbules and Arcilla move us toward an educational position already embodied within James's performance. Burbules's admirably argued suggestion is that, in the realm of education, we best move through the despair of tragedy, not merely by way of a pragmatic hope concerning outcomes but, rather through a sense of one's integrity as an educator. Arcilla, building on Burbules' work, defines this further as a Pascalian faith in the power of love and witness. Commenting on Wordsworth's performance of tragedy in his "Intimations Ode," he writes, "Such a redemptive transformation of the memory of loss into presence, the miracle of the present, of splendor should be a focus of our educational endeavor" (Arcilla, 1992, p. 480). My remarks have been meant to suggest that in VRE one can, given the presence of grace as well as one's own effort, find, enjoy and benefit from a beautifully realized example of such an endeavor. Education, in Arcilla's words, can: "serve as the dramatic stage, so to speak, where we become the tragic spectators of the protagonists (including ourselves) whose deeds have historically scarred our lives" (ibid.). Following Arcilla's discussion of Wordsworth, I would suggest that VRE also "invites us not only to acknowledge how our educational endeavors are given to tragedy, but especially to explore how tragedy is itself an educative force. . . ." (ibid.). In this way philosophical education can, again be "education of the spirit." Philosophical education as a way of life can enact tragedy. It can, in the words of Socrates, help us "learn how to die" (Neiman, 2000).

Finally, in his chapter on "The Value of Saintliness," after referring to the metaphysical mystery for which the cross acts as a solution, James (1985) says: "No matter what a man's frailties otherwise may be, if he be willing to risk death, and still more if he suffer it heroically, in the service he has chosen, the fact consecrates him forever" (p. 364). Whatever this death of the self means, this meaning can not, in actuality, be said. For if it could be said, would not the Prometheans be right in condemning James as a metaphysician? In order to resist the Promethean catechism's "take" on James, in order to be true to the spirit of Poirier's tale of pragmatism, the meaning of the self and its death would need to be embodied in the structure of the text which VRE is, in the form which was the drama of the life of William James, that adorable genius and ironist, Promethean and sick soul, that remarkable yet elusive hero, a singer of faith beyond the minor island of hope.

May you catch at least a glimpse of him, the man there, as I have, if only God wills it.

Notes

1   It is difficult not to discuss Peirce's semiotics and his notion that we cannot think without signs, that we ourselves are signs, and that, as Peirce ([1868] 1992) suggests, these signs might turn round and say "You mean nothing which we have not taught you" (p. 54). Since everything is potentially a sign, including technologies, social institutions, and especially other persons, this statement has immense implications. We cannot develop this idea in the space available. It is just one of the pragmatic resources we hope the reader will wish to investigate.

2 The influence of Peirce, who was on Dewey's doctoral examining committee, is evident in Dewey's work, but never explicitly acknowledged.
3 Rorty (1982) is right to point out the similarities between Dewey and Foucault on the topic of how society seizes the body.
4 This reading of Poirier is influenced by Susan Huddleston Edgerston's highly instructive discussions of teaching as a literary genre, and of autobiography as a condition of knowledge (Edgerston, 1997).

Recommendations for Further Reading

Hook, S. (1974) *Pragmatism and the Tragic Sense of Life*, Basic Books.
Rorty, R. (1980) *Philosophy and the Mirror of Nature*, Blackwell.
Thayer, H. S. (1981) *Meaning and Action: A Critical History of Pragmatism*, Hackett Publishing Co.
West, C. (1989) *The American Evasion of Philosophy: A Genealogy of Pragmatism*, University of Wisconsin Press.

Chapter 2

Critical Theory and Critical Pedagogy

Nigel Blake and Jan Masschelein

Characteristics and Development of Critical Theory

We refer here to Critical Theory as the tradition of thought associated with the Frankfurt School of philosophy and social theory, which originated in the late 1920s, flourished in the 1930s in Germany and 1940s in the USA, and continued to develop through the 1950s and into the 1960s. Jürgen Habermas claims to continue the tradition of the Frankfurt School, though some authors (e.g., Jay, 1973) apply the name of Critical Theory only to the Frankfurt School proper, and exclude Habermas. We will include him.

Critical Theory may be thought of as, in the first instance, a critical reappropriation and revision of Marxism, albeit one which has traveled a long way from these roots. And as such, its relevance to education might seem initially dubious. However, one of the commitments from Marxism that remains most potent in Critical Theory is, loosely speaking, that of liberation from "false consciousness," though certainly not in the classic Marxist formulation of that idea. Inasmuch as this inevitably brings in train an interest in critique of ideology, or in critique of the "taken for granted" otherwise conceived, it should be no surprise that an overlap has been found between the concerns of Critical Theorists and of those educationists who take seriously any emancipatory role for education. The only surprise is that Critical Theorists, as philosophers, have taken less direct interest in education than educationists have taken in Critical Theory, notwithstanding the indirect influence that Horkheimer and Adorno exerted on educational reform in Germany (Albrecht et al., 1999).

However, there is no such thing as "the" Critical Theory. There are many lines of thought relating to the different thinkers (not all of them philosophers) who were affiliated to the School (Horkheimer, Adorno, Benjamin, Marcuse, Fromm, and later Habermas, to name the best known of them) and these thinkers certainly changed their minds over time. This history of Critical Theory and of the Frankfurt School is well documented (Jay, 1973; Dubiel, 1978; Held, 1980; Friedman, 1981; Honneth and Bonss, 1982). Although it is difficult to identify authoritatively "the" ideas of Critical Theory, we can indicate some motives and a principal theoretical interest that inform the tradition. Among their motives, we can point to their critical stance toward society in its actual and developing forms, informed by a strong ethical concern for the individual and a rejection of all possible excuses for hunger, domination, humiliation, or injustice, and a longing for a better world. Herein lies one of the main reasons for educationists to talk about Critical Theory.

Of course, any good theory and any serious theorist can be supposed to be critical. But Critical Theory is distinctive in claiming that the theorists' involvement and engagement in the reality under investigation is not an obstacle to, but a prerequisite of, their "objectivity." Objectivity is not achieved by theoretical distance from phenomena, but by personal closeness to them. Critical Theory views society from the position of the "injured" and the "vulnerable." Nor does Critical Theory find objectivity in disinterestedness. It is not itself "value-free," but interested. It usually conceives itself as a "moment" in a transformative practice directed toward creating a more humane world.

However, in the classic works of the Frankfurt School, this longing for a better world manifested itself almost exclusively in a negative way – though as we shall notice, Habermas is an important dissenter from this negativity. As Peukert says, the negativity of Critical Theory is its most irritating characteristic and yet also one of the most penetrating challenges that Critical Theory offers to Western thought; the challenge of making real our humanity and of striving continuously for a better world, but in the absence of any *telos* or meaning for human history which we could know or grasp or formulate (Peukert, 1983, pp. 204–17). (Habermas later"discovers" a *telos* – of consensus – in language.) The tradition of Jewish thought is probably the inspiration for this approach (even though Critical Theory certainly intended to avoid direct association with Jewish thought – Walter Benjamin's explicit reference to Jewish theology is an important exception). Indeed, rather than an empty nihilism, as some suppose, it is arguably the Jewish prohibition against making an image of God that is reflected in the refusal of the most important thinkers of the Frankfurt School to name a positive ideal or utopia. Any such an ideal might too easily be used to justify violence and injustice, for any attempt to realize some represented ideal seems almost necessarily to involve some exercise of terror. And a second religious lesson is also crucial. Horkheimer characterized the doctrine of "original sin" as a call on us to remember that every moment of happiness was and is bought with the suffering of others (*"Die Lehre von der Erbsunde,"* Horkheimer, 1972, p. 167). And therefore, our happiness and joy should always remain connected to sadness and mourning. With these thoughts in mind, we might characterize critical theory as a form of utopian pessimism (Gur Ze'ev, 1998).

As for its main theoretical interest, Critical Theory has always tried to investigate the relationship between the individual and social and cultural developments, and always used a variety of theories and disciplines to develop a framework for understanding. Critical Theorists also investigated empirically how social and economic structures were produced and reproduced, through and in the concrete action and thought of individuals and collectives and in relation to culture (not least in empirical studies which have had great influence in different disciplines, such as *"Studien über Autorität und Familie"* (Horkheimer et al., [1936] 1987) and the five volumes of the Studies in Prejudice, including the famous volume on "The Authoritarian Personality" (Adorno et al., 1950).

Following Peukert (1983), we can distinguish three phases in the development of Critical Theory and relate them to its influence on the theory, practice, and philosophy of education accordingly. In the first phase, a Marxist analysis of social relations was integrated with Freudian psychoanalysis into a social-psychological theory, formulated in the 1930s by Horkheimer (Horkheimer, [1937] 1977) and Marcuse (Marcuse, [1937] 1972). This synthesis allowed the Frankfurt School to clarify the relationship between psychological and social deep structures, and to see even dissatisfaction and rebellion as forces that reproduce the dominant order. The program of this phase finds expression in the empirical studies mentioned above. It was informed by an all-emcompassing notion of reason that stood in the Enlightenment tradition of reason and its promise of social justice. Yet the same writers also denounced the historical development of reason into a scientific and social positivism, which repudiates the capacity of reason to transcend "given" reality.

Although this research program could obviously have been of great relevance to educational theory, it had no contemporary reception at all in educational studies, and we have to wait until the 1970s and early 1980s to see how these analyses are taken up, after their rediscovery by the student movement and by antiauthoritarian parents of that period. Philosophy of education in Germany eventually assimilated Horkheimer's thoughts on epistemology and philosophy of science (*Wissenschaftstheorie*) through the work of Habermas, differentiating Critical Theory from both positivism and hermeneutics. And in the USA, the early Frankfurt School was taken up by Giroux in his *Critical Theory and Educational Practice* (Giroux, 1983a) and *Theory and Resistance in Education* (Giroux, 1983b).

The second phase is the period of the critique of instrumental reason. Its key texts were *Dialectic of Enlightenment* (Horkheimer and Adorno, [1947] 1991), *Negative Dialectics* (Adorno, 1966), *Eclipse of Reason* (Horkheimer, 1974), and *One-dimensional Man* (Marcuse, 1964). Here we find the most radical analyses of the complicity of Reason itself (and of culture too) in the catastrophic events of the first half of the twentieth century, analyses in which Reason is viewed as intrinsically instrumental. It was during this period that Adorno also formulated the Theory of *Halb-Bildung* (Adorno, [1959] 1972), in which he argued that *Bildung* had come to be stripped of its normative content, its relation to a good and just life. It had thus been reduced to a good that could be owned, like many other goods, and offered on the market of well-being and happiness. *Halb-Bildung* merely made people competent and fit for the existing social order, whereas originally, *Bildung* had also been meant to equip them to radically question that order.

This decline in the scope of individual autonomy is disguised by progress in science and technology. Accordingly, Horkheimer and Adorno radically changed their mind as to what is at stake in Critical Theory. With other Critical Theorists, they came to believe that the existing order was almost immunized against critique by the mass media, which rendered people insensitive to injustice. In this situation, they argued, revolution was inconceivable and all that remained was to rescue the individual from a totalitarian world, totally bureaucratized, totally economized. There remained nothing but the vulnerability, loneliness, and abandonment of the individual to call us to solidarity and resistance – a view in contrast to Habermas's later commitment to the potential of unconstrained dialogue and intersubjectivity for emancipation and solidarity.

But Critical Theory could only have a negative task in such a context. It could no longer be a positive moment in a transformative practice, but only remind us of the "totally other" and insist on its importance, appealing first to the vulnerability of the individual. Horkheimer summarized this stance as a theoretical pessimism and a practical optimism (Horkheimer, 1972, p. 175), related to an understanding of history from the standpoint of the weak and the victims. Thus Horkheimer and Benjamin emphasized that (future) progress could not justify the past victims (of history), so that a "true" perception of history should entail unreconcilable mourning.

It has been questioned whether it is really possible to do any work in educational thought with the analyses of this "dark" period, since it seems, in these interpretations, that education could only ever contribute to the reproduction of social and individual alienation. However we will later argue that critical philosophy of education has maybe too easily passed over the radical analyses and profound motives of this period.

The third period is characterized by Habermas's attempt to reinstate the original emancipatory program of Critical Theory, by reformulating the concept of *praxis*. At first, he took up the Marxist idea that science is a part or moment of the transformative economic *praxis* of material production, enabling the "species being" Man to transform the material context in which he survives and flourishes. But since science is a discourse, Habermas differentiated this *praxis* (unlike classic Marxists) into labor on the one hand, linguistic interaction on the other. And on this basis, he further distinguished three "species-general interests" – not the subjective interests of individual humans, but the objective interests of Man as a species. To the "technical" interest in economic reproduction recognized in Marxism, he added a "practical" interest in normative discourse. And on this basis, he further posited a species-general "emancipatory interest" – a necessary interest in emancipation in both social and psychological forms, and thus an interest in a critical understanding of society.

In his mature work, after taking a "linguistic [and pragmatic] turn," Habermas redeveloped the idea of an emancipatory interest within a theory of communicative competence. He argued to the necessity in human affairs of open and undistorted linguistic interaction, which he called communicative interaction. Undistorted communicative action could be contrasted with strategic interaction, defined by a suppression of true motives and an enactment of manipulative social relations. With this move, Habermas could demonstrate the necessity of communicative, as opposed to strategic, interaction for socialization, social integration, and cultural reproduction, and consequently also theorize the pathologies of society under late capitalism, in terms of a "colonization of the lifeworld" by the "strategic" discourse of dominant social forces, by the media of money and power. These analyses gave him both the motive and the means to posit a "discourse ethics" as the normative core of Critical Theory and thus make the break that he sought with the negativity and pessimism, or negative utopianism, of the earlier Frankfurt School. For insofar as the social necessity of communicative interaction entailed a social interest in open and undistorted communication, he could now posit emancipation as the *telos* of human life, implicit in the very necessity, structure, and ethics of communicative action itself, and thus of course a universal norm. However, these developments make it contestable whether Habermas is still working in the tradition of Critical Theory. He "forgets" too easily the longing for the absolute other, which, we will argue, can express itself only in a negative way.

Notwithstanding, this third period played a major role in Critical Pedagogy in Germany, Belgium, and the Netherlands between 1965 and the end of the 1970s. Critical Theory in the line of Habermas now seemed to offer a way to formulate emancipation and self-determination as the general aims of education. "Ideology critique" and analyses of communicative interaction were taken up by educationists. But the central question remained whether educational theory could describe convincingly a form of educational practice that could include moments of personal transformation and intellectual critique, without reproducing the basic instrumental logic of all traditional concepts of education that remain closely tied up to means – end reasoning. Arguably, it has not yet succeeded. We believe that success would require a reconsideration of the negative and messianic elements of the Frankfurt School, and new thinking about the concept of action and practice (see our final section).

The Educational Relevance of Critical Theory

Considering the scope and depth of Critical Theory as social theory and philosophy, and given its noneducational roots, it is easy for the skeptic to view Critical Theory of Education as importing extraneous sociopolitical considerations into educational theory, at least with partial and sectarian ambitions, or even as a kind of subversion. But to think this is to misunderstand both Critical Theory and the history of educational theory itself. The legacy of Enlightenment thinking informs the modern tradition in education quite comprehensively. Its deep influence extends far beyond educational progressivism. Rousseau's concern at least to respect the "natural" freedom of man and Kant's response, to attempt to ground respect for persons as a categorical imperative, inform liberal and even conservative attitudes to education no less than the progressive or radical. They are the moral *lingua franca* of modernity. Thus, Kantian and Enlightenment moral thinking more generally inform not just progressivism but also the traditional German educational concern with *Bildung*; while, remarkably, when Peters, Hirst, and Dearden sought to establish a mildly conservative analytic philosophy of education in Britain, it is Kant they took for inspiration, going quite against the empiricist grain of most British philosophy. What seems fundamental to modern educational thought is the post-Kantian emphasis on ideals of autonomy and critical reason as ultimate educational goals.

Typically, modern theories of education rest on some theory of the individual, usually informed by some theory of society. In fact the emergence of autonomous theories and philosophies of education, as well as of "educational sciences" and educational research, cannot be separated from the emergence of modern societies and nations; and the development of education as a field or discipline has to be related to their problems and concerns. In this context, most major theories of education have tried to resist pure instrumentalism in the service of particular and utilitarian interests and have included a plea for individual and social self-realization and self-development, over and above such interests. Given the central concern of Critical Theory with ideals of enlightenment and emancipation and its analyses of their social preconditions, it is hardly surprising that it has commended itself to many educational theorists, not as extraneous to education in the modern world but as quite fundamental to it.

Furthermore, the engaged (or "interested") theoretical position of early Critical Theory and the universalism of the later thought of Jürgen Habermas both speak clearly to modern concerns for justice in the educational arena. Moreover, notwithstanding the Marxist, and thus radical, inspiration of much earlier Critical Theory, it has never lacked a commitment to exacting intellectual standards, a concern to defend high culture and an understanding of the importance of cultural tradition. Adorno's aesthetics and the sociology of the Culture Industry developed by different members of the Frankfurt School (Adorno, Marcuse, Fromm, Benjamin) are informed by commitment to art as a sphere of demanding intellectual engagement as a last bastion against the normalizing vulgarities of capitalist modernization. (For Benjamin, the subversive aspects of modern art were also crucial.) Habermas's proposal, in his earlier work, of a basic knowledge-guiding interest in historical-hermeneutic understanding, grounded a legitimate concern for intelligent engagement with cultural tradition and its sustenance. Similarly, the erosion of the "life world" by expert cultures, which he addresses in his later work, is an area of concern where radical and conservative impulses meet. Thus the conservative address of Critical Theory is much stronger than a matter of a shared but distant Enlightenment heritage.

Has there been any actual engagement, then, between Critical Theory and conservative or analytic traditions in education? There was certainly engagement in Germany, most importantly with respect to Habermas's fruitful debate with Gadamer, in which the radical conceded much to the conservative. In the English-speaking world, however, differences of tradition have seemed like reasons to disregard telling similarities of interests and commitments. Echoes are loud between Richard Peters and Habermas. Peters' Transcendental Argument attempts to demonstrate an intrinsic human interest in enlightenment through initiation into culturally given Forms of Knowledge. Similarly, Habermas argues to an intrinsic communicative, and therefore universal, interest in maximum communicative rationality; and this, for him, entails the liberalization of interaction (and the radicalization of argument) in open and unconstrained intellectual discourse. But echoes such as these have seemed excuses for one tradition to ignore the other as much as a reason to make contact, as if to say "We can make these points better our own way."

And of course, whatever the points of similarity and however strong the aims of both schools to deal with fundamental questions for education, differences are also vivid. There are three in particular that we wish to highlight.

Distinctive Insights and Contributions

Nontransparency

First, of course, and in contrast to both the rationalist and empiricist strains in modern culture, Critical Theory questions the transparency of society to the individual consciousness, and with it, the transparency of self to self. The Frankfurt School is of course informed by two of the Masters of Suspicion, Marx and Freud.[1] In work such as Freud's *Civilisation and its Discontents*, psychoanalysis attempted to theorize the bridge between the economic base of capitalism and its reproduction through the concrete actions and thoughts of individuals. Neither Marx nor Freud accept any picture of contemporary, and in particular, modern society as in any sense natural for man or in any way to be taken for granted. Whilst both have conceptions of human nature, neither views modern society as well-adjusted to the needs of the "species being" of Man. And in this, they are both informed by historical observations on the one hand (including those of Freud), and observations of individual human misery on the other (including those of Marx). The Frankfurt School share similar perceptions and intuitions of the disgrace of modern life.

To the Enlightenment ideals of transparency, autonomy, and authenticity, both Marx and Freud in their different ways counterposed the actual delusions fostered by alienation, anomie, and fetish – psychological failings constituting false consciousness both of society and of self. It is particularly striking that Marx and Freud both make important use of the anthropological concept of fetish – of the substitution of false relationships for real ones, concealing from view those which are painfully unsatisfactory yet difficult to alter, for instance thwarted sexual attachments or exploitative labor relations. The idea of "false consciousness" formulates the insight that the truths of both society and self can be too intolerable for us to acknowledge, yet that we have to carry on living in acceptance of them.

These Marxist and Freudian concepts have recommended themselves strongly to dissenting theorists of education and indeed to cultural theorists, who have much to say to education. (For instance, they informed theories of ideology in educational thinking, particularly in the neo-Marxist "new sociology of education" of the 1970s and 1980s.) Early Critical Theory itself took over the notion of ideology critique, more or less unaltered, from Marxism, and the German Critical Pedagogy movement and Anglo-Saxon versions of Critical Theory of Education then received the idea from Frankfurt. The Freudian legacy has been less enthusiastically taken up, outside Critical Theory, except for its significant influence on the hermeneutics of Gadamer and Ricoeur. Its main educational manifestations are independent of Critical Theory, for instance the extreme and inchoate (and ultimately un-Freudian) libertarianism of A. S. Neill and the influence of child psychiatrists like Winnicott on theories of educational play.

By contrast, the original Frankfurt School was much inspired by Freud, and indeed also one could say that, *via negativa*, Adorno and others cherished a post-Freudian idea of unconstrained dialogue, indirectly referring to a post-Freudian notion of intersubjectivity. And arguably, their acknowledgment and respect for irreducible Otherness was analytically inspired. But the most distinctive feature of the reception of Freud in Critical Theory is perhaps also its most influential for education: Habermas's reconception of the process of emancipation. In Habermas's work, Critical Theory took from psychoanalysis the insight that it takes a human being to emancipate a human being (Masschelein, 1997, 1991b). His insight was that ideology critique involves a particular kind of discourse, a particular kind of interpersonal interaction, and could not be identified simply by reference to the content or subject matter of the discourse. Since personal or social truth is prey to false consciousness, monological contemplation is necessarily too vulnerable to delusion to uncover it. Only a dialogue whose participants strive for optimal mutual understanding can hope to release the subject from unconscious tutelage, whether to neurotic fantasy or to ideological illusion – and even then, only given an understanding of the dynamics proper to successful dialogue. And here we find the roots both of Habermas's later formulation of ideal speech conditions as conditions for radicalized argument, and of his later intersubjectivist and postfoundationalist epistemology. (There is seemingly here an unemphasized but useful compatibility with Wittgenstein, regarding the logical impossibility of a logically private language.) Where truth is sytematically veiled, it takes two at least to strip the veil away – no monological appeal to foundational, and thus supposedly canonic, knowledge can do so.

The implications for education of the value of unconstrained dialogue have seemed patent to many. And for all the notorious problems involved in both classic Marxist and Freudian theory, the Frankfurt School seems to some writers to have rescued from each at least some of their most valuable and enduringly defensible insights. However, we shall also point out later that, not unlike (indeed not unconnected with) postmodernism, Critical Theory (certainly in its second phase) has actually impugned the modernist ideal of authenticity and questioned the limits of autonomy. Arguably, educational theory has still to respond intelligently to these challenges.

History and philosophy

We alluded just above to a traditional strategy in philosophy, to enact critique of any view of the world by comparing its claims with those sanctioned by an appeal to the foundations of knowledge, those irrefragable "givens" which rigorous analysis may disclose in ontology, epistemology, or ethics. Accordingly, foundations are necessarily conceived in such a strategy as immune to historical change and its contingencies. (Thus philosophy supposedly secures its pre-eminence within the humanities.) So just as Habermas locates the emancipatory potential of critique in its form rather than its content, so too does his Critical Theory rescind, in critique, from appeal to foundations of knowledge. (We return, in our last section, to the question of foundations in earlier phases of Critical Theory.) In fact, insofar as it is useful to speak at all of foundations of knowledge in Critical Theory, it is only in the restricted sense of "foundations" which are contingent and historically situated. And insofar as neither society nor self are transparent, either to themselves or to each other, the discernment of situated "foundations," in science, ethics, or psychology, can only result from critical analysis – it cannot precede it. (It might of course have a later use in critique, once it has been established in critique itself.) This inverts precisely the typical stance of analytic philosophy and entails a more equal and reciprocal relationship between philosophy, culture, and education than an analytic approach would lead one to expect.[2] In fact, the process of analysis itself is seen as situated.

This may seem to bring us close to the theories of ideology in the radical educational theory of the 1970s and early 1980s. But here, critique typically appealed implicitly to positive utopian commitments wholly incompatible with the pessimistic utopianism of the Frankfurt School. Habermas, by contrast, shares the positive commitment to emancipation. But what distinguishes his position, and seems to save it from the impotence of relativism, is his insistence on the salience of dialogue in any critical exercise. Within his account of dialogue, the possibility is patent of raising meaningfully, and attempting, collaboratively but critically, to address higher-order questions in relation to any debate, or its more fundamental presuppositions; a "radicalization of argument" that makes possible both the critique of the putative "given" and a search for the historically contingent "givens" of any discourse or practice. It is in this radicalization of argument that he locates the reflexivity which, for him, is characteristic of specifically modern discourse (and for which he explicitly reserves the term "discourse"). And modernity, therefore, is explicitly a value for Habermas, because it involves this form of emancipatory reflexivity. This is one important reason for taking modernity as a criterion for educational value, distinctive not least in avoiding and indeed repudiating economistic appeals to modern instrumentalism, and the reduction of education to a technology.

Ironically, Habermas in particular is often himself accused of foundationalism (and this is sometimes taken to vitiate his universalism in ethics). But this is to blur his own distinction between form and content and to mistake his historicizing analyses of conditions of production of knowledge for an ahistorical epistemology. As he wrote,

> The universalist position does not have to deny the pluralism and the incompatibility of historical versions of "civilised humanity"; but it regards the multiplicity of forms of life as limited to cultural contents, and it asserts that every culture must share certain formal properties of the modern understanding of the world, if it is at all able to attain a certain degree of "conscious awareness." (Habermas, 1981b, p. 340)

It is sometimes alleged that, for Habermas, "West is best." Those who make this criticism take it for granted that cultural modernization is either an exclusively Western process or that it leads inexorably in the direction of Westernization. But they overlook the strong influence of Weber on Critical Theory, and in particular on Horkheimer and later, on Habermas. For Weber, modernization is an epochal historical process, whose first stirrings may be identified with monotheism and the rise of the great world religions. Habermas, drawing on anthropology, locates the origin of modernization with the decentering of consciousness into its cognitive, normative, and affective spheres, and thus with the move from a prehistoric to historic culture. Thus, as the quotation above indicates, cultural modernity is, for him, available within any culture that shares the appropriate formal properties established in this early move beyond a "magical" to a "disenchanted" form of consciousness. But no culture is impeded from modernization by its substantive cultural "foundations." On the contrary, the purely formal nature of these conditions allows many versions of modernity to be possibilities. And this in turn suggests that modernization need not be equated with cultural imperialism (Blake, 1992). This point is particularly relevant to problems in the current globalization of education, which rides on the back of the explosion in information technologies. (Habermas's concept of history and his "reconstruction" of the idea of modernity are by design very different from the critique of modern rationality offered by Horkheimer, Adorno, and Benjamin.)

The centrality of critique

Analytic philosophy of education certainly does not preclude an interest in the emancipatory potential of critique and the potential of, and for, critique in education. But this approach is most likely to value critique as a support for personal autonomy, itself valued as either an aim or a condition for education. But Critical Theory, we can now see, places critique nearer the center of educational concerns. In repudiating social or psychological transparency, while historicizing and problematizing any appeal to foundations, Critical Theory strongly repudiates any form of empiricism or rationalism. Yet the analytic tradition in educational theory has at times been complicit with them. Thus, it is possible in the analytic tradition to gloss "emancipation" as quite simply "emancipation from ignorance"; and to treat comparatively gently any "bucket theory" of knowledge (to use Popper's term for empiricist epistemology). Although analytic theorists generally now repudiate such theories of knowledge, this is arguably a later development of their basic position, rather than an integral part of it, and thus vulnerable to the kind of practice that picks and chooses from educational theory, rather than respecting its integrity. In particular, the analytic tradition is not too well equipped to repudiate contemporary redefinitions of the curriculum in terms of "information" rather than knowledge (under the influence in education of information and communications technology), and is obliged to rely on value claims here more readily than on epistemological analysis.

By contrast, Habermasian Critical Theory recognizes how fundamental are reflexive processes of critique to the development of modern forms of knowledge and the danger to the production of knowledge where processes of critical debate are subverted or baulked. Thus the value of emancipation is not one that we might choose to impose on a modern curriculum (construing "modern" in Habermas's normative sense) but one that is constitutive and central to the very processes by which that curriculum has been furnished in the first place. So in a further inversion, rather than justifying critique by appeal to the value of autonomy, autonomy itself is validated by its value for participation in critique.

Differing Receptions of Critical Theory

It seems clear that the reception of Critical Theory has differed in different national contexts; and nobody, of course, will be less surprised by this than adherents of Critical Theory, which underlines more firmly than most the significance of social and historical context in determining the reception and meaning of general ideas. We will confine ourselves to an outline of differences between Germany, Belgium, and the Netherlands, the USA, and the UK, though we should also acknowledge significant work in Italy, Spain, and South America. But beneath the differences, we also descry a common pattern of failure in reception. We will argue in our final section that the true import of Critical Theory has yet to be realized in education, and requires address to other thinkers than those mentioned so far.

In Germany, educational theory received Marx and Freud from the Frankfurt School through the mediation of the influential Critical Pedagogy movement. The influence of Habermas was vital to the process, and Marcuse also made an impact, in particular in connection with the Student Movement of the late 1960s. Progressive social movements of the time demanded of education the aim of "individual auto- nomy in a just society." Put thus broadly, this program might seem no different from that proposed in Britain by Richard Peters in *Ethics and Education.* But the difference lay in the post-Marxist concern to avoid the reproduction of alienation, and to "cash" this ambition in terms of a critical understanding of the specific historic moment. The key figure here, besides Wolfgang Klafki (Klafki, 1976), was Klaus Mollenhauer (Mollenhauer, 1972). He saw the task as resisting conceptions of education that pre-empt the legitimate interests that individuals have in understand- ing their world by prioritizing the extraneous requirements of state, economy, church, "society," or culture.

Mollenhauer's first attempt at Critical Pedagogy drew on Habermas's early philo- sophical anthropology to demonstrate an immanent developmental direction in his- tory. If, according to *Knowledge and Human Interests* (Habermas, 1971b), Man as a species is driven by a knowledge-guiding interest in emancipatory critique no less than by any interest in hermeneutic-historical and technical-scientific understanding, then education could justify a critical orientation without begging any particular, substantive, and sectional norms. In this light, both the idealist and ahistorical hermeneutic tradition in pedagogy and the new, positivist, supposedly value-free empirical orientation seemed revealed as self-subverting in their willful disregard of their own historical conditioning, as products themselves of emancipatory critique (see W. Carr, 1995, pp. 104–7 for a useful discussion of positivism in this respect). Critical education could be conceived as a process of self-reflection modeled on the psychoanalytic paradigm of emancipation. The catch was, however, that education needs a curriculum. Thus the emancipatory dialogue would be pre-empted, in prac- tice, by specific and substantive positions in ideology critique. The dialogue of emancipation had to lead to a politically predetermined terminus.

This was a problem for Critical Theory, no less than for education. Mollenhauer later reformulated Critical Pedagogy in the light of Habermas's first attempt at a revision, his introductory remarks to a theory of communicative competence

(Habermas, 1971a, translated as Habermas, 1970b). Like Peters and Hirst, he now saw the task as to specify a goal intrinsic rather than extrinsic to the educational engagement. For Mollenhauer, the goal is unconstrained (and therefore emancipatory) understanding between student and teacher. This requires undistorted communicative interaction, which has its own intrinsic norms – norms that moreover provide criteria for distinguishing between unconstrained, and therefore genuine, consensus and a false consensus of submission to pressure. (Unhelpfully, Habermas's translators call the latter a "moral" consensus. But what is meant by this, in fact, is a consensus coerced by the pressure of moral conformism, and thus to be repudiated.) True consensus recognizes only "the 'unforced force' of the better argument" (Habermas's often-used phrase), and is thus intrinsically educative.

This version of pedagogy has been criticized at least in two aspects (see Masschelein, 1991a, 1991b, 1998; Blake, 1992). We can first point to the inapplicability of this ideal to the education of children and to its still inherently instrumental character. No such dialogue is possible unless the child both wants understanding and can be known in fact (and not just supposed in principle) to want understanding. Yet this knowledge of the child's genuine wishes presupposes the autonomy of the child, necessary for communicative transparency. But according to Mollenhauer this autonomy and transparency is precisely what education seeks to achieve. So the conditions are circular. Moreover, communicative interaction is understood not as constitutive of education but as its goal, and therefore remains caught in an instrumental logic – an "end" of educational action, requiring appropriate "means." Moreover, the very idea of transparency as a possible ideal of human dialogue can be questioned.

Furthermore, drawing on Habermas's position in the Theory of Communicative Action (Habermas, 1981b), we can object that communicative action should not be conflated with discourse, a critical form of interaction that may make a reflexive appeal to higher-order questions. Most communicative action does not require to be discursive in character or benefit from being so. Thus, while educative interaction should be communicative rather than "strategic" (or manipulative), it does not follow directly that it should be modeled on discourse – a specific form of interaction typical of high modernity in the realm of culture, science, and law.

American theorists developed their own critical pedagogy from the beginning of the 1980s (see Giroux, 1983a; McLaren, 1989). The first of these was Giroux, who was inspired by the early critical theory of Horkheimer and Adorno but principally by Marcuse's analyses of dominant ideology as reified consciousness. Giroux's *Theory and Resistance in Education. A Pedagogy for the Opposition* (Giroux, 1983b) can be considered as the most important and only extensive American pedagogical study which uses the analyses of early Critical Theory in a fruitful way. Giroux emphasized first a concrete analysis of how education reproduced the actual social capitalist order and therefore had to be seen as alienating and repressive. He was interested mainly in the ways in which schools produced a "false consciousness," that reproduced the dominant ideology and in this way helped to make the system immune from critique. Giroux insisted that schools can play a different, critical, and even revolutionary role to the extent that they are conceived as democratic public spaces of action and dialogue, in which false consciousness is dissolved and students learn to reflect on social and political questions. In some of his later work, therefore, he emphasizes that critical pedagogy has to develop not only "a language of critique" but also "a language of possibility" and a positively formulated vision of democracy (Giroux, 1989).

Here, the later line of development of American critical pedagogy becomes clear, and Critical Theory plays only a marginal role in it. The project was mainly determined by Paolo Freire's *Pedagogy of the Oppressed* (Freire, 1973) and the so-called "New Sociology of Education" (which included Bourdieu and Bernstein), which worked against a background of Deweyan pragmatism, Marxist historical materialism, and Gramscian antihegemonism. These were also strong influences on other representatives of American critical pedagogy such as Aronowitz, Apple, and McLaren. All these authors emphasize that the school is a place of social reproduction and of possible social and political change. In Freire's analysis of depository education and in the (Marxist) sociological analysis of the hidden curriculum, they find schemes that clarify how schools are reproducing existing power constellations. Out of this came (and still come) very interesting and detailed studies of the mechanisms of reproduction at work in schools, like McLaren's much praised study on educational rituals *Schooling as Ritual Performance* (McLaren, 1999) or Gee, Hull, and Lankshear's study on the language of new capitalism in education, *The New Work Order* (Gee et al., 1996). A strong engagement in concrete political action and liberation movements, mainly in South America (see recently McLaren, 2000), is very typical for American critical pedagogy, and in this it is different from critical pedagogy in Europe.

However, like its European counterparts, American critical pedagogy remains attached to a strongly instrumental and functional concept of educational practice, because it has not questioned the very concept of educational *praxis* itself but conceived it as an *instrument* for liberation or repression. Educational *praxis* still receives its meaning from the goal or end at which it should aim, here conceived as a utopia. Education then becomes the realization or execution of this ideal or program (see Masschelein, 1998). Critical pedagogy thus formulates essentially and fundamentally a technological project. Its first step is the formulation of an ideal or utopia, which it uncritically supposes both possible and necessary. It thus remains itself subject to the same instrumental logic that it deplores at the heart of the capitalist system.

There has been no genuine tradition of Critical Theory of education in Britain. In sociology of education, the Marxist influences of the 1970s and 1980s flowed rather from the Althusserian orthodoxies of left-leaning social sciences in Britain at that time, typified in the writings of the circle around Michael F. D. Young, with their unacknowledged yet controversial philosophical skepticism. Here, the emphasis is on education as a form of social control, in versions philosophically more "advanced" than that of, for instance, Bowles and Gintis. For cultural theory, by contrast, the influence of Gramsci was again important, particularly in its concerns with language and culture, hegemony and the possibility of counterhegemonic change (especially from within popular culture). This influence, with others from the disparate field of "Western Marxism," filtered especially through the work of the literary and media scholar Raymond Williams (e.g., Williams, 1977, 1981), and was manifest most directly in the work of the Birmingham Centre for Cultural Studies.

In philosophy of education itself, Marxism in general made no impact in Britain (but some in Australia, for instance in the work of Kevin Harris), and this beyond doubt is explained by a profound academic and political mistrust of Marxism, not least in the wake of the student disturbances of 1968. With regard to Critical Theory, this nonoccurence also arguably reflected not just the past potency of the analytic tradition within a small field, but perhaps too the similarities already noticed between the positions of Habermas and Peters. These similarities, and perhaps in particular their shared roots in the Kantian tradition, opened up a route into Critical Theory, even as they weakened motives for actually following that route. However, the writings of Wilfred Carr (with his colleague Stephen Kemmis) were an important dissenting voice in the 1980s, drawing on both Critical Theory and a reading of Gadamer, for an important critique of the role and nature of educational theory itself (Carr and Kemmis, 1986; Carr, 1995). Carr questioned the theory/practice dichotomy from a position usefully distinct from Action Research. His neo-Aristotelian analysis of educational practice has been particularly influential, not least in South America, and his insistence on its necessary historical dimension marked the earliest appearance in British philosophy of education of the historical emphases so important for both Critical Theory and hermeneutics. In the 1990s, dissatisfaction with the classic British paradigm became manifest in a wide variety of new departures, addressed elsewhere in this book. Of this group, it is Blake who has taken an interest in Critical Theory, while trying to balance this interest with some aspects of post-structuralism (particularly from the work of Lyotard and Foucault). For Blake, it is Habermas's account of modernity and modernization, his postfoundationalist pragmatics, and his account of the role of critique in a distinctively modern social production of knowledge, which are fundamental (Blake, 1992, 1995a, 1996b). Blake also re-examines the implications for pedagogy of the idea of ideal speech conditions, emphasizing the difference between Habermas's two distinctions, communicative/strategic and discursive/prediscursive (Blake, 1995b).

Critical Theory and the Student Movement

Arguably, the most potent influence of Critical Theory on education has been ironically through its "mis"reception by the student movements of the late 1960s. While political and academic reaction against those movements was violent, few would deny that the contemporary educational landscape, at least in higher education, now bears their deep imprint. Heightened emphases on student autonomy and independent learning, interest in processes of group learning, a much broadened curriculum (now including such new disciplines as Cultural Theory and Women's, Black, or Gay Studies), and an attack on "the canon" all have roots in the student movements, not least in their heightened sensitivity to the role of power in education. Obviously, the influences of Foucault and feminism have also been important here. But arguably, the student reception of Critical Theory in Berlin, during 1965–7, provided the original matrix in which these new influences managed to emerge and exert themselves in Paris and throughout the West in 1968. Yet ironically, the new vocationalist managerialism of the 1990s has suborned many of these educational developments for instrumental purposes functional for globalized capitalism, while antithetical to Critical Theory. That this has been possible may be related to the nature of the "mis"reception of Critical Theory by the student movement.

Significantly, the German student movement erupted at the Free University of Berlin, the first educational flower (founded in 1810) of the German Enlightenment. Justifiable complaints about both underresourcing and a deadening academicism of the curriculum swiftly merged with worries about the suppression of free speech in Cold War conditions. And yet representatives of the Frankfurt School recoiled from these protests, notwithstanding shared Left political agendas. Adorno reacted in horror to a perceived desecration of high culture and its authority, which the students seemed to legitimate by reference to Critical Theory. Similarly, Habermas fiercely repudiated what he saw as a dogmatization of ideology critique, detached from any commitment to open and undistorted discourse. Famously, if excessively, he branded the student leaders as "Red Fascists."[3] But we may wonder whether we can see here in retrospect some early forms of an opportunistic instrumentalization of critique that arguably has been coopted into contemporary managerialism in education.

In the UK, while the student movement knew about the Frankfurt School, they lacked the intellectual roots in German philosophy to receive it intelligently (the British philosophical tradition being even more rigidly empiricist than the American). British students equated Critical Theory with Marcuse's utopianism, while his notion of "repressive tolerance" was vilified by reaction as just a contradiction in terms.

We find it surprising and regrettable that Habermas's contemporary analyses of the Student Movements (see Habermas, 1969, for three important essays on these events, collected in English in Habermas, 1987b) has had so little impact even on Critical Theory in Education. Given the importance of history to Critical Theory, it is ironic that his historical analysis has been obscured in education by his more abstract theory.

An "Other" Critical Pedagogy?

So does Critical Theory still matter now? Does it still make sense to listen to its representatives? We think it certainly does. We now live in a world that tries to teach us that, after the demise of most communist regimes, it is no longer meaningful or necessary to long for a radically different and better world, since the new social order is itself based on the value of freedom; and remaining inequalities and injustices arise not from fundamental shortcomings of that order, but either from temporary problems that will be solved by future social "research and development" or from the merely personal inadequacies of those who suffer through their own fault. In such a world, it seems crucial to us to recall a teaching that lies at the heart of Critical Theory. It teaches that past and present suffering and injustice have always affected and do always affect singular beings, and therefore cannot be resolved (or answered) *without any deficit* by *future* development. This means that wise thinking always implies a certain sadness and a certain burden of experience, which nonetheless speaks to us of the possibility of a radically different order of things. This deep motive should be at the heart of any critical pedagogy or critical philosophy of education that feels the need to question the current triumph of a "realism" that seems to neutralize every form of utopian longing. As stated before, the challenge posed by Critical Theory is to keep alive this critical utopian motive and critical questioning in the absence of any *telos* or meaning for human history that we could know or represent.

In our view, taking up that challenge has to imply a re-examination of the notions of critique and of action that currently inform most of our thought about education and educational practice (see also Masschelein and Smeyers, 2000). In this latter tradition, thought and action are identified with the representation of a better world and its consequent realization or accomplishment. Therefore it is always prone to involve an instrumental or functionalist logic.

In fact, this implicitly technical and instrumental tradition of educational *praxis* has, as we have seen, been continued by most of the educational theorists who have been inspired by Critical Theory (such as Mollenhauer, Giroux, McLaren, etc.) and who distil from their analyses some kind of educational program to be executed in the future, in order to improve society. They use Critical Theory to "found" or "ground" the ideals that are stated as educational goals or end-states to be achieved, marginalizing the negativism of Critical Theory and reproducing an instrumentalist notion of education.

This raises the question in what sense either the First or Second Frankfurt Schools were foundationalist and also how the "utopian moment" of Critical Theory became instrumentalized, so that educational programs (those of critical pedagogy and of the Critical Thinking movement) substituted a positivistic ameliorism for critical awareness of the "intolerable" experience of injustice. We think that this is at least partly a consequence of the unclarity of the notion of *praxis* in Critical Theory.

As noted earlier, Critical Theory conceived itself as a moment in a transformative *praxis*. But as Habermas has rightly seen, the notion of *praxis* is either very unclear or simply identical to a notion of Labor as Man's transformation of nature. (In Habermas's terms, this notion of Labor overlooks the distinction between labor and communicative action or interaction; in Arendt's terms, it misses the distinction between speech and action and identifies work with mere labor). The concept of *praxis* as labor/work informs what is paradoxical in the thinking of Critical Theorists concerning education. Although Horkheimer and Adorno fulminate against a total "scientification" (*Verwissenschaftlichung*) and technologization (*Technologisierung*) of society, they themselves are looking for ways in which results of social-scientific research can determine the development of practice, and so they fall back into very instrumentalistic thinking. So in his foreword to the "Studies in Prejudice," which highlighted the sociological and social-psychological backgrounds of prejudice, Horkheimer expressed his hope that these studies would lead to a new "scientific" planning of education (in Adorno et al. 1950, p. vii). Similarly, Marcuse at one point pleads for an "educational dictatorship" that educates the population, starting out from socialist ideas (Marcuse, in Korthals, 1981, p. 45). Even Adorno in his famous essay "Education after Auschwitz" concluded that people "enlightened" by the social sciences should go out "to the countryside" to instruct the people about the true state of affairs (Adorno, 1971a, p. 94).

It is clear to us, then, that if we want to take Critical Theory seriously, we have to analyze this concept of *praxis* critically and follow Habermas in his initial differentiation of it into labor and language. However, we also think that it is necessary to radicalize his analysis of communication and human interaction by taking up the analyses of, for example Levinas and Arendt (Levinas, 1987; Hand, 1989; Arendt, 1958). Habermas's move from content to form shines no light on the radical contingency and nonreciprocity that lie at the heart of communication and action. He dissolves the contingency of communication in a new determination of it as (rational) procedure, stripping communicators of their irresolvable difference and singularity without which "human" communication is not human. And he "forgets" too easily that reciprocal recognition in communication between persons cannot simply be conceptualized in terms of the economic and rational logic of performance and counterperformance (I recognize you when you recognize me), but that the gift of "trust" also has to include a noneconomic aspect, a gift to the other with no certainty of reciprocation, a gift without which there would be no recognition to begin with. It is this noneconomic element (which impedes a too facile conception of reciprocity), together with the absolute difference that relates human beings to each other (precisely in their difference which makes them not indifferent), which is crucial for a reconception of action in noninstrumental or nonfunctionalist terms.

Starting from a noninstrumental concept of action, it should be possible to begin to develop a critical philosophy of education and a critical pedagogy "without foundation." This critical pedagogy could also take on from Critical Theory its research interest in relationships between the individual and social and cultural developments. As we have seen, Critical Theorists always used a variety of theories and disciplines to develop a framework for understanding and for investigating empirically how social and economic structures were produced and reproduced, through and in the concrete action and thought of individuals and collectives (and in relation to culture). In this regard and in our view, one theorist whose work could be of much use is Foucault. He offers interesting theoretical tools that could allow us to shed a light on the contemporary construct of the "learning society" and to demonstrate that this construct, which appeals to supposedly inescapable logics, in fact remains merely a contingent development. By the same token, we could repudiate those critical pedagogical approaches that see education as merely an expression (or failure of expression) of some principle (for example, the ideal of autonomy) or as bound by the logic of capital, and conceive of it rather as an aspect of a new kind of "governmentality" (see the very promising attempt in this direction by Hunter, 1996). Together with other resources offered by Lyotard, Arendt, Levinas, and others, it could also allow us to address once again another important issue of society's anesthetization to injustice.

In fact, critical pedagogy, as it has developed until now, seems in a certain sense rather to have contributed to the immunization of society against critique. It has contributed to the way that "critical competence" and "communicative competence" have become standard ends of education and even standard prerequisites of operating and functioning within the given order, thus robbing critique and communication of their element of transcendence of the given order. It has substituted a positivist ameliorism for a critical awareness of the "intolerable" experience of injustice. We agree with Foucault that any program is destined to reproduce injustice, even as it tries to eradicate it. The problem is not just that any instrumental approach to social engagement (including education) will inherently fail to treat persons as ends in themselves. More fundamentally, social action (including educational action) is itself realized in speech, so that educational speech need not be seen as a means to some end already specified – yet this is the picture presupposed in the idea of an educational program. Educational conversation is neither tutor-centered nor student-centered (nor subject-centered) – it is not "centered" at all. If it were, it would cease to be dialogue.

But has the "linguistic turn" of Critical Theory made it easier for us to repudiate instrumentalism, acknowledge difference and nonreciprocity (as noneconomic relations), to abandon any appeal to foundations and to formulate a decentered account of education? We doubt whether the linguistic turn is sufficient. The deeper failure has been to overlook the most serious motive behind Critical Theory, its negative aspect and Messianic impulse, transforming it into a positivistic form of ideology critique and program building. But the point of Critical Theory is not that it envisages a "positive utopia" but that it is informed by a sharpened experience of the actual and intolerable injustice of the world as it currently exists. Current revivals of Critical Theory arguably have lost a grasp of this critical potential. (Nonetheless, the Messianic impulse in Adorno and Horkheimer and in Benjamin has been received by Masschelein and Gur Ze'ev, though in different ways – the issue between them is foundationalism.)

Capitalism promotes indefinite and inexhaustible change. Yet nonetheless, the parameters of capitalism still exclude more than they include. Critical Theory seeks to show the possibility of change beyond these parameters (and of a change of the accepted parameters themselves), but without falling into the trap (again best described by Foucault) of prespecifying what changes may be desirable. To the positivist mind, no call for change is credible unless the alternative can be plausibly described in advance. Yet to respond to the negative aspect of Critical Theory is to accept as valid the cry, "I don't know what, but not this!" – and thus to repudiate the fatalism of a seemingly compulsory acceptance of the present. (Compare Foucault's alleged "nihilism" as a form of Nietzschean self-assertion and resistance, enacted within the circuits of power/knowledge via "techniques of the self.")

If Critical Theory is not to be read in an instrumental spirit, and yet is to be seen as important to the education of teachers, then teacher education must be treated as more than just a form of teacher training (even one characterized by a deeper understanding and reflective consciousness). Teacher education in the spirit of Critical Theory must have a transformative aspect. A teacher might perhaps come to be seen as being as good as her or his own sense of dissatisfaction.

Notes

1 The reception of Nietzsche in Critical Theory is more equivocal. Habermas has famously objected to what he sees as Nietzsche's nihilistic influence on post-structuralism in particular. But Horkheimer and Adorno strongly appreciated his critical attitude.
2 For an account of this different relationship, see Habermas (1990a).
3 For an account of this episode, see Robert Holub (Holub, 1991, chapter 4).

Recommendations for Further Reading

Carr, W. (1995) *For Education: Towards Critical Educational Enquiry*, Open University Press.

Giroux, H. (1983) *Critical Theory and Educational Practice*, Deakin.

Habermas, J. (1987b) *Towards a Rational Society*, Polity Press.

Horkheimer, M. (1972) Traditional and critical theory, in *Critical Theory: Selected Essays*, trans. Matthew J. O'Connell et al., Seabury Press.

Chapter 3

Postmodernism/
Post-structuralism

Michael Peters and Kenneth Wain

The Meanings of "Postmodernism"

There has been such a huge outpouring of literature in education on both post-modernism and post-structuralism in the last decade that it is now intimidating in its scope and depth of scholarship. If we are also to count the parallel literatures in the social sciences and the humanities, then the overlapping literatures assume immense proportions, defying the activities of any one scholar to summarize or to synthesize. Indeed, various scholars have now begun to chart and periodize aspects of "post-modernism" in terms of its historical development. Charles Jencks has recorded 70 such related uses, including "post-industrial," "postminimalism," "post-Marxism" and "post-liberal era," and charted a genealogy of "postmodernism" in terms of its prehistory (1870–1950), its positive definition (1950–80), and its final phase characterized by attacks upon it and its anthologization (Jencks, 1996, pp. 14–15).

There are notorious difficulties with pinning down the meaning and origins of the word "postmodern." Several attempts have been made at both. Ihab Hassan (Hassan, 1993), who inspired Lyotard's use of the term in *The Postmodern Condition* (Lyotard, 1984), cites Federico de Onis as the first to use it in 1934, while Docherty (1993) cites Toynbee as its originator, in 1939. Best and Kellner, on the other hand, locate it much earlier (Best and Kellner, 1991). Their "genealogy" of the term takes them back to Rudolf Pannowitz who, following up on Nietzsche's announcement of the dawning of a new age of nihilism, used the term "postmodern" in 1917 in relation to what he saw as a historical collapse of values in contemporary Europe. Pannowitz remarked that this "collapse" had produced a fascist generation of "postmodern men." Best and Kellner describe how, in the 1950s, postmodernism came into focus as a cultural phenomenon when, in reaction to the self-referential formalism of the Bauhaus, it was theorized by such as Robert Venturi, Denise Scott Brown, and Charles Jencks as architectural philosophy. From architecture, they say, the debate about postmodernism quickly proliferated through the other disciplines in the United States, also becoming controversial. Hassan refers to the "rather disconsolate" way in which the word was related to "the falling off of the great modernist movement" in the late 1950s. But he goes on to describe its rehabilitation at his and Leslie Fiedler's hands during the 1960s when, he says, they used it with "premature approbation, and even with a touch of bravado" (Hassan, 1993, p. 147). By the 1980s, "the postmodern discourses were split into cultural conservatives decrying the new developments and avant-gardists celebrating them" (Best and Kellner, 1991, p. 15).

Best and Kellner explain the French openness to postmodern suggestions as resonating well with the old counter-Enlightenment, antirationalist, romantic thread running through French literary and intellectual culture from de Sade to Bataille and Artaud, and including also Baudelaire and Rimbaud. We might also mention the German antirationalist tradition, contemporary with and oppositional to the high Kantian/post-Kantian tradition, running from Hamann through Herder to Fichte, and taking in Kierkegaard and Nietzsche.[1] The influence of this tradition, they contend, grew in strength following World War II when, like many other Western countries, France went through a rapid process of destabilizing modernization. This experience produced a spate of social theories designed to articulate the dynamics of change. And the key expression of this discourse, developed simultaneously by Daniel Bell and Alain Touraine, was the expression "postindustrial," although the term might be better used for the kind of modernization process that France underwent during the 1980s. But the decisive philosophical influences on the French writers who subsequently came to be referred to as "postmodernists" were German, namely Nietzsche and Heidegger. So was the social theory, which was mainly Weberian and Frankfurt School. With this kind of pedigree, it is unsurprising that their "postmodernism" presents itself not as a homogeneous but as a very complex discourse. The way social theorists define it, however, is as a general cultural *ethos* marked by an attitude of deep "suspiciousness towards metanarratives," as Lyotard famously put it.

Lyotard insists that postmodernism be regarded not as a radical break with the modern, a total cultural rupture signifying a brand new epoch, but as that which "in the modern, puts forward the unpresentable in presentation itself" (Lyotard, 1984, p. 81): that which defies the categorization or judgement of the present because it operates outside its rules and criteria and has the character of an event. The unpresentable, in short, is sheer creativity. It is, as Lyotard's own example from the history of modern art illustrates, the avant garde. Who, then, are the postmodernists? Hassan provides a huge and heterogenous list, but the term is usually used today, in philosophical circles at least, for French writers like Lyotard himself, Derrida, Foucault, Deleuze, Guattari, and Baudrillard. And, in the Anglo-Saxon camp, Richard Rorty. It does not help much, in terms of stabilizing a definition, that most have, at different times, disclaimed the title. But this means that we should be careful to distinguish postmodernism from "post-structuralism."

The so-called "critique of reason" and of the *grand récits* of the Enlightenment and the Renaissance – Lyotard's focus in *The Postmodern Condition* – is still the central question for critical philosophy: the legitimation of knowledge in face of the emergence in "the modern" of both a "technical" and "administrative" reason. National education systems in the contemporary era are still caught between satisfying these twin demands: the administrative reason of the state apparatus and the technical reason promoted by the market and industrialism in general. Certainly, as everyone who has a fleeting familiarity with the on-going debate knows, one of the classic statements comes from Jean-François Lyotard's *The Postmodern Condition*, first published in France in 1979 (Lyotard, 1984).

We ought not to be surprised that the term "postmodernism" should eventually face its own linguistic limit – its own narrative endgame. Indeed, if we take Jean-François Lyotard's insight given in the essay "Answering the Question: What is Postmodernism?" that postmodernism is "not modernism at its end but in its nascent state and that state is constant" (Lyotard, 1984, p. 79), then, culturally speaking, we should *expect* it. Lyotard raises the question of "the postmodern" in his discussion of the Kantian sublime (that overwhelming aesthetic experience which defies artistic representation) and the attempt to *present the unpresentable* that he considers as a characterization of the history of successive avant-gardes, whose impulse is now exhausted. His observation is worthy of repeating here once more:

> What, then, is the postmodern? What place does it or does it not occupy in the vertiginous work of the questions hurled at the rules of image and narration? It is undoubtedly a part of the modern. All that has been received, if only yesterday (*modo, modo*, Petronious used to say), must be suspected. What space does Cézanne challenge? The Impressionists'. What object do Picasso and Braque attack? Cézanne's. What pre-supposition does Duchamp break with in 1912? That which says one must make a painting, be it cubist. And Buren questions that other presupposition which he believes had survived untouched by the work of Duchamp: the place of presentation of the work. In an amazing acceleration, the generations precipitate themselves. A work can become modern only if it is first postmodern. (Lyotard, 1984, p. 79)

The "post" considered as an indicator of "what comes after" is a classic modernist trope that, historically, has come to define philosophy after Kant: a break or "rup-ture" with the past that is "in fact a way of forgetting or repressing the past, that is to say, repeating it and not surpassing it" (Lyotard, 1992, p. 90). Yet in respect of art, literature, philosophy, and politics, Lyotard argues:

> the "post" of "postmodern" does not signify a movement of *comeback, flashback* or *feedback*, that is, not a movement of repetition but a procedure in "ana-": a procedure of analysis, anamnesis, anagogy and anamorphosis which elaborates an "initial forget-ting." (Lyotard, 1992, p. 93)

Clearly, when we come to understand postmodernism in relation to the field of education, we must come to terms with both features: *postmodernism* as a movement in the arts – *high* modernism – insofar as it becomes significant not only for the arts curriculum, for education considered as an art, but also for the range of new approaches that have developed in the modern tradition of criticism; and, also postmodernity, the ethos, the attitude, even the style characteristic of a historical valuation of "the modern."

In one of the earliest statements in relation to education, Henry Giroux, in an article published in 1988 "Postmodernism and the Discourse of Educational Criticism" (in Aronowitz and Giroux, 1991), addressed the issues in terms of a problematics involving three themes: the crisis of totality and foundationalism; culture and the problematic of otherness; the crisis of language, representation, and agency. While Giroux still used the language of "crisis" – a reflection of his attempt to weld "an emancipatory postmodernism" to "a critical and reflexive modernism" – his statement of the major themes as they involve education shows considerable foresight. Since Giroux's statement in 1988 there have been many books and articles published in the field of education dealing with postmodernism (see our Recommendations for Further Reading below).

The Meanings of Post-structuralism

As we have argued, there has been a tendency in the literature to conflate postmodernism and post-structuralism. In this section we want briefly to make the case for the differences between the terms and to outline quite schematically some of the main features of post-structuralism, finally commenting upon their significance for education.

Post-structuralism will be resisted in the domain of educational theory and research for some time to come, not only for the reason that this domain, at least in the mainstream, is inherently conservative, being largely state or federally funded and still strongly imbued with the positivist ethos it inherited during its historical development and professionalization as a legitimate field of study, but also because post-structuralism – if we can both risk and indulge a singularization – at the broadest level carries with its philosophical reaction to the scientific pretensions of structuralism, a critique of the very Enlightenment norms that "education research" today prides itself on: "truth," "objectivity," "progress." Post-structuralism as a contemporary philosophical movement offers a range of theories (of the text), critiques (of institutions), new concepts, and forms of analysis (of power) that are relevant and significant for the study of education, but also it offers a range of writings explicitly devoted to education.

Post-structuralism is a difficult term to define. It has often been confused with its kinship term, postmodernism, and, indeed, some critics have argued that the latter term, through patterns of established usage, has come to subsume post-structuralism. We can distinguish between the two terms by recognizing the difference between their theoretical objects of study. Post-structuralism takes as it theoretical object "structuralism," whereas postmodernism takes as its theoretical object "modernism." Post-structuralism can be characterized as a mode of thinking, a style of philosophizing, and a kind of writing, yet the term should not be used to convey a sense of homogeneity, singularity, and unity. The very term "post-structuralism" is not uncontested. Mark Poster remarks that the term post-structuralism is American in origin and that "post-structuralist theory" names a uniquely American practice, which is based upon an assimilation of the work of a diverse range of theorists (Poster, 1989, p. 6).

More generally, we might say that the term is a label used in the English-speaking academic community to describe a distinctively philosophical response to the structuralism characterizing the work of Claude Lévi-Strauss (anthropology), Louis Althusser (Marxism), Jacques Lacan (psychoanalysis), and Roland Barthes (literature) (see Gadet, 1989). Manfred Frank (1988), a contemporary German philosopher, for his part prefers the term "neo-structuralism," emphasizing a continuity with "structuralism," as does John Sturrock who, focusing upon Jacques Derrida the "Post-Structuralist" – indeed, "the weightiest and most acute critic Structuralism has had" – discusses the "post" in "post-Structuralism" in terms of "coming after and of seeking to extend Structuralism in its rightful direction" (Sturrock, 1986, p. 137). He continues: "Post-Structuralism is a critique of Structuralism conducted from within: that is, it turns certain of Structuralism's arguments against itself and points to certain fundamental inconsistencies in their method which Structuralists have ignored" (ibid.). Richard Harland (Harland, 1987), by contrast, coins the term "superstructuralism" as a single umbrella based on an underlying framework of assumptions common to "structuralists, Post-structuralists, (European) Semioticians, Althusserian Marxists, Lacanians, Foucauldians, et al." (Harland, 1993, pp. ix–x). All of these locutions "post-structuralism," "neo-structuralism," and "superstructuralism" entertain as central the movement's historical, institutional, and theoretical proximity to "structuralism." Yet post-structuralism cannot be simply reduced to a set of shared assumptions, a method, a theory, or even a school. It is best referred to as a movement of thought – a complex skein of thought – embodying different forms of critical practice. It is decidedly interdisciplinary and has many different but related strands.

Post-structuralism, then, can be interpreted as a specifically philosophical response to the alleged scientific status of structuralism – to its status as a meta-paradigm for the social sciences – and as a movement which, under the inspiration of Friedrich Nietzsche, Martin Heidegger, and others, sought to decenter the "structures," systematicity, and scientific status of structuralism, to critique its underlying metaphysics, and to extend it in a number of different directions, while at the same time preserving central elements of structuralism's critique of the humanist subject. Its main theoretical tendencies and innovations can be summarized in terms of its affinities and differences with structuralism.

Affinities

1 *The critique of Renaissance humanist philosophy and the rational, autonomous, self-transparent, subject of humanist thought* (e.g., Foucault, 1972). There is a shared suspicion of phenomenology's and existentialism's privileging of human consciousness as autonomous, directly accessible, and as the sole basis of historical interpretation, understanding, and action.
2 *A general theoretical understanding of language and culture in terms of linguistic and symbolic systems.* The interrelations of constituent elements are regarded as more important than the elements considered in isolation from one another. Both structuralism and post-structuralism take up the Saussurean belief – and innovative methodologies based upon its insights – that linguistic signs act relationally rather than referentially (see Saussure, 1959).
3 *A general belief in the Unconscious and in hidden structures or sociohistorical forces that, to a large extent, constrain and govern our behavior.* Much of the innovation of

structuralism and post-structuralism is directly indebted to Freud's study of the Unconscious and his clinical investigations which undermined the prevalent philosophical view of the pure rationality and self-transparency of the subject, substituting a greater complexity that called into question traditional distinctions of reason/unreason (madness).

4 *A shared intellectual inheritance and tradition based upon Saussure, Jacobson, the Russian formalists, Freud, and Marx, among other thinkers.* This shared intellectual history is like a complex skein that has many strands. We might call one aspect of it European Formalism, beginning in pre-Revolutionary Russia, in Geneva, and in Jena, with simultaneous and overlapping developments in linguistics, poetics, art, science, and literature.

Differences

1 *The reintroduction of history.* Where structuralism sought to efface history through synchronic analyses of structures, post-structuralism brings about a renewed interest in a critical history through a re-emphasis on diachronic analyses, on the mutation, transformation, and discontinuity of structures, on serialization, repetition, "archeology," and, perhaps most importantly, what Foucault, following Nietzsche, calls genealogy (Nietzsche, 1967; Foucault, 1977). Genealogy is a form of historical analysis that inquires into the formation and structure of value through a variety of techniques, including both etymological and conceptual scrutiny. Genealogical narratives are seen to replace ontology or, to express the same thought in a different way, questions of ontology become historicized.

2 *The challenge to scientism in the human sciences, an antifoundationalism in epistemology, and a new emphasis upon perspectivism in interpretation.* Post-structuralism challenges the rationalism and realism that structuralism continues from positivism, with its Promethean faith in scientific method, in progress, and in the capacity of the structuralist approach to discern and identify universal structures of all cultures and the human mind.

3 *The rediscovery of Nietzsche and Heidegger's interpretation of Nietzsche as the "last metaphysician."* Nietzsche's work provides a new way to theorize and conceive of the discursive operation of power and desire in the constitution and self-overcoming of human subjects. Heidegger, in his multivolumed *Nietzsche* (Heidegger, 1991), first published in 1961, focuses upon *The Will to Power* – a work assembled from notes and first published posthumously by Nietzsche's sister – and interprets Nietzsche as the last metaphysician. Derrida, in particular, takes issue with Heidegger's "reductive" interpretation, and translates Heidegger's "destruction" of the history of Western metaphysics as "deconstruction." "Deconstruction," the term most famously associated with Derrida, is a practice of reading and writing, a mode of analysis and criticism that depends deeply upon an interpretation of the question of style. In this Derrida follows a Nietzschean–Heideggerian line of thought that repudiates Platonism as the source of all metaphysics in the West from St. Paul to Kant, Mill, and Marx. Where Heidegger still sees in Nietzsche the last strands of an inverted Platonism, tied to the metaphysics of the *will to power*, and pictures himself as the first genuinely

post-metaphysical thinker, Derrida, in his turn, while acknowledging his debt, detects in Heidegger's notion of Being a residual and nostalgic vestige of metaphysics. He agrees with Heidegger that the most important philosophical task is to break free from the "logocentrism" of Western philosophy – the self-presence, immediacy, and univocity – that clouds our view and manifests its nihilistic impulses in Western culture. And yet "breaking free" does not mean overcoming metaphysics. Deconstruction substitutes a critical practice focused upon texts for the ineffable or the inexpressible. It does so, not by trying to escape the metaphysical character of language, but by exposing and undermining it: by fixing upon accidental features of the text to subvert its essential message and by playing off its rhetorical elements against its grammatical structure. Heidegger's strategy for getting beyond "man" will not do the trick: Derrida suggests that "a change of style" is needed.

4   *A critical philosophy of technology.* Much of the history of post-structuralism can be written as a series of innovative theoretical developments of or about Heidegger's notion of technology. Heidegger's philosophy of technology is related to his critique of the history of Western metaphysics and disclosure of being. The essence of technology is a *poiesis* or "bringing forth" that is grounded in such disclosure (*aletheia*). He suggests that the essence of modern technology shows itself in what he calls "enframing" and reveals itself as "standing reserve," a concept that refers to resources that are stored in the anticipation of consumption. As such, modern technology names the final stage in the history of metaphysics (nihilism) and the way in which being is disclosed in this particular epoch: a stockpiling in principle completely knowable and devoted entirely to human use. He suggests that the essence of technology is nothing technological; it is rather a system (*Gestell*), an all-embracing view of technology, described as a mode of human existence that focuses upon the way machine technology can alter our mode of being, distorting our actions and aspirations. Heidegger is careful not to pose as an optimist or pessimist. He sees his own work as preparation for a new beginning that will enable one to rescue oneself from nihilism and allow the resolute individual to achieve an authenticity.

5   *A deepening of democracy and a political critique of Enlightenment values.* Post-structuralism criticizes the ways that modern liberal democracies construct political identity on the basis of a series of binary oppositions (e.g., we/them, citizen/noncitizen, responsible/irresponsible, legitimate/illegitimate), which has the effect of excluding or "othering" some groups of people. Western countries grant rights to citizens – rights are dependent upon citizenship – and regard noncitizens, that is, immigrants, those seeking asylum, and refugees, as "aliens." Some strands of post-structuralist thought are interested in examining how these boundaries are socially constructed, and how they are maintained and policed. In particular, the deconstruction of political hierarchies of value comprising binary oppositions and philosophies of difference, are seen as highly significant for current debates on multiculturalism and feminism, and as issuing from the post-structuralist critique of representation and consensus.

6   *Governmentality and political reason.* Foucault's later work based on the notion of "governmentality" (Foucault, 1991b) has initiated a substantial body of contemporary work in political philosophy that deals directly with political reason. Foucault coins the term "governmentality" in an analysis of liberalism and neoliberalism,

viewing the former as originating in a doctrine concerning the critique of state reason. Foucault uses the term "governmentality" to mean the art of government and to signal the emergence of a distinctive type of rule that became the basis for modern liberal politics. He maintains that the "art of government" emerged in the sixteenth century, motivated by diverse questions: the government of oneself (personal conduct); the government of souls (pastoral doctrine); the government of children (pedagogy). It was around the same time that "economy" was introduced into political practice as part of the governmentalization of the state. What is distinctive about Foucault's approach is that he is interested in the question of how power is exercised and, implicitly, he is providing a critique of contemporary tendencies to overvalue problems of the state, reducing it to a unity or singularity based upon a certain functionality. Both Foucault and Derrida, returning to Kant's cosmopolitical writings, have addressed themselves to the prospect for global governance, and Derrida has talked about both deepening democracy and – entertaining developments of new technologies – a "democracy to come" (see, e.g., Derrida, 1997).

7 *Philosophies of difference.* If there is one element that distinguishes post-structuralism it is the notion of difference that various thinkers use, develop, and apply in different ways. The notion of difference comes from Nietzsche, from Saussure, and from Heidegger. Gilles Deleuze, in *Nietzsche and Philosophy* (Deleuze, [1962] 1983), interprets Nietzsche's philosophy according to the principle of difference and advances this interpretation as an attack upon the Hegelian dialectic. Derrida's notion of difference can be traced back to at least two sources: Saussure's insight that linguistic systems are constituted through difference, and Heidegger's notion of difference. From the first mention of the notion of difference (in 1959) to its development as the concept *différance*, takes nearly a decade. *Différance*, as Derrida remarks (Derrida, 1981, pp. 8–9), as both the common root of all the positional concepts marking our language and the condition for all signification, refers not only to the "movement that consists in deferring by means of delay, delegation, reprieve, referral, detour, postponement, reserving" but also and finally to "the unfolding of difference," of the ontico-ontological difference, which Heidegger named as the difference between Being and beings. As such, *différance* is seen as plotting the linguistic limits of the subject. Lyotard, by contrast, invents the concept of the *différend* which he suggests establishes the very condition for the existence of discourse: "that a universal rule of judgement between heterogeneous genres is lacking in general" (Lyotard, 1988b, p. xi), or again, there is "no genres whose hegemony over others would be just" (ibid., p. 158). A *différend*, as Lyotard defines it "is a case of conflict, between (at least) two parties, that cannot be equitably resolved for lack of a rule of judgement applicable to both arguments" (ibid., p. xi). Post-structuralist notions of difference, pointing to an antiessentialism, have been subsequently developed in relation to gender and ethnicity: the American feminist philosopher Iris Marion Young writes of *Justice and the Politics of Difference* (Young, 1990) and the Afro-American philosopher Cornel West speaks of "The New Cultural Politics of Difference" (West, 1993).

8 *Suspicion of metanarratives.* Lyotard's definition of the "postmodern condition" characterizes a feature of post-structuralism that we can call the suspicion of transcendental arguments and viewpoints, combined with the rejection of canonical

descriptions and final vocabularies. In particular, "suspicion toward metanarratives" refers to the question of legitimation with reference to the modern age in which various grand narratives have been advanced as a legitimation of state power. There is no synthesizing or neutral master discourse that can reproduce the speculative unity of knowledge or adjudicate between competing views, claims, or discourses. The "linguistic turn" of twentieth-century philosophy and social sciences does not warrant the assumption of a metalinguistic neutrality or foundational epistemological privilege.

9   *The diagnosis of "power/knowledge" and the exposure of technologies of domination based upon Foucault's analytics of power.* For Foucault, power is productive; it is dispersed throughout the social system, and it is intimately related to knowledge. It is productive rather than repressive and also creates new knowledge (which may also liberate). It is dispersed rather than located in any one center, like the state, and it is part of the constellation "power/knowledge," which means that knowledge, in the sense of discursive practices, is generated through the exercise of power in the control of populations. Foucault develops this thesis through his genealogical study of the development of modern institutions like the prison and the school, and the corresponding emergence of the social sciences that helped devise new methods of social control.

10   *The politics of the global knowledge/information society/economy.* Post-structuralism provides intellectual resources to philosophers of education for unpicking the ruling assumptions currently used to construct the dominant neoliberal paradigm of globalization as a global economy/society allegedly based upon a conception of knowledge and "free trade." The new production of knowledge and the global knowledge economy, together with classical assumptions of rationality, individuality, and self-interest, are important construction sites for knowledge deconstruction and critique. They are also conceptual sites for alternative conceptions.

Education and the Politics of Post-structuralism

Foucault defines *ethos* as a mode of relating to contemporary reality, which takes the form of both an attitude and a commitment (Foucault, 1984) The postmodern *ethos*, as a *mature* "point of exit" from the modern world, is marked by a deep suspicion of modernism's master narratives of emancipation and progress. We suggested that post-structuralism can be understood in part as a rereading of structuralism. Yet neither genealogy, nor deconstruction, nor paralogy (the kind of writing recommended by Lyotard), constitutes the writing of theory. To use Rorty's useful distinction, all are *reactive* ways of writing rather than *constructive* (Rorty, 1980).

Reading post-structuralism as simply a retheorizing of structuralism also runs the risk of losing sight of the crucial role Nietzsche and Heidegger play in post-structuralist thinking. In short, if we are using post-structuralism to refer to the writings of Derrida, Foucault, Lyotard, and others, describing their writings as "a specifically philosophical response to the alleged scientific status of structuralism" fails to do justice to this complexity and, possibly, misleads on their mode of writing. Moreover in France during the 1950s and 1960s, Deleuze, Derrida, Foucault, and Lyotard, among others, started reading Nietzsche and Heidegger and used these thinkers as a means of questioning the "scientific" and universalist pretensions of structuralism and of passing beyond both structuralism and Hegelianism (see M. Peters, 1996, 1997). This French reception of Nietzsche (so influentially mediated through Heidegger's *Nietzsche*) proved decisive in the intellectual formation of what became known, particularly in the United States, as "post-structuralism" and, more specifically, after Derrida, as "deconstruction."

We referred earlier to the new practices of reading and writing that constitute deconstruction. It is these new critical practices that quickly became institutionalized as the Yale School of literary criticism that blossomed in the work of Harold Bloom, Paul de Man, Hillis Miller, and Geoffrey Hartman, among others (see Bloom et al., 1979). The work of the Yale school has generated much criticism and focused attention on both the construction of the so-called Western canon and on the higher education curriculum. Allan Bloom, the conservative critic, in *The Closing of the American Mind* (Bloom, 1987), argues strongly that the social and political crisis of twentieth-century America is really an intellectual crisis caused by the vulgarization of Continental ideas of nihilism and despair, of relativism disguised as tolerance. He alleges that the American university is closed to the principles of the Western tradition, and that it is especially closed to the spiritual heritage of the West, which gave rise to the university in the first place.

There are clear dangers of reducing French post-structuralism to a reading of the French reception of Nietzsche (see M. Peters, 1998a, pp. 6–18). The relationship of each of these contemporary French thinkers to Nietzsche, and the use to which they put his work, is very different, and some, like Lyotard, deny the importance of Nietzsche in their thinking, emphasizing rather, the importance of Kant (who is also important to Foucault). We must actively resist the kind of (French) reductive "neoliberal" reading of post-structuralism as "French Nietzscheanism" given by Ferry and Renaut on a number of grounds (Ferry and Renaut, 1990, especially pp. 15–17; see also M. Peters et al., 2000).

Moreover there are grounds for not referring to post-structuralism as a "movement," even if the "ism" seems to suggest it. Or rather we might use the notion of "movement" to refer to "post-structuralism" not in the sense of a *project*, which is modernist, but rather more as a *movement* in music: a series of repeated refrains or motifs, even harmonies (and discordances), that has a distinctive structure of its own. The notion of a social or political movement belongs to the language game of modernist politics rather than the postmodernist. But concrete post-structuralist political activism addresses local and specific issues that demand only temporary solidarity in the group and refer to no long-term emancipatory agenda. It could be argued that there is no theory of action, cause, or political program that the post-structuralists consciously hold in common or subscribe to. Indeed, one tendency, as suggested earlier, is to regard post-structuralism as a postmodern *ethos* of Nietzschean inspiration. This is how Habermas sees it also, as a "revitalization" of Nietzsche (Habermas, 1990b). Nietzsche influences such focal post-structuralist views as those on power and the play with knowledge, on freedom as ludic transgression, on poetic irony and self creation, and on the key agonistic political principle of engaging in struggle without the ambition to overpower completely or dominate the other.

French thinkers wish *"to repudiate the dream of an innocent language"* and specifically to call into question Habermas's modernist, universalist vision of a "noise-free," fully transparent sphere of communication. As Wellbery writes:

> Whereas Habermas adheres to an ideal of transparent communication, the French investigate the opacities inherent in speech itself. Whereas Habermas stresses the harmonious aspects of consensus, the French hold that consensus can only be established on the basis of acts of exclusion. And whereas Habermas seeks in such notions as truth, truthfulness, and correctness criteria that, as it were, stand above language and give it its validity, the French interpret such notions as strategies for the control of speech, and through speech, of others. (Wellbery, 1985, p. 233)

Stephen White notes that Habermas's recent work (i.e., since 1971) is captured in "the commitment to a universalistic perspective on rationality and ethics," and that this commitment has become increasingly contestable as the decade of the 1970s drew to a close:

> The universalist, rationalist tradition of the Enlightenment came under increasing fire from various quarters. Contextualist and relativist positions were articulated by analytic philosophers, moral and political theorists, social anthropologists, feminists and post-structuralists. (White, 1988, p. 1)

Under this pressure, White maintains, Habermas has shifted his position "from assertions about what is implicit in speech actions of all actors to assertions about 'the intuition of competent members of *modern* societies'" (White, 1988, p. 2, White's emphasis). In the new millennium, with the increasing recognition of forms of value pluralism, the acceleration of decolonization, the revitalization of indigenous cultures and traditions, the increased recognition of the gendered nature of Western philosophy and science, and the re-assertion of Chinese, Indian, Islamic, and African philosophies, Habermas's universalist claims have come under further scrutiny for their Eurocentrism.

Such criticisms would also apply to those educational theorists wanting to base a model for higher education on Habermas's theory of communicative rationality (e.g., Barnett, 1990) or on "learning processes" that seek to exploit the *telos* of communicative rationality said to be inherent in ordinary discourse and redeemable at the level of discourse. There are a series of criticisms here that are aimed at a Habermasian interpretation of the unity of the university. Is the notion of communicative rationality strong enough to prevent the fragmentation of knowledges and the generation of new academic language games? Can the notion of consensus really serve, even in its Rawlsian "overlapping" nature, to advance the liberal ideal of the university? To what extent has the notion of consensus served to exclude other than mainstream interests and disciplines? (see M. Peters, 1999).

Our description of the political orientations of post-structuralism is accurate but does not mention the criticism it has been subjected to over the years *because* of its politics. We raise it because this criticism has crucial implications for the credibility of post-structuralism as a discourse about education. Reactive post-structuralist writers, in fact, are very clear about what they are against but not quite so clear about what they are for – if, in fact, as their critics have remarked, they are *for* anything. Their attack on Western Reason has earned them the well-known charge of irrationality. The parallel charge made against them with regard to their ethics and politics is that of gross irresponsibility, that they are nihilists and anarchists, as well as intellectual vandals. What can writers of this ilk possibly contribute to education?

Let us describe the criticism and the problems it raises for education. Bertens says that Derridean deconstructionism was the decisive influence right into the early 1980s but, by roughly the middle of the 1980s, Foucault came to the fore. His "influence materialised imperceptibly until it is suddenly very much there, like a fine drizzle that to your surprise has managed to get you thoroughly wet after an hour's walk" (Bertens, 1995, p. 7).

Deconstruction was criticized by its critics, including Bertens, for absorbing itself in the self-reflexivity of language and limiting its interest to texts and intertexts. "In its firm belief that the attack on representation was in itself an important political act," Bertens remarks, "it was content to celebrate the so-called death of the subject, and ignored the important political questions that this event raises" (ibid., p. 7). Foucault's genealogical analyses shifted deconstructionism's emphasis on language and the text onto power/knowledge and its constitution of the modern subject. Merquior, who is an otherwise hostile critic, echoes Bertens in describing Foucault as "the man who tried to place post-structuralism on an ethico-political ground at a far remove from the textual navel-gazing of 'deconstruction'" (Merquior, 1985, p. 14). Concern with power/knowledge did not, however, protect Foucault from the charge of ludic irresponsibility leveled also against Derrida. This charge comes from their refusal to take up positions on matters of freedom and justice, and to allow themselves to be positioned in any way on "the political chessboard." Derrida, in particular, was criticized for refusing to take a position on Marxism during the time of the Paris uprisings. Foucault was criticized for the impression he gave of being neutral about the power/knowledge regimes and disciplinary technologies he described so harrowingly in *Discipline and Punish* (Foucault, 1991a) and elsewhere.

Foucault's account of power was criticized by Charles Taylor and others as incoherent because, Taylor said, it equated power with domination and had no counternotion of freedom (Taylor, 1985b). While his "refusal to specify either a prescription or a prognosis for the social illnesses he diagnoses," Hoy remarked, "suggests to the reader that genealogy is as unserious and irresponsible as archeology" (Hoy, 1986, p. 67). Michael Walzer (ibid., p. 51) dismissed his politics as a form of "infantile leftism," and Richard Rorty described them as "self-indulgent political chic" (ibid., p. 71). Merquior went further, describing Foucault's impact on continental philosophy as "unfortunate" and referring to him as a revolutionary "spontaneist" and a bad anarchist to boot (Merquior, 1985, p. 154). In sum, it was claimed by his critics "that he was normatively confused or that he deprives himself of any basis for criticism of the social phenomena he describes" (Patten, 1989, p. 22).

Rorty, post-structuralist in his philosophic sympathies, at least since *Philosophy and the Mirror of Nature* (Rorty, 1980), has described French post-structuralism in general as philosophically right but politically silly (Rorty, 1992). His political stance in favor of the "politics of hope" of the social democracy, however, has not saved him from the flack of his critics either. The problem with trying to reconcile his intellectual attraction toward postmodernism with his politics is experienced by a lot of others of the left, including a number of feminists. Rorty (1990a) is particularly interesting to us because he takes the post-structuralist outlook to lead to the conclusion that philosophy is irrelevant to both education and politics (see Peters and Ghiraldelli, 2001).

It is also important to specify that the adjective "postmodern," besides describing the intellectual outlook or ethos mentioned above, is used also to refer to the contemporary sociocultural reality of Western societies, which Giddens (1991), Beck (U. Beck, 1992), and other social theorists, have described as "risk societies" characterized by existential disorientation (though they have been referred to also in other ways besides postmodern, as "high modern," "late modern," "reflexive modern," and so on). The distrust of the master narratives of modernity referred to by Lyotard partly explains the disorientation. To put it succinctly, postmodern refers to an ethos, and it also refers to the contemporary reality of the Western world. In the latter sense, one necessarily lives in a postmodern world but one need not embrace a postmodernist outlook or commitment. This suggests that our learning institutions, practices, and policies must, for the sake of relevance, react to the postmodern world but could resist its politics.

This is the position taken by Kiziltian, Bain, and Canizares who observe that "contemporary education, as an institutional constellation of a variety of practices (e.g., teaching, disciplining, testing, tracking, etc.) largely intersects with the broader society," which is postmodern (Kiziltian et al., 1990, p. 353) but find that in "disclosing education's inwrought partiality and exposing the fragility and the insubstantiality of its epistemic and metaphysical presuppositions," postmodernism threatens the very possibility of public education in a radical way. It should, therefore, be resisted (ibid., p. 355). Usher and Edwards, for their part, do not think there is any immediate danger to public education because, in actuality, "education is particularly resistant to the postmodern 'message,'" since the influence of modernity on our educational systems is still strong (Usher and Edwards, 1994, p. 2). But the danger of being seduced by the "message" of postmodernism is taken up by different writers. Andy Green, for instance, echoing Habermas, warns that "taken to its extremes, postmodernism can only lead to moral nihilism, political apathy and the abandonment of the intellect to the chaos of the contingent" (Green, 1994, p. 74). Moreover, the logic of its argument, he contends, "points towards an individualistic educational consumerism in many respects similar to that advocated by the free-marketeers of the new Right" (ibid., p. 76).

This is where Rorty is led in *Contingency, Irony, and Solidarity*, by turning it into a political program for a liberal utopia (Rorty, 1989). Otherwise, Rorty says, the kind of aestheticized outlook poststructuralism encourages should be limited to one's private life. He then asks us (Rorty, 1990b) to think of education not as one continuous process but as two distinct ones, lower and higher, with the first, schooling, consisting in the straightforward enculturation of pupils, and the second, the non-vocational university, edifying them or, later, promoting their radical individuation.

A lot of objections have been made against this suggestion to bifurcate individual existence into radically separate public and private spheres and to divide education, equally radically, into separate phases of enculturation and individuation. Paul Standish has raised another problem with the post-structuralists' way of representing the self, as a seamless web of experiences and the denial of a core self or ego (Standish, 1995). It makes it difficult, he observes, to identify the subject to be educated when the self is proposed in this way. It also renders the common assumption that education is of "the whole person" meaningless. One could add that it also runs contrary to the long-standing liberal view that education is about the achievement of a rationally autonomous subject. Standish was one who, otherwise, approved of the way postmodernism problematizes the kind of socialization to which individuals are exposed in modern societies.

Aronowitz and Giroux once claimed to have uncovered a postmodernism other than the "right wing" or nihilistic kinds identified by Habermas, referring to it as an "emancipatory" postmodernism (Aronowitz and Giroux, 1991). Apart from raising crucial questions about certain hegemonic aspects of modernism which are reflected in contemporary schooling, they claimed, postmodernism offers the radical promise of deterritorializing modern society and redrawing its political, social, and cultural boundaries, while affirming a politics of racial, gender, and ethnic difference. It thus resituates us within a world that little resembles the one that inspired the grand narratives of Marx and Freud, and calls attention to the shifting boundaries related to the increasing influence of electronic mass media and information technologies, to the changing nature of class and social formations in our postindustrialized capitalist societies, and to the growing transgression of the boundaries between life, art, high and popular culture, and image and reality. The sociologists of the "risk society," however, refer to our postmodernist resituation in the world as disoriented. Some would argue that, following Lyotard's definition of postmodernism, "emancipatory postmodernism" is a contradiction in terms, although it is by no means clear that small narratives of emancipation are excluded. In line with this way of thinking, Green criticizes Aronowitz and Giroux for seeking "to annex some of the ideas of postmodernism to the unashamedly modernist project of radical democracy and social justice," which they support (A. Green, 1994, p. 75).

Like Aronowitz and Giroux, Bayer and Liston mark down as positive the fact that "postmodernist" writing draws our attention toward the problems of marginalization and the exclusion of particular social groups and minorities in schools and society. All this is undone, however, in their view, by postmodernism's distrust of all forms of commonality and of all kinds of emancipatory discourse, as well as by its emphasis on the need to engage in local rather than global issues (on not creating movements). This, they concede, may be fruitful in some circumstances, but "makes problematic significant contributions to alternative social and educational actions" (Bayer and Liston, 1992, p. 371), undermining, in particular, the kind of collaborative social action, which alone, they contend, makes change or reform in favor of the marginalized themselves possible. Finally, they express another worry: that postmodernism poses serious problems for educators "for whom both intellectual engagement and transformative practice are mandatory," personally, not just in terms of its general politics (ibid., p. 371). Rob Gilbert also has positive things to say about postmodern writings, but worries that they threaten the idea of citizenship in general and political education in general (Gilbert, 1992). Even more fundamentally, they threaten, in his view, the notion of democracy itself. In sum, though many would not share Green's unequivocal negative judgement that "postmodernism proper (i.e., as propounded by Lyotard, Baudrillard, et al.), has contributed little that is distinctive or theoretically fruitful and it seems unlikely that it will," most have their worries about it (A. Green, 1994, pp. 74–5).

We are not sure what Green means by "postmodernism proper," but it is a needlessly harsh and contestable conclusion to make of post-structuralism. Green himself concedes that the contributions in Stephen Ball's book on Foucault and education (Ball, 1990) are good examples of how Foucauldian discourse analysis, for instance, could prove a "useful tool for decoding ideologies, policies and power relations at the macro and micro levels" of school and classroom (A. Green, 1994, p. 74). Other writers, like James Marshall, have demonstrated the relevance of Foucault's work on punishment, and his account of the subjectification of the self through the power of the different disciplinary mechanisms of governance and domination, created by modern practices of surveillance in modern institutions (typified by the panopticon) as different technologies of examination (the confession, the gaze, pastoral care, therapeutic practices of self-disclosure etc.) to the practices of schooling (Marshall, 1996).

Rorty consigns the more positive of Foucault's reflections on self-creation to the university and, as we have seen, denies any part in educating to the school. We disagree both with this move and with its premise that we should regard education as two distinct stages instead of one continuous one of open-ended growth. Foucault also provides an excellent resource for exploring the implications of defining education as a process of self-creation in a postmodern age. Numerous books and articles have also been written relating Lyotard's notion of *performativity* to contemporary educational practices and institutions, including not just schools but also universities and adult education. And his account of the state of knowledge and technology in postmodern societies and of the future of the "professor" have equally challenged the contemporary debate about the future of education (see M. Peters, 1995; Dhillon and Standish, 2000; Blake and Standish, 2000). Finally, in a text strongly influenced by Lyotard, Nigel Blake, Paul Smeyers, Richard Smith, and Paul Standish, reflecting a lot of people's belief that educational theory is currently at an impasse, offer the post-structuralist writers as a resource for revitalizing it again, and show how the deconstructive reading of educational and literary texts can be truly edifying (Blake et al., 1998). These authors see themselves addressing, in part, the very need for "intellectual engagement and transformative practice" within a postmodern framework that rightly concerns Bayer and Liston (mentioned above).

When we begin to think through educational issues from the perspectives that "post-structuralism" offers, we believe it provides a greater political awareness of contemporary realities and problems: "the logic of performativity" (Lyotard) that drives the system that thrives upon the annihilation of difference; the "power/knowledge" of the human sciences that often domesticate and control us while at the same time purporting to make us free; the commodification of the systems of knowledge and education; the "technologization" of education and of the self that springs from a logocentric metaphysics of presence; the assimilation of others as part and parcel of liberal consensus-making that seems incapable of detecting or of even witnessing "difference."

Of course, these ideas and the philosophies that develop them are not fixed and stable theoretical entities to be chosen as one might chose a new commodity or even a set of beliefs or values; they are positions to be "worked through," trajectories to be explored, arguments to be developed. Only with considerable hindsight is it possible, if at all, to determine the strengths and weaknesses of "movements" and rarely can one pass final judgement. We urge caution in our present assessments for these reasons and because the positions we have described under the label of "post-structuralism" are still very much in the making; these positions await our engagement. One line of inquiry for educational philosophy is to work through similar themes to post-structuralism but from the viewpoint of a Nietzschean–Wittgensteinian perspective that attempts to weave an intersection between aspects of the Anglo-American tradition and post-structuralism, focusing upon pedagogy of the self (see, for example, Peters and Marshall, 1999; Peters et al., 2000). A post-structuralist pedagogy of the self might be understood as one based on assisting individuals toward a transgressive form of self-creation responding, in our postmodern risk societies, to the Nietzschean notion of *amor fati*, and tempered with an ethics of care for the other.

Note

1   We are grateful to the editors for this point and a number of other editorial suggestions that we have adopted.

Recommendations for Further Reading

Lyotard, J.-F. (1984) *The Postmodern Condition: A Report on Knowledge*, trans. G. Bennington and Brian Massumi, Foreword by F. Jameson, University of Minnesota Press.
Kellner, D. and Best, S. (1991) *Postmodern Theory: Critical Interrogations*, Macmillan.
Peters, M. A. (ed.) (1995) *Education and the Postmodern Condition*, Bergin & Garvey.
Usher, R. and Edwards, R. (1994) *Postmodernism and Education*, Routledge.

Chapter 4

Feminism, Philosophy, and Education: Imagining Public Spaces

Maxine Greene and Morwenna Griffiths

Introduction: Not Philosophy-as-Usual

We begin by explaining ourselves, if we can. This chapter is not "philosophy-as-usual," as ordinarily conceived. Perhaps it would be strange if it were, since, as we mean to show, feminism is precisely a way of rethinking the "usual."

We need to explain ourselves, however, because our individual voices, perspectives, positions, locations, and social relationships – *our situations* – are irreducibly part of the ways we do feminist philosophy of education. We are fully aware that there is no one "feminism"; there are multiple points of view described as "feminist." Feminist theories, or clusters of theories, are not united by some overarching principle of "essence," still less by any single set of beliefs, but rather by the way they generate or infuse actions in the world. As someone in pursuit of a project, each individual actor originates her own undertakings, launches her own beginnings, and articulates her own perceptions, ideas, and purposes. Striving to actualize the givenness of her being as a woman, to "make articulate and call into full existence what otherwise they would have to suffer passively anyhow" (Arendt, 1958, p. 208), each of us feel ourselves to be not only women but distinctive beings, whose uniqueness must be taken into account by any theory that is made or story that is told. The form of the chapter reflects this. Much of it is in dialogue; and the whole arose from dialogues carried out in letters and (often taped) conversations. After this preliminary introduction we present a short, assertive overview of feminisms in relation to philosophy (of education). This is followed by our two personal narratives of identity and philosophy of education. The last section is a brief demonstration of what a feminist approach to philosophy of education might be: we undertake this in relation to social justice.

In the dialogue sections, Maxine Greene's subsections are headed by odd Roman numerals and Morwenna Griffiths' subsections by even ones.

Both coauthors are women, and each one's life history is distinctive, different from the other's. Both have shared experiences of marginality, one through her being introduced at a young age to a dominant Protestant reality at odds with her experiences growing up in a secular Jewish family. The other, like so many of her compatriots, has a family which has migrated (in her case for several generations). She was born in colonial East Africa and came "home" (as we called it) to a foreign country, England, when she was 10. Although one of us was born and reared in New York City (the birthplace of her parents as well), she never felt herself to be at the "center." Her boundary engagements, like those of her colleague, cannot but infuse her approach to philosophy and to education. It goes without saying that, although the authors are of different generations, their universities were governed by male administrators and officials, who did not willingly usher them "inside." A mere taste of being an outsider or a stranger tends to make one reflective upon one's origins and less likely to be so submerged in the ordinary as to take for granted ethnicity, gender, even one's materiality. One of us chose, after a long involvement with John Dewey and other experientialists, to come to the doing of philosophy through her readings of literature, existential writings, drama, and film. All these affected her posing of questions, perhaps particularly with regard to the tensions of trying to reconcile a desire to be free and "outside" and her longing to be part of the dominant group. The other comes from and through the sciences and has moved (taught by her students) from a preoccupation with knowledge, skills, and rationality to problems of authenticity, selfhood, and identity. She too has been much preoccupied with questions of "wanting and not wanting to belong."

For all their differences, both writers share a concern for social justice. Both are concerned with the shifting relations between the public and the private, and with the possibility of weaving what Hannah Arendt has called a "web of relations" that is woven when human beings, people experiencing a common interest, come together in "agent-revealing" ways, presenting themselves as "who" not "what" they are. Like other women (e.g., de Beauvoir, Haraway) and certain male philosophers (e.g., Kierkegaard, Merleau-Ponty, Dewey) we have come in different ways to the doing of philosophy from the vantage point of situationality, rather than as uninvolved spectators, offering "news from nowhere."

For the males, the discovery of that vantage point did not draw their attention to the crucial role of the gendered body when it comes to perceiving, imagining, valuing, knowing, seeking meaning.[1] Unlike them, we are aware of our gendered bodies; of having what Battersby (1998) describes as "bodies that bleed." That is, we are aware that we women are capable of giving birth, may have given birth to one or several children. We are aware that in the social context in which we grew up, women assume responsibility for seeing to everyday imperatives of food, shelter, love, care, support, friendship, neighborliness, and kinship. Indeed few women can be unaware of their physical selves (their mothering selves, their housecleaning selves, their cooking selves, their supporting selves). And few women can be unaware of the significance attached to the appearance and then changing appearances of their bodies and the effects of the ever-present male gaze. All this cannot but keep them in touch with the actualities, the physical and material actualities, of lived lives.

We are agreed that perceptions of what this signifies when it comes to thinking, knowing, or understanding cannot simply result in new pathways through the forests of philosophical thinking. It means, it should mean, an almost total reconception of the doing of philosophy. Clearly it is impossible to encapsulate recent (or future) treatments of "feminism" (or even particular feminisms) within philosophy of education, since feminist approaches permeate all branches of philosophy but also escape them. Each philosopher marked by feminism makes her own trajectory.

We come from a position that recognizes links and also disjunctions between women within and between different parts of the world. We continue to assert the relevance of gender and feminism but claim no universal sisterhood of sameness, no "essence of femaleness." We both see gender as a construction; and we think of the multiple meanings gender has taken on or been given over the centuries. Think of the typifications – maternal images, infantile images, servile images, the dark lady (like Scott's Rebecca) and the angelic lady (like the blonde Rowena), the many diversifications – along with the controls and constraints. And think particularly of those connected with ethnic and racial differences. Our minds edge toward and then away from what gender meant under slavery – during the auctions, during the time the white planters indulged themselves with so-called concubines. We remember that "strange fruit" hung in living memory in the United States and that white women were known to have participated in the lynching of their black lovers. Mindful of Caroline Steedman's (1986) auto/biography of her mother, we observe the complexities of what gender might have meant to working-class women. And mindful of Radha Kumar's (1993) careful discussion of movements for women's rights in India and Yasmin Alibhai-Brown's (1995) autobiography of growing up in Uganda, we consider what gender might have meant to all classes of women under British colonialism.

We continue to endeavor to uncover links and to forge new networks with other women *as* women, in all their specificities of social class, ethnicity, religion, sexuality, age, nationality, and (dis)ability. We find ourselves confronted with experiences of oppression and mutilation still suffered by women in many parts of the world, including our own. We find ourselves confronted at the same time with the examples of women's power when it comes to rebuilding shattered community structures and a "domestic economy" (as in Paraguay, Bangladesh, South Africa, the UK, the USA, and the former Yugoslavia). We have tried – we continue to try – to be pluralist in our own reading and listening. As we write we try to be pluralist in imagining you, our audience. We also know that we almost certainly fall short in these endeavors, that knowledge or understanding of the other is always incomplete.

An Overview of Feminisms in Relation to Philosophy (of Education)

This section can only be a brief summary of a large subject. Therefore it is both short and assertive. Let the reader beware: it is important to notice that there is no such thing as *the* gendered or *the* feminist position, nor is there any content that is specifically feminist (care, parenting, birth, or anything else highlighted as a "women's issue"). Nor is there any philosophical position that is specifically feminist. Feminists routinely "go pearl fishing," to use Arendt's phrase (Young-Bruehl, 1982, p. 95), from male or from nonfeminist female philosophers. We do so ourselves. Arendt, to use one example, was most certainly not a feminist philosopher. She has been sharply criticized by feminists, for instance by Adrienne Rich, as a "female mind nourished on male ideologies" (in Seller, 1996, p. 102). We find plenty to criticize ourselves. Yet she is one of the heroines of this chapter. Most especially there is not anything that can be added on to philosophy-as-usual to get the woman's angle on it. That is, taking any feminist perspective changes all of philosophy-as-usual but not to any single recognizable end.[2]

So is there anything that holds "feminisms" together, with all their differences? Any short, assertive suggestions are bound to be met with objections. That said, it is always possible to make some general comments that would be recognized as reasonable (though not universally agreed). We put forward the following in that spirit, and commend the interested reader to follow up some of the references. (It may be remarked that it is just as difficult to say what holds "philosophy" together – or "liberalism" or "postmodernism.")

Bodies and gender

Bodies and gender matter in understanding the world. Neither men nor women are disembodied pure rationalities, and their bodies leave their marks on the kinds of understanding they have. This is not, of course, to say that anatomy is destiny, although some feminist philosophers come close to saying so. We ourselves would want to remark on other bodily and material marks on knowledge and understanding, such as those of ethnicity, poverty, geography, and (dis)ability. Like gender, they are all social distributions that are constructed by/through power. When we ourselves think of the marks of poverty and too much childbirth and the cases of mutilation, and so on, it seems to us that we ought to take into account the lived body, as experienced by the living person, and the body as looked at (or the woman feeling herself to be an object of someone else's gaze). We would also remark that attention to the body (like so much else) is not exclusively female or feminist. We think of Merleau-Ponty, for instance, who brought the body to the foreground and has proved useful to some feminist philosophers.[3]

The salience of gender

Gender is salient and significant in all known societies; it affects ways of interacting, and so of doing philosophy. Most starkly, throughout history women have been told to stop thinking and get back to their real, womanly tasks. Hypatia, a philosopher in Alexandria in the fourth century, provides one of the earliest examples (told to get back to her loom) (Le Doeuff, 1991). Other well-known ones are Harriet Martineau (go back to your needle) and Mary Wollstonecraft (the hyena in petticoats).[4] We remark on more modern examples from our own experiences of struggling with prejudice later on in this chapter.

Doing situated philosophy

It is necessary to acknowledge the place of experience/subjectivity and of concrete practical example in doing philosophy of/in/for education or educational philosophy (for both sexes). It is clear to us that situatedness is so much clearer for women and that it affects our doing of philosophy. We cannot be the unmoved movers, or take the view from nowhere. We cannot be Joyce's indifferent God "paring his nails" as he looks at the universe. We agree with Arendt that "thought itself arises out of incidents of living experience and must remain bound to them as the only guideposts by which to take its bearings" ([1961] 1993, p. 14).[5]

Untidy disciplinary divisions

A strength of feminist scholarship is that there are few tidy disciplinary divisions. Therefore feminist educational philosophy could not be a category to be tidily pinned down. It is loose cloth woven from philosophy, feminist theories, feminist practices and politics, educational theorizing, and educational practices.[6] To take this further, it means that feminist work does not have to fit into specifically feminist academic spaces either. We have both been frightened, on occasion, by the degree of feminist *scholarship* needed by some journals, while on other occasions we have also both been glad to find feminist publishing outlets.

Two Personal Narratives of Identity and Philosophy of Education

In sum, feminism is less a theory – or a set of theories – and more a perspective, a lens, a handle on the world and its ideas, a way of acting and speaking. It is less a belief system or a faith; it is more a serious project of identification with real consequences. One way of seeing this is to trace the paths that have led particular persons to take a feminist perspective in philosophy of education and which still draw them on into unknown, unknowable futures.

One of us has been much affected by existential thinking as well as by Dewey. The other remains marked by her early love of analytic philosophy, for instance the work of Wittgenstein, Quine, and others, but now finds most help in relatively recent work focusing on perspective and power – and the play between them. But we at least reach related conclusions when it comes to the achievement of social justice as one of the purposes of public education.

What made us realize how much was excluded or denied by dominant male epistemologies was the personal discovery of experiential and existential approaches to teaching, to the shaping of a project, to the search for identity, and to shaping self-expression. Also there was the impact of certain works of literature (the Western canon, dating from Greek tragedy, and newer Anglophone literature from Africa, America, Australia, Britain, the Caribbean, the Indian subcontinent, and New Zealand) that suggested a shallowness in ongoing objectivist ways of viewing life, not to speak of the positivist split between facts/values and facts/politics. We saw ourselves rather than our male colleagues engaged in what Susan Bordo (1987) called "the flight to objectivity." We were engaged in a philosophical exercise that did not require us to "take leave of our senses" (Woolf, [1938] 1977, p. 83). In a way we flew; in another way we experienced the world as an adventure in sensuality, in imagination, yes, and in perception. We found ourselves on a roller coaster ride of politics, solidarity, pleasure in the sharpness of mind; and then pleasure in using all the riches of language to express ourselves. We enjoyed the exhilaration of logical and careful thought but by remaining mindful of its personal, political significance we were not tempted to indulge in the endless repetition of five-finger mental exercises in logic and argument.

I

I remember my earliest paper, I think, or one of the earliest, when I was trying to get into philosophy of education under the cold hand of analytic philosophy (with those analysts – all male, all big drinkers and smokers, all nice guys – holding private meetings in hotel rooms, talking Ayer and Ryle, as if they were in a locker room telling dirty jokes). Anyway, the paper I had in mind was "The meaning of meaninglessness." It showed people I was "soft," too "literary," and by implication, too "female." And I was scared to death, thinking back nostalgically to the days when I liked being introduced as a woman who "thinks like a man" – and felt like curtseying in gratitude for the compliment. It once happened in Hawaii, and I can still smell the heavy scent of the lei around my neck – and feel the guilt washing over me.

At Barnard, I had majored in history, minored in philosophy, never thought for a single minute of education, but what the hell. Next year I was assistant in that class, suddenly teaching big classes mostly in history of education, realized I could get my doctorate without charging my husband. I guess it was there that I first read Sartre, began my philosophical marginalization. I did a long thesis trying to please my fatherly sponsor (oh spare me) on "Naturalist Humanism in Eighteenth Century England, 1750–1780: An Essay in the Sociology of Knowledge," only because he wanted me to do a thesis on Henry Fielding whom he had just discovered, and I did want to please him but go beyond – way, way beyond – into all kinds of interdisciplinary stuff, art, philosophy, politics, even rotten boroughs, believe it or not, and Coleridge on romanticism. Anyway, a woman in philosophy of education in 1955 did not have a chance of a job. So I took one (a long, long drive from home) teaching World Literature in New Jersey. I had never taken a course in English, and had a marvelous year doing self-study in world lit. from Homer on, learned much, left partly because the club where Faculty ate would not admit Jews, nor would the golf club, etc. I went back to NYU part-time, got kicked out of philosophy because of being too literary, soft, et al. (again), finally got to Brooklyn College teaching Foundations, then to Teachers College to be editor of the *TC Record*. I had been president of the Philosophy of Education Society by then but Teachers College's Department of Philosophy and the Social Sciences had never hired a woman, so I took a job in English (seduced by false promises) with permission to teach one course in Philosophy. I won't go on. It took 10 years, I guess, before I was allowed into that Department, was given a chair, had huge courses. When in the English Department, because I wanted to keep one foot in philosophy, I asked to teach a course in Philosophy and Literature. The Chair asked, "Philosophy-and or philosophy-of?" I said (luckily) "of" and there I was teaching myself aesthetics and education, helping invent the Lincoln Center Institute,[7] writing, speaking in the field.

II

When I started philosophy of education it was with very little self-consciousness of myself as a woman or as a woman philosopher. That came later, just as I was completing my thesis as a doctoral student, when I found I was beginning to take feminist arguments seriously. More by good luck than good management, I became a founder member of the Society for Women in Philosophy in the UK. It began as a group of women (if "group" does not sound too definite: I would hate to be asked to draw its boundaries) who came together, almost experimentally, as "women in philosophy," not necessarily "women in university philosophy departments," you understand. We began meeting in the early 1980s when it was wonderful just to find anyone else who could be described as both woman and philosopher. We could meet without apologizing to other women for this arcane, apparently elitist, academic interest, and without being the only woman in the group among other philosophers. About half of us thought we were not even "real" philosophers, since we were academically situated in other departments like Education, French, Politics, and Theology.

There were only a few of us, and if we did not talk to each other, who could we talk to? So this became a group that held together with all its many philosophical and feminist differences and enjoyed and built on those differences, not to produce consensus but to explore and build on them. I might describe our discussions as "Yes! Yes! But . . ."

Being a part of this group changed my relationship with philosophy of education and other philosophers of education. I was marginal, yes, but then I think I always had been; the men at our conferences would have been very much at home at the conferences that Maxine describes. But now I could name my marginality, and better build on it. I was freed to talk to other sets of people, including other feminists, other educators and other feminist educators. After all, if I was not centrally a philosopher of education, then I need not fit any of their norms. By the beginning of the 1990s I was one of only two or three British philosophers of education who were as much at home at the British Educational Research Association as at our Philosophy of Education Society. On the other hand, I was not that much at home at either: always too theoretical, too abstract for one; but too practical, too political for the other.

III

I find myself often perplexed by what feminism signifies for me today – although I am fearfully aware of the old men of the sea, the survival of patriarchal warnings underlying and often crowding out the sound of whatever little story I have to tell. Some is guilt at belittling my father and my doctoral sponsor, still wanting them (both gone of course) not to feel their manhood diminished (for all my wonder at the continually exposed frailties). At once, there is the situatedness and the particularity I associate with the feminist outcry or story, the laughing refusal to be Joyce's indifferent God paring his nails, wanting to include Molly Bloom's "Yes" somehow (from *Ulysses*) – for all Joyce's evil behavior towards his women. Included in my gropings (because I had a child before most of my academic colleagues, because that child is now dead – having died in London some years ago of cancer, in a hospital in Harley Street, dead at age 35) were the contradictions of motherhood, the hopes, guilt, disappointments, memories of quarrels with her, impossibility of real understanding. I used *The Scarlet Letter* in a recent feminist paper, including Hester's occasional wish that she could kill her little daughter Pearl. Anyway, for me, feminism, definition of myself-in-process, myself at all the intersections, includes my puzzlement about myself as mother, mother of a daughter. I also have a son, younger, by another husband, with a formal kind of intellectual relationship. He has had epilepsy most of his life (until very recent surgery, which may – we hope – stop the seizures). But he has lived a life, studied, gone to Berkeley, hitchhiked alone across the country, kept a good job, married, adopted little Rumanian Danny – and I have said my proudest memory is of letting him go, encouraging him to go on (maybe like an African-American mother), hiding my anxieties. Happened my husband could never show up at moments of seizure, hospital, ambulance – was too scared, I guess.

So, yes, feminism and philosophy have much to do with that self in process, in shifting situations, changing relationships, refusal of any idea of "essence" (connected with my existential leaning as well). The other day Hazel Barnes asked me what it was about Sartre, what with my feminism, what with my knowing what a bastard he was. And I told her I felt like a *Doppelgänger* with Sartre. And what does that mean? But my notion of feminism has much to do with existential ideas of dreadful freedom and with the notion that women as well as men can be described in the light of a "futile passion." If I had time I would also need to add what I have learned about feminism from my lesbian friends, from queer pedagogy, about the relation between private and public, about the stern heterosexuality of public space. You can see how and why "point of view" is so important to me and so perplexing. Me, who had had two husbands, both gone, the second one two years ago, and two children, one gone. I cannot detach my Molly self, my Hester self, my Maxine self from all that.

IV

Maxine wonders what feminism means for her, today, after years of "myself-in-progress." I wonder how much my points of view change over all my years, for all my thinking and rethinking about them, for all my own "myself-in-progress." I know that they do change because, having worried about this question, I have spent some time looking for evidence about it. So I can say that I have gone on from thinking – and acting on the thought – that values, meanings, principles, plans, definitions, all those, could be pinned down and clearly expressed once and for all. Or at least if they had not yet been so pinned down it behoved us collectively to try because it would be better if they were. It would help everyone to know where they were, I thought. We could be sure it was all consistent, coherent, logical, and fitted the facts. Now I do not think that. I think that revisability in ethics, epistemology, and politics (which are all interconnected for me) is not only inevitable but to be welcomed. The kind of revisability I'm talking of comes about through open, critical encounters with others (their arguments, their little stories). Indeed it is just this view of revisability that made me question how far my own ethics, epistemology, and politics had been revised by me, in response to others.

On the other hand, maybe the revisions have been less than I think. For instance, as a young woman I was, explicitly, *not* a feminist. Instead, I proclaimed my belief in the importance of human beings, all of them, and their needs and freedoms. It was later, when I was in my late twenties (what a late developer I was, what a slow learner) that I found it was all very well me thinking myself a human being equal to other human beings, but there were others, powerful, significant, mostly male, others who persisted in thinking of me as female, and so unequal, and so inferior (however nicely and politely it was expressed). This dawning realization made me think again. But now I wonder if that rethink was less than radical. I could say that I never lost that initial passion for justice for human beings, all of them, whatever their needs and freedoms. So it is not surprising in retrospect that it was a socialist feminism that I embraced. "Radical" feminism for me was useful, but merely as a short-term political solution. (For a clear exposition of these terms see Jagger, 1983.) It was something that enabled women to begin to recognize some of their own interests and perspectives but that would never be enough on its own. So, finally, here I am carefully and passionately including issues of social class, sexuality, ethnicity, religion, and nationality in my feminism, whether or not these issues are exemplified by women or men, boys or girls; whether or not it is men or women, girls or boys who are stigmatized, unfairly constrained, oppressed, by them. Though I still think there are short-term, occasional uses in addressing the world only in gender terms.

So not much revision there then? Or is there? Well yes, there is. From a clear, uncompromising "only human beings, no feminism," I find that ambiguity and inconsistency seem built in (as Maxine also says). Sometimes I see the world in stark gender terms, sometimes in more patchy human ones. And as the context changes I move from one to the other, and back again. I consciously make alliances with women. I express and support feminist points of view in committees. I write from an explicitly feminist perspective, using women's feminist writing rather than the better-known men's works. But, on the other hand, these days I am less likely to react to men wanting to know "If I am excluded from the meetings of women and philosophy, how can I learn and contribute?" with a shrug and a "Well, you should have been a woman. I can't really help you." Though I am just as likely to respond sharply to those who think it is the job of various excluded groups to educate the included.

Like Maxine, I have to acknowledge the influence, indeed the power, of my personal history, myself-in-progress, of living every day, day after day, in a relationship with a (most beloved) man, in another one with my (much loved, very old, forgetful, sharp-witted) mother; of my reliance on, or falling out with, friends, my stepdaughter, and my brothers; and also with my personal history of having battled with the Deans and Heads of Department of my last institution about sexism, of having been the "Equal Ops" person there, and so having listened to dreadful tales of exploitation and injustice within that nice, liberal, academic environment. I have also learned (continue to learn) from my students in all their differences of class, gender, sexuality, nationality, and race.

V

Morwenna starts me wondering how I have changed – moving from a distinctly falsified kind of feminism (I would fight those scary men with their pipes and their gin and their raunchy jokes by myself – trying to find a language they could not understand, wanting at once to be as good as they were, admitted to that grungy hotel room). When I was president of the Philosophy of Education Society, I found it impossible to muster up the courage to go to the evening party after the speechifying, the dinner; and I remember lying on the bed in a presidential suite, listening to the boys singing, reciting ballads to one another, and I thought in my infantile shyness that I never should have ventured out in the first place – and, at the same moment, I would show them, I would speak to really large audiences who would finally understand me, whatever that might come to mean.

It might be said as well, that being a secular Jew (marginal on two counts) has affected my sense of engagement. There is the focus on "the law," which certainly led to formalism and objectivism; but there is also the kind of desperate search for principles, even laws, required to make a case for equity, equality, the end of "social suffering," of torture, massacres. (I remember the first chapter of Vonnegut's *Slaughterhouse Five*: "I have told my sons that they are not under any circumstances to take part in massacres.") Again, I think of how being a secular Jew comes into my (critical) response to Nel Noddings, how it contributes to my wariness in some domains: being a New Yorker, an American. I remember Julia Kristeva saying that the experience of freedom in this country makes it impossible really to understand the European experience after World War I – not only the holocaust, but the fate of the Workers' Councils Arendt writes about, the ghosts of the Weimar Republic, the Bauhaus. I was just thinking how on one end of the spectrum are the vicious Balkan wars, the histories of ethnic and tribal hatred and of anti-Semitism, anti-Romany – and at the other end, my short little grandmother who spoke and thought in Hungarian, who said she was still loyal to her emperor, sitting on a park bench with little feet swinging – trying to mark us all, holocaust despite, with the gilt, the panoply, of – for God's sake – the Austro-Hungarian Empire. And there she was, an orthodox Jewish widow in Brooklyn, having escaped the holocaust because some of her relatives had come over earlier, and she was trying to wed all the heritages, and I wonder now if my late-blooming feminism was affected by all that – although my Grandma died before I was 14. I am pretty sure that some vestige of the immigrant story affects us all. It is a hot, hot Sunday morning as I write, and the Puerto Rican parade is starting to take over in the street outside, and I am looking at the contrast of mamas and daughters cooking steaming things on portable stoves – while others ride the floats.

A Joint Preoccupation with Social Justice and Politics in Education

Our personal narratives were told for a reason. Yes, part of the reason was mentioned earlier: they show some of the paths that might lead a woman (and, perhaps, some men too) to a feminist perspective in philosophy of education. But there is another reason. We may have used the metaphor of a roller coaster ride, but it was not a ride we took just for fun. Indeed not – there are easier ways of having fun. It was a roller coaster precisely because we keep alive the feeling that philosophic choice matters, that we should do more (and try to move our colleagues to do more) to look through our philosophic lenses at the lacks, the losses, the unfairnesses in the work we try to share. The narratives point up why we share a preoccupation with questions of social justice and political action in relation to education. They also point to some reasons why we would call our approach to such questions *feminist*. It remains to show what such an approach might look like in practice, even if only briefly.

Over the years each of us has explored justice and freedom in relation to education, in a series of books and articles (for instance, recently, in Greene, 1988, 1995, 2000; Griffiths and Davies, 1995; Griffiths, 1998, 2000). We show how the political abstractions of justice and freedom work themselves out in educational practices and contexts. We link them to social imagination, fairness, equality, subversion, and the establishment of spaces free of cruelty, torture, harassment, and bullying. No doubt there are significant differences between us of emphasis or of detail. Nonetheless, we concur that a just society is one in which we all contribute (or could contribute) and benefit. Influenced by Arendt, we use ideas of coconstruction, of the in-between. With Arendt, too, we see freedom as related to that "in-between" (Greene, 1988, esp. ch. 1). Freedom is to be found in action *with* others. It is not simply the negative freedom of interference *from* others, nor again is it simply the freedom to make individual choices (Arendt, [1961] 1993, p. 151). There is an equality of recognition of the presence of the other as *who* as well as *what* she is. This is not, we would emphasize, an equality of sameness; it is an equality that "is the result of human organization insofar as it is guided by the principle of justice" (Arendt, 1968, p. 301). This kind of organization must be one which we all create – and continue to create – by working *with* (not *on* or *for*) others (Griffiths, 1998). It is much more than the equal distribution of benefits. And it is a project that is never finished; nor could it be.

Women in Public (and Noticing Them When They are There)

The principles of justice and freedom imply the existence of some kind of public space: a space, a place, where people can meet, discuss, argue, throw out ideas, work out their common concerns, and decide what to do for the best. So it is not surprising that, since the Greeks, Western political philosophy has been concerned with the nature of such a space. The Greeks themselves imagined their own such space to be the public square, the agora. They distinguished it from their private households in the city and its surroundings.

This idea has kept a hold on political philosophy ever since. Even though the city state has long since disappeared, even though public face-to-face meetings have not been the usual way for a polity to talk to itself for a long time, the idea of the agora (or the forum, or the public arena) has retained its hold. It is an idea that continues to have a strong influence today. In particular, modern Liberalism,[8] which is still the dominant influence on political discourse in the West, depends on a notion of "the public" – a public arena open to everyone – which is sharply distinguished from "the private."[9] At the same time, liberalism is not the only source of political ideas, merely the dominant one. Nor is it the only theory to distinguish private and public. Arendt, for instance, does so, but is certainly no liberal (Young-Bruehl, 1982; Benhabib, 1992). Dewey (1927) says a public space is opened when people with a shared interest take action to repair deficiencies or fill in the empty spaces – spaces often defined by irony, by ambiguity.

Over the last few decades feminist theorists have identified the mainstream under-standing of "the public" as a problem for women. They have pointed out that what counts as a proper subject for a public airing has been defined by men. The slogan "the personal is political" encapsulated this insight, and heralded public discussion of matters like housework, domestic violence, and sexual harassment, previously deemed to be private concerns. Feminist theorists have also pointed to the narrowly male-defined, male-assumed, rules of argument and to the silencing or erasure of women's voices. Liberal theorists have been uncomfortable with such challenges because liberalism prides itself on making no assumptions about the individuals who enter public space. They are meant to be equal in their humanity. As Jeremy Bentham put it, "Each man shall count for one and no more than one." How often these individuals are, in fact, tacitly male, has been the subject of a series of devastating (now classic) critiques by feminist philosophers, notably Benhabib, Irigaray, Jagger, Lloyd, Martin, and the women of the Milan Women's Bookshop. These critiques by feminists overlap with similar critiques from perspectives rooted in experiences of both women and men facing exclusion on the grounds of their being, for instance, black or Jewish, or gay/lesbian, or born in a poor part of the world.

A further problem with the notion of "the public" springs from its conceptual opposition to "the private." This opposition has sexist effects (rather more than racist or social class-based effects) because the ideas of "public" and "private" are themselves gender-inflected for Westerners. In an early piece of feminist philosoph-ical analysis, *Public Man and Private Woman*, Jean Elshtain (1981) traces the effects of that gender inflection through the history of Western philosophy. Susan Okin

(1995) points out how even a liberal like Rawls, writing so recently, assumes households of whom only the "heads of households" take part in the polity. Somebody, after all, has to mind the baby and put hot dinners on the table.

Is all this still relevant? Rawls wrote his main work 30 years ago now. Surely since then we have experienced such a "genderquake" that men now rock the cradles and help to look after their elderly relatives as well as ironing their own shirts. Doesn't what would have been thought personal and private now routinely appear in public life (childcare, cooking, maintaining the home)? And don't women so routinely take their place in public life that nobody expects otherwise? It would seem not as much as they might. The reports of the genderquake have been exaggerated. Much of the apparent appearance of the personal in public space is just that: apparent. All the public kissings of spouses and photo opportunities of public figures engaged in family activities could well be described as performance, as a simulacrum, as fetishization. Current citizenship debates make us realize that the old exclusions are alive and well in school (for instance, see Arnot and Dillabough, 2000; Enslin and White, this volume). More widely, another concrete effect of continuing exclusion is the way women still barely figure in national and international decision making (for instance, see Brine, 1999; Hutchings, 1996; Okin, 1995).

There is another possibility. Maybe the reports of a genderquake are not only exaggerated but continue an inaccuracy that has persisted for decades, perhaps for centuries? Women do "do politics" and they always have. As Siltanen and Stanworth (1984, p. 185) pointed out, years ago, "The fact that women's political capacity has been underestimated and undervalued in male-stream literature is now well established." How else did the feminist movement not only get going but keep going? Somehow the public space that women have inhabited has been overlooked by orthodox perspectives.

Metaphorical thinking

Our suggestion is that the old categorization, the old vision of "the public," has become frozen, and clouded with age. We need to rethink, to think differently: to use our imaginations again.[10] This is a highly metaphorical statement but we make no apology for that. Rather, in this section we go on to consider metaphorical language as a way of rethinking and questioning orthodox thinking.

I

A metaphor is what it does. A metaphor, because of the way it brings together things that are unlike, reorients consciousness, which customarily connects things that are like. Poetry, obviously, is made of metaphors. I keep asking teachers to think more metaphorically, not so straight ahead.

Toni Morrison's *Jazz* could be thought of as a metaphor. It is a very peculiar book in a way, because of the way it starts out. The narrator, the *I*, is never identified. You do not know who it is or what it is, though people make assumptions. It was somehow that unknown narrator that opened it for me. It was one of the metaphors that was so powerful for me in that book, though I'm not sure how many other people saw it that way. It is about a man who is married to Violet but is forever in search of his mother and of the young girl he loved – and killed. Violet and Joe had been migrant workers in the South. They came up to Harlem, where he falls in love with a girl, and she plays around with other guys and he kills her. She will not say that he is the one who killed her. Then Violet, his wife, runs into the funeral parlor during the funeral and tries to slash the dead girl's face. The story is like jazz. It keeps introducing the themes over and over. It sums it up by talking about how it was snowing, and how Violet opened the window and pushed everything out the window, including the parrot that said, "I love you." Later on the book goes back in time. Violet's mother is evicted in the South. The men come in. The mother has got her coffee on the table, and they take the table away. She doesn't get up and they tip her onto the floor. Then, it says, she commits suicide a little while later. That became the metaphor for me, the parrot on the verge, and the women on the verge. So I read the book in terms of always being on the verge, as black people are. The book is an example to me of how you can come on a metaphor like that and it makes you see what you did not even suspect before. In a larger sense it is saying that black people, then, in the 1920s, were always on the edge, always on the verge of being killed or lynched. And, later on, in our own time, discrimination, sometimes veiled, continues to harm and isolate African Americans.

II

I am interested by Maxine's thought that a metaphor is what it does, which is to open up ways of seeing, because I began this joint piece of work on the public and political from a contrary perception. I have long been impressed by the way that metaphors can close down the imagination, especially when they are used uncritically for too long. The language is crammed with "dead metaphors." I learned this from feminists like Maryann Ayim (1987). She pointed out how the philosophical literature so abounds in metaphors of violence to describe arguments ("between a rock and a hard place" or "to go for the jugular," and so on) that it becomes difficult to think of an argument as anything else but a violent contest. I also think of many feminist critiques of the metaphors of science: for instance (male) scientists dominating, marrying, or raping (female) Nature. In feminist critiques of science the frozen metaphors of science are seen as constricting. Once a metaphor is frozen it is very hard to stop thinking with it. An influential book by Lakoff and Johnson (1980) has unearthed a lot of dead – or perhaps just frozen – metaphors that constrict how we speak and act. For instance they demonstrate that we think with the metaphor "Argument is war" rather than, say, "Argument is conversation."

III

The metaphor is associated with the imagination rather than with any kind of linguistic structure. For Max Black, metaphors were schemata. Sartre talks about them in terms of images but I think they cannot be in images. We might expand our perspectives and think about metaphors in terms of meanings. Metaphors make us see things differently. Hawthorne's *The Scarlet Letter* is full of metaphors and so are his stories, and the questions they raise are not the ones you could get from even the most elegant reports of Horace Mann. For instance, the story of the maypole is a metaphor. Again, Hawthorne writes that Hester Prynne sees the world "like a wild Indian"; there is a metaphor of the effect of her ostracism at the verge of the wilderness. It is then she begins to engage in speculative and emancipatory thinking that would have scared the elders more than her adultery.

Morwenna talks of feminist science. Think about Barbara McClintock. She was the most wonderful one for metaphor, with her ideas of jumping genes and how instead of exploiting the earth you're friends with it. And what about Donna Haraway and her work on cyborgs?

IV

Maxine is right. Fox Keller (1985) shows us how McClintock's use of metaphor helped engender her distinctive approach to science. And it is true that Donna Haraway uses metaphors as a way of opening up our thinking about science. The cyborg is an imaginative metaphor. She uses it to turn upside down the idea that women (and the feminine) are associated with the "natural," unlike men (and the masculine) who are associated with science and technology. She invites us to use our imaginations to see that we can embrace the connections that we already have to science and technology. We are already cyborgs and that is to be celebrated. Her purpose was that her readers end up with a new way of looking at things.

However I still think that metaphors can close down thinking as much as they can open it up. McClintock's metaphor of "listening to the material" is powerful in opening it up. However it is significant that we read about it in the context of Fox Keller's criticisms of scientists. She points out that they rejected McClintock as eccentric, and reacted to her metaphors with incomprehension. Similarly, Haraway (1991) creates new metaphors in her work about the cyborg but she does it partly to work against the old frozen metaphors that close down thinking: woman is natural and organic; man is technological. However, these metaphors remain alive and well. Maxine, on the other hand, unlike me, might want to say that if a metaphor does not make us see differently then it has stopped being a metaphor. But if so, what would we call the imagery that stops thinking – but which plainly came from the use of somebody's imagination years ago – like "the public arena," or "going for the jugular" or "the rape of nature"?

My suggestion now is that a metaphor is something that frames ways of understanding. Some frames open up your world, make you look again, look differently. They invite you to try new frames of your own. Other frames constrict your world. They close it down, discouraging the use of any other frames. They become fixed, rigid, frozen, and cloudy with age. It should be possible to turn the second kind into the first by being creative – by playing – with the frames we have. There is an example in Arendt's (1961) Preface, "The Gap Between Past and Future." She draws on an image of Kafka's of the past as an assailant pushing forward and of the future as another assailant pushing backwards. She then goes on to play with this vivid image as a way of making us see (human) time differently. This seems to be one of Maxine's "opening up" metaphors. (Though I do not at all want to suggest that Kafka's image was constricting. The point is what Arendt did with it.)

A play for public space: using metaphor

We see that the Greek idea of the polis that Arendt talks about can be understood as a metaphor, but a frozen metaphor. We remarked earlier how people talk about the agora, the forum, the arena. However we do not live in small warring city states supported by a peasantry any more. It is only in villages like those in modern Greece and Turkey that we can still see the men drinking coffee in the main square while the women work in the fields and at home. In our own familiar world of connurbations and mass communications there is no parallel to such village squares where all the men can congregate. So why should we talk about *the* public arena, as if it were only one and as if we could all take our place in it? In this respect it is an unhelpful metaphor. On the other hand, as Maxine has argued (Greene, 2000), it can be helpful because of its connotations of enclosure. She discusses Melville's view of space in *Moby Dick*: the image of the great sea and its openness, the resonance of this image in the American imagination with the one of the wide open prairie. She goes on to argue how a contrary image, enclosure, is needed for a polis, understood in the Arendtian sense of a "space between," which is created and maintained by links with other people.

The need for other people in a polis, in all their lovely and intractable variety, is another reason that metaphorical thinking is so important in the creation of a public space as an in-between. Metaphor allows you to imagine the familiar face of the stranger. In other words, imagination makes empathy possible. It provides one means for particularity to get expression and to be communicated. The in-between is created by people speaking in terms of *who* they are, and not *what* they are; speaking in "agent-revealing voices." This is important because social justice on a purely abstract plane without room for the particularity of human beings does not mean anything.

I

I am interested in ways to create the spaces through the arts to see differently, to break through the crust. The alternative to fixities, to reification, is seeing differently, by all means available. To continue to struggle for all this, for the arts, for social justice, is to continue to struggle to protect the spaces where people can come to be. Relevant here is my long connection with the Lincoln Center Institute for the Arts in Education and the "Center for Social Imagination," in which I relate my concern with the arts and aesthetics to a concern for social justice and social action. I suppose these are both concerns with what Freire calls the process of "conscientization," which I call "wide-awakeness" a lot of the time. I have been the "philosopher-in-residence" at the Lincoln Center Institute for the Arts in Education, mostly a three-week summer program in which teachers work with professional artists in workshops, see exhibitions, see/hear performances, hear me on a kind of rudimentary aesthetics – and, in winter, artists come to schools to invent relevant multicultural, multiage programs.

One of the things Dewey talks about in *The Public and Its Problems* is domination by technology, where technology is controlled by experts. And then he talks about the importance of the arts. He says that they help you to break through the crust of conventionality and to reach below it. He talks about the triviality and superficiality of so much public opinion. He says that if the arts can undo the conversation then you touch a level of desire and memory that you would not be able to touch otherwise. The point of the dancing teachers at the Lincoln Center is not that they know more about the subject but that they open new modalities of getting in touch with people, feeling, knowledge, and so forth. So the teachers who attend the courses learn something of the language, something of how to do the dance. The teachers say things like, "Look at the light! Don't just follow the story." This is not "art education." It is more like the constructivist approach of making sense of the world, teaching people how to notice. At the Lincoln Center we see there are connections between the obsessive kinds of education talk that go on about zero tolerance, the criminalization of children, single standards, a preoccupation with testing four year olds, and the attacks on freedom that arts education makes possible. This is freedom found in a space where children and adults can make choices and act on them. Those other things narrow those choices.

II

Playing with metaphor seems a good way of dealing with a frozen metaphor. One way is, as Maxine says, through the creative play of the arts. Another way is to play imaginatively with the metaphor itself. Rethinking its meanings can free up the imagination to create new ways of speaking and acting. I suggest we take the metaphor of the agora and stretch it, unfreeze it, reframe it. There are any number of ways of doing this, limited only by our imaginations. We could think using the examples of the arena audience and the players (Is it a theater? A television? Does the action involve the audience directly? Is it perhaps a sports field?). We could think of chat rooms on the Web. We could imagine where the secret resistance movements, schools, education for teachers might have met in or out of the agora. We could think of the squares of bigger cities than Athens or Sparta (New York? Nottingham?).

Of these let us plump for the last of these (regretfully looking back at the others, but space is pressing): city squares. For instance we might notice that there are many city squares, connected by roads. Or again, we might notice that public squares are surrounded by houses with their rooms, gardens, and garden fences. (Or their New York equivalents – I do not know what these are! Cafes? Clubs? Salons like Maxine's?) So, to extend this metaphor of the agora and the spaces in between: what about talking about pavements and gardens? Talking over the garden fence, for instance. Or sitting in the garden. And I suppose the men in the agora come and sit in those gardens from time to time. So ideas travel both ways. Even if the men (mostly) do not stay long nor actually plan, buy, cook, set out, fetch, nor clear away the drinks and nibbles, women's talk of subversion can continue while doing the dishes afterwards.

This helps us think about real political actions. Walker (1998) describes the influence on nineteenth-century education policy of some Victorian women who plotted their moves into power while appearing to be staying respectably at home. At one university where I worked, we organized very informal "women and lunch" meetings at which real career moves and strategies against harassment were plotted, most successfully. And it is not only women who have needed to find other spaces to plot liberation. There are also the barber shops for men who cannot dare to walk in the agora: they were potent for leftist men in pre-war Spanish villages (R. Fraser, 1972).[11] And in apartheid South Africa in the 1980s, I am told:

> Private homes were critical to our ability (men and women, Black and some white) to keep building civil society. Public spaces were far too dangerous in all sorts of ways (although we used them too).
>
> The other intriguing example of this is the idea of the "street" as linking the private and the public and this made me think of the Black women who worked as servants in our Natal homes. There were all kinds of restrictions on having friends in their rooms so private space was very carefully controlled. But it was also traditional for Thursday afternoons to be the "maid's day off" so all the "nannies" would gather on the pavement on the boundaries of the white bosses' houses and who knows what then went on! (Melanie Walker, e-mail communication)

In 2000, black children in one British secondary school successfully used the invisible public spaces of the school to combat racism to act in response to their head teacher's racist remarks. Within a couple of hours of the remarks being made, all the black children in the school were present in class but on strike, refusing to take any part in the lesson. The head teacher apologized.[12]

An Indeterminate Ending

For social justice we need children who grow up to have attitude; children who speak up, act up and contribute rather than get their perspectives smoothed out in consensual agreements. That is, we need children and adults with the confidence and ability to make their voices heard, however those voices are expressed. Voices that contribute to social action need not only speak in rational prose. We need children and adults to "release their imagination" in order to release the imagination of others; to participate in a dialectic of freedom; to be themselves, together with others, and to create public spaces in which to exercise power in the world. The result would be radically indeterminate.

We have been arguing that feminist approaches to philosophy of education cannot be pinned down into any determinate system. Just so, we argue that a future of social justice would be new, radical, and currently unimaginable.

Notes

1 As the long history of misogyny in philosophy shows, many males only noticed gender as a marker of inferiority from their own universal humanity (Hughes, 1988; Shanley and Pateman, 1991).

2 Feminist philosophy focuses on, among other areas, language, rationality, logic, science, ontology, epistemology, ethics, politics, law, self-identity, as well as on gender itself. Standard collections include: Harding and Hintikka (1983), Griffiths and Whitford (1988), Gunew (1990), Lennon and Whitford (1994), Garry and Pearsall (1996), Nicholson (1990), Pateman and Grosz (1986), Bar On and Ferguson (1998) and some sections of Bono and Kemp (1991). (As in other academic areas, the size of the USA market means that USA-based feminists dominate the field though there is also plenty going on in the rest of the world.)

3 Feminist philosophers have had a lot to say about the body, and the sex/gender system. Even a short list leaves out some of the best known but here is one: de Beauvoir ([1949] 1972), Bordo (1993), Braidotti (1994), Butler (1990, 1993, 1997), Battersby (1998), Haraway (1991, 1996), Grosz (1994), Arthurs and Grimshaw (1998), Irigaray (1985a,b), Whitford (1991), Young (1990b), Diprose (1994), Gatens (1996).

4 Assiter (1996), Dickenson (1997), Martin (1985, 1994), Le Doeuff (1991), Cavarero, (1995), Lloyd ([1984] 1993), Kourany (1998), Okin (1979).

5 Discussions of situatedness are found in: Lennon and Whitford (1994), Benhabib (1992), Scheman (1993), Haraway (1991, 1996), Harding (1991), Martin (1994), Noddings (1984), Barr (1999), Griffiths (1995), Greene (1988, 1995), Narayan (1997).

6 Stanley (1997), Martin (1985, 1994), Barr (1999), Nussbaum (1997), Milan Women's Bookstore (1990).

7 Working in the tradition of Dewey, James, and the Existentialists, the Center brings schoolchildren, artists, academics, and social activists together in conferences and workshops to explore possibilities of reform and transformation in schools and social communities.

8 By "Liberalism" we mean the tradition largely derived from JS Mill: the pre-eminence of the right over the good and the defense of individual liberty against interference from others (see Berlin, 1969, pp. 164–5). To say this is merely to draw a rough boundary round a range of different kinds of Liberalism.

9 Other theories which are influential elide the distinctions altogether. Examples are versions of communitarianism, lifestyle politics, or politics based on post-structuralist/ postmodern theorizing about regimes of truth, resistance, border skirmishes, deployments of discourses, and discussions of hyperrealities. The stormy relationships of feminist activism and theory to all of these makes a complex story but this story is not our concern here. We focus on the influential and, we would say, still fertile, concepts of private and public.

10 We gratefully acknowledge other attempts to shift the vision, to melt hard-frozen frames, and to illuminate the field in regard of the relations between private, public, and political, especially: Young (2000), A. Phillips (1993), Benhabib (1992), P. Williams (1993), Pateman (1988) N. Fraser (1997).

11 This book is an oral history of Manuel Cortez, whose life was shaped by the 1930s conflicts in Spain. It shows how barbers' shops were a center for political discussion. He also relates how resulting political meetings were held in private houses. Cortez learnt his passion for justice in school, in spite of school: "The first time I saw social injustice was at school. Of course it was around me all the time, it was the air we breathed. But when

I saw the favoritism the schoolmaster showed the sons of the rich it made me more rebellious than ever. Despite that, I loved school" (Fraser, 1972, p. 78).

12 Personal communication from Tony Sewell.

Recommendations for Further Reading

Greene, Maxine (1995) *Releasing the Imagination: Essays on Education, the Arts, and Social Change*, Jossey Bass.

Griffiths, Morwenna (1998) *Educational Research for Social Justice: Getting off the Fence*, Open University Press.

Martin, Jane Roland (1994) *Changing the Educational Landscape: Philosophy, Women and Curriculum*, Routledge.

Milan Women's Bookstore Collective (1990) *Sexual Difference: A Theory of Social-Symbolic Practice*, Indiana University Press.

Part II

Politics and Education

Chapter 5

Liberalism and Communitarianism

Eamonn Callan and John White

I

Philosophy of education came into its own in the twentieth century, finding its first and still most influential voice in John Dewey and flourishing as a many-faceted, international pursuit after 1950. That pursuit is a critical enterprise, and by bringing basic assumptions and conceptual schemes to the bar of critical scrutiny, it can find no secure place in authoritarian regimes, except occasionally among their dissidents. It is thus hardly surprising that philosophy of education throughout the century frequently turned its attention to the basic political principles that make a free society possible. Since the last quarter of the twentieth century this development in the discipline's political self-awareness has been most marked. Yet as a critical enterprise, the philosophy of education has not satisfied itself simply with understanding its liberal pedigree. This too is properly subject to critical assessment.

What has been happening in the philosophy of education in recent years has mirrored a wider self-examination in liberal societies themselves. The challenge of communism until the last decade of the century, the defeats of colonialism and the emergence of new tyrannies in their aftermath, and finally, the persistence of national, religious, and ethnic conflict throughout the world have all heightened consciousness of the contingency of liberal politics. Political philosophy from the early John Rawls of the 1950s and 1960s onward has systematically addressed the foundations of liberalism, seeking to discover how secure these are. This body of work has spurred parallel inquiry within the philosophy of education, and critiques of liberalism in political philosophy have often been inseparable from critiques of liberalism in philosophy of education. Perhaps the most influential challenge of this kind has come from communitarianism. The basis of communitarian philosophy is the idea that liberal political principles rest on too thin a view of good lives and the good society. An implication of the idea is that liberal conceptions of education must militate against individual and social well-being. The debate between liberals and

Section I written by John White; Section II written by Eamonn Callan.

communitarians is far more than a theoretical diversion for philosophers and political scientists. At stake are rival understandings of what makes human lives and the societies in which they unfold both good and just, and derivatively, competing conceptions of the education needed for individual and social betterment.

The liberty at the heart of liberalism is the freedom of individuals to lead lives of their own. From the end of the nineteenth century this ideal, sometimes also called "positive liberty" or more recently "personal autonomy," became more clearly disentangled from the "negative liberty" that consists in the absence of certain impediments to doing what one wants. A prisoner free from jail is called "free" in the latter sense. But whether or not the freed prisoner is author of his or her own life is a further matter. Furthermore, contemporary liberalism is more emphatically egalitarian than its historical antecedents. Although no specific conception of justice unites liberal theorists, a common assumption is that all citizens are deserving of equal concern and respect. In securing conditions for the development and exercise of autonomy, the liberal state weighs the interests of all equally.

The ideal of an autonomy to which all people of normal cognitive capacity are in some sense entitled is not unique to the twentieth century. Both Kant and Mill developed conceptions of autonomy that were fundamental to their political theories, and each remains a powerful influence on contemporary liberal theory. But before 1900 liberalism as a political idea was more often associated with opposition to state power used to constrain market relations or arbitrarily favor hereditary elites. This emphasis on a negative liberty whose chief enemy is the state has persisted on the right wing of liberal democratic politics, where it now bears the label of "libertarianism." Libertarian political and educational philosophy remains an important scholarly genre. But from the perspective of contemporary liberalism, the libertarian fixation with limiting state power seems arbitrary. People need state support to become and remain authors of their own lives as often as they need freedom from the authority of an overweening state. According to liberals, negative freedom is not valuable in its own right but only as a necessary condition of autonomy.

How has liberalism affected educational philosophy? Historically, the story begins in the late eighteenth century. Early modern philosophers who had views on education, such as Descartes, Hobbes, Locke, and Leibniz, wrote about a disparate array of topics: the cultivation of the intellect, the aims of universities, the upbringing of gentlemen, the education of princes. Not surprisingly, they scarcely ever referred to anything any of the others wrote. But from Condorcet, Adam Smith, and Rousseau onwards, through Kant, Schiller, Herbart, Humboldt, J. S. Mill, and Nietzsche to Dewey, Russell, Percy Nunn, and writers of our own times, we find something like a continuous tradition of philosophical thought – with vastly different emphases, to be sure – about the education of citizens under conditions of political freedom (Rorty, 1998).

This tradition of liberal philosophy of education has to be distinguished from another, more ancient, line of thought on "liberal education" that remains influential today. That more ancient tradition, which begins with Plato, identifies the human good with the disinterested achievement of knowledge. Philosophical accounts of "liberal education" in this sense were prominent in the 1960s and early 1970s, for example, in the works of R. S. Peters (1966, 1975) and P. H. Hirst (1974b).

But these were based on different core values from those with which we will be concerned. A "liberal education" in the sense under discussion is an initiation into a range of forms of thought valuable for their own sake rather than for some extrinsic, for example, vocational, reason. But it is not a liberal conception as understood in the present chapter. Indeed, there are grounds for seeing it as an antiliberal conception. This version of liberal education is paternalist. Pupils brought up under its aegis are encouraged to see the pursuit of intellectual activities for its own sake as central to the good life. But why should such activities be privileged, given the great variety of other pursuits around which an autonomous life can be built?

A more genuinely liberal argument is this. Autonomy depends on the existence of options. Education cannot supply these, but it can make students aware of them. Its job is partly to open up horizons on different conceptions of how one should live – ways of life, forms of relationship, vocational and nonvocational activities. But a broad understanding of options is not enough. Autonomous agents also need to understand themselves. They need to interpret their major goals and establish priorities among them, and to discern possible psychological obstacles arising to their self-directness. In addition they need to understand the main features of the society in which they live and among whose options they will choose.

They need also to be equipped with qualities of character. They have, for instance, to be able to withstand pressures to conform to what authority or public opinion want them to do. For this they require the critical independence of thought to assess others' arguments, as well as the moral courage to stand up for their own views. Exercise from as early an age as practicable in making choices and reflecting on these is a further requirement – as is a whole-heartedness of commitment to activities of their own choosing.

How should such aims be realized? There are tasks here for both families and schools. With regard to the latter, philosophers of education have paid considerable attention to the kind of school curriculum best suited to promote autonomy. To some extent opening up horizons on options must draw on traditional academic subjects, but the project goes wider than these. A personal/social, including civic, element in the curriculum is also important for the further aims outlined in the previous two paragraphs.

But the curriculum is not the only way of realizing aims. Whole school processes also play a role, many would say a more important one. An authoritarian ethos is unlikely to encourage autonomy, except perhaps in a few rebels. Neither is a school day tight-packed with constrained activities. Seeing how much is learned by example, children need teachers who both think for themselves and are self-directing in the conduct of their lives.

Liberal educational thinking has taken other directions than this. Sometimes egalitarian values have been played down: education is for personal autonomy, but not personal autonomy for all. Nietzsche's account of self-creation has been one source of inspiration for elitist thinking of this sort.

Sometimes, as has been said, the focus has been on negative liberty, especially on diminishing the power of the state to fund, manage, or determine the content of school education. This has been intended to give more power to parents or to communities. Since it does not guarantee that every child will be educated for personal self-directedness, it may lead to conflict with the mainstream liberal ideal discussed above.

Sometimes liberalism has taken a "child-centered" turn. Of course, the mainstream view is child-centered in that it aims at every child having a fulfilling life of his or her own – rather than, say, being more centrally focused on subject-learning. The mainstream view sees autonomy as an ideal for mature persons, and children as being gradually prepared for an autonomy that lies substantially in their future rather than their present. But this presupposes a distinction between children and adults that some would reject or at least blur substantially. On this latter view, the compulsory curriculum to which children are normally subjected may be as unjustified as any other of the constraints on free choice that liberals have traditionally deplored.

Sometimes the child-centered view has taken a specifically biological interpretation. On this view children develop mentally just as they grow physically. The educator's task is to facilitate this development rather as gardeners create the best conditions in which their plants can grow. Nature, not parents, teachers, or the state, sets the direction toward which education should proceed. Once again, this makes the compulsory curriculum anathema.

Variants of this kind of theory have appealed to liberal educational thinkers from Rousseau through to Nunn and beyond. In Nunn (1945), it was harnessed to the specifically Millian ideal of individuality, the purpose of education being the fullest possible development of the student's individuality. This was tied to a psychological theory positing that the individual differences so important in Mill's social ideal had innate roots. Contemporary ideas of intelligence, as measured by IQ, were woven into this story.

From the mainstream liberal point of view, the biological approach is both misconceived and counterproductive. It underplays the role of social standards in shaping the content of children's minds, not least in their acquisition of concepts. Children need, for instance, to be inducted by others into what "cat" or "triangle" or "grateful" mean and corrected when they make mistakes. If the main directions of young children's intellectual and ethical learning are not firmly laid down by adults already initiated into these, the children will be hindered in acquiring the prerequisites of an autonomous life. (For further discussion of the role of social standards in the formation of individuals, see the following section on communitarianism.)

Nevertheless, child-centered theory is not inevitably tied to an untenable biological view about the course of autonomous development. Egalitarian liberalism is in principle suspicious of the idea that the moral standing of one group of persons (for example, men rather than women, members of one ethnic group rather than another, etc.) differ from those of another in ways that justify greater coercion toward one rather than the other. That being so, the child/adult distinction is an appropriate object of philosophical scrutiny for liberals, and even when it is conceded that the distinction is often morally relevant, its relevance is not so clear to the extent that a compulsory curriculum on the mainstream view has been conclusively justified.

Let us look more deeply at some problems in the mainstream position. First, if one allows influences from one's society and people around one to help shape one's identity, how can this be the self-creation that the autonomy ideal seems to demand? Liberalism appears to point to the rejection of anything that has helped to shape one

– the character formed in one in childhood by one's parents, the traditions of one's society. But what would remain of one if all the layers were removed? Is liberalism coherent?

Again, how are we to take the idea of self-creation? One strand in liberal educational thinking, coming to us via Schiller and Nietzsche with overtones of Plato, is aesthetic. On one view, human life is modeled on a work of art, fulfillment being seen in terms of a harmonious relationship between disparate elements. In Nunn's case, following a different aesthetics, this was seen in terms of "expressiveness": children's individuality is most adequately developed when their powers of self-expression, again explicitly modeled on the expressive abilities of the artist, are given fullest rein.

Critics would point to dangers in tying liberalism too closely to ideas of self-creation taken in these senses. Autonomy does not imply the rejection of the influences that have shaped one, only by certain reflective attitudes toward them compatible with embracing them if they are in line with one's main goals and ideals. The aesthetic version of self-creation veers toward illiberalism if learners are steered toward having to turn their lives into a kind of art-work. This is only one way of conceiving a human life, and most self-directing people lead lives full of unresolved conflicts and psychic loose ends, which puts the artistic analogy under unbearable strain.

A second problem is perhaps more serious. A central concern of the liberal educator is to promote the learner's personal autonomy. But is this itself not just another form of illicit steering, as antipathetic to the liberal ideal as that mentioned in the last paragraph? Why should learners have to conform to what their educators think good for them?

A first response on the liberal's part may be that the learners don't have to conform. If at the end of their apprenticeship in autonomy they decide to forgo a life of their own in favor of, say, strict adherence to a religious code, then that is their decision. But is this answer good enough? For these and other students have already been molded as autonomous persons. How can liberals justify this given their own assumptions?

Critics will urge the need to distinguish between the autonomous life and the flourishing life, or the life of personal well-being. The liberal position seems to run these two together, taking it as read that autonomy is and must be the road to well-being. But not all societies and not all groups within them have taken this line. A religious group may locate personal well-being in strict obedience to God. If the defender of liberalism is a secularist, he or she may dismiss this as based on an inadequate metaphysics. But what is he or she to say about the following argument?

A life of well-being is one in which, among other things, one's basic biological needs are met and one's major goals in life are broadly achieved. Take a tribal community that has never known personal autonomy. The goals that its members aim at – being a good farmer, warrior, parent, and so forth, by the standards of the tribe – have all been laid down by immemorial custom. It is possible to distinguish between a tribesman who is successful in all the tasks ascribed to him and is held in high esteem by his fellows from another who for whatever reason – weakmindedness, ill-luck, ill-health, or whatever – fails in most of what he undertakes, is reviled by the tribe, goes blind early in life, loses all his children in childbirth. The former surely leads a more flourishing life than the latter. Yet neither is in any way leading an autonomous life. So well-being and autonomy need not go together.

The upshot for liberalism is this. If autonomy is not necessary for personal well-being, what can justify the liberal's insistence on it? There are practical issues of educational policy that arise at this point. In multicultural, multifaith societies, some groups will see the cultivation of autonomy as a threat to ideals they cherish, such as traditional conceptions of the family or customary religious practices and doctrines. Should the liberal state impose its values through the educational system on children from these groups? If the answer is "yes," its justification will hinge on finding a compelling reason to link the development of autonomy to the well-being of these children, even when the development may put severe strain on family attachments and cultural identity. But one influential school of thought in contemporary liberal philosophy – so-called "political liberalism" – would seem to suggest that the right answer is a qualified "no." According to political liberalism, our commitment to tolerance should trump our commitment to autonomy.

By far the most influential liberal philosopher in the last half of the twentieth century, John Rawls, has embraced political liberalism in his most recent work (Rawls, 1993). Here personal autonomy does not have the central place it had in what is now called the "comprehensive liberalism" of the earlier book (Rawls, 1971). That is because that kind of liberalism, premised on the ideal of personal autonomy for everyone, is only one kind of "comprehensive doctrine" about how one should lead one's life; since in a pluralist society there will be many comprehensive doctrines of religious and other kinds, room must be found for all of them to flourish without privileging ones based on autonomy. Followers of the later Rawls, like Kenneth Strike, would argue that aims of education deriving from particular comprehensive doctrines have a legitimate place in a liberal society and are not to be trumped by civic aims – to do with promoting autonomy and democratic character – arising from ethical liberalism (Strike, 1994).

The merits of political over comprehensive liberalism remain heavily contested (Callan, 1997). One powerful objection is that if state-mandated education on the political liberal account must defer to cultural practices that instill patterns of subordination – the deference of women to men, say – then the state would become complicit in the perpetuation of oppressive cultural practices. That cannot be a welcome outcome for anyone who takes the egalitarian aspect of liberalism seriously.

And what if children are socialized into the beliefs of their families and groups without being encouraged to reflect on these and shape a life of their own? Would this matter? As we have seen, some stress that there can be fulfillment without autonomy. But others will ask why the group's paternalist preferences should win out. Who is right?

This leads us back to the justification of autonomy. If the liberal is to win the argument, she or he will have to provide convincing reasons why autonomy should be an aim in every child's education. Joseph Raz has argued that, although well-being does not in general require autonomy, in the modern, industrialized societies in which so many of us live it is not possible to lead a flourishing life unless self-directing (Raz, 1986). This is because the major institutions in these societies all presuppose autonomous agents. Marriages are based on consent, not parental prearrangement; it is taken as read that people are free (in theory) to live where they want (unlike the citizens of the former USSR, who needed a license to live in certain cities), choose their job or their religion rather than being directed into it, and so on. In an "autonomy-supporting society" of this sort one would be severely hampered in attaining one's major goals if one were not autonomous.

On this view, education policy concerning nonautonomy-favoring groups might depend on whether, like many children from such groups in Britain, the expectation would be that when adults they would live at least partly in the mainstream, autonomy-supporting, society, or whether, like children from the Amish community in America, they are likely to remain wholly within their own group. Whereas the latter, on Raz's argument, could lead a fulfilled though heteronomous life, this would not be possible for the former. But would this be enough to justify educating children from, for example, the Amish community totally within its values? Or does every child have the right of exit from its original community?

There are large, and as yet unresolved, issues in all this. One has to do with the adequacy of Raz's justification. What kind of autonomous life does it justify? Many people in Britain and comparable countries choose their jobs, partners, leisure pursuits, town where they live, vacation destinations, and so on. Some of these make their choices pretty unreflectively, perhaps guided by some simple utilitarian considerations which they have picked up from those around them about what is likely to yield most in terms of comfort, wealth, power. Are they, too, autonomous? If we insist on tighter criteria, involving greater critical reflectiveness about possibilities, the bases on which choices are made, the framework values of the society in which they live – do we not have to go beyond Raz's justification?

A further problem facing the mainstream liberal position has to do with the place of personal autonomy among other values. If it is given absolute priority, what is there to stop a liberal society becoming a mass of self-seeking self-creators, a society in which, in Herbart's (1806) words, "each brags of his individuality and no one understands his fellows"?

There is an answer to this from within the liberal tradition. We have already touched on it. If autonomy is an ideal for every citizen, then it would make best sense to bring children up with some interest in promoting other people's self-directedness as well as their own. This would mean cultivating in them the public virtues associated with negative liberty, of tolerantly leaving people free to lead their own lives, not breaking promises to them, physically abusing them, stealing their property. But it would also point to something more positive than this, to helping to provide other necessary conditions of autonomous well-being like good health, education, material resources.

There are few liberals who would not see their liberalism as bringing with it moral/civic educational prescriptions of this sort. A theoretical issue that might divide them is: to what extent is altruism already embedded in the autonomy ideal itself, rather than constraining it from without? The basic issue here about autonomous well-being is really about well-being rather than autonomy. Can a concern for one's own well-being be conceived in total abstraction from a concern with the well-being of other people?

II

As a political philosophy, liberalism grounds the political organization of society on the exclusive values of individual choice and well-being. That is the substance of "liberal individualism." To accept liberal individualism is not to be indifferent to community. But it does mean that the community liberals can encourage or tolerate must be adapted to the worth of individual lives and the freedom of choice that properly gives each life its distinctive course. Communities that violate the rights of individuals may be subject to the coercive intervention of the liberal state, even if coercion threatens the survival of the group over time. Groups that curtail the individual right to exit, for example, or restrict education in ways that impede the ability freely to choose a way of life are liable to run foul of the liberal state's authority. The question then is whether these constraints on the kinds of community worth promoting or tolerating are defensible. Communitarians think not.

Communitarian arguments are best understood as defining a reactive philosophical stance that liberalism has episodically evoked since the early nineteenth century. The reaction is motivated by questions that are both ethical and metaphysical. Might not liberalism exaggerate the place of individual choice and well-being in its interpretation of the good and just society? Much of what enriches our lives is found in associations of family, culture, and creed that we do not initially or perhaps ever choose. And if the good society is a place where our lives are woven together by shared adherence to a common good, does not liberalism sponsor attitudes that alienate us from one powerful source of human fulfillment and social cohesion? Similarly, it may be doubted that liberalism rests on a metaphysically coherent conception of the individual, given the constitutive role of social practices in forming any self. Communitarians believe that liberals have no satisfactory way of answering these questions. A different political philosophy is needed to give community its due. And a different educational philosophy is necessary too since liberal educational thought is said to be infected with the same politically corrosive and metaphysically false individualism that its political philosophy expresses.

Communitarian arguments are sometimes adduced in support of a diverse array of particular educational policies, including religious exercises in state-sponsored schools, school choice for parents, and cooperative learning in classrooms (Haldane, 1986; Bricker, 1988). But trying to understand what is at stake between communitarian and liberal philosophies by dwelling on their implications for educational policy is often more confusing than enlightening. Many versions of communitarianism are not so sharply distinguished from liberalism that they will not often yield convergent policy implications; for example, there are liberal as well as communitarian arguments for school choice and the civic importance of cooperative learning. Furthermore, the internal diversity of both liberalism and communitarianism means that within each category there might be sharp differences among theorists that generate divergent implications for policy. Communitarians differ on the question whether the nation-state can be construed as an object apt for communal identification, and their differences have an obvious bearing on questions about the desirability and content of a national curriculum and the proper scale and ends of state regulation of schools. Nevertheless, the distinction between liberalism and communitarianism is of immense practical consequence, notwithstanding these complexities. Whether the best argument for school choice is liberal or communitarian, say, is likely to make a profound difference to the purpose and design of the policy. A liberal argument might stress the importance of enforcing strong safeguards on children's rights in any choice scheme, even when these have damaging consequences on the survival of cultural groups across generations. Communitarians would likely be skeptical of arguments for robust safeguards on children's rights in the regulation and funding of schools since these might weaken the effectiveness of school choice as a means of empowering communities to inculcate their values more successfully in the young. But we cannot be clear about who would have the better argument in that or any similar dispute without an understanding and assessment of the rival political philosophies to which the arguments implicitly or explicitly appeal. Liberal and communitarian theories articulate ideals that have long had a powerful hold on our political imagination, and these ideals permeate our thinking about the state's role in education even when we pretend to be indifferent to philosophical abstractions.

For two decades much Anglo-American political philosophy has revolved around the comparative strengths and weaknesses of liberal and communitarian theory. Yet the basic terms of the debate go back much farther than that. The paradigm communitarian argument remains Hegel's critique of Kant's moral (and his derivative political) theory. Kantian ethics celebrate the sovereign rational agent, who ascertains the moral law by abstracting from the accidents of history and the claims of allegiance that any existing social group make upon him or her. Hegel argued that Kant's moral conception empties the ethical life of substance because the abstraction it enjoins would blind us to the particular obligations we incur as members of ongoing communities, with distinctive histories and conventions that inform our very identities (Taylor, 1975, pp. 365–88). The success of the Hegelian critique is contestable, and in any event, the viability of the liberal tradition does not stand or fall with Kant's moral philosophy. But Kant has remained a vital influence on liberal theory, and the Hegelian critique opened up a vein of argument against liberalism that continues to be exploited.

Hegel's elevation of received roles and obligations over the imperatives of autonomous reason might be taken to suggest that communitarianism is necessarily complacent about social practices in their current forms. That is not so after Hegel. Anxiety about the moral decay and fragmentation of existing communities is a pervasive theme of communitarian discourse in the twentieth century. But the resources for political renewal must be found within established social practices that vary greatly from one time or place to another, and liberal politics discards these resources, or so communitarians would claim. Nevertheless, if liberal values are part of a public culture – and they are a part even in societies where the influence of liberal thought might be fairly recent and weak – a communitarian account of politico-moral argument cannot rule out altogether the appeal to liberal values. Thus the flourishing society that communitarians seek to create through educational and other means might embody many things that liberals also cherish – for example, respect for freedom of conscience and speech. The justification of these values would have to avoid the supposed individualistic errors of liberal philosophy. Thus liberties of conscience, speech, and the like would have to be interpreted and limited by an overarching commitment to the good of society as a whole, and the proper place of communal identification in the lives of individuals.

A case in point is John Dewey's political and educational theory, developed over a remarkable career that began in the 1880s and only ended at his death in 1952. Dewey's is perhaps the most substantial attempt to construct a communitarian theory of democracy and democratic education that absorbs important liberal elements. Although he is often classified in the USA as the liberal philosopher of education par excellence, this ignores the deeply communitarian currents in his work that endured long after his early intellectual infatuation with Hegel.

The unifying thread in Dewey's philosophy is an understanding of democracy that extends beyond familiar notions of political self-rule and comes to signify an ideal way of living in community. That way of living would be realized through the proliferation of shared interests across existing social fissures, and a collective deployment of a critical intelligence that could only succeed through cooperative endeavor (Dewey, 1916). Dewey believed his democratic ideal was latent in American culture and inseparably tied to the progressive tendencies of modern science. But he also knew that the struggle for democratic community contended with powerful opposing pressures which included the atomizing effects of industrial capitalism, the persistence of premodern forms of religiosity, and the shallow individualism that liberal thought had traditionally encouraged. Dewey believed that the school was the principal site for the realization of democratic community. If democratic community required a convergence of interests and a widely diffused critical intelligence that existing institutions only faintly anticipated, social progress depended on what and how students learned in the one formative institution all held in common – the public school. The public school should aspire to be a microcosm of democratic community at its best. There cooperative habits and the sharing of interests would be nurtured, learning would proceed through collaborative problem solving in a scientific spirit, and the servility and domination that traditional pedagogy embodied would give way to more egalitarian relations.

The ideal of democratic community that Dewey articulated certainly seems to express some important liberal values. The language of liberty resonates throughout his writing. What is more doubtful is whether his democratic ideal successfully reconciles communitarian concerns with our intuitions about the full significance of individual liberty and cognate values. For Dewey, democratic education rightly operates as an overwhelmingly powerful centripetal force in the formation of identity. Lives become melded together through an increasingly dense network of shared interests that blur the distinction between private and public life as the rancorous conflicts of imperfectly democratic societies gradually give way to the cooperative dialogue of scientifically minded citizens, working together to surmount common obstacles. Their shared interests and scientific worldview forecloses serious disagreement about ends. Science also operates as a powerful engine of consensus about the means to achieve those ends and affords boundless prospects of success in their achievement. In Dewey's flourishing democracy, liberty becomes something other than the bulwark of individual dignity against invasive states or intolerant cultures: it is simply the absence of impediments to the realization of democratic community.

Respect for rights and liberty matters (only) so far as the consequences of respect bring us closer to authentic democracy. This seems to run counter to something deep about what a humane politics would be under modern conditions of diversity, something that was evident in Dewey's era but is now more obvious than ever.

The "fact of pluralism," as Rawls calls it, is the persistence of conflicting creeds, cultures, and ethical beliefs within shared political structures. The germinal idea of liberal politics in seventeenth-century Europe was religious toleration, and that toleration signified a limited acceptance of the fact of pluralism: no just state could force a religious orthodoxy on all citizens. As liberalism has developed in ways that widen acceptance, and sometimes foster celebration of other sources of diversity, the vocabulary of individual rights and liberties have often been a potent way of giving voice to criticism of oppressive measures against dissident individuals or despised groups. The vocabulary has had that potency precisely because it presupposes that people have interests we must honor even when their conduct is in conflict with a given community's or state's received understanding of "the common good." This is a point worth emphasizing. For although "the fact of pluralism" is commonly invoked as if it referred to the existence of monolithic groups, pluralism character-izes the inner workings of groups as well as oppressed subgroups, such as women or heterodox religious believers. These may stand in need of the state's protection against discrimination or intolerance as much as the larger group to which they belong.

But all this gives us reason to worry that Dewey's democratic education and its communitarian rationale do not adequately accommodate the fact of pluralism. The only diversity worth having, on Dewey's account, is whatever can survive the massive diffusion of shared interests and the triumph of scientific intelligence, conceived as a comprehensive worldview rather than a specialized form of reasoning. To be sure, his democratic education is not coercive. But the scope of the assimilation it warrants is completely open-ended, and his political theory leaves no room for any appeal to individual rights and liberties to limit its pursuit. For if rights and liberties are only means to the end of democratic community, nothing that conduces to democratic community could be coherently condemned on their basis. The larger question Dewey's project raises is whether any version of communitarianism can be reconciled to the compelling moral relevance of "the fact of pluralism."

The question of how communitarian theory might be a morally plausible alternat-ive to liberalism under conditions of diversity surfaces again with the communitarian revival of the early 1980s. The most influential texts of the revival, Alasdair MacIntyre's *After Virtue* and Michael Sandel's *Liberalism and the Limits of Justice*, each developed a somewhat different indictment of liberalism (MacIntyre, 1981; Sandel, 1982). But both arrived at broadly similar conclusions. According to MacIntyre, liberalism made a life of authentic virtue impossible because it sundered moral judgement from the sustaining context of shared practices and coherent traditions. For example, liberal talk of human or natural rights appeals to sheer "fictions" because it falsely purports to employ a moral reason that transcends historically situated communities and the substantive common goods that give focus to the development and exercise of virtue. Such talk merely obscures the amoral character of the liberal individual, who learns to see social cooperation as adherence to a contractual system of rules in which self-interest alone can motivate parties to the contract. Moral education is thus impossible within the ethos of liberal modernity, and it could only be renewed through the revival of communities in which premodern ideas about how virtue and shared goods are internally related still have some purchase.

MacIntyre says nothing about how that renewal might be accomplished. But a reasonable inference would be that its success must depend in part on a scrupulously insular education, in which children learn to conceive their own good in terms of the established practices of their communities of birth and acquire the virtues that sustain these practices from one generation to another. Insularity would be necessary to protect that delicate process of learning from the moral toxins of modernity and pluralism. But this inevitably raises questions about how rights to exit on their most modest interpretation could be respected in the conduct of education. MacIntyre might be indifferent to such matters since his rejection of liberalism is unqualified. But for anyone with an attachment to rudimentary liberal values – a much larger group than those who embrace (or even know about) liberal theory – these conclusions are scarcely tolerable.

Sandel's *Liberalism and the Limits of Justice* (1982) is a sustained communitarian critique of Rawls's *A Theory of Justice* (1971). Metaphysical considerations predominate in the way the argument is framed: Rawls is accused of presupposing an untenable view of the self as an abstract rational chooser, "unencumbered" by the social ties and attachments that must constitute the being of any self. Liberals could easily show that Rawls's theory (and liberalism in general) presupposed no such thing. But Sandel's argument also invited an ethical rather than a metaphysical reading that had obvious affinities with MacIntyre's strictures on liberalism. Suppose we think of the (relatively) "encumbered" and the (relatively) "unencumbered" self not as rival metaphysical theories of the person but as marking a distinction between different kinds of socially situated selves. Encumbered selves are closely tied to others in ways that potentially enrich their lives and those of others. Relations to others in community are experienced as part of the very fabric of identity, rather than external possessions we abandon or discard according to the vagaries of preference. Then Sandel might be taken to argue that only encumbered selves can participate in the construction and maintenance of a good society, and only they can escape the anomie and mutual estrangement that afflict our lives under a liberal dispensation.

As in MacIntyre's case, education is not Sandel's primary concern, but in his more recent work, *Democracy's Discontent*, the role of the state in the formation and malformation of identity moves to the center of the stage, even though schooling is given scant attention (Sandel, 1996). Sandel depicts the USA as a country where an ideal of republican freedom was once firmly rooted in the encumbered identity of citizens who found a compelling common good in the exercise of democratic self-rule. But that ideal has gradually been eclipsed by the thin values of the "procedural republic," which claims to function only as a neutral arbiter of private ends. Sandel wishes to revive the "formative project" of republican freedom. In that project, the powers of the state are directed to the formation of citizens who bear the responsibility and enjoy the intrinsic good of collective self-rule.

But Sandel's project has to be adapted to the realities of an America very different than the one in which republican freedom was equated with the solidarity of white, propertied, Protestant males. Among these realities are the vast scale of American pluralism in the wake of twentieth-century immigration, the moral repugnance of any ideal of republican community that would strengthen traditional social hierarchies and exclusions, and the potency of liberal rights as a means of discrediting them. Sandel's formative project is thus closely akin to Dewey's and is beset with comparable difficulties. He needs to find a way of reconciling two demands that pull hard in contrary directions. First, he needs to depict an attractive and feasible model of civic community significantly different than liberal politics can sustain, even on the best interpretation of liberalism. Second, the model must somehow accommodate liberal values given a world where oppression in the name of community has a long history, a history that seems unlikely to be countervailed by anything other than the appeal to liberal values.

Whereas Dewey at least drew the rough contours of a community in which he thought that reconciliation might be achieved, Sandel does not. In fact, the contrast between republican community as he construes it and liberalism depends largely on a caricature of liberal politics as a merely procedural conception that rules out any serious interest in the formation of citizens' identities. On the other hand, responsibility for that caricature – which is pervasive in the communitarian revival – cannot fairly be laid only at the door of communitarians. The formative project of liberalism has not until very recently received the attention it merits by liberal theorists, and once it does receive serious attention, questions about community and its importance to the development of the liberal individual must move to the foreground of liberal theory (Macedo, 1990, 1999).

Recall that what divides liberal and communitarian political theories at the deepest level is disagreement about the terms on which community warrants public endorsement or toleration. For liberals, the critical issue is whether the community is in keeping with the worth and fulfillment of the freely choosing individual. The characteristic communitarian objection to all this is that by taking autonomy too seriously liberals fail to take community seriously enough.

To take the measure of the objection we need to ask about how community is entwined with the educational formation of liberal individuals and the conditions necessary to the flourishing of their autonomy over time. An education for autonomy depends critically on associative ties that begin in families that nourish a basic sense of self-worth and personal efficacy. These ties extend outward to more inclusive communities defined by neighborhood, creed, common ethnicity, or the like, and perhaps embrace the liberal polity itself as a particular object of identification. Moreover, freedom of association will be necessary to the many ways of life that people come to autonomously embrace since it is through identification with established communities (and sometimes the invention of new ones) that many find their good.

The coherence and plausibility of this account must depend on a conception of autonomy remote from the bizarre amalgam of emotional repression, narcissism, and calculating reason pilloried by many communitarians. Autonomy in the sense relevant to liberal politics requires the ability and inclination to think critically about the good and the right, as well as the self-respect and confidence to act on the basis of critical thought in making choices. Why should communitarians see autonomy in this sense as a threat to the community worth having? A good answer cannot merely be that those who are taught to be autonomous will reject communities they have come to regard as unfulfilling or unjust. First, if the moral renewal of currently weak or corrupted communal life is the very object of communitarianism, that purpose cannot be squared with the thought that evil is done whenever an existing community is rejected as unfulfilling or unjust. Second, if life in union with others answers to a profound human need, as communitarians claim, then we should expect that learning to think critically about the good and the right would in general lead to the revision of existing communities or the creation of new ones rather than lives of solitary, rootless egoism. That expectation could only be otherwise on the assumption that people who think critically for themselves about the good and the right will generally tend to think less well about their deepest needs than they would as unreflective conformists. The assumption is coherent, but it bespeaks an aristocratic rather than any recognizably liberal or democratic view of human nature and authority.

The liberal theory that emerges in response to the communitarian revival treats questions about the formation of identity as central rather than peripheral, and it registers the decisive role of associative ties in the formative process (Macedo, 1990, 1999). If individual autonomy is indeed the touchstone of free government, then liberals must worry about securing the stable cultural context that individuals need to grow into autonomous adults (Kymlicka, 1989). Families become an important focus for study as the "first school" of individual autonomy and the sense of justice (Okin, 1989). Moreover, the cultural diversity of so many contemporary liberal states (and especially multination states) means that liberal theorists must ask whether group rights are sometimes a necessary means of securing equal respect and consideration for all citizens. The question arises because in many societies the identity of individuals is often bound up with particular groups who have been traditionally discounted or oppressed, and a uniform package of individual rights for all citizens may not suffice to overcome their oppression or marginalization. Group rights to education – for example, in particular languages or religions – are inevitably an important part of this new debate in liberal theory (e.g., Callan, 2000). Whether liberal arguments for group rights can succeed is an open question. But their salience in recent debate attests to the fact that liberals must now confront problems about the communal setting for the development and expression of identity that had been badly neglected since Dewey. The liberal theory that emerges from these debates will have far more to say about education and culture than it did before the communitarian revival, and it will be none the worse for that.

Communitarianism has made liberalism more aware of the communal horizons within which its own claims must be vindicated. This is as true for educational philosophy as it is for political philosophy. Among the issues it has drawn scholarly attention to is the phenomenon of nationalism and the role of education in nation-building. Between the end of World War II and the end of the 1980s, the promotion of national sentiment or patriotism had been widely seen as fundamentally at odds with liberal principles. This was understandable in the light of the excesses of nationalism in the first half of the twentieth century. The reassessment of ideas about nationality is among the most important fruits of the communitarian revival.

Political and educational philosophers in the liberal tradition are currently deeply divided about whether, or to what extent, the fostering of national sentiment is compatible with liberal ideals. National identity is commonly contrasted with a sense of cosmopolitan political identity, and the divergence between the two is registered in conflicting visions of civic education (Nussbaum, 1999). Whatever the outcome of that debate, it has already deepened our understanding of civic education in free societies.

Recommendations for Further Reading

Bell, D. (1993) *Communitarianism and its Critics*, Oxford University Press.
Callan, E. (1997) *Creating Citizens*, Clarendon Press.
Levinson, M. (1999) *The Demands of Liberal Education*, Oxford University Press.
Mulhall, S. and Swift, A. (1996) *Liberals and Communitarians*, 2nd edn., Blackwell.

Chapter 6

Democratic Citizenship

Penny Enslin and Patricia White

Introduction

If there were charts for topic popularity in political theory, citizenship would certainly have been at the top of them since the early 1990s. It was not always so. In the late 1970s it was suggested that the topic had "gone out of fashion" (van Gunsteren, 1978, p. 9), so what caused this change? Increased interest in theories of citizenship and citizenship education are probably attributable to several factors arising in different contexts: perceptions of political apathy and declining levels of participation (Frazer, 1999); tensions resulting from the resurgence of nationalism and from the presence of multicultural populations in Western European societies (Kymlicka and Norman, 1994); regional political and economic restructuring, for instance, in moves towards an integrated Europe; and problems of democratic consolidation in societies in transition to democracy. Unsurprisingly, these concerns frequently provoke attempts to re-examine the notion of citizenship.

Topical and practical concerns lie behind the various philosophical issues discussed in the first section below. Those in the first part of the section have been on the agenda for some time, though they continue to raise questions still to be resolved, to which this treatment draws attention. In the later subsections relative newcomers to the agenda are explored in rather greater depth.

Common to many writers is their perception of the need to bring some order into the growing field of work and to this end various dichotomies are introduced. Notable are the maximal/minimal and active/passive distinctions where the assumption is usually that the first of the pair of terms represents the desirable state to which democratic citizenship should aspire. As emerges in the discussion of the substantive issues, matters may not be so straightforward. The distinctions are applied in a number of ways which need to be distinguished so that it may be that it is not possible to say that maximal/active citizenship, despite its positive ring, is always to be preferred to the apparently unattractively negative minimal/passive citizenship. How these distinctions are applied and how useful they are, are themes running thorough both the first section and the educationally oriented second section.

Drawing the Boundaries

Whether maximal or minimal, active or passive (in any of the several senses of those terms), citizenship is a legal status conferred by a state. As such it transforms people. The people living in the Fifth Republic and the Vichy regime were physically the same people but different citizens (cf. Shklar, 1995, p. 8). The same might be said of the Weimar Republic and the Third Reich. The rights offered, the duties required, the civic aspirations encouraged, and the conception of the good citizen, all changed as the later regimes replaced the earlier.

Since citizenship is conferred, rather than biologically or socially given, the political community determines who gets it and who does not. Historical and contemporary exclusions are familiar. To note just some, women were only admitted to citizenship status in the last century in many putative democracies, guest workers are currently excluded from citizenship in several European states and children for varying periods of time in most states have remained outside the citizenship body.

What might be the grounds for these exclusions? Can any of them be defended in a democratic community? Can an inspection of the grounds for exclusion throw any light on the appropriate criteria for citizenship?

Traditionally women were excluded, ostensibly because they had no recognized role in the public life of society and thus lacked the relevant knowledge to participate in the affairs of state. They were similarly placed to children and both groups had their interests looked after by masculine heads of households. Guest workers give temporary economic support in societies where there is a lack of desire on the part of its citizens to do degrading and sometimes dangerous work and, as if they were tourists, they do not have citizenship rights extended to them (Walzer, 1983, chapter 2).

The qualifications that are allegedly lacking are knowledge and mature judgement in the case of children and, historically, women, and something like long-term commitment to others in an ongoing community in the case of guest workers. Leaving aside the justice of these particular exclusions, are these appropriate criteria for a democratic community to employ in granting and withholding citizenship? Are the crucial qualifications knowledge and commitment? If so, does this have implications for education? Do democracies need a civic education promoting relevant knowledge and some fostering of the civic virtues of commitment to a democratic polity? And should there then be tests for this knowledge and commitment before citizenship is granted?

Or is pursuing the assumption that citizenship requires appropriate qualifications taking us in an unwelcome direction? Rather than seeing citizenship as something to be earned, an alternative view is that it should be seen as the granting of a status which all in the democratic polity share, an embodiment of the democratic ideal of political equality. To do otherwise is to put some people literally beyond the bounds of the polity. "Not to be heard is not to exist, to have no visibility and no place politically" (see Shklar, 1995, for an eloquent statement of this argument).

What follows from the view that democratic citizenship is a status shared by all in the polity? To recall the example of children, what does not follow is that as soon as toddlers can make a cross, they can vote. They can, however, share many other rights of adult citizens, like the right not to be abused. The case is similar with guest workers. Is there any reason for them not to enjoy most of the rights of other citizens, so that they in fact have something like dual citizenship, in their country of origin and the country in which they work? If, however, these claims can be upheld, do they lead to the counterintuitive conclusion that education and commitment are not required for citizenship?

Not at all. What they highlight is the dual nature of citizenship. On the one hand it is a shared status, on the other it is a normative ideal. Citizens can aspire to be good citizens, and good citizens can come in a variety of forms. Sometimes the citizen/good citizen distinction is marked by versions of the minimal/maximal and passive/active distinction but, as we shall see, this can be too rough and ready a distinction to catch all the important possibilities.

Thus, having citizenship status provides the occasion and the impetus for education and commitment. This point is familiar from the arguments used to justify extending the vote to black people in the USA (see Shklar, 1995, p. 52ff.) and from the work of others who have urged the educative function of democracy (cf. J. S. Mill).

Citizens as bearers of rights

What is this status that is bestowed on all citizens? What rights does it extend to citizens? Nothing demonstrates more clearly the nature of citizenship as a developing institution in predemocratic and aspiring democratic societies than the changing and expanding scope of the rights offered. Marshall, in a seminal account, noted a progress from the eighteenth to the twentieth centuries in Western democracies from civil rights (for example, the right to own property), to political rights (for example, the right to vote), to social rights (for example, the right to a minimum level of health care and social security) (Marshall, 1950). But this suggestion of a march of progress toward a justifiable extension of the rights of the citizen has not gone uncontested. It has been argued that the only legitimate rights to be attached to citizenship are "liberty" rights (for example, freedom from arbitrary arrest, the right to vote, to free speech). So-called "welfare" rights are overly demanding and perhaps even impossible of realization (see Cranston's statement of this position, 1967, pp. 50–3 and Waldron's response, 1995, p. 580).

So within the (according to one perspective, minimal) notion of the citizen as rights bearer (Kymlicka and Norman, 1994, p. 354) the minimal/maximal distinction gets further application, distinguishing between a minimal notion of citizenship based on liberty rights and a maximal one based on welfare rights.

But from another point of view a maximal conception of citizenship including welfare rights can be seen as minimal if it fails to be gender-sensitive. It may be, as we discuss below (see "Feminist theory and active citizenship"), that in a society with a whole panoply of welfare rights the constraints of domestic responsibilities effectively curtail women's political participation to a brief appearance in the polling booth every few years (Phillips, 1991, p. 157f.).

The notion of the individual citizen as rights bearer has been challenged on another front in the interests of greater justice. Cases which might arguably be seen to embody a more expansive conception of citizenship have been made for group rights (Phillips, 1996; Kymlicka, 1996) and even for the power of veto for oppressed groups over matters that affect the group directly (Young, 1990a, pp. 183–91). If representation is to be based, in part at least, on identity, this introduces a host of problems (for example, of forcing an undesirable essentialism of identity on individuals) of which advocates of some group representation are all too aware. Nevertheless, rather than abandon the project of attempting to realize group representation, their advocates feel that these problems have to be grappled with in the interests of social justice.

Do citizens need civic virtues?

Seeing the conception of the citizen as a bearer of rights *per se* as constituting a minimal notion of citizenship is, then, too simplistic. Matters are, as we have seen, more complex. The notion of the citizen as rights bearer can itself be given broader or narrower interpretations. Leaving aside these more finely drawn distinctions, however, perhaps one of the major uses of the minimal/maximal distinction is to mark the difference between a conception of citizens as passive bearers of rights and one of citizens actively virtuous in the public arena.

This distinction, however, can be variously understood. In its starkest form the contrast is between citizens as bearers of rights – welfare rights as well as liberty rights – and citizens of robust republican virtue. For the latter, participation in political affairs has an intrinsic value and playing an active part in the political life of one's society is held to be superior to the private pleasures of family, personal relationships, and work. Civic republicans contrast our currently impoverished political life with the active citizenship that characterized ancient Greece, and tend to assume that such a weighting of public life against private life is unarguably the appropriate stance for any citizen (Shklar, 1995, pp. 11–12; Oldfield, 1990). Skinner offers a rather more subtle defense, arguing that the republican vision of civic virtue is actually the best route to individual liberty. As he puts it "if we wish to maximise our personal liberty, we must not place our trust in princes; we must instead take charge of the political arena ourselves" (Skinner, 1992, p. 219ff.).

Citizenship as the most valued activity in a person's life is to be contrasted with the more common modern view of citizenship as one aspect of a person's life that may be variously weighted by different individuals, and that in the end exists, as does politics, to support individuals in their personal and shared projects. In an extreme form this view sees the citizenship role as little more than a nominal adjunct to a person's private roles. In contrast to the citizen replete with republican virtue this individual need do little of a civic kind because necessary democratic vigilance over the political process is assured by democratic institutions (for example, a legal opposition, free press, an independent judiciary) honed over centuries for this purpose. So there need be no shaping of the loyal citizen, with its undertones of totalitarian coercion and the "character standardization" of citizens (Holmes, 1995, p. 75). Sophisticated democratic machinery replaces civic virtues.

This however is a bit quick. Whereas perhaps unswerving political loyalty may be a quality happily dispensed with, it is not clear that democracy can be achieved by a totally virtue-free population. Citizens who have to support and operate the democratic machinery that Holmes rightly favors need to have certain dispositions if that machinery is not to be open to misuse. Free speech, for instance, will not flourish in a society whose citizens do not want to give a hearing to unpopular views. Not only legal bans but also self-censorship and public indifference can inhibit free speech. Thus even in a society with well-developed political machinery citizens will need basic political virtues like trust and distrust (P. White, 1996, pp. 52–65) and a sense of fairness.

A further question is how far it makes sense to divide civic virtues into the necessary and the desirable and how precisely one draws that distinction (Kymlicka, 1999). Is hope, for instance, necessary? And what about decency or civility? If such a distinction makes sense, this could be another application of the maximal/minimal distinction with implications for education.

Nationality and citizenship

If citizenship entails membership of a political community, does it also require national identity as a basis for a shared sense of community with one's fellow citizens? National identity has recently undergone a revival of support as the basis for the social unity that underpins citizenship. This development has prompted a reconsideration of nationalism, which some have associated with chauvinism, xenophobia, and militarism, as well as irrational mythologizing of historical origins and events.

Supporters of national identity as a defensible grounding for citizenship argue that it should not be equated with organic conceptions of citizenship, which can be ethnically based and aggressive toward those who are not members of the nation. For Miller (1992) citizenship and nationality complement each other; citizens need a shared national identity to hold them together and provide them with a sense of community. This common identity enables them to work together to shape their world as active citizens. It is claimed that such a conception of nationality can be rationally believed and can be separated from the forms of aggression that have given nationalism a bad name (Miller, 1992, p. 86). Similarly, Tamir (1993) defends a theory of nationalism that is not ethnocentric but polycentric, recognizing the possibility of a plurality of nations within a political community. Tamir, like Miller, rejects organic interpretations of nationalism. Emphasizing the value of context, roots, and belonging for human flourishing, Tamir (1993, pp. 79–82) bases her defense of nationalism on liberal recognition of particular cultures as well as on universal human rights. In defending the promotion of national sentiment in education, John White (1996) argues that it need not necessarily be chauvinistic or incompatible with liberal democratic values. As there is a need for members of a community to identify with one another, national sentiment "can be desirable for reasons of personal and cultural identity" (1996, p. 327). Individuals need a framework in order to exist. Following Miller (1989), White observes that national sentiment can also provide a motivation for redistribution of resources among citizens.

Yet while defenders of nationalism, national identity, or national sentiment, wish to separate it from those expressions that have been organic, ethnocentric, and aggressive toward nonmembers, there remain actual manifestations of nationalism that are different from the depictions of nationalism described by Miller and Tamir, such as in the Balkans and Central Africa. Even without the excesses of ethnic cleansing and ethnic genocide, where traditions of liberal democracy are weak or absent, as in many of the states with multiethnic populations in transition to democratic citizenship, national identity has a volatile presence that threatens to undermine the democratic values of autonomy and equal respect (see Enslin, 1999). Here the nation as an item of invention, with its manufactured myths of origin (Smith, 1986) is less likely to be an object of rational belief, critically understood, than is possible in the national communities presupposed by Miller.

Miller's conception of citizenship adopts an avowedly minimal sense of national identity, together with an endorsement of active citizenship. But as globalization accelerates and the national community as a locus of political, cultural, and economic activity weakens, active citizenship tied to a national community may be overtaken by the pace of globalization and the development of transnational citizenship. The significance of these developments for citizenship is clarified by their treatment in recent work on deliberative democracy.

Citizenship as deliberation

Deliberative democracy, a recent development in democratic theory, has wide implications for our understanding of citizenship, in its conception of the practice of citizenship, its potential for inclusiveness, and in creating new spaces for democratic citizenship as well as new citizen identities. It sets out to regain some of the quality of citizenship in ancient Greece, recreating the model of addressing one's fellow citizens in a public assembly. This model of democracy (see, for example, Benhabib, 1996a) takes as its starting point deliberation among free and equal citizens, committed to collective decision making in which fellow citizens share an obligation to propose reasons for settling questions that they can persuade others to accept as compelling. Deliberative democracy is based on the premise that if individuals are to be subject to decisions, they ought to be justified in terms that all could be reasonably expected to accept (Thompson, 1999, p. 120).

In its communicative version deliberative democracy offers ways of making citizenship more inclusive. For Young (1996) an overemphasis in most deliberative theories on the importance of presenting and being willing to accept reasons based on the best argument favors those most adept at argument and excludes those less versed and confident in the skills of critical argument, like some women and members of minorities and non-Western cultures. In Young's communicative model of deliberation, argument is supplemented by the emotional and embodied talk more likely to come from those previously excluded from public deliberation. Difference is a resource for reaching understanding through democratic discussion, including other forms of interaction among citizens, such as storytelling.

A deliberative assembly of all citizens, as in ancient Greece, is not viable in modern conditions. Instead, deliberative theorists envisage a wide range of contexts in which deliberation should be practiced. This "plurality of modes of association" (Benhabib, 1996a, p. 73) comprises a network of various associations and organizations in civil society, like political parties, pressure groups, social movements, voluntary associations, trade unions, and, presumably, educational institutions. But deliberation can also characterize the conduct of formal political institutions and of citizens' relationships with them.

Gutmann and Thompson argue that "the resources of deliberation provide more justifiable ways of responding to the challenges of representation than do other conceptions of democracy" (1996, p. 132). In deliberative democracy representatives are required to provide moral justifications for their actions and policies, giving reasons to justify them that could be accepted by those affected. Here representative government requires reiterative deliberation, in which representatives present their proposals, to which citizens react, and representatives respond, in an ongoing exchange. In this way representatives can enhance democracy by providing opportunities for citizens to deliberate, and representation itself is also enhanced by being constituted in a more deliberative way. Public officials are obliged to account not only to those who elected them, but also to their "moral constituents" (Thompson, 1999, p. 120), anyone bound or likely to be affected by the decisions made by public representatives.

Instead of requiring that political decisions always be the result of wide public participation, democratic authority in large modern democracies means that there is the possibility of challenging authority, while citizens suspend judgement much of the time, relying on "attentive publics" (Warren, 1996) to scrutinize the claims of experts. This role will be played by a range of pressure groups, NGOs, and the media. Deliberative democracy does not depend on every decision being the result of deliberation by all citizens, leaving them instead to suspend judgement much of the time, focusing attention on those issues that are important to them and about which they might have some expertise.

Cosmopolitan citizenship?

In some versions of deliberative democracy (for example, Benhabib, 1996a; Bohman, 1997, 1998), deliberative exchanges between citizens are not confined to separate nation-states, but are open to all who are potentially affected by a decision. While democratic citizenship is commonly considered to be practiced within the national boundaries of sovereign territorial states, under conditions of globalization deliberation crosses the old boundaries, undercutting the traditional location of democracy within separate states (see Dryzek, 1999). As decisions taken within particular states increasingly affect those located outside their boundaries, and as advances in communication make deliberation across boundaries much easier, a new framework for citizenship and its exercise emerges.

Speculation among deliberative theorists about the institutional implications of this blurring of national boundaries, about the potential of deliberation under conditions of globalization to foster new forms and sites of democracy, takes several different directions. One sees the moral constituencies of public officials within individual states as going beyond territorial borders, as noncitizens are affected by some decisions made by individual states, for example, on immigration, trade, and environmental policies, but without going so far as to argue that all those potentially affected by a state's decision be included in making it (Thompson, 1999, p. 120).

Another direction in which cosmopolitan deliberation is creating new opportunities for democratic citizenship lies in the growth of a transnational civil society (Dryzek, 1999), most obviously in environmental campaigns and movements such as those against whaling and biopiracy. In the emerging international civil society, a cosmopolitan public is using the growing network of communications among associations and organizations like those campaigning for human rights to expand democracy through publicity, enhancing human rights internationally and so citizen rights transnationally. This has the potential to influence the shape, organization, and actions of existing political institutions (Bohman, 1997, p. 180). But while these cosmopolitan networks are beginning to enable those who have access to them to deliberate in pursuit of the longer term goal of public agreements acceptable to all affected, deliberative theorists do not yet envisage the emergence of world government in a universal state (Bohman, 1997). Indeed, the influence of international civil society so far should not be overestimated, to the neglect of the role of national and local governments in promoting decision making for the common good, rather than in the interests of the often sectional goals pursued by organizations in civil society (Thompson, 1999, pp. 116–17). While the 1990s did see the emergence of an international human rights culture, it remains the case that it is largely on the governments of existing states that the international public focuses in campaigning for the recognition and respect of those human rights.

Apart from the potential that deliberative democracy poses for expanding citizenship, it also requires and promises to develop a set of democratic capacities and virtues. As well as the deliberative skills of presenting arguments to others and being able to judge which argument carries the greatest force, deliberation requires a disposition to reciprocity, a willingness to recognize others as free and equal participants in deliberation. A commitment to communication across difference demands that deliberators behave not as bearers of interests, but as willing to recognize calls for justice from those both differently situated and whose speaking styles are different too. In participating in deliberation across a wide public, citizens need to acquire knowledge of when to suspend judgement and when not, keeping themselves informed about issues and following public deliberation vigilantly. As deliberation is conducted more and more through electronic media, citizens will need to acquire and exercise knowledge of information and communications technology . This complex and demanding range of skills and dispositions is likely to mean citizenship that is maximally informed but – much of the time – minimally active. Under such conditions, a simplistic distinction between active and passive citizenship is unlikely to be useful, and the more nuanced distinction between minimal and maximal citizenship needs to be reconfigured.

Deliberative democracy casts a different light on the distinction between participation and representation, which is sometimes associated with the distinction between maximal and minimal citizenship. As a model of democracy it accommodates both, requiring the citizen to participate where possible in deliberation, but also making representation more deliberative. Democratic vigilance may be exercised in both forms of activity. But transnational deliberation, while adding a new dimension to democratic citizenship, also raises problems for participation as well as representation. Deliberative participation may be limited for most citizens to smaller, more local contexts. In the absence of democratically elected institutions of government across boundaries of national states, who represents the interests of citizens? As the significance of territoriality in organizing interactions among citizens is reduced, traditional conceptions of democratic representation may become less relevant (Rosenau, 1998, p. 40). It remains to be seen what new mechanisms of representation and accountability might emerge.

These considerations warn us against taking a naively optimistic view of the potential for democratic citizenship to be enhanced under more deliberative conditions, transnationally expanded. A negative consequence of globalization, in which politics crosses national boundaries, could be "that there is nowhere in particular to exercise the privileges of citizenship" (Bohman, 1998, p. 200). And while globalization promises the growth of citizenship on an international scale through greater scrutiny by an international critical public, if the democratic powers of organized citizens in those societies most threatened by globalization are not developed, their access to the benefits of citizenship may be hampered rather than fostered.

What bearing do these considerations have on the location, like Miller's, of active citizenship within a national community? While it would be reckless to predict that globalization will inevitably foster an inclusive, cosmopolitan, democratic citizenship, there are grounds other than concerns about the irrational and aggressive potential of national identity to argue against a conception of democratic citizenship founded solely on the territorial national state. Under conditions of globalization, citizens who assume an exclusively national identity may, in spite of active citizenship, fail to engage with forces that really do influence their circumstances. In a globalized world the citizen as member of a single nation-state offers a limited conception of citizenship.

The notion of European citizenship has prompted a reconsideration of the idea of a single national identity as the focus of citizen identity. Habermas (1996) takes the view that in the transition of the European Community to a closer political union the classic form of the nation state is disintegrating. Envisaging the emergence of a "postnational identity" he posits in its place a "constitutional patriotism" (1992, 1996), a form of political union based on a shared commitment to a constitution or a common political project. An increasingly common political culture may differentiate itself from the national traditions of the member states. At the same time, Habermas (1996) is concerned about the "chauvinism of affluence," as a fortress Europe is inclusive of a wide membership of European citizens while excluding those of the East and the South who wish to immigrate. Much of this is quite speculative and perhaps unrealistic. Perhaps a more plausible assessment is that European citizenship will grow alongside a persisting set of national citizenships

reflecting local, national, and supranational identities (see, for example, Delanty, 1997, p. 299). But a single maximal European citizen identity seems unlikely and would be an unrealistic goal of citizenship education.

Feminist theory and active citizenship

A consideration of feminist theory also prompts second thoughts about the desirability of maximal over minimal citizenship. It seems likely that feminist theory would support a notion of citizenship located on the participatory, active, maximal side of the distinction between maximal and minimal citizenship (for example, Arnot, 1997, p. 289). Given women's initial exclusion from the franchise, from eligibility to stand for election to public office, to apply for work on equal terms with men, and in some countries restrictions on their freedom to be out unescorted in public, from one point of view it seems obvious that participatory citizenship is valuable both for its own sake and for the further gains that it promises for women as they share in decision making.

Yet a number of feminist writers have expressed reservations about the usefulness of the very notion of citizenship, for example as in Pateman's indictment of citizenship as "made in the male image" (1989, p. 14). For Jones (1990, p. 811) the question of whether the concept of citizenship can be reconstructed so that it can play a role in a redefined polity that is friendly to women and their experiences remains open. Noting the republican assumption that citizenship is to be interpreted as public participation, which is valued above the concerns of the private, domestic sphere, Okin (1992) takes the view that women should indeed claim the right to citizenship and the participatory ideal, but that the classical ideal has to be subverted and considerably modified (along with other political concepts) so as to include rather than exclude women. A modified ideal of citizenship would, she claims, also provide a better ideal for men. Crucially, democratic citizenship will be strengthened by social changes in the domestic realm. While feminism has contributed a substantial critique of the male-centeredness of politics and political theory, it has also focused attention on the significance of the private. Regardless of the support that many theorists of citizenship, feminists and others, give to a vision of participatory citizenship, the reality of many women's lives restricts much of their activity to the private, where they carry a disproportionate responsibility for the care of children, the elderly, and the sick, and for domestic labor, thus reducing opportunities for public participation.

A crucial flaw in traditional conceptions of citizenship is their exclusive focus on the citizen as active in the public sphere. A danger in this emphasis is that it implies that what people do at home is not a part of their activities and duties as citizens. What we do in the private realm by way of reproduction and care of dependents does not qualify as active in the same ways as participation in the public, even though domestic labor may be exhaustingly active. We cannot, it seems, be citizens when we are at home – at least beyond a minimal sense of citizenship.

But feminist criticisms of theories of citizenship suggest that the configuration of citizenship as appropriately maximal and public rather than minimal and private should be reconstructed. Focusing one's activities in the private is not necessarily a minimal form of citizenship in the sense of declining to show an interest in public affairs. Confinement of many women to the home, especially when single and poor, can be argued to oblige the state to concede a maximal obligation on its part to recognize and meet welfare rights. Meeting such rights by providing child support and publicly funded day care that enables mothers to earn a living wage, competing for work on equal terms with men in the public sphere of the workplace, can provide the means for women to be able to participate in the public. To interpret demands for such rights as a sign of passivity by minimally active citizens would be to impose on such women a conception of citizenship whose achievement would be beyond their reach. For women heading single-parent families in conditions of poverty such rights are both more important than opportunities for active citizenship, as well as a precondition for the very possibility of active citizenship. Women's socialization into the idea that it is natural for them to assume domestic responsibilities, and an accompanying assumption that the public realm and politics is more suited to men, makes participatory involvement an intimidating prospect.

Recognizing these constraints and the consequent reconstruction of the idea of citizenship that they require has led feminist writers to make two central proposals to bring about equal democratic citizen status for women. These proposals call, first, for a reordering of relations within the household, and second for a reconsideration of the relative value of representative and participatory arenas of democracy.

Both Okin (1992) and Phillips (1991) argue that a reordering of domestic relations is a prerequisite for equal citizenship. Okin argues that equal citizenship requires that the relationship between the public realm and the personal-domestic realm be changed, pointing out that: "Feminists have argued quite persuasively that the division of labor between those who have reproduced and nurtured life, and those who have ordered society and determined its meanings, has greatly encumbered both politics and political theory" (1992, p. 63).

Hence the transformation of citizenship requires that inegalitarian families be changed so that they may become places in which future citizens learn to treat one another as equals. If women are to achieve equal citizenship: "The ancient assumption that the responsibilities of domestic life – caring for children and the aged – are 'naturally' women's, must finally give way to assumptions and policies that will facilitate the equal sharing of these things by men and women" (Okin, 1992, p. 70). Allied to an active notion of citizenship, then, a maximal conception presents some problems for a feminist perspective on democratic citizenship. A feminist reading of the maximal/minimal distinction suggests that the permutations on the continuum between active/passive and public/private in relation to equal, democratic citizenship ought to be reconsidered by those who favor a maximal, active version of citizenship along with its implications for education for democratic citizenship.

Citizenship and Education

When, after its period in the doldrums, political philosophy began to revive in the 1970s, not least with Rawls's (1971) and Nozick's (1974) large-scale and wide-ranging treatments of social justice and rights, one topic failed to make it onto the agenda –, children. Political philosophy seemed to assume a world composed solely of adults. Indeed some would say it assumed not just adults but articulate, rational barristers with settled views and preferences. No one seemed to want to consider how the rational political citizens of their liberal theories might have developed from the amoral and ignorant children they once were. In a sense this was odd since for the great political philosophers like Plato and Rousseau civic education was a central topic. Gradually, however, the education of citizens began to make its way onto the political philosophy agenda, first in single chapters (see, for example, Ackerman, 1980; Walzer, 1983) and then in whole books (Gutmann, 1987; Callan, 1997; Levinson, 1999).

What should be the aims of citizenship education?

Increasing attention to the question of citizenship education has not, however, produced a consensus on its aims and procedures in a liberal democracy. This is in part because in the first forays into this field political philosophers tended to concentrate on broad issues like the need for a basic education and how it might be provided in a socially just way (see especially Ackerman, 1980; Walzer, 1983; Gutmann, 1987) rather than focusing on details of the nature of citizenship education. Our earlier survey of the issues raised by the nature of citizenship, however, suggests further reasons why consensus might not be readily forthcoming.

Matters start promisingly enough. It seems uncontroversial that one aim of citizenship education must be to give young people some understanding of their status in the democratic society and how that will change as they grow older. This will cover the criteria for citizenship and the rights citizens enjoy. In calling this uncontroversial we have in mind the understanding of one's status and rights as a matter of fact. Where, as we have seen, controversiality comes in is in the criteria for inclusion and exclusion from citizenship and the nature and extent of rights enjoyed, and these will properly be matters of debate during citizenship education. Thus, fully stated, the aim is to give an understanding of what constitutes citizenship in any given society while subjecting that conception to critical scrutiny. Even with the rider, however, we are still on reasonably uncontested territory.

Matters get more complex with the question of whether the promotion of active citizenship should be an aim. Here, as we have seen, there are two contrasts that are germane: (1) citizens as merely passive recipients of rights as distinct from citizens who are alert to the responsibilities sometimes required by those rights (like, for example, voting, writing to the newspapers, joining protests etc.) (2) citizens as bearers of rights and aware of, and committed to, the related responsibilities as distinct from citizens actively virtuous in the public sphere which activity they rate more highly than private concerns.

Active citizenship as vigilance, as in (1), would seem to be necessary if the continuance of democratic government is to be safeguarded. The promotion of democratic vigilance of this sort cannot be simply an option. Whether, however, the education of citizens needs to have as its goal, as in (2), that they should give the highest priority to the responsibilities of citizenship at every stage in their lives, always rating them more highly than private concerns, is problematic. It raises questions on at least two scores. First, it seems to run counter to the value pluralism that is the *raison d'être* of liberal democracy to insist in the absence of compelling reasons that everyone should give priority to participation in political matters. Second, it raises far-reaching questions about the way in which the public/private distinction is made, whether all aspects deemed to fall into the "private" are indeed private, in the sense of being justifiably beyond the reach of the public sphere, or whether some of them, like, for example, the upbringing of children, should actually be conceived as part of citizenship. Connectedly, it raises questions about the kind of reordering of domestic life that would be required if everyone were to make participation in the public arena their highest priority.

Answers to these questions have significant implications for how citizenship education ought to be tackled. Inadequacies begin to emerge in an approach that envisages citizenship education as encouraging participatory citizenship in the republican tradition, with its emphasis on activity in the public realm. If citizenship education is to promote equal citizenship for girls, it ought to pay at least some attention to encouraging changes in the ways in which girls as well as boys understand their roles in the private as well as the public. To continue to treat the private as beyond the legitimate scope of educational intervention is to ignore a major obstacle to the acquisition of equal citizenship. For boys, this means turning attention at least partly away from the public sphere, from the importance of involvement in associations and organizations – and politics itself – toward citizenship in the private.

The feminist call to reconsider the importance of representation, often neglected as a result of enthusiasm for participatory versions of democracy, also has implications for a reconsidered approach to citizenship education. Okin points out the need to improve the representation of women, without which discrepancies between "representatives" and those they purport to represent will continue (1992, p. 71). Phillips proposes that we need "to develop representative mechanisms that explicitly acknowledge gender and gender inequality," which "may ensure a new proportionality between the sexes in those arenas within which political decisions are made" (1991, p. 7).

As Kymlicka and Norman argue, "emphasizing participation does not yet ensure that citizens participate responsibly – that is, in a public-spirited, rather than self-interested or prejudiced, way" (1994, p. 361). Those citizens who are empowered by participatory democracy can use their power in irresponsible ways, to obtain the greatest advantage for themselves at the expense of less powerful groups whose needs are greater. This view is endorsed by Parry and Moyser (1994), who point out that just increasing levels of participation by citizens can increase inequality, as the more advantaged make more effective use of making themselves heard. Similarly, teaching the knowledge, skills, and attitudes that make for effective participation, without bringing about other social changes, is likely to enable boys to exercise active citizenship more effectively in maintaining male dominance.

What does this reconsideration of democracy as representation and a concomitant awareness of the limitations of the participatory variant of democracy suggest about how we might reconsider education for citizenship? Perhaps one of the most salient points of contrast for educational processes concerns the degree of critical under-standing and questioning that is seen as necessary to citizenship. Maximal concep-tions require a considerable degree of explicit understanding of democratic principles, values, and procedures on the part of the citizen, together with the dispositions and capacities required for participation in democratic citizenship generously conceived (McLaughlin, 1992a, p. 237) There is a substantial overlap between the capacities that citizens need to acquire in order to engage in an educated way with participat-ory and representative forms of democracy. Recognizing both the differences in opportunities for active participation available to different citizens, and that there will also be those who simply do not wish to be particularly active citizens, citizen-ship education ought to approach its task as encouraging both participation and engagement with representative processes. Encouraging better representation, even if active participation by some is rare, should be seen as enhancing democracy.

If it is not justifiable to try to shape peoples' preferences so that political particip-ation trumps other valued activities, does this mean that any aim involving the shaping of desires and preferences is out of court? What about the civic virtues? Should they simply be laid before students to practice if they feel attracted to them? Here again, as we have seen, matters are not straightforward. It may be that some virtues, like justice and toleration, are integral to the living of the democratic life, while others, like decency, are more peripheral. It might be argued that the liberal democratic society will not be in serious danger of collapse without the peripheral virtues even if life is less commodious than it would be if the majority of people possessed them. Without the core virtues of justice and tolerance, however, there is no recognizable liberal democratic society (Callan, 1997; Kymlicka, 1999).

The aims of civic education so far considered all concern matters of democratic rights, principles, and attitudes, and some would judge that these comprise the possible field of democratic aims from which to construct a democratic civic educa-tion. But it has been suggested that such shared political principles and rights are not sufficient for social unity. Social unity requires not only shared principles but a sense of shared membership in the same community. Thus there is a sharing of identity. In some states this would be supplied by a shared religious faith or ethnic origin but in a pluralist democracy these things are not shared. So there is the question of what might supply this shared identity and whether it is necessary. Does the forging and supporting of a common identity need to be an aim of civic education? And if so, in the absence of a religious or ethnic basis, how far might nationality fill this role? Also, how might it cohere with the citizen's membership of other democratic groupings, like, say, membership of the European community for those belonging to its member states? And can it to be related to a notion of cosmopolitan citizenship?

Given the contemporary state of the debate on citizenship the aims of citizenship education have to be seen as varying in the support they can currently reasonably command. A strong case can be made for giving people an understanding of their status as citizens in a liberal democratic state, encouraging them to be active citizens in the sense of maintaining democratic vigilance, and fostering the core virtues, like attitudes of justice and tolerance. Over and above these aims there are aspirations that might be offered, rather than urgently pressed, like the possibility of more active citizen involvement and the cultivation of more wide-ranging civic virtues. Beyond these aspirations lie the aims connected with the unresolved issues of the kind of social unity that might be desirable.

Realizing aims: procedures and institutions

As the school in a liberal democratic society is the only institution that all young people are likely to attend, it seems that this must be the major site for citizenship education. What might this involve?

To answer the demand for knowledge about the rights and status of democratic citizens, courses in citizenship will be needed, particularly for older students. These cannot be merely straightforwardly instructional, as we have seen, but need to take on issues like the justifiability of possible reasons for exclusion from citizenship status.

As an institution the school, like any other institution in the society, will be expected to be organized and run on democratic lines. In this sense the ethos in all schools, however old or young their students, will be democratic and the arrangements, characteristic ways of doing things, and the attitudes of staff and students will, thus indirectly, mutually encourage in the members of the school the qualities required for living in a democratic community. It will include an education in civic virtue, covering virtues like justice, tolerance, trust and distrust, honesty, hope, decency, gratitude, loyalty, mercy, and so on. But what, then, about the differentiation mentioned earlier between the core and peripheral virtues? How will this be conveyed to students? It seems reasonable to assume that, for the most part, this will emerge in living the life of the school and will only need here and there to be discreetly underscored where the message seems somehow to have got distorted. Concretely, the attitude taken toward racial abuse will be different from that taken to a surly expression of gratitude.

Encouraging active participation in the life of this school will again prepare the way for a reasoned choice to be made about active participation in the adult society. Every student can be encouraged to see what is involved. At first hand they will come to appreciate the personal and social costs and benefits of involvement and what demands the participation of some may make upon others. The fact of participation along gendered lines is an obvious issue for consideration.

We have talked about *the* school as though the assumption must be that citizenship education demands a common school, and this seems a not unreasonable assumption if we are concerned with an education that is going to help all members of the community to live together. A common school will acquaint any individual child with the variety of views abounding among future fellow citizens and also provide a site where these can be debated and, where necessary, practical arrangements can be negotiated. This view is challenged, however, and it has been contended that a solution is separate schools for ethnic or religious groups with a common curriculum. This may suffice for the teaching of the facts of government but it can hardly provide the experience of learning to live with others who differ from us in their race, class, religion, and so on. If there are felt to be compelling reasons for separate schools the solution may be an education which is partly offered in common and partly in separate institutions (Kymlicka, 1999).

No curriculum area has a neat set of uncontested aims. Education for citizenship is no exception. This stems in part, as we have seen, from the fact that the nature and many aspects of the citizenship role are still very much matters of political and philosophical debate. This is not, however, an obstacle to the construction of a robust education for citizenship. This itself can, and should, reflect the tensions between competing aims by making the critical question of the nature of citizenship and what it is to be a good citizen a leitmotif of any citizenship program.

Recommendations for Further Reading

Callan, E. (1997) *Creating Citizens: Political Education and Liberal Democracy*, Clarendon Press.

Gutmann, A. (1987) *Democratic Education*, Princeton University Press.

Kymlicka, W. and Norman, W. (1994) Return of the citizen: a survey of recent work on citizenship theory, *Ethics*, 104, pp. 352–81.

White, Patricia (1996) *Civic Virtues and Public Schooling: Educating Citizens for a Democratic Society*, Teachers College Press.

Chapter 7

Education and the Market

David Bridges and Ruth Jonathan

Introduction

Both the authors of this paper first wrote about the application of market principles to education in the Thatcher/Major years and in the United Kingdom (Jonathan, 1983, 1989, 1990, 1993, 1997a, 1997b; Bridges, 1994; Bridges and Husbands, 1996). At the time educators might have been forgiven for supposing this cause to be a particular feature of the Anglo-American liberal conservatism which held sway for a period across North America, the UK, and Australasia, an approach to social policy and in particular to the management of public services that might be overthrown, in some countries at least, with a swing to the left in their politics and a change of government. Jonathan argued, however, that the competitive individualism which legitimates a quasi-market in education was an unacknowledged feature of that form of liberalism that informed both the social expansion of liberal education from the mid-twentieth century and the liberal philosophy of education that developed at that time for its analysis. The popular appeal of many quasi-market "reforms" rests in part therefore, paradoxically, on unresolved contradictions in an earlier ostensibly egalitarian public project (Jonathan, 1995, 1997).

A longer perspective of time has indeed demonstrated that the policies are both more deep-seated and more widespread than some expectations might have suggested. In the UK, Blair's "New Labour" government has shown no less a passion for market principles than its Tory predecessors – extending rather than limiting parental choice of schools and the assessment and league tables that are supposed to inform such choice; enabling popular schools to expand; introducing student fees in the context of higher education, and showing some favor toward universities that wish to introduce differential charging; and taking on the teachers' unions in a battle over performance-related pay. Meanwhile, on the global scene, regimes in such diverse political environments as Russia, Ethiopia, and Vietnam are all sending government ministers and officials on courses in market economics and wrestling

Section I written by David Bridges; Section II written by Ruth Jonathan.

with the application of market principles to social policy. All of this makes it particularly relevant to understand the persuasive attraction of these principles and to locate them in a broader historical and political perspective, as well as to set out and develop some of the counterarguments, which we are at risk of losing under the weight of fatalistic as much as enthusiastic endorsement of the market ideology.

The first part of this chapter reviews these arguments and counterarguments against the backdrop of educational policy in the UK. The second part broadens the context of discussion and examines the roots of contemporary controversy in the philosophical analysis of the policies and practices and preoccupations of the recent past. Key current issues for theory are then highlighted and a future agenda for research indicated.

I

The application of market principles to education

Social policies do not operate in a historical vacuum; nor are we looking at the creation of an educational market from nothing. In most contexts market principles have been applied against a background of an established public education service managed in some way through the apparatus of the state. Thus the application of market principles is nearly always at the expense of a nationally or locally administered state bureaucracy which, in the UK at least, was subject to national and local forms of democratic accountability. Critics of such systems highlight the predominance of the role of the state bureaucracy in their operation (cf. Tooley, 1994, p. 138, on "state-supplied, state-regulated, and state-funded schooling"), while their defenders emphasize the feature of local democratic accountability. Not surprisingly, then, the introduction of market principles to education rests in part on the destruction of "the state monopoly" or, as Flew (1991) preferred, "the LEA [Local Education Authority] monopolies" of schooling.

The main conditions that seem to be required for the "marketization" of education are, on the supply side of the educational economy, the creation of diversity and choice and, on the demand side, the placing of information and purchasing power in the hands of "consumers." More fully, there are five main ingredients to these developments:

1   *The breaking up or weakening of state monopolies so as to provide a choice of service provider for customers and competition between providers.* In the UK this principle has been primarily expressed by "freeing" schools from the control of local education authorities, first by the creation of grant maintained schools (which received their funding direct from government) and then by insisting that local authorities passed on the vast majority of funding that came through their hands directly to schools, which could then purchase local authority services like catering, in-service training, and maintenance if these offered best value for money. More recently private educational organizations have been brought in to replace "failing" local authorities on the basis of competitive tendering.

2   *The creation of real opportunities for choice and an appreciation of that opportunity for choice among consumers.* This principle has been used in the UK to defend the preservation of selective schools and private schools, the establishment of city technology colleges and grant maintained schools outside the control of local education authorities, and the establishment of religious schools by Muslim communities. It is part of the motivation for the creation of schools with a special focus on, for example, languages, technology, or sport.

3   *The provision of reliable information for consumers to inform their choices.* The 1991 Parents Charter (DES, 1991) promised five key documents that would provide information for parents: a report about the parents' own child at least once a year, regular reports on the school by independent inspectors, performance tables for all local schools, a prospectus or brochure about individual schools, and an annual report from the governors of their school. The league tables based on national test results and the OFSTED inspector reports have proved especially significant in informing parents about the relative merits of schools (judged at least against the criteria of success implicit in their particular forms of assessment).

4   *The encouragement to educational providers to "free themselves" from dependency on state funds by becoming entrepreneurial and generating alternative sources of income.* This imperative is especially well marked in higher education. Oxbridge has long had its independent financial resources drawn from a rich history of private endowments, but newer universities like Warwick now claim that more than half their revenue comes from sources other than government. Schools have perhaps fewer opportunities for generating private income, but many are at least supplementing their state provision through, for example, voluntary donations from parents, charges for activities like individual music tuition that fall outside state-funded provision, leasing premises to local banks, or somewhat controversially in the United States guaranteeing a TV audience for a particular commercial TV channel (see Harty, 1994).

5   *The enabling of consumers to secure the option of their choice, whether from a public or private provider.* In practice this tends to result in the development of either a voucher system (see Naismith, 1994) which consumers can use to purchase educational services from any (approved) supplier – as developed in Milwaukee in the USA and in a late and abortive experiment with nursery education under John Major's regime – or, in the case of higher education, in the placing of purchasing power directly in the hands of the student consumers.

As is perhaps already clear, educational systems that meet these criteria still fall short of a pure market model. "There is no such thing as a 'free market,'" warns James Tooley, one of the more radical advocates of the application of market principles to education, "but there are 'markets' . . . with lesser or greater degrees of state intervention, and with lesser or greater imperfections (in terms of information of the consumers, transaction costs etc)" (Tooley, 1997, p. 139). Even Tooley's fairly radical model of the application of market principles to education leaves a significant role for the state: in setting the standards for what will be regarded as a minimum adequate education; in licensing an inspectorate to ensure that educational establishments meet these standards; in assisting families who cannot otherwise afford to send their children to school; and in compelling those children who do not partake of the minimum acceptable educational opportunities to do so. The state is given in fact the minimal role that is commensurate with the obligation that John Stuart Mill argued it had to protect children from harm (Mill, 1867).

Set against Tooley's vision, we can see that the practice that even the Thatcher/Major administrations endorsed was a pretty half-hearted attempt at the "marketization" of education. It was one in which the state was expected to continue to be the main provider of education, through schools that were either directly funded by central government or indirectly through local authorities; in which the state defined in detail (greater detail than ever before) the curriculum that all these publicly funded schools were required to follow; in which the state provided for the training of teachers – again on a tightly and centrally defined curriculum; and in which all these requirements were carefully policed through a combination of nationally defined tests, benchmarks of achievement, and a state-controlled system of inspection. Those with a care for precision were anxious to describe this particular "market" as a "quasi-market": more cynical observers, faced with the juxtaposition of liberal rhetoric on the one hand and, on the other, a huge concentration of power in the hands of government and the systematic undermining of such oppositional institutions as the teachers' unions, local education authorities, an independent inspectorate, and "the teacher training establishment," might have been excused for feeling that it could equally appropriately have been described as a "quasi-Stalinist" social economy. In the educational sphere, what Michael Power refers to as "a pathologicality of excessive checking" (Power, 1999, p. xii) has replaced more traditional systems of centralized control to ensure the conformity of "self-managing institutions" to the will of government. It is a Red Riding Hood market in which illusory or trivial freedoms are given – "the better to control you by"!

Nevertheless, the rhetoric of the marketplace was everywhere, and this was reinforced by the simultaneous application of the discourse of business to educational management (the language of management itself replaced the earlier style of leadership and headship). Headteachers' conference bars rang to the sound of "marketing strategies," "mission statements" and "business plans," "performance measures" and "performance-related pay"; parents became "customers" or "clients"; heads of department were constituted into "senior management teams" and became "line managers." Schools "delivered" "products" in the most "cost-effective" ways they could invent. Students, if they dwelt on the matter at all, might have been excused for feeling a little unsure where precisely they were positioned in this new economy: "consumers," "customers," "raw materials," "products," or numbers in the accountants' tables of the schools' "achievements against targets"?

What, then, was or is the case for the marketization of education, or, at least, the application of quasi-market principles to education? The arguments rest on a mixture of empirical claims and points of principle. Central among them were four types of claim.

First, the context of the initiative was one in which there was evidence of the failures of the state-controlled systems, most evidently in the low levels of achievement and the high rates of truancy in urban schools in the United States and the UK. It was possible (and perhaps convenient) to argue that these failures were the consequence of overbureaucratic systems that were insensitive to the preferences of customers on the ground. Chubb and Moe most famously claimed considerable success for market-based school reform in addressing these problems in East Harlem (Chubb and Moe, 1990, but see also 1992).

One more particular, and to many headteachers, attractive form of this argument related to the delegation of budgets from local education authorities to schools. It was argued that schools could make more locally sensitive and intelligent decisions about their expenditure than "remote" administrators, could save money where its expenditure was not really necessary, and could focus expenditure where they see it as doing most good (see, e.g., Morris, 1994).

Second, and more positively, market systems were held to have inherent means for achieving the most cost-effective delivery of a service. Gerald Grace describes the two remarkable doctrinal rather than scientific assumptions of economics that underpinned, among others, the New Zealand government's advocacy of these policies – "the assumption that there is such an entity as a 'self steering ability' and that this entity when operating in a market situation for education will deliver 'optimal solutions'" (Grace, 1994, p. 130). The free market is held to have an almost magical power to generate the best solution to a problem, the best response to a perceived need, at the lowest possible cost. Indeed so strong is this particular faith that "the best solution" becomes defined as that produced under ideal market conditions, with the result that the claim becomes virtually tautologous.

Third, there are arguments of an essentially liberal kind that suggest that marketization extends consumer choice and empowers those at the receiving end of educational provision. The New Zealand Treasury brief to which Grace was referring above argued that "the key element . . . is empowering, through choice and through maximizing information flows, the family, the parent, or individual as the customer of educational resources" (New Zealand Treasury, 1987, p. 42). This empowering of the individual under market conditions is sometimes contrasted with the "dependency culture" that is said to be cultivated by (a favorite phrase of the Thatcherite circle) "the nanny state." Thus the development of such virtues as self-reliance, independence, individualism, and enterprise become a product of the extension of market practices to the areas of traditional public service. In different ways, then, markets contribute to the development of the autonomy of customers (who enjoy greater freedom of choice) and of suppliers (who are freed from bureaucratic constraints and become more independent and self-reliant).

Fourth, there are arguments that the very competition that markets create among providers to attract and retain customers provides an incentive for them both to do more, to be more successful, and to meet more closely the preferences of these customers. (In an environment in which there is flexibility in the prices that can be charged this competition produces additional benefits in terms of the reduction of cost for services.)

Briefly, and no doubt crudely, the claim was and remains that market conditions allow the application of local and individual preference and individual intelligence to decisions about educational provision and practice and thus the more responsive, successful, and cost-effective delivery of the services that customers want. Quasi-markets that leave with the state a role in the determination of quality thresholds, monitoring, and inspection provide additional security against any particular mave-rick tendencies to which an entirely free market might be exposed.

Additional material making the case broadly in favor of markets can be found in Coons and Sugarman (1978), Cox et al. (1986), Flew (1991), D. G. Green (1991), Seldon (1986), and Tooley (1992a, 1992b, 1993a, 1994). In practice, however, given that government policies have presented the educational hypothesis in con-crete and powerful terms, the bulk of the philosophical commentary has been critical and it is to this criticism that we shall now turn.

Critiques of the application of market principles to education

Critical responses to the application of market principles to education have been many and varied – and, as in the defense of these policies, it is sometimes difficult to untangle what are essentially empirical claims about the consequential benefits from more strictly philosophical argument. For present purposes I will outline four sets of these critical approaches.

The rationality of market choice

The first set of criticisms challenge what is in a sense the logic or rationality of choice within a market environment, or more particularly the view that it is the sum of independent individual choices that produce the "best" aggregate judgement. A central part of this debate focuses on the so-called "prisoner's dilemma" (see Jonathan, 1990; Tooley, 1992a). At one level, this discussion boils down to consideration of whether or not individuals who make decisions of what is in their interests from, as it were, their individual cells, can make what is in fact the best decision in terms of the aggregate benefit as might be seen from a wider viewpoint. Against the market standpoint, it is argued that the best aggregate benefit for a population is achieved from a perspective on the consequences of different options that is broader than that provided by the sum of individual choices made out of self-interest. Jonathan (1990) argues a stronger thesis, suggesting that choices exercised individually cannot be fully rational with respect to social goods. Individual choosers may be able to weigh up the best course of action from the point of view of securing individual positional advantage, but only by at the same time surrendering the greater influence on the shape of the social future itself that he or she previously had under the terms of a democratic negotiation of the aggregate choices of a community.

In an argument derived from the prisoner's dilemma, Bridges (1994) first ob-serves the distinction between the *positional* advantages that education can bestow and that can only be achieved by one child at another's expense (e.g., higher grades in a norm-based assessment system, better preparedness for employment) and the *nonpositional* benefits that education can contribute to a community and that can be spread widely without loss to anyone (e.g., understanding of history or the natural environment, enjoyment of the arts, intellectual curiosity). The problem is that there are differences between the rational course of action that parents and schools might take depending on which of these sets of benefits they focus on. As custodians of their own children's interests parents will naturally seek to advance their access to the positional advantages that education can bestow, even at the expense of other people's children. It will suit them to have unequally distributed educational provision provided they can secure for their own children the better end of the deal. Though they and their children may benefit from the wider distribution of the nonpositional contributions of education, concern for these will naturally tend to be secondary to the immediate benefits that parents can see in gaining positional advantage for their children. Thus:

> The consequence of this dilemma is that the more a system of schooling offers the opportunity for parents to secure positional advantage for their children, the more they will (quite rationally) exercise their custodial responsibility to secure that advantage for their own children and the less they will concern themselves with ensuring that the system provides non-positional benefits to all. The richer, educative and universally beneficial purposes of schooling will become subordinate to the narrower, self-interested function which can benefit some only at the expense of others. (Bridges, 1994, p. 77)

The nature of education

A second set of arguments against the application of market principles to education is almost ontological in character, that is, it suggests that the marketizers are confused as to the sort of thing that education *is* – and that this confusion leads to all sorts of errors in the systems that are devised for its "delivery." Sergiovanni, for example, following Tonnies' classic distinction, contrasts what he identifies as "the *Gesellschaft* transmission model (of teaching) where experts create instructional delivery systems as a way to transmit their expertness to clients" with something that is much more reflexive, much more informing of and informed by relationships within a community or *Gemeinschaft* (Sergiovanni, 1994, p. 143). Arguments have thus been addressed against the wider range of commercial and production line language which has come to be applied to every aspect of education, so that education becomes a commodity and schools production lines, "educated" students the products, and teachers rewarded on the basis of their productivity. Such language, it is argued, systematically distorts our understanding of the nature of education and the relationship between students, teachers, and the selections from culture with which both are engaged. It turns intrinsic values and essentially moral and humanistic relations into instrumental ones. It is no doubt possible to separate some of the worst excesses of this language from arguments about, for example, parental choice of schooling or the ways in which funding might be channeled to schools, but advocates of markets have perhaps been their own worst enemies in enjoying the provocation of their excesses in extending this language across the field of education. They have, however, in the process helped to clarify some of the radically different values and premises that underpin the broader debate.

A more specific instance of arguments about the nature of education is reflected in the debate about education as "a public good." Grace argued from a view of education as a public good to the conclusion that it should therefore be provided directly by the state and without direct charge to its citizens. Grace defines public goods as follows:

> Public goods are intrinsically desirable publicly provided services which enhance the quality of life of all citizens and which facilitate the acquisition by those citizens of moral, intellectual, creative, economic and political competencies, regardless of the individual ability of those citizens to pay for such services. (Grace, 1988, p. 214)

(It is perhaps already evident that a good deal of the conclusion as to how such "public goods" should be provided is thus prefigured in their definition.) Grace goes on to ask, rhetorically:

> Might not education be regarded as a public good because one of its fundamental aims is to facilitate the development of the personality and the artistic, creative and intellectual abilities of all citizens, regardless of their class, race or gender status and regardless of their regional location? Might not education be regarded as a public good because it seeks to develop in all citizens a moral sense, a sense of social and fraternal responsibility for others and a disposition to act in rational and cooperative ways? (ibid.)

Jonathan points out ways in which education operates both as a public and a private good and concludes that "the over-simple dichotomy between the public and the private most obviously breaks down in the case of education" and that this explains "the apparently schizoid neo-liberal approach to educational reform, whereby content and process merits closer state supervision whilst distribution merits deregulation" (Jonathan, 1997b, p. 79).

Tooley provides a helpful commentary on both the "public good" arguments in the mainstream literature of economics and its educational applications (Tooley, 1993b, 1994). The conclusion of Tooley's 1993 paper is that: "education is an (impure) public good in the economist's sense, but that conclusion alone does not tell us whether or not markets, internal or free, are appropriate mechanisms for educational provision" (p. 121). This conclusion was no doubt informed by Malkin's and Wildavsky's shrewd observations (to which he refers) that "A public good is one that the public decides to treat as a public good" and that "It is the moveable boundary between public and private that makes it essential to analyse public policy with our values up front, not hidden behind the seemingly technical concept of public goods" (Malkin and Wildavsky, 1991, pp. 372–3).

This part of my discussion serves two purposes. First, it illustrates a section of the wider literature that addresses the question of how education should be managed in society through consideration of what sort of a thing it is. While the debate about "public goods" does not offer a great deal of encouragement for this project, we have nevertheless some sympathy for the view that the application to education of a discourse derived from manufacturing and commerce risks distortions in our treatment of something that is arguably of a very different kind. Secondly, Malkin and Wildavsky's conclusion, in particular, highlights the need "to analyse public policy with our values up front" – and it is to the confrontation between the values of the market place and those of its critics that we now turn.

Competing social values

If the advocates of markets admire freedom of choice, individuality, self-reliance, and enterprise (let's call these the *neoliberal* virtues) and see conditions of competitiveness as conducive to their development, then at least some of their critical adversaries extol the virtues of community, fraternity (or sorority, though this does not have the same political/historical resonance), and equality and see conditions of collaboration in a public service as conducive to their development (let's call these the *social democratic* virtues). In other words we can observe in this debate a conflict not just about which means are best conducive to a particular set of outcomes (judged perhaps by reference to the aggregate of children's achievements on some measure of their learning of school subjects) but about the social values that are expressed in and through the means of providing the education that results in these outcomes, including in this the value-laden behavior and beliefs that are properly to be counted among those outcomes. Thus Noddings argues:

> We do not ask how we must treat children in order to get them to learn arithmetic but, rather, what effect each instructional move we consider has on the development of good persons. Our guiding principles for teaching arithmetic, or any other subject, are derived from our primary concern for the persons whom we teach, and methods of teaching are chosen in consonance with these derived principles. An ethic of caring guides us to ask: What effect will this have on the person I teach? What effect will it have on the caring community we are trying to build? (Noddings, 1986, p. 499)

It is not difficult to see how this approach can be extended both to the organizational arrangements within a school and to those that govern the relations between schools in a democratic society. Arguably – and this is the position taken by Fielding (1996), for example – the values of the market are incompatible with the values broadly understood as associated with community (he recognizes that this is a contested concept). Fielding quotes with approval Cohen's observation that:

> The immediate motive to productive activity in a market society is typically some mixture of greed and fear, in proportions that vary with the details of a person's market position and personal character. In greed, other people are seen as possible sources of enrichment, and in fear they are seen as threats. (Cohen, 1994, p. 9)

Not only, observes Fielding, are these "horrible ways of seeing people" (Cohen 1994, p. 9) but they are utterly inappropriate within the context of an educational undertaking. "Insofar as the market imprints its moral, psychological and procedural imperatives on the work of schools and colleges it constantly threatens to undermine what is specifically educational in it" (Fielding, 1994, p. 166).

This review does not provide us with space to explore the differences between (and within) these different ideological positions in any detail. What is plainly the case, however, is that the debate about the application of market principles to education is not just about the connection between alternative technical management systems and agreed ends, but very importantly about different ideological positions which include contrasting views of both human virtue and social values.

Differentiation, difference and equality

Markets require differentiated products: without them they lose their *raison d'être*. We have already seen how successive governments in the UK have attempted to provide for this differentiation by, for example, encouraging private sector provision alongside state provision; by supporting the foundation of religious schools; by encouraging schools to take on a specialist complexion as a technology, languages, or sports center of excellence.

The trouble is, however, that market conditions contain several dynamics which create first differences of quality (and not just of character) and then unequal access to the best. First, it is evident that in market conditions success breeds success and failure just as surely breeds failure. Early achievement encourages custom, which brings additional resources and commitment, which enables further success, and so on: early failure opens the way to a precipitous drop down a less virtuous circle. Markets produce Ratners as well as Cartiers, street corner groceries as well as Fortnum and Mason – and while such extreme differences will be constrained to the extent that government sets system-wide levels of funding (the private sector lies outside such constraints), state schools have a variety of means of raising funds and the increase in student numbers that comes with success in market conditions brings its own financial reward.

Further, the notion that parents or children can then flock to the more successful schools, the schools of their choice, leaving others to close, is an unrealistic one in practice. Children with the most ambitious and geographically mobile parents (which on the whole also means the wealthiest) will best be enabled to profit from this par-ticular competition. Those living in rural areas with geographically immobile parents may have no choice but to stay in an increasingly beleaguered and depressing environment. Thus the dynamic of the market operates to create a system that is not just differentiated in terms of marginal features of the character of the schools, but increasingly by the quality of the provision they are able to offer. As Miliband has argued:

> It is not the imperfections of the market that make it dangerous, but rather its potential to do damage where it works most effectively ... "Success" according to the logic established in the ERA's [Education Reform Act's] educational market is precisely what society requires that we avoid – namely an education system marked by (narrowly-based) excellence for an elite but sub-optimal provision for the majority of children. (Miliband, 1991, p. 13)

Jonathan makes the connection between these inequalities and what she argues is the illusory nature of the freedoms that are vaunted as the particular benefits of a market regime:

> The language of rights, choice, control and individual responsibility appeals to public intuitions about the conditions for formal distributive justice. However, that same rhetoric leads the public to overlook the fact that these are also the very conditions for substantive injustice in distribution when the goods in question are social and the

context of distribution is competitive . . . *Formal free choice for all necessarily entails curtailed possibilities for some.* (Jonathan, 1997b, p. 42)

II

"Marketization" issues and themes in the philosophical study of education

The previous section of this chapter reviewed the raft of policy "reforms" which over the past two decades have arisen from or accompanied the introduction of quasi-market mechanisms, disciplines, and practices into education, and highlighted and commented on some of their underlying themes. This section will consider how treatment of these themes and the philosophical issues and debates that lie behind them has evolved within philosophy of education. For just as "social policies do not operate in a historical vacuum," as Bridges notes in section I, so neither do the changing values and understandings making up the climate of opinion against which radical policy shifts take root in mature democracies.

The shift from a strongly state-regulated to a quasi-market distribution of educational goods and their positional value, which was reported and analyzed in the previous section, was clearly not conceived by policy makers as a specific remedy to particularly educational ills. Had that been the case we would not also have seen, over the same period, similar policies implemented for the distribution of health care, as well as the introduction of "market discipline" into a broad range of previously social provision through the privatization of public assets and the "outsourcing" of public services. Nonetheless, education has had a peculiarly central place in both the rhetoric and the reality of what has amounted to a radical change in the social settlement. It was the first social practice to be targeted for "reform" by the deregulators (and the social practice that has been most insistently re-presented as a social service); it is the social practice where citizen ambivalence concerning the rights and wrongs, gains and losses, of a major shift in political values and resulting policies has been greatest; and it seems likely to be the last social practice where a wholesale reversal of "marketization" would receive electoral mandate. Clearly, there is much here that requires elucidation, with three avenues for enquiry, in addition to the analysis of relevant policy principles and themes, immediately recommending themselves for philosophy of education.

The first is an enquiry into the complex nature of educational goods, their diverse forms of value and the varying constituencies that expect their benefits. The second is an enquiry into the relation between education and social change: into the complex of practices and understandings that give rise to (or inhibit) both individual and societal aspiration and achievement. The third is an archeological exercise: to excavate the roots in educational debate of those normative, epistemological, and ontological disputes whose shifting settlements frame a society's understandings about worthy educational aims and legitimate means to their achievement. For without such an exercise, large-scale changes in the educational landscape and in public expectations of society's most fundamental social practice – changes which would have been unimaginable a generation earlier but now seem unexceptionable to many – can be neither fully understood nor adequately addressed. I shall confine myself in this brief contribution to the last of these enquiries both because there would be insufficient space for either of the others and because I have addressed them elsewhere. (For the first, see Jonathan, 1997b. For the second, see Jonathan, 2000.) What follows will therefore be an exhumation of the origins of those concerns which, coming together with political and material circumstance, provided some of the backing for the policies discussed in section I. This should be more illuminating than a "literature review" of analyses directly aimed at either defense or critique of the general trend of "quasi-marketization" or of particular policies such as parental choice of school, local management of schools, or the adoption of "league tables." Literature reviews of that kind, while useful in mapping the current state of debate, cannot reveal the complexity and scope of departure from the prior educational consensus and political settlement that these changes reflect. Nor can they remind us of how such shifts in popular and political understandings and values arise and gain currency.

The societies that were the first to embrace what might usefully be called "the individualist turn" – with the United Kingdom in the vanguard – were long-established democracies. Such polities do not experience sweeping political reversals imposed from above over the heads and against the inclinations of the populace, whether by an internal power clique or by external pressures. When far-reaching changes of political settlement and social ethos occur in such polities – as they did in Britain after World War II and again three decades later – they result from a cumulative build-up of dissatisfaction with the previous settlement which tips the scales of popular and political opinion when circumstance (whether of particular crisis or marked stasis) prompts new direction. And when such a shift occurs, as evidenced at each of those watersheds, the social practice of education becomes a primary focus for change in policy and practice, again not without the support of diverse sections of the public. Thus British education legislation of 1944/5 responded to popular demands for more equitable access both to education's intrinsic goods and to its social exchange value, while at the same time answering the needs of commerce and industry for the more effective use of human capital in the project of postwar reconstruction. And the correspondingly sweeping changes reflected there in the legislation of 1988/9 answered political perceptions of a need to raise the stakes of social competition, promoting entrepreneurship for growth in a global market, while at the same time they appealed to popular disappointment with the personal pay-off of those formally equal opportunities whose extension had been the primary focus of the settlement then under challenge.

Given, then, that major shifts in ethos and policy do not come as bolts from the blue, and, further, that in democracies they do not result from simple changes in the distribution of brute power, we would expect that under conditions of modernity, with a generally literate electorate having access to widespread media of communication, such shifts would be presaged by a slow build-up of changing ideas, attitudes, and values as well as of evolving circumstances. We would further expect that philosophy in general, and philosophers of education in particular, would play a significant role whether in actively propelling the changing current of thought; in analyzing and commenting on evolving ideas, values, and attitudes; or in offering insight into the assumptions implicit in the changing current of social and educational preoccupations and aspirations. We would expect these roles for philosophers of education in particular precisely because education is the social practice that both reflects and reconstructs ideas and circumstance. Thus any review of the part played by philosophy of education with respect to that broad swathe of questions signaled by the topic "education and the market" is required to range much further than examining analyses of issues such as parental rights or professional accountability, or of particular policies such as school choice or selective entry.

For the role of philosophers of education, as of social and political philosophers, is not merely that of reactive commentators *ex post facto* to changes in intellectual climate. While it would be hubris to overstate their influence in a world of mass communication and media manipulation, and while philosophers, too, are creatures of their time and circumstance, they are explicitly charged with the task of at least clarifying the concerns of the day and at best moving forward the agenda of interest. It is not surprising, therefore, that we find many of the issues that underlie the shift in political ethos and educational consensus that began some two decades ago to have formed the foci of interest for some philosophers of education more than a decade before that – and before the cracks in the existing settlement had become publicly visible. Among those theoretical issues we could include (an exhaustive list would be unwieldy here) the relation between education and politics, or the permissible role of education as an instrument of social change; debate over the relative roles of parents and the state with regard to the welfare of children; dispute concerning the proper balance in educational policies between the requirements of individual liberty and the claims of social equality; the cultural implications of "mass" public education extending beyond schooling; analysis of the defensible extent of professional control over the choices of individuals, and so on. Unless we look back to those growing preoccupations of the 1960s and 1970s (with reference here particularly to the UK context), we can understand neither the roots and scope of the current "individualist turn" which underpins and gives popular legitimacy to the quasi-marketization of public education nor the role of philosophy of education in the present analysis and prospective modification of that latest settlement. For that shift, in which market-type mechanisms and disciplines have been powerfully influential in affecting both the distribution and the constitution of educational "goods," has now been with us long enough for both popular and political cracks to open up, offering space and voice again for informed analysis and critique.

If we look back to the resurgence of philosophy of education in the 1950s and 1960s, two things are evident. One is that in its procedures that field of study, not surprisingly, gained new impetus as a theoretical child of its times, with the dominant liberal neutralism of the day presenting highly politically contestable principles such as "justice," "liberty," "equality," and so forth as suited to apolitical analysis grounded in a universalistic Kantianism, and key concepts of educational policy and practice as ripe for elucidation through an agnostic study of linguistic usage. The other is that the substance of its concerns, again unsurprisingly, reflected the issues and understandings of the prevailing educational dispensation. The major preoccupations of philosophy of education in the UK for 20 years from the 1950s were thus threefold. First, much attention was devoted to analysis of the moral principles that should inform the aims and procedures of a liberal education then to be made available to all, irrespective of social or economic circumstance. (The work of R. S. Peters is seminal here, notably Peters, 1966, 1967, 1973a.) Secondly, a sound epistemological basis for the content of that education was sought, as was an educationally informed understanding of those capacities such as rationality and autonomy which such content – legitimized no longer by the social origins or destinations of learners but by the nature of knowledge itself – was designed to foster. (The work of P. H. Hirst is seminal in the first of these areas, notably Hirst, 1974b, and that of D. W. Hamlyn, notably Hamlyn, 1978.) Thirdly, analytic attention focused both on the proposals then emerging (child-centered education, creativity, etc.) for the revitalization of pedagogy and on those aspects of development they were claimed to foster. (R. F. Dearden's contribution is seminal here, notably Dearden, 1968.)

The philosophical task was thus the elucidation of morally acceptable and pedagogically well-grounded means of extending to all the benefits of that liberal educational experience which, prior to the postwar settlement, had only been available to the privileged. That settlement envisaged a fairer social world of expanding opportunity, with public education understood as having a key role to play. However, the public education project itself, though socially funded and state-regulated, was still conceptualized as a means to the emancipation of individuals: the hoped-for social benefit being predicated on the implicit assumption that the welfare of all would accrue from the sum of the welfare of each. Though taken for granted in that period of postwar optimism and liberal neutralism, with hindsight this was clearly a highly contentious assumption requiring endorsement either of "trickle-down" theories of economics or of neoliberal normative priorities for its support. While the contradictions inherent in a *social* project for the emancipation of (increasing numbers) of *individuals* through the distribution of a good that was positional in important respects were not explicitly confronted through the 1950s and 1960s – at a time when politicians, public, professionals, and philosophers of education in the main treated the social practice of education and its analysis as a fundamentally apolitical field – the underlying strains, both in the project and its analysis, were there from the start.

Thus even in those three most mainstream currents of newly resurgent philosophy of education, early indications can be discerned of preoccupations that would come to the fore in the closing decades of the century as hidden strains became more insistent. For in the first of the three strands I have highlighted, it was "equality" (whether "in" or "through" education, whether of access, of process, of outcome or merely of opportunity) that excited most continuing debate;[1] in the second strand the search for an epistemological rationale for common curricula evidenced awareness that, failing this, instrumentalism and "use-value" would allow interest-group disputes into the universalizing narrative of "liberal education for all"; and in the third strand pedagogical innovation was as much about democratizing learning as revitalizing it and as much about a questioning of professional and cultural authority as about fostering cognitive and emotional development.

Within and beyond these strands, particular writers showed more explicit attention to those questions that would later come more strongly to the fore. Thus in relation to the first strand – elucidation of the (politico-) moral principles that must inform the aims and procedures of liberal education – two countervailing tendencies could be seen developing through the 1970s and at the start of the following decade. On the one hand, the debates around "equality in education" soon no longer confined themselves to conceptual clarification of the concept, analyses of defensible or unjustifiable grounds for the identification of differences relevant to education, and examinations of the relations between educational equality and equality of opportunity and between that latter and social equity. Additionally then, some philosophers of education began to raise queries about the very desirability of "equality" as an organizing principle for public education. In this, they were reflecting that growing current in political and social theory that argued that the claims of individual liberty were becoming eclipsed by the demands of social equality, with consequences for individuals and society that were both morally objectionable and practically damaging. (Notable political theorists here are Hayek and Nozick, notably in Nozick, 1974.) Thus the egalitarian emphasis began to be examined by some in relation to its consequences for individual desert or merit and for educational "standards,"[2] while others revisited the virtues of competition and of individual responsibility (whether student or parent) for educational outcomes. Such challenges to an originally egalitarian impetus informing the postwar educational settlement are clearly analogous to – and politically significant instantiations of – the general individualist or neoliberal turn whose political moment came in the 1980s.

At the time, however, such challenges seemed highly contentious, educationally as well as politically, and were presented as defenses of standards by their proponents and of elitism by their detractors, rather than as the populist demands for rights to secure personal relative advantage into which they were later transformed. Moreover they were in stark contrast within philosophy of education to a countervailing societal emphasis which developed during the same period. That "societal turn" urged that such debates – and indeed the analysis of educational questions in general – required reconnection with social context[3] and took two forms. On the one hand attention was focused on the relation between education and politics and hence on the beginnings of a developing concern with the complexity of education's "goods," the diversity of its beneficiaries, and the relation of educational value (both intrinsic and exchange) to social context. Such enquiries belatedly reinstated awareness of clashes of interest into the previously universalizing narrative of educational analysis. On the other hand, a growing questioning of the claimed neutrality of the procedural values at the heart of philosophy of education (and a growing unease with "conceptual clarification" as primary method and role) paralleled developments in philosophy in general where conceptual analysis became seen as a contingent methodological feature of neutralist liberalism, with that form of liberalism becoming challenged from the one side by neoliberals and from the other by ethical liberals and proto-communitarians. Indeed, the revival of interest in social and political philosophy that gained momentum through the 1970s set the stage for some redefinition of the scope of philosophy of education, paving the way for later direct analyses of "education and the marketplace."

In relation to the second major strand within philosophy of education through the 1960s and early 1970s – the search for an epistemological rationale for curricula appropriate to the "neutral" aim of fostering rationality and autonomy – dissenting work was more diffuse. The epistemological grounding of curricula was overtaken (in theoretical debate if not in practice) by social developments from feminism to decolonization. These objections to what was (mistakenly) interpreted as a justification for cultural hegemony would have had less persuasive force without the simultaneous calling into question of the neutrality of "rationality" and "autonomy" themselves, again under the influence of widening cracks in the underpinning philosophical consensus around the claimed neutrality of liberalism and its central values and tenets. While Hirst, the philosopher most readily associated with that epistemological work, has subsequently revised much of his early analyses, that work has remained indirectly very influential in relation to later analyses of concepts of "skills" ("core," "transferable," "generic") and their extension ("problem-solving skills," "life skills," "moral skills" – see analyses by, for instance, Smith, 1987; Barrow, 1987); to notions of "competence" and learning profiles (see, for instance, Winch, 1996; Davis, 1998); and to the renewed debates over the relation of content to process that they prompt. Though the 1980s and 1990s emphasis on the acquisition by individuals of marketable skills and social attributes deemed necessary for particular economic circumstances seems at first sight a far cry from the goal of developing rational and moral autonomy, which drove curriculum analysis in the 1960s and 1970s, paradoxically the "skills-talk" of the later period gains much of its plausibility from apparently extending the universalizing, common-goals-for-all ethos of the earlier settlement. Indeed, apparent continuity with that ethos – with the shift ostensibly only from commonality of method to that of process – is required to gloss the diversity of provision that Bridges notes in the preceding section to be both a prerequisite and a consequence of an educational quasi-market.

In relation to the third major strand in philosophy of education noted above – analysis of proposals for the revitalization and democratizing of pedagogy – we see not so much divergence and dissent through the 1970s, as branching developments. As the early challenges to professional authority implicit in "child-centeredness" gathered momentum among public and politicians, philosophers of education turned to analyses of accountability in teaching (among the earliest analyses being Sockett, 1976), to debates over who should control the curriculum (see, for instance White et al., 1979), and to critique of emerging notions of "the needs of society" which had overtaken earlier concern with the needs and interests of the child. It was a short step from this to analyzing the nature of the educational consumer and addressing the shaping of educational priorities by economistic choices, both private and public (as in Jonathan, 1983). It is noteworthy that these were the very concerns to which policy makers made appeal when circumstance prompted the individualistic turn in practical politics. We thus see that earlier work in this strand, as in the others described above, both presaged and paved the way for philosophers of education to address the individualistic turn directly when, in the 1980s, it became explicit.

It is not coincidental, therefore, that the period of work in philosophy of education reported above saw the terminal decline of the "end of ideology" thesis that had underpinned not only conceptual analysis as methodology but also the substantive understanding of education as a social practice ideally immune from political interference – a practice through which all could benefit equally provided only that defensible groundings of policy and practice could be adequately revealed by analysis. In philosophy of education, as in revived social and political philosophy, it became gradually apparent again over that period that fundamental disputes about normative priorities colored both the framework and the elaboration of debate. From this brief and necessarily incomplete survey of developing concerns among philosophers of education through the 1970s, it should be clear then that this field of enquiry is neither separate from nor merely reactive to the current of ideas that flows at both theoretical and popular levels, a current which, together with potentiating circumstance, issues, at particular watersheds, in shifts in social consensus and educational settlement.

One such, as no readers of this volume need reminding, occurred some 20 years ago, prompting many philosophers of education to enlarge or redirect the focus of their concerns and some to redefine their role. Again, to attempt a literature review of philosophical contributions to a 20-year debate around the policies, practices, consequences, values, and assumptions of the quasi-marketization of education, even when this is largely confined to one society, would be both unwieldy and invidious in the compass of this section. It may be useful nonetheless to indicate three trends. The first flows from a renewed awareness of the necessary connection between educational consensus and political settlement, and the relation between educational arrangements and social structure. The second – associated – trend results from a willingness to engage philosophically both with the implicit assumptions and values inherent in policy "reforms" and with the substance of those policies themselves. The third results from a *rapprochement* between philosophy of education and a revitalized social and political philosophy. (This latter is just one aspect of a blurring of the boundaries around "philosophy of education" where much recent work relevant to our topic "education and the market" consciously incorporates historical, sociological, and policy analysis perspectives.)

That first trend has produced a growing body of work that questions the presuppositions of the twentieth century project of public education, with its emphasis on the intellectual emancipation – and social advancement – of individuals. From that project, social progress in terms of greater equity as well as prosperity was assumed to follow, provided only that education could be appropriately ordered, on the neutralist liberal belief in a link between freedom, reason, and the good. The "individualist" turn represented by the introduction of quasi-market practices and disciplines into the governance and distribution of public education has prompted two kinds of response to loss of confidence in those sanguine expectations. One has been to recontextualize public education's role in democratization (Carr and Hartnett, 1996); to trace philosophy of education's part in underplaying the societal aspect of the public education project; and to offer critiques of the assumptions and implications inherent in policies that explicitly individualize those aspects of the constitution and distribution of educational goods that hitherto were the subject of democratic negotiation (Bridges and McLaughlin, 1994; Jonathan, 1989, 1990). Further aspects of this focus have been renewed interest in relations between equality of educational opportunity and social equality, and between that latter and equity. Extensions of that work have seen renewed interest in education and citizenship, with that conceived as a matter of shared values and common interest rather than as mere consumer participation in a social market. Meanwhile, this corpus of critique has not gone entirely unchallenged, with some philosophers celebrating the proper reward of merit that accompanies a more competitive environment and others, much influenced by both public choice theory and a Hayekian social epistemology, arguing that while equity may have suffered under the deregulatory policies of the past two decades, this is only because the state has not been removed far enough from the provision and regulation of education which rather requires full privatization (see many papers by Tooley, culminating in Tooley, 2000).

The second trend sees philosophers engaging with the substance of policies, their assumptions and implications. Much of this is far more interesting than a simple defense of the *status quo ante*. For example, recent analyses of what should count as educational quality have taken account of the democratizing tendency behind educational consumerism at the same time as they have highlighted its dangers (Winch, 1996); analyses of the rights of parents have revisited the proper limits to the role of the state in safeguarding the interests of the rising generation (see many papers on religious and moral education by Terry McLaughlin, Colin Wringe, and Mark Halstead); investigations into the conflation of education and training resulting from consumer pressure have problematized earlier understandings of both (Jonathan, 1990); and reconsiderations of the legitimate scope of professional autonomy in matters of content and pedagogy have thrown new light on the costs and benefits of both personal and cultural deference.

The third trend seems the most significant departure from the work of philosophers of education of the 1950s and 1960s, but when examined more closely can be seen as its analogue, distinguished only by *"autres temps, autres moeurs."* This is the work that reconnects philosophy of education quite explicitly with political and social philosophy, with the intent of informing not merely the policies, theory, and practices of education, but also of contributing to current debates within liberal philosophy around the social construction of autonomy, the formation of preferences, and the nature and social interdependence of personal freedom – debates that are currently part of the reconstruction of liberalism (Jonathan, 1997b). Nothing could be more salient for this chapter's topic, "education and the market," since the policies and their rationale that Bridges describes in section I represent nothing less than the playing out in the arena of educational policy of the currently ascendant version of liberalism – a version of that worldview in which the rights of the individual are paramount and the duties of the individual are those of self-development, of informed choice-making, and of social contribution through individual effort to personal advancement within the framework of a deregulatory state in which social justice is understood primarily as the removal of barriers to free and fair competition between citizens.

It is in the educational context that the inherent contradictions of that vision are the most apparent, for while it is obvious that each of us should expect to benefit from our own educational experience, it is equally clear that all of us also benefit (or suffer) from the educational successes (or failures) of others, socially, culturally, and economically. If the currently ascendant vision of a desirable social ordering is inconsistent with the ordering of our key social practice then, clearly, continued philosophical scrutiny of that practice is central to today's climate of contestation, both with regard to defensible interpretations of liberalism and to legitimate social arrangements. It is perhaps not surprising, then, that philosophical analysis of our educational arrangements should once again draw closer to political philosophy. If that should seem a far cry from the concerns of *Ethics and Education* (Peters, 1966) we might recall that the substance of that work was the pertinence to public education of the core *political* principles of justice, freedom, and equality. If those principles, then, were treated as of *moral* significance in a project which, though public, was primarily concerned with the emancipation of individuals through education, that emphasis was a reflection of its times, and of the prevailing philosophical consensus and sociopolitical settlement of the day.

Today, in very different times, as Bridges showed in section I, a preponderance of philosophical work on aspects of "education and the market" has focused to date on the implications of the individualistic turn for the *distribution of educational goods*. A more competitive model of distribution is shown in such analyses to have significant impact both on the distribution of social opportunity and on the variable distribution of educational quality through the system. Whether changes to those two distributions are to be welcomed or regretted depends upon competing conceptions of the good society and of a worthwhile life for individuals within it. Much needed attention is now beginning to be focused also on the implications of a quasi-market in education for the *constitution of educational goods*. Within philosophy of education therefore, we might expect over the coming years a growing research agenda in relation to education and the market, which draws less on moral and political philosophy and more on epistemology and philosophy of mind. In any event, we can anticipate that when we look back in 20 years to the philosophical concerns of today, we will discern prefigurings of a changed educational settlement in that future time which today we cannot foresee.

Notes

1 Particular contributors to these debates in the philosophy of education literature being too numerous to list comprehensively, only contributions of particular salience for those later developments that concern us here will be noted below.

2 Some of the work of J. Wilson, A. Flew, D. J. O'Connor, and D. Cooper represents the focus on desert and merit here, consolidated in Cooper (1980). That journal articles of this sort reliably generated replies and rejoinders showed early signs of the imminent shift in practical and political consensus. The focus on threats to educational and cultural "standards" animated the work of contributors such as A. O'Hear and D. J. O'Connor.

3 Philosophers of education in Australia, meanwhile, notably K. Harris and M. Matthews, re-emphasised social context through a neo-Marxist perspective which in the UK remained largely a focus of interest for sociologists of education.

Recommendations for Futher Reading

Bridges, D. and McLaughlin, T. (eds.) (1994) *Education and the Market Place*, Falmer Press.

Carr, W. and Hartnett, A. (1996) *Education and the Struggle for Democracy*, Open University Press.

Chubb, J. and Moe, T. (1990) *Politics, Markets and America's Schools*, The Brookings Institute.

Jonathan, R. (1997) *Illusory Freedoms: Liberalism, Education and the Market*, Blackwell.

Chapter 8

Multicultural Education

Pradeep A. Dhillon and J. Mark Halstead

Multicultural education came into being initially as a pragmatic response, based on broadly liberal principles, to a number of practical educational issues that surfaced in the last 30 to 40 years as a result of the increasing cultural and ethnic diversity within Western states. Subsequent philosophical attention to the concept has begun to explore its social and political ramifications more fully and to link it to more recent cultural theory, and as a result a more substantial body of theory is beginning to develop around the concept. As we shall see later in this chapter, it is now widely accepted that there are good grounds for arguing that multiculturalism is internal to the very idea of education.

In the first section of this chapter we examine the origins and development of multicultural education and attempt to clarify some of the key issues, debates, and theoretical perspectives. The second section presents a contemporary liberal vision of multicultural education, and examines some practical challenges to this perspective. The third section considers the implications of notions of common humanity and cultural relativism. The fourth section develops a more critical multicultural perspective, drawing insights from feminist criticism and exploring the permeability and interrelationality of cultures. The final section takes forward the idea that multiculturalism can involve alliances related to a mutual concern for the welfare of those who are vulnerable rather than reinforcing action along lines of unified ideological commitments. We argue in conclusion for a new vision of liberal multiculturalism that is enriched by this kind of "deep humanism."

Origins and Issues

The issues that lay behind the development of multicultural education in many Western countries over the last 30 years or so include the following: what use schools should make of the variety of mother tongues spoken by children from ethnic minorities; how schools should respond to the racism and other forms of discrimination and disadvantage experienced by the children and their families; whether and how schools should teach about religion in schools in view of the increasing religious diversity in Western states; how schools should ensure that the culture of ethnic minority children is not ignored in the curriculum and general running of schools; and how schools should respond to the specific demands of ethnic minorities (including demands for single-sex schooling, for freedom to wear the turban or the *hijab* in school, for permission to be absent from school on religious festivals, for facilities for Islamic prayers in school, and so on).

The development of multicultural education as a practical response to such issues has been far from smooth. The inadequacies of earlier approaches to cultural diversity such as assimilation or the "melting-pot" theory were easily exposed, but liberal values did not always provide clear answers to the question of what policies and practices should replace them. For example, both collecting racial statistics and refusing to collect them have at various times been challenged as racist, and as Kirp (1979, p. 40) points out, in Britain intentional racial mixing (as instanced in the policy of "busing" black children to white suburban schools) has been condemned and eventually abandoned as racially discriminatory – exactly the reverse of the earlier American practice of "busing." In an early book, Wellman captures the irony in the dilemmas and uncertainties facing the well-intentioned American white liberal:

> Just as she was coming to evaluate black people as individuals, they demanded to be treated as a group. When she came to recognize that black people needed equal opportunities, they were demanding political power. As she began to locate the causes of discrimination in individual prejudice, black people were referring to the entire society as racist. By the time she recognized that black people needed help, they rejected it. (Wellman, 1977, p. 118)

Thirty years ago, the problem in developing a coherent approach to multicultural education was that there was an inadequate foundation of theory on which to base policy and practice. Today multiculturalism occupies a central place in discussions of social justice, democracy, and human rights; indeed, there is an embarrassment of riches as far as theory is concerned – Kincheloe and Steinberg (1997), for example, set out five major theoretical perspectives – and endless argument over terminology as well as over the principles that should underpin multicultural education. One of the main problems with the concept of multicultural education is that it contains a wide range of issues – political, social, cultural, moral, educational, religious – all tangled up together. An important initial task therefore is to find some way of disentangling them, and in what follows we identify four distinct strands.

First, there are issues relating to the concept of culture itself, including questions about the nature of ethnic and cultural attachments, the notion of cultural identity, and links between culture, power, and inequality. It is clear that there is a wide diversity of human activity to which the term "culture" is applied. At one level, the term is used to describe the fundamental meanings, beliefs, standards, and values of a community or group, as evidenced in the group's religion, language, nationality, history, or politics. At a second level, the term refers to the group's customs, traditions, and patterns of behavior (such as food, clothes, celebrations, festivals, leisure activities, and attitudes to health care). At a third level, the term refers to activities or achievements that the group recognizes to be of particular interest or worth, such as the arts, painting, or music, though it is worth noting that what one group defines as the pinnacle of human achievement may be a matter of indifference to another. These three levels interact in a number of ways, so that they are not always easy to distinguish; for example, particular customs and human achievements are normally associated with the shared consciousness of particular nationalities or ethnic groups.

However, there is a danger that multicultural education in schools concentrates on the second level at the expense of the first. Cultural assumptions exist at all three levels that are often taken for granted by the members of the groups concerned, such as the assumption that the culture is something fixed, external, and objective, which children need to learn and be initiated into. But cultural theorists often claim that culture exists only within the consciousness of the members of the group, that it evolves as a way of helping "social groups to cope with the problems of living in a particular habitat" (Bullivant, 1986, p. 43) and that it is therefore subject to development and change over time. We need to explore the implications these claims and assumptions have for education. Should schools be more concerned with the preservation and transmission of traditional cultural values and practices, or with encouraging an approach to culture that allows for criticism, development, and change (cf. May, 1999, p. 33)? Is it possible to encourage children to engage critically with a range of different cultural identities, including their own, to explore connections and differences and to exchange experiences in creative dialogue with people from different ethnic backgrounds, without potentially undermining the children's existing cultural commitments? But if children's existing cultural commitments are being undermined, how can it be claimed that this process demonstrates recognition and respect for different cultures? There is clearly a need to clarify the role of schools in the development and transmission of culture, and the way this relates to broader power relations in society (cf. Giroux, 1997).

Secondly, "multiculturalism" has become an increasingly important issue for political theorists and philosophers. Work on political and cultural pluralism in the first half of the twentieth century tended to depict groups as voluntary associations which individuals could freely join or withdraw from, or else as pressure groups vying with each other in a struggle for power (see Nicholls, 1974, 1975), but since the increase in migration to Western states following World War II, the term "pluralist" has more frequently been applied to states made up of different ethnic groups living side by side but distinguished by language, culture, race, or religion. The "peaceful coexistence of diverse lifestyles, language patterns, religious practices and family structures" which is said to characterize contemporary pluralist societies (Wlodkowski and Ginsberg, 1995, p. 17) masks very significant socioeconomic and political inequalities between groups, and the coexistence is very much on terms set by the majority. It is often maintained that the price minority groups must pay for general toleration in a pluralist society is the acceptance of a public order at odds with its fundamental ideals. But what alternatives to such apparent cultural domination are possible? In the last decade, a number of political philosophers (see, for example, Taylor, 1992; Kymlicka, 1995) have begun to explore topics such as the degree of public recognition the state should accord to ethnic minority cultures, the conditions that minority cultures must satisfy in order to merit such recognition, and the adaptations that should be made to structures in the public domain to take account of cultural diversity. A crucial question is whether the state itself should endeavor to adopt a neutral stance with regard to culture, or whether there are any circumstances in which the state can justifiably align itself with the culture of the majority, and promote this through legislation and through public institutions. Questions such as these have clear implications for the development of multicultural education.

Thirdly, debates about the right of ethnic minority groups to use education to preserve and maintain their distinctive beliefs and values and transmit these to the next generation take place alongside broader discussions about group rights. One problem about the notion of "group rights" is that it is difficult to justify restricting it to disadvantaged minority groups, but once it is extended to dominant or powerful groups it tends to undermine equality (cf. Vogt, 1997, p. 38). A further problem is that the distinction between group rights and individual rights is not always clear-cut: for example, the provision of state funding for religious schools may be claimed as a group right by Catholics or Muslims, but the choice whether or not to send their children to such schools is exercised by parents as individuals. Ethnic minorities typically claim two kinds of rights relating to their cultural aspirations (cf. Halstead, 1995a). The first is equity of treatment with other groups within the state, which involves on the one hand the right to see the barriers of discrimination and institutional racism broken down so that full social integration can be achieved, and on the other the right to see their own cultural identity as a source of pride, loyalty, and personal identity and as something worthy of celebration; as already implied, this would involve a shift in power relations within the state and an end to the sense of powerlessness among minority groups as a result of the cultural domination of the majority. The second is the right to give priority on occasions to their cultural or religious commitments over their responsibilities as citizens. Into this second category fall the claims of Sikhs to wear turbans rather than helmets when riding motorcycles, the claims of Hindus to cremate their deceased on a funeral pyre and scatter the ashes in rivers, the claims of some Africans to inflict permanent scars on their children as part of an initiation ceremony, the claims of the Amish to withdraw their children from school before the age of 16 in order to restrict their knowledge of the outside world (cf. the much discussed case of *Wisconsin v. Yoder* in the United States), and the claims of Muslims to apply Muslim personal law in Western states (cf. Lustgarten, 1983; Parekh, 1999). The group rights claimed here are not dissimilar in many cases to those claimed by other minority groups, notably national minorities like the American Indians or the Kurds in Turkey and Iraq, linguistic minorities like the French speakers in Canada, or other marginalized or disadvantaged social groups identified in terms of disability, sexual orientation, gender, class, or religion (cf. Kymlicka, 1995, pp. 17–20; Vogt, 1997, p. 188). We argue below for a concept of multiculturalism that depends more on shared concern for those who are vulnerable than on narrow lines of unified ideological commitments based on any particular kind of grouping.

Fourthly, the question arises who has the right to make fundamental decisions about the way children are educated. There is clearly a potential clash between the right of parents to bring up their children in their own culture and religion, and the right of children (perhaps protected by the state) to be liberated from the constraints of the cultural background of their parents (cf. Bailey, 1984). But it may be claimed conversely that children have a right to a degree of cultural continuity in their education. The question therefore arises whether schools have a duty to encourage all children to develop into autonomous individuals, even if this generates a clash of loyalties and may result in children casting off their cultural heritage, or whether they should give priority to emotional security and stability by ensuring that there is some continuity between the cultural values to which children are exposed at home and those of the school.

Finally, questions about the rights of children merge into more general questions of educational theory and practice. In particular, if it is accepted that children should receive a common educational experience, it is necessary to consider the values on which that common educational experience is based (cf. McLaughlin, 1995a). This might involve the search for a highest common factor of values, in other words, a framework of values that is shared as a matter of empirical fact by all the major cultural groups within the state. This would probably cover agreement on a basic social morality and acceptance of a common system of law, but the framework would probably be too thin to support any substantial system of education. However, any attempt to provide a thicker framework of values is bound to run into problems in a multicultural society. One possibility is to root the framework in the culture, history, and traditions of the dominant group, but this might be seen by minority groups as cultural domination. Another possibility is to establish the framework through democratic negotiation, but this may end up again in a form of majority domination, and in any case many religious groups may not consider their values to be matters for negotiation. A third possibility involves the claim that all cultural values have their roots in religion, and that it is only by exploring "those fundamental absolute values that all religions share" that an adequate conceptualization of "shared values" can be reached (Ashraf, 1986, p. vi); but such an approach is unlikely to prove popular in an increasingly secular age. However, it is hard to see how any form of multicultural education can be developed without some agreement over the shared values on which it is to be based.

It is only by looking at the complex interaction between all of the factors listed above – including the concept of culture, the role of education in the development of cultural identity, the nature of pluralism and the recognition of ethnic minorities, the right of minorities to maintain their distinctive culture, the right of parents to some involvement in educational decision making, and the problem of shared values in a pluralist society – that we can start to find a way of responding to the fundamental questions that multicultural education raises. Our aim in this chapter is to reflect on some of these questions and on the nature of multicultural education more generally in the light of recent work in social and political philosophy and the philosophy of education. We take liberalism as our starting point because it provides the general framework within which multicultural education policies were first developed and because it provides a substantial set of principles within which the concept of multicultural education and all the complex interacting issues outlined above can be discussed.

A Liberal Vision of Multicultural Education

Kincheloe and Steinberg caricature liberal multiculturalism as based solely on the belief that individuals from diverse cultural backgrounds "share a natural equality and a common humanity" (1997, p. 10). However, it seems more reasonable to claim that just as liberalism as a political theory takes its origin in the tension between the two fundamental values of liberty and equality (Halstead, 1996, pp. 18–20), so liberal multiculturalism is built upon the tension between similarity and difference. Emphasis on similarity in an educational context may help the development of racial tolerance within the broader society, but too strong an emphasis on similarity may lead to charges of cultural insensitivity and oppression (Halstead, 1995a, p. 267); conversely, diversity may be presented as something that is culturally enriching, but too much emphasis on difference may perpetuate stereotypes and encourage segregation and social rejection. In the liberal vision of multicultural education, therefore, there is an equal stress on two main principles: on the one hand, respect for difference and, on the other, the equal need of all children for education for life in a pluralist society.

The principle of respect for difference manifests itself in schools in attempts to respond positively to the cultural needs and sensitivities of children from minority groups wherever possible. This may take a variety of different forms:

- welcoming and making educational use of the different cultural experiences that children bring with them into the classroom, such as linguistic diversity;
- respecting the cultural integrity of children from ethnic minority groups by avoiding putting them into a position where they are expected to act against their own deeply held cultural or religious beliefs (e.g., by requiring Muslim children to wear a school uniform that does not meet their own standards of modesty and decency, or requiring them to attend school on major religious festivals);
- combating cultural, racial, and religious prejudice and discrimination, and condescending and patronizing attitudes toward cultural difference;
- recognizing the need for courses that support the cultural identity of children from ethnic minorities.

The principle of education for life in a pluralist society is based on the belief that all children, irrespective of their own cultural background, share the same need to develop tolerance, respect, and cross-cultural understanding if they are to live together harmoniously as adult citizens. Like the principle of respect for difference, it combines a number of elements affecting both the ethos and the curriculum of the school:

- It involves educating children from different cultures together in a safe, inclusive learning environment where the staff, values, structures, teaching practices, and curriculum reflect the cultural diversity of the children, so that the school becomes a microcosm of the broader society and children have opportunities to learn to interact naturally with others from different cultures. If schools do not serve a multicultural neighborhood, they will still emphasize the multicultural nature of the broader society through the careful choice of resources.

- It rules out the uncritical presentation of any particular worldview or concept of the good, but rather encourages children from all groups to question their assumptions, to engage in rational debate, to develop as autonomous individuals, to respond critically to a range of different worldviews, and to value the diversity of outlooks that makes such critical engagement possible.
- It encourages students to develop tolerance toward beliefs and worldviews they do not share, and a sensitive respect for people from different cultural backgrounds.
- It seeks to prepare students for citizenship in a democratic, pluralist society, and challenges all forms of racism, prejudice, bias, and ethnocentrism (whether direct or indirect, personal or institutional), and anything else that denies any students equal access to their rights as citizens.
- It entails studying the literature, art, music, history, and religions of different cultural groups and coming to see cultural diversity as a source of enrichment and breadth of perspective. The aim of this approach to education is to encourage all children to develop a spirit of enquiry in relation to other cultures, an openness to and sympathetic understanding of a variety of ways of looking at the world, and a willingness to enter into the spirit of different civilizations and societies.

These two principles – respect for difference and education for life in a pluralist society – are of course closely connected. Both welcome cultural diversity, both reject cultural domination, and both place a strong emphasis on combating cultural prejudice and racial injustice. And in any case schools can hardly encourage children to respect other beliefs and cultures (the principle of the equal need of all children for education for life in a pluralist society) if they do not model such respect in their own dealings with ethnic minority students (the principle of respect for difference). But it is also true that together the two principles form a distinctively liberal approach to multicultural education, in that they are based on a clear framework of liberal values (cf. Parekh, 2000).

Of course, liberalism is a broad canvas which contains many entwined themes and which it is possible to interpret in many different ways, as Eamonn Callan and John White make clear in chapter 5 of this volume. But let us agree for the moment on some broad brushstrokes. The rejection of ethnocentrism, cultural domination, racism, stereotyping, and discrimination is based on the core liberal values of justice, freedom, and equality (Halstead, 1996). So too is affirmative action, wherever it is taken as a rational response to perceived inequalities. These fundamental liberal values also generate many of the key principles that underpin multicultural education, including tolerance, respect for persons, and in particular the notion of rights. As we have seen, the right of parents to bring their children up within their own worldview and the right of groups to maintain their distinctive cultural identity are central to any concept of multiculturalism, but liberal individualism also protects the right of children as they grow older to free themselves if they choose from the cultural practices and worldview of their parents. The liberal refusal to align itself with any determinate version of the good ensures that the liberal state accepts pluralism as an underlying principle, welcomes diversity, and adopts a stance of neutrality on controversies to do with the good life, while at the same time support-ing the value of personal autonomy by leaving individuals free to pursue their own vision of the good, and free from both cultural domination by the majority and cultural ghettoization within a minority group.

Parekh (1986) has argued persuasively that the concept of multicultural education is not only compatible with, but also a logical extension of, liberal education. Monocultural education, he claims, is not only alienating to children from ethnic minorities but is also a narrow and impoverished education for children from the majority culture: it restricts the growth of imagination, curiosity, and critical self-reflection and provides fertile ground for the development of arrogant, insensitive, and racist attitudes. Multicultural education, by contrast, by encouraging children to go beyond the framework of their own culture and beliefs, helps them to develop open, lively, enquiring minds and a rational critical faculty; it is therefore

> an education in freedom – freedom from inherited biases and narrow feelings and sentiments, as well as freedom to explore other cultures and perspectives and make choices in full awareness of the available and practical alternatives . . . If education is concerned to develop such basic human capacities as curiosity, self-criticism, capacity for reflection, ability to form an independent judgement, sensitivity, intellectual humility and respect for others, and to open the pupil's mind to the great achievements of mankind, then it must be multicultural in orientation. (Parekh, 1986, pp. 26–9)

On this view, the case for multicultural education does not ultimately depend on the presence of ethnic minority children in a state's schools, although their presence has proved a catalyst for its development. But quite apart from the ethnic makeup of the school, good education based on liberal principles will always strive to free students from the straitjacket of ethnocentrism and introduce them to the rich diversity of other cultures and the plurality of ways of life and thought that form our human heritage.

However, the liberal vision of multicultural education presented in this section leaves many issues open to debate. Tamir (1995), for example, discusses whether liberal multiculturalism encompasses only the diversity of broadly liberal cultures, or whether it includes illiberal cultures as well. Another problem is that liberal values do not always point to clear courses of action. In the Rushdie affair, for example, there was a clash between those who prioritized the value of freedom of expression and those who prioritized respect for minority cultures. For some liberals, wearing the *hijab* in school is an issue of freedom of expression whereas for others it is a symbol of unacceptable cultural constraint and the oppression of women. In addi-tion to these internal debates, liberal multiculturalism has come under attack from a variety of positions. Critics on the left have argued that liberal multiculturalism pays inadequate attention to the structures of power in society and thus fails to get to the root of racism, oppression, and inequality in all its manifestations. Critics on the right have argued that multicultural education is an unpalatable "mishmash" of cultures, and that children's biggest need, if they are to succeed in an increasingly competitive job market, is for a high level of literacy in the dominant culture of their society (Hirsch, 1988). Critics among religious fundamentalists have argued that liberalism lacks an adequate spiritual and moral foundation and that it denies them the freedom to pursue their own vision of what is good for their children. However, our aim in the remainder of this chapter is not to discuss specific criticisms such as these in more detail, but to develop a more nuanced approach to thinking about culture in general and multicultural education in particular. This will involve, for example, an understanding of liberal civic virtues that is enriched by postmodern insights and goes beyond mere tolerance and recognition toward a deeper view of shared human values. We will argue finally that this enriched perspective ultimately converges on the way in which multiculturalism and multicultural education have been treated within the liberal analytic tradition.

Shared Concerns: The Possibility of Universal Moral Action

It was asserted in the previous section that liberalism comprises the core values of justice, freedom, and equality. What remains unstated is the ways in which these values are understood, for it is clear that these are not the sole preserve of the liberal. Indeed it is doubt about liberal construals of these terms and their metaphysical underpinnings that lies at the heart of problems with liberal multiculturalism as it is currently conceived. Perhaps most salient of the values of justice, freedom, and equality in this respect is equality. For the liberal, whatever individual or cultural differences manifest themselves, there is an underlying humanity that is common to all. It is above all in this respect that we are equal. It is in virtue of this that all should be treated as ends-in-themselves. It is on the basis of this that concern with rights has become so prominent a feature of contemporary politics.

If the idea of a common humanity received its most powerful expression in the modern world in the thought of the Enlightenment, it is probably the substantive forms that European expansion took that have elicited the strongest reactions against it. This is not to deny that there have always been groups to whom the idea is totally alien. It is not the place here to rehearse the various ways in which relativism has emerged, in realms well beyond the political. A particular issue is the refusal of cultural groups to be judged by or to live by standards alien to themselves. The liberal principle of respect for difference then comes to be seen as a political gesture based on assumptions that impose a subtle hegemony on nondominant groups. The danger in the liberal point of view is then that it may treat other cultures in a tokenistic way, failing to respond fully to the quality and extent of their otherness. Liberal respect for difference can thus maintain a society in which forms of behavior or values are sanctioned or promoted that violate the beliefs of nondominant groups.

A degree of cultural relativism has been to the fore in many respects in discussions of multiculturalism, and this has drawn somewhat promiscuously and gleefully on the supposed loss of certainty in ethics and epistemology. We do not propose to rehearse these relativistic arguments here. Rather we want to consider reactions against such cultural relativism from two principal sources. On the one hand, these concern individual rights and welfare; on the other, commitment to gender equity. A concern for a group's right to fairness and respect, it is feared, might lead to the suppression of the rights of individuals and subgroups within them. The welfare and cultural integrity of the group is often offered as a reason for overriding individual rights on the grounds that attention to those rights might weaken the momentum of the group's movement toward political and cultural equity. These latter rights, it is argued, are ascribed a lower priority because they might weaken the momentum of a movement that seeks to promote its political and cultural ends within an environment of inequity. Feminists have been similarly and increasingly insistent in pointing out that multiculturalism might present a problem for gender equity (Okin, 1999), a worry shared by such different philosophers as Martha Nussbaum and Gayatri Spivak. Meanwhile, some contemporary approaches to the politics of multiculturalism, as represented, for example, by Ella Shohat, refuse this hierarchy of priorities. One way in which the tension between, on the one hand, concerns for individual rights and gender equity and, on the other, respect for different cultures, can be eased is by addressing the idea of cultural integrity itself.

Cultural Integrity and Complexity

The dominant approach to multiculturalism and educational practice keeps in focus the very many ways from the psychological, through the linguistic, to the legal, that individuals are excluded from full participation within national cultures in particular and international culture in general because of their membership of groups formed along such lines of difference as race, class, and gender. The main concern in these discussions is about the demands for equity among diverse groups within the classroom and in the wider society. Moreover, it is often assumed that references to culture point to collective group identity and that membership in groups determines personal identity. On this view, culture is not merely a set of settled practices but rather is constitutive of people. This view rests on the assumptions that there is an undeniable link between an individual and a culture and that there is individual moral value to be derived from the recognition of such a link. Such a view of identity depends on, and draws moral force from, a certain notion of authenticity based less on an individual's characteristics and agency than on that individual belonging to a particular people. One danger of such a deterministic view of culture is that it sustains moral and political practices in such a way as to render them impervious to criticism, both internal and external. It is as well to remember instances of fascism in modern history that depended precisely on such a linkage. Furthermore, the idea that culture constitutes identity makes the concept of culture interchangeable with quasi-biological and highly problematic concepts of "race," "gender," and "ethnicity." Stereotypes regarding the abilities of individuals and practices of discrimination are generated from such a collapsing of the concepts of "identity" and "culture," as also is an unreflective identity politics.

One fallacy here is the idea that cultures are hermetically sealed. Cultures have always exerted mutual influence. Such mutual influence is noted even under conditions of colonialism where the colonizing culture changes even as it effects changes on the cultures that are brought under its power (see, for example, King, 1984). Following the work of historians like Fernand Braudel (1981) and Janet Abu-Lughod (1981), and their studies of cultural exchange within the contexts of modernity and in premodern societies, the claims for uniqueness regarding contemporary processes are placed in doubt. One has only to think of the libraries of Alexandria or the Moorish gardens of the Alhambra in Spain.

We can find a vivid way of realizing the logic of what we might call a deep humanism through some consideration of the nature of language. This works less as an analogy than as an example, even the epitome, of what is important in cultural coherence and interaction. There is no such thing as a universal language; there are diverse *languages*. But these are neither unchanging nor unaffected by each other, and translation between them is possible. There is no such thing as perfect translation, but neither is there any language that is sealed off from others: translation works and in the process it changes, and often enriches, the languages involved. While contemporary theories of intertextuality suggest something of the inevitably multicultural nature of our lives, it was Merleau-Ponty especially who recognized the special significance of language in identifying human connections of a different order than those typically designated by ideas of a common human nature. In contrast to the essentialism of such a conception of the human, Merleau-Ponty draws attention to the lateral nature of these cross-cultural elements and to their fertility in the realization of a better political order (Dhillon, 1994, p. 173).

The cultural complexity of which we speak is not a new condition within the world economy. What is new is that changing technologies of travel and communication, the near universalization of radio and television, have made the effects of processes of cultural interpenetration quickly and deeply noticeable. Current conditions of globalization have folded regional economies into the global economy in a manner that makes it difficult to maintain the distinction between core and peripheral regions of the world economy with quite as much ease as has been done in the past.

Yet the prevailing discourse on multiculturalism and cultural diversity, with its concern for the welfare of subgroups or of individuals within marginalized groups, takes cultural groups to be both undifferentiated and hermetically sealed. In other words, most discussions of cultural diversity rest on an idealized view of what a culture is. The approach suggested by Shohat, in contrast, assumes that:

> genders, sexualities, races, classes, nations, and even continents exist not as hermetically sealed entities but rather as parts of a permeable interwoven relationality. Instead of segregating historical periods and geographical regions into neatly fenced off areas of expertise, it highlights the multiplicity of community histories and perspectives, as well as the hybrid culture of all communities, especially in a world increasingly characterized by the traveling of images and sounds, goods and people. (Shohat, 1998, p. 1)

In her introduction to *Talking Visions: Multicultural Feminism in a Transnational Age*, Shohat tells us that contemporary feminist multiculturalism aims at a "feminist reimagining of community relations and cultural practices," articulated not in isolation but rather relative to each other. "It does not exalt one political concern (feminism) over another (multiculturalism); rather, it highlights and reinforces the mutual embeddedness between the two" (Shohat, 1998, p. 1). Such an approach calls for pedagogical, curatorial, and organizational practices that place diverse gendered/sexed histories and geographies in dialogical relation in terms of the tensions and overlappings that take place "within" and "between" cultures, ethnic groups, and nations. The claims Shohat makes for multicultural feminism in the post-Cold War period could be made for multiculturalism in general. This is a departure from the version of multiculturalism that has come to dominate much contemporary educational discourse within the United States (see, for example, Banks and McGee-Banks, 1999). Yet this postmodern, multilayered, complex approach to thinking about culture in general and multicultural education in particular converges with the way in which multiculturalism and multicultural education have been treated within the liberal analytic tradition.

Thus, Michele Moody-Adams (1997) argues that an idealization of group cultures can be found in the discourse of both those outside a group and those who are members, and that the idealization of cultural groups often turns on making a distinction between "modern" and "traditional" cultures. The former are taken to be dynamic, differentiated, and open-ended, and the latter stagnant and closed. Such views of "traditional" cultures mistakenly suggest that their members have holistic systems of meaning tied to seamless webs of belief. Bernard Williams, attempting to break down the distinction between "us" and "the other," argues that "because cultures constantly meet one another and exchange and modify practices," it is implausible that "social practices might come forward with a certificate saying that they belonged to a genuinely different culture" (Williams, 1985, p. 158). Moody-Adams makes a similar point: "there is no conception more mystical or unreflective than the doctrine of cultural integration, along with its usual companion, the assumption that beliefs and values of 'traditional' or 'primitive' societies must be more integrated than those of any other" (Moody-Adams, 1997, p. 53). To the extent that relativist positions rest on the assumption that cultures are hermetically sealed, they are undermined by this recognition of complexity.

Mary Midgley takes the example of the Samurai practice in medieval Japan of testing a new sword's worth – its ability to cut a person in half – on random passers-by. While such a practice seems abhorrent to us from a modern standpoint (as it also must to contemporary members of Japanese society) there is no reason for us to think that the practice was universally accepted by medieval Japanese culture. Arguing so would lead us to the uncomfortable conclusion that the random passers-by – and their families – would not have questioned the morality of the practice. The medieval period, Midgley goes on to remind us, was a contentious, troubled time in Japanese history (Midgley, 1991). Let us consider also the practice of female infanticide still widely practiced in certain parts of India. This practice has received a new twist with the availability of technologies like amniocentesis that are being used in deciding which pregnancy is to be brought to term and which terminated. Needless to say, these decisions overwhelmingly favor male fetuses. In both these cases, a relativist view relying on an undifferentiated and bounded view of culture would miss the criticisms of these practices by Japanese historians of modern sensibility and Indian feminists informed by Western theories of gender oppression and equity. It would also miss internal criticisms of such practices, such as those in favor of gender equity that can be found in early, sixteenth-century Sikh thought. Even the most well-intentioned of theorists, themselves located within institutions of power, can miss the irony attendant on arguments of this kind. The fact of cultural complexity does not necessarily destroy the relativist's claim that there is no ground outside particular cultures from which to judge the worth of a culture. What it does do is to weaken the belief that a culture's values are determined, and are also to be judged exclusively, from within. As already argued, "within" is not as tidily sealed as some, including many relativists, might have thought.

But surely, it might be objected, it is difficult to deny that there are some practices that are so alien from our standpoint and yet so accepted within a certain, usually traditional, culture that we can have only "notional" confrontations with them. Bernard Williams (1981) calls such a position "relativism at a distance." While he suggests that this applies primarily to the past, it applies also to cases like the veiling required of Muslim women, the recent case of sati in contemporary India, the persistence of the practice of female clitorectomy. Consider also the sentence of stoning to death, on a certain interpretation of Islamic law, passed and carried out by the Taliban while in power in Afghanistan. In each of these cases arguments are made, often by women themselves from within these cultures, for the value of these practices. Yet the cases are quite different in the extent to which they take the interests of those directly affected into account, and perhaps in the way they con-strue those interests. In the case of veiling it is argued that in a patriarchal society where women are placed under the masculine gaze within the public sphere, the veil offers the freedom to move and participate in these public spaces. In the absence of these practices women would be completely restricted to the domestic sphere. It may be, as argued by certain Islamic feminists such as Fatima Mernissi (1987), that such veiling actually privileges the female gaze because the *chador* or the *burqua* are constructed in a manner that allows women to look around them while remaining hidden themselves as they move through the marketplace, for example. Moreover, when these practices are followed within Western society they are easily tolerated and criticisms tend to come only from those preoccupied with Western conceptions of women's rights. Hence the possibilities of hybridity extend in varied and fluid ways, with a corresponding reduction in the plausibility of the idea of "relativism at a distance."

Such reflection draws our attention to several presuppositions of our inquiry. For example, in noticing that the local criticisms that are on offer tend to come from individuals influenced by Western feminism we acknowledge not only that cultures are differentiated but also that they are not bounded. Hence alliances tied to issues related to a shared concern for the welfare of those who are vulnerable offer greater potential, it becomes apparent, than action in accordance with unified ideological commitments. Furthermore, the recognition that cultures are not bounded encour-ages us to treat the absence of criticism, perhaps even the celebration, of a practice such as that seen in the case of *sati* in north India with greater subtlety and responsibility than Williams's idea of "notional" confrontation, or relativism at a distance, might suggest. Postcolonial feminist theorists, such as Lata Mani, have shown how the practice of *sati* sharply increased as a result of the outlawing of such practices under British colonial rule (Mani, 1998). These theorists argue that the increase in instances of *sati* was a retaliatory reaction linked to a context of unequal power relations. Separating a concern for the welfare of women from concerns regarding cultural equity, these feminists point out that such contestations are played out on the female body. At the very least the taking up of such arguments based on the recognition of the relationality between cultures would indicate that we should look at how judgement tied to power might result in an increase in practices that make the already vulnerable even more so. The implication is that the persistence, even intensification and celebration, of such practices could be causally connected to the permeability of cultures and the relationality of cultures within national and international contexts. However ironic this may be to the well-intentioned (and naive), the politics of knowledge within the context of colonialism should make this no surprise at all.

In other words, any understanding of cultural practices that rests on a division between "us" and "them" needs to be examined further. In the first place, such forms of understanding should be scrutinized closely in order to determine whether any unacknowledged sense of moral supremacy lurks within. Second, we would need to educate ourselves in the traditions whose practices are in question in order to find ways of making alliances with members of such a culture who uphold traditional values. We would do so in order to make the lives of women, and others who are vulnerable, a little easier, perhaps even less dangerous. That is, we would be acting thus for reasons of a universal democratic humanity (Nussbaum, 2000).

To put it somewhat baldly, critical multiculturalism demands, whether the context is local or global, that we ask ourselves if our predominantly secular and often Eurocentric criticisms of Muslim, Christian, and Hindu values, or latent Eurocentric values, are in any way implicated in practices that violate our deepest humanistic values (Murungi, 1994; Shohat and Stam, 1994). Critical multicultural education requires a sensitivity to the internal coherence of the values of a culture, to the different kinds of rationality that are in operation, and a recognition of the way that everyday actions thereby have their sense. While anthropological or sociological approaches may now have acquired something of that sensitivity, these disciplines have characteristically in the past been vulnerable to the kinds of criticism Wittgenstein makes in his remarks on Frazer's *Golden Bough*: the anthropologist approaches the practices of the tribe from within the unquestioned metaphysics of the West, and so the rain-making ceremony is seen simply as bad science. What is needed is a more holistic conception of the part that the practice plays in the life of the community, of a ritual or symbolic function that Western perceptions are apt to occlude (see Wittgenstein, 1979).

It is the analogy of language itself that should be recalled. There is no universal language: there are languages. And these interpenetrate and are translatable. So in our understanding of other cultures the removal of the illusion of a universal human nature helps us toward a proper humility in the witnessing of difference, while recognition of the complexity of cultures and the overlaps between them saves our critical judgement from a disabling relativism (Dhillon, 2001).

Toward a Deep Humanism

This is a turn to what we have called a deep humanism. While this is not merely a return to common values, the novelty of this formulation must not be a means of evading criticism. Rather, when offered as a Kantian regulative ideal for the work of multicultural education – an ideal that remains vigilant against the encroachment of dogmatism – it enables us to remain alert to all the ways in which we might stray from this ideal through presumptions of normality derived from notions of supremacy themselves derived from identifications with nation, class, race, gender, sexuality, and so on. In other words, even the most abrasive of criticisms would find a place within such multiculturalism when motivated by a commitment to a kingdom of ends. As Ella Shohat (1998) reminds us, critical multiculturalism has moved from an anticolonial stance to the more complex postcolonial position that can find expression within a fully liberal state (Dhillon, 1996).

Perhaps no contemporary philosopher captures the ethics reflecting the deep humanism of this idea as well as Thoreau did in the nineteenth century:

> Those who have not learned to read the ancient classics in the language in which they were written must have a very imperfect knowledge of the history of the human race; for it is remarkable that no transcript of them has ever been made into any modern tongue, unless our civilization itself may be regarded as such a transcript . . . That age will be rich indeed when those relics which we call Classics, and the still older and more than classic but even less known Scriptures of the nations, shall have further accumulated, when the Vaticans shall be filled with the Vedas and Zendavestas and Bibles, with Homers, and Dantes, and Shakespeares, and all the centuries to come shall have successively deposited their trophies in the forum of the world. By such a pile we may hope to scale heaven at last. (cited in Cavell, 1972, p. 14)

Thoreau – if we extend these thoughts to include the full range of cultures and subcultures that preoccupies contemporary multicultural education – can be taken to be calling for a kind of multilingualism, or transnational literacy, that is helpful in thinking about a nonmetaphysical universalism. If, as argued earlier, we wish to resist a reductive view of identity while leaving open the possibility of a critical collectivity then we can call on the critical reformation of curricula so that they reflect not only the diverse cultures that are present and have contributed toward the making of a certain "tradition" or "civilization," but the relations between them.

While the focus of the bulk of this discussion has been on the United Kingdom and the United States in a national and international context, similar arguments could also be extended to other contexts such as India where the contestation between religious, linguistic, caste, and gender identifications is being raised with a new energy and influence. The arguments of a responsibly critical multiculturalism brought to bear on these situations would enable the forging of robust new cultural identities that are not based on exclusionary practices tied to reductive identifications, themselves endorsed by nostalgia or resentment. In this chapter we have attempted to explore the possibilities of a refinement of liberal multiculturalism in a way that avoids the problems of facile universalist assumptions but that uncovers a deep humanism. It is in such a vision that the future of increasingly diverse societies throughout the world seems most secure.

Recommendations for Further Reading

Midgley, M. (1991) *Can't We Make Moral Judgements?* St. Martin's Press.
Parekh, B. (2000) *Rethinking Multiculturalism: Cultural Diversity and Political Theory*, Palgrave.
Tamir, Y. (ed.) (1995) *Democratic Education in a Multicultural State*, Blackwell.
Williams, B. (1985) *Ethics and the Limits of Philosophy*, Harvard University Press.

Part III

Philosophy as Education

Chapter 9

The Activity of Philosophy and the Practice of Education

Pádraig Hogan and Richard Smith

Introduction

Views differ widely about how philosophical reflection can inform the conduct of educational practice, and also about the extent to which it should do so. For instance, if one follows Plato's lead, especially that shown in the *Republic* (apart from Book I) and also in his *Laws*, one is pointed toward the conclusion that education is a practice that stands sorely in need of direction from the most sophisticated and embracing metaphysics. In the course of Plato's own writings, this metaphysics became a body of doctrines on a grand scale which included theoretical accounts of the human soul, the nature and purpose of the arts, the nonworldly origins of goodness, the changeless nature of goodness itself, the requirements of authority and obedience, and the regulation and control of public affairs, especially education. A theoretical conception of truth, achieved through advanced philosophical reasoning, is the guiding inspiration.

In our own time a similar conception of philosophy of education has been held by such writers as Paul Hirst, John White (*Towards a Compulsory Curriculum*, 1973), and Allen Brent (*Philosophical Foundations for the Curriculum*, 1978). This well-known approach consists in the attempts to distinguish various "forms of knowledge" (ethical, empirical/scientific, deductive/mathematical, and so on) as the basis for the various "curricular activities" that are to make up the school timetable and thereby furnish the mind of the educated individual.

By contrast, if one follows a prominent contemporary philosopher like Richard Rorty, a conclusion of the opposite kind is canvased. Rorty's adverse stance toward both metaphysics and its "successor discipline," epistemology, leads him to take a distinctly skeptical view of philosophy's contribution to education. Far from viewing education as standing in need of direction from any philosophical conception of truth, Rorty (1990a, p. 41) frankly declares: "I am dubious about the relevance of philosophy to education." And he continues: "Insofar as philosophy has a social function, it seems to me a therapeutic one – helping people get out from under outdated philosophical ideas, helping break the crust of convention" (ibid.). In keeping with this, he presents a two-stage conception of public education. The socialization of pupils into the communal historical narratives of their nation would be the main purpose of primary and secondary education. Secondly, higher education of a nonvocational kind would then be concerned with enabling students to "reinvent themselves," and in such a way that they could aspire to "an open personal future for themselves and an open social future for their society" (ibid., p. 43). Rorty's argument is informed, then, not by the fruits of any philosophical investigation into the notion of truth, but by something more commonplace: in the case of primary and secondary education by "what is held to be true by the society to which the children belong," and then by the critical "redescribing" of this during higher education (ibid., p. 42). Although the raising of critical questions is accommodated by this second stage, Rorty's account makes explicit no criteria for distinguishing better redescriptions from inferior ones, apart from periodically invoking the narrative of American history as a story of increasing freedom and uncompleted reform (ibid., pp. 42–3).

These deeply contrasting conceptions of education (or at any rate of schooling) – Plato's being historically far more influential, though Rorty's provokes much contemporary debate – have an underlying feature in common which the contrast serves to obscure. Each in its own way is a good illustration of a widespread view that public education is not an autonomous practice but is primarily a part of the machinery of some higher office, or dominant outlook, whether authoritarian or democratic, religious or secular, or other in character. The prevalence of such an outlook, and the managerialist assumptions that typically accompany it, are not things that can be quickly tackled and effectively disposed of by logical argument. Yet in this exploration we want to take a longer-term view and argue that it is the responsibility of the philosophy of education to show that education is a distinctive practice with an integrity of its own, and that this entitles that practice to a decisive measure of autonomy in carrying out its work. Accordingly, we also want to explore promising ways in which philosophy of education might be engaged so as to uncover the most appropriate understanding of that practice and to nurture its fruitful and defensible conduct.

Circumscribing the Claims of Theory

A suggestion to start with: philosophy of education can do much to put its own house in order by discarding both metaphysical claims to objective truth and epistemological ones to certainty. To begin with such a bold suggestion is not to side with Rorty against Plato, or with late modernity against antiquity. Nor is it necessarily to embrace the antifoundationalist "postmodern turn," though as we shall later note it is a similar move. The suggestion does not imply, moreover, that truth can be dispensed with in teaching and learning, in favor of Rortyan socialization plus redescription. Rather, its implication is that both metaphysics and epistemology overestimate what is humanly achievable. Both make the human concern with truth a prisoner of the kind of thinking we shall here call *theoretical*, meaning by this that it severs something called "theory" from something else called "practice" and then attempts to reconnect them by having the former direct the latter. This dichotomy thus in turn attenuates the experience of learning and disfigures that of teaching. To eschew metaphysics is not to recommend any dismissal of Plato, though it is to decline the all-embracing answers his later writings supplied to the cardinal questions he raised. Nor is it to side whole-heartedly with Rorty, who is one of the most prominent advocates in contemporary philosophy of just such a recommendation. The implications of Rorty's abandonment of metaphysics and epistemology are very different from the argument that will be explored in this chapter. We are wary of following Rorty too far, partly because his position involves an almost cavalier disregard of criteria of justification: a disregard that encloses his philosophy within a new parochialism, albeit one of a North American liberal, pragmatic, and democratic cast.[1]

Our own conception of the philosophy of education, then, turns against metaphysics and epistemology on the grounds of the *theoretical* character, conceived as above, of their enquiries. Education is a *human* practice, as distinct from a natural phenomenon or a biological process. This practice cannot be theorized about in the same objective way as the objects of physics or biology or chemistry can, because what is being investigated when education is submitted to reflection is nothing other than human experience itself. In such reflection the investigator is already a part of that which is being investigated. Theory here cannot have the independence from its object that the natural sciences claim in their own fields. One may of course attempt to gain a critical distance from one's own experiences of understanding and learning, but the very exercise of this disciplined reflection reveals that such experiences, unlike the order of nature disclosed by scientific theory, have an ever-emergent character, an inherent unpredictability, and an unsurpassable contingency. All of this order of experience is governed probably less by demonstrable regularity than by surprises, disappointments, accidental encounters, contingencies, and everything else to which human circumstance and history are heir.

If theorizing about human experience cannot have the methodological independence that theorizing can have in the physical sciences, neither can it have science's coherence, or adequacy, or predictive validity in relation to its object of investigation. In short, to *theorize* about human experience is to render it lucid at the cost of wresting it from its embeddedness in social and historical circumstance. It is to obscure the particularity, the contextuality, the embodiment in language and idiom, that is essential to experience itself. The gain in understanding is secured at the cost of recasting experience as something else, of losing what is particular to experience *qua* experience, as distinct from experience as the object of theoretical explanation.[2]

Plato's Reversal of the Precedence of Practice

If philosophical thinking is properly to inform how education is to be understood and carried out, then that thinking must itself be practical rather than theoretical in character. A reflection on practice that remains true to its task is a different *kind* of thinking from that which characterizes theory in any of its modes. Some of the best examples of such practical reflection can be found in the early dialogues of Plato – those nonmetaphysical writings which give dramatic accounts of the historical figure, Socrates of Athens, and of the kind of educational work in which he engaged. These dialogues include the *Gorgias, Protagoras, Euthyphro, Republic* (at least Book I), and especially the *Apology*, which contains Socrates' reflection on his life's work as a whole. In each instance here, since all these earlier dialogues are themselves exploratory experiences of learning, the reader is not presented with anything theoretical, but is invited to join the exploration as a specific instance of practice. The dialogues actually show that the participants' attempts run into intractable difficulties wherever they seek, or more precisely *insofar* as they seek, to establish theoretical definitions that would thereafter serve as *a priori* directions for thought and action.

Plato's own solution to these difficulties experienced by Socrates and his students was to break (in his middle and later works) with the ever-provisional, ever-uncertain, character of Socratic understanding and to build instead a metaphysical theory of majestic scope and finality. Thus he attempted to make practice itself, and its predicaments, amenable to explanation and control by theory. This can be gathered from the way in which the spontaneous to-and-fro of the earlier dialogues yields to the more contrived exchanges of Plato's middle and later writings. In these writings, Socrates becomes less the living Socrates of Athens and increasingly a literary device for the often poetic articulation, but always the authoritative accomplishing, of Plato's metaphysics. Socrates' lively interlocutors of the early dialogues are largely replaced by his consenting listeners in the later ones. In one of Plato's last works, *Laws*, the character "Socrates" has finally disappeared and the central place is given to a strikingly didactic figure, the "Athenian Stranger," whose thoughts on education are issued more with the certainty of edicts[3] than with the openness to critical response that marks the contributions of Socrates in the early dialogues.

A Lesson about Learning

The apparent inconclusiveness of the debates on various questions of practice in Plato's early dialogues – justice, civic duty, goodness, pleasure – suggests that an absence of finality, an incompleteness of insight, may attend even the best human efforts to discern and to act. Metaphysics can be understood as the intellectual attempt to overcome these debilitating limitations and to secure an objective and conclusive account of all that *is*, beyond the deceptive perception of the human senses. If one resists this flight into theory, which Plato himself took in his later writing, and attends more closely to what actually befalls human understanding itself during the dramatic encounters of the early dialogues, the limitations just referred to take on a different significance. It cannot be denied that the venturing of contrasting perspectives during a serious dialogue may arouse partisan passions as well as sometimes calling forth fresh insights. And thus it might be objected that dialogue generates more heat than light: that it fails to escape the bounds of prejudice, while theory reaches beyond partisanship to a more pure, more incisive, kind of thought.

It must be pointed out however that the most important lesson to be gleaned from the practices of Socrates is that such "pure" knowledge lies beyond the range of human *achievement*, though not beyond the ability of humans to imagine in principle: that is, as some kind of ideal or superhuman knowledge. Or to put it another way, the limitations of perspective that metaphysics tries to overcome through objective theorizing are in fact *inescapable features of human understanding itself*. On this account, then, the most imposing metaphysics would still remain a perspective: something to be argued for and upheld in the face of contrasting perspectives.

To pursue this lesson a bit further, the significance of the Socratic dramas in the early dialogues of Plato lies in their disclosure of how human understanding becomes gradually – and sometimes painfully – enlightened about its own possibilities and limitations; of how it becomes disciplined toward a discerning modesty concerning its own capabilities as it becomes, in practice, a re-education of one's own perspectives. This applies to the careful reader of the dialogues as much as to the participants being read about. As dialogues like the *Gorgias, Protagoras, Euthyphro, Republic I*, and *Apology* show, none of this is accomplished in accordance with a program laid down in advance, but by allowing one's own perspectives as a reader of the dialogues – that is, as a vicarious participant in the drama – to engage with the contrasting perspectives ventured therein on the issues under discussion. Taking the dialogues just mentioned, these issues under discussion include: the relative claims of power, pleasure, and justice and how these might be understood (*Gorgias*); one's understanding of moral action and the question of its teachability (*Protagoras*); one's understanding of civic duty and its practical responsibilities (*Euthyphro*); the intractable nature of justice itself (*Republic I*); the limitations of human knowledge and the dangers in human pretensions to certainty or to absolute knowledge (*Apology*).

If Socrates seems to have a more incisive perspective than any of the other participants in these early dialogues, it is not because he is in possession of an objective theoretical knowledge that enables him to expose the subjectivity of the other participants' arguments. Rather it is because he has already gone over these questions continually in his own reflections and in earlier discussions with others. During these he has encountered many pitfalls and wrong turnings, from which chastening experiences he has learned a lot. But he has not arrived at anything like "the full picture" or "the final truth." It is in the light of such invaluable – but also fallible – experience that he ventures in each new encounter *his best understanding to date*. His understanding then is never that of an expert in possession of incontrovertible insight. It proceeds, rather, from his own presuppositions, and from the consequences of his own best efforts to have these presuppositions unearthed and criticized in exchanges with others.

As recounted by Plato, Socrates himself is explicit on this point in the *Apology*, the story of his conduct of his own defense before a jury of 501 fellow-Athenians. He explains to the jury that when he heard that the oracle of Apollo at Delphi had declared that Socrates was the wisest of men, he himself was perplexed and had then continually sought to refute the oracle's declaration (*Apology*, 21). But in meeting and interviewing those with the highest reputation for wisdom – particularly the sophists of Athens and other Greek city-states – in order to disprove the oracle's claim, Socrates relates in evidence that he invariably found, sometimes to his own amazement, that it was invariably those renowned sophists' claims that fell victim to refutation, thus upholding the oracle's declaration. Eventually, as Socrates explains to the court, he was forced to the following conclusion about the true significance of the oracle's declaration.

> Real wisdom is the property of God, and this oracle is his way of telling us that human wisdom has little or no value. It seems to me that he is not referring literally to Socrates, but has merely taken my name as an example, as if he would say to us "The wisest of you is he who has realized, like Socrates, that in respect of wisdom he is really worthless." (*Apology*, 23)

Socrates is not suggesting here that the search for knowledge or truth is a worthless undertaking, or that ignorance is a virtue. On the contrary, he devoted his life's work to this search, but he also continually warned, by his own example, that it was the greatest illusion to think that any human could arrive at the final goal. He is calling attention to the point that humans should not allow themselves to assume a God's-eye-view of all of reality. This might aptly be described as Socrates' anti-metaphysical warning. It is one of the greatest ironies of Western philosophy that Plato, to whom Western learning is incalculably in debt for its acquaintance with Socrates, came to turn his back on this warning, or underestimated its significance. Far from advocating ignorance, Socrates' actions embodied certain virtues of learning which follow from having an *educated sense* of one's own ignorance, and of the relative ignorance of humankind as a whole. Such virtues are to be made explicit then, as a close study of the events in the early dialogues discloses, through a reflection on what befalls experience during practices of teaching and learning. They are not to be found in any theory, understood as something that might be applied to these practices from above, as it were. They are chiefly to be understood as *emerging within* teaching and learning, and as *embodied in* teaching and learning, as a reflectively experienced way of life.

Philosophy as a Way of Life and as the Pursuit of a Specialism

The distinction between philosophy as a theoretical activity and as a reflection on one's own practices features as a major theme in Pierre Hadot's book, *Philosophy as a Way of Life*. Hadot's historical investigations lead him to the conclusion that in Greek and Roman antiquity philosophy was "above all the choice of a form of life, to which philosophical discourse then gives justifications and theoretical foundations" (Hadot, 1995, p. 281). He argues that it is not as an explanatory discourse about reality, but as a "therapeutics of the passions" in order to transform the conduct of one's life, that ancient philosophy from Socrates to the Epicureans and the Stoics should be understood (p. 82). In a bold argument which anticipates objections from those who might wish to defend philosophy as a theoretical enterprise, Hadot includes Aristotle among those ancients whose conception of philosophy was primarily practical:

It is sometimes claimed that Aristotle was a pure theoretician, but for him, too, philosophy was incapable of being reduced to philosophical discourse, or to a body of knowledge. Rather, philosophy for Aristotle was a quality of the mind, the result of an inner transformation. The form of life preached by Aristotle was the life according to the mind. (Hadot, 1995, p. 269)

A crucial point about this conclusion is that it could in important respects apply with even greater force to Plato, who has appeared in earlier paragraphs above as a chief patron of *theoretical* philosophy. This suggestion gains in strength if one could ignore, or excise from Plato's works, his draconian provisions relating to education, the arts, and the affairs of public life, especially those contained in the *Republic*, Books II–X and in the *Laws*. In this event Plato's philosophy might be significant chiefly as a powerful and poetic exhortation to personal spiritual aspiration, for instance as exemplified in dialogues such as the *Symposium, Phaedrus*, and *Theaetetus*. But where education as a major undertaking is concerned, it was the hierarchical and exclusionary features of Plato's philosophy that were to prove the most influential in subsequent history. Such features, including those of medieval as well as ancient metaphysics, were eventually to provoke a critical stance toward metaphysics as such (as found, e.g., in Hume and Kant), not least on the grounds that metaphysics confounds matters of personal conviction, or moral vision, with matters that are supposedly theoretically compelling and then, somehow, legitimately enforceable on others.

For his part, Hadot identifies the ascendancy of the theoretical in philosophy not with Plato or Aristotle, nor with the philosophers of the Hellenistic or Roman periods, but with the European Middle Ages. He suggests that the medieval universities, as creations of the Christian church, drew philosophy under the rule of theology, which was in turn "founded on the rule of faith" (Hadot, 1995, p. 270). Philosophy, he points out, thus ceased to be a way of life and became the "servant of theology," supplying it "with the conceptual, logical, physical, and metaphysical materials it needed." The vital connection between philosophy and one's own life thus became secondary, or even severed. Taking a longer historical perspective on this development, Hadot concludes:

Education was thus no longer directed toward people who were to be educated with a view to becoming fully developed human beings, but to specialists, in order that they might learn how to train other specialists. This is the danger of "Scholasticism," that philosophical tendency which began to be sketched at the end of antiquity, developed in the Middle Ages, and whose presence is still recognizable in philosophy today. (ibid.)

The reference, in one of the brief quotations cited before this passage, to the *rule* of faith, as distinct from the *experience* of faith, or the *practice* of faith, betrays something further about medieval scholarship, which Hadot does not make explicit. From the handling of the controversies that attended the study of theology in the twelfth and thirteenth century, most notably in Paris, it becomes evident that where teaching and learning were concerned, the rule of faith was largely the rule of the monastic orders, the papacy, and its ecclesiastical councils. This rule often established in fact the austerity (though not the scrupulosity) of the reign of the philosopher rulers that was merely contemplated by Plato in the *Republic*, Books II–X.[4] So in addition to losing the vitality of being a way of life, philosophy – as philosophy-cum-theology – became a branch of something that was now conceived as a science, or, more precisely, the supreme *scientia*. In the conduct of this science moreover, important scriptural passages and themes were to feature as axioms,[5] thus altering their character as teachings that were originally addressed to *practice*, or, more specifically, addressed to personal spiritual aspirations. As metaphysics, philosophy in medieval times became important chiefly as a specialized field of study within a larger enterprise of academic theology: an enterprise that was itself overseen by and answerable to ecclesiastical authority. And thus, for the most part, it remained until the Enlightenment.

From Epistemology Back to Practice

It is familiar that Enlightenment philosophers like Hume and Kant criticized metaphysics for its lack of rational foundations and, with Descartes, were influential in promoting epistemology to the place of prominence enjoyed for centuries previously by metaphysics. But the Enlightenment's new emphasis on rational analysis deepened further the rift between philosophy as a way of life and philosophy as a specialized theoretical undertaking. It intensified rather than dissolved its academic preoccupations. As epistemology, philosophy became a dedicated search for the foundations of certain knowledge. One of the educational and more broadly cultural consequences of this new orientation was that anything less than certain knowledge was to be seen as a deficiency. This stance still remains influential in many fields of Western philosophy. It influences educational thought and action by giving pride of place to the "transmission" of what is taken to be certain knowledge and officially prescribed competences. In consequence, what we have called above the integrity of education, the reciprocal engagement of sensibility and understanding in teaching and learning, gets relegated to the margins or even dropped from active consideration.

The supremacy of the foundationalist stance has been successfully challenged by a number of notable philosophical figures however. In the first half of the twentieth century these included Dewey, Heidegger, and Wittgenstein. To the radical currents of thought flowing from these thinkers were added, during the middle and later twentieth century, further antirationalist voices, from thinkers as diverse as Hannah Arendt, Paul Ricoeur, Michel Foucault, Richard Rorty, Alasdair MacIntyre, Donald Davidson, Richard J. Bernstein, Jean-François Lyotard, Charles Taylor, Jacques Derrida, and Seyla Benhabib, to mention just some. But of particular significance for the contribution of philosophy to education as a practice are the investigations of Hans-Georg Gadamer, over most of the course of the twentieth century, into the encounters between inheritances of learning and the efforts by new generations to understand them. This is so because these investigations are concerned, like those of Wittgenstein, with discovering what befalls human experience, "over and above our wanting and doing" (Gadamer, 1975, p. xvi) as understanding itself takes place.[6]

Gadamer's researches thus include within their scope investigations of misunderstanding, failures in understanding, and the propensities to illusion to which understanding is ever prone. Gadamer's chief conclusions, presaged to one or other degree by the thinkers in the first group above, and echoed in one respect or another by most of those in the second group, mark an important bridge to the Socrates of the early dialogues of Plato. To recall a point made earlier, these dialogues show that as understanding is drawn into play during the course of engagements with others who hold different perspectives, presumptions from previous experience are brought to light and challenged. More importantly, however, the early dialogues also disclose that a final overcoming of the partiality of perspective proves resistant even to the best efforts of dialogue. Hence of course Plato's dissatisfaction with this recurring outcome, which was at least partly responsible for his decision, *contra* Socrates, to make dialogue yield pride of place in his thinking to metaphysics.

Gadamer's bold formulation, "it is not so much our judgements as it is our prejudices that constitute us as human" (1977, p. 9; 1975, p. 245), now makes explicit, through its striking reconceptualization of the idea of prejudice, a conclusion that is already implicit in the early dialogues of Plato. This is a conclusion that Plato either failed to see or declined to contemplate, and one that was inadmissible for metaphysics and unthinkable for epistemology. It is a conclusion, however, which most teachers already know intuitively from their own way of life – from their daily experience with pupils, students, parents, school principals, school managements. In summary, the import of Gadamer's point, which underlies hermeneutics as an orientation towards learning, is threefold. First, prejudgements, presuppositions, preconceptions, and other such predisposing influences are invariably at work already in anything that can be called human experience. Secondly, these constitute the medium – the inescapably *interpretative* medium – through which human understanding itself takes place. Thirdly, though one may never fully break free of such predisposing influences, one may learn to subject them to a discipline of criticism: by opening them to other perspectives than those in which they have acquiesced to date.

Bearing this in mind, where one's occupation involves a commitment to teaching and learning, one is now confronted in a new way with a choice between philosophy as a way of life and philosophy as a theoretical enterprise. Let us briefly consider both alternatives, taking first the standpoint of philosophy as a theoretical enterprise. Here, any attempt to uphold the traditional claims of philosophy as theory would be confronted with the dismal conclusion that radical relativism is ultimately unavoidable. On this account, if education can no longer be guided by concepts of objective and foundational truth as something humanly achievable, then it must be conceived as a battle for the supremacy of certain perspectives over others, inevitably of the more articulate over the less so, of the stronger over the weaker. On the other hand lies the choice to decline this foundationalist reading and its relativist consequences, and to orient one's learning in the critical light of *the best of one's knowledge*, to use a popular but perceptive phrase. This is where the Socratic notion of an educated sense of one's own ignorance comes into its own. Far from any capitulation to relativism, its awareness of its own partiality (in the twofold sense of bias and of incompleteness) becomes decisive in a fruitful way. It promotes an orientation toward learning where dialogue as a pedagogical discipline brings together three things: first, a rich understanding of the limitations and possibilities of human understanding itself; secondly, an informed but fallible conviction or (convictions) about how human understanding might now best be advanced. This confluence of insights thus features as an imperative of educational practice. Thirdly, in the attempts to adapt this imperative to the different circumstances encountered in teaching as a way of life, the integrity of education as a critical and constructive practice is distinguished from both theoretical and coercive undertakings.

Questions of Interpretation

Hermeneutics of course has its origins in the interpretation of texts, especially Biblical texts. Philosophy as a hermeneutical activity thus bears comparison to the interpreting of, say, a poem, and this comparison is a fruitful one for the conception of philosophy of education that we are advancing in this chapter. In reading a poem, *meaning* is a question largely of the relationship between the text and the reader. The reader responds to the poem and justifies that response in terms of identifiable features of the poem: the way that the image running through the first six lines of the sonnet is inverted in the last eight, for example, or the ambiguity of a series of metaphors or similes. In literary criticism the structure of our interpreting is that we say: *this is so, isn't it?*[7] We offer our reading to the critical community, who may challenge our interpretation and respond with one of their own. This is not an entirely subjective procedure, for we can ground what we say on elements of the text before us. Yet there are no *conclusive* answers here either, as there might be if interpretation were rather a matter of uncovering the relationship between the author and the work of art. If Chaucer were "trying to say," as the naive student is prone to put it, were trying to express some doctrine, perhaps, for which we had anterior evidence, then the meaning of the text could be largely fixed once and for all (with some relatively minor dispute possible about quite why he said it like *that*).

All this is disturbing to the kind of reader who wanted an (the) *answer* to the question of the poem's meaning, perhaps so that the poem could be decisively laid to rest and another poem dealt with in turn. On this account literary criticism (which here stands for any intelligent response to art) is indeed a continuing activity. No expert will ever emerge to tell us, from on high, how many children Lady Macbeth had, the true meaning of *Hamlet*, or precisely what is moving about the fate of Anna Karenina. It is of the nature of art that matters should be thus, art being art and not science; and Gadamer for one is clear that the hermeneutic approach stands in clear opposition to the methodological assumptions of our age. It defends practical and political reason against the domination of technology-based science. It resists the idolatry of scientific method and encourages the citizen virtue of decision making, instead of delegating it to experts.

So too philosophy as an activity stands opposed to our characteristic modern (and modernist) assumptions: that any worthwhile discipline of thought will deliver *answers*, will tell us "what works," will prove its merit by the criterion of effectiveness. It is at odds – and we need to be clear that this is so – with an age that seems to believe that nothing has value unless it has demonstrable, quantifiable outcomes. It does not only fit ill with, *but constitutes an act of resistance to,* what we have learned to call, following Lyotard, the culture of performativity: a culture that behaves as if in education as in everything else the highest good is to maximize the ratio between input and output, as if economy with resources (larger class sizes and standardized lessons) and better results (as measured by test scores and examinations) automatically means better education. To the mentality that fetishizes the performance-indicator the Socratic dialogue is likely to remain a lasting puzzle. Could its conclusions not have been reached more quickly, without the interminable scene-setting and digressions into mythology? Or at least with a larger cast of interlocutors (a more efficient staff–student ratio) to benefit from its effects?

There is a further dimension to the comparison between literature and philosophy, which is that on the view of philosophy that we are espousing there is no sharp distinction to be made between a work of literature and one of philosophy. The early Platonic dialogues of course exemplify this to the highest degree. They are carefully wrought literary artefacts in which much attention is paid to the setting (the banquet, the banks of the river Illisus, the house of Cephalus and what brought the interlocutors there) and the characters of those who can properly be called the *dramatis personae.* Nor are these merely the *vehicles* of the philosophy, as if they are sugar to the medicine of the distinctively philosophical ideas (what Plato, like the poet, is "trying to say"). Rather they are intrinsic to the kind of activity that is here being enacted, in which fleshed-out persons, subject to the contingencies of love, drink, war, and disease, find their prejudices challenged and their notions changed, are thrown into confusion, are offered inspiring and thought-provoking visions. A Platonic dialogue is thus not very different from one of Jane Austen's novels,[8] or Iris Murdoch's. The imperfections of human life are not irrelevant to it, to be transcended in the journey toward timeless metaphysical truths, the perfect (if bloodless) dance of categories.

Reinterpreting Theory

This marks a decisive break with philosophy of education as it has generally been practiced in the West in the last half-century. At its worst (we would say) students of education, trainee teachers for the most part, have been introduced to the ideas of Plato, Kant, or Dewey and to the appropriate conclusions, as if these were simple recipes for what should go on in schools. A naive version of progressivism, supposedly based on Rousseau with dashes of Dewey, was one unfortunate consequence. While this approach is now far less common, it is still not difficult to find contemporary writing that attempts to summarize Nietzsche's thinking, or Lyotard's, as a body of *doctrine* with educational *consequences* of one sort or another.

Analytical philosophy of education, of the kind that flowered in the late 1960s and 1970s in the English-speaking countries, tended to reject that approach, of course, in favor of the "underlabourer" conception of philosophy as a business of removing conceptual clutter and rubbish. In this respect it followed the analytic conception of philosophy criticized by Peter Winch in *The Idea of a Social Science*: philosophy clears the ground for empirical science to proceed on its characteristically effective and productive path. So too, it was felt, analytical philosophy of education would serve as the handmaiden to policy, or to other, more empirical kinds of research. And this of course means that the discipline, having done its necessary work, retires from the scene until the next overgrown patch of ground is discovered to require its services; in the meantime perhaps it keeps its hand in with a few traditional philosophical problems, sharpening its tools from time to time. Philosophy exists to achieve its results; having achieved them, it stops. As Wittgenstein put it, "The real discovery is the one that makes me capable of stopping doing philosophy when I want to" (*Philosophical Investigations*, 133). Thus philosophy, of education or otherwise, becomes for the student largely a spectator sport (and surely a rather dull one): a matter of seeing how philosophers have disposed of various thickets and thorns.

Given such a conception of philosophy, it is scarcely surprising that its explicit role in the training of teachers (in the UK at least, and developments elsewhere have often followed the same pattern) has become progressively attenuated to the point where it is now virtually nonexistent. It may seem paradoxical that that role was greatest during the heyday of analytical philosophy of education, gripped as it was by both the overweening ambition to uncover the foundations for the curriculum and at the same time by the humble, underlaborer conception of its task. The common factor in both cases was that philosophy tended to be offered to the student, even if it was not practiced by the expert, as a product: as a set of conclusions to be learned rather than as a practice to be engaged in. And this is of course what our age understands: that there should be outcomes and conclusions, and that these are the important thing. Just as consumers are interested in the quality of the car or burger turned out by the factory or restaurant (though they may acknowledge from time to time that there may be ethical issues to do with the exploitation of the worker or the destruction of the rain-forest), so they are supposed to conceive education as a product – to be *delivered*, in that most revealing of contemporary phrases.

Here we see how much is at stake in our conception of philosophy, for our vision of education is closely bound up with it. As a *practical* activity, in the Socratic, and indeed Aristotelian, sense we have used in this chapter, neither philosophy nor education is like producing artefacts whose quality can be tested and assured in much the same way as the output of a factory. Education marks those who pass through it – whether students on the one hand, or teachers of various kinds on the other – with its characteristic ways of working. Along with mathematics or geography children learn a good deal about what it is to be fair or unfair, grudging or generous-spirited, attentive to other persons or detached and distant. Teachers too learn similar lessons together with the elements of their craft. Perhaps they learn that teaching is a matter of acquiring and exercising *techniques* which can be safely ticked off the list of officially prescribed competencies; or then again they might learn that teaching has a lot in common with forming other human relationships, where openness, honesty, a willingness to give of oneself, are of the essence. This is not to say that techniques are not useful, only that they are not the same as the qualities of persons. Our instrumental age, obsessed with delivery, outcomes, and audit, finds that distinction, and its importance, hard to grasp.

For the same reason, there is a danger that the recommendation of philosophy as a *practice* may seem to chime too readily with the popular idea of education as an eminently *practical* business, a matter of doing rather than thinking, as reflected in the common phrase "busy teachers." All round the world in recent years, with only a few exceptions, governments have reshaped the preparation of teachers to increase classroom practice at the expense of academic elements of training, often to the accompaniment of a stream of propaganda against the academic institutions themselves.[9] At one stage the UK government came close to removing the training of teachers from colleges and universities altogether and making it completely school-based. Of course insofar as the philosophy being taught was *theoretical* rather than *practical*, in the senses we have outlined, there was a case for marginalizing it. But equally clearly this is not to make a case for thinking of education as a wholly atheoretical business, in which the practitioner proceeds by seeing "what works" in the classroom and doing likewise, or simply implementing curriculum prescriptions issuing from government and its agencies as they attempt to render teaching "teacher-proof" by ensuring that as far as possible it is not colored by the thinking of the individual teacher.[10]

The Uses of Practical Philosophy

It is no particular part of our intention here to make a case for philosophy of education in the initial or in-service training of teachers. In fact it can be argued that philosophy of education has suffered by being too closely linked to such training: the books and journals show only too clearly how the range of topics covered 30 or so years ago was circumscribed by a narrow conception of what was thought relevant to the concerns of practitioners. But it is nevertheless worth concluding this chapter by spelling out the manifest importance of practical philosophy to teachers of all kinds, not least as a way of showing in some detail how, thus understood, philosophy goes about its work.

First, no teacher, beginner or experienced, is wholly innocent of theory, of having an underlying philosophy. It is clear enough, watching their lessons, that this teacher thinks learning can only take place in an atmosphere of calm and quiet, while that teacher holds that a murmur of activity is a necessary prerequisite for achieving understanding. It is common for a teacher to justify the former as simple common sense, or the latter with reference to some variation on the adage "I hear and I forget, I do and I remember," as if this represented an unquestionable truth. Trainees arrive for their courses quite full of educational theories and philosophies, well before they have opened their first book on education or attended their first lecture. Asked to describe their personal views on education they will often make such declarations as (and these are all real examples): "Learning is fun," "Nobody ever learns anything unless somebody makes them," "Teachers have no right to impose their values on kids." Such philosophical assumptions need to be brought into the open, questioned, and challenged. Often their holder is quite astonished to find that others hold very different opinions. One of us recalls a recent seminar on moral education in which the following exchange (reported here as accurately as memory allows) took place:

> A: One of the best ways of teaching morals is through children's books – you could use *Harry Potter*, for example, it's all about the struggle between good and evil.
>
> B: Oh, I don't think you could use *Harry Potter*: he's a bad example to children, he's always breaking the school rules.
>
> A: You mean you shouldn't break the school rules if you're trying to overcome evil? Suppose you had had the chance to prevent the First World War by diverting the Archduke's car at Sarajevo so he didn't get assassinated. Would you have refused to do so on the grounds that it would have meant driving through a red light?
>
> B: So the end always justifies the means, does it?
>
> A: Of course it does, sometimes, otherwise you're in the position where you don't make any distinction between trivial rules and really important things. And that's what moral education is for, to help children learn to make that distinction.
>
> A: You say *sometimes*. So when does the end justify the means, and when doesn't it . . . ?

Here is the Socratic dialogue, showing its enduring power and importance as two students in their early twenties tried to clarify their understanding of morality and moral education.

Secondly, there is usually held to be something distinctive about *education*, such that we can ask about what goes on in schools, universities, and other institutions whether it is properly educational. We can ask whether it measures up to our best understanding of something that enlarges our horizons, inspires us with moments of insight, or helps us grasp the nature of the human condition. Precisely because those and other such formulations are controversial and contestable it is important that teachers be equipped and encouraged to develop their own philosophy of education and not simply accede to whatever notion of delivery, transferable skills, or preparation for the world of work happens to be fashionable at the time. No set of ready-made ideas will do here, precisely because such a philosophy must be the teacher's own, thought through and internalized. Here it is crucial that teachers have a lively awareness of the problems or costs associated with any conception of education. For example, education as the expanding of our horizons and our liberation from "the present and the particular" may cut us from our roots, leaving us with no culture to call our own. This is no mere *theoretical* problem but a tension likely to be experienced in the life of anyone who has enjoyed an education worthy of the name.

Thirdly, practical philosophy reveals that the world of education is not a "given" but something on which there is a variety of perspectives: it is not so much that there is *the* world, but that there are views of the world. Characteristically student teachers begin by supposing there must be an answer to the question of how children learn to read, for example, and expect that answer to be supplied to them. Then later there comes the point where they see that there is a *debate* about reading, colored by all kinds of considerations including political ones: to become absorbed by this debate, and not just find it an obstacle to discovering "what works," is to see education as *interesting*. It is also to acquire a measure of respect for other people's perspectives and interpretations, and to learn the ways in which it is legitimate to challenge and try to change them. Student teachers learn to seek and give reasons, to test an argument against their own intuitions, to be touched (but not over-whelmed) by the reasons and intuitions of others. Thus they do more than find their way to certain conclusions, or acquire a set of techniques. They become a particular kind of person, both able and eager to combine "the rigour of speculative argument with sensitive responses to the particulars of human experience" (Nussbaum, 1986, p. 227): and this can stand as a good definition of the practical philosophy we have here described and recommended.

Notes

1 See for instance Rorty 1985; see also chapters 3 and 4 of Rorty 1989.
2 This is to raise problematic questions about the nature and scope of "empirical" social sciences, such as, in some of their manifestations, sociology and psychology. And this in turn carries important implications for the validity of practices of management, not least in education, which draw on these social sciences. It is important to add however, that none of this is to deny that these sciences can play a certain part in explaining human behavior, as distinct from the larger undertaking of understanding human experience.
3 See, for example, *Laws* 643–644, 765–766, 798.
4 A good instance of this austerity and lack of scrupulosity is the handling by ecclesiastical authorities of the controversy between Peter Abelard and Bernard of Clairvaux. Abelard's condemnation at the council of Sens in 1140, chiefly at Bernard's instigation, revealed the awesome ecclesiastical powers that could be marshaled against the efforts of a thinker who struck out, in good faith it must be said, on new pathways. In relation to the point about scrupulosity or its absence, Betty Radice cites the following from a satirical con-temporary account of the prosecution of Abelard at the Council of Sens: "the bishops were half asleep and drunk after a heavy meal, mumbling *namus* (we swim) instead of *damnamus* (we condemn)" (Radice, 1974, p. 41).
5 In his monumental work, *Summa Theologiae*, Thomas Aquinas raised this kind of proce-dure to new heights of influence. He underpinned the procedure itself moreover with a rationale such as the following: "As our faith is founded on infallible truth it is imposs-ible to use any truth to prove anything that contradicts our faith. For this reason 'evidence' adduced against the faith must be invalid evidence, arguments which can be dismissed" (*ST*, Ia, q1, a8).
6 Curiously, given his deep interest in inheritances of learning and what befalls human understanding in its encounters with them, Gadamer has written very little explicitly about teaching.
7 This way of putting it is particularly associated with the literary critic F. R. Leavis.

8 A point made with great force and elegance by Maskell (1999).

9 Perhaps the example that best deserves to be remembered is a speech in 1991 by the then UK Secretary of State for Education, Kenneth Clarke: he described educational theory as "barmy" and said teachers should ignore it.

10 In the UK, for instance, government prescribes in detail not just what teachers are to do throughout the "numeracy hour" and "literacy hour" in the primary school, but how they are to do it (so many minutes in direct teaching, so many in group or individual work, etc.). These prescriptions are now being introduced into secondary school teaching.

Recommendations for Further Reading

Dunne, J. (1995) What's the good of education? in P. Hogan (ed.) *Partnership and the Benefits of Learning*, Educational Studies Association of Ireland.

Hadot, P. (1995) *Philosophy as a Way of Life. Spiritual Exercises from Socrates to Foucault*, Blackwell.

Rozema, D. (1998) Plato's *Theaetetus*: what to do with an Honours student, *Journal of Philosophy of Education*, 32.2, pp. 207–23.

Vlastos, G. (1991) *Socrates – Ironist and Moral Philosopher*, Cambridge University Press.

Chapter 10

Critical Thinking

Sharon Bailin and Harvey Siegel

The Nature of Critical Thinking

Critical thinking is, first and foremost, a variety of *good* thinking. As such, any adequate account of it must explain the sense in which it is good. We begin by emphasizing this *normative* character of critical thinking. This emphasis distinguishes our conception, and philosophical conceptions more generally, from psychological conceptions, which are essentially descriptive – describing psychological processes, procedures, and/or skills thought to be central to critical thinking. Such process accounts are problematic in that (1) it is impossible to determine whether particular mental operations correlate with particular cases of good thinking; (2) there is no particular set of procedures that is either necessary or sufficient for critical thinking; and (3) terms denoting thinking (for example, classifying, observing, hypothesizing) refer not to mental operations or processes but rather to different tasks requiring thinking (Bailin, 1998).

In contrast to contemporary psychological accounts of it, philosophical theorists of critical thinking are agreed that the concept is essentially a normative one. To characterize thinking as "critical" is, accordingly, to judge that it meets relevant *standards* or *criteria* of acceptability, and is thus appropriately thought of as "good." Extant philosophical accounts of critical thinking emphasize such criteria. Robert H. Ennis, for example, defines critical thinking as "reasonable reflective thinking that is focused on deciding what to believe and do" (Ennis, 1987, p. 10), and offers a detailed list of abilities, skills, and dispositions that thinking (and thinkers) must manifest if it is (they are) to be critical. Siegel characterizes the critical thinker as one who is "appropriately moved by reasons" (Siegel, 1988, p. 23), and emphasizes the critical thinker's mastery of *epistemic* criteria that reasons must meet in order to be rightly judged to be good reasons, that is, reasons that warrant beliefs, claims, and actions. Richard Paul similarly conceives of critical thinking in terms of the ability and disposition to critically evaluate beliefs, their underlying assumptions, and the world views in which they are embedded (Paul, 1990). Matthew Lipman defines critical thinking as thinking that facilitates judgement because it relies on criteria, is self-correcting, and is sensitive to context (Lipman, 1991). Other authors, including John McPeck (1981, 1990), similarly emphasize this normative dimension of the concept. While these authors' accounts of critical thinking differ in many respects, and have their own emphases, they are nevertheless agreed on the essential normativity of the concept.

While some early treatments of critical thinking defined it only in terms of particular skills – for example, Ennis's early definition of it as "the correct assessing of statements" (Ennis, 1962, p. 83) – almost all philosophical discussion of it regards critical thinking as involving both skills or abilities and dispositions. We turn to this combination next.

Critical Thinking: Skills/Abilities and Dispositions

On most philosophical accounts of it, critical thinking involves two related, but conceptually distinct, aspects or dimensions: the *ability* to reason well and the *disposition* to do so. We discuss these in turn.

Skills/abilities

Thinking is critical just to the extent that it manifests due attention to, and concern for, the probative strength of relevant reasons (such strength being determined by the degree to which such reasons meet the epistemic criteria mentioned above). In this respect critical thinking is, as one of us puts it elsewhere, the "educational cognate" (Siegel, 1988, p. 32) of rationality, since both rational thinking and critical thinking are "coextensive with the relevance of reasons" (Scheffler, 1965, p. 107). Beliefs, judgements, and actions are rational just to the extent that the believer/actor has good reasons for so believing, judging, or acting;[1] having the ability to think critically requires, then, having the ability to ascertain the goodness of candidate reasons. Consequently, a central task involved in educating for critical thinking is that of fostering in students the ability to assess the probative strength of reasons.

This of course raises many questions – mainly epistemological in nature – concerning the criteria by which the goodness of candidate reasons is determined. How are these criteria chosen, and who chooses them? How are they themselves justified? – and indeed, can they be justified, even in principle, in a way that is neither circular or question-begging? What is the source of their epistemic authority? Are they "absolute" or "relative"? Are they really "epistemic" or rather political, constituting tools of power and oppression? And so on. Both of us have addressed one or more of these issues at some length elsewhere (Bailin, 1992a, 1995, 1998; Siegel, 1997); we return to several of them below.[2] Of particular note is the question of the extent to which such criteria (and so critical thinking itself) are *generalizable*: are the criteria in accordance with which the goodness of candidate reasons is determined the same in all contexts? Or do these vary from context to context? This question has divided critical thinking theorists like no other; we take it up in the next section.

Dispositions

Having the ability to determine the goodness, or probative force, of candidate reasons for belief, judgement, or action may be necessary, but cannot be sufficient, for critical thinking, since a given thinker may have the ability but not (or not systematically or routinely) use it. Accordingly, most theorists of critical thinking argue that, along with the skill or ability to assess the probative force of reasons, critical thinkers must also have relevant *dispositions*. The primary disposition consists in valuing good reasoning and being disposed to seek reasons, to assess them, and to govern beliefs and actions on the basis of such assessment. In addition, most theorists outline a subset of dispositions that are also necessary for critical thinking, including open-mindedness, fair-mindedness, independent-mindedness, an inquiring attitude, and respect for others in group inquiry and deliberation. (Bailin et al., 1999; Hare, 1979, 1985) This "two-component" conception of critical thinking – according to which critical thinking encompasses both a reason assessment compon- ent and a dispositional component[3] – is endorsed by most theorists.[4]

Problems with "skill talk"

Some theorists have criticized the use of the term "skill" in conceptualizing critical thinking, on the grounds that, when used as a noun, "skill" can be seen to refer to something within individuals, some inner entity or ability or inner possession. The problems that result from conceiving of skills as "mental operations" have been noted above (and outlined more fully in Bailin, 1998). However, references to skills, particularly in the adjectival and adverbial forms, can be understood as indicating, not inner entities or possessions, but rather thinking that meets relevant criteria. For most philosophical theorists of critical thinking, then, saying that Jones "has the skills of a critical thinker" would be taken to indicate not that Jones possesses an array of inner mental entities of some sort, but rather that Jones's thinking is skilled in the sense that her thinking meets relevant criteria (ibid., pp. 210–11). Talk of "critical thinking skills" is thus ambiguous, and can be misleading, particularly with respect to the issue of generalizability, as will be argued below. The present authors do not agree about the degree to which this ambiguity is philosophically troubling. Bailin would prefer to avoid the noun form "skills" altogether. Siegel finds such "skill talk" acceptable as long as it is taken as referring to thinking that is skilled in the sense that it meets relevant criteria. In this sense the critical thinker is rightly conceived as a thinker who has both the skills or abilities, and the dispositions, mentioned above. Our use of "skill" in what follows is to be understood in this way.

Critical Thinking and the Problem of Generalizability

Perhaps the most controversial question concerning critical thinking is whether or not it is rightly conceived as something *general*, or should be understood rather indeed as domain-, discipline-, or context-*specific*. It has seemed to many that critical thinking is rightly conceived as a set of generalized skills, abilities, and dispositions, in the sense that these can be utilized or applied across a broad range of contexts and circumstances. On this *generalist* view, it would make sense to regard (for example) the ability to detect an ordinary fallacy like begging the question, basing a generalization on too small a sample, or appealing to an illegitimate authority, as general in the sense that it is applicable across many different reasoning contexts. A critical thinker, on this view, would be able to detect such fallacies generally, that is, without regard to the particular contexts in which they occur. Parallel remarks would be made for all, or at least many, such abilities.

The *specifist* view, on the contrary, denies any such general ability. The most prominent exponent of this view, John McPeck, holds that there cannot, in principle, be any critical thinking skills or abilities that can be applied generally across subject-area domains, because thinking itself is always tied to a particular content and subject: "thinking is always thinking *about* something. To think about nothing is a conceptual impossibility" (McPeck, 1981, p. 3, emphasis in original). Consequently, McPeck argues, conceiving of general critical thinking skills, and developing courses intended to enhance students' critical thinking generally, are mistakes:

> In isolation from a particular subject, the phrase "critical thinking" neither refers to nor denotes any particular skill. It follows from this that it makes no sense to talk about critical thinking as a distinct subject and that it therefore cannot profitably be taught as such. To the extent that critical thinking is not about a specific subject X, it is both conceptually and practically empty. (ibid., p. 5)

The "specifist" view defended by McPeck has many adherents. However, it also has been subject to much criticism. A particularly telling criticism, in our view, is that while it is true that particular acts or episodes of thinking always have particular content, and so are about some particular thing or other, it simply does not follow that nothing general can be said about the activity of thinking, conceived as the general activity of which all particular episodes of thinking are instances (Siegel, 1988, p. 19). That particular episodes of thinking always have particular content is perfectly compatible with there being general thinking skills or abilities that are applicable to a wide range of domains, subjects, or contexts.[5]

A second issue raised by McPeck is that of the place of context-, domain-, or subject-specific content knowledge in critical thinking. McPeck insists – rightly in our view – that such knowledge is very often essential for critical thinking. This is, we think, the correct insight of specifism. But it doesn't upend generalism, for the latter view makes full room for the role of subject-specific content knowledge in critical thinking. As William Hare conclusively demonstrates, advocates of critical thinking who conceive it in generalist terms have systematically acknowledged the essential role of subject-specific content knowledge in any educationally adequate effort to foster students' critical thinking (Hare, 1995).

So how then should we think about the generalizability of critical thinking? On this point the present authors agree to a certain extent. We both agree that if the question is broken down, so that we ask not whether critical thinking as a whole is generalizable, but rather whether each component of it is generalizable, we find the following. First, the reason assessment component – which has in effect been the subject of most of the discussion of generalizability – is *partly* generalizable. Here both the specifists and the generalists are importantly right. The specifists are right to insist both that subject-specific knowledge is often (Bailin would say always) necessary for critical thinking, and that many of the criteria in accordance with which reasons are appropriately assessed are indeed domain- or subject-specific. The generalists are right to insist that some criteria of reason assessment (for example, those that determine the constitution of valid or fallacious forms of reasoning) are not domain-specific, but are general in that they are applicable across widely varied contexts. Moreover, the *epistemology underlying critical thinking* – according to which there is a rejection of relativism, an important distinction to be drawn between rational justification and truth, and a recognition that rational justification, though distinct from truth, is a fallible indicator of it – is itself fully generalizable. Finally, the "critical spirit" component, that complex of dispositions, attitudes, habits of mind, and character traits, characteristic of the critical thinker, is also fully generalizable.

The present authors differ on some points, however. Bailin emphasizes the centrality of subject-specific knowledge, while Siegel emphasizes the generalizability of abilities constitutive of critical thinking (for example, the abilities to recognize and detect particular fallacies, valid forms of reasoning, and types of good reasons) as well as the highly general applicability of many criteria of reason assessment. Bailin believes that the generalizability issue has been on the whole unhappily characterized by focusing on skills or abilities. She urges that it be reframed so as to focus on the understandings (intellectual resources) required in order to make reasoned judgements in particular contexts. This move reframes the issue of generalizability from the question of whether certain skills transfer to a variety of contexts to the question of what constellation of intellectual resources is required in particular contexts in response to particular challenges and what the range of application is for particular resources (Bailin, 1998, pp. 211–16). (As argued above, some resources are quite narrow and others quite broad.) The problem, then, becomes one of determining the range of use and application of the principles and criteria that underlie our public traditions of inquiry rather than looking for general skills or abilities within individuals, with its attendant conceptual problems. Siegel regards these problems as straightforwardly handled by making clear, as we have above, that the skills and abilities in question are those that, when exercised, result in thinking which is skilled in the sense that it meets relevant criteria. He is also wary of couching the matter in terms of the principles and criteria that underlie public traditions of inquiry, since those principles and criteria are themselves always open to critical scrutiny and revision (a point on which we are agreed). On his view critical thinking is mainly, though not fully, generalizable; the generalist view is correct on the whole, but the specifist view is also correct in important respects (Siegel, 1997, chapter 2).

Despite our disagreements concerning how best to frame the question of generalizability, the necessity of subject-specific knowledge for critical thinking, and the viability of "skill talk" in its characterization, we hope the substantial agreement between us concerning generalizability is clear. In particular, we are agreed that some principles and criteria of reason-assessment are quite narrow, and others quite broad; we are agreed as well that the dispositions and habits of mind that characterize the critical thinker, and the epistemology underlying critical thinking, are fully generalizable (Bailin, 1998; Siegel, 1997). We are agreed, finally, that both generalism and specifism are correct in the important respects just indicated.[6]

The Relationship Between Critical Thinking and Creative Thinking

An issue frequently raised in discussions of critical thinking concerns the relationship between critical thinking and creative thinking. The assumption is generally made that they are two different and distinct kinds of thinking. Critical thinking is viewed as strictly analytic and evaluative, an algorithmic process that consists in arriving at the correct evaluations of ideas, arguments, or products. It is considered to be necessarily noncreative since it involves a fairly mechanical process of following existing rules and thus is not able to transcend frameworks or result in new ideas. Creative thinking, on the other hand, is seen as strictly generative, the kind of thinking that allows for the breaking of rules, the transcending of frameworks, and the creation of novel products. As such, it is considered to be noncritical, since criticism must take place according to prevailing criteria but being creative involves violating these criteria (for example, de Bono, 1970).

The relationship between the two kinds of thinking is a subject of debate. Some theorists view critical thinking and creative thinking as distinct but complementary, while others believe that they are in opposition to one another – that the generation of new ideas requires the abandonment of the logic and criteria of assessment that characterize critical thinking (de Bono, 1976).

It is our view that the dichotomy between critical thinking and creative thinking is ill-founded. There are evaluative, analytic, logical aspects to creating new ideas or products and an imaginative, constructive dimension to their assessment. A conceptualization in terms of two distinct types of thinking, critical and creative, is seriously problematic.

First, consider the claim that creative thinking is strictly generative and nonevaluative, that the creation of new ideas and products is a result of a type of thinking that does not involve logic or critical assessment but involves the unconstrained generation of ideas. This claim is incompatible with the fact that creativity involves not simply the generation of novelty but rather the generation of products that constitute improvements or innovations, products that have significance in terms of the context of the domain. Analysis, logic, and evaluation are necessarily involved in such creative production. Critical judgement is central to the identification of problems, the recognition of inadequacies in existing solutions, the decision that a new approach is required, the determination of directions for investigation, and the recognition of possible solutions. The thinking that leads to creative achievement can best be seen, then, not in terms of unconstrained generation, but rather in terms of a reasonable and critical response to a problem situation (Bailin, 1987, 1992a).

The characterization of critical thinking as strictly analytic, selective, and rule-determined is similarly problematic. Thinking that is directed primarily toward the evaluation or criticism of ideas or products is not algorithmic but has a generative, imaginative component. The application of criteria is not a mechanical process but involves both some interpretation of circumstances, and imaginative judgement as to the applicability of criteria in different circumstances and to whether the criteria have been met. Similarly, inventing hypotheses, generating counterexamples, constructing counterarguments, and envisioning potential problems are all important aspects of critical thinking that have a generative dimension. Finally, arriving at an overall assessment in any complex circumstance requires constructing a view based on the questioning, weighing, rejecting, reconciling, and integrating of numerous divergent points of view, and may lead to the questioning of assumptions and the redefinition of a problem (Bailin, 1990).

Both the constraints of logic and the inventiveness of imagination are evident in all instances of serious thought. There is a creative dimension in all critical thinking, and in some cases, critical deliberation leads to the questioning of assumptions, the breaking of rules, the rearrangement of elements – and thus results in products that exhibit considerable novelty.

Some proponents of the dichotomy between critical thinking and creative thinking accept the idea that both critical and creative thinking are necessary to all complex thought, but maintain that they are distinct and take place at different stages of the thinking process. An individual first researches a problem in a logical, analytical way (critical thinking), then suspends critical judgement and generates large numbers of ideas (creative thinking), then reactivates critical judgement to evaluate the proposed solutions (critical thinking). We would argue, however, that one cannot really distinguish two different kinds of thinking. The very process of generating ideas involves evaluation since it is constrained by various criteria related to the problem situation and to what would constitute an effective and innovative solution. If this were not the case, the result would be chaos rather than creation. Nor is it possible to identify an evaluative phase of thinking that lacks a generative dimension. The terms "critical thinking" and "creative thinking" can be used to refer to the generative and to the evaluative aspects of thinking for purposes of analysis and discussion, but it is important to be clear that these are not really two different kinds of thinking that can be engaged in separately.

"Critical Thinking" and Other Terms Referring to Thinking

Also of interest is the relationship between critical thinking and other terms referring to thinking. Some theorists offer taxonomies of thinking that categorize critical thinking alongside such terms as *problem solving, decision making,* and *inquiry* (for example, Swartz and Perkins, 1989). Thus critical thinking is seen as one form of thinking among many. We would claim, however, that terms such as problem solving, decision making, or inquiry refer to different contexts in which thinking is required, while critical thinking is a normative term that refers to how such thinking is carried out. Problem solving emphasizes the need to deal with a particular problem or problematic situation; decision making involves the making of choices; inquiry refers to an attempt to answer a question or explore an issue. Any of these activities can be carried out in a critical or an uncritical manner. When they are carried out in accordance with the relevant criteria, they would all constitute instances of critical thinking. Thus critical thinking does not describe one type of thinking among others, but is an umbrella term that refers to the quality of thinking, whatever the context or activity.

The term *higher-order thinking* can also usefully be contrasted with critical thinking. Higher-order thinking generally refers to advanced or complex thinking in contrast to simpler, less sophisticated, forms of thinking. Bloom's taxonomy illustrates well the type of hierarchy of kinds of thinking upon which the idea of higher-order thinking is based, with knowledge at the bottom, progressing through comprehension, application, analysis, and synthesis, to evaluation at the top (Bloom, 1956). Other schemes view sensing in the lowest category, with remembering, recognizing, and recalling next, and comparing, classifying, interpreting, and evaluating in the highest category (Judd, 1936). One major difficulty with this type of scheme is its mischaracterization of activities such as analyzing, evaluating, or interpreting as kinds of thinking. As argued above, such terms do not refer to thinking processes at all but rather to particular outcomes that result from the application of certain critical standards, and the nature of what is involved in achieving any one of these will vary with the context. Moreover, the notion of a hierarchy of kinds of thinking is itself problematic. Knowledge, for example, if viewed as something more than the accumulation of isolated and unproblematic pieces of information, might well be seen as the pinnacle of thinking rather than as the base, as might the comprehension of certain highly complex and difficult understandings. We would argue, then, that rather than attempting to categorize thinking into different kinds to be placed on a hierarchy, it is much more fruitful to focus on what is involved in fulfilling the relevant critical criteria, no matter what the task or context – that is, to focus on critical thinking.

Critical Thinking and Education

Critical thinking (and so rationality) is often, and in our view rightly, regarded as a fundamental aim, and overriding ideal, of education. To so regard it is to hold that educational activities ought to be designed and conducted in such a way that the construction and evaluation of reasons (in accordance with relevant criteria) is paramount, throughout the curriculum. As Israel Scheffler puts the point: "Critical thinking is of the first importance in the conception and organization of educational activities" (Scheffler, [1973] 1989, p. 1). "Rationality . . . is a matter of *reasons*, and to take it as a fundamental educational ideal is to make as pervasive as possible the free and critical quest for reasons, in all realms of study" (ibid., p. 62, emphasis in original). So to take it is to regard the fostering of the abilities and dispositions of critical thinking in students as the prime educational directive, of central importance to the design and implementation of curriculum and educational policy. This is not to say that other aims and ideals might not also be of serious importance, but that none outrank the primary obligation of educational institutions and efforts to foster critical thinking.

Why should the fostering of critical thinking be thought to be so important? Siegel offers four reasons for so thinking (Siegel, 1988, chapter 3). First, and most importantly, striving to foster critical thinking in students is necessary if they are to be treated with *respect as persons*. The moral requirement to treat students with respect as persons requires that we strive to enable them to think for themselves, competently and well, rather than to deny them the fundamental ability to determine for themselves, to the greatest extent possible, the contours of their own minds and lives. Acknowledging them as persons of equal moral worth requires that we treat students as independent centers of consciousness, with needs and interests not less important than our own, who are at least in principle capable of determining for themselves how best to live and who to be. As educators, treating them with respect involves striving to enable them to judge such matters for themselves. Doing so competently requires judging in accordance with the criteria governing critical thinking. Consequently, treating students with respect requires fostering in them the abilities and dispositions of critical thinking.

A second reason for regarding critical thinking as a fundamental educational ideal involves education's generally recognized task of preparing students for adulthood. Such preparation cannot properly be conceived in terms of preparing students for preconceived roles; rather, it must be understood to involve student self-sufficiency and self-direction. In this the place of critical thinking is manifest. A third reason for regarding the fostering of critical thinking as a central aim of education is the role it plays in the rational traditions that have always been at the center of educational activities and efforts – mathematics, science, literature, art, history, and so forth. All these traditions incorporate and rely upon critical thinking; mastering or becoming initiated into the former both requires, and is basic to the fostering and enhancement of, the latter. A fourth reason involves the place of careful analysis, good thinking, and reasoned deliberation in democratic life. To the extent that we value democracy, we must be committed to the fostering of the abilities and dispositions of critical thinking. Democracy can flourish just to the extent that its citizenry is able to reason well regarding political issues and matters of public policy, scrutinize the media, and generally meet the demands of democratic citizenship, many of which require the abilities and dispositions constitutive of critical thinking.

These four reasons can and should be spelled out at greater length, but they are sufficiently powerful, we think, to justify regarding critical thinking as a fundamental educational ideal. As suggested above, efforts to foster critical thinking aim at the promotion of independent thinking, personal autonomy, and reasoned judgement in thought and action; these particular aims are in turn justified in terms of broader conceptions of knowledge, reasons, and persons: for example, that all knowledge is fallible, that it is possible to objectively evaluate the goodness of reasons, and that personal autonomy is an important value (Bailin, 1998, p. 204). These aims, and the broader conceptions in terms of which they are grounded, are philosophically contentious; it is no surprise, then, that they – and the educational ideal of critical thinking itself – have been challenged. We turn to these challenges next.

Critiques of Critical Thinking

Much recent discussion about critical thinking has taken the form of challenges to prevailing conceptions and their justification. These criticisms, which emanate primarily from postmodern and feminist perspectives, charge that critical thinking favors the values and practices of the dominant groups in society and devalues those of groups traditionally lacking in power (for example, T. Bridges, 1991; Garrison and Phelan, 1989; Martin, 1992; Orr, 1989; Thayer-Bacon, 1992, 1993). These criticisms include: that critical thinking privileges rational, linear thought over intuition; that critical thinking is aggressive and confrontational rather than collegial and collaborative; that critical thinking neglects or downplays emotions; that critical thinking deals in abstraction and devalues lived experience and concrete particularity; that critical thinking is individualistic and privileges personal autonomy over community and relationship; and that critical thinking presupposes the possibility of objectivity and thus does not recognize an individual's situatedness (Bailin, 1995).

These criticisms are, generally, of two sorts. One type of criticism challenges particular aspects of critical thinking theory and practice but leaves intact its foundational underpinnings. Some of the criticisms of this type have provided useful correctives to problems, omissions, or elements that have not been sufficiently emphasized in critical thinking theory and practice. Others, however, are misdirected in failing to recognize aspects that already exist in much contemporary critical thinking theory, or are problematic in suggesting revisions that might undermine important aspects of critical thinking. Consider, for example, the charge that critical thinking neglects or downplays emotion. Contrary to this complaint, many critical thinking theorists explicitly acknowledge a role for emotions in critical thinking, enjoining us, for example, to be sensitive to the feelings of others (Bailin, 1995) and to understand other perspectives (Paul, 1990). Indeed, emotional aspects are central to Siegel's notion of the critical spirit (Siegel, 1988) and to Scheffler's account of critical thinking (Scheffler, 1991). And Ennis has added caring to his list of critical thinking dispositions in response to some feminist critiques of critical thinking (Ennis, 1996, p. 369). What most critical theorists would caution against, however, is a reliance on emotion without critical assessment. What is advocated is an appropriate role for emotion, one which enhances rather than detracts from one's assessing and acting upon reasons. A similar point can be made with respect to the charge that critical thinking is aggressive and confrontational and devalues collegiality and collaboration. Although it may be the case that critical thinking has sometimes been practiced in a confrontational manner, there is nothing in critical thinking theory that requires or even suggests that it must be so practiced or understood. Many theorists in fact acknowledge that critical thinking can be practiced in a collegial, collaborative manner, and argue that such practice may better serve our purposes as critical thinkers.[7] And although autonomy is generally advocated as a value central to critical thinking, this does not preclude an acknowledgement of the role of joint and communal inquiry (Bailin et al., 1999, p. 289).

The claim that critical thinking privileges rational, linear, deductive thought over intuition bears further examination. First, it must be pointed out that the equation of rational thought with linear and deductive reasoning is problematic. Deductive reasoning represents only a narrow subset of rational thinking; the latter also encompasses (at least) inductive, probabilistic, analogical, and abductive ("inference to the best explanation") reasoning. In addition, as pointed out previously, critical thinking does have a generative, imaginative component. It is the case, however, that critical thinking theorists do advocate rational thought (conceived of in this broader way) over intuition as a means of deciding what to believe or do, and the challenge to this position represents a more radical type of critique of critical thinking than the ones discussed to this point. The previously mentioned critiques offer challenges and correctives to the manner in which critical thinking is currently, or has been, conceptualized or practiced but nonetheless accept its role and importance. This second type of criticism challenges the very foundation of critical thinking theory and practice.

According to this type of criticism, critical thinking is only one mode of understanding – that of the dominant groups in society – but it has been privileged as the only legitimate mode of understanding. Such privileging, it is alleged, is biased in excluding the modes of understanding of those groups traditionally lacking in power and status (women and minorities, for example). Critical thinking is seen, then, as one ideology among others. Its principles and criteria are seen as arbitrary, and the promotion of critical thinking is seen as an act of cultural hegemony. Andrea Nye, for example, argues that logic (which includes critical thinking) is an invention of men that structures speech situations that occur between men and thus excludes many voices, while it falsely presents itself as universal (Nye, 1990). This type of criticism goes much deeper than a critique of certain contingent and remediable biases in critical thinking. It puts into question the validity of the entire enterprise and its claims to universality. If accepted, it would necessitate a recognition of the partiality of the enterprise of critical thinking and the recognition of other modes of understanding, intuition for example, as equally valid.

We find this second, more radical type of criticism seriously problematic, however. One problem is that the charge of arbitrariness is based on a misrepresentation of the nature of critical criteria and principles. These principles are not simply the products of group interests but are embedded in traditions of rational inquiry and are closely tied to purposes – for example, predicting and explaining natural phenomena, recovering and understanding the past, developing and appreciating works of art, and so forth – that are not group-specific. Moreover one of the defining characteristics of rational inquiry is that it is self-correcting (Lipman, 1991; Scheffler, [1967] 1982). Thus the criteria themselves can be, and regularly are, modified in the face of criticisms and our purposes as thinkers. And the traditions themselves are dynamic, open-ended, plural ones that contain alternative or competing streams (Bailin, 1992a). Thus critical modes of inquiry provide for the possibility, and actuality, of alterations of the traditions themselves, in the light both of new evidence, arguments, problems, and limitations discovered during the course of inquiry and also in light of criticisms from competing streams within the tradition and insights from other traditions and frameworks. Rational inquiry gives rise to criticism, and criticisms of a tradition inevitably grow out of the traditions that they criticize, appeal to values inherent in these traditions, and presuppose rationality by appealing to reasons. Indeed, it could not be otherwise, since any attempt to engage in questioning, criticism, and inquiry presupposes rationality and a recognition of the force of reasons. Criticism rests on rationality, including the criticisms of rationality itself, and any proposed alternative would ultimately have to be assessed on the basis of critical thinking principles and criteria (Siegel, 1988, 1997).

Conclusion

We have offered an account of critical thinking that emphasizes its normative character. According to that account, critical thinking involves both the ability to assess the probative strength of reasons and the disposition to do so. We have indicated potential problems with talk of critical thinking skills, and urged that such "skill talk" be understood not as referring to inner entities or processes but rather as indicating that thinking which is critical is "skilled" in that such thinking satisfies relevant criteria. We have discussed the difficult question of generalizability and offered our own somewhat distinct approaches to it. We have urged that critical thinking not be conceived as radically distinct from creative thinking, but rather that there are evaluative, analytic, logical aspects to creating new ideas or products and an imaginative, constructive dimension to their assessment. We have discussed the relationship between critical thinking and other terms referring to thinking, suggesting that placing these terms in hierarchical schemes is less helpful than focusing on the way in which critical thinking, with its emphasis on the meeting of relevant criteria, is applicable to them all. We have argued that critical thinking is rightly regarded as a fundamental educational ideal, and have offered reasons for regarding it as such. Finally, we have addressed several recent critiques of critical thinking, suggesting that while there is considerable merit in some of them, the more radical challenges fail in that they in the end rely on the very critical thinking they aim to challenge.

There is obviously much more to be said about all of this. But we hope that enough has been said to indicate what critical thinking it, what it is not, why it is valuable and why it is educationally basic.

Notes

1 An important epistemological issue is: do believers/actors have to be *aware* of the goodness of their reasons in order for their beliefs/actions to count as rational, or to be (to the relevant extent) justified? For brief explanation of this "internalism/externalism" controversy, see Siegel (1998, p. 33, n. 7).

2 We particularly recommend the discussions of Nicholas Burbules (1995) and Mark Weinstein, which defend views in important respects opposed to ours (and which are critically examined in chapters 7 and 8–9, respectively, of Siegel, 1997); we enthusiastically recommend as well Emily Robertson's (1995, 1999) penetrating discussions of these matters. Broad, very helpful discussions of many of these issues from the perspectives of

the allied fields of informal logic and argumentation theory may be found in Johnson and Blair (1994) and van Eemeren et al. (1996, chapter 6).

3 Virtually all the major theorists of critical thinking, including Bailin, Ennis, Lipman, McPeck, Paul, and Siegel, make dispositions central to their accounts of critical thinking. The latter characterizes them as part of the "critical spirit," which includes attitudes, dispositions, habits of mind, and character traits (Siegel, 1988, pp. 39–42), and offers an account of them in Siegel (1999).

4 One theorist who challenges the inclusion of dispositions in an adequate conception of critical thinking is Connie Missimer (1990). This paper (and subsequent discussion by Missimer) are discussed in Siegel (1993), expanded and reprinted as chapter 4 of Siegel (1997).

5 These and other criticisms of McPeck's case for "specifism," and references to many critical discussions of McPeck's book, are given in Siegel (1988, pp. 18–30). Engaging recent defenses of it include Johnson and Gardner (1999) and Gardner and Johnson (1996).

6 There is of course much more to the generalizability debate than we have indicated here. The papers collected in Norris (1992) provide a fuller picture of the many strands of the debate.

7 For example, one of the habits of mind recommended by Bailin et al. is "respect for others in group inquiry and deliberation (commitment to open, critical discussion in which all persons are given a fair hearing and their feelings as well as their interests are taken into account)" Bailin et al. (1999, p. 295).

Recommendations for Further Reading

Bailin, S., Case, R., Coombs, J. R., and Daniels, L. B. (1999) Conceptualizing critical thinking, *Journal of Curriculum Studies*, 31.3, pp. 285–302.

Ennis, R. H. (1987) A taxonomy of critical thinking dispositions and abilities, in J. Boykoff-Baron and R. J. Sternberg (eds.) *Teaching Thinking Skills: Theory and Practice*, W. H. Freeman.

Robertson, E. (1999) The value of reason: why not a sardine can opener? in R. Curren (ed.) *Philosophy of Education 1999*, Philosophy of Education Society.

Siegel, H. (1988) *Educating Reason: Rationality, Critical Thinking and Education*, Routledge.

Chapter 11

Practical Reason

Joseph Dunne and Shirley Pendlebury

Introduction

Over the past few decades "practical reason" has come to feature prominently in much philosophical discussion in ethics, political theory, and the philosophy of mind. Over this period, too, writers on education have been drawn to the same topic in attempts to clarify the kind of knowledge operative in good teaching, the orientation best fitted to programs of teacher education seeking to cultivate this knowledge and, more broadly, the contribution that education may properly be expected to make in helping students to become practically wise persons – especially in terms of the deliberative dispositions required for citizenship in democratic polities.

Practical knowledge has not always been highly regarded by philosophers. In the ancient world a lofty conception of theory – and of philosophy itself as theory's fullest realization – diminished its epistemic status and its relative significance in a flourishing human life. And in the modern period it fared no better, eclipsed by a kind of theory that, though all too clearly different from philosophy, much philosophy sought to canonize.

In section I of this essay Joseph Dunne first sets the scene for the recent recovery of robust notions of practical knowledge by showing how much the latter was occluded by a picture of knowledge accredited by the dominant outlook of modern epistemology – and seemingly sanctioned by the rise of science – so that what was needed in its regard was precisely a recovery. "Recovery" of course also implies that recent articulations of practical reason have had something to appeal to in an earlier philosophical tradition. And so the analysis of practical knowledge under the rubric of "judgement" offered in the next subsection is followed by an account of Aristotle's pioneering account of *phronesis*, a practical wisdom that he defended despite his esteem for the contemplative pursuits of a life of theory and his anticipation (through his conception of *techne*) of the kind of scientific-technical attitude that, in its later modern realization, would powerfully overshadow practical judgement.

Section I written by Joseph Dunne; Section II written by Shirley Pendlebury

Recognition of the enduring significance of Aristotelian *phronesis* has been helped by a revolution in twentieth-century philosophy that has brought a new appreciation of engaged agency as the irreducible mode of human being in the world. This larger philosophical background to recent preoccupation with practical reason is sketched in the following subsection, while section I concludes with some reflection on the question (heavy with consequence for educational studies and teacher education) of how theory is to be reconceived if it is to offer any illumination to practical knowledge.

Broad outline in section I is followed by closer analysis in section II. There Shirley Pendlebury shows how any contemporary reclamation of Aristotelian *phronesis* is challenged by the exigent standards of justification required by more critical, judicial conceptions of practical reason; she reveals the variety and complexity in the responses to this challenge of several different Aristotelian commentators; and she unpacks in more detail the implications of all this for central issues in education. How exactly practical reasoning relates to ends and means, whether it is primarily an individual ("I") or shared ("we") activity, and how it negotiates the boundaries between private and public: these questions, with their upshot for education, are outlined in the first subsection. Next, the contrast in various readings of Aristotle between an insistence on argumentative rectitude (via the "practical syllogism") and an emphasis on sensitive discernment of salient features of action-situations is analyzed. The merits of the latter – not least for understanding the requirements of good teaching – and its involvement with the kind of dispositions of character canvassed in a recent renaissance of "virtue theory" are analyzed in the following subsection. This analysis then extends to a consideration of the discursive and dispositional qualities required for (and hence falling within the remit of public schools as the reproductive agents of) democratic citizenship. The essay concludes with some reflections, in the light of the earlier analysis, of the kind of practical reasonableness exemplified in competent pedagogy.

I

The new science and the triumph of technical reason

A conception of reason that is quite inhospitable to practice arose within the purview of modern epistemology and became dominant on the basis of its seeming to articulate the defining features of the scientific revolution of the seventeenth century. It puts a premium on detachment and "objectivity," suppressing the context-dependence of first-person experience in favor of a third-person perspective which yields generalized findings in accordance with clearly formulated, publicly agreed procedures. The procedures insist on strict quantification, formulation in interpretation-immune language, replicability of operations and findings, and modes of testing that specify precisely what can count as counterevidence. The aim of such procedures is to establish nomological knowledge: law-like explanations establishing correlations within the phenomenal field that hold reliably under conditions precisely specified in the laws. This knowledge then has predictive value: given conditions a, b, and c, it can be reliably predicted that x, y, and z will occur.

The success of the modern sciences and their superiority over their pre-Galilean, still largely Aristotelian, predecessors could be ascribed to a new experimentalism and to new ways of exploiting mathematics in the service of natural inquiry. The seal of this success was the *power* delivered by the new knowledge. From now on – and in strong contrast to the contemplative bias of earlier forms of inquiry – power was to be the defining criterion of knowledge; *scientia*, in Bacon's slogan, was now *propter potentiam*. This power, already inscribed in the new science, *qua* predictive knowledge, was to be realized through the *application* of the latter to the material environment – an application that has given us unimagined technological transformations of the natural world. But the object of this new kind of explanation and control was not to be limited to the material universe. It would include human behavior too, the new physics presaging a new psychology and politics – as early as the seventeenth century with Hobbes, for example, or with Holbach and La Mettrie in the full glare of eighteenth-century Enlightenment.

Conceived along these lines, scientific knowledge came to define the only kind of rigor that could claim *rational* status. And this rationality came to be translated into a new standard of effectiveness through the application of scientific knowledge in more and more domains of action. In the nineteenth and twentieth centuries, this standard achieved enormous prestige, reinforced in complex combination by positivist philosophy, aspirations to social control and pursuit of economic interests (see Habermas, 1971c and "Overcoming epistemology" subsection below). It was against this standard – what can be called that of *technical rationality* – that older forms of practical knowledge came to seem hopelessly inadequate. The new paradigm seemed to confer objectivity (no distortion by merely subjective prejudices), generalizability (no confinement to merely local or particular contexts), replicability and control (no exceptions or unpredicted outcomes), transparency and publicity (no reliance on personal gifts or inarticulate intuitions), and clear-cut criteria for assessing success and establishing accountability (no ambiguous interpretations or interminable disputes). In the light of these attractions, merely practical knowledge was vulnerable to charges of being unreliable, makeshift, unaccountable, and elitist. It seemed reasonable then that it should be supplanted – or, in other words, that the practical should be absorbed into the *technical*.

It is in the face of this attempted absorption that the defense of practical reason, and the counterattempt to articulate its irreducible otherness, has become a striking leitmotif in recent philosophy. Two developments had given substance to the ascendancy of technical rationality. First was the emergence of a kind of knowledge with real productive efficacy: the new science yielded deep-structure explanations that informed and made possible a new harnessing and transforming of matter. Second, an attempt was made to extend this same kind of theory to the personal and cultural worlds, searching for the same kind of regularities in human functioning – and hence the same basis for prediction and control – that had been found in the material universe. The first of these developments may seem unproblematic: the huge discrepancy between later and earlier levels of technological advance is itself evidence enough of the power of the scientific knowledge that has brought it about. Still, *technical feasibility*, which can indeed be assured by scientific advance, does not necessarily coincide with *practical desirability*. The latter weaves the former into a fabric of human purposes and needs, the fulfillment of which calls for a kind of deliberation that is neither identical with nor deliverable by scientifically certified knowledge. This fact can be accepted, however, while an attempt is made to retain primacy for nomological knowledge. A division is made between "means" and "ends" and, while ends are conceded to "deliberation," the organization and deployment of means to these ends is still claimed to fall exclusively within the competence of technical – or, as it now appears, *instrumental* – reason. "Deliberation," however, all too often turns out to be no more than an assertion of some personal but ultimately unjustifiable commitment, a positing of some brutely given preference, or a mere plumping for one of several imponderable options. This manifest absence of reason from the determination of ends (or "values" as they are now called) then leads to a strange inversion: the most rational calculation of means is made normative so that a combination of efficiency and economy becomes, in itself, the single overarching end. Technical reason is taken, by default, to be equivalent to reason *tout court*.

Even if this triumph of technical reason seems assured by the history of the past century – with the relentless and apparently irreversible replacement of older modes of production by newer, more powerful and efficient, ones – greater resistance may perhaps be expected with respect to the second development mentioned above. Here it is a question not of controlling matter but rather of directing human action and interaction in all the multifarious domains of "common sense" residing in family and community as well as in more specialized, increasingly professionalized, enclaves such as law, medicine, business management, psychotherapy, and education. But here too technical reason has exerted its fascination or, what amounts to the same thing, there has been a strong tendency to consider "practice" as "merely an expression of embarrassment at the deplorable but soon overcome condition of incomplete theory" (Bubner, 1981, p. 204). Theorizing a practice has tended to involve attempts to disembed the knowledge or skill implicit in the performance of its characteristic tasks from the immediacy and idiosyncrasy of the particular situations in which they are deployed, and from the experience and character of the practitioners in whom they reside. Through this disembedding it is supposed that what is essential in the knowledge and skill can be encapsulated in explicit, generalizable formulae, procedures, or rules. The latter then are to be applied to the various situations and circumstances that arise in the practice so as to meet the problems that they present. These problems are supposed to have nothing in them that has not been anticipated in the analysis that yielded the general formulae, and hence to be soluble by a straightforward application of the latter, without need for insight or discernment in the actual situation itself. Control – and efficiency – seems to be made possible here by the fact that the system is minimally dependent on the discretion or judgement of individual practitioners, with all the hazard and lack of standardization that this might entail. The ideal to which technical rationality aspires, one might say, is a practitioner-proof mode of practice.

Judgement and the texture of practical domains

In the face of all this, the philosophical defense of practitioner's knowledge has involved attempts to articulate some cognate of what may be called *judgement* (Smith, 1999). This is knowledge not as a possession (a kind of dead capital) but as invested in action. It is knowledge brought into play in the concrete, dealing with this situation now, that may be perfectly standard and typical – that is to say, of a type that has often been met previously and for which there is an already established and well-rehearsed procedure – but that may *not* be exactly to type but rather may deviate in an indefinite number of respects from what is standard or conventional. Judgement, then, is in the first instance an ability to recognize situations, cases, or problems of this kind (which are precisely of *no* clearly specifiable kind) and to deal adequately with them. A person of judgement respects the particularity of the case – and thus does not impose on it a procrustean application of the general rule. At the same time, such a person will try to find a way of bringing this particularity into some relationship, albeit one yet to be determined, with established norms or procedures in the area. Thus a person of judgement is not a maverick with a nose for the unusual, who is indifferent to the body of general knowledge codified in rules, formulae, and procedures (without familiarity with these, how could she or he even recognize the atypicality of the present instance?). To the contrary, a person of judgement is a keen student of the general stock of knowledge, all the better to find a fit (perhaps of an unusual shape; see Aristotle on the Lesbian rule in *Nicomachean Ethics*, 5, 10) between it and the particular case. The adeptness of the person of judgement, then, lies neither in a knowledge of the general as such nor in an entirely unprincipled dealing with particulars. Rather, it lies precisely in the mediation between general and particular, in bringing both into illuminating connection with each other. This requires perceptiveness in one's reading of particular situations as much as flexibility in one's mode of "possessing" and "applying" the general knowledge (Schön, 1983).

The exercise of judgement, then, requires resourcefulness and a kind of fluency. It involves creative insight insofar as it has to prove itself afresh in being equal to the demands of each new situation. Outstripping what has been formulated, it exhibits ability to actuate knowledge with relevance, appropriateness, or sensitivity to context (Polanyi, 1964). Experience, and the intimate exposure to particulars that comes with it, seems to be a necessary condition for acquiring it. Still, raw experience is not a sufficient condition: crucially, one must learn from one's experience – perhaps especially from one's mistakes – so that one's experience is constantly reconstructed. Openness to learning brings in a reference beyond experience to character: personal qualities and not just cognitive abilities are in play. There are virtues such as patience in sticking with a problem, a sense of balance that keeps both details and "big picture" in focus, a sobriety that keeps one from being easily swayed by impulse or first impressions, a courage that enables one to persist in a truthful though otherwise unprofitable or unpopular direction. Something impersonal is involved here that frees one from traps of the "ego"; and yet it is quite personal in that one's judgement ramifies into the recesses of one's mind and being, expressing the kind of person one has become (for the convergence here between analyses of practical reason and "virtue theory" see subsection on action situations below).

While each practical field has a specific texture of its own, the need for judgement arises in each of them because of an intricacy and frailty, inherent in human affairs, that is rife in all of them. They often present us with a problematic situation where there is no discrete problem already clearly labeled as such; insofar as the issue is largely one of identifying just what the problem is, we might better speak of a "difficulty" or "predicament" rather than a "problem" (Dunne, 1999a). Here several lines of consideration and priority run in different directions, interwoven tightly in a complex web. Attempts to unravel any one of these strands (the classic task of analysis) may only reinforce tangles in the others. Moreover, the material considerations may not all be internal to a particular discipline as a strictly circumscribed domain. In a business situation, for example, not only may production issues pull against financial ones but both may be curtailed by legal considerations; and at any point psychological or ethical factors may obtrude.

Attempts to resolve problematic situations of this kind, then, deviate from the standard instrumentalist paradigm. For the task is not one of calculating the efficiency of different possible means toward an already determined end. It often involves, rather, deliberation about the end itself – about what would count as a satisfactory, or at least not entirely unacceptable, outcome to a particular "case." And it may only be by action – and not, in the end, by any purely analytic process – that this deliberation can really be followed through. Strategically orientated action will provide new feedback but it can also set off its own chain of unintended consequences. And so one is involved in an experimental process. There is a significant difference, however, between the kind of experimentation that may occur in a practical field and that which goes on in a laboratory. Whereas in the latter case, a "negative" or disconfirming result may be celebrated by the skeptical spirit of the scientist as a step in the onward march of knowledge, in a practical field it may have to be regarded as an error that was simply too costly. And yet the situation may be such that to hazard no experimental probe is itself an error, if not an outright impossibility. It is in such situations that one needs the art of judgement.

An Aristotelian background

If this cardinal distinction between *technical* reason and judgement as the defining power of *practical* reason is intuitively recognizable to many practitioners, it has taken something of a revolution for it to find philosophical expression. This revolution has involved an attempt to move beyond the kind of canonization of natural science derived from the opposing but often mutually sustaining viewpoints of Cartesian rationalism and empiricism; and in one significant aspect it has been an attempt to get *behind* (or before) these viewpoints through a retrieval of Aristotle's "practical philosophy" (Dunne, 1997). Technical reason had in fact older and deeper roots in a tendency of classical Greek thinkers – pre-eminently Plato and Aristotle himself – to see in the act of fabrication (e.g., by housebuilder or cobbler) the most powerful resource against the capriciousness of nature and fate, and so to regard the kind of knowledge possessed by the master-fabricator as the privileged exemplar of rationality. This knowledge resided in *techne*, a concept they elaborated in terms of a set of related dualities that remain part of our linguistic stock-in-trade and still animate our conception of technical rationality: matter and form, means and end, planning and execution. Matter (e.g., stone or leather) is at the disposal of the producer, who can masterfully construct a design or blueprint (the "form"), which is then to be impressed on the matter to yield the finished product. This formed product is the end that the fabricator's productive activity is set to achieve; and the activity, together with the materials and whatever tools are needed, are the means that are used for its achievement. There is a clean separability here both between form and matter and between end and means; and this is reflected in a further separation within the productive process itself between a planning phase and an implemention phase. Rationality here resides in the planning: it is just to the extent that this planning can be abstracted from the nitty-gritty of the actual productive activity (to the point of being independently formulable as the content of rules and procedures), while at the same time being capable of subordinating the latter to itself, that the whole activity qualifies as "rational."

As articulated by the philosophers, *techne* did not accurately reflect the reality of what actually went on in some arenas of fabrication – think, for example, of the amount of know-how in the hands of a potter that is irrecoverable in any explicit propositions. Moreover, there were other areas of activity that were also seen as falling within the competence of *techne* although, as nonfabricating – that is to say, as not issuing in a substantial, durable, product – they seem to run athwart the philosophical conception of *techne*. Familiar examples in the Greek world were military strategy, rhetoric, and politics or statecraft. Far from being stable or passive (awaiting the impress of an already devised form), the materials here include volatile constellations of human passions and motivations; and, lacking the clearly defined boundaries of the workshop or laboratory, sites of engagement are shifting and protean. Rather than imposing a design on materials to bring about a product, adepts here intervene in a field of forces or immerse themselves in a medium, in which they seek to bring about a propitious result; and insofar as the play of chance and the vagaries of timing are ineliminable, they need a kind of opportunism, or talent for improvisation, that responds to the dynamism in the materials themselves. Against the bright light of Reason, there remained something shady and discreditable about these areas for classical Greek thinkers; and the latter's heirs today, devotees of technical reason, find them and the kind of intelligence they entail no more acceptable. There is, for example, a good deal of sophisticated rational choice- and decision-theory now available – but still a striking mismatch between it and the kind of perceptions, insights, and deliberative judgements of a skilled manager, advocate, psychotherapist, or teacher.

I have implicated Aristotle in the formative Greek occlusion of irreducibly practical modes of knowledge. But the great significance of Aristotle lies in the fact that he also set limits to the sway of *techne* and, through his novel conception of *phronesis*, provided a rich analysis of the kind of knowledge that guides, and is well fitted to, characteristically human – and therefore inescapably ethical – activity (*praxis*). For him, the prestige of *method* does not override resistances in different *materials*: to the contrary, a kind of epistemological pluralism follows from differentiations brought to the fore through sensitive phenomenological reflection. The materials of human affairs, he believes, are subject to such variety and fluctuation that they do not lend themselves to exceptionless, universal formulation: true rigor entails due appreciation of the kinds of rigor that are and are not available in disparate domains (*Nicomachean Ethics*, 1, 3). Arising from his understanding of the nature of *praxis*, then, Aristotle's treatment of *phronesis* incorporates the interrelated elements identified above under the rubric of "judgement": the open texture of the deliberation it sets in train; its need for fresh acts of perception or insight to meet the particularity of each action-situation; its irreducibility to general propositions and its hence inextinguishably experiential character; its being not only directive of present action but also itself shaped by the history of one's previous actions as these have become layered in one's character (Wiggins, 1980; Nussbaum, 1985; MacDowell, 1996; Dunne, 1999b).

"Overcoming epistemology": the hermeneutical turn

The conspicuous revival of interest in Aristotle's ethical-political thought has both contributed to and itself been motivated by a more general revolution in philosophy. "Overcoming epistemology" (Taylor, 1995a) is perhaps the best characterization of the common project of a wide range of disparate thinkers whose work has accomplished this revolution. In the twentieth century the major figures have been Heidegger and Wittgenstein: Heidegger through his attack on disengaged subjectivity and his emphasis on the temporal forestructure of human understanding, and Wittgenstein through the emphasis (in his later work) on practical forms of life and already functioning "language games" as the unsurpassable background of all knowledge. Subsequent thinkers, variously influenced by these two masters, have developed these themes.

For Hannah Arendt (1958), for example, action (as distinct from behavior) discloses and realizes the agent in her uniqueness at the same time that it inserts her into a web of relations with others; unpredictable in the consequences it unleashes and the reactions it evokes, it enmeshes her in a story that can never be foretold by herself but only retold afterwards by others. Or Hans-Georg Gadamer (1975) shows how large is the role of *interpretation* (as distinct from explanation) in understanding human affairs; how "objectivity" in our interpretations is never possible, if it is taken to imply an unprejudiced standpoint outside the flux and turbulence of actions and events; how the interpreter is rather always already situated within a particular historical horizon that has to be acknowledged rather than suppressed; and how these "limitations" on our knowledge – pertaining both to our anticipation of the future and our understanding of the past – lie at the level of our ineluctably human mode of being-in-the-world, beyond the purchase of methodological strategy or prescription. Or again Alasdair MacIntyre (1981, chapters 7 and 8) offers a powerful set of arguments to show that managerial expertise in modern bureaucratic institutions trades on the fiction rather than the reality of scientific generalizations about human functioning, giving us "not scientifically managed social control, but a skilful dramatic imitation of such control" (p. 107). Counterposed to this masquerade (which can exercise power while concealing the interest it serves beneath the glamour of "science") MacIntyre provides an influential account of "practices." A practice is a specific set of coherent activities – say, teaching, farming, architecture, chess – embedded in a tradition of ongoing collaboration, with goods and standards of excellence that are internal to itself and can thus be properly achieved and furthered only by those who have become practitioners, that is to say, who have developed that combination of practical virtues, of intellect, and of character, that are quite specific to the texture and integrity of the particular practice.

"Overcoming epistemology" has entailed not a repudiation of science but rather a correction of a positivistic misconception of it. Influential accounts of the scientific enterprise (e.g., Kuhn, 1962; MacIntyre, 1977) have shown that it is itself tradition-bound and endures crises that are resolved through commitments that cannot be justified in advance but only vindicated retrospectively through the place they find in a narrative of progress that trumps alternative rival narratives. Conversely, accounts of human agency and practical knowledge (e.g., Taylor, 1995a) show not only that the latter does not accord with the technicist picture of it but that it *does* in significant respects resemble what goes on in the conduct of the sciences. Scientific inquiry *is itself a practice* – whose affinities, moreover, with the kind of inquiries conducted in a law court, for example, or in establishing the authenticity of an artwork, or indeed in resolving a practical difficulty in one's life, must be recognized. And so the "physics envy" of technicist attempts to enhance the status of practical domains appears as truly foolish when not only its mimeticism but its distorted perception of the object of its attempted emulation is exposed.

While this discussion has entered the philosophy of science still its main heartland lies in ethics, political philosophy, and the philosophy of education, where "practice" and "practical knowledge" have become central to critiques of instrumentalism and "managerialism" in the institutional culture of modernity. The resources for such critique identified above might be broadly characterized as "hermeneutical." But quite apart from marked differences among the thinkers mentioned, there are other philosophical perspectives which, while finding common ground with hermeneutics in opposition to instrumental reason, still differ from it in their conceptions of practical reason itself. On the one hand critical theorists, most influentially Jürgen Habermas, emphasize the properly emancipatory role of genuine praxis and the consequently critical intent of the knowledge that must inform it (see chapter 2 of this volume). On the other hand, and in contrast with the strong notion of rational justification espoused by Habermas, neopragmatists such as Richard Rorty reject any rational foundation for norms – to the point of replacing "truth" by "what works for us" – while post-structuralists such as Jacques Derrida argue that the unavoidability within discourse of "deferral" and "dissemination" destabilizes the knowing subject and imposes a certain "undecidability" on all his or her judgements (see chapters 1 and 3).

Practice and the right kind of theory

All of this has of course a very direct bearing on central issues in education, especially with respect to conceptions of teaching and the kind of knowledge that properly informs it. Recent work in philosophy of education has taken up these issues, exploring their implications for pedagogy, assessment, curriculum, teacher training, and research (e.g., W. Carr, 1995). Responding to political and economic pressures on education, much of this philosophical analysis has taken the form of advocacy and critique; its purpose has been to defend the integrity of educational practice while contesting the technicist bias of a great deal of government policy on education in industrialized societies and of officially sponsored attempts to export this policy to developing countries. Since it is not possible here to do justice to the full range of this work, I shall conclude by briefly addressing, from the hermeneutical perspective to which my own philosophical sympathies incline, one important question raised by the emphasis on practical knowledge in teaching: does it, as is sometimes suggested, have antitheoretical implications?

To be sure, the philosophy that provides such a strong defense of practical knowledge is itself a kind of theory. But does it impoverish practical knowledge by denying the relevance to it, and therefore the power to enlighten it, of any theory? There are of course patterns of recurrence and of reliable expectation and projection without which social life in general, as well as within a more specialized enclave such as teaching, would collapse into incoherence. While some of these patterns are sedimented in our habitual stocks of tacit knowledge they may also be elucidated by social scientists as behavioral regularities. There are at least two important respects, however, in which these regularities need to be distinguished from law-like theories in natural science. First, they establish what is the case only "for the most part"; because of the open-textured character of action-situations already alluded to, they cannot reliably predict in individual cases. Second, whereas physical laws, for example, give us deep-structure knowledge that is radically discontinuous from the deliverances of common sense, thereby opening doors to previously unimaginable technical advances, the generalizations of educational (and indeed all social) science are rarely counterintuitive and so typically they corroborate rather than substantially reorientate the judgements of experienced practitioners.

The price that generalized empirical findings in the social sciences have to pay for their very generalizability, then, is a certain thinness of content. They can be complemented however – and here there is an opening for a different kind of "theory" – by thickly descriptive studies. The latter will embrace a variety of narrative modes and be strongly hermeneutical in character. In other words, they will tell stories about particular projects or episodes in the history of an individual teacher or school, and they will do so with the kind of interpretative skill that can bring out the nuances of plot and character; the dense meshing of insights and oversights, of convergent or contrary purposes, motivations, and interests; of anticipated or unanticipated responses from students and other relevant agents, all conspiring to bring relative success or failure. If these studies, with their deep embeddedness in a particular milieu, renounce the generalizing ambitions of wider-gauge research, they are not on that account condemned to a narcissism of the particular. To the contrary, when they are well done, they possess what might be called epiphanic power: they disclose an exemplary significance (Løvlie, 1997) in the setting they depict so that it proves capable of illuminating other settings – without need for rerouting through abstract generalities and, indeed, with greatest potential effect for those most deeply in the throes of the very particularity of another setting. (This is close to the power of all literary art which, as Aristotle suggests, can instruct and move us precisely because, in its depiction of individual cases and characters, it reveals – without necessarily stating or explaining – universal themes.) If our aim is to enlist theory in aid of the kind of practical knowledge outlined above in the analysis of judgement, it is to "theory" such as this that we must look.

II

Practical reason

Recent accounts of practical reason differ not only in their diagnosis of wise or rational action and in how they characterize the related agency stance. They differ, too, in their understanding of the relationship between an end and what pertains to an end, and in whether they take practical reason as primarily concerned with means or with ends, or both. Against instrumentalist accounts, which take practical reason to be primarily concerned with choosing efficacious means to an end, David Wiggins (1980) argues that in hard cases the problem is less a matter of deciding on the best means than to see what really constitutes an appropriate end. Hard cases demand what might be called constituents-of-end reasoning rather than mere means-to-end reasoning. Teaching, like other complex human practices, depends crucially on constituents-of-end reasoning (see D. Carr, 2000; Pendlebury, 1990a).

Two further dimensions of difference are discernible in recent work on practical reason: one concerning the distinction between individual and shared or communal questions; another concerning the distinction and relationship between public and private or personal spheres. The practical question is commonly taken as one that arises for and is answered, explicitly or implicitly, by individuals – "What should *I* do?" But rich accounts of teaching as an ethical practice suggest that the individual question cannot properly be posed or answered outside of the community of practice in which the practical question arises (see, for example, Sockett, 1987; Pendlebury, 1990a). Not every conception of a community of practice takes the ethical dimension seriously. Alasdair MacIntyre's conception of a community of practice is intrinsically ethical; Lave and Wenger's conception is not (Lave and Wenger, 1991; Wenger, 1998). Nonetheless both conceptions shift the emphasis in practical reason from strictly individual to communal concerns and criteria. In work on deliberative democracy and its enabling educational conditions, the communal question – "What should *we* do?" – is typically the more important, although questions about wise or appropriate individual action may also arise in public deliberative contexts.

While practical reason in the domain of deliberative democracy is largely concerned with public choice, it is not clear where to locate a teacher's practical reasoning, which is concerned neither with purely personal (or private) nor with purely public (or impersonal) choices, actions, or ends. Here the notions of role responsibility, vocation (Blum, 1993), community of practice (Pendlebury, 1990a), and epistemology of practice (Sockett, 1987) have been proposed as more illuminating and accurate ways both of locating and appraising teachers' practical reasoning.

Interpretations of Aristotle

Aristotle remains a primary source not only for those engaged in reclaiming *phronesis*, as Joe Dunne has argued, but also for those mining a narrower and analytically exacting justificatory vein. What different writers make of Aristotle is revealing. Some begin with the practical syllogism and from there develop an analytical account of how an agent chooses appropriate or effective means to an end. Others begin further back with the sort of character and characteristics required for seeing when an occasion calls for practical reasoning and for seeing what would constitute an appropriate set of ends in each case.

Writers working in a justificatory vein tend to be primarily interested in Aristotle's account of the process of practical reasoning and its relationship to the practical syllogism. Also, in addressing matters of appraisal, they are more concerned with how to judge the *reasoning* than the *reasoner*. Consider, for example, Robert Audi's reading of Aristotle: "A rational person characteristically answers a practical question by deliberation and, given sufficient knowledge, by producing a practical syllogism which yields a conclusion in favour of an action that is judged, in the light of the end governing deliberation, to be suitable" (Audi, 1989, p. 37). Working from interpretations of practical reasoning in Aristotle, Hume, and Kant, Audi proposes that practical reasoning is an inferential process with cognitive and motivational premises and which instantiates a basic schema represented by the practical syllogism. At its simplest the schema consists of a major (motivational) premise, a minor (cognitive) premise, and a conclusion (the practical judgement about what should be done). A practical judgement is directive, in content and in causal potential, and so provides a reason for action. Agents do not, of course, always act on their practical reasoning – inability, incontinence, intervention, or a change of mind may halt action or turn it in a different direction. Nor is every intentional action based on explicit practical reasoning. Nonetheless an agent may reconstruct a run of practical reasoning as a partial explanation of, and prima facie justification for, any intentional action performed in order to further an end.

Like others working in a justificatory vein, Audi is interested in the appraisal of practical reasoning. How can we judge the quality of a piece of practical reasoning? Audi proposes four appraisal standards: inferential, logical, epistemic, and material. The first two rest on a distinction between inferential processes (what we do when we reason) and inferential content ("arguments as what reasoning instantiates"). Whereas logical standards concern relations of entailment between propositions, inferential standards concern the justificatory and psychological relations between beliefs of the premises on the one hand and beliefs of the conclusion on the other. Inferential standards depend partly but not entirely on logical standards. Even when the corresponding argument is logically unobjectionable, practical reasoning may be inferentially deficient. This is so in cases of rationalization, where an agent produces an argument that *corresponds* to, but does not *underlie*, a judgement in favor of some or other conclusion. One could say, although Audi does not, that the inferential criterion reminds us that good practical reasoning is not a resource for those rationalizing practices in which sound argument serves self-deception, incontinence, and other failures of character. The second two assessment standards relate to the notion of justified true belief: epistemic standards call for justified belief in each constituent proposition in the corresponding argument; material standards concern the truth of these propositions (that is, the premises and conclusion). In order to meet the epistemic conditions for cogent practical reasoning, a person must justifiably believe both premises and must on the basis of them conclude with a practical judgement warranted by those premises.

While full compliance with these standards may be the mark of a good piece of practical reasoning, it is no guarantee of success. As Audi reminds us, a run of practical reasoning may be *defeasible* even when it meets all four standards. In other words, even when a person's reasoning expresses a good underlying argument and the person holds the relevant related beliefs, that person may not on balance be justified in holding the conclusion. This is because the conclusion to follow a particular line of action may be *overridden* by considerations that make a different line of action preferable. Alternatively, it may be *undermined* by considerations that have yet to emerge or that lie in the background and so escape notice. So even when a teacher's practice is richly informed by cogent practical reasoning, it is vulnerable to defeats of one kind or another.

Writers engaged in reclaiming *phronesis* argue that a proper account of practical reason cannot begin, or end, with an analysis of the practical syllogism, largely on the grounds that to do so ignores or underplays the inseparability of practical reason and character (Sherman, 1989). In matters of appraisal, these writers attend as much, if not more, to the character of the *reasoner* than to his or her *reasoning* as represented in a practical argument. Practical reasoning about a particular set of circumstances begins with our perception of the ethically salient features of those circumstances. An appropriate and discerning reaction to circumstances is itself part of a wise or virtuous response. Making choices is not simply a linear process of promoting efficient and effective means to single ends, but a process of promoting some ends in the light of others so as to integrate different interests and ends into a unified life over time. And this is not simply an individual matter: the ends of a good life are shared, as are the resources for promoting it. Accordingly, collaboration and a concern for the well-being of others mediate practical reason's perceptual and deliberative aspects.

Careful attention to the practical syllogism need not imply either an instrumentalist account of practical reason or a neglect of perception, character, and shared ends. For example, David Wiggins (1980) offers an interpretation of Aristotle's practical syllogism that is simultaneously a formal description of the practically wise person or *phronimos*. A person of the highest practical wisdom is one who brings to bear upon a situation a full range of authentically pertinent perceptions, concerns, and considerations commensurate with the deliberative context. The best practical syllogism is one whose minor premise arises from such discernment and it records what strikes such a person as the most salient features of the context calling for action. This activates a corresponding premise that spells out the general import of the relevant concerns. Competing syllogisms and their claims are not open to comparison or assessment according to some formal set of criteria. They cannot be, since the syllogism arises in a particular context and the major premise must thus be evaluated for its adequacy to the situation, not for its unconditional acceptability or for embracing a greater number of considerations than its rivals. Adequacy to the situation depends crucially upon the agent's situational appreciation or what other writers have called perception or discernment.

Action situations

For Wiggins (1980), Sherman (1989), A. Rorty (1988), Nussbaum (1986, 1990) and others working to reclaim the insights of an Aristotelian conception of practical reason, perception is perhaps the primary character mark of the practically wise person. Salient features of situations calling for practical reason do not spring to the eye already tagged for easy recognition, as Joe Dunne has already argued above. Rather we have to pick them out, and this involves the ability to see fine detail and nuance and the ability to discern the differences between this situation and others that to the inexperienced eye might seem the same. If we are wrong in our identification of the special features of a case, the result will be inappropriate action, no matter how tight the internal coherence of the arguments we give to justify what we do. Without finely tuned habits of salient focusing – and sometimes even with them – internally tight arguments can be used to rationalize inappropriate actions and so serve long-term projects of self-deception or weakness of will.

Herein lies the risk of too great a dependence on the practical argument as a device for helping teachers use defensible theory and good research to advance their pedagogical competence (see Fenstermacher, 1987; Fenstermacher and Richardson, 1993). Even if defensible theory and reliable, pertinent research do play an important part in good teaching, they are not sufficient for vigorous, well-directed practice. If teachers have a distorted view of the goods (or ends) of the practice or lose sight of them, or if they misjudge the salient features of situations – regardless of how defensible the theory or how reliable the research they rely upon – their deliberations cannot result in wise practice. Teacher education, then, is at least as much a matter of developing an understanding of the goods or ends of teaching as it is about "the theory of education." And it is at least as much about developing such aspects of character as insight and discernment as it is about exposing teachers to relevant and reliable research.

Once character and practical reason are seen as mutually dependent – as they are in various efforts to reclaim the insights of *phronesis* – it comes as no surprise that so much contemporary writing on practical reason falls roughly within the category of virtue theory. Even writers like Amy Gutmann (1995) who are not committed to virtue theory use the language of virtues in connection with practical reason and democratic deliberation. Conceptions of virtue vary widely in their detail but share a common core. Few are likely to contest Zagzebski's definition of a virtue as "an acquired excellence of the person in a deep and lasting sense" (Zagzebski, 1996, p. 135). Virtues and vices, she suggests, are among the more enduring of a person's qualities, and "come closer to defining who the person is than any other category of qualities" (ibid.). In short, virtue is a quality of character. For Sherman (1989), one cannot talk about character without talking about practical reason. Practical reason integrates, refines, and assesses the different ends of character. A foray into virtue ethics would take us well beyond the limits of this chapter. Suffice it to remark that the virtues relevant to the exercise of practical reason are both virtues of intellect and virtues of character, and that reflective, critical habituation plays an important part in their formation.

Among the primary virtues for sound practical judgement and appropriate action is what Amelie Rorty (1988) calls the habit of salient focusing. The habit goes together with, and is partly constituted by, a set of tropic cognitive dispositions. They are tropic because they organize a person's perceptions of and emotional responses to situations so as to elicit appropriate actions. People of practical reason, as Rorty (1988) describes them, have habits of salient focusing "that are corrigible without being distractible, imaginative habits of association that elicit a wide range of relevant material without being volatile, thresholds that are sensitive without being hypersensitive" (p. 316).

What is involved in becoming a practical reasoner (or a person of practical wisdom) and what is the role of education in developing the relevant qualities and capacities? Views like Audi's suggest that one of education's tasks is to teach critical thinking, conceived primarily as argument analysis, tempered with an understanding of defeasibility and those features of the world and our own psychology which make rational action a precarious accomplishment. For educational writers who accept or advance a contemporary version of *phronesis*, the habituation of character and development of discernment are primary tasks of education, if not its definitive end.

Democratic citizenship

Are there special dimensions of character, special virtues if you like, that are needed for citizenship in contemporary democracies? What forms of practical deliberation are most crucial for democratic practice? What role can and should education play in promoting them?

The recent surge of interest in deliberative democracy carries with it a renewed interest in practical reason in the public domain and in the role of education in nurturing deliberative citizens. Amy Gutmann (1995) argues that public schools are a democratic government's single most legitimate and powerful means for teaching democracy to young citizens and that they have a special obligation to do so. A central part of this obligation is to teach respect for reasonable public disagreement. Citizens also need an understanding of and capacity for the kinds of reasoning that underpin reasonable public disagreement (Gutmann, 1987, 1995). This is primarily moral reasoning of the practical kind – moral because it concerns questions of good and bad, right and wrong; practical because it ensues in action or in policies for action. It cannot be developed, Gutmann (1987) suggests, without attention to the character of deliberative democratic citizens.

What are the distinctive virtues of a deliberative character? An initial list might include reciprocity, mutual respect, openness, a willingness to give reasons and to listen to the reasons given by others in a deliberative interchange. The common thread here is the idea of give-and-take, an idea that runs through all current models of deliberative democracy but with a distinctive reach, range, and tenor in each different model. In some – for example, in Rawls's (1993) model of public reason – deliberative give-and-take operates within the parsimonious boundaries of conversational constraint and overlapping consensus. In others – for example, communicative democracy (Young, 1996, 1997) – deliberative give-and-take ranges wide in manner and matter to include a lively acceptance of dissent and difference.

The idea that difference and dissent in public deliberation are to be welcomed for their educative possibilities also lies at the heart of Martha Nussbaum's (1997) work on curriculum reform in liberal education. Her contemporary reading of the Stoics extends the range of public deliberation beyond the confines of a nation-state to global concerns. Accomplishing membership in the world community requires our willingness to doubt the goodness of our own ways and to participate in the give-and-take of critical argument about ethical and political choices. Increasingly refined exchanges of experience and argument enable participants gradually to acquire "the ability to distinguish, within their own traditions, what is parochial from what may be commended as a norm for others, what is arbitrary and unjustified from that which may be justified by reasoned argument" (Nussbaum, 1997, p. 60).

Like Young, Nussbaum (1997) regards the willingness to work with difference as a deliberative virtue with rich educational possibilities. The good citizen is a citizen of the world because thinking about humanity in its many manifestations is a valuable source of self-knowledge. Seeing our own ways in relation to those of other reasonable people enables us to see ourselves and our customs more clearly. Over and above its role in enabling self-knowledge, the awareness of the world citizen enables imaginative public deliberation, unconstrained by "cramped partisanship." Stories, and other art forms, cultivate the powers of imagination and those capacities of judgement and sensitivity that are essential to citizens' exercise of practical reason. Nussbaum pursues a similar line of argument through her earlier work on Aristotle. People of practical wisdom, in public and in private life, "will cultivate emotion and imagination in themselves and in others, and will be very careful not to rely too heavily on a technical or purely intellectual theory that might stifle or impede these responses" (Nussbaum, 1990, p. 82). For both Young and Nussbaum, narrative has a crucial role in public deliberation. Young's work suggests that one of the tasks of education is to help young people learn how to supplement formal arguments with narratives presented as grounds for claims of entitlement or need (see Enslin et al., 2001).

Different models of deliberative democracy, together with Nussbaum's argument for a global perspective, suggest an expanding educational agenda. Working strictly within the limits of the model of public reason (for example, Rawls, 1993), the educational task is to develop a respect for and capacity to apply rules of evidence and principles of reasoning, with due regard for accepted general beliefs. A related task is to nurture forbearance, mutual respect, and the exercise of conversational constraint. While Seyla Benhabib's (1996b) discursive model builds on several of these educational imperatives, it expands the educational agenda to permit and encourage wide-ranging deliberative topics. Deliberation itself becomes the means of enabling students both to understand themselves better and, through guided critical reflection, to order their views coherently, and perhaps change them, in the light of the range of perspectives brought to bear in deliberative interchanges.

Young's communicative model and Nussbaum's project of cultivating citizens' humanity expand the educational agenda even further to include the development of narrative imagination, emotional attunement, a sensitivity to the dialogical demands of different situations and situational moments, and the capacity to act in the light of these sensitivities. Here an education for practical reason in the public domain comes close to being an education of character.

Practical reasoning in pedagogic practice

Can an account of practical reasoning enhance our understanding of teaching as a practice and, if so, what kind of account and how? How can the quality of teachers' practical reasoning be appraised and improved and why, if at all, is it important to do this? What constitutes wise practice in teaching and what is the role and nature of ethical judgement in teaching?

During the 1980s and early 1990s, Gary Fenstermacher's work on practical rationality was largely responsible for putting the notions of practical reason and practical arguments back on the agenda for educational research and debate (Fenstermacher, 1986, 1987; Fenstermacher and Richardson, 1993). Much of the debate turns on the question of whether practical arguments can be used as a device for understanding and improving teaching. If practical arguments are taken to be restricted to means-to-end reasoning and so to represent what Schön (1983) calls technical rationality, then the practical argument is too barren and inappropriate a device for illuminating either teachers' thinking or the "reasonableness" of their classroom practice. Teaching is a moral practice that depends crucially on constituents-of-end reasoning, situational appreciation, and the capacity to respond to a range of cognitive uncertainties that arise from three related features of the world of practice, namely mutability, indeterminacy, and particularity (see Nussbaum, 1986).

Practice is mutable because it changes over time, presenting us with new configurations which cannot be ignored if our deliberations are to result in wise action. For example, on a fairly large time scale, the practice of teaching and its special challenges and dilemmas change with the institutions that contain and support it. Practice is indeterminate because practical questions necessarily arise within particular contexts. Appropriate actions are thus context-relative. To give just one example: the choices that are available and fitting to a teacher in a well-equipped urban school with a long-standing academic tradition are seldom available or fitting to teachers in the ill-equipped, overcrowded rural schools in many parts of Africa. Under such circumstances, situationally attuned practice may require the adjustment not only of means but also of ends. For these reasons, and those mentioned by Joe Dunne, practical deliberation in teaching is not accessible to a set of general rules governing a procedure for selecting the most effective means to a neat and easily specifiable end. A wise and competent teacher is surely one who has a rich understanding of the internal goods and definitive ends of the practice and a realistic, clear-sighted perception of what is possible and fitting under different circumstances.

If practical argument elicitation can help teachers to see the richness and complexity of practical deliberation in their practice then perhaps, and only then, can it serve as a device for appraising and improving teaching. But improving teachers' practical reasoning cannot simply be a matter of improving their practical arguments. Good practical reasoning, as we have said several times and in several ways in this chapter, depends on the capacity for discernment. An important question for teacher education, then, is how to develop the capacity for discernment. The cultivation of imagination and finely tuned emotions have a role here (Nussbaum, 1990), but so too does the development of moral reasoning concerned with the pursuit of the good (Carr, 2000). Much recent work in teacher education fails to grasp the nature of discernment and its necessity in wise practice. As a result, the development of teachers' practical reasoning becomes little more than a training in the procedures and "skills" of reasoning and reflection. Even writers who recognize the relationship between discernment, imagination, and wise practice still tend to leave these central concerns at the periphery of their accounts of teacher education and wise practice.

Recommendations for Further Reading

Dunne, J. (1997) *Back to the Rough Ground: Practical Judgment and the Lure of Technique*, University of Notre Dame Press.

Fenstermacher, G. and Richardson, V. (1993) The elicitation and reconstruction of practical arguments in teaching, *Journal of Curriculum Studies*, 25, pp. 101–14.

Pendlebury, S. (1990a) Practical reasoning and situational appreciation in teaching, *Educational Theory* 40, pp. 171–9.

Wiggins, D. (1980) Deliberation and practical reason, in A. O. Rorty (ed.) *Essays on Aristotle's Ethics*, University of California Press.

Part IV

Teaching and Curriculum

Chapter 12

Higher Education and the University

Ronald Barnett and Paul Standish

I

One does not get far in contemporary discussions of the university before one is caught up in complex questions of social justice. Differences in participation rates – between countries, between social classes, between ethnic groups – raise important questions about the justice of systems of higher education. There are complex practical problems about funding and related issues concerning inequalities that limit access to opportunity. In a mixed economy questions arise not only in relation to the respective responsibilities of individual and state but also concerning the roles of private (commercial) and state sources of remuneration. These questions relate, it is clear, to the issue of the autonomy and independence of universities, and these have direct academic import. For students in many countries, compelled to support themselves, a university education can no longer provide "the space of an interval," in Michael Oakeshott's celebrated phrase, but is rather an experience that must be juggled, perhaps not entirely to its detriment, with work and other commitments. The issue of social justice does not stop with the issue of opportunities to participate, however. There are questions about the content of a university education which, in their classic form, are expressed in terms of the nature and justifiability of the canon. Clearly in some subjects these questions have greater purchase than in others.

With the dramatic increase in scale of higher education, and with the relative decline in direct funding, which were generally features of the closing decades of the twentieth century, universities and other providers found themselves facing increasingly complex managerial tasks. There has been the seemingly inevitable tendency to see these tasks in quasi-technical terms as if this might avert attention from the real ethical issues that they almost always involve. Where the ethical has been more directly broached, this has generally been in terms of these questions of distributive justice. It is, however, not these issues that I shall pursue here. Rather I take as my starting point the curious character of the discourse of education, and of higher

Sections I and III written by Paul Standish; Sections II and IV written by Ronald Barnett.

education especially. For all the earnestness of the main protagonists here, there is a perplexing absence of an appropriate language within which to speak of the university. It is not just that there is no J. H. Newman or Von Humboldt now but that one can scarcely imagine anyone writing in this way.

Important voices have been raised in recent decades addressing the question of the university in terms beyond the managerial and political ones that have become the norm. Thus, in a number of essays some 30 years ago, Michael Oakeshott provided a moving defense of the importance of the university and of a liberal higher education. John Anderson and Alastair MacIntyre both wrote of the kinds of conditions that must be met if the academic pursuits of the university are to thrive. In what was to become a surprise bestseller Allan Bloom (1987) presented a provocative defense of the values of the elite university, and in the process spawned a sometimes heated debate. At a slightly different and in some ways metatextual level, Jaroslav Pelikan (1992) sought to pose again Newman's questions. Texts such as these have been accompanied by a stream, though never a torrent, of articles that have explored philosophical issues in higher education. At the same time there has developed a burgeoning literature, which positions itself somewhere between philosophy, sociology, and policy studies, within which the several books of my collaborator in this chapter have an exceptionally high profile.

In a number of essays, Jacques Derrida has addressed especially the place of the humanities in the university, and in one case in particular (Derrida, 1992) has provoked an eloquent and sometimes profound set of responses (Rand, 1992). Perhaps the more salient figure here, however, is Jean-François Lyotard who, notwithstanding his denial that this text is strictly philosophical, produced in *The Postmodern Condition* a work that showed remarkable prescience regarding the development of the university in an era dominated by the rise of information technology. The remainder of this section outlines a main theme of Lyotard's critique and then explores developments of that critique.

The key insight that Lyotard presents in *The Postmodern Condition* is captured by a term that has become common parlance in the criticism of contemporary educational practice: "The true goal of the system," he writes, "the reason it programs itself like a computer is the optimization of the global relationship between input and output: performativity" (Lyotard, 1984, p. 11). The term aptly exposes the jargon and practices of efficiency and effectiveness, quality assurance and control, inspection and accountability, that have become so prominent a feature of contemporary educational regimes. Whatever is undertaken must be justified in terms of an increase in productivity measured in terms of a gain in time. Computerization could become the "dream" instrument for extending the application of the performativity principle.

Performativity is particularly insidious because of its imperviousness to conventional opposition. It has the ability to tolerate and incorporate criticism, and so to strengthen the system, in such a way that both traditional and radical theory lose their force, reduced as they are to token protest or utopian hope. Central to the supposed credibility of its practices is the presumption of a kind of scientific status, of objectivity and rigor, but, as Lyotard shows, this amounts to a serious misunderstanding of the nature of science. Science does not expand by means of the positivism of efficiency. It proceeds rather by inventing counterexamples, by looking for "paradox" and legitimating it with new rules in the game of reasoning (ibid., p. 54). It was the emergence of a science that concerned itself with undecidables – he cites Benoit Mandelbrot and René Thom – that in particular gave Lyotard hope that the limits of performativity must eventually be exposed, but it is evident from the work of the range of scientists that Lyotard refers to that scientific research does not in fact operate in quite the way that the positivism of efficiency imagines. The views of Peter Medawar are illustrative: *having ideas* is the scientist's highest achievement; there is no "scientific method"; a scientist is before anything else a person who *tells stories*, albeit stories that there is a duty to verify (p. 60). The imaginative advancement of knowledge then is not facilitated in a regime where those responsible for the management of universities and for the quality of their curricula are agents of performativity.

Of course, the response to this text has sometimes been hostile. A disastrous misunderstanding of the tone of the text has led some to believe that Lyotard is advocating precisely the performativity that he condemns. Some have found the vocabulary of totalitarianism excessive and melodramatic, but it is worth remembering that Lyotard sees performativity as deriving from the cultural imperialism, no less, of Western civilization, governed as it is by the demand for legitimation (ibid., p. 27). Acknowledging the risks of scandalizing the reader, Lyotard speaks of the severity of the system, of the terroristic tendencies of a "scientific" establishment that is governed by homeostasis. "Adapt your aspirations to our ends – or else" is perhaps not a very great exaggeration of the threat that educators find themselves under in some Western liberal societies today (pp. 62–4).

Whatever the cogency of the negative aspects of Lyotard's critique, however much he is correctly seen as concerned to sustain the best traditions of academic enquiry, there is something deflating about the hope that Lyotard offers in this text. Elsewhere in his work, there are richer suggestions for ways in which higher education might develop. Let us then consider accounts of the university that take off from those suggestions.

Bill Readings' sensitive reading of the range of Lyotard's work is turned towards higher education in his *The University in Ruins* (Readings, 1996). His characterization of the modern university in terms of the idea of excellence serves in part to emphasize the dominance of the institution by performativity but also to point up a contrast with earlier incarnations: the (Kantian) University of Reason, the founding discipline for which is philosophy; and the (Humboldtian) University of Culture, which replaced philosophy with literature, thereby tying more closely the development of the modern university to the rise of the nation-state. The ideal of excellence is unlike its predecessors in that it conceals a kind of vacuity. Globalization and the decline of the nation-state create conditions where the currency of excellence can function ideally for a knowledge economy. Homogenized systems of transferability and commensurability enable the free flow of cultural capital, and these are realized through a downgrading in importance of content and a weakening of cultural attachments. The modern university is dominated by procedural reasoning – in its emphasis on skills and on management systems, and in an incipient reduction of knowledge to information (all accelerated by computerization) – to the detriment of a proper attention to content and to traditions of enquiry.

In the University of Excellence academic freedom is not so much threatened as effaced. Radical and subversive research need not be feared because it can "count" in the next research assessment exercise – the more outrageous, the more the citations. And in a newly democratized curriculum, it is possible to be excellent in . . . well, anything. The danger here is not despotic control or repression but rather the kind of semblance of freedom that de Tocqueville anticipated in American society, a semblance whose most recent name is perhaps "social inclusion." In our teaching, Readings claims, we are more free than we used to be, but we can no longer see what it is that our freedom is freedom from because alternative conceptions are effectively neutralized (Readings, 1996, p. 164).

Far from giving up on the university, however, or attempting to turn this clock back, Readings' suggestion is that we might live well in the ruins of the university if the ideal of excellence is displaced by a restoration of the name of thought. He argues for "a pedagogy that refuses to justify the University in terms of a metanarrative of emancipation, that recognizes that thought is necessarily an addiction from which we never get free" (ibid., p. 128). The apparently substantial though in fact vacuous referent of excellence must give way to the overtly empty *name* of thought. When the frameworks of our understanding cannot contain the events that confront us, when we have neither received ideas, nor formulae, nor rules to guide us, when there are rules but the rules conflict, the thinking that we most need is empty. Our temptation is to accommodate events within our existing frameworks. The imperative on us not to give into this temptation is especially acute in the university in view of the fact that the university is the place where the languages we have for understanding the world are to be pushed to their limits. This is an exercise of judgement and justice.

Readings acknowledges that he writes as a university teacher but that he does not know in any absolute sense what the signification for the name of teacher is: indeed, if there were a clear signification, if the role and duties of a teacher, the nature of the job, were cut and dried, this would imperil precisely that bracing uncertainty and challenge that should be at the heart of education: "We must seek to do justice to teaching rather than to know what it is. A belief that we know what teaching is or should be is actually a major impediment to just teaching" (1996, p. 154). And one might say as much for many of the other contestable terms that characterize education: "Thought is one of many names that operate in the pedagogic scene, and the attribution of any signification to it is an act that must understand itself as such, as having a certain rhetorical and ethical weight" (ibid., p. 160). Neither sanctified nor invoked as an alibi, thought cannot redeem us from the ruins nor can it provide formulaic ready responses for the inevitable occasions for judgement that confront us. It requires a pedagogy that is agonistic, one where the *aporias* of enquiry are exposed. Its absolute requirement is an attention to the Other, where what is other is not represented as the opposite pole in a binary coding, where, in fact, it is not to be *represented* at all – the metaphysics of presence and of representation are indeed the backdrop to the creation of the University of Excellence. Thought responds to an incompatibility in ways of speaking that is not dissolvable by any philosophy, system, or practice.

That a degree of pessimism and caution here is wise is very much a tenor of Lyotard's later writings:

> The decline, perhaps the ruin, of the universal idea can free thought and life from totalizing obsessions. The multiplicity of responsibilities, and their independence (their incompatibility), oblige and will oblige those who take on those responsibilities, small or great, to be flexible, tolerant, and svelte. These qualities will cease to be the contrary of rigor, honesty, and force: they will be their signs. Intelligences do not fall silent, they do not withdraw into their beloved work, they try to live up to this new responsibility, which renders the "intellectuals" troublesome, impossible: the responsibility to distinguish intelligence from the paranoia that gave rise to "modernity." (Lyotard, 1993b, p. 7)

The muted hope expressed here is tied to a clear imperative regarding the assumption of responsibility. The theme of responsibility, so prominent in Derrida's work, recurs in his recent "The Future of the Profession, or The Unconditional University" where it is examined in terms of "the profession of faith of a professor" (Derrida, n.d.). Just as Readings stresses that thought must be understood *as an act*, Derrida here revisits J. L. Austin's celebrated distinction – involving a term that is not be confused with the Lyotardian notion of performativity – between the constative and the performative to explore ways in which the idea of profession requires something tantamount to a pledge, to the freely accepted responsibility to profess the truth. Professors enact this performative continually in their work: what they say is testimony to the truth. The academic work of professing must then be something more than the (purely constative) statement of how things are.

The humanities are not to be understood without reference to questions of man, of humanity and of freedom. They relate to a certain conception of public space. This is now undergoing fundamental changes with a new virtual topology and perhaps with the puzzling contemporary preoccupation with an array of cognate performatives involving profession or confession. This role of the humanities, Derrida claims, cannot be properly played if they are restricted to the description of what is. The emphasis on the performative entails a change of modality: if the description of the world relates to the way *it is*, the work of profession involves the performative putting to work of the *as if*. The responsibility of the professor extends beyond the performatives of criticism to an openness to the event. The irruption of the event disturbs the sovereign authorities of the disciplines of enquiry, it breaks through their horizons, and, rightly received, it puts into "deconstructive ferment" the settled oppositions that have structured so many aspects of the modern world. If disciplinary borders are crossed here, however, they must not be dissolved in a confused interdisciplinarity. Openness to the event is a way of honoring the commitment to the truth that is any discipline's concern. Something beyond the range of a purely autonomous control, this openness is essential to the exercise and growth of the imagination that this professing requires. The alternative would be to rest complacently within the settled ways of one's thought, with the presumption that one could simply represent what is, in what would amount to a relinquishing of the very responsibility the university must require. And that responsibility holds out the best hope for democracy, which is always a working toward a democracy *still to come*.

What needs to be noticed especially here, in Derrida as in Lyotard, is the trajectory of the idea of judgement toward a certain operation of the imagination. We must turn to a different reading of Lyotard, however, to deepen and extend this. This requires us to see in the emphasis on the aporias of enquiry and silent witness of the sublime in Readings' account a latent negativity. A way beyond these limitations is offered in a recent essay by Gordon Bearn (2000). "Lyotard mistakenly turns," he writes, "to a version of the sublime – projecting an ideal University of the Sublime – when he should have turned to the beautiful – projecting an ideal University of Beauty. The difference is the difference between double negation and full fledged affirmation" (Bearn, 2000, p. 237). It is the alternation or vibration between two moments, which Lyotard refers to as "an affective 'no' and 'yes'" (Lyotard, 1994, p. 68). And it is the negative dependency of this alternation that Bearn wants to resist. His account is resonant of Lyotard's *Libidinal Economy*, the spirit of the ideas Dionysian.[1]

Bearn's exploitation of the classic contrast between the beautiful and the sublime serves to turn the attention to questions of rhythm and intensity. In a flagrant violation of the principles of "outcomes based education," beauty becomes linked to an ideal of *pointlessness*. Intensity is achieved via two routes. It can come most obviously through the kind of subtraction or lack of connection that is involved in concentration – as perhaps in absorption in a problem in pure mathematics. But it can also occur through something like addition where the object of the study is connected in countless ways:

> Formlessness and pointlessness move us in this direction not toward emptiness, but toward a beauteous intensity. This is what the other side of representation is: swarms of differences, swarms of intensities, a world without identity. And in its pointlessness, beauty will recover its autonomy, but this time not by negation. This time beauty's autonomy derives not from its lack of connection, but from the myriad lines connecting it from here to everywhere. (Bearn, 2000, p. 246)

There is something about our representational practices and genres of discourse that regiments and stifles this intensity, that stages it and stops its flows. In contrast, Bearn imagines beauteous intensity in terms of the intersecting lines of a multi-dimensional graph, the lines pulling their intersections along multiple dimensions. He pictures Leonardo's studies of water, vortices, and deluges, in one of which

> water from a single source pours into a turbulent pool producing a swarm of swirls ejecting flows in all directions . . . We can imagine maximally intense activities in terms of water pouring in from all directions producing swarms of almost Cartesian vortices, then ejecting flows in all directions, to begin the cycle again. The University of Beauty is dedicated to the cause of releasing the lines of that intense graph, the powerful turbulent flows which Leonardo depicts, sometimes even breaking apart mountains . . . (ibid.)

Such a vision would characterize study in terms of intense fascination in the work at hand. It would disrupt, indeed render ridiculous, it is plain, any attempt tidily to specify learning outcomes or curricular objectives. It would expose the poverty of a curriculum based on the conjunction of skills or competencies with banks of information. One can anticipate any number of workaday objections here. But what is so valuable is the finding of a language for that beauteous intensity that should be the quality of university study.

The argument bypasses the hackneyed dichotomies of liberal and vocational education, and of intrinsic and extrinsic value. For the kind of beauty that is at issue here is found across the range of academic engagement. Vocational education inevitably involves theory, practice, pleasure, and function. In the building of a bridge or road connecting two communities, for example, there is a site of investigation that can be approached from multiple points of view: population flows, concrete chemistry, the aesthetics and physics of bridge design, costs to the communities, and the social change it effects.

> It is simply a matter of not hiding this multiplicity of purposes behind the desire to seem either gruff and practical or sophisticated and theoretical. Unveiled, this multiplicity is a fine example of positive pointlessness, of beauty. Pointlessness is not to be restricted to the humanities, generalized or otherwise, it is the key to progress and excitement in every field. The university of beauty is not mourning anything; it is a place where the intrinsic and extrinsic values of a university education are both ordered by the quest for the positive sense of pointlessness: beauty. (ibid., p. 255)

There is now widespread recognition that over the course of a life the importance of technical training fades while that of an inventive imagination increases. It is then our duty to encourage "those features of higher education (in whatever field) that ignite the fires of the imagination, radiating 'light without heat,' burning with a fire that does not consume (Freeman, 1999)" (Bearn, 2000, p. 247). Positive pointlessness may be the secret to intensifying the life of that imagination, in any field.

The vitality of the imagination that runs through Bearn's article helps to concentrate a line of thought that has been emerging progressively in this chapter so far. It frees this from the melancholic tones that color Readings' higher education. But there is, I think, no necessary incompatibility here. In other words, the witnessing of the sublime could exist alongside the exuberance of beauteous intensity and be part of the same student's experience. All these accounts are committed to the maintenance of disciplinary traditions of enquiry, and all see these as under threat.

II

The end of the story?

What is it to try to understand the university? There has been a long line of seminal texts about the idea of the university, at least, from Cardinal Newman onwards but now, as my fellow discussant, Paul Standish, notes: "one can scarcely imagine anyone writing in this way." One reason is that even if anyone was to write in that tradition, he or she would probably not be taken seriously, for such writing was essentially an ideological project. It was an attempt to persuade us that the university should not only be understood *as* such and such but that it should set itself up *to be* such and such.

There were two other aspects to those writings. First, they were value-laden. They took largely for granted that goals such as civilizing gentlemen (Newman) or developing an intelligent professionalism (Jaspers), or promoting the "culture" of society (Ortega, 1946; Arnold, 1932), or finding a Christian-compatible set of values (Moberly), or promoting a particular kind of "intelligence" (Leavis), or maintaining a separate academic life (Minogue), were both possible and desirable.

Secondly, texts such as these were written in a relatively straightforward style. Indeed, they were written *with* style. Doubtless this was partly because those texts were the product of a particular commitment in favor of a particular view of human development and of society *and* of the contribution that the university might play in bringing about those larger ends. Partly, too, those texts were written in a setting free of the felt constraints that result from the institutionalization of a field of study within modern higher education. These writers were often not writing as academics for an academic audience but were writing for a general audience. Their writings were open-textured, accessible, and even pleasurable to read.

These three characteristics of the seminal texts on the idea of the university – (1) their advocacy of a particular kind of university, (2) that vision stemming from a set of values and beliefs, and (3) their views being developed in a nontechnical language – immediately mark out the kind of text that would be likely to be repudiated today in the academic world. With the emergence of competitive disciplinary groupings and with the arrival of national evaluation mechanisms, the tacit rules of what it is to be an academic have tightened. As a result, academic speaks unto academic. The dual risk of being thought too old-fashioned or nonserious has put paid to texts that reached out to publics.

In short, for a number of reasons – to do with the structure of academic life, its discourses and its modes of communication – the lineage of John Henry Newman seems to be at an end. The story of the idea of the university appears to have run its course (cf. Rothblatt, [1988] 1997a, 1997b).

The end of universality – and the end of the university?

As well as the sociopolitical reasons, there are, as I have hinted, philosophical reasons for entertaining suspicions that a new Newman is no longer possible. Postmodernism has, it may seem, undermined any project that looked to advance a general view or theory concerned with human life. Postmodernism and universality are polar opposities: they exclude each other, or so we are told. It is hardly surprising, therefore, that Derrida (1992), raising the question as to whether the university has a responsibility today, was unable to answer his own question in any positive way. To do so would have meant coming forth with some large general idea, even a universal idea, and just such a move is ruled off-side within his genre.

Postmodernism presages, indeed, a double undermining of the Western university. For the Western university has come to stand both for progress *and* for universality.

The two are connected, of course. The project of universality *is* one of implicit progress. There are, in fact, several projects of universality wrapped up in the idea of the Western university; but each is associated with the idea of progress.

First, there is a sense that the criteria of the reason sustained by "universities" are universal. Its truth claims are universal; they do not reflect partial "Western" takes on the world. Secondly, universities are social institutions that are communicatively open; if any institution in the world approximates to Habermas's idea of an "ideal speech situation," this is it (Habermas, 1981b). Any one of its members can contest any claim by any other one of its members. Thirdly, its truth claims presuppose and speak to a universal audience. Fourthly, universities are open to all comers. No one is to be excluded *or admitted* on irrelevant grounds – such as gender, ethnicity, or physical capacities. Fifthly, universities are universal in the sense that all forms of valid cognition are open to them: there are no *a priori* boundaries to the domains of reason that they might pursue. Indeed, in principle, any issue that they pursue could open up inquiries in any domain.

One way of expressing this universality of the Western university is to say that it is a nonideological institution. It is a social institution that is open-textured in its activities, its truth claims, and its relationships with the wider world. Its mottoes could variously be: "nothing is ruled in and nothing is ruled out"; or, simply, "no bias here." This, at least, is the self-understanding of the Western university. It is an institution intended to advance universal reason and, in the process, to assist in the wider project of human progress.

As a set of interconnected beliefs, all this, as I have already indicated, is now in jeopardy. In the postmodern age, it is not only difficult to sustain a belief in universality; it is also that the very concept has become suspect. The idea of progress, in turn, is put in doubt, for any sense of universal progress or universal standards against which progress might be monitored itself dissolves. In the process, the planks on which the Western university has developed its self-understanding appear to have collapsed. Far from being representative of a universal set of ideas as to the character of reason, the Western university is in the dock as being representative *of* a particular form of reason, namely the instrumental reason that sustains a technological-bureaucratic society. (This is not a new argument; it was made in a more straight-forward way, and trenchantly so, by Leavis half a century ago.) The more modern twist is the sense that, in a global age, the university is becoming a key institution in the development of the networked global economy. The project is now global instead of universal; global economy as against universal reason.

The argument as to the undermining of the Western university as a source of universal reason is not just theoretical but is also empirical. Universities have been coopted by the host state to fulfill state agendas, especially those connected with economic development and, although less evidently, social integration. The state has also intensified its surveillance techniques to ensure these agendas are being fulfilled. At the same time, higher education is required to take on many of the characteristics of a market, in which its services are costed and made available to consumers to whom, in turn, universities are obliged to be responsive. Connections with industry have been encouraged, in research, teaching, and in more entrepreneurial income-generating activities (cf. Clark, 1998; Slaughter and Leslie, 1997). In the process, the power of the academics as a social class is reduced. Some even talk of the "loss of academic dominion" and even of the "proletarianization" of the "dons" (Halsey, 1992).

As an unintended consequence of these developments, the university can no longer be considered as a site of universal reason, for reason has been commandeered by extramural interests. These extramural interests also are themselves heterogeneous, often evincing conflicting responses. Apparently unifying discourses, such as that focused on "excellence," turn out either to be empty (Readings, 1996) or, again, serving to embrace and, thereby, neutralize competing definitions of higher education.

The end of the idea of the university?

There are, it is apparent, two alternative readings of the contemporary university. On the one hand, the university is understood as becoming an instrument in the hands of the state for advancing the interests of the state in the global knowledge economy. On the other hand, higher education is simply part of a market economy, putting its services at the disposal of anyone, or any constituency, that finds an exchange value in its commodities. *On either reading*, the university has abandoned any calling to pursue universal reason and has given itself up to local or national agendas, to the exigencies of the moment, and to the particular (even if, in some forms, the particular is also global in character).

There is, however, a third reading to the effect that universities are becoming part of an interconnected global world. Since their medieval inception, they have always been international, taking their members from around the world and making their knowledge claims available to worldwide publics. Now they are becoming global in character, networking globally and acting globally, independently of their host society. A university is no longer primarily a physical site but is a set of open-ended relationships and communications, in "virtual" reality. But such a set of reflections opens the door for the possibility that new spaces are opening for the university to reclaim an interest in universal reason (Zembylas, 2000). The severing of the close ties between the state and the university which, for some (Readings, 1996) is a cause of regret, may be freeing the university to reclaim some lost ground. The global age is potentially not just an age of a global knowledge economy but can also be seen as an age of global communicative reason.

Is it then possible to find common cause with the great tradition of the literature on the idea of the university? Is there any way of writing, any way of espousing a thesis, that might be felt to stand in the line of Newman, Arnold, Jaspers, Ortega, Leavis, and Moberly? The difficulties, as we have seen, are considerable. The university, as an idea, faces three substantive forms of undermining: philosophical, sociological, and ideological. Perhaps, too, as Scott (1995) has hinted, it faces also a cultural undermining.

Philosophically, the key ideas for which the university has stood – of knowledge, truth, and reason – are now even more slippery than they ever were. The university cannot be assumed to be their ultimate safeguard any more. Sociologically, the university has become a state apparatus, as societies see in the university vehicles for advancing their interests in the global economy, in developing high level human capital. Ideologically, the university fragments as it positions itself in relation to its multiple possible client groups. The university that Clark Kerr (1972) captured in his evocative phrase "the multiversity" has split even further, as the university becomes entrepreneurial and finds different markets for itself in relation to its separate epistemic communities *and* as the wider world interpenetrates universities such that they are now caught in global webs of relationships with various societal domains. Culturally, too, the university becomes unsure of itself, hesitant of all things "elitist." Bloom's (1987) lament was just this: high culture in the university had given way to no culture at all.

The impossibility of a manifesto?

Given these apparent underminings, it is perhaps hardly surprising that it is felt that the university is "in ruins." The key question is simple, therefore: do we just shrug our shoulders and accept that the story of "the idea of the university" is at an end *or* can we continue the lineage? The sheer production of a text that seeks to espouse an idea of the university is not in itself a sufficient condition of that hope being realized. Such a realization requires that the idea set forth is feasible as a project; and, here, feasibility involves both a practical *and* a communicative feasibility as much as an intellectual one. The argument has to reach out to multiple audiences and it has to contain an action plan (of a kind). What is required, therefore, is a manifesto.

The manifesto also has to be serious in the sense of being adequate to its context. There can, therefore, be no pure philosophy of higher education. Any such "philosophy" has to take account of the wider social, political, and policy context within which higher education finds itself. Any serious philosophy of higher education has to be a social philosophy. Without such a reckoning, emerging proposals are bound to run the risks of being naive and even of being ideological. That was one of the strengths of Lyotard's (1984) extended essay and one reason, perhaps, why it has been so influential: the analysis of higher education was placed firmly within a broader analysis of moving epistemologies, computer networking, and discourse dynamics that characterize the modern world as such.

Such a situatedness, however, is neither a necessary nor a sufficient condition of there emerging an appropriate conception of the university. Lyotard was both misleading and self-contradictory. He was misleading in declaring that the modern world is faced with "an incredulity towards grand narratives." To the contrary, the world is *saturated* with multiple, expanding, and conflicting narratives, many of them large in scope and even claiming to be universal. He was self-contradictory in, having declared that we are bereft of grand narratives, then going on tacitly to indicate that "performativity" *de facto* is becoming a grand narrative through its assimilatation via a state-orchestrated discourse. Lyotard was also unhelpful in that he failed seriously to analyze "performativity" and its manifold manifestations. An apparently single teaching act may itself be a complex of competing performativities.

Despite these difficulties in Lyotard's account, it retains a particular value in perhaps demonstrating that a manifesto for higher education, in proferring a set of large ideas or even a clear unifying vision of it, is no longer possible. Lyotard's account wore on its sleeve the technical nonfeasibility of such a project: large unifying ideas are now *outré*. Postmodernism has apparently put paid to all that. His account also demonstrated *implicitly* its nonfeasibility. Few, I suggest, are going to pick up Lyotard's book and find themselves in the presence of an accessible text, and be able to hold a ready dialogue with it, as is possible with those authors of the great tradition (Newman, Jaspers, Moberly, Leavis, and so on). Not many will be reading Lyotard for pleasure. We are, it seems, in a postmanifesto age.

A terrible beauty is born?

This challenge, of supplying some kind of substantive thinking about the university, in an age of contending frameworks, is tackled by Paul Standish. Standish apparently endorses the Readings–Lyotard effort in drawing attention to the kind of thinking that is called for when "the frameworks of our understanding cannot contain the events that confront us." He goes on, too, to quote Lyotard's suggestion that "the decline, perhaps the ruin, of the universal idea can free thought and life from totalizing obsessions. The multiplicity of responsibilities, and their independence (*their incompatibility*) oblige . . . those who take on . . . responsibilities . . . to be flexible, tolerant, and svelte" (my emphasis). However, even against this background of a multiplicity and incompatibility of frameworks that exceed our comprehension, Standish goes on to urge a unifying idea, namely that of moving towards what Bearn calls "a beauteous intensity." Through this idea, "the University of Beauty" may "recover its autonomy" from "the myriad lines connecting it from here to everywhere."

Surely, this does not stack up. We are pointed to multiple frameworks and then are offered a unifying framework (here, over the caption of "beauteous intensity"). We are given to understand that our frameworks exceed our comprehension but we are given an image (of a water flow) in which our comprehension is considerably enhanced and even unified. We are reminded of a "multiplicity of responsibilities" but this University of Beauty is to take on a new overriding responsibility, that of creating, through "an inventive imagination," a "positive pointlessness." In short, we are being offered a new universalism in a situation in which we are being cautioned against all universalisms.[2]

The frameworks with which we now interpret the world, even in our everyday understandings, are multiple, proliferating, and incompatible. This is a world of supercomplexity (Barnett, 2000), in which the frameworks not just abut against each other but collide with each other. The assumption that there is a beauteous pattern or even patterns within this interplay of frameworks has to be suspect: it is a sign of hope attempting to triumph over reason.

In a fast-changing global age, ideas, values, and frames of interpretation multiply chaotically and it should not be assumed that such chaotic patterns possess some underlying order or system or beauty. Nor, yet, should the university be shy of recognizing this situation. For the university has itself been party to the production and proliferation of competing frameworks. That the university now has the responsibility of developing the educational capacities for prospering in such a world of expanding and competing frameworks is only a form of justice: the university is simply helping to meet the bill that it has landed us all with.

The claim, therefore, that there lies to hand a form of beauty, intense or not, multifaceted or not, can be seen as a form of wishful thinking, in which "necessity is aestheticized into the beauty of the eternal order" (Rosen, 1997, p. 269). It is an attempt to make intelligible that which is unintelligible. It is the creation of a myth so as to ease the troubled mind. That the mind might be troubled here is readily understandable. As our frameworks expand and compete with each other, so our hold on life appears to be ever more tenuous. It is not quite true to say that we are being faced with an "ignorance explosion" (Lukasiewicz, 1994) but what is true is that our capacity for deriving overarching orderly frameworks is fast diminishing. If there is a beauty to be observed in this world, it is more the beauty of a Hieronymous Bosch than of a Leonardo da Vinci.

A new manifesto

It is understandable if the great tradition of "the idea of the university" is at an end since, on one level, the idea of the university is itself at an end. We live not just in a global age but in a knowing age. In the knowledge society, everyone – by definition – is a producer of knowledge (Stehr, 1994). Corporate universities arise, knowledge officers are appointed in major corporations, and professional life comes to be understood as sustaining a complex of knowledges ranging well beyond the propositional knowledge given high marks in universities. Knowledges are understood as complex processes, as problem-solving in situ, as tacit knowledge, as calling on all the human senses, and as action learning. That knowledges expand is itself an inevitable concomitant of fast globalization: worlds collide and, in the process, new worlds are formed.

In this milieu, unless it is careful, the university stands condemned to being behind the game. It is confronted not just with a complex world but with a supercomplex world, in which the frames by which we might understand the world multiply and compete with each other. There is no order, no pattern, no system to any of this. But the university is not bereft of purpose.

The purposes of the university in such an age are threefold: first, to go on expanding the frameworks with which we might comprehend our world. The university is epistemologically challenged: it is threatened with being displaced as the primary producer and disseminator of high level knowledge. Unless it is prepared to be more epistemologically generous and imaginative, it will find itself epistemologically outflanked (cf. Gibbons et al., 1994). Secondly, the university has the challenge of providing the wherewithal for living at ease with this epistemological and ontological mayhem. It becomes a therapeutic university. To stop there, however, would produce voyeurs who were able only to contemplate the craziness of the world. Thirdly, therefore, the university has the challenge of developing the competences of living purposefully and even of prospering in the world. Of course, "purposefully" and "prospering" hide value judgements and there would be dispute as to what such terms might imply. But, in an age of supercomplexity, such conflict over basic frameworks has to be accepted and lived through.

There can be no new Newman in the sense of our being offered a clear unifying vision of the university. The world, knowledges, and universities are too complex to allow for that. It is a world in which there are no stable frameworks. It is a world in which the university has continually to remake itself. In such a world, therefore, in developing a sense of the idea of the university, there can be no falling back on any unifying idea, and certainly not an idea suggestive of order and pattern. There can be no liberal idea of the university in any straightforward sense.

Yet, as we have seen, we can still talk meaningfully of the university. As well as as adding to the epistemological and ontological mayhem of the world, the university has a responsibility to enable us to live purposefully in that world. Understanding, creativity, reflection, and discussion are all implied in this new set of ideas and are, thereby, retained from past traditions. Now added, too, is the dimension of enlightened and engaged action. All in all, this is a very large agenda. The university has nearly one thousand years behind it; there is no reason to suppose that it cannot have another thousand years before it.

III

"There can be no liberal idea of the university in any straightforward sense." Let us – setting aside the nature of this impossibility and the question of how far the idea of the liberal university has ever had a straightforward sense – agree thus far: it is no good simply trying to revive Newman. Barnett wants us to face up to the stark reality of the changing sociopolitical context. The university, he suggests, must be more epistemologically generous and imaginative in the range of knowledge frameworks it admits, live at ease with epistemological and ontological mayhem, and develop in its students the competences necessary for purposeful living and prosperity. Sometimes, through its subjugation to the state's interests or through its willing submission to market forces, the contemporary university seems to have severed any commitment to universal reason. But Barnett suggests a more sanguine reading of the situation: that the interconnection of the globalized world may herald an age of global communicative reason.

A certain starkness of tone here, however, prompts us to see the situation in unduly polarized terms. Resistance to the economic imperative should not prevent us from recognizing that private or entrepreneurial institutions sometimes succeed not only in promoting academic excellence but in sustaining the best liberal education. Neither private interests nor those of the state need necessarily be so constricting.

Stark also is the discussion of the loss of faith in universal reason and the suspicion toward metanarratives. Postmodernism and universality, Barnett writes, are polar opposites. When Derrida ponders the nature of responsibility, the very possibility of any fruitful – that is, general or universal – idea is ruled out in advance by the very terms of the genre in which he is working. Yet some nonuniversal practices – customs and traditions, for example – scarcely make sense without some responsibility being incumbent on participants. It is a metaphysical presupposition, as Wittgenstein amply illustrates, to suppose that there must be some underlying universal that makes sense of such responsibility. Furthermore, recognition of the coherence of local practice casts light on the diversity of subjects, orientations, and paradigms within the academy, and the conflicts between them. What is critical for Derrida (or Lyotard) is the avoidance of that passing up of the responsibility for judgement in favor of reference to settled rules and edicts. This should surely be true of the kind of responsibility that is held by teachers and researchers in the university. There are rules to be learned and practices into which one must become initiated, but they must be directed towards the focusing of particular critical questions, questions that are the dynamic and *raison d'être* of what is taught. Criticism implies judgement.

There is a starkness also in the diagnosis of the situation that confronts us as mayhem or supercomplexity. On the face of it these two do not appear the same, but in *Realizing the University* Barnett makes clear what he has in mind. While hypercomplexity is an expansion, supercomplexity is a higher order of complexity in which our frameworks for understanding the world are themselves problematic or conflicting, our strategies for handling that complexity are themselves in question, and our frameworks are continually tested and challenged. In conditions of supercomplexity metanarratives do not disappear but proliferate and compete. The retreat to rules, both epistemological and operational, is then for the faint-hearted. Barnett's avowed realism about these challenges becomes almost gleeful, it seems, in the acceptance of such egalitarian mayhem. The chaos and pandemonium that characterize this condition require that the university should in some degree be chaotic in response (Barnett, 2000, pp. 130 ff.). Yet competition between frameworks, their being put in question, is not tantamount to chaos or mayhem. Responsibility in Derrida and Lyotard suggests something less dramatic but more subtle and rigorous.

In spite of the boldness of Barnett's approach to these problems, however, there is apparent in the text a certain equivocation over questions of value that seems to echo the widely held contemporary belief that, in the absence of universality, all value judgements are merely subjective. Thus, the explicitly value-laden[3] nature of Newman's writing would be unlikely to be taken seriously today; the recommended competences to live purposefully and to prosper "hide value judgements"; and the change that is heralded from universality to global communicative reason, a movement from the *a priori* to the empirical, reflects a willing deferral of such matters. Epistemological generosity becomes disabling relativism when it requires us to see everyone as a producer of knowledge (or "knowledges"?) and arbiter of her or his own values. *Without value judgements the university would disappear*, as for that matter would all our institutions. While these cannot and should not always be made explicit, their absence leaves the way open to usurpation by ideology (in the derogatory sense of that term).

Barnett rightly draws attention to two features of texts such as Newman's – their accessibility to the general reader and their freedom from the constraints that subsequent institutionalization and specialization were to impose. But it is another discourse that currently threatens the university. This is a technicist language that extends through policy and into research in education, whose ardent claims of rigor and reasonableness constitute a bland yet insidious rhetoric. Buttressed too often by hastily adopted theories in the psychology of learning, by managerialism, by glib notions of quality and accountability, and by an evangelical and largely uncritical approach to the possibilities of information and communication technology,[4] these texts adopt a characteristically inclusive tone – "widening participation and excellence," "social inclusion and standards" – designed to "take on board" (and therefore neutralize) any possible objection. And they have their characteristic graphic forms: numbered paragraphs, bullet points, appendices, and summary sections, the only ones that busy people are likely to read. A complement to these rhetorical forms is found in the efforts of educational research to affirm its credentials as a fully fledged technology of teaching and learning. Academics today in both the sciences and the arts generally line up against this new discourse; understandably it deepens their skepticism about educational theory and research.

To diagnose a prevailing malaise in the university (performativity) is not to erect a new metanarrative, any more than is the attempt to characterize some of its best practice in terms of the University of Beauty. This latter term takes off from the contrast between the beautiful and the sublime (and hence by contradistinction to the University of the Sublime that Lyotard's later work might be thought to recommend). It has nothing to do with "the beauty of the eternal order." Rather it is Dionysian in spirit: not cool contemplation but the intensity that can sometimes be found – in the fascination of the engineer, the student's absorption as the metaphysical conceit unfolds, rapt delight in a mathematical proof, the characteristic puzzlement of philosophy. Such experience may be high points in the kind of study that goes on in a university. It could not always be like this. I have already said that I see no necessary incompatibility between the kinds of experience alluded to here and that more somber experience of the sublime. No incompatibility, that is, in the sense that such experiences can coexist within the same course or in the same student's experience, alongside no doubt more humdrum but sometimes necessary aspects of study. Thoughts such as these are readily obliterated in the homogenized language that is fast becoming the norm in the discussion of higher education. But they should not remain silent when it comes to deciding what is to count as a standard or as quality, what is fit for study in higher education.

IV

The Western university is eight hundred years old. As many are happy to point out, Clark Kerr drew attention to the fact that European universities constitute together the largest social institution that has substantial longevity. Of the hundred or so social institutions that survive since medieval times, some 70 are universities. Against this background, it is hardly surprising if those whose identities are constituted by and in the world of universities come to consider that universities sustain traditions and values that are worthwhile. Such members of that world have, by definition, rather a lot invested in it. It is not surprising, too, if it is felt, in the face of apparent forms of destablization, that the traditions and values of universities nevertheless are worth retaining and defending.

This picture of the sociohistorical context of contemporary texts about the university conjured from *within* the university is certainly crude but it helps us here, I think. There are many points of agreement between Paul Standish and myself but the points of disagreement can be understood through a sociohistorical reading as much as through a philosophical one.

Let me pick out a few phrases from my codiscussant's contributions. In his rejoinder, we find the following: "there must be some underlying universal"; "without value judgements the university would disappear"; "[the] discourse that currently threatens the university"; "a prevailing malaise in the university"; "the intensity . . . in the fascination of the engineer, . . . rapt delight in a mathematical proof"; "the coherence of local practice . . . within the academy"; and "sustaining the best liberal education."

The messages are surely clear. The contemporary university is beseiged by malevolent forces that would destroy it. It appears that, too, we should beware of assuming that the university is uniform and has an integrity *in toto* but, even so, the different disciplines contain their own "customs and traditions" that contain coherent "local practices," and these practices – for their incumbents – can provide sources of personal delight and wonder. By hanging on to those local traditions, a University of Beauty can be maintained, even against the forces of chaos that threaten it.

I should like to buy this argument but I cannot do so as it stands. It would be good to believe that the university can still provide an epistemological haven where different disciplines can be pursued, their internal coherence and standards generating delight and beauty. Unfortunately, this is a picture that has to be abandoned. Standish takes me to task for saying it but I shall repeat the point: a liberal higher education is not straightforwardly available any longer, either conceptually or empirically. But this is not to jettison the idea of a liberal higher education altogether. It is just possible to hang on to the idea in other ways.

First, though, the picture that we are given does have to be abandoned. Empirically, we can point to the weakening of the boundaries with which disciplines have surrounded themselves. The boundaries are not yet dissolved but they are weakening. As the university has come into the world, and has run against the practical problems of the world, epistemic resources are now culled as such to meet the challenges posed. The challenges may be theoretical in nature but call for cross-disciplinary resources. Genetics as a knowledge practice, for example, becomes a hybrid, poised between biology, microbiology, chemistry, agriculture, and even sociology, philosophy, and economics. Knowledge becomes knowledges: the practices of the midwife, to take another example, are interrogated to reveal a manifold of knowledges of a personal, ethical, emotional, interpersonal, and dexterous character alongside more cognitive knowledges. Nor is it the case that these are held separate from each other: an understanding of them as midwifery knowledges can only be gained by understanding their intersections and exchanges.

Gibbons and his colleagues (1994) have spoken of Mode 2 knowledge – knowledge-in-situ – coming to rival Mode 1 – knowledge-in-the-academy. The story is right in principle, namely that there are more knowledges than those that are recognized in the academy and that many of them have their own worthwhileness. The story, however, is deficient in that it does not go far enough. First, in a knowledge society, there are multiple knowledges, not just two. Secondly, in a knowledge society, by definition, knowledge is produced universally, and the resultant knowledges interact with those in the academy. Inevitably, therefore, the boundaries of knowledge within the academy weaken. This is hardly surprising for the processes of boundary creation and boundary maintenance in the university are symptoms of an age (in the UK, most of the twentieth century) in which the academics were licensed by the state to order their affairs in their own interests.

Conceptually, too, the picture that Paul Standish offers us has to be placed in question. It relies on a sense that the Western university remains sure of its foundations. The phrases are telling: "There must be some underlying universal"; there are "certain critical questions" to be asked; "[the] discourse that currently threatens the university"; and "sustaining the best liberal education." These phrases are surely an indication of a hanging-on (in the context of the university) to an interlinked set of conceptual underpinnings that Standish has elsewhere himself, with others, done much to demolish. The idea that "there must be some underlying universal" is now at least so much in question in contemporary philosophy that the safety of the "must" is no longer available to us. We do not have to declare that we are in a postfoundational age in a bold assertive sense; but we are in a postfoundational age in that any metaphysical assuredness is now denied to us if only because we live in a literate age, an age of mass higher education indeed, in which de facto there are numerous competing philosophies, some of which *are* postfoundational in character.

Correspondingly, the notion that there might be a "discourse that . . . threatens the university" assumes just that which is in question, namely that there is a discourse with which we can identify the university, but one of the stories of poststructuralism is that no discourse can claim superiority. Further, the notion of "the *best* liberal education" implies a pretty determinate idea as to the character of liberal education and what it might look like in its highest form. The idea of liberal education may still be able to serve as a regulative ideal but we should be cautious before implying that there is a consensus as to its character and that it is still available to us in the contemporary world (even granted such a consensus).

Rorty's (1999) notion of hope is perhaps alluring: let us live in hope; let us read the world *as if* liberal education were possible. Such an orientation, however, is not going to be adequate to its task. The age of supercomplexity that now surrounds us is an age not just of proliferating, messy (and often ugly), and competing discourses; it is an age in which those discourses are of unequal weight. Many are also ideological in the pejorative sense: they would seek to vanquish liberal agendas. Mere hope is a recipe for nonliberal forces to capture the high ground.

Realizing the university in an age of supercomplexity calls for resilience, courage, and a determination to continue to work in support of an ideal of the university, even if it can never be either fully grounded or achieved. In turn, this means taking the fight outwards, engaging with the wider society, and partly on its terms. The drawbridge cannot be pulled up. The Western university, insofar as it stood for a total institution, sure of itself and of its powers to delight through its internal discourses, is at an end, its discourses awash with those of the wider society. The options are either to be overrun or to engage in the messy ground of society's discourses and expanding knowledges and ontologies. It is for the university to become itself supercomplex in character not only in its epistemologies but also in its ontologies. It is for the university to live neither in hope nor in internal aesthetic wonder but in a creative, persistent, and open endeavor of engagement with all around it.

Notes

1 For an elaboration of the idea of the Dionysian in relation to teaching and learning, see Blake et al. (2000).
2 A parallel view of the university was developed by Marjorie Reeves (1988) in laying weight on the idea of "delight."
3 Barnett also uses the term ideological "in the positive sense of that term."
4 See, for example, the MacFarlane Report (CSUP, 1992).

Recommendations for Further Reading

Bearn, G. (2000) The university of beauty, in P. Dhillon and P. Standish (eds.) *Educating after Lyotard*, Routledge.

Delanty, G. (2001) *Challenging Knowledge: The University in the Knowledge Society*, Open University Press.

Readings, B. (1996) *The University in Ruins*, Harvard University Press.

Wortham, S. (1999) *Rethinking the University: Leverage and Deconstruction*, Manchester University Press.

Chapter 13

Information and Communication Technology

David Blacker and Jane McKie

Educational Technology as Revealing and Concealing

Educational technology can extend our capabilities. It can enable us to teach larger numbers over greater distances online, gain economic efficiencies for local educational authorities and entrepreneurs, and provide wider and more meaningful access to larger and more diverse populations. Such goals are important and they rightly partake of a great deal of the public spotlight. Yet technology can do much more than quantitatively extend what we already do. Heightened technological innovation and implementation – particularly of the pervasiveness and pace with which we are experiencing it today – raises the stakes for education even more fundamentally through its effect upon basic questions of value. Any technology has the potential to raise questions and alter the answers we give (implicit or explicit) concerning the nature, meaning, and moral worth of the educational enterprise itself.

We say "potential" because technology does not always have such illuminative effects. In a given setting, technology may just as easily obscure and stultify as enlighten and educate. The design ideal of "user-friendliness," for example, may require less and less skill and effort from its "interfacing" human beings, as value choices and conceptual horizons are to a greater extent prestructured into the tools. After a few icon touches, the high tech cash register at McDonald's calculates and dispenses customers' change all but automatically. Yet in doing so it requires very little from the employee, far less than did the less efficient machines of yesteryear, some of which called upon the mathematical skills of the user. Such technological effects may be antieducative, complicit in a situation of deskilling or, in a classroom, a mind-numbing rote transmission of information to the exclusion of all else. So there is nothing *inherently* educative about technology, high-tech or low; it is an entirely contingent matter whether or not a given technology is educative or not. Consequently, we submit that the phrase "educational technology" should be understood less as an objective description of some inert feature of the world – the hardware and software lying about – and more clearly as an *aspiration*, a prescription whose realization depends upon the skill of teachers and the will of learners to bring the "educational" and the "technology" together. Insofar as education itself has value, technology enters into the philosophy of education as both an intellectual and moral challenge.

John Dewey and Martin Heidegger help us to see key aspects of this challenge. Dewey writes: "A tool is a particular thing, but it is more than a particular thing, since it is a thing in which a connection, a sequential bond of nature is embodied. It possesses an objective relation as its own defining property. Its perception as well as its actual use takes the mind to other things" (Dewey, [1925] 1981, p. 101; see also Blacker, 1993). This insight into how technology affects the quality of our experience – how it "takes the mind to other things" is strikingly complementary to Heidegger's often-discussed "existential analysis" of everyday activities involving tools that are "ready-to-hand." As one hammers along in order, say, to build the children a dollhouse, the project is given significance by the end in view (the dollhouse), its primary goal (delighting the kids), along with secondary goals (e.g., saving some money as compared to the toystore version, savoring a rare moment or two alone as one works, etc.). In a sense, one is lost for a time within these experiential horizons, a world of one's own *personal* functional relations, the relays being connected via these "in-order-to's" (Heidegger, 1962, pp. 116f.). The point is that the materiality of the hammer recedes from conscious awareness in favor of a dynamic world of meaningful involvements, ever expanding and contracting. One strives to make one's children happy because being a father demands it, as does one's place within the family. Perhaps, as one hammers along building the dollhouse, one is driven by guilt for having forgotten a birthday last week, or by fear of being branded a bad parent. Ultimately, according to Heidegger, if pursued tenaciously and far enough, a questioning of these in-order-to's will help highlight what one cares most deeply for, one's larger purposes. However far down this road one may travel, though, the activity of hammering along (or whatever one does, from arranging the furniture to teaching kindergarten to contemplating one's own death) is necessarily ensconced in a web of involvements whose significance is limited only by one's capacity, perhaps one's courage, for self-reflection.

This in essence is how technology presents its moral challenge to educators. The key Heideggerian–Deweyan insight is that technologies essentially "hide" themselves in their functioning, insofar as they are actually functioning. When they are working smoothly toward their assigned ends, they neither present themselves as problems nor even, really, as *things* at all. My word processing program does not stand out for me as an object of my explicit attention unless I encounter some problem with it, or maybe if I aestheticize or fetishize it upon a new purchase (gazing lovingly at the packaging and so on). It may stand out as an object for me, but it does not insofar as it is functioning within the context I have circumscribed for it, that is, insofar as it is truly behaving like a tool, rather than some *thing* that needs to be made (or returned) to proper tool status. When it is working, one doesn't bother oneself with the tool as such. Rather, one bothers oneself with the project at hand, whatever that may be. Thus technology "takes the mind to other things." The job of the educator is to examine this mind-taking, the manner in which it is conducted, the "things" to which it is taking those minds. All teaching involves at some level drawing attention to something in particular, which necessarily means drawing attention to that particular thing to the exclusion (at least for that moment) of certain other things. And this is precisely what it means to say that technologies simultaneously reveal and conceal, and that in this they are inextricably tied to education. By structuring experience, they educate (or miseducate) whether we intend them to or not.

As Don Ihde has described, utilizing technologies – from the simplest to the most complex – at the same time both extends and atrophies our experiential range (Ihde, 1990, pp. 74–80). Consider using a stick to shake loose apples from a tree. The stick extends one's reach while also diminishing the tactile and other sensations surrounding unaided apple picking. The telephone obviously greatly extends our communicative range, but at the cost of diminishing many germane features of face-to-face conversation: gesticulations, facial expressions, other subtle bodily and visual cues. (Anyone whose humorous, sarcastic, or ironic intentions have been misread in an e-mail message is familiar with a current manifestation of this phenomenon, the proliferation of sentence-concluding "emoticons," so placed to avoid misunderstandings that would have been unlikely had the conversation been face-to-face or via telephone.) This revealing-concealing structure of technology is inescapable and it is basic to considering the educative use of technology. One's blackboard-written graphic may help the lesson along. But even so, in order to use the technology, one has to turn one's back on one's students to write, interrupt the flow of a conversation in order to "freeze" some element of it on the board, or draw students' minds to a spatial representation of something that some of them may have been conceiving (or on the way to conceiving) differently. More dramatically, consider the listening systems often used in classrooms to assist hard of hearing students. These devices "take" the hard of hearing students' minds to the auditory world rather than the visual world of sign language. This is not to say that students cannot become fluent in both worlds, but only that the choice of the assistant technology is also a pedagogical choice of which world to emphasize at that moment for that child.

For the educator, there is presumably a strong imperative toward the revealing moment of this dual revealing-concealing phenomenon rather than the concealing one, though both moments are always present in some measure. Encountered in the proper way, even simple technologies can catalyze self-understanding to unforeseen depths, while they simultaneously conceal much from view. This double aspect of technology is a central insight around which may be built not only descriptions but also a normative account that links technology with educational experience. For it shows how certain pedagogical directions are always being taken, consciously or not: what to reveal and conceal, in what measure and by what method. In the manner of the Platonic noble lie, should some things be hidden from the children "for their own good"? Or, perhaps in the name of "freedom," should the educator eschew all concealments and pursue an unmitigated commitment to pure revelation: *any* information to *any* children at *any* time? Either extreme is of course problematic. But if one grants that, on the whole, education, as opposed to training, indoctrination, and the like, has much more to do with revealing worlds of involvement than it does with closing them off (certainly in the long run), one may generate an imperative for educators to orient themselves toward technology such that the latter are allowed to reveal worlds in as open-ended a manner as possible, with the qualification "as possible" a necessary recognition of the undesirability of absolute revelation. Teaching is not simply opening the faucets full blast. We may, for example, want to use a software program to filter pornography and violence from the screens viewed by our seven year olds, just as reasonable parents filter the experiences of their children in reasonable ways generally. Yet at the same time, we worry about concealing too much from the learner, a censoring of experience that may atrophy or otherwise diminish especially young learners' future capabilities. Good educators must see now more clearly than ever how central is this problem if assessing whether, in the long run and considering the whole of what people value in their lives, a given educational technology reveals more than it conceals.

Philosophy can help educators find a more compelling vocabulary for faulting, say, a curriculum too laden with software "drill and practice" programs on the grounds that, while they may well effectively disclose how to accomplish certain narrowly defined tasks, the overall effect may be to shut out much, much more – largely by concealing the predetermined pathways along which such programs must run. One may learn to factor quadratic equations like a pro while also "learning" that education itself is accumulating information, has end-points, and is generally something to be got over with. The problem here lies not with the transmission of useful information *per se*, but with the mode of transmission's diminishment of one's ability to initiate learning in wider and alien contexts; no sum of overly narrow microworlds can match the dynamic, ever-expanding and edifying capacity to go on revealing one's own life-world. Educators cannot be neutral about this. Though it is always necessary to make strategic pedagogical choices regarding the proper time, place, and manner of the revealing, the educator has to take sides and favor the revealing side of the equation. Norms internal to the enterprise demand this moral stance. The educational process ceases to be such insofar as it is geared toward such things as deception, obfuscation, or a lessening of the learner's capacities for further learning. Yet this moral allegiance to the revelatory aspect of technology is underappreciated and underdeveloped among educators. We need, in a way, to catch up normatively with what the technology is showing us about ourselves.

We believe there are two main initial orders of business along these lines, and philosophy is crucial to both of them. First is taking conceptual stock of the basic assumptions we have allowed to undergird our understanding of educational technology – the conflicted ways in which we have come to think of what technology really *is* at bottom, our ontological assumptions about it, in a phrase. Second, and more urgent, is that of examining how our own sense of what we are doing as educators is changing along with the new technologies, even altering such basic matters as how we view the relationship among education, work, and play. We will pursue both of these agendas to explore in turn, first, how inherited ontological assumptions have framed our understanding of educational technology and, second, how a fuller realization of the nature of technology may invite a reconsideration of much that we have taken for granted about education's social and moral purposes.

Ontological Assumptions

Theoretical accounts of technology generally may be characterized as adhering in varying degrees to what we will call a *structural ambiguity of common sense*.[1] Our common-sense intuitions regarding technological phenomena are beset with a deep and internal contradiction, an underlying ambivalence that oscillates within our everyday practices and attitudes. On the one hand, we experience tools as things that we *use*; we regard them as morally neutral in the sense that they seem to await a human purpose to animate them with moral life (e.g., a sharp blade may injure me as well as dice my carrots). Someone or other is always at the helm, so it seems, deciding through some willful act the uses to which the tool is put. Though intentions and outcomes vary tremendously, human beings are, in the final analysis, behind it all, somewhere and somehow.

But on the other hand, it also seems that we are positively awash with technologies that we must constantly keep up with by adjusting our lives to *them* rather than the other way around. We may make superficial consumer choices about, say, an office computer, but today's businesses do not need first to determine whether or not to have one at all, any more than they do about their telephone system. It is not up to us personally – or to anyone in particular – whether or not networked computers are increasingly necessary to mediate everyday human interactions. One becomes acquainted with the relevant devices at work, at home, or in school, in order to keep pace. It seems as if the technology is doing the advancing and that we, the human beings, are the ones hopping alongside trying to keep up; the technological tail wags the human dog. In such experiences, and undoubtedly against our more considered judgement, we begin to endow technology with a certain agency, proceeding as if *it* does things in the world, things that we must react to in various ways. Technologies are thus often regarded as the bearers of intentions and are encountered via what Daniel Dennett calls the "intentional stance" (e.g., "my car doesn't want to start," "the computer won't let me do that") (Dennett, 1987, pp. 13–34, 49–53, 69–80). But all the while we go on *using* tools and techniques, for somehow it still seems that they are simply at mine or someone's service. Hence the relevant intuitions conflict and, until they are sorted out reflectively, our overall attitude is justly characterized as profoundly ambiguous.

Much of the thinking on technology and education reflects this underlying ambiguity. To borrow from the schema Albert Borgmann uses to classify theories of technology generally, the relevant educational literature may be classified into two main groups, corresponding to the two poles of common sense and the ontologies implicit in them: "substantive" and "instrumental" (Borgmann, 1984, pp. 9–12). As we will illustrate, important further distinctions are to be made within both categories.[2]

Substantive theories of technology stem from the common-sense intuition that technology is to a great extent an autonomous force, one that shapes us much more than we shape it. Substantivism often betrays a commitment to a kind of technological determinism in providing a picture wherein technology itself is the primary motive force within most, if not all, spheres of human activity.

An uncompromising proponent of substantivism is the French theologian and sociologist Jacques Ellul, who regarded *la technique* as an all-embracing and evil power that has come to enslave all our endeavors, from art and politics to education (Ellul, 1964, pp. 3–22). In contemporary educational theory, a view of this sort was first defended by C. A. Bowers, who holds that "the technological mindset" – a "unique configuration of thought and social practice that emerged in the West over the last two to three hundred years" – is now so deeply seated in our culture that it determines almost every aspect of contemporary pedagogical practice (Bowers, 1982, p. 530).[3] This technological mindset is so pervasive that major school reform movements have been all but helplessly contained within it, doomed merely to advance "its" cause. For Bowers, in order to recover or even imagine a truly human vision of education, it is first necessary somehow to step outside this mindset. (The question of how one "steps outside" of a pervasive mindset is unanswered.) An earlier and more general version of this view derives from the Frankfurt School and describes the root cause of technology's dominance as a creeping "instrumental reason," a *sub rosa* ideology that increasingly dominates all forms of social and personal life by subverting the legitimacy of public discussion concerning the *ends* of human activity, leaving only talk about *means*.[4]

Substantive theories of technology, however, also admit of a very different attitude toward this allegedly autonomous force, one that welcomes it with an often messianic fervor. Possessors of this attitude include the breathless technology advocates so heavily represented among the news media, the software designers who dream of "teacher-proofing" instruction, the odd self-anointed "tech guru" (academic or not), and, increasingly, the "true believer" academic administrator responding to consumer demand. These protechnology substantivists hold that technology is the key to better schools and better education; it can and will break down traditional barriers to effective and successful school reform (including, conveniently, teacher unions and the like). If we only would follow wherever technological innovation leads, we cannot go astray. One such jeremiad at the beginning of the networked age in schools exhorts, "Some can regret the change, but they cannot reverse it; and others . . . can welcome it and work to fulfil it" (McClintock, 1988, p. xiii). A popular critic during the same period insists, "[t]echnology is the most purely human of humanity's features, and it is the driving force of human society," predicting that "the nations that stop trying to 'reform' their education and training institutions and choose instead to totally replace them with a brand-new, high-tech learning system will be the world's economic powerhouses through the twenty-first century" (Perelman, 1992, pp. 25, 20). Technology can and should end schooling as we know it. For educators, there is not even really a choice: either we tag along as closely as we can, or we lose individually and nationally in the global marketplace.

Neither worshipful nor fearful, the second major category, instrumentalism, builds upon the founding common-sense intuition that technologies are merely tools that human beings use in order to achieve the purposes we assign to them. Powerful proof for this is that technologies have always been and are everywhere part of the human story to extend the capacities of given individuals or cultures, for good or ill. The bumper-sticker slogan "guns don't kill people, people kill people" hits the mark. Individual or collective human agency is the locus of all valuation and therefore not the device itself, but its causal ensconcement in a social context, is the proper target for inquiry.

In education, instrumentalism may be described as protechnology when it is relatively sanguine about the beneficial uses to which various technologies can be put. A prescient early exponent of this view was Seymour Papert, developer of the seminal LOGO programming language for use in school classrooms. In his classic book, *Mindstorms*, Papert argues that children learning to program in LOGO can develop "powerful ideas" for problem solving that can, he contends, transfer to many other areas of life: "What is most important in this is that through these experiences the children would be serving their apprenticeships as epistemologists, that is to say learning to think articulately about thinking" (Papert, 1980, p. 27). Despite his enthusiasm about his invention, however, Papert is no substantivist. He does not believe that the pedagogical benefit of LOGO resides in what it *does to* children, but rather in the kind of control it requires children to take over it. Children should encounter computers in the classroom as "objects to think with," and he argues explicitly against what he calls "technocentric thinking." One must attend to the culture suffusing the classroom first, and on that basis train teachers to use classroom technologies properly.

As distinct from Papert's more sanguine view, instrumentalism is driven by a suspicion about technology insofar as it considers present usage to be overwhelmingly driven by morally suspect motives; technology is problematic, but *only as it is currently employed*. Technology's liberatory potential awaits significant societal change. Most instrumentalism of this type in education has been Marxist in provenance and takes the form of sociopolitical critique. Following Andrew Feenberg's philosophical statement of this general position, it might be called a "critical theory of technology" (CTT) (Feenberg, 1991).

CTT typically regards all other views of technology as so many smokescreens behind which certain social groups, usually identified as the patriarchy, the capitalists, or some other cultural elite, advance their agendas of domination. A focus on the tools themselves aids in maintaining privilege by deflecting critical scrutiny away from the real motive forces of society, namely, the economy and those who control it.

In educational theory, two more or less distinct levels of CTT may be identified. First-level CTT corresponds to a straightforwardly unreconstructed Marxist analysis. The most direct statement of first-level CTT in education, Bowles and Gintis's classic *Schooling in Capitalist America*, suggests that, like schooling, technology essentially functions as a superstructural variable dependent upon the economic base of society and those who control it. Though allowing for a certain amount of dialectical interplay between base and superstructure, Bowles and Gintis nonetheless counsel that technology itself is mostly beside the point: "If meaningful educational reform requires a transformation of production relations, as we believe, we must begin by creating a new social structure, not a new technology" (Bowles and Gintis, 1976, p. 69). One does not liberate today's oppressive classroom by altering its physical structure, but rather by teaching liberating things for tomorrow's liberated society. Second-level CTT shares with the Marxist view the contention that at present technology serves elite groups and that the task of a radical pedagogy is to uncover how and why this happens. But it differs markedly by not regarding tech-nology as a *neutral* tool in the service of hegemonic power; technology as currently constituted is nonneutral in its demonstrably prejudicial *effects* that privilege some groups at the expense of others.[5] Elites not only use technology as a club, but also to conceal that there is any clubbing going on at all. It provides a perfect weapon, effective yet invisible. And the more value-neutral we regard it, the more invisible it becomes.

Consider ostensibly innocuous notions such as "technological" or "computer literacy." What harm could come from learning to use computers? As it turns out, a great deal: to take just one example, the aim of educating for high tech fosters a climate of bogus credentialing providing the ideological cover for the disenfranchise-ment of certain groups. Yesterday's reading test for custodians is today's "computer experience" for all types of employment. Yet, there are ample grounds to challenge the idea that on the whole work in a high-tech society requires any substantive notion of "technological literacy" at all. Given the "user-friendly" trajectory of business machines and the deskilling and further fragmentation of labor in the wake of automation (not to mention unemployment in areas outside the corporate loop, such as many inner-city and Third World regions), in the vast majority of cases, working "in contact" with high tech does not really demand knowing anything much about it. The above-noted McDonald's cashier indeed "works with" high-tech cash registers, but this hardly entails a higher degree of knowledge about technology. If anything, it demands *less*. That there are so many such examples adds evidence that the drive toward technological literacy seems not to serve any legitim-ate economic need. Rather, some other agenda, a deep ideological one serving certain identifiable interests, must be driving it. It is not as simple as "change society and technology will follow," for the latter has become too thoroughly interwoven with the former.

Despite its revelatory potential, however, second-level CTT harbors significant dangers. These have mostly to do with the outlook's potential for slipping into a more or less indoctrinating stance. Consistently framing one's role in the classroom as one of unmasking power relations implies that one possesses an unassailable social ontology "up" to which one must educate one's students. Yet as one liberates from a putatively false consciousness toward the truth, one also tends to disable a more open-ended and, in our view, richer pedagogy – one that remains in a meaningful way open to students' differing and even deeply challenging interpretations – in a word a more truly *dialogical* pedagogy, where entering into a dialogue while pre-supposing the correct answer tends to limit the experience. Presupposing the truth in this manner, particularly when it comes to inherently controversial sociopolitical critique, tends to commit one to a deeply conservative transmission-of-truths-oriented pedagogy, short-circuiting a richer, more open-ended notion of what edu-cation can be.

The ontologies implicit in instrumentalism and substantivism locate them on opposite ends of the ambiguous spectrum of our culture's common sense. While both stances yield insight, driving them further also reveals their limitations. Each position has its strengths: the substantive conviction that technology can, in a man-ner of speaking, take on a life of its own, as well as the instrumentalist impulse to contextualize it within the intentions and effects it mediates. But it is also necessary to avoid the excesses and lacunae to which the two views are prone: the take it or leave it *en bloc* blackmail of substantivism, and instrumentalism's blinding zeal to name *the* one and only force behind it all. A better account of technology in education must incorporate the strengths while also avoiding the corrupted counterparts. Such an account would develop a more open-ended view that recognizes how our worlds of involvement have changed without sacrificing the conviction that actual human beings will continue to define the significance of those changes in all their nuance and contradictoriness. Tools *per se* will never provide our reasons, hopes, and fears. But they are in deep alliance with our attempts to make sense of ourselves and our educational endeavors.

Critical Themes for Education

It is time to turn more directly to the specific significance of this technology for education. The questions raised by information and communication technology (ICT) in education are multiple, and there are two main dangers in the way that they are currently addressed. Among practitioners there is a tendency toward an evangelism that accepts uncritically the potential of the computer as a tool in the classroom. The pages of the educational press carry endless articles and special supplements that exhort teachers and educational managers to exploit the new technology and that sometimes seem bewitched by its technical appeal. A different tendency is found in more theoretical writings on education where the focus is longer term and inevitably more speculative. Here the literature seems to have picked up on a *fin de siècle* anxiety (or perhaps a new millennial euphoria) regarding the ways in which the Internet changes personal identity. Our aim here is to emulate neither of these tendencies but to highlight matters of more immediate practical importance in a critical way. We highlight here six main facets of ICT in education that require philosophical examination, following which we proceed to a more extended consideration of the significance of ICT for our conceptions of work and play.

First, what happens to knowledge when it becomes information? There is now an extensive literature addressing the prominence of information in late modernity. While some have appeared to accept this as part of the sea-change of late modernity, others have drawn attention to reductivist tendencies at work here (for example, Midgley, 1989). In terms of its impact on education, Jean-François Lyotard's *The Postmodern Condition* (1984) is widely read though it is arguable that the theme is pursued in more depth elsewhere in his writings. Criticism of the performativity of contemporary educational practice that highlights its reduction of knowledge in this way is now familiar enough (see, for example, Lankshear et al., 2000). Similarly, the naivety of imaging that the World Wide Web is something like a superlibrary has been clearly exposed (see Conlon, 1997). The conception of learning as centrally involving information and the skills to access it has been a feature of contemporary conceptions of lifelong learning. This has been given a specifically political color in the idea of the "digital divide," a new rift in society between those who are computer literate and have online access and those who do not. One dimension of this political prominence can be seen in Microsoft's great interest in making us believe that we must be educated to compete in the newly globalized world with its knowledge economy. The marketing of Microsoft becomes a factor in the political: there is political mileage in being seen to be in favor of ICT because such a stance borrows some of its appeal from the advertisements themselves. Access to the technology undoubtedly is important, but these particular orientations of learning and social inclusion involve in turn, we suggest, a reductivist conception of the political.

A second related factor concerns the so-called "attention economy." This is germane not only to the capacity for learning of children (and older students) but to the ways in which we have increasingly to cope with all the information that calls for our attention in our ordinary lives. It places a premium on novelty and militates against contemplation and concentration, and the intense absorption that can, as we shall argue below, be a crucial part of rich educational experience. Educational practice colludes with this in its anxiety for greater effectiveness, understood as quicker throughput.

A third aspect concerns more or less metaphysical problems related to the phenomenology of Internet use. The screen is instantly refreshable and framed, and concentration on what it shows amplifies the visual sense to the comparative neglect of the others. Surfing, so-called, is nothing like surfing on the sea-waves: the flow is not continuous but punctuated by clicks and hence sudden changes, along paths that are predetermined (at some level) by the designers of links (see Burbules, 1997). It may be that this more frenetic experience usurps the place of flow that is found in some aspects of our lives with profound effects on the kinds of thinking and being that are available to us. (Think of Wordsworth as a boy running through the woods at Tintern Abbey, and as an adult recreating that experience in the imagination.) The use of the Web might then make us come to see the world as always already marked with its pathways and gates and windows. (Degenerate forms of computer use in education reduce the experience to programmed learning.) Moreover, there are more obvious questions to be addressed about the kind of social experience that is had – at home in solitude at a computer, in a "learning center" surrounded by scores of other learners working alone at computers, socially with others online. The possibilities here defy easy classification and they depend on the detail of the engagement that is taking place.

A fourth facet has to do with the dovetailing of ICT with the rhetoric of student-centeredness. ICT makes it possible to provide individually tailored learning paths that are available to students as and when they want to follow them. This is part of the burgeoning industry of open learning. But the progressivist impetus to this is oddly in line with the agenda of "efficiency" and "quality control." ICT then seems to meet the aspirations not only of educators committed to student-centeredness but also of managerialism. It hastens the commodification of education and, in a further reduction, the conversion of the student into a customer. The point is not that it inevitably does this but that this is the way that it is being taken up, and the reasons for this are fairly easy to see.

Much contemporary discussion of the educational potential of ICT tends to focus on the World Wide Web, but the Internet is broader than this. Accordingly our fifth concern is with the obvious educational potential of e-mail (including chat rooms, bulletin boards, lists, and the like). It is worth acknowledging the special possibilities of communication and conversation this seems to generate, possibilities that should not be overlooked by the designers of curricula. To what extent is the playful open-endedness of e-mail to be exploited in education? How far, in contrast, will tightly controlled forms of quasi-programmed learning prevail? There are economic pressures here and these must not be allowed to decide the issue.[6]

The final point relates to a strand in philosophical thought concerning the Internet that connects with a deeper current of thought that can be found in Nietzsche. Cyberfeminism has explored the possibility that ICT is ill-construed along masculine lines, that the technology of computing has always had a different side to it.[7] It is Nietzsche's account of the Dionysian (as opposed to the Appolonine) in *The Birth of Tragedy* that constitutes the deeper current of thought here, a current that is found also in the work of Lyotard (in *Libidinal Economy*) and Gilles Deleuze.[8] The emphasis in this thought in overcoming dialectical oppositions is a powerful antidote to many ways in which the modern world and its values have become structured, not least those in education itself. As such it is valuable in disturbing the relationship between work and play that has formed such a mainstay of the ways in which both modern industry and the institution of modern education have developed. It is to a closer examination of the dichotomy that we now turn.

Work and Play

These considerations point to the conclusion that there has been a reconfiguration of work and play in the contemporary world sufficient to redefine political forms of circulation and exchange. How would such changes affect the ways in which people come to define themselves? How would they affect education's relationship to democracy? That some sense of these changes waits in the wings of public consciousness, as it were, is perhaps suggested by a prominent article in the color supplement of *The Observer* in which Pat Kane calls for a new ethic for a new millennium – one founded in notions of play rather than work:

> This we know: we're stressed out, debt-ridden, exhausted. We have less time for our families than we feel we should have. We take fewer pleasures from our entertainments and consumptions than we expected to take. We feel less connected to our communities than we ever did. In our workplaces, we subject ourselves to routines and duties which at best seem pointless, at worst unethical or immoral. Yet we also feel like hollow citizens, too weary to respond to any political entreaty with anything other than a shrug. In short, we are workers.
>
> Yet why do we meekly accept this condition, when our brave new technological future – the amazing potential still to be unleashed in computers, genetics and molecular engineering – could change it utterly? Why, with all this power at our disposal, do we still feel like mere objects ourselves? (Kane, 2000, p. 20)

Kane attributes the potential to undermine the work ethic to technology, and in so doing picks up on a trend toward an association between technology and the legitimacy of play. This is partly a common-sense connection: computer games and networked sociability equal play. And it is partly a convergence with academic theory: the play within language exposed by post-structuralist theory is perhaps even more marked in an online context with its characteristic iconography and hyperlinks, and with the kind of word-play it facilitates.

We would like to ask two questions concerning the association between new technologies and play at the outset. First, to what extent are new developments in technology a precondition for undermining the work ethic? Second, might the way that the technological is bound up with everyday life also have the paradoxical and deleterious effect of rendering work inescapable?

In partial reply to the second question, Sherry Turkle acknowledges that the possibilities for self-reflection and transformation inherent in online engagement are profound. She singles out online role-playing: MUDs (multiuser dungeons or domains) blur the boundaries between self and game, self and role, self and simulation (Turkle, 1996, p. 192). On the face of it, they are quintessentially a moratorium, literally "time-out" to play: "Vacations give a finite structure to adult moratoria. Time in cyberspace reshapes the notion of vacations and moratoria because they may now exist in always available windows" (ibid., p. 204). However, apart from being a host to in-built moratoria, a home computer has potential to be a virtual office. Turkle implies that time out from our daily lives is enhanced by access to time online when we might be engaged in different activities with various time-frames associated with them. A varying intensity of focus may result in a disjunction between the perception of time passing and real (clock) time. Turkle has in mind particular sociable activities such as chat room style conversations and also solitary activities such as gaming. When we focus intensely on activities of this nature time seems to speed up and passes without our noticing. But is virtual game-time as fulfilling as time spent in real life diversions? Many questions about the quality and richness of interaction are raised and left unanswered.

The relation between work and play has structured our everyday sense of time. What we do, and when and where we do it, is fundamental to the construction of the lifeworld, and to our development as ethical beings. Specific values are accorded to activities depending in part on their definition in terms of this dichotomy. This is not just a matter of the moralism associated with an excessive emphasis on good time-keeping. Such values as utility, duty, effort, and perseverance, on the one hand, and pleasure, indulgence, imagination, and liberty, on the other, are clustered according to the dialectic between work and play. Although not opposites (effort can be a pleasure or be imaginative, for example), they are nevertheless placed in opposition according to the schism between work and play *in the abstract*. Their tension is inherent in their meanings. In reality, work can be playful or effortless, and one can work very hard at play in sporting and other arenas. Musicians work hard in order to play better, as do amateur and professional footballers alike. The bank manager comes home to do some work in the garden in the evening. The key insight here is that they dwell within each other, that the opposition deconstructs.

However, the polarity is not to be collapsed completely. If work simply becomes play, our categories cease to hold meaning for us. This is not to say that we should not accord more value to forms of play than we currently do; indeed we are going to argue for this later. But to turn work *into* play, to make no distinction between play and work *time*, would jeopardize the integrity and variety of our experiences.

A disruption or transformation of the dialectic between work and play would have repercussions in all arenas, including the educational. Can we imagine what some of the repercussions might be? Are they to be welcomed? Will new digital technologies in particular blur their boundaries? In order to address to what extent technological developments herald a redefinition of play, it is necessary to look more closely at modes of engagement with networks and applications, and, in particular, at the spirit in which these activities are carried out.

Educational software is sometimes referred to as "edutainment." The concept implies that educational "work" can be fun by marketing it as hybrid work/play. It trades off the dichotomy between work and play, but also undermines it. It is particularly pertinent that such software is frequently designed and marketed for home use. The domestic realm is the domain of play. But the fact that work masquerading as play is taking place within the home reinforces the popular view that an educationally rich environment at home supplements, or provides the background for, the type of learning that takes place at school (and by extension the adult workplace). This conflation of work and play in the home life of the child blurs the boundary between home and school as the site of education.

The construction of the domestic setting in such software is significant. The large text of the 1995 print advertisement for *Microsoft Fine Artist* reads, "if i tidy my room, can i be Picasso?" A joke that runs through the advertisement is the "trade-off" between a mother and son. "Mum" utilizes *Microsoft Fine Artist* as bargaining power: "If you want to play cubist and primarily concern yourself with abstract forms rather than lifelike representation that's fine with me," Mum says, "but only after you've tidied your room." Throughout the text there is the juxtaposition of childlike preoccupations and conventions with specialized art historical knowledge. "Play" here extends, as the smaller text tells us, to the way that the boy "became" an artist "for an hour or so." With the aid of his computer, the boy can slip in and out of identities at will.

This usage of "became" reinforces the suspension of disbelief common to childhood play: one *becomes* a cowboy or a trapeze artist or a doctor, one enters fully and joyfully into the scenario of the day, and this characteristically involves the play of the imagination. This suspension of disbelief is evocative of the fluidity of identity that Turkle (1996) experiences when she selects how best to represent herself on a personal Web page, "cycling through" different identities. It evokes the sea imagery of Robert Jay Lifton's (1993) notion of the *protean* self with its connotations of online navigation and immersion. "Multiple, differently experienced realities," in John Fiske's phrase (1996), somehow *come into focus* in an on-screen context. Phenomenologically, it reveals more about the nature of our presentations of self when we interact with others, and makes us pay attention to how this is realized in textual form. Life on or in the screen provides us not only with a new metaphor but with a new realization of the ambiguity of felt experience. The presence or absence of others, mood, context-specific behavioral norms – a variety of factors affects the foregrounding and concealing of aspects of personality, a revealing and concealing that is mirrored or even amplified in e-mail correspondence, chat rooms, and online cooperative games.

The advertisement for *Microsoft Fine Artist* introduces a "muse" in the eccentric and comic figure of McZee, " . . . who wears a Hawaiian shirt and a Davy Crockett hat and a kilt and plays the bagpipes." This muse "runs" the Fine Artist Museum and Gallery, acting as companion and commentator. McZee also presides over an allied software package called *Microsoft Creative Writer*. "And when I'm in the mood to be Shakespeare and write Hamlet 2, McZee helps me there too." When I'm in the *mood* to *be* Shakespeare – you can slip in and out of identities as the mood takes you, you can *be* Shakespeare.

Imagine a now familiar sight: a child in front of a monitor engaged in an "educational" computer game. She is held in thrall by the flickering images, much as a cinemagoer is entranced by a film. There is the same posture of absorption, the same openness to the play of sound and motion. But her involvement will be different in terms of the level and the nature of the interaction. What is the nature of this interaction? A number of different possibilities emerge – of intensity of focus, of frenetic activity, of listless browsing or frustrated searching, of clearly channeled or rigidly programmed activity, of creative play. Let us delineate two broad possibilities.

First, the package can be regarded as a substitute for a tutor, imparting knowledge and facilitating understanding. The user may make her own mistakes and receive either prompts or gentle admonishments. She may make "correct" assumptions on the basis of what she has been told and receive praise and admittance to the next stage. In this interpretation, the medium is also the message. The child is able to learn only by listening to her tutor present data drawn from a "storehouse" of knowledge. A second interpretation might cast the computer as an environment in which to encounter "objects to think with."[9] That computers are something more than tools is particularly evident with the development of CD ROMS and the Internet. We can then think of such environments as offering possibilities of experience in which discovery and play will be to the fore. Of course, these "instructionist" and "child-centered" interpretations of the interaction are arbitrarily separated. Elements of both are to be found in much educational software. What is clear, however, is that there are critical curriculum decisions to be made about the nature of the education that is desired in the incorporation of ICT into teaching and learning practices, and it should be recognized that the imperatives of efficient management may well seem to militate in favor of more programmatic methods. The revealing and concealing effects of technology, which we have emphasized throughout this chapter, suggest that a blindness to alternative possibilities may easily develop. It is important, therefore, to look beyond these possibilities to a deeper level at which the Internet may surreptitiously affect us.

With respect to the Internet specifically, the computer can be seen not as *the* medium, but almost as a (spiritual) medium: images drawn on the screen are eldritch communications from an etherealized beyond (where information "resides"), and the computer acts as amanuensis in transcribing the words and images that trigger understanding. The potency that the interface holds for the user can be read as an example of what Don Slater, writing of the diorama, describes as the successful magic of modernity:

> What we experience in successful magic is a sense of the power of technique over appearances, the ability to transform the material world (both representations and real objects) into a new reality. Yet, in a final twist, the technical achievement of realistic illusions itself mystifies technique: the magic show (or the diorama) is a demonstration of technical power, but not an explication of it. Two simultaneous senses of wonder are invoked: wonder at the experience of being transported into a fully realised unreal world; and wonder at the (incomprehensible, hidden) technology which makes it possible. (Slater, 1995, p. 219)

There is, then, something mysterious about the possibilities of connectivity that computer usage seems to promise. But it is easy to overlook the ways in which nontextual elements – the graphics and iconography and the operation of links[10] – themselves have subtle effects in contributing to the seductiveness of computer use. This seduction slips from an initial fascination with color, animation, sometimes sound, to a more anesthetizing familiarity as where the technical instrument "disappears" with accustomed usage. The icons themselves, with their friendly efficiency, draw us into engagement but gradually become less visible. Rarely do we question how they appear on our screens, what mechanisms are at work. Turkle (1996) describes how the inner workings of the machine – the code – are *concealed* from the user. We live in a world where sealed black boxes of electronics, operating in ways we do not understand, provide the user-friendly devices on which we have come to rely. Having grown accustomed to and colluded with this concealment, we more readily suspend disbelief and succumb to the magic of the spectacle.

Imagination

There is a curious ambivalence in the ways in which these patterns of concealment impact on our lives in terms of our freedom. At a later point in the *Observer* article referred to above, Kane recalls Sartre's assertion that "play is what you do when you feel at your most free, your most voluntary" (Kane, 2000, p. 22). The Internet is a tool – better, an environment or environments – that makes possible the forging of emotional, social, and professional relationships, extending possibilities in "real life": it offers ways of being in which we can be free or unfree.

It is surely the materialistic and instrumentalist cast to culture that permits a work ethic to persist with its mechanistic attention to productivity, targets, and (observable) outcomes, so often lamented in educational research. A narrowing of focus that promises "fitness for purpose" diminishes the prospects for a liberal education, for the freeing of the mind that this implies. And that freeing is crucially related to a certain development of the imagination. Suspicion of a means–ends approach is not new. Many have written about the pervasive reductionism inherent in many arenas of human activity, including the educational. Walter Pater (1889), for example, in a critical essay engaging with the poetry of Wordsworth, is despairing:

> Contemplation – impassioned contemplation – that is with Wordsworth the end-in-itself, the perfect end. We see the majority of mankind going most often to definite ends, lower or higher ends, as their own instincts may determine; but the end may never be attained, and the means not be quite the right means, great ends and little ones alike being, for the most part, distant, and the ways to them, in this dim world, somewhat vague. Meantime, to higher or lower ends, they move too often with something of a sad countenance, with hurried and ignoble gait, becoming, unconsciously, something like thorns, in their anxiety to bear grapes; it being possible for people, in the pursuit of even great ends, to become themselves thin and impoverished in spirit and temper, thus diminishing the sum of perfection in the world, at its very sources. (Pater, 1889, in Jones, 1990, p. 83)

For Pater, many people function as if they were automata, going about their daily business without any profound satisfaction, without any real absorption, and with dulled sensibility. The economistic language that pervades contemporary educational settings – targets, delivery, performance, and so on – is ubiquitous. It is rooted in relentless future-orientation. As we expend our energies in proceeding onwards we seldom stop to notice how we feel about where we are in the here-and-now, or if we do notice it is through the lens of postponement. In contrast, the end-in-itself of "impassioned contemplation" requires conditions in which the imagination is allowed to flourish.

Traditionally, leisure and work have been distinguished by the normative parameters, the diurnal routine, of the conventional job. The parameters are changing hand in hand with changing demographics (for example, an aging population in many Western countries, a proliferation of part-time and temporary contracts). Work and play are forced into an unstable relationship, because of the development of ICT and broader economic change to which this contributes. Is there space to resist economic determinism, and to shape the evolution of work/play in favor of a more authentic (and liberal) education? In other words, might we be able to shape what we do out of a desire to feel profoundly connected to it rather than offering ourselves up unthinkingly to the exigencies of the day? Perhaps attention to the spirit in which any activity is performed is a first move toward a greater sense of connection and fulfillment:

> Whether an activity should be considered work or play is to be determined not only by the external description of the activity, but also by the internal spirit in which it is carried on. This is clearly seen in the way young children will often carry out in a spirit of joyous play tasks that would be regarded as work by an adult. The mental attitude determines whether the task is done because of the compulsion of the outcome or because of a free enjoyment of the activity. There is danger in many contemporary pedagogical activities because they concentrate so fully on the results of the work. This may induce the student to produce more in the short run, but it often leads eventually to a loss of zest, to dullness, and to boredom. (Nash, 1966, p. 52)

What constitutes work and what constitutes play is determined partly by the nature of the activity and the context and discourse in which it takes place, and partly by the spirit in which the activity is carried out. In ICT these conditions and discourses proliferate. It is neither necessary nor desirable to attempt to dispense with work and play as mutually defining modes of being. To develop an ethic of play, one perhaps needs to reclaim the word "play" so that it is no longer the poor cousin of work. Technology, within which modern notions of work have developed, is a mode of revealing that is unique in its tendency to crowd out all others. It is as a result of this that modern concepts of play and leisure have come to be understood negatively, as time off, as recuperation from the real business of work. Can there be a reclaimed conception of play that provides a different mode of revealing, one that holds notions of what is productive and unproductive in tension? Can we have productive play without undermining unproductive but nevertheless valuable play?

Study can be intrinsically rewarding. Eclecticism can be an antidote to over-specialization and excessive future-orientation in education. The eclecticism and interdisciplinarity that ICT can encourage are consonant with an attitude of play; they require the play of the imagination. And the imagination, as we have implied, is internally related to the kind of absorption and impassioned contemplation that education can provide.

But surely, it might be objected, there is something in play that resists seriousness. It is true that the virtues characteristic of the work ethic – worthiness and earnest-ness, not to mention the moralism of good time-keeping alluded to earlier – are not evident in what is advocated here. There is something incongruous in the idea of "worthy play." But this is not to say that play is parodic, parasitic, frivolous, or superficial. It accrues depth through our explicit acknowledgement of its centrality to our being and becoming, and in this the imagination is central. Richard Kearney (1988) suggests that we have two related types of imagination, the *poetical* (playful) imagination and the *ethical* imagination. This latter imagination reminds us always of our relationship and duty to the *other*, which is paramount. But the ethical and poetical are mutually constitutive:

> Otherness is as essential to the life of *poiesis* as it is to that of *ethos*. In both cases it signals a call to abandon the priority of ecological existence for the sake of alternative modes of experience hitherto repressed or simply unimagined. Indeed without the poetical openness to the pluri-dimensionality of meaning, the ethical imagination might well shrink back into a cheerless moralizing, an authoritarian and fearful censorship. And, likewise, a poetical imagination entirely lacking in ethical sensibility all too easily slides into an irresponsible *je me'en foutisme*: an attitude where anything goes and everything is everything else because it is, in the final analysis, nothing at all. This is where the poetical readiness to tolerate the *undecidability* of play must be considered in relation to the ethical readiness to *decide* between different modes of response to the other. (Kearney, 1988, p. 369)

It is possible to trace some of the phenomenological characteristics that an ethic of play might entail. As we have seen, the spirit with which an activity is pursued is intimately related to its purpose. In recognition of this, teachers might encourage their students to harness their curiosity to projects in which the goal is either secondary or – if it is to assume as much significance as the process – is of genuine interest to them. Of course, play has the potential to be as goal-oriented as work but, in this characterization, it is never purely instrumental.

There are benefits in clearly articulating objectives, and assessing the progress of students (for the development of teaching as well as for the students themselves). What might be required is not so much a reversal of what is currently held to be "good practice," but a reconfiguration of the relationships between outcome and process, depth and breadth, work and play. These reconfigured relationships, whether the result of disruptions achieved through the medium of new technologies or not, have their own distinctive potential to reveal or conceal aspects of the life-world.

As we said at the start of this chapter, educational technology can extend our capabilities, but it can also – does also – do much more than this. It raises new questions for us and modifies the kinds of answers we are able to give. It reveals and conceals the world in multiple new ways. It raises the stakes for education in ways that amplify the significance of currents of performativity and that can render in stark relief the instrumentalism that has in so many ways characterized the modern technological world. We have tried to show that these raised stakes call for a reconfiguration and reconception of play and work, in which the fundamental importance of the imagination to human beings, and hence to education, is newly recognized. ICT has the potential to exercise and extend the imagination in new ways, but it can also stifle it. The ways in which it is allowed to flourish in education will have a critical bearing on how far this potential is realized.

Notes

1 This phrase has been used by Don Ihde (1990, p. 76), though our own usage here is slightly different.

2 Portions of this section are drawn from David Blacker (1995).

3 Bowers extends the argument in *The Cultural Dimensions of Educational Computing* (Bowers, 1988).

4 See Max Horkheimer and Theodor Adorno, *Dialectic of Enlightenment* (1991, p. 121); and Jürgen Habermas's earlier writings, where modern technology is considered a distinctive force in social life that must be countered by a noninstrumental "communicative action" (Habermas, 1970a, pp. 50ff.).

5 Feminist theorists have begun to show how these groups may be constituted via patriarchy as well, asserting, for example, in the manner of second-level CTT, that the

> model that represents technology itself as neutral, and asserts that it is the human application of technology that determines whether it has beneficial or destructive effects, does not go far enough. By contrast, the social shaping approach insists that technology is always a form of *social* knowledge, practices and products. It is the result of conflicts and compromises, the outcomes of which depend primarily on the distribution of power and resources between different groups in society. (Wacjman, 1988, p. 162)

6 For exploration of these matters see the essays by the editors in Blake and Standish (2000). Bertram Bruce's essay in the collection contains some vivid examples of ways in which ICT can facilitate forms of learning that fruitfully go beyond planned targets. See also his website: http://w3.ed.uiuc.edu/facstaff/detail.lasso?netid=chip.

7 In what was to become something of a cult essay, Donna Haraway (1985) coined the term "cyberfeminism" as a means to identify these different possibilities. See also Sadie Plant's *Zeros + Ones* (1997). Both are discussed in relation to education in Standish (1999) and in complementary essays by Ilan Gur Ze'ev and by Kenway and Nixon in *Educational Theory* (1999).

8 For interesting explorations of the educational significance of such themes in Lyotard's work, see the essays by Gordon Bearn and James Williams in Dhillon and Standish (2000, pp. 215–29, 230–58), and for the Nietzschean background see Blake et al. (2000, pp. 96–117).

9 For a valuable discussion of ICT in terms of environments, see David Kolb's excellent essay "Learning places: building dwelling thinking online" (in Blake and Standish, 2000, pp. 135–48).

10 For a helpful discussion of the significance of links see Burbules (1997).

Recommendations for Further Reading

Blake, N. and Standish, P. (eds), *Enquiries at the Interface: Philosophical Problems of Online Education* (Blackwell, 2000, and *Journal of Philosophy of Education* 34.1, 2000).

Borgmann, A. (1987) *Technology and the Character of Contemporary Life: A Philosophical Inquiry*, University of Chicago Press.

Burbules, N. and Callister, T. (2000) *Watch It: The Risks and Promises of Educational Technologies For Education*, Westview Press.

Feenberg, A. (1999) *Questioning Technology*, Routledge.

Chapter 14

Epistemology and Curriculum

Andrew Davis and Kevin Williams

I

In Plato's haunting allegory of the Cave, light is linked with knowledge and truth: those who emerge from the Cave, leaving behind them an awareness of mere shadows, passions, and prejudices grow accustomed to the light and may gaze at intelligible reality. For Plato education enables the young to make progress from the darkness, and to be saved from error and ignorance of true values. Hence from its inception epistemology embodied profound reasons for humans to take action.

Twentieth-century analytical philosophy continued to pursue epistemology with unabated vigor. In one fundamental way it turned away from its Greek origins. It rarely discussed the possibility that its results might provide reasons for *action*. It concerned itself rather with meeting the traditional skeptical challenge, with accounts of the nature of knowledge and of its justification and with the kinds of knowledge that there are. However, it did not claim to occupy a value-free zone. Many epistemologists appreciated that attributing knowledge to a person involved a positive evaluation of that person's belief, or perhaps a positive evaluation of that person (Greco, 1999).

In contrast, when philosophers reflected on educational issues in the 1960s, epistemological concerns were seen to be of the first importance for curricular decision making. Paul Hirst drew directly on the Greek origins of epistemology in portraying human minds as so constituted that the pursuit of knowledge was for the good of the mind. Knowledge had a significance in the determination of the good life as a whole. A liberal education, concerned with the pursuit of knowledge, was "essential to man's understanding of how he ought to live, both individually and socially" (Hirst, 1974b, p. 31). Knowledge could be divided up into seven "forms" and it was essential for the development of mind that students were initiated into all of them. Many engaged in the "forms of knowledge" debate had no hesitation in assuming that its outcome would have fundamental implications for the curriculum.

Section I written by Andrew Davis; Section II written by Kevin Williams

However, robust arguments for detailed prescriptions for the way school subjects should be divided up were not forthcoming. Hirst himself made a sharp distinction between the "logic" of a subject and its psychology. How best to teach a subject was a matter for empirical investigation. The "forms of knowledge" did not provide "a pattern for curriculum units" (Hirst, 1974a). Nevertheless the broad objectives for education were covered by the forms of knowledge, and so in that sense they were held to "define" the content of the curriculum.

Scheffler, in his writings of that period, also appeared to take it for granted that particular views of knowledge at least "suggested" curriculum features. The empiricist view of knowledge as arising from experience pointed to an education that "supplies abundant and optimally ordered phenomenal experiences." It "trains the student in . . . traits requisite for learning from experience – accurate observation, reasonable generalization, willingness to revise or relinquish purported laws which fail to anticipate the actual course of events." On the other hand, a pragmatist version of knowledge implied an education that "connects general ideals with real problems and that stresses their practical bearings" (Scheffler, 1965, in McCormick and Paechter, 1999, p. 4).

Philosophers of education at this time certainly were convinced of epistemology's "importance" for education. That is not to say that they believed in any simple justificatory relationship between accounts of knowledge and curricular decision making. This is an issue that is addressed in the second subsection of this chapter.

Contemporary philosophy of education has in some measure turned away from epistemology. Current debates are dominated by social and political issues, together with a range of postmodernist concerns. Rorty and Derrida are much more likely to be discussed than Goodman, Quine, or Davidson. Needless to say there are fundamental epistemological reverberations. Rorty denies that knowledge represents reality (the correspondence theory of truth), the quest for certainty, and foundationalist epistemologies. He believes that there is no privileged position from which reality can be accurately "known": "Goodman is right to say that there is no one Way the World Is, and so no one way it is to be accurately represented" (Rorty, 1999, p. 33). This resembles the claim that there is no privileged spatiotemporal framework determining the "real mass" of an object; mass is relative to a choice of spatiotemporal framework (Harman and Thompson, 1996).

In response writers such as Harvey Siegel (for example, Siegel, 1995) have targeted what they see as the epistemological relativism within some brands of postmodernism. Siegel is motivated not only by a philosophical impatience with the posture of contempt for metanarratives, but with *the implications of the results of the debate for decisions about the curriculum*. In this sense, for him epistemology is not "neutral."

While many philosophers of education have seen curricular implications in the insights of epistemology, there are also those who have suggested that we should be looking at matters the other way round. The advent of the Internet and "digital ICT" more generally is felt to raise questions about traditional epistemology's construction of knowledge as "something that is carried linguistically and expressed in sentences/propositions and theories" (Lankshear et al., 2000, p. 35). It is arguable that suggestions of these kinds are made in ignorance of advances in epistemology during the twentieth century in the wake of Quine's holism and the "radical inter-pretation" debates, but discussion of such issues is beyond the scope of this chapter.

Epistemology's role in the justification of decisions about the curriculum

Wittgenstein remarked that philosophy "leaves everything as it is" (Wittgenstein, 1953, 124). We have seen that many philosophers of education do not hold that epistemology leaves curriculum as it is. In this subsection I want to explore the logical character of proposed movements from epistemology to curricular decision making. For the results of epistemology are *prima facie* not value judgements in any sense. How then can epistemology even "suggest" curriculum content or organiza-tion, let alone justify it or "imply" it?

Some of the key assumptions behind the purportedly "curriculum-neutral" nature of epistemology are as follows:

1   The results of epistemological investigation are not "evaluative." Now epistem-ology may be held to explain the uses of "know" and related terms. Or again, it may be thought to deliver insights into the nature of knowledge, justification, and truth. A number of other accounts are available. Most would agree that epistemology does *not* inform us of what is important or valuable. It does not tell us what we ought to do, about any aspects of human flourishing, or about how human societies should best be organized.
2   The justifications for curriculum decisions necessarily rest in part on judgements about human flourishing and the rest. Such support will be indirect, being routed through accounts of educational aims. These accounts will themselves rest on fundamental value judgements about persons and societies.
3   Suppose we were in a position to combine the most robust justifications for such value judgements with a complete and definitive epistemology. Even this would not suffice for watertight curriculum implications. We would also need insights from empirical research into child development and learning generally before we could justify curriculum recommendations.
4   Assumptions (1) and (2) rely on a conventional Humean gulf between "is" and "ought." On this view we cannot justify claims about what we ought to do (or about which actions are right, which situations are morally good or valuable in some other way) by reference to value-independent facts. Epistemological insights are being seen as "value-independent."
5   Underlying (4)'s way of thinking is the further assumption that we can *distin-guish clearly* between moral claims on the one hand and "descriptive" claims of an empirical, metaphysical or epistemological character which purport to charac-terize value-independent facts on the other.

Discussion of the assumptions

It is many years since Hume's position on the "is"/"ought" gap was subjected to fundamental criticisms.[1] Indeed, those who believe that it is possible to justify value judgements may insist that in pursuit of such justification appeal must ultimately be made to value-independent facts. One crude argument for this position might run as follows.

Suppose a given value judgement *V* was supported by referring to other value judgements. If we were seeking some kind of ultimate justification for *V* this move would not help unless either (1) these other value judgements are justified *per se* without the necessity to appeal to further value judgements to justify these in turn, or (2) the other value judgements in turn are justified by appeal to yet further value judgements, and so on and so on until we reach value judgements that are "justified in themselves" or self-evident in some way. The notion of a self-evident value judgement has not been much favored since the demise of intuitionist accounts of value judgements. Hence the whole project of justifying value judgements by appealing to other value judgements may be held to be fatally flawed.

An alternative understanding of justification might reject the Humean fact – value gap. It might be argued that value judgements can after all be based on nonevaluative justified claims about reality, whether these are provided by scientists, the deliverances of common sense, or even philosophers themselves. Are we better able to provide justifications for claims concerning value-independent facts than we are for claims involving values? If not, such an alternative program for justifying value judgements may in its turn be found to be equally flawed.

If value claims can ultimately be supported by appeal to value-independent facts then curriculum recommendations might for example be based on epistemological insights. For instance, suppose scientific claims are aptly characterized as conjectures that makes it as clear as possible what kind of evidence would count against them. Here we have a putative value-independent fact about the nature and status of science. It represents an account of science in the tradition of Popper, rejected by many philosophers of science. However, imagine if only for the sake of argument that it could be defended convincingly. It would appear to imply that the science curriculum should include at least some opportunities for students to form hypotheses and to construct testable predictions from these.

The logical character and strength of such an alleged "implication" can of course easily be questioned. Evidently there is no deductive relationship between a Popperian account of science and a Popperian science curriculum. Moreover, not only have I failed to establish any kind of implication, but it is at least theoretically possible that the best long-term teaching strategy for imparting a conjectural conception of science is to transmit a diet of scientific facts to passive recipients, at least up to the age of 16.

So, if any relationships *could* be established between epistemological insights into the nature and status of a subject and the curriculum for that subject they would be nondeductive and complex in character. They would be *defeasible* in the sense that epistemological features of a subject might provide a strong *prima facie* justification for handling it in certain ways within the curriculum, but this justification could be undermined by other considerations. If Popper is right about science, this points (it might be argued) to a recommendation that science is handled in a "Popperian manner" on the curriculum. However this move could be overset, for example by empirical discoveries about the Popperian outcomes of an authoritarian science curriculum.

In discussions of any move from value-independent epistemological insights to curriculum decisions we need to distinguish between decisions *about* a subject and decisions *within* a subject. A decision to have science on the curriculum at all is a decision *about* science. I would want to accept the neutrality of epistemology at this level, and argue that such a decision cannot be based on the epistemology of science *per se*, but must also appeal to conceptions of the good life for individuals and societies. On the other hand, curriculum decisions *within* science, I am suggesting, might rest in some fashion on value-independent epistemological features of science.

Epistemology is not necessarily curriculum-neutral: a negative illustration

Even if epistemology *taken alone* were necessarily curriculum-neutral it does not follow that a set of soundly justified aims for education, together with relevant empirical knowledge about learning and child development, is always *sufficient* to support particular curricular recommendations. Indeed the findings of epistemology may conflict with recommendations made on this basis. I now explore one illustration of this. I *assume* a particular set of values embodied in instrumental educational aims. These aims are believed to entail that the curriculum should contain some quite specific content. I show that *if* we properly understand certain insights offered by contemporary epistemology then instrumental educational aims do not after all have the curriculum implications often attributed to them.

The version of an instrumental aim for education I have in mind is crudely as follows. Education should prepare students to take their place in an industrial economy. I put to one side all questions about how this aim might be further justified in terms of conceptions of human flourishing and of a vision of how people should live together.

"Preparing students to take their place" needs unpacking. Note just two possible interpretations out of several. It could be construed as a preparation in which students were imbued with appropriate attitudes and moral values. On reaching adulthood they are committed workers who concentrate on the task in hand, are not disposed to demand too much money for their efforts, are disinclined to take sick leave unless they are really ill, and seek to support fellow workers in the aim of maximizing the profits for the enterprise in which they are employed.

This highly controversial reading builds in value judgements. A second construal may be easily generated given a *different* set of values. On this version, students should, when reaching adulthood, be disposed to review critically tasks given by their employers, and be sufficiently informed to weigh profit against other values, for example, environmental values, or the benefit of employing more people rather than extracting the maximum possible productivity from a smaller number.

The first reading suggests curriculum content significantly different from the second. To debate the merits of each would need the resources of moral, political, and social philosophy. This will not be pursued here. For the purpose of this discussion I deploy a set of values firmly associated with the first reading. If these values are assumed, then employers may well hold education responsible not only for developing the "right" attitudes but also for ensuring that their prospective employees arrive in the workplace *with appropriate sets of cognitive and practical skills.* Industrial requirements in that sense may be felt to have strong and direct curricular implications. The curriculum should include the cognitive content and practical skills in question.

A proper consideration of the nature of knowledge, belief, and practical skill undermines employers' assumptions as summarized above. It becomes clear that education simply *cannot* frame curriculum content and style of delivery in such a way that it unambiguously prepares students for the workplace in this direct fashion.

A necessary condition for knowing that *p* is believing that *p*. A familiar theme of holist analyses of belief is that the stock of beliefs held by an individual should not be regarded as a collection of atomistic beliefs, but rather as a "whole" which is not divisible into individual "components." A full rehearsal of the relevant arguments is beyond the scope of this chapter, but we need to look briefly at the justifications for holism, and at why anyone should have thought that beliefs *can* be regarded as psychological items each of which are capable of independent "existence."

If it is both true that Jones believes that Faraday discovered the dynamo and that Smith believes that Faraday discovered the dynamo then Jones and Smith share a belief. Indeed, if this is not an example of shared belief, then it is difficult to see what is. The trouble begins when we try to offer an account of *what it is to share the belief.* This is because we apparently are able to identify a particular belief by using a sentence to which any believer would assent if they held the supposed belief in question. In the example under discussion, each would assent to "Faraday discovered the dynamo." The ready production of a relevant sentence may be taken to imply that sharing a belief is having the "same" piece of content in each of their heads, and that the sentence somehow refers to this specific element of content and indicates its nature.

In opposition to this picture, Donald Davidson remarks: "We identify thoughts, distinguish between them, describe them for what they are, only as they can be located within a dense network of related beliefs" (Davidson, 1985, p. 475). "The identity of a thought cannot be divorced from its place in the logical network of other thoughts" (ibid.).

What it is for Smith to have the Faraday belief will depend on what beliefs he has about dynamos, electricity, and the Victorian scientist Faraday himself. The nature of these beliefs in turn depends on others. If Jones's stock of related beliefs differs at least to some extent from Smith's, as it certainly will, then we can easily see that the sentence "Faraday discovered the dynamo" cannot make a precise identifying reference to an item of "content" that they both share as such. "Faraday discovered the dynamo" does not refer to a "fact," a "true proposition," or "content" in any fashion that resembles the way "The man in the green hat under the clock at Charing Cross Station" could refer to a particular person at a particular time. Of course we often *say* that a sentence such as "Faraday discovered the dynamo" may be used to state a fact or express a true proposition. Holists have no need to claim that such ways of speaking lack respectability. The point is rather to argue for a particular account of what these ways of speaking can possibly mean.

Some philosophers may think that there must be something wrong with these kinds of holist arguments. For example, we can surely acquire, *or lose,* beliefs one at a time. Stich represents this point as a basic tenet of "folk psychology." "When Henry awoke from his nap he had completely forgotten that the car keys were hidden in the refrigerator, though he had forgotten nothing else." Stich's "folk psychologist" could acknowledge that the belief in question could not be acquired by a primitive tribesman "who knew nothing about cars, keys, or refrigerators," but once the "relevant background" is in place "a person may acquire (or lose) the belief that the car keys are in the refrigerator while the remainder of his beliefs remain unchanged" (Stich, 1996, p. 96).

One response to this is to concede that the connectedness of belief content varies in quality and strength. The content of the belief that the average temperature in London in December 1890 was –1°C cannot be separated from material about calendars, weather, scales, and so on. At the same time, this content is "separate" from the corresponding fact about the same year's average November temperature. Henry could forget a December fact of this kind without disturbing his hold on the corresponding November fact. Henry cannot "lose" his basic belief about car key functions without considerable disturbance to very many "connected" beliefs about cars, transport, crime, and the modern world in general. Yet he seemingly can lose a particular belief about the key's current location. We might admit to the opponent of holism that some beliefs are "relatively discrete."

Even if this is granted, it does not undermine the holist account of belief content being defended here. The content of Henry's belief *that the car keys are in the refrigerator* is not separable from the complex background of other beliefs and ideas with which the content of the belief in question is inextricably linked. The holist denial that "The car keys are in the refrigerator" can pick out a piece of stand-alone content holds good.

Precisely the opposite of this result seems to be held by those who advocate that the school curriculum should ensure that students acquire knowledge that they will use as workers in the industrial economy. It is assumed that at least some of the knowledge required in the workplace can be clearly identified, and that this can then be used to determine some elements of the school curriculum. Employers, it may be held, know perfectly well what their employees need to know, and expect the schools to deliver it.

I am claiming that holism undermines the possibility of such direct and naive instrumentalism about the curriculum. (There are of course other arguments that establish a similar conclusion: the interest here is in an *epistemological* argument for the conclusion.) This holist argument could be understood as an epistemological "take" on claims made by writers in the situated cognition tradition. If the workplace requires knowledge, for instance of fractions, there is simply no straightforward and detailed relationship between what is called knowledge of fractions within a school curriculum and the mathematical knowledge required in the workplace. The latter has a distinctive identity; it is "situated." An employee's fractions knowledge will be linked to much other knowledge about "workplace phenomena." The fractions knowledge will be "modeled" in specific ways that enable it to be used in the contexts concerned, and perhaps also allow communication with fellow-employees about the nature of the tasks. There will be many connections, most of which could not be made explicit, with beliefs about relevant practices, habits, and "cultural elements" relevant to the employment context in question. Such links provide workplace fractions knowledge with a distinctive identity. We cannot in principle assert a straightforward identity between "school fractions knowledge" and "workplace fractions knowledge." Indeed the latter phrase fails to capture a specific "type" of knowledge.

As Wittgenstein so often warned us, we are bewitched by our own language here. For this reason, many will respond to these holistic considerations with incredulity, and even hostility. It is quite obvious, they may argue, that if workers need knowledge of fractions at work, then schools should teach their students about fractions, once the legitimacy of instrumental education aims is accepted. There must be *something* common to fractions knowledge in the workplace and a practicable curriculum treatment of an area that we will call *fractions* for want of something better.

Admittedly the argument from holism should not be taken too far. It does not entail that there is *no* relationship between the curriculum and workplace needs. However it does imply that the relationship is indirect and difficult to express with any precision. Finer curriculum details cannot be justified on this basis. If employees are going to use mathematics in the workplace then this suggests that the curriculum should include some mathematics. If written English is required of many workers, then they should cover aspects of written English at school. However, these points hardly contribute to detailed curriculum planning.

It is important to understand how a parallel skeptical argument can be conducted if we conceptualize knowledge in another way. The first argument just outlined refers to "knowledge," "content," and "belief." Now some may prefer to think of the curriculum as fostering abilities, competences, and in particular as encouraging students to acquire sets of rules that can later be employed when they are adult employees. Here is a second argument that shows that the idea of a rule cannot do the work required of it. An advantage of this second argument is that it includes practical skills or "know how," whereas the first argument from holism as stated seems only to refer to "knowledge that," or what some refer to as propositional or declarative knowledge.

The first move in developing the second argument is to express in words the rules felt to be important for the workplace. A list could be made. Some would be idiosyncratic to particular employment contexts, and so they would be excluded. We are not at present considering *workplace learning*, which might take place in the specific physical and cultural contexts provided by a particular kind of employment. Rather we are reflecting on a more general curriculum to be offered in schools and elsewhere for *all* students before they join the world of work. So the instrumentalist might urge that at least part of this general curriculum could be framed in terms of rules the mastery of which all students should acquire at school, and then apply as appropriate when they are adult employees.

Wittgenstein treated the topic of rule following extensively. One of his main points is that the *words* or *symbols* in which a rule may be expressed are never sufficient for a unique interpretation to be secured. If someone is trying to teach me to follow a rule they will always have to rely on a vast unspoken shared set of contextual elements. These will include aspects of the natural and cultural world, together with knowledge about habits within that culture, patterns of behavior, and about human capacities and potentialities. John Searle took up this Wittgensteinian theme, referring to it in a number of his writings as the "Background," which is essential for all communication. Words are never enough. If we seek to interpret them by using other words, these too will depend on the Background for a particular construal.

Space does not permit me to do more than summarize Searle (1992, 1995). I discuss this at greater length in Davis (1998). Searle considers occurrences of "cut" in sentences such as "Sam cut the grass," "Bill cut the cake," and "I just cut my skin." He contends that "cut" has the same literal meaning in each sentence. Nevertheless the word is interpreted differently in each sentence. We are clear that cutting the grass does not involve rushing out and stabbing it with a knife, and that cutting the cake does not involve mowing it with the lawn mower. Each sentence, Searle contends, is interpreted against a Background of "human abilities to engage in certain practices, know-how, ways of doing things etc . . ." The Background determines different interpretations of "cut" even though it retains its literal meaning from one sentence to the other. Searle argues that this is not a matter of ambiguity. We could not block the "wrong" interpretation of "cut" by specifying further what appropriate cutting was in the context in question. We would never come to the end of our attempts at interpretation, and, moreover each qualification would itself be subject to the Background for a particular interpretation.

If we fail to take proper account of the insights of Wittgenstein or Searle, we may believe that once we have a rule expressed in words then its application in future cases is fixed. We may feel that we can read off types of situations from the range of likely workplace contexts, that we can define the performances required of workers in these kinds of situations, and then frame the rule whose applications would result in the said performances. Given all this, it is only another step to designing the curriculum in such a way that students are taught to follow the relevant "rules."

My appropriate application of any rule requires much other knowledge and the making of a range of value judgements. Following my treatment in Davis (1998) I explain this argument through an example. Suppose we thought that every employee needs a certain competence in written English, and attempted to identify some of the rules that make up this competence, hoping ultimately to draw out a particular implication for curriculum content in English. One particular "rule" might be that you should begin a sentence with a capital letter and end it with a full stop. This rule now needs to be tested against a range of workplace contexts in which people might be writing English. When entering data into a computer the field concerned may permit complete sentences. However it may well not be appropriate for the user to use full stops at the ends of these sentences. On the other hand, the entry in a particular field may consist of a string of words that is not a complete sentence, and yet it may be appropriate to begin the first word with a capital letter. It is true that the rule did not say *only* begin sentences with capital letters. However, we can go on. Someone might be compiling an index for a book, or an exercise for students into which missing punctuation must be inserted, or completing an application form. In many contexts it may be appropriate for the user to refrain from beginning sentences with capital letters and ending them with full stops. The rule taken alone simply cannot fix its application in future cases. In each case generated by the workplace, the user must draw on a complex field of knowledge about language, audience, and many other matters in order to decide whether to use the rule or not. In short, the successful user is located within, and is aware of, the Background.

To sum up, both skeptical arguments point to the same conclusion about attempts to relate the curriculum to the demands of the workplace. It is simply not possible to conceptualize in any precise manner the knowledge elements required. So, from a proper account of the nature of knowledge and understanding, a task of epistemology *par excellence*, we can undermine one currently fashionable set of arguments for particular curriculum content. Epistemology is shown to be fundamentally relevant to policy decisions in education.

Such a move from epistemology to curriculum is a negative one, and it is of course remote from Plato's commitment to truth and goodness and the positive educational vision held to flow from this. It nevertheless has the merit of being *argued for* in contemporary analytical terms.

II

In writing about what it is to "share a belief," Andrew Davis draws attention to the necessarily public nature of knowledge. Let us move now from the notion of sharing a belief in the sense of having a belief in common to the kind of sharing that is involved where a teacher wishes to share understanding with a learner – in short, to teach. As well as a commitment to the pursuit of truth, being a teacher involves the further commitment to share knowledge, and much (although obviously not all) learning is communicated within this context of relationship. We are not speaking here simply of a relationship between a motivator and the person to be motivated – what is involved is rather a relationship between a teacher and a learner that makes possible the latter's relationship with shareable knowledge. Concern with pedagogic sharing extends the focus of epistemological inquiry from consideration of the logic of subject boundaries to addressing the potential of knowledge to be shared with learners. This fruitful approach presents us with a conception of learning involving a triadic relationship of teacher, activity to be learned, and learner.

Central to the defense of such pursuits as science, history, literature, and other subjects is some sense of the quality of the experiences that these areas offer and their connection with notions of richness. Such learning can take rich forms that highlight the impoverishment of the managerial view of the curriculum illustrated by Andrew Davis. To take this form learning must first exhibit "thickness," that is, depth of understanding that is appropriately located within a network of justified true beliefs. To count as being "rich" the learning must contribute to an enhanced quality of life. (This distinction will be illustrated later.) The aim in pedagogic sharing is to secure richness in learning and this demands personal commitment on the part of teachers both to the value of what they are teaching and to the learner.

Emphasis on the significance of the centrality of sharing to pedagogy, which is threaded through Plato's work, has remained an enduring concern in philosophy of education. It is to be found, for example, in Oakeshott's conception of the teacher as the "agent of civilization" (Fuller, 1989, pp. 46, 48) committed to ensuring that the experience of education should be for young people an entrée into a world of "wonder and delight" (ibid., p. 40; see Williams, 1996). For Oakeshott the teacher is a "custodian" of part of a culture in whom "an inheritance of human understanding survives and is perpetually renewed in being imparted to newcomers" (Fuller, 1989, p. 70). Teachers have a mastery of, and a commitment to, some aspect of civilization so that in them a part of a culture is "alive" (ibid.). To ensure that this inheritance comes to resonate in the heart and mind of the learner and assume the character of an "encounter" rather than a mere "recognition" (ibid., p. 32), the teacher first "studies his pupil" (p. 47). Pádraig Hogan uses the suggestive metaphor of a "cultural courtship" (Hogan, 1995, p. 170) to refer to the relationship between teacher and taught in the school context. Teachers are the conduit of the "authentic voice of the subject" which they must enact in an "engaging yet faithful idiom; an idiom which addresses the sensibilities of the pupils in an inviting and challenging manner" (ibid.) Gerry Gaden has also done helpful work in characterizing the kind of learning that can connect with children's experience and engender in them a shared commitment to the activity being taught. He speaks of this in terms of identification between learners and what they are invited to learn. The teacher's task is to promote what Gaden refers to as "a degree of identification or a relationship of some personal significance" (Gaden, 1990, p. 36) between learners and their chosen pursuit, which can contribute to "the sustenance and enjoyment" of their lives (Gaden, 1983, p. 52). At the heart of his account of teaching and learning is also the triadic relationship of teacher, learner, and activity to be learned.

Let us consider in more concrete detail what is involved in the sharing of rich learning.

Pedagogy as sharing

Mathematics, for example, can prompt the kind of rich learning that can "joyfully excite the mind" (Murdoch, 1992, p. 338) and usually, although not always, this richness and excitement are routed via a pedagogic sharing. This point is well made in the following comments from Sharon, an 18-year-old young woman, in an interview with psychologist, James Day. Sharon's story, explains Day, is a "narrative of relationship" (Day, 1999, p. 270) and it highlights the salience of receptivity, responsivity, and relationship in rich learning. Although she had a solid grounding in mathematics, she then encountered "a teacher who loved algebra, and made me feel that it meant the world to him and that I could come to love it too. He made algebra into a wonderland, and me into an algebra fanatic" (ibid., p. 266). Everything about algebra "became fascinating, everything about the world was involved in it, algebra was suddenly important to other things that mattered in the world" (ibid., p. 267). Now, she tells us: "(w)hen I . . . think of algebra, I think of him. I see his face, I hear his voice . . . (I)t doesn't seem so separate to me now, what is algebra and what was the relationship" (pp. 267–8). She has learned to use the subject since, in her own life and for her own purposes, but, she continues:

I can't say that my thinking about it or my sense of its importance are at all independent of him . . . Maybe Mr. Norton as a person made algebra lovable because of how it was just to be there with him and us. But I think, anyway, that love is involved there, that when you care for something, when you believe in it as I have come to feel about algebra, there is a kind of love involved . . . some kind of deep appreciation, some kind of seeing the thing in its several dimensions, seeing its uses yet being in awe of what remains beyond you about it – what it is you still have to learn . . . I can love algebra, or even I think sometimes other people . . . because of the way Mr Norton treated me in his class, and kind of gave algebra to me as a gift. (Day, 1999, pp. 268–9)

Sharon's father thinks that her love for the subject is tied up with a romantic crush on the teacher. But she knows that her love for the subject and relationship with the teacher are in fact distinct. Mr. Norton is not a mere motivator – rather he is the one who through his relationship with Sharon makes possible her relationship with the public and inexhaustible object that is algebra. The public character of algebra points to an interesting feature of this narrative. While Sharon's understanding of algebra has acquired its own temper in terms of her life history, it can count as knowledge only in virtue of this public character. This understanding is in no sense therefore merely a personal construct or an individual "way of world-making" – no more than the proof of the theorem of Pythagoras that I learned through English has a different logic from the proof learned through Irish by some of my contemporaries.

Nonetheless, algebra itself has become highly significant in Sharon's life, taking on what Day wishes to call "a human even a sacred character" (ibid., p. 271) in that it is:

irreducible to the sum of its parts, it is knowable only through fascination, desire, respect, commitment and responsible use, it remains something other and mysterious that, if approached properly, will give us more than we could otherwise ever hope to understand about it. Its being loved is the condition whereby it yields both its secrets and its powers. Its being loved is the possibility of its being known . . . algebra stands as a metaphor for our longing and our inability to know, save for the relationship we enter with the thing we want to understand. (Day, 1999, p. 271)

Through the quality of his teaching, writes Day, Mr. Norton has given the students the "gift" of "connecting algebra to their desire" and introduced them to the "possibility that knowledge doesn't have to be a matter of possession, but of respect, of relationship . . . [and] that education could be about love" (ibid., p. 272). Through this teacher, she has, says Sharon, come to an appreciation "of what education, at its best, *could* be" (p. 269).

This notion of teacher and taught sharing in a love affair with knowledge is not unusual. The recent biography of distinguished linguist, Eric Hawkins, abounds in examples of how, through a sharing with teachers, he was enabled to journey into the "song of other languages" (Hawkins, 1999, p. 278). Of his teacher in his final years at secondary school, he writes: "He was not passing on to us second hand opinions from his university notes, but engaging in a shared voyage of discovery. I can remember how this sensation, of sharing his excitement in the reading, whetted my appetite" (ibid., p. 48). Nor is pedagogic sharing limited to the academic sphere. Engineer and scientist, Mike Cooley, speaks of a particular "great gifted" teacher of metalwork who used to give "a vision of what engineering and metalwork could be like" (Cooley, in Quinn, 1997, pp. 59–60) and who perceived the teacher as a conduit in "the transmission of a great culture" (ibid., p. 60). Students tend to respond to teachers who live their craft in these ways.

What is also striking is the propensity of learning to be unproductive where relationship is absent. In the novel, *The Woman Who Walked into Doors*, Roddy Doyle demonstrates this very well through the contrasting experience of Paula, the main character, of different kinds of educational relationship. Paula has treasured and cherished memories of her primary school days: "I was good in school, especially at stories . . . [The teacher] always got me to read mine out to the class . . . I loved that . . . I don't remember any of the stories . . . But I remember the applause after and the smiles. I was good in school; she made us think that we were good" (Doyle, 1996, p. 25). Her encounter with second level schooling is very different. Demoralized by being allocated to a class in the second lowest stream, her encounters with her teachers reinforce the negative image that the school authorities have imposed upon her. She feels particular anger toward her English teacher who treats the class dismissively, provoking the students with rhetorical questions about their indifference, indeed inviting them to affirm hostility towards learning. "What's the point? What's the point? You don't care about poetry, do you; any of you?" (ibid., p. 33). This prompts the chorus response of "No, Sir" (ibid.). Paula deplores both insensitive treatment and the failure genuinely to try to teach her. "I was good at English until he came along with his Brylcream head. He never let us forget that we were dense, that we were a waste of his time" (ibid.). The mathematics teacher humiliates her with a disparaging reference to her elder sister and by making her stand up in class. The experience of being shamed by the teacher has serious consequences. Efforts to learn the teacher's subject ended in failure: mathematics never came to "make sense" (p. 31) . In saying that the teacher "didn't care" (ibid.), Paula is affirming her indifference to her as a person and as a learner. Unfortunately her encounter with school leads her to get "worse and worse" (ibid., p. 31) at all of her school subjects and she asserts: "I don't think I learned one new thing after I went to that school" (ibid.).

Nonetheless, rich understanding can be acquired despite, rather than because of, a teacher. A short story of A. S. Byatt's, for example, shows how engagement in learning can be absorbing, fulfilling, and stimulating, even addictive. In the story, Emily, a student, becomes so drawn into the study of the plays of Jean Racine that she becomes "a secret addict of Racine's convoluted world, tortuously lucid, savage and controlled" (Byatt, 1995, p. 17). Emily enters wholeheartedly into the imaginative universe of the playwright whose characters "were gripped wholly by incompatible passions which swelled uncontrollably to fill their whole universe, brimming over and drowning its horizons. They were all creatures of excess, their secret blood burned and boiled and an unimaginably hot bright sun glared down in judgment" (ibid.). Having originally "shared" the "reluctance" and "near-apathy" (ibid.) of the other students towards Racine's *Phèdre*, she has come to respond to its characters with a combination of terror, pity, and aesthetic appreciation. "They were all horribly and beautifully interwoven, tearing each other apart in a perfectly choreographed dance, every move inevitable, lovely, destroying" (ibid.). Yet the teacher herself was entirely lacking in enthusiasm for Racine, a lack of enthusiasm which would be reprehensible only if it were a feature of all of her teaching. She "clearly despised a little herself" the classical dramatic unities "as though the Greeks and French were children who made unnecessary rules for themselves" and failed to "see wider horizons" (ibid.). Obviously pedagogic sharing is not the only route to learning.

Nor is this sharing always benign. Manipulative and disabling forms of sharing do exist which are instruments of power rather than of emancipation and inimical to any attempt by young people critically to assimilate their culture or to enable them to find themselves in its heritage. The following example from Edith Wharton's short novel, *Madame de Treymes*, serves to illustrate everything that is miseducative in learning. Madame de Malrive, an expatriate American, who is estranged from her philandering husband, explains that her husband and his family refuse to consent to a divorce for fear of losing custody of the couple's son. Wharton offers a memorable account of the closed and manipulative nature of "upper-class" French family life and of its predatory designs on the son. Like other children of the upper class, the boy is enclosed in a "network of accepted prejudices and opinions":

> Everything is prepared in advance – his political and religious convictions, his judgments of people, his sense of honour, his ideas of women, his whole view of life. He is taught to see vileness and corruption in everyone not of his own way of thinking, and in every idea that does not directly serve the religious and political purposes of his class. The truth isn't a fixed thing: it's not used to test actions by, it's tested by them, and made to fit with them. And this forming of the mind begins with the child's first consciousness; it's in his nursery stories, his baby prayers, his very games with his playmates! (Wharton, 1995, p. 11)

The purpose of this form of social education is to appropriate the child "to his race, his religion, his true place in the order of things" (ibid., p. 80). Noteworthy is the appearance of the metaphor "network," showing Wharton's subtle awareness of the embedded quality of all thinking "within a dense network of beliefs" (Davidson, 1985). Although the learning being offered to children could in a sense be described as a sharing, it is an imposition rather than a sharing of beliefs. This program of learning also discloses the distinction between thick and rich understanding. Thick understanding is involved in the sense that the underlying beliefs are complex and networked or interconnected and rooted in a "whole view of life" (Wharton, 1995, p. 11). The understanding sought, however, is not rich because it does not enhance life; it is contaminated by bias and fatally compromised by association with the interests of the sociopolitical establishment.

Pedagogy and Realism

We must not romanticize or sentimentalize what learning a subject entails and so become carried away by Oakeshott's well-known metaphor of education as a "conversation" (Oakeshott, 1981, pp. 199/200, 304, 311–12). The sharing involved in this conversation is more like that entailed in learning a new language rather than the less arduous sharing involved in acquiring one's mother tongue. For most of us to arrive at a point where we can read Racine involves hard work and application to the basics. Let us stay a little with this point. One important reason, which is sometimes overlooked, for the lack of success of so many in learning foreign languages in school is the actual difficulty of learning another language, particularly in the context of the classroom rather than by living in the country where the language is spoken. Even in the latter context, prior study of the basics prepares learners for what to listen for and what to expect (see Hawkins, 1999, p. 85). For most people hard work is needed, first, to master the basics of a language, subsequently, to acquire fluency in it. Similar effort is required to develop fluency in the exercise of any complex human art or skill. Although learning may at times be a gift, it is more often a challenge that demands what Oakeshott describes as a "discipline of inclination" (Fuller, 1989, p. 68). This applies very much to the algebra example where the teacher is "simultaneously very demanding, caring and extremely competent" and where his relationship to his subject and his students is "at once an exacting and profoundly inviting one" (Day, 1999, pp. 271–2). The same point is echoed in the treatment by Joseph Dunne of the effort which is a feature of much learning. Incidentally Dunne also succeeds in cutting out the dross from, and thus in giving force to, such cliches as "enablement," "empowerment," "self-esteem," and even "finding oneself." Learning, writes Dunne, requires "a submission that imposes a discipline," but it is precisely this discipline that, in a "very real sense" of these "overused" terms, "enables or empowers people" (Dunne, 1995, p. 72). Through "real engagement with, and in, a practice a person's powers are released, directed and enlarged" (ibid., pp. 72–3). By offering the way to a "real, deeply grounded 'self-esteem'"(ibid., p. 76), this submission allows people to find themselves.

Making demands of learners does not mean forsaking the principles of respect for the world of the learner. The sharing involved in teaching and learning is not a sharing between equals in terms of knowledge but is rather a sharing of an unpatronizing character between two people who are equally learners but at different stages of mastery. The spirit of the kind of ecology of knowing and learning involved in educational sharing requires an ability on the part of teachers to stand outside of their subject and in the shoes of a learner in order to perceive it as a learner perceives it. The teacher then is something like George Eliot's good preacher who has "the wonderful art of preaching sermons which the wheelwright and the blacksmith can understand; not because he talks condescending twaddle, but because he can call a spade a spade, and knows how to disencumber ideas of their wordy frippery" (Eliot, 1976, p. 48). In exercising this art, the preacher must bring:

> his geographical, chronological, exegetical mind pretty nearly to the pauper point of view, or of no view; he must have some approximate conception of the mode in which the doctrines which have so much vitality in the plenum of his own brain will comport themselves *in vacuo* – that is to say, in a brain that is neither geographical, chronological, nor exegetical. It is a flexible imagination that can take such a leap as that, and an adroit tongue that can adapt its speech to so unfamiliar a position. (Eliot, 1976, p. 21)

Rather than skills of "facilitation" or "learning management," what the preacher, like any good teacher, really requires are the qualities of a "flexible imagination" and an "adroit tongue." Significant too is the link that Eliot makes between these qualities and a capacity to engage in a personal relationship with learners. Reverend Cleves, the example of a good preacher, has also an ability to teach that is associated with his "hereditary sympathies with the checkered life of the people" and his evening classes are described as "a sort of conversational lecture on useful practical matters" (ibid., p. 48). His audience, she remarks, would characterize him (unburdened with the quality-appraisal schedules in some adult education classes) as "a uncommon knowin', sensable, free-spoken gentleman; very kind an' good-natur'd too" (ibid., p. 49).

The limits of pedagogy

None of the foregoing should be understood to suggest that a pedagogy based on effort and most scrupulous commitment on the teacher's part will always lead to success. A former teacher, who had spent much frustrated effort in trying to gain the attention and interest of a very difficult student, recounts the following story. The boy decided to leave school without taking any examination. On leaving the school, the young man proudly announced that the teacher had never succeeded in teaching him anything. When asked why he continued to come to class, the young man replied, "I simply wanted to see if you would ever give up" (Halpin, 1997, pp. 2–3). It is not difficult to see that pedagogic failure does not then necessarily mean incompetence or lack of commitment. In the novel, *Agnes Grey*, Anne Brontë also writes of an experience that will strike a chord with many frustrated teachers. "The task of instruction was as arduous for the body as the mind" and, despite "unremitting patience and perseverance," the "best intentions and most strenuous efforts" of the teacher, the eponymous Agnes Grey, "seemed productive of no better result than sport to the children . . . and torment" to herself (Brontë, 1994, p. 20).

It is one thing then to prescribe a curriculum based on a rich conception of knowledge; it is another to ensure the richness of this learning. We cannot guarantee a minimum education, let alone a rich quality of engagement with curricular pursuits or practices. We can prescribe a right or entitlement to receive schooling and do our utmost to ensure that young people profit from it but it is impossible to ensure the success of our efforts. Analogously, perhaps, we can prescribe a minimum wage but we cannot guarantee a minimum quality of life; we can prescribe minimum standards of health care but we cannot guarantee health. Educational expectations must not therefore be extreme and unrealistic.

This also applies to the business of assessing learning. We should admit the impossibility of assessing in an exhaustive way the quality of a learner's achievement. Definition of outcomes and assessment of these have a certain thinness; they cannot include the comprehensive context in which rich understanding is embodied. Our access to the contents of other minds is, thankfully, limited. As long, however, as we do not think that what we are assessing is the whole picture, we should be reconciled to living with this. There is a danger that philosophers' fear of the curriculum becoming "transmission of a fixed content – be this information, skills or received opinion" (Blake et al., 1998, p. 190) will become an obstacle to the use of any educational measurement. George Eliot herself seems to believe that conventional examinations inevitably frustrate "the inward bent toward comprehension and thoroughness" (Eliot, 1970, p. 175). But this need not be the case (see Williams, 1998) and we should not allow an impossible best to become the enemy of a possible good.

The limits of epistemology

There is one point to be made in conclusion. Philosophical inquiry alerts us to the complexity of knowledge and enlarges and enhances our epistemological maps, teaching us, in the words of Louis MacNeice, that the world is "(i)ncorrigibly plural" and that there is "more of it than we think" (see Allott, 1968, pp. 191–2). Such inquiry has obvious implications for curriculum design and should serve to make the theories of knowledge of curriculum planners finer and more discriminating. But it cannot tell us how and at what approximate age knowledge should be imparted. Even theologically inspired conceptions of knowledge, which purport to offer comprehensive pictures of the world, cannot imbue this knowledge with imperatives about how to teach children. George Eliot, as we have just seen, makes fun of ministers of religion who cannot make the leap of the imagination necessary in order to communicate theological knowledge to their congregations. Possession of knowledge equips neither preachers nor teachers with the "flexible imagination" and "adroit tongue" (Eliot, 1976, p. 21) required in order to enable learners to share in the "vitality" of this knowledge. In making decisions about teaching methods and the sequencing of learning, we need to draw on the wisdom of experienced teachers as well as on contributions from empirical research.

The relationship of epistemology to the curriculum is well captured in Oakeshott's celebrated essay, "Political education." In this essay, Oakeshott rightly alerts us to the folly of endeavoring to construct a curriculum of civic education without prior, deep reflection on the nature of civic culture. "The more profound our understanding . . . , the less we shall be at the mercy of plausible but mistaken analogy, the less we shall be tempted by a false or irrelevant model . . . , the less likely we shall be to embrace the illusions that wait for the ignorant and the unwary" (Fuller, 1989, p. 155). The kind of searching inquiry practiced by Oakeshott in respect of political education is undertaken with regard to other topics in a number of chapters of this volume. These analyses shows that the more extensive and subtle our philosophical investigations into the nature of knowledge, the better will be our understanding of the subject, area, or skill that we wish to teach. Such inquiry is a necessary preliminary to the achievement of coherence in curriculum design and to the promotion of richness in learning. But the role of epistemology in theorizing about the curriculum extends beyond conceptual underlaboring. It can also alert us to the personal qualities required in successful teaching and remind us that teachers who are inspired by the "beauty of a thought or a science" (Plato, 1979, p. 93) will be likely to be animated by a commitment to share this with their students.[2]

Notes

1 For instance, John Searle in *Speech Acts* (Searle, 1969).
2 This chapter has benefited greatly from the comments of Paul Standish.

Recommendations for Further Reading

Blake, N., Smeyers, P., Smith, R. and Standish, P. (1998) *Thinking Again: Education after Post-modernism*, Bergin & Garvey.

Greco, J. and Sosa, E. (eds.) (1999) *The Blackwell Guide to Epistemology*, Blackwell.

Searle, J. (1995) *The Construction of Social Reality*, Penguin.

Walsh, P. D. (1993) *Education and Meaning: Philosophy in Practice*, Cassell.

Chapter 15

Vocational Education and Training

Paul Hager and Terry Hyland

Introduction

If educational processes are viewed in broad, nonformal terms as aspects of "up-bringing" (J. White, 1997, p. 83), then vocational studies are as old and, since they are vital to survival and reproduction, arguably older than any other form of education. The concept of apprenticeship – an historically important component in accounts of vocational education and training (VET) – provides a useful entry point here. If apprenticeship is conceived in terms of teaching/learning processes whereby a novice or initiate is enabled to achieve mastery in a particular sphere of activity, then such vocationalism must date back to the very earliest times when humans first organized themselves into distinct communities. As Coffey observes, all early education can be said to have had an "explicit vocational function" in that: "Economic life was primarily sustained by the passing on of manual skills from one generation to the next. Most people were educated 'on the job', in particular by experiencing some sort of formal or informal apprenticeship" (Coffey, 1992, p. 11).

Both the formal and informal educational practices of early societies – with a specifically vocational function of inculcating knowledge, skills, and values required for survival and reproduction – must have included passing on to young people the key elements of hunting, fishing, making food and clothing, and caring for the young. Harold Benjamin's famous "saber-tooth curriculum" ([1939] 1975) – consisting of the skills of fish-grabbing, horse-clubbing, and saber-tooth tiger-scaring – though self-evidently factitious, is probably a reasonably accurate account of how these early VET practices would have eventually been formalized and systematized as tribes and communities developed religious, puberty, and organizational/leadership mores and rituals (Wilds and Lottich, 1970). Since such vocational practices seem both natural and crucial in terms of survival and progress, the intriguing question is why these processes came to be differentiated, with different forms and strands distinguished in terms of prestige and status in ways that generally disfavor and disvalue vocational studies.

Lewis, for instance, refers to the "historical problem of vocational education" which he outlines in terms of its subordinate status in relation to general academic studies and the fact that it "has traditionally been viewed in class terms" (Lewis, 1991, pp. 96–7). Similarly, in examining the historical development of vocational studies in British schools, Coffey noted that its "place and scope . . . has been sparse, limited in intent and fragmented" (Coffey, 1992, p. 2), and Maclure has commented upon the "historical failure of English education to integrate the academic and the practical, the general and the vocational" (Maclure, 1991, p. 28). Moreover, Lewis suggests that "whether in the developed or developing world . . . vocational education has been conceived of as being unworthy of the elite, and more suited to the oppressed or unprivileged classes" (Lewis, 1991, p. 97). In like vein, observe that, in England and Wales, the "educational tradition has been inhospitable to a broad and comprehensive vocational philosophy" (Skilbeck et al., 1994, p. 138).

As Silver and Brennan have commented, "education and training, theory and practice, the liberal and the vocational – the polarities have centuries of turbulent history" (Silver and Brennan, 1988, p. 3). This history goes back at least to ideas about knowledge and education originally espoused by Plato and Aristotle, though more recent formulations owe much to the development of compulsory schooling at a time when societies were industrializing and conceptions of work, labor, and production were being shaped in the popular consciousness (Hyland, 1999). Distinctions between "work" (linked to autonomous activity) and "labor" (associated with heteronomous activity) have, as White (1997, chapter 2) has argued, played a crucial role in determining the values surrounding different notions of vocational learning. Against this background it will be argued later that, although the concept of productive work linked to vocationalism through applied knowledge may have contributed to the subordinate status of VET in the past, the idea of workplace learning provides an excellent means of transcending the bifurcated reasoning in this sphere and establishing a cogent reconceptualization of vocational studies for the post-Fordist society of the twenty-first century.

Vocational–Academic Distinctions

All the hierarchical curriculum differences outlined above – eventually linked to social stratification in which disinterested knowledge came to be associated with a leisured elite and applied knowledge with the mass of people who had to work for a living (Schofield, 1972) – were later to be codified precisely by Dewey in his attempts to break down the "antithesis of vocational and cultural education" based on the false oppositions of "labour and leisure, theory and practice, body and mind" (Dewey, 1916/1966, p. 306). As a result of these developments, educational arrangements in the English-speaking world have been powerfully shaped throughout their history by a series of related and overlapping dichotomies inspired by the ancient Greeks, viz. body vs. mind, hand vs. head, manual vs. mental, skills vs. knowledge, applied vs. pure, knowing how vs. knowing that, practice vs. theory, particular vs. general, and training vs. education. We say "dichotomies" rather than "distinctions" because dichotomies more clearly go beyond the linguistic in having material consequences in social and political realities. The power of this series of

dichotomies is reflected in the ongoing institutional separation of vocational education and training from the educational mainstream.

Of course some university education is clearly vocational and always has been
(Carr, 1997). For example, a major role of universities from their beginnings was to
produce leaders in areas such as the church and the law. Since the industrial revolution, the vocational scope of universities has expanded continually. However, this
expansion has been justified as educational rather than narrowly vocational by the
perceived predominance of the mental over the manual in such studies, a feature not
seen as shared by those sub-professional occupations excluded from university study.
As Ashby succinctly put it:

> Here is the criterion for determining what subject or what parts of a subject should be
> taught at a university. If the subject lends itself to disinterested thinking; if generaliza-
> tion can be extracted from it; if it can be advanced by research; if, in brief, it breeds
> ideas in the mind, then the subject is appropriate for a university. If, on the other hand,
> the subject borrows all its principles from an older study (as journalism does from
> literature, or salesmanship from psychology, or massage from anatomy and physiology),
> and does not lead to generalization, then the subject is not a proper one for a university.
> Let it be taught somewhere by all means. It is important that there should be opportun-
> ities for training in it. But it is a technique, not an exercise for maintaining intellectual
> health; and the place for technique is a technical college. (Ashby, 1946, p. 81)

Ashby's suggestions have a certain plausibility. For a start they incorporate the
idea that institutional arrangements validate the dichotomy – universities for general
education, technical (or further education or community) colleges for vocational
education. Ashby's suggestions also seem to explain a range of historical facts about
the development of particular university courses. In law and medicine general principles underlying the profession are the province of the university, whilst specific
vocational skills are learnt away from the university as an articled clerk or intern.
Certain subjects faced a long battle to gain a place in universities. For example,
pharmacy was typically an apprenticeship course at technical or further education
colleges until it could finally breed enough ideas in the mind to move to the universities. Likewise, the struggle of engineering to gain acceptance within universities
was long and complex (Ashby, 1966, chapter 3). The dichotomies have had crucial
material consequences at the social and political levels as they significantly shaped
what counts as knowledge, who delivers it and who certifies it. According to this
received "grand narrative" of education derived from Plato and Aristotle, theoretical
knowledge is superior to both practical and productive knowledge. For Aristotle,
theoretical knowledge was linked "to certainty, because its object was said to be
what is always or for most part the case" (Aristotle, 1976, p. 207). According to
Aristotle, it thereby had a share in the divine. He held that practical knowledge was
inferior to theoretical knowledge because it involved "choice among relative goods"
and productive knowledge was even more inferior because it involved "the making
of things out of contingent matter." For the Greeks this hierarchy of theory/
practice/production was not only epistemological, but also social in that a person's
place in the city state reflected the kind of knowledge that was their daily concern.

It is arguable that this epistemology creates several problems due to its impoverished notions of knowledge. Knowledge is quarantined from emotion and will. Although this influential view of knowledge may have origins in the thought of Plato and Aristotle, its influence became greater via the legacy of Descartes (Schofield, 1972). If humans are essentially minds that incidentally inhabit bodies, then development of mind remains the focus of education. If thinking is the essential characteristic of minds, it can be treated in isolation from non-essential emotion and conation.

This elevation of theoretical knowledge underpins the front-end model of education for work: that is, a structured dose of appropriate education prior to entering an occupation is sufficient basis for a career. The main business of preparatory courses is then to supply novices with the knowledge that they will apply later on to solve problems in their workplace practice. However, such dichotomous theory/practice thinking prevents serious consideration of knowledge peculiar to the workplace, or of the possibility that the workplace might be an important and distinctive source of knowledge. If workplace practice merely involves the application of general theories (taught through formal education), then the details of workplace problems remain of little interest to formal education.

Criticisms of the Vocational Education/ General Education Dichotomy

Over the years the vocational education/general education dichotomy has attracted a diverse range of critical comment (Skilbeck et al., 1994; Avis et al., 1996). Three broad types of arguments against this dichotomy can be distinguished readily – economic arguments, technological arguments, and educational arguments (see Hager, 1990). From the economist's point of view the vocational/general dichotomy is a false one, not only because graduates of supposedly general higher education courses end up in relatively well paid jobs, but also because the same result is found in all countries where schooling offers alternatives of general education or vocational education. In addition, underdeveloped countries that set out to achieve economic growth and development by deliberately making their education system specifically vocational have fared less well than those whose education system focused on basic general education (Green, 1997). So in both cases there remains the paradox that general education appears to be more vocational than vocational education. Hence the dichotomy appears a spurious one, at least in terms of distinguishing education that prepares people for work from education that serves other purposes.

Technological arguments against the dichotomy center on the capacities needed to deal successfully with rapid technological change (Lewis, 1997). The main claim here is that while specific skills are quickly rendered redundant by the pace of technological change, more generic attributes remain relevant and, indeed, are the key to adapting quickly and easily to ever new circumstances. The major impact of microelectronic technology on work is an oft-quoted example of the creation of a demand for the broad attributes that general education provides. Hence a major interest in generic attributes has become evident at all levels of education in the last decade. The aim has been to identify, teach, and assess generic attributes thought to be common to performance in both education and the workplace. In the United States these generic attributes are known as "workplace competencies" or "foundation skills" (SCANS, 1991), in England and Scotland as "core skills," in Australia as "key competencies," and in New Zealand as "essential skills" – all reductive expressions and all leading to confusion. However, generic attribute approaches are not without their problems. Their proponents are often naively optimistic about the transferability of such attributes (Hyland, 1999). Research evidence that generic attributes are acquired best in authentic practice situations further emphasizes the limitations of the front-end model of vocational preparation.

The educational arguments against the vocational education/general education dichotomy are more diverse. Perhaps one thing that they broadly have in common is a rejection of the theory/practice dichotomy, which is a close relative of the general education/vocational education dichotomy. Although the educational arguments against the vocational education/general education dichotomy are diverse, a common theme is well presented by Whitehead. In arguing for the view that "the antithesis between a technical and a liberal education is fallacious" (Whitehead, 1950, p. 74), Whitehead offers the following basic challenge: "Pedants sneer at an education which is useful. But if education is not useful, what is it?" (ibid., p. 3).

The educational arguments against the vocational education/general education dichotomy usually turn on epistemological considerations. For one thing, knowledge and competence are not as disparate as some commentators assume. Wolf argues "that there is no bifurcation between competence and education." She takes this to mean that competency-based education "is perfectly compatible with the learning of higher-level skills, the acquisition of generalizable knowledge (and understanding), and with broad-based courses . . . Competence is a construct, and not something that we can observe directly" (Wolf, 1989, pp. 39–40). But so too is knowledge. (We infer whether a student's knowledge is adequate from their performance on various tests and assignments.) What we know of the structure of mind shows the importance of a variety of cognitive abilities. Knowledge recall is only the start. Far from involving practice without theory, as some higher education critics fear, what competence does is to take us beyond lower cognitive abilities, such as recall, to higher cognitive abilities, such as application and synthesis of knowledge. Not just that something is done, but why it is done is crucial, that is, "'knowing' something involves knowing when to access it, and being able to do so when appropriate – even if it is only in an examination room" (ibid., p. 42).

There are still other epistemological arguments against the vocational/general dichotomy. For instance, Wilson (1992) has argued that by shunning the vocational, universities risk inhibiting the growth of knowledge. His argument, briefly, is that knowledge is a social product and so are the ways that we package it. He discusses various sorts of boxes in which it might be packaged, and suggests an initial four-fold division: (1) enabling disciplines (philosophy, mathematics, computing, etc.); (2) disciplines concerned with the natural world (physics, chemistry, biology, etc); (3) disciplines concerned with the human world (the arts, the social sciences); and (4) disciplines concerned with practice in the human world (engineering, medicine, law, education, etc.). Wilson argues that all categories of the disciplines make valuable contributions to knowledge advance. Increasingly, he suggests, significant advances require interdisciplinary and multidisciplinary input. He further suggests that disciplines concerned with practice in the human world offer unique skills, such as design, diagnosis, and pattern recognition, and should not be neglected in favor of the first three categories. Many of these characteristics are now incorporated in contemporary programs of work-based learning in universities (Symes and McIntyre, 2000).

Given these criticisms of the vocational education/general education dichotomy, it is unsurprising that the model of education that has been inspired by this dichotomy is experiencing increasing difficulties.

The Front-end Model and its Increasing Problems

The term "front-end model" refers to any instance of vocational preparation that is based on a period of formal education and/or training that needs to be completed by entrants to the occupation before they can be regarded as qualified workers. This usually takes place in classrooms remote from the workplace. This model is called "front-end" because it implies that all of the learning that is needed for a lifetime of practice has been completed. The model has been dominant in vocational preparation of all kinds, especially in professional and subprofessional occupations where a period of some years study in a formal educational institution is typically a prerequisite for entry into the occupation. However, the front-end model has been influential also in trades and other skilled occupations in spite of their greater recognition of the importance of on-the-job learning for novices. In these occupations a mandatory period of formal education or training has been common, and is becoming even more so. In Australia, for example, a system of one year traineeships including a formal education component has been instituted over the last decade for a wide range of occupations not covered by apprenticeships. Thus, in the recent past, approaches to vocational preparation have nearly always centered around formal and structured learning in classrooms and training settings.

This front-end model has, however, been the target of much recent criticism. Three main sets of doubts – outlined and discussed in the following sections – signal a sharp decline in confidence in it. In response to these doubts, some seek to refurbish a model that they argue has served us well. Hence they regard the problems as internal ones. For others, a new and unstable external environment is what renders the model obsolete.

Doubts generated by perceived failures of the front-end model

During the 1990s there has been growing international public dissatisfaction with the professions and with the performance of particular professionals, fueled by an increased willingness on the part of the media to expose professional incompetence and malpractice, by the increasing sophistication of consumers, and by general demands for greater accountability. The professions have reacted to this situation in various ways – by implementing more rigorous assessment and certification of professionals, by increasing continuing professional education (CPE) requirements, and by reforming assessment procedures in professional preparation courses. All of these, but especially the second, have raised doubts about whether the front-end model is still viable.

Doubts about its efficacy are not confined to the professions. In the last decade, various countries have introduced occupational competency standards (Arguelles and Gonczi, 2000) and, in America, the 1990 Carl D. Perkins Act set out similar standards. These represent an attempt to specify the main attributes and skills required in the competent performance of an occupation. One of the clear lessons from this experience is that vocational preparation courses are unable to produce graduates who fully meet the competency standards (Hager, 1998). At best, the front-end model produces novices requiring significant on-the-job learning. Typically this limitation of the model has been ignored, though in some cases recently it has received at least tacit recognition. It is no accident surely that many of the professions have long required that completion of the formal course be followed by an internship, a professional year, a probationary year, and so forth. Likewise the traditional path from apprentice to fully qualified tradesperson can be seen as recognizing the ongoing on-the-job learning that high level performance requires. Typically, the formal vocational education component is completed in the early years with subsequent workplace practice leading to full qualification as a tradesperson. While poorly planned arrangements have understandably led some to raise charges of "time-serving," this should not be allowed to obscure the significant role that informal on-the-job learning plays in all apprenticeships.

Doubts about the received understanding of the nature of workplace practice

A prominent "common-sense" assumption underpinning the front-end model is that the theories taught in the formal course subsequently play a major role in workplace performance. Various writers on the preparation of professionals have drawn attention to the inadequacy of this "common-sense" assumption, which Schön (1983, 1987) calls "technical rationality." He characterizes it as the view that professionals need to have command of a body of disciplinary knowledge, mostly scientific, which they then draw upon to analyze and solve the various problems that they encounter in their daily practice. This approach does not fit well, he claims, with what is known about the actual practice of professionals. For one thing, it is typical of real life practice that ready-made problems do not simply present themselves to the practitioner. A major role of professionals is to identify what the problems are in a given set of circumstances.

The front-end model of professional education typically reflects this technical rationality in its curriculum emphases: knowledge acquisition, together with practice at applying knowledge to professional problems. Even if the technical rationality critique is not compelling, the front-end model can be seen as a fairly hit-and-miss affair in its own terms. The extent of transferability and application would seem to depend on the cognate proximity of the workplace to the intellectual core of the formal learning. Sometimes proximity is regarded as ideal – for example, banking is underpinned better by a Bachelor of Commerce than by an arts degree; sometimes the opposite is favored – for example, in the diplomatic corps, or even in the public sector. Thus there has been, traditionally, a spectrum of beliefs about the best model of transfer and application. Little wonder, then, that the nature of professional practice and ways to improve induction into it have recently become major concerns.

The critique of technical rationality has the effect of raising questions about the types of knowledge that practitioners actually require. These questions have been sharpened further by debates about whether or not competency or performance standards incorporate knowledge adequately (see, e.g., Hager and Beckett, 1995; Davis, 1998; Lum, 1999). In Western culture universities have become the knowledge creation and development centers of society. The vocational education and training sector, however, has been geared to knowledge users as opposed to knowledge producers. The emerging rhetoric suggests that the workplace of the future is one that will also be a knowledge creation and development site, opening an age-old debate concerning the relationship between theoreticians and practitioners. The classical elevation of the academic over the practitioner has dominated the relationship between the two groups within our culture. Practice-based knowledge and the knowledge developed through formal education exist independently of one another, and each is relatively unrecognized by those in the other domain. Large areas of know-how are therefore frequently either omitted from educational programs or described and codified differently. Practice-based know-how is, in itself, often imprecise, implicit in nature, contextualized, and therefore difficult to explain. In contrast, the knowledge base in education programs lends itself to codification and generalizability. This appears to be the position in both professional and nonprofessional situations (Eraut, 1994).

Doubts about the capacity of the front-end model to deal with rapid change

The very real impact of unprecedented and accelerating change on work and on vocational preparation courses cannot be ignored. One clear effect has been to place pressure on the front-end approach. Increasingly, a formal two, three, or four year course at the start of a career is seen merely as the necessary foundation for the early years of practice, rather than as the sufficient basis for a lifetime of practice.

One upshot is an increasing openness to a reconceptualization of the role of knowledge in the workplace. Declining confidence in received understandings of the nature of professional practice have, however, not been enough to convince everyone of the need for an alternative model. This is so because, while the front-end model is founded on the dubious theory/practice view of the nature of professional practice, no rival theory has gained sufficient support to replace decisively the theory/

practice view. Schön's well-known theory of "reflecting-in-action" has been widely influential, not least in attempts to revivify the front-end model by incorporating the practice of reflection into it, but it has been subject to an increasing range of criticisms. A major criticism is that it is much clearer what Schön is against than what he is for. His proposal for "reflecting-in-action" is variously charged with being too vague. Gilroy (1993) challenges it on general epistemological grounds. Beckett (1996) goes further and questions the very existence of "reflecting-in-action," particularly in those professions where the action is typically "hot." "Hot" action is a characteristic of professions where the "pressure for action is immediate" (Eraut, 1985, p. 128). This includes much of the work of teachers, surgeons, lawyers in court, nurses, and so forth. By contrast the work of a lawyer preparing a brief, of an architect developing a design, or of a doctor in a consulting room, is much "cooler." Beckett's point is that while "reflecting-in-action" might have some plausibility in these latter cases, it is simply inapplicable in situations of "hot" action. He argues that "anticipative action" is a better explanatory concept for these cases, though itself not without its difficulties.

While Schön's theory has failed to gain widespread assent, so have many others (Hager, 1996). Although various theories offer interesting insights into the nature of occupational and professional practice, our overall understanding of this important topic is still rather primitive. We are left in an unsatisfactory situation. The familiarity and commonsensical plausibility of the front-end model have not saved it from criticism, and attempts to renovate it have not removed doubt about its capacity to produce graduates who deal effectively with change. This has led to a strong interest in the idea of lifelong learning.

Vocational Education and Training: Developments and Strategies

Although the vocational/academic divisions outlined in earlier sections have persisted in educational developments over the last half century, the changing nature and demands of capital and the labor market have meant that the language and terms of reference have developed apace. Changes in the meanings and popular conceptions of the key notions of "class" and "skill" have paralleled developments in capitalism in the move from Fordist to post-Fordist production (Ainley, 1993) and these transformations – particularly since the 1970s oil crisis, recession, and growth of mass youth unemployment – have been matched by reformulations of the role of VET (Flude and Sieminski, 1999).

The "new vocationalism" – a term that commentators use to characterize the vocationalization of all aspects of education since the 1970s (Avis et al., 1996; Hyland, 1999) – may be defined in terms of the "ideal of practical relevance: applicable knowledge and skills" (Skilbeck et al., 1994, p. 18). The recent "resurgence of interest in the world's industrialised countries in the vocational dimension of education" (ibid., p. 22) has not, however, been prompted by educational considerations linked to the need to reconcile or create parity of esteem between the academic and the vocational, but by the changing nature of the global economy and labor markets. Since the period of the so-called Great Debate in Britain and the beginning of the new vocational initiatives in the 1970s there has been a tendency (unfortunate since, as argued later, it is grossly mistaken) to correlate VET and economic/industrial performance in a direct and often causal manner (Hyland, 1994; Raggatt and Williams, 1999). This sort of interpretation was encouraged by analyses of the problems of the British economy such as Barnett's *Audit of War* (1986) and Wiener's *English Culture and the Decline of the Industrial Spirit* (1981) which, as Whiteside et al. noted, "contributed to the development of a set of beliefs among politicians and industrialists that one of the central causes of Britain's prolonged economic decline lay in its education and training system" (Whiteside et al., 1992, p. 4).

Consequently, throughout the 1980s a view emerged that schooling was not just an inadequate preparation for working life for a substantial number of students, but that the poor economic performance of Britain in those days was somehow caused by the deficiencies of school leavers. Such a representation of the problem has been exposed as a crude and dishonest "vocationalist ritual," a tissue of misinformation that attempted to "juvenalise and personalise the problem ... understate more parsimonious causes ... equate simplistically education and economic success and deflect attention from youth unemployment" (Stronach, 1990, p. 173). The irrationality of this discourse "had the effect of distorting public policy debate about the relationship between economic change, education and employment" (Esland, 1990, p. 5). Even more damage was done to the cause of upgrading vocational studies by the practical implications of such policies, particularly the development of a number of Youth Training Schemes (YTS) – most of which, under the guise of the "enterprise" label, immorally "sold unemployment relief as training" (Lee et al., 1990, p. 195) – which, by concentrating on narrow job skills and competences (Hyland, 1994; Green, 1997) effectively downgraded VET in general and work-based training in particular.

In recent years public policy for postcompulsory education and training has moved away from skill-talk and competences toward the notion of lifelong learning as a model for reform. Appropriated from the adult education tradition with the purpose of breaking down the so-called "front-end," conventional model of schooling, the slogan of "lifelong learning" is now being used in Britain primarily as a means of popularizing a particular view of VET. In commenting on *The Learning Age* (DfEE, 1998) – the New Labour government's definitive policy document on education and training – the then Secretary of State observed that "for individuals who want security in employment and a nation that must compete worldwide, learning is the key" (Blunkett, 1998, p. 18).

Although there are references to broader perspectives on education – for example, emphasizing active citizenship, personal development, and social inclusion – in the more recent New Labour policy documents, the overriding thrust of current policy is economistic and concerned principally with upskilling the workforce to gain a competitive advantage in the global marketplace (Hyland, 1999). However, the emphasis on *learning* – as opposed to skills or competence-based training – has been welcomed by adult educators and VET providers for the scope it offers to transcend the narrow, task-based occupationalism which characterized education and training in Britain in the 1980s and 1990s.

Two examples of the impact of such policy on practice – the University for Industry (UfI) scheme and the New Deal programs for unemployed people – are worth mentioning since, in addition to being flagship government programs, they serve to illustrate contemporary strategies for VET. Both of the programs are characterized by the "third way politics" whose aim is the "social investment state" which "defines equality as inclusion and inequality as exclusion" (Giddens, 1998, p. 102). The commitment to social inclusion leads to objectives concerned with bridging the "learning divide between those who have benefited from education and training and those who have not" (DfEE, 1998, p. 11). To this end both the UfI and the New Deal initiatives are informed by ideas of extending opportunities and access to VET programs for traditionally underrepresented individuals and organizations.

The UfI is a "virtual" organization which – by exploiting existing resources and facilities through information and communications technology (ICT) and the Internet – seeks to establish a network of learning centers that will "broker" services and sources between users and providers of VET (Hillman, 1997). Targeting individuals who lack basic skills and small and medium-sized enterprises (SMEs) that have historically been excluded from VET networks, the new organization intends to open up opportunities and stimulate the demand for lifelong learning.

The New Deal Welfare to Work (WtW) programs (DfEE, 1997) are also concerned with social exclusion in the sense that they are designed to provide the skills and wherewithal to help unemployed people (especially 18–24 year olds) to find sustained jobs. A key element in WtW schemes is the initial "Gateway" phase, a period of intensive guidance and counseling by which unemployed people are directed toward various options in the public, private, and voluntary sectors of employment. There is also a full-time VET option and all job placements are linked to part-time education and training for which employers receive government subsidies. In its two years of operation, New Deal has helped 230,000 young people into jobs and another 148,000 have been guided into work experience or training (*Educa*, 2000, p. 5).

Although such lifelong learning policies are currently operating primarily on the deficit model in remedying past VET shortcomings, their populist ethos and determination to widen and extend access for traditionally underrepresented groups is highly significant and promising. Lifelong learning versions of vocational studies are still influenced rather too much by the technicism and narrow instrumentalism characteristic of former strategies but, in forging links between the short-term work-relief schemes and traineeship, modern apprenticeship, and general VET provision in Britain, they demonstrate a potential for generating the sort of reforms necessary for solving the historical problems in this sphere (Hyland, 2000a).

Conclusion: Enhancing Vocational Studies

It has been argued that developments in VET during the last quarter of the twentieth century in Britain and elsewhere not only failed to heal the historical divisions between vocational and academic studies but, through narrowly defined skills and competence-based strategies, actually served to deskill and downgrade many VET programs. Current lifelong learning programs are only likely to have a limited impact on this historical problem since their main purpose is directed toward relieving unemployment, upskilling the workforce, and enhancing the employability skills of young people. In order to create parity of esteem for vocational studies, enhance work-based learning, and achieve the principal lifelong learning objectives, such short-term relief projects need to be supplemented by substantial reform measures.

There have been many strategies – both theoretical and practical – for reconciling the vocational and academic strands of educational provision. In the nineteenth century, the ideas of philosophical idealists such as T. H. Green and utilitarians such as Mill were used to construct elaborated conceptions of liberal education that purported to incorporate the scientific and technological advances of the Industrial Revolution (Gordon and White, 1979). In response to the same technological revolution, Dewey's writings have been highly influential in arguing for an education that stresses the "full intellectual and social meaning of a vocation" (Dewey, [1916] 1966, p. 318) with the aim of breaking down the "antithesis of vocational and cultural education" (ibid., p. 301).

An interesting version of revisionism in this sphere is illustrated in Adams's *Modern Developments in Educational Practice* which insists that "all education must affect our future life either adversely or favourably, and to that extent all education is vocational, preparing us for the vocation of life" (Adams, 1933, p. 50). A more recent example of this sort of approach is Silver and Brennan's (1988) advocacy of "liberal vocationalism" in higher education, which involves both the introduction of "hybrid" courses combining arts and science subjects, and the incorporation of liberal/general education elements into vocational programs in engineering and business studies degrees. The key principle here seems to be that of demonstrating that liberal and vocational studies have many characteristics in common. R. S. Peters makes a similar point in observing that both theoretical and practical activities can be engaged in "for their own sakes" (Peters, 1978, p. 9) and, in the same vein, Walsh argues that "once the real values of liberal pursuits are stated and classified . . . we can find the same values in practical pursuits" (Walsh, 1978, p. 62).

A danger with all such reconciliation strategies – whether they seek to show that liberal education can include the vocational, or that vocational education can be liberal – is that of reinforcing the original divisions and sources of differentiation. Pring alludes to such difficulties in his observation that in many such formulations: "'Liberal' is contrasted with 'vocational' as if the vocational, *properly taught*, cannot itself be liberating – a way into those forms of knowledge through which a person is freed from ignorance, and opened to new imaginings, new possibilities" (Pring, 1995, p. 189, original italics). There is now a growing consensus about what needs to be done (Avis et al., 1996; Raggatt and Williams, 1999) – at both practical and theoretical levels – to upgrade vocational studies and bridge the academic/vocational divide. By way of a conclusion it is worth examining the emerging discourse in this sphere in terms of three key categories: learning, curriculum, and values.

Learning

Although Pring recommends a form of *teaching* as part of a vocational/academic reconciliation strategy, in truth the emphasis really needs to be placed upon *learning* (while accepting the connections between learning and teaching), particularly the sort of learning directed toward student autonomy and empowerment which figures prominently in conceptions of "studentship" and "learning careers" (Bloomer, 1997). It is surely worth noting that the one common element in relation to the main dualisms in this sphere – vocational–academic, theoretical–practical, education–training – is precisely and crucially the process of *learning*. What matters in terms of enhancing the quality and status of VET, therefore, is that this learning is rich and deep, allowing for the progression and continuity that is essential to working careers and lifelong learning objectives.

This focus on learning also raises the challenge of recognizing that worthwhile learning often occurs outside of formal education settings. Earlier sections have indicated why the workplace has been viewed as uninteresting from an educational perspective. Thus any learning that occurs during the practice of work has been held to be of little significance compared to knowledge acquired by other means, particularly formal education and training. Quite simply, informal learning, which by definition largely lies outside of the political and social processes by which societies organize, transmit, and accredit knowledge, is thereby rendered invisible. The widespread acceptance of this view becomes understandable when the major differences on many criteria between informal workplace learning and traditional "educational" activities are noted. Owing to the influence of the vocational education/general education dichotomy, formal on-the-job training is widely viewed as of dubious educational status. But, on many criteria, structured on-the-job training is much more like traditional "educational" activities than it is like informal workplace learning. This is because both share many features common to all formal learning. Hence, there is a paradigm shift implied in any suggestion that informal workplace learning should be taken seriously as part of someone's education. The vast differences between informal workplace learning and formal learning activities of all kinds can be appreciated from the following considerations:

1 Teachers/trainers are in control in both formal learning in educational institutions and in on-the-job training, whereas the learner is in control (if anyone is) in informal workplace learning. That is, formal learning is intentional, but workplace learning is often unintentional.

2 Learning in formal education and in on-the-job training is prescribed by formal curriculum, competency standards, learning outcomes, and so forth. Informal workplace learning has no formal curriculum or prescribed outcomes.

3 In both educational institutions and on-the-job training, learning outcomes are largely predictable. Informal workplace learning outcomes are much less predictable.

4 In both educational institutions and on-the-job training, learning is largely explicit (the learner is expected to be able to articulate what has been learnt, for example in a written examination or in answer to teacher questioning; trainees

are required to perform appropriate activities as a result of their training). Informal workplace learning is often implicit or tacit (learners are commonly unaware of the extent of their learning).

5 In formal classrooms and in on-the-job training the emphasis is on teaching/ training and on the content and structure of what is taught/trained (largely as a consequence of 1–4). In informal workplace learning, the emphasis is on the experiences of the learner-as-worker: not a concept to be taken lightly, given the power of self-directed learning in making sense of one's workplace as well as one's own life at work.

6 Formal classroom learning and on-the-job training usually focus on individual learning. Informal workplace learning is more often collaborative and/or colle- gial, despite the current policy and rhetorical emphasis on self-direction and individual experience, noted in point 5. This sociality occurs because work- places are by definition socioculturally located, and their consequently shared and site-specific experiences collectively available for educative purposes. Thus workers invest much of their personal identities in work, and find these defined and redefined by the local work culture – by "the way we do things here."

7 Learning in formal classrooms is uncontextualized, that is, it emphasizes general principles rather than their specific applications. While on-the-job training is typically somewhat contextualized, even here the general is emphasized, for example, training for general industry standards. But, informal workplace learn- ing is by its nature highly contextualized, as outlined in point 6, and must include emotive, cognitive, and social dimensions of workers' experiences in advancing their learning.

8 Learning in formal education and in on-the-job training is seen typically in terms of theory (or knowledge) and practice (application of theory and knowledge). Informal workplace learning, though, seems to be appropriately viewed as seam- less know-how, a close relative of the Aristotelian notion of *phronesis* or practical wisdom.

9 In educational institutions and in on-the-job training, learning knowledge typ- ically is viewed as more difficult than learning skills (thus, e.g., more teaching effort is invested usually in the first as against the second). Informal workplace learning, as the development of competence or capability via a suitably structured sequence of experience, does not operate with the knowledge/skills distinction.

Given 1–9, it is hardly surprising that formal learning/education is valued much more than informal learning (including workplace learning). Informal workplace learning is a paradigm case of informal education which is undervalued particularly by all levels in the formal education system. Historically, training has been viewed as the antithesis of education. Training as mindless, mechanical, routine activity has been contrasted with education as development of mind via completion of intel- lectually challenging tasks (Winch, 1995). Yet despite this "chalk and cheese" con- ception of education and training, 1–9 above show that they have more in common with one another than either has with informal workplace learning. No wonder, then, that for many involved in education the idea of informal workplace learning as genuine education is beyond the pale. Despite this, for several reasons discussed in this chapter, such as the growth of interest in lifelong learning and the advent of the University for Industry, informal learning at work is suddenly starting to receive significant attention.

However, for informal workplace learning to be viewed seriously as a legitimate adjunct to mainstream educational activities, traditional dichotomies would need to be discarded and the notion of education itself reconceptualized. This remains a major challenge for philosophy of education as evidenced by J. White (1997). In this book White provides excellent analyses of various philosophical accounts of work, but his own theory has the effect of preserving the traditional dichotomies. White defines both education and work in such as way as to rule out any significant overlap between the two. Thus the outcome, perhaps unintentional, of White's intellectual framework is that work is educationally uninteresting, and hence learning at work of little value (Hager, 1999).

What contemporary work in philosophy of education clearly goes beyond the traditional dichotomies? Perhaps the most promising is that seeking to develop new understandings of learning based on the later Wittgenstein (e.g., M. Williams, 1994; Winch, 1998). Despite the bad press that training has received in traditional philosophy of education, this work suggests that the basic form of learning is being trained into pattern-governed behaviors, that is, learning to engage in activities licensed by practice or custom. This work stresses learning as a normative social practice avoiding the mentalistic presuppositions that have shaped most philosophical thought on these matters.

Curriculum

Skilbeck et al., in comparing a broad range of national VET strategies, note the differences between the "schooling" and "working life" approaches to vocational studies. On the schooling model (operating, in different degrees, in the USA, France, and Britain) the "primary responsibility for vocational education lies with the school authorities," whereas on the working life model (characteristic of VET systems in Germany, Austria, Switzerland, and Denmark) the "primary responsibility for vocational education lies with employers or in a shared arrangement with school authorities"(Skilbeck et al., 1994, p. 64). After examining all the various systems, the authors conclude by suggesting that – whatever their location on the schooling–working life continuum – there is "an acceptance of the need for improved quality and relevance of programmes that aim to embrace all youth up to and beyond the age of 18" (ibid., p. 105). In order to achieve this goal, they argue that: "The idea of a core of common, fundamental learnings for working life, and their definition, organisation and delivery to students in appropriate settings, provides a means of interrelating the traditionally, and dysfunctionally, separated domains of general and vocational education" (p. 60).

In a similar vein, Green has identified two major strategies used for ensuring that VET is underpinned by the general educational foundation necessary for adult and working life. The "general technical and vocational education" paradigm (which operates in France, Germany, Japan, and Sweden) is based on the "precept that vocational learning rests on a common foundation of general education, or *culture generale* as it is termed in France" (Green, 1997, p. 92). Linked to ideas of citizenship and minimum cultural entitlement, this approach assumes that all forms of vocational study require a general foundation to support the knowledge and skills required for working life. Against this, the "core skills" paradigm (characteristic of the American and British systems) assumes no general educational or cultural entitlement but, instead, bases VET on technical and essentially utilitarian considerations linked to employment and labor market requirements.

Reflecting on the skills and competence-based developments in British VET referred to earlier, Green observes that with the "decline of time-served apprenticeship, and the advent of competence-based learning, this already 'lean' notion of skill has become more minimalist, both culture- and theory-free" (1997, p. 93). He concludes that:

> the core skills paradigm represents an impoverished form of general education which is neither adequately delivering the minimum basic skills normally associated with an effective general education . . . nor even attempting to impart a foundation of scientific and humanistic culture adequate to the demands of active citizenship in modern societies . . . However, the critique must go wider than this, since core skills fall short on another count central to the reform of post-16 education, which is that they fail to provide the basis for a workable unified curriculum. (ibid., p. 100)

There is now a broad consensus on the need for a unified curriculum for students aged 14 to 19 that avoids specialization until the later years and allows for a mix of general and vocational subjects (Hodgson and Spours, 1997). The abolition of the divisions between vocational and academic studies at this stage can effectively bridge the historical divide and foster the learning culture that is required to support contemporary lifelong learning policy and practice.

Values

Green's reference to the impoverishment of VET through skills-based and competence-based strategies is paralleled by an impoverishment in the values domain. The new vocationalist initiatives referred to earlier generated a VET system that was excessively technicist and individualist – suggesting that students were nothing more than receptacles needing to be filled with skills and competences for a competitive labor market – and that reduced all values to the qualities desired by employers. There is now a growing critique of this ethically vacuous approach to vocational studies (J. White, 1997; Hyland, 1999) which – in the spirit of Dewey – insists that VET programs should be underpinned by the social, moral, and aesthetic values that are an integral part of all working lives.

Such a values dimension for VET would seek to go beyond the utilitarianism and neoliberal notions that characterized the "enterprise culture" of the 1980s and 1990s (Hyland, 2000b) to construct a framework of communitarian and public service values within which a reconstructed VET can be located. Pring expresses the position well in his observation that in

> trying to reconcile different traditions of liberal education and vocational preparation . . . we need to ask more fundamental moral questions about what it is to live fully human lives and what the connection is between personal development and the wider social framework in which that development might take place. (Pring, 1995, pp. 194–5)

Gleeson makes a similar point in calling for a "new educational settlement" which embraces an "active view of citizenship which links partnership and empowerment in personal education and economic relations beyond market, qualifications and employer-led considerations. . . . It also involves realisation that education, learning, society and work are synonymous, not separate entities" (Gleeson, 1996, p. 15).

Recommendations for Further Reading

Hyland, T. (1999) *Vocational Studies, Lifelong Learning and Social Values*, Ashgate.
Pring, R. (1995) *Closing the Gap: Liberal Education and Vocational Preparation*, Hodder & Stoughton.
Symes, C. and McIntyre, J. (eds.) (2000) *Working Knowledge: The New Vocationalism and Higher Education*, SRHE/Open University Press.
White, J. (1997) *Education and the End of Work: A New Philosophy of Work and Learning*, Cassell.

Chapter 16

Progressivism

John Darling and Sven Erik Nordenbo

Introduction

Progressivism is the name of a broad practical and theoretical approach in education. It should today be viewed, at least in its classical form, as a historical phenomenon that flourished particularly in the first half of the twentieth century. This claim needs certain qualifications, however, regarding time and place. It applies first and foremost to central Europe, particularly Germany and Scandinavia, and North America, while progressivism did not become significant in Great Britain until some decades later. At the same time, this is not to say that today, at the beginning of the twenty-first century, schools do not run along progressivist lines. Indeed it might be argued that classical progressivist approaches and methods, at least in some school systems, have become the new orthodoxy. And this raises the delicate question of whether such approaches and methods still merit the term "progressivism."

Progressivism, or *Reformpädagogik*, arises in contexts in which major educational crises exist in the form of significant gaps between existing arrangements and perceived societal and cultural needs. Either practitioners or theorists, or both, then begin to devise new educational ideas and procedures as alternatives to the prevailing ones. According to Benner and Kemper (1993; cf. also Benner, 1998) such crises have occurred three times in the modern history of education: the first in the second half of the eighteenth century and around the beginning of the nineteenth century when J. J. Rousseau (1712–78) and W. von Humboldt (1767–1835) among others played so prominent a role; the second in the last decade of the nineteenth century and the first third of the twentieth century when a new interest in the nature of the child took its point of departure from the movement *"vom Kinde aus"* – a name taken from a German translation, published in 1900, of a collection of essays with the telling title *Barnets Århundrade* (The Century of the Child) by the Swedish author and feminist Ellen Key (1849–1926); and finally, there is the period from the 1960s onward in which it has become a commonplace to think of things as being in crisis. To understand progressivism, and the nature of these responses to crisis, requires a prior grasp of the defining features of the traditional education to which it reacts.

In the following the discussion will be divided into three main sections. First, we provide a short account of the historical background of, and main contributors to, the development of the classical progressive movement. Second, we identify five main themes that characterize progressivism in its most prominent version. Each of these themes will then be scrutinized. Finally, we discuss briefly the viability of progressivism today. It will be claimed that the three movements of deschooling, children's rights, and antieducation can all be considered to be early contemporary reactions to "postmodern" conditions in the late twentieth century.

Historical Perspective

The history of progressivism could be written either as an account of progressive schools and practitioners or as an account of theorists and advocates of progressive ideas. As philosophers of education, our principal concern will be with the latter. In German history of education, the conventional view has been that *Reformpädagogik* began in 1890 and ended in 1933 (cf. Nohl, 1970). Recently, however, Jürgen Oelkers (1989) has shown that progressivism, understood in terms of a definite period of time, turns out after detailed examination to be the product of a fixed historical tradition. Progressivism did not begin at a specific date but crept in during the nineteenth century until it became the most dominant feature in the world of education at the beginning of the following century. Neither did it, as already mentioned, flourish at the same time in the different European countries. To be more precise, progressive or *reformpädagogische* considerations were at a peak up to the 1930s in northern Europe and Scandinavia with Germany as the main bastion, whereas the heyday of progressivism in Great Britain came in the 1960s and 1970s, only to decline in the Thatcher and Reagan years.

As a prerequisite for identifying an educational movement as progressivism, a certain number of themes or arguments have to be present. The traditional way of introducing these is by telling the story of the precursors of progressivism. In this historiography, this *courant mystique* (Cousinet, 1950), there is a significant group of figures – Comenius, Rousseau, Pestalozzi, Froebel, and Dewey – who are inevitably referred to when the narrative of progressivism is presented. The Czech theologian Johan Amos Comenius (1592–1670) introduced some of the features that later were valued in progressivism. For years he worked on his main educational work *Didactica Magna* (1657) "in which is presented a generally valid art of teaching all things to all men," as its subtitle claims. Comenius later developed this ambitious revival of curricular encyclopedism under the title of "pansophism." The work presents a logical and systematic plan for a reorganization of the whole educational system. Its fundamental philosophical principle is that Nature everywhere can be considered an example for all aspects of teaching: for its phases, progression, manner, and matter. For what Nature writes in capital letters is written in Man in small letters. It is in the light of this that the child's nature has to be respected and kept free to unfold in play. Comenius turns against humanistic linguacentrism and, apart from religion, includes in the curriculum "the real things," or science. Here, it is the children's own experience that is important. In matters of discipline, Comenius advocates gentleness: the sun should be the ideal for the teacher – it is always light and warm, brings sometimes rain and wind, but rarely lightning and thunder.

Despite all this, Comenius remains nothing more than an overture to the first of the classics in the history of progressivism: Rousseau. By any standards, Rousseau is one of the intellectual giants of the Western world and perhaps the first writer to advance the idea of what we now sometimes call a child-centered approach to education. In *Émile* (1762) Rousseau stresses that the educator needs a proper understanding of the child's nature and the way in which this develops. This knowledge should then be used to consider what the child should be taught. In the book's preface, Rousseau argues that the key question is not what we think a child ought to know, but what a child is capable of learning; and he later warns against the facile assumption that children's thought processes are the same as ours: "Childhood has its own ways of seeing, thinking and feeling; nothing is more foolish than to try and substitute our ways" (Rousseau, 1911, p. 54).

Rousseau's armchair psychology, which strikingly anticipates the conclusions of Jean Piaget, claims that reason is absent until the age of 12. Earlier than this, children are incapable of grasping any ideas beyond those that are rooted in, and discovered through, their own experience. Attempts to teach any other ideas should therefore be delayed until the youngster is older, since we know from first principles that such material is beyond the child's understanding. Of course, says Rousseau, it is easy for traditional teachers to convince themselves that it is otherwise; and he gives the following illustration. We can imagine a conventional lesson in which the teacher conveys an idea verbally to the student. To check that this has been received, the teacher asks a question and the student formulates an answer using the same words as the teacher. From the teacher's point of view, the reply appears to confirm that the lesson has been successful but, according to Rousseau, this is a mistaken conclusion. What is really happening in this kind of standard classroom interaction is that the student's mind is functioning only as a mirror. The teacher beams a series of words in the direction of the mirror, and the same words are bounced back to the teacher. But, as Rousseau puts it, the message does not penetrate behind the mirror: the idea is not actually received or internalized. In this early piece of progressive writing we can immediately note two typical features. The first is the critical account of traditional teaching here, arguably providing a plausible and insightful analysis. The second is the assumption that real learning only takes place when the student understands what has been taught. Rousseau's insistence on the importance of understanding is now so generally accepted that it may be hard for people today to appreciate why it was that Rousseau had to press the point so vigorously.

If a book can be said to possess charisma, *Émile* certainly had it. Quickly translated into several different languages, it exercised a powerful influence on various groups and individuals throughout Europe. In Denmark, for instance, significant parts of the book were discussed within months of its publication in *Den patriotiske Tilskuer*, the Danish equivalent of the British *Spectator*. Rousseau was widely read, especially among the upper classes, and even the Danish crown prince was brought up according to Rousseauesque principles in the early 1770s. In the translation of J. H. Campe's entire *Revisionswerk* into Danish in the years 1799–1806, the complete

Émile was included in the 16 volumes along with Locke's *On Education* (Nordenbo, 1984).

One educator who fell under the spell of *Émile* was Johann Heinrich Pestalozzi (1746–1827), who ran several schools and produced many papers and books on education. The most celebrated of these, *Leonard and Gertrude* (1781), was reprinted three times within a decade. Following the elements of fiction in *Émile*, *Leonard and Gertrude* took the form of a novel; but unlike Rousseau, Pestalozzi was able to endow his educational writing with the authority of experience gained as a reflective teacher and father.

Pestalozzi was instrumental in developing another progressive theme, the education of the whole person, summed up in Pestalozzi's phrase "head, heart, and hands." His argument proceeds by suggesting that we should first try to identify what constitutes an ideal man; and then if we can find such a person, we should question him about his education. We will then be told "that the characteristic of his education was that it did not aim solely or predominantly at producing intellectual attainments" but at assisting in the self-fulfillment of man's many-sided abilities (Pestalozzi, 1805, in Green, 1912, p. 58).

For practical educators, one of Rousseau's limitations is that he had so little patience with the idea of schools that he had no interest in how to practice the art of school teaching. Pestalozzi was thus the first progressive to point to the possibility of reconstructing schooling in a more imaginative and participative way, while at the same time recognizing (as some less practical progressive writers later failed to do) that this might make the job more difficult:

> The teacher must enter wholly into the child's point of view, identifying himself completely with the purpose in hand, and march in company with the child from truth to truth, discovery to discovery. This is admittedly much harder than to stand at a desk with a text-book in your hand, dictating or demonstrating its content to the boys. (Pestalozzi, 1807, in Green, 1912, p. 350)

One of Pestalozzi's schools was visited by Friedrich Froebel (1782–1852), who went on to develop his own theory about children's awareness and understanding. These are said to be actually innate, though undeveloped. They become "unfolded" through the practical and creative activity that children naturally want to engage in. Unfortunately this instinct is often checked by misguided adults who fail to realize that such activity is part of the design of a divinely ordered nature. Thus, in his pedagogical interventions the educator has to proceed with great sensitivity:

> If we take account of divine action and consider man in his original state, it is clear that all teaching which prescribes and determines must impede, destroy, annihilate. To take another example from Nature – the vine has to be pruned, but pruning as such does not bring more wine; however good the intention, the vine may be entirely ruined in the process or its fertility destroyed unless the gardener pays attention to the plant's natural growth. In our treatment of natural objects we often go right, whereas we can get on to an entirely wrong track in dealing with human beings. Yet forces are at work in both which flow from one source and obey the same law – and this is an aspect of Nature which it is important for man to observe. (Froebel, 1826, in Lilley, 1967, p. 52)

Froebel's conception of educational development as an unfolding process brought about by practical activity and creativity provided a fresh rationale for the importance of play and of art and craft work, which today are prominent features of classroom life in progressive primary schools. It has been argued (Darling, 1994, p. 24) that what made the impact on schools was not Froebel's writing, but the setting up, after his death, of organizations that aimed to promote Froebelian (and also Pestalozzian) practice. Teachers undoubtedly appreciated the availability of practical material through which such organizations attempted to promote the kind of play that could be seen as having educational value.

John Dewey (1859–1952) was, notwithstanding the year of his birth, "a man of the twentieth century" (Murphy, 1990, p. 59). His best philosophical work, published in the period from World War I to the end of the 1930s, includes the following books: *Democracy and Education* (1916), *Reconstruction in Philosophy* (1920), *Human Nature and Conduct* (1922), *Experience and Nature* (1925), *The Quest for Certainty* (1929), *Art as Experience* (1934), and *Logic: The Theory of Inquiry* (1938). In 1919 he lectured in Japan, and then, for two years, in China. In 1924, he made an inspection tour of schools in Turkey, in 1926 those in Mexico, and in 1928 those in the Soviet Union. All this reflects the fact that Dewey was an internationally known educational theorist. It is thus not surprising that Carr and Hartnett claim that "John Dewey is undoubtedly the most influential educational philosopher of the twentieth century" (Carr and Hartnett, 1996, p. 54). There is, however, a question concerning how much impact on progressivism and *Reformpädagogik* Dewey's philosophy of education had in Europe, at least in the earlier part of the twentieth century. Studies in Germany, England, and the Netherlands suggest that to the extent that Dewey had influence, and was not simply disregarded, his work was passed on second-hand by national progressive educationists (Biesta and Miedema, 1999). In Germany, knowledge of Dewey was scanty even among academic educationists (Bohnsack, 1976), although he influenced the well-known architect of the activity school principle, Georg Kerschensteiner (1854–1932), and a German translation of his main work in philosophy of education, *Democracy and Education*, appeared in 1930.

In England J. J. Findlay, who had studied education in Germany, introduced Dewey at an early stage in two edited anthologies of Dewey's texts, *The School and the Child* (1906) and *Educational Essays* (1910). He also tried to establish a school in Manchester, based on Dewey's Laboratory School in Chicago, but without much success. In spite of the creation of the organization New Education Fellowship (founded 1921) with its journal *New Era*, and of the fact that the American Progressive Education Association (founded 1919) became the American section of the former in 1932, little is heard of Dewey in the United Kingdom between the two World Wars (Brehony, 1997). It is not until after World War II that "Deweyesque" positions, ideas conforming with Dewey's thinking and writing, come into prominence (Darling and Nisbet, 2000). And his work was of undoubted influence during the 1960s on government reports on primary education, and on a generation of trainee teachers, in the United Kingdom. As a curiosity, it is worth noting that this influence later gave rise to comments by Keith Joseph, the first Secretary of State for Education in Margaret Thatcher's government, to the effect that Deweyan theories had been responsible for what had gone wrong in education. Something of these sentiments was echoed in the early 1990s with Prime Minister John Major's adage: "The progressives have had their say and they have had their day."

In the 1990s a sustained revival of interest in Dewey's view of education and democracy has taken place both in the USA and in Germany. With reference to Dewey, Amy Gutmann (1987) stresses political education as the school's main aim in a deliberative democracy and Nel Noddings argues for renewing democracy in schools (Noddings, 1995), while Jürgen Habermas (1998) and Hans Joas (2000) see Dewey as a precursor of deliberative democracy.

Dewey's epistemology, his pragmatic instrumentalism, was inspired by the challenges of Darwin's theory of evolution to philosophy. Dewey wanted to replace the prevailing view that knowledge can be uncovered as a definite and permanent truth, with a new understanding: that knowledge is individual, teleological, instrumental, and relative. The prevailing view was, according to Dewey, based on the mistaken assumption that the world is fundamentally eternal and unchangeable. If that were the case it would make sense to believe that knowledge about the world could be passed on from one generation to another as packages of knowledge labeled "history," "mathematics," "geography," and so on, *without* introducing the new generation to the way this knowledge is created. On the other hand, if the world is a stream of ever-changing phenomena, knowledge is very quickly made obsolete. According to Deweyan understanding, to know the world is to face endlessly new problem situations; it is to apply the individual intellect instrumentally to cope with problems relative to given contexts. The aim of education is consequently to prepare the child to live in such a world together with other human beings.

One way of doing this is to teach the child how to think in a scientific manner. Dewey stresses in his writing that the systematic and methodical acquiring of knowledge demands a definite procedure, first named a "logical theory" and later, in its most elaborated form, a "theory of inquiry" (Dewey, 1938). In *How We Think* (1910) Dewey presents the theory in five steps, with special reference to education (Dewey, 1991, 77ff.). There is in principle no difference between how we make science and how we acquire experience in our day-to-day life. Both are fundamentally to be seen as problem-solving situations in which we continuously reconstruct our experience. Therefore, if we organize schools as places where everyday life problems, *en miniature*, have to be encountered and solved in an active and socially responsible way, schools will not only prepare for life but be places of life in their own right. One important consequence of this for Dewey is that traditional philosophical dualisms between body and soul, action and thought, consciousness and activity, reason and emotion, individual and society, dissolve into a situation in which the total organism is in a continuous interaction with world and society. The child becomes an actor who, out of interest in democratic cooperation with others, actively solves genuine problems encountered in life. Thus, following Deweyan principles, the cross-curricular approach realized in the project and problem method become the stock-in-trade of school teaching. Yet Dewey's writing is full of vagueness, ambiguity, and even inconsistency on the question of practice; perhaps it is these very qualities that have fed the huge academic interest in publishing discussions of his work. Indeed, Dewey himself seems sometimes to have been positively evasive toward questions about the practical implications of his thinking, preferring to confine himself to general suggestions.

In general, with regard to the more specifically philosophical writers, including Dewey, it is not always easy to know what to say about their relationship to classroom practice. To claim a relationship between the development of progressive classroom practice and Rousseau's *Émile* is obviously even more problematic. The book is not known to many teachers, or even today to teachers of teachers, however enthusiastic they may be about the value of discovery learning. In any case, attributing practical innovations to one eighteenth-century work would involve inherently implausible assumptions about how social change can be accounted for. The inclusion of major philosophers in histories of the development of progressive education, particularly those histories constructed by advocates of progressivism, may perhaps be explained as having iconic significance. It is, after all, reassuring to believe that one's preferred style of teaching has an impressive pedigree and is apparently endorsed by thinkers of the highest intellectual standing.

Progressivism: Five Themes

It is generally agreed that progressivism is a movement that includes various features not necessarily embraced by everyone characterized as "progressive." In a recent German paper, Kleinespel and Tillmann (1998, pp. 719–20; cf. also Tenorth, 1994) have set up five arguments that characterize progressivist discourse in general. First and foremost, they mention the Copernican revolution – that is, that education in all aspects has to take its point of departure from children, their nature and perspective, including making the child the author of his or her own learning processes. Second, they underline the widespread critique of the state-governed school, the overcrowded curriculum, and the pressure to achieve, its distance from "real life" and its ritualized and hierarchical management. Then these two arguments are followed by three others that all have a social aspect: that the school has to be a school-community (*Schulgemeinde*) in which all participate on an equal footing; that the internal organization of the school and school classes has to be reformed to involve different kinds of group work; and that the school in its entirety should be an autonomous social unit within the wider society.

In a different account, Sveinung Vaage (2000, pp. 9–10) emphasizes in a Norwegian introduction to John Dewey that progressivism is connected with three features: the emergence of the new child psychology at the end of the nineteenth century; the great importance attached to activity, self-activity, and experience in learning; and the changing of teaching methods toward the project method and other forms involving greater student activity. Vaage especially stresses that John Dewey took up an independent position within the progressive movement with his idea that the final aim of education is to contribute to the development of a better quality of democracy known as "deliberative democracy."

Although we agree with the view that progressivism cannot be precisely defined owing to the fact that many inconsistent responses have been made to the educational crises that have been experienced (cf. Biesta and Miedema, 1999, p. 99), the nature of progressivism can be grasped, nonetheless, with the help of five themes that echo through its history. These are discussed under five headings below.

Criticism of traditional education

As noted above, dissatisfaction with traditional approaches in education has provided the stimulus for the development of progressive educational theory. Expression of this dissatisfaction has taken many forms, some of them quite unphilosophical. The spirit that prevailed over the way in which some young people were at one time educated is memorably portrayed in Charles Dickens's crusading novel, *Hard Times* (1854). In this he sets up a caricature of a private school owned by a Mr. Gradgrind who has recruited a recently trained teacher called McChoakumchild:

> Orthography, etymology, syntax, and prosody, biography, astronomy, geography and general cosmography, the sciences of compound proportion, algebra, land-surveying and levelling, vocal music, and drawing from models, were all at the ends of his ten chilled fingers. . . . He knew all about all the Water Sheds of all the world (whatever they are), and all the histories of all the peoples, and all the names of all the rivers and mountains, and all the productions, manners, and customs of all the countries, and all the boundaries and bearings on the two-and-thirty points of the compass. Ah, rather overdone, McChoakumchild. If he had only learnt a little less, how infinitely better he might have taught much more!

Dickens is here ridiculing an approach to education in which the highest importance is attached to the direct transmission of information and where the value of imagination is deliberately downgraded. When Gradgrind informs his own daughter that a friend of his proposes to marry her, he enquires if she is emotionally involved with someone else. Louisa replies:

> "What do *I* know, Father, . . . of tastes and fancies; of aspirations and affections; of all that part of my nature in which such light things might have been nourished? [. . .] You have trained me so well, that I never dreamed a child's dream. You have dealt so wisely with me, Father, from my cradle to this hour, that I never had a child's belief or a child's fear."
> Mr. Gradgrind was quite moved by his success, and by this testimony to it. (ibid., pp. 101–2)

Knowledge ("facts") is here valued for its utility. But Dickens is pointing to a broader view in which rich experience should be valued not just for its own sake but for its ability to prepare us for the rest of life. There are two objections to Gradgrind's attempt to disparage anything to do with "fancy." One is that this devalues the experience of the child, when a more fruitful approach would be to try to enrich it. The second is that a focus on the world of fact does not actually constitute an adequate preparation for life: since love and marriage are central features of many people's lives, it would be useful for education to attend also to matters of emotional development.

The centrality of the transmission of knowledge has been a feature of traditional education before and after Dickens. The 1947 guidelines for teachers in Edinburgh advised that children should be acquainted with historical figures and episodes that are today largely unknown, and that would now be regarded as difficult for children to comprehend. Eight year olds were to learn about the union of the Scottish and English parliaments; seven year olds had to know of Sir Andrew Wood[1] ("brief references will be sufficient"); and six year olds were to study Peter the Hermit and the Capture of Jerusalem. Influenced by some of the progressivist arguments that will be discussed later, we have now changed our ideas about what constitutes suitable curriculum material for children, and, more radically, our way of understanding what a curriculum is.

In fact, much of the traditionalist conception of education seems strangely unfamiliar today. Yet the approach is not wholly irrational, despite contrary suggestions from the progressivists. It stems from a time when what was seen as being known was accepted on authority and consequently went unchallenged. Where there appeared no need to test the authenticity of claims about the world, knowledge was most appropriately seen as consisting of facts to be inculcated in the young mind. Understanding of the young mind itself was rudimentary, limited by a failure to appreciate the possibility that it might differ significantly from the mental operations of the adult. A student's failure to assimilate the knowledge that the teacher presented was generally explained in terms of the child's inattentiveness or indolence, and hence as something culpable.

We could possibly state traditionalism's implicit theory of human nature in the following way. Human beings are by nature gifted with a certain number of mental powers or faculties such as memory, imagination, fantasy, will, reason, feeling, perception, and so on. All of these powers are essential for the smooth functioning of the mind but develop during a lifetime in different ways and directions. When children are small, some of their powers are underdeveloped, while others are at their peak. For instance, the young child has an excellent memory and seems to be able to store piles of information, both meaningful and otherwise. The older we become the more is our memory impaired. Our reasoning ability, on the other hand, undergoes a development reminiscent of the answer the future king Oedipus gave to the sphinx's riddle: which creature starts walking on four, then two, and finally three legs? In this case the answer is our rational power, which works poorly in the early and late stages of life. For our proper functioning in society it is then necessary that we make the best possible use of our human powers and abilities at the right time, and it is the object of education to fulfill this aim. Given these premises, a child (or, more rightly, the teacher) has to derive advantage from good memory and learn or memorize as much as possible by heart even when what is learned by rote is incomprehensible to the child. Then, as time advances, the child's reason will find available a full warehouse of useful knowledge to draw on. As it is natural that young children take no interest in incomprehensible noise, they have to be forced in their own best interests to learn a lot without understanding why. The teacher and the whole school system are in this way justified in applying the necessary means, including corporal punishment, to catalyze the learning process.

The child's understandable aversion to taking part in this process makes it obvious why discipline and control were considered unavoidable elements in the art of teaching. Teaching the child was not a question of finding the child's spontaneous motivation for learning, but of providing the necessary external motives to get children to work in defiance of their own wishes.

Since the teacher functioned as the medium through which instruction was received, attention had to be focused on the teacher. The classroom was designed to give the teacher a dominant position, with students' desks arranged so that they all faced the teacher, who was placed at the "front" of the room with his or her own desk sometimes positioned on a raised platform. This arrangement facilitated the exercise of authoritarian control by the teacher. Such kinds of seating arrangements, often seen by those who were educated in this manner as "natural," have clear pedagogical implications in terms of who speaks to whom and on what terms. The teacher addresses the students, and is in a position to permit direct responses from student to teacher. The students are expected to adopt tunnel vision so that all they see of their peers is the backs of their heads. No student is facing another student because interaction between students is an unacceptable distraction in a place of instruction. The teacher is placed in a dominant position so that he or she can ensure that communication of this kind does not take place.

At the same time it can be seen that, since it can never have held much attraction for students, this approach to education again underlined the need for such control. There was no place for students to become actively involved in their own learning: they were merely expected to absorb what was seen as established knowledge and to reproduce it when required, either orally or in writing, as evidence of successful memorization. For example, religious knowledge, for long periods the most highly esteemed form of knowledge, particularly in societies where schools were controlled by religious bodies, generally stressed the need for the rote learning of catechisms. Further, there was no doubt among educators about what other kinds of knowledge were of most value: literacy and numeracy, plus the academic disciplines of the day (see the following subsection). All important knowledge was contained within "subjects," a system of classification whose validity went unquestioned. The duty of the educator was therefore to insist that the children cease to attend to what they were really interested in, and attend instead to what adult authority believed they *ought* to be interested in, namely a curriculum made up of "school subjects." The tensions inherent in such an ambitious project cannot be contained without a strong element of coercion.

In the following subsections we review in more detail the main lines of criticism made by progressives of such traditional approaches.

The nature of knowledge

As is often the case, an understanding of the conception of knowledge held by progressivists is best understood against a background of what they see themselves as rejecting. Here we can usefully quote the American reformer, John Holt, not just to indicate what he sees as unacceptable, but also to illustrate the tendency among some progressivists to present the traditionalist position in terms of grotesque lampoon, a habit that is more likely to enliven the discussion than to illuminate it. Holt sees schooling as underpinned by three main ideas:

> (1) Of the vast body of human knowledge, there are certain bits and pieces that can be called essential, that everyone should know; (2) the extent to which a person can be considered educated, qualified to live intelligently in today's world and be a useful member of society, depends on the amount of this essential knowledge that he carries about with him; (3) it is the duty of schools, therefore, to get as much of this essential knowledge as possible into the minds of children. (Holt, 1969, p. 171)

Why? A good answer would have to rely on an understanding of the nature of knowledge that does not fit Holt's picture. Some appreciation of the place of knowledge in school teaching from the Middle Ages to the present day could help to provide such an answer.

If we take a broad view of educational trends and approaches, they can be divided into three phases on the basis of a small number of viewpoints. They represent ideal types: reality can never be reconciled with rigid categories. If the understanding of the nature of knowledge is linked to the educational problem of how people learn, the central problem of education can be formulated as a problem concerning the relation between the subject who learns and reality, the object, the matter to be learnt (cf. Gustavsson, 1996, p. 248). A continual shifting of balance between these two poles can be observed throughout the history of education. This movement can be described in spatial terms, from outer to inner.

Traditional educational practice is historically founded on the assertion that there exists a ready-made body of knowledge, a set of objective truths, which it is essential for the individual to acquire. In the first phase, the establishment of the beginnings of the modern school in the Middle Ages, the objective truth is of a divine nature and the job of education is, put simply, to transport the divine truth to the human soul from beyond, for the sake of the salvation of this inner soul. In the second phase, which appears from the Renaissance onwards, the existence of a ready-made body of knowledge is still asserted; now, however, this knowledge is no longer a divine revelation from beyond but is established in the secular realm during a continual process of scientific development. The school's job is still to ensure that the truth is transported into young people, but now it is for the sake of the salvation of the existing world. What is central both here and in the first phase is the mimetic. The job of education is to help transfer already established truths. Traditional education, as shown in the first two phases, has its origin in the Church, the mother of the school. In these phases the practical job of education is not to help discover truths, for they have already been revealed or uncovered, but to ensure their reproduction in a form as close to the original as possible. In the third phase the possibility of retaining the mimetic principle is contested. Knowledge is seen now as a personal acquisition, obtained by learning from experience. The idea of connecting knowledge and learning to the student's own experience is found in the works of the kind of classical prophets already discussed above. As explicitly formulated by William H. Kilpatrick ([1918] 1961), this way of thinking assumes that personal experience is a precondition of real learning and bears fruit for the learning process itself. Although a number of reasons can be adduced for not accepting this assertion unconditionally (cf. Ennis, 1961), it is a central element in the third phase of the development, which from the early twentieth century is called "progressivism" or *Reformpädagogik*. Here the aim is for the student to be transformed into a new person or, as is sometimes said, brought to true humanity by virtue of his or her achieved experience. While the focus in the first phase was on the other world, and in the second phase on the outside world, in the third phase it is on individuals and their personal growth.

It should now be clear that the traditionalist system, which progressives have criticized, is not incoherent but has a rationale of its own not only concerning manner or "method" but also matter or "content." Holt's account of it as the teaching of "bits and pieces of knowledge" is manifestly a travesty. A relatively recent attempt to re-establish a nonprogressivist understanding of knowledge is to be found in the widely influential writing of Richard Peters and Paul Hirst, who are probably the best known British philosophers of education in the last 50 years, noted both for their attempt to restate the principles of liberal education and for their antiprogressivist views. Hirst and Peters advocate seeing "knowledge" as an umbrella term for a number of quite different ways of understanding, each with its own methodology. The development through time of different forms of knowing is a central feature of our civilization: these different ways of understanding are the tools that make sense of the world. However, these kinds of understanding cannot be acquired by young people thinking for themselves. Students need to be *shown* how to think in the ways that are known to be fruitful: this is what teachers are for.

On this kind of account, any sound educational program must involve familiarizing students with a full range of the different forms of knowledge. Without such breadth in the curriculum, the young are prevented from achieving a balanced mental development. Consequently, as John White once argued, no form of knowledge should be regarded as optional. No one should normally leave school without having attained a basic understanding of the disciplines. If they are "less able" at one of them, mathematics say, then, far from being allowed to give it up in favor of something with which they can cope, they should be given *more*, perhaps differently oriented, teaching in the discipline, so that they *become* able at it.

Underlying this kind of thinking is an assumption that the school curriculum should in some way reflect the nature of knowledge; and it is not hard to see how various school subjects can be seen as related to Hirst's forms of knowledge. Progressivists have challenged this idea in two different ways. The first is to accept the assumption that the school curriculum should be largely determined by epistemological considerations, but to challenge the account given above, replacing it with a progressivist analysis similar to the Deweyan one mentioned above or perhaps of the kind outlined in the following paragraph.

What passes for knowledge in traditional schooling is often not really knowledge at all: it makes no impact, is not permanent, and involves no understanding. Where knowledge is acquired under pressure – perhaps because students need to assimilate it to pass examinations – it makes little impression on the life of the learner, for this is only likely to happen when students want to learn or need to learn. But this in turn depends on many factors like the nature of their previous experience, their ways of making sense of experience, the kinds of things they find puzzling or which they want to explore. These are all factors that may vary from one individual to another, and that would have to be taken into account if a curriculum were to prove effective. Here we can usefully turn to two British reports, The Primary Memorandum in Scotland (SED, 1965) and the Plowden Report (Central Advisory Council for Education, 1967), which are generally recognized as embodying a classic modern statement of progressivism, one that was hugely influential in Britain in promoting an informal pedagogy in primary schools. Few other official reports generated by a nation state have received a comparable amount of attention from other countries. Plowden was even translated into German (Belser, 1972). Its opening declaration is that:

> At the heart of the educational process lies the child. No advances in policy, no acquisitions of new equipment have their desired effect unless they are in harmony with the nature of the child, unless they are fundamentally acceptable to him. (Central Advisory Council for Education, 1967, p. 7)

On this view, satisfactory learning cannot be provided for through a fixed curriculum of subject matter defined by adults as valuable.

The second challenge to the idea that the curriculum should reflect the nature of knowledge rests on the argument that taking into account the child's needs and interests does more than promote more effective learning: it also shows some respect for the student-learner as a person. A preoccupation with providing compulsory menus of knowledge tends to transmit a negative message to the learner: this is what you ought to know (but don't), and this is what you ought to be interested in (but aren't). Plowden commends flexible methods of curriculum organization "designed to make good use of the interest and curiosity of children, to minimise the notion of subject matter being rigidly compartmental, and to allow the teacher to adopt a consultative, guiding, stimulating role rather than a purely didactic one" (p. 198).

Human nature

This subsection begins by attempting to unpack the last argument in the previous subsection. Progressivists insist on seeing children as natural learners and reconcile this with their belief that traditional schooling has proved unsatisfactory by identifying a mismatch between what children actually want to learn and what the traditionalists insist that they ought to learn. The suggested solution is to reconceptualize the curriculum so that there is correspondence between what is to be learned and the directions taken by children's active curiosity and their drive to understand their situation and surroundings. Can such a program be carried through, and what would it look like?

The Plowden Report embraces much of the thinking indicated in this paper's earlier section on progressivism's precursors though without much explicit acknowledgement (see Darling and Nisbet, 2000). However it does recognize the influence of Piaget on its view of learning (Central Advisory Council for Education, 1967, p. 192). Since Piaget saw the learning process as an interaction between an individual and the physical environment, this served to weight the main thrust of the report towards the more individualistic European version of progressivism. It is significant that one of the benefits of "group methods" is said to be that students have opportunities of "learning to share in co-operative enterprises" (ibid., p. 68). If human life were seen as naturally social, surely such an aim would be superfluous. Children's earliest experience, after all, is of interacting with at least one other human being; they do not grow up on their own.

Similar uncertainty arises elsewhere about Plowden's understanding of the nature of the learner: "one of the main tasks of the primary school is to build on and strengthen children's intrinsic interest in learning and lead them to learn for themselves rather than from fear of disapproval or desire for praise" (ibid., p. 196). But there appears to be significant internal tension in this claim. For if children are indeed intrinsically motivated to learn, why would they need to be "led" to pursue their own learning without rewards or sanctions? The progressive belief in the child's natural curiosity and capacity for learning by discovery requires a much more searching examination of the role of the teacher. Here Plowden gives an intellectually slack response to the apparent implications of this view of the nature of the child. It is assumed that schools and teaching should continue, that what is required is an appreciation of how children's understanding develops, and that this will allow a benign and supportive paternalism to replace an authoritarian approach.

There could be no better illustration of this paternalism than the recommendation noted above, at the end of the last subsection, that "good use" should be made of children's curiosity. This manipulation of what is said to be the child's instinctive nature is also evident in progressivist discussions of play. Since it is in the child's nature to play, the curriculum should accommodate this. First, the kinds of opportunities that progressive teachers provide in fact exclude many of the kinds of games actually pursued by children when they are away from the classroom: games that involve chasing, capturing, kissing; games that are vigorous and even violent. When progressive teachers allow or encourage children to play, what is usually envisaged is commonly a sedentary and sedate affair; but more importantly, it is to have a learning outcome that the teacher sees as valuable. Here again, "good use" is being made of children's play.

The issue of play can be used to underline the point already made that there exist significant differences of opinion between different progressivists, both practitioners and theorists. A. S. Neill was both, running a school for 70 years and authoring many books and articles. His ability to translate theory into institutional practice and to enrich theory by drawing on his experience with children makes him a figure of particular interest in the development of progressivism, and he will be used here to illuminate several progressivist themes. On play he was clear: play should be pursued for its own sake because it is a natural thing for a child to do. Play requires no educational justification and should not be exploited for the promotion of learning. Neill's school, Summerhill, is chiefly known for the amount of freedom its students enjoyed. They were not required to attend lessons, and could, if they wished, decide to play all day.

Perhaps Neill could be seen as taking progressivism to its logical conclusion. Progressivists characteristically take a very positive view of the nature of the child: children are lacking in malice, if not positively virtuous, and they are natural learners with an instinctive desire to make sense of the world around them; further, they are already programmed to develop in a way that is admirable. Yet in Neill's eyes, many progressivists lack the courage of their convictions. Surely such beings do not require guidance and stimulation. What they should be given is freedom.

Democracy and Schulgemeinde

The notion of *vom Kinde aus* is frequently deployed to underline the need to try to understand how children see the world. While a sensitivity to the child's perspective is essential if a lesson is to be successful, there is an even more fundamental need to see the child not just as an actively intelligent learner but as a human agent. Children are entitled to a say (perhaps the main say) in how their lives proceed; indeed it might be claimed that instead of having to argue this, the onus to produce a convincing case lies with those adults who would assume the right to make decisions on behalf of children. In education as conventionally understood, such paternalistic decisions are made all the time. Indeed it might be said that compulsory schooling as an existing policy is itself blatantly in conflict with the right of the child to be self-determining (cf. Nordenbo, 1986). One way to escape this dilemma is to turn schools into democratic communities. Within the progressive schools the relation between education and democracy had a remarkably parallel development in the UK, Germany, and the USA.

It is clear that children's rights are more generally respected at schools like Summerhill. But of course no individual can enjoy an unqualified right to do as he or she pleases: there have to be constraints in any society. At Summerhill (cf. Neill, 1960), since the exercise of adult authority is seen as harmful, rules are decided upon by an assembly consisting of all students and teachers, with each member having one vote. The agenda appears to consist primarily of social issues, particularly the curtailment of antisocial behavior. The curriculum does not seem to be discussed. Given each student's entitlement to opt in or out of classes, this may seem reasonable, since each student's decision may be argued to be his or her concern alone. But the reality is that such choices can be constrained by what classes are on offer: you cannot choose to attend a class on a particular subject if, say, staffing arrangements are such that it is not practicable to mount such a class. So in principle the curriculum should be considered by the Summerhill assembly. But in schools where lesson attendance is compulsory there would clearly be an even stronger case for students to influence, if not to control, the nature of the curriculum on offer.

Neill did not get the idea of the Summerhill assembly out of the blue. In a short note on Summerhill in 1928 he actually used the German word *Schulgemeinde* to characterize the relationship between the school's students. He says: "Children are ideal when they deal with humans. The tolerance and sympathy shown in our

Schulgemeinde are wonderful. It is where children deal with inanimate things that they differ from (and, alas, with) grown-ups" (Neill, 1928, pp. 70–1). In his youth Neill worked as a teacher for several years before and after World War I at various progressive schools in Austria and Germany. In Germany one of the main features of progressivism or *Reformpädagogik* was a belief in the educational benefit of living in the countryside, away from the big cities, close to nature, and in a school community taking the family as a model (Scheibe, [1969] 1994, pp. 111–37).

A number of *Landerziehungsheime* – that is, boarding schools in the countryside – became a substantial ingredient of German progressivism. These schools, some of which are still in existence, did not stress formal teaching of subjects but focused on the personal and social aspects of upbringing. To live at the school was to be a member of a community that strived to obtain harmony among individuals. Two objectives were achieved by placing the schools in the countryside. The schools were protected from the undesirable effects of urban life, and the very environment offered good opportunities for children to experience and cultivate an appreciation of nature. The schools also offered work in farmhouses, workplaces, and gardens, not only for training the body but also in the belief that this would strengthen the character. They also had a faith in the independent value of youth culture, for which the schools provided good opportunities.

One of the main objectives was to develop the ability to live in a community. Coeducation, family-like relationships in a homelike atmosphere (the schools were in fact called "homes," not "schools"), a friendly, informal educational relationship between students and teachers – these things made the school community (*Schulgemeine*) into a place where students and teachers regularly met to discuss and decide on common issues. In this form of self-government, the students themselves laid down the rules on matters of common interest in an independent school assembly (*Volksversammlung*). It has finally to be mentioned that part of this character-forming education also included a number of characteristically progressive activities such as music, amateur theatricals, folk dance, and art and craft. A lot of free talk, discussion, and debate went on, and in teaching an interdisciplinary approach to subjects was dominant, with little importance being attached to the transmission of knowledge. What was thought to matter was that the students were working with pleasure. In many ways this picture was not far away from the one Neill draws of Summerhill.

In more general terms, it is worth taking note of Dewey's observation that, as an institution, the school has a social life of its own, and social life is itself educational. The school is in this way a conservatory for promoting deliberative democracy. Disregarding considerations of entitlement and rights, it may plausibly be argued that its educative potential may depend substantially on the extent to which the school community is self-governing. A degree of institutionalized student power is clearly likely to encourage the development of thoughtfulness and responsibility, as well as transmitting the message that students are seen by adults as having significant capabilities and good sense. Conversely, where student power is minimal, a contrary message is surely being conveyed, and an important educational instrument is being neglected. With their positive view of children, progressivists are unlikely to make this mistake.

Development of the whole person

An important thrust of progressivism has been to discourage too much emphasis on the educational process as a preparation for later life. We can illustrate this with two different kinds of point.

After World War I, British and German progressivists felt that the educational system had, by teaching unquestioning obedience to authority, prepared a generation of young men to defend their country unquestioningly with their lives without any criticism being leveled at the unintelligent direction of the generals and politicians. At other times, progressivists have strongly resisted regarding students as tomorrow's labor force, with all that this might mean for their curriculum and the way in which children are schooled. It is hard for the state not to view education as a conveniently powerful mechanism for fulfilling its own requirements – especially if the state is itself financing a very costly school system.

The second kind of point is Dewey's insight that rather than school being a preparation for life it is itself an important part of life. Instead of thinking exclusively in terms of the quality of future life as an adult, we should be thinking more about the quality of the child's present existence. A variant of this is to suggest that, by concentrating on providing an enriching educational experience for children, one is in fact, even if unintentionally, giving them the best possible chance of a fulfilling future. In England's Hadow Report (1931), which was later to inspire Plowden, it is argued that a fully lived childhood constitutes the best possible preparation for adulthood. For children, according to Hadow, schooling "will best serve their future by a single-minded devotion to their needs in the present." Clearly no educator can properly be without concern for a child's future. So progressive arguments here must be interpreted not as urging such neglect, but as counseling a different perspective on adulthood. In negative terms, as we have already noted, adults are not just wage-earners or, in more current parlance, wealth-creators. They dream, form friendships, read literature, play games, drink, fall in love, listen to music, wonder about the meaning of life . . . Much of this is of course continuous with the activities of childhood, which is why enabling a child to live fully is indeed, as Hadow suggests, likely to promote a rich adult existence.

But there is a further kind of consideration that should discourage a simplistic understanding of education-as-preparation: it is impossible to foresee what kind of future a child will have. There are two kinds of reason for this. The more superficial is the phenomenon of accelerating social change: we do not know what kind of adult society children will be entering. It has become a commonplace to see this as a new problem, but of course it is hard to imagine a society where this has not been true. Rousseau, for example, used anticipated social change to explain why it would be wrong to educate a prince's son to perform the role of a prince — such a role might simply disappear. More significantly, however, human beings have to make their own lives, not just in the sense that they have to find a role but that they have partly to create themselves. They will develop their own ideas, their own perspectives, their own values; and these will influence what kinds of persons they want to be and what kinds of lives they want to lead. The centrality of agency in this typically individualistic account is incompatible with any mechanistic understanding of education as preparation for the future. And the breadth of understanding of human life, coupled with a belief in an open future, has led to recent variants of progressive education, such as that developed by Carl Rogers, being called "humanistic."

The implication of all this is that, in the final analysis, the aim of education for progressivists is the unfolding of all aspects of the child's nature. Education is thus seen as a contribution to the development of the child's whole person. Wilhelm von Humboldt crystalized this aim in the German concept of *Bildung*. In this way it is possible to find a vague similarity between "progressive" reactions to the first and the second crisis in modern history of education discussed above in the introductory section.

Progressivism Today

Does progressivism exist today? In a trivial sense we could claim that it is the prevailing orthodoxy, that today we are experiencing a new "progressivism." Many of the demands that progressivism has made on traditional education during the twentieth century – to consider the child's nature, to care for learner-centeredness, to adapt the lessons to the child's "natural" motivation, to promote children's personal growth and creativity – belong today to the standard equipment of modern teachers' vocabulary and practice. These educational approaches form part of a common knowledge in education embraced by nearly all. Student activity methods, paradigmatically represented by the project method, cannot any longer arouse aston-ishment or provocation, equally disseminated as they are in educational and work-ing life. Likewise student participation and democracy in one way or another is taken for granted by everyone. Progressivism has triumphed through being the victim of repressive tolerance. For the prevailing orthodoxy of new "progressivism" focuses on the procedural, on the manner rather than the matter of education. What has recently been written about higher education applies in broad outline to existing education systems, not only in the UK but also in Scandinavia, Northern Europe, and the USA:

> The new "progressivism" in higher education has only a veneer of the concern with personal growth and creativity that characterised the primary education of the *Plowden Report* and the *Primary Memorandum*. Underneath this can easily be seen the drive to prepare people "effectively" for work. The language of learner-centredness has readily been harnessed to a consumerist conception of empowerment, where the position of learners as isolated choosers renders more achievable the streamlined flexible systems upon which managerialism thrives, and the surreptitious creation of desire. (Blake, Smith, and Standish, 1998, pp. 43–4)

New "progressivism" has, by putting the educational style of the traditional progress-ivism to the service of educational managerialism, turned the relationship between the individual and society, as it originally appeared to the progressivists, upside-down. The question today is how we should arrange the school so that individuals meet societal needs – *not*, as it used to be for the progressivists, how we arrange society so that schools meet the individual needs of the child. Educational instrumentalism has thrown the baby out with the bath water.

But new "progressivism" cannot be "progressivism today." In the introductory section above, we argued that progressivism or *Reformpädagogik* are not just names for a distinctive body of opinions about educational theory and practice. The kind of progressivism we are talking about has to be related to the historical situation from which it arises, and we accepted the idea that progressivism arises in contexts in which major educational crises exist, that is, that each crisis provokes its own kind of progressivism. We also claimed that from the period of the 1960s onwards it has become a commonplace to think of education as being in crisis. Although the educational systems since then have been constantly expanding, the focus has not been on the individual learner, child or adult. Instead educational theories and ideas have more and more turned themselves into technicalities about how to turn the learner into an efficient tool of the economic system. Individuals have become not the subjects but the objects of their own development. Under these conditions, the understanding of the relationships between the individual, school, and society is threatened. Where progressivism sees the relations between individual, school, and society as an interaction that attaches the greatest importance to the contribution of society, via the school, in promoting the development of the individual, contemporary crises show that the individual is to be regarded now as the loser in this game.

We can, then, from an educational perspective, conceive the interaction between individual, school, and society in at least three possible ways. First, we can hold that the dominating power has to emanate from society such that society both designs and determines what kind of influence schools exercise over individuals. The task here is to ensure that individuals conform to the wishes of society. In broad outline this is the view of traditional education. Second, one can locate the pre-eminent power in schools, whose role is to change society via the individual, in the direction of greater democratization. This in general has been the view of progressive education in the twentieth century. Finally, we can hold that the school as a public institution has been so compromised by society's dominating influence that it is no longer morally or politically justifiable, and should wither away as a public institution. New and emerging circumstances favor this last viewpoint. Since the 1970s schools' (and universities') monopoly on knowledge has been heavily contested by the new media and consumer society more widely. At the same time, as remarked by Charles Taylor (1992, p. 25), a number of strands in contemporary politics have turned on the need, indeed the demand, for *recognition*. "The demand comes to the fore in a number of ways in today's politics, on behalf of minority or 'subaltern' groups, in some forms of feminism and in what is today called the politics of 'multiculturalism'" (ibid.). One such group consists of those representing the interests of the child.

Hence it is that three independent but related movements – deschooling, children's rights, and antieducation – share a profound moral indignation at the way modern society treats children. They see children as victims: of sexual abuse at one extreme, but at the other of the soft paternalism operated in all kinds of contexts of care, even by well-meaning teachers.

These movements differ in critical focus and political radicality.The deschooling movement arose around 1970 with the publication of the books of Ivan Illich, especially *Deschooling Society* (1971), and Everett Reimer's *School is Dead* (1971). Its main target is the – then – accepted view of schools as benign institutions. They claim that beneath the surface, a hidden curriculum indoctrinates the students to endorse existing societal values and class divisions. The remedy for this is to abolish compulsory schooling and to allow learners to take control of their own education, for instance by joining educational networks and webs.

The children's rights movement appeared almost at the same time as the deschooling movement, inspired partly by student militancy in connection with the events of May 1968 at various European and British universities (cf. Wringe, 1981). In the USA the movement followed the general trend to fight for the rights of various minority groups such as Afro-Americans and women. It was claimed that young people are the most oppressed of all minorities:

> They are discriminated against on the basis of age in everything from movie admissions to sex. They are traditionally the subjects of ridicule, humiliation, and mental torture of adults. Their civil rights are routinely violated in homes, schools and other institutions. They often cannot own money or property. They lack the right to trial by jury before being sentenced to jail. (Gross and Gross, 1977, p. 1)

The movement against education (*Anti-pädagogik*) also came into existence in Germany in the 1970s. Inspired by psychoanalysis and antipsychiatry, its main target was schools considered as "total institutions" in Goffman's sense. Philosophically this movement represents a radical, antipaternalist position, rejecting every form of education and every established kind of upbringing.

What entitles us to describe these three movements as descendants of traditional progressivism? If we look at the five themes with the help of which we attempted above to grasp the nature of progressivism, it can easily be shown that the three movements embrace them all, but in a more radical version. (1) The three movements condemn the prevailing traditional education and do so to such a degree that they favor the abolition of all schools and all upbringing. (2) They are all sensitive to the child's distinctive and special needs and demand that children's learning activities follow from their own experienced needs. (3) The three movements are united in the belief that educational intervention cannot be justified by even the softest version of educational paternalism. (4) They embrace the view that every child is entitled to participate in democratic cooperation. (5) Finally, they consider educational institutions as one of the main obstacles preventing the unfolding of the child's potential and growth as a whole person.

By identifying the three movements as representative of "progressivism today" a more profound lesson can perhaps be learned. The three movements take the traditional progressivist program to its extreme. That reveals that progressivism contains a perhaps intractable conflict between on the one hand the individuality of the child and on the other hand the organizational unity of the institutionalized school. "*Vom Kinde aus*" or child-centeredness is deeply ingrained in progressivism and in the last resort rejects every kind of educational paternalism. If progressivism is taken to its logical conclusion it results in the repudiation of the educational enterprise itself.

Note

1   i.e., the fifteenth-century Scottish naval commander.

Recommendations for Further Reading

Cremin, L. (1961) *The Transformation of the School: Progressivism in American Education 1876–1957*, Alfred A. Knopf.

Darling, J. (1994) *Child-Centred Education and its Critics*, Paul Chapman Publishing.

Oelkers, J. (1989) *Reformpädagogik. Eine kritische Dogmengeschichte*, Juventa.

Scheibe, W. ([1969] 1994) *Die reformpädagogische Bewegung*, Beltz Taschenbuch.

Part V

Ethics and Upbringing

Chapter 17

Adults and Children

Paul Smeyers and Colin Wringe

The "Traditional" Picture

It was once notoriously said (Central Advisory Council for Education, 1967) that at the center of the educational process is the child. The titles of relatively few well-known philosophical works explicitly refer to "the child" or "childhood" and one writer (M. Peters, 2000) has commented on the conspicuous absence of the child from analytical philosophy. Yet the said child is of necessity present by implication, often unseen as well as unheard, in the wings at any serious discussion of upbringing or education. Learning implies a learner and where the learner is a child, any theory of education implies a particular conception of the child. It will scarcely be necessary to say that "the child" and "childhood" are, like all role-words, protean social constructs varying from age to age (Aries, 1973), from place to place (Bronfenbrenner, 1970) and, as becomes all too evident if we compare the concept of the child in legal statutes with that to be found in, say, Victorian children's literature, from discourse to discourse. The present chapter will focus upon the varying concepts of childhood and the relationship between childhood and two particular adult roles (parents and teachers) from what we term the "traditional picture" as originally conceived by educational thinkers of the Enlightenment, through its changing representations during the twentieth century down to the inspiration postmodernists find in the concept of the "child."

To begin with the traditional picture, such (eighteenth or nineteenth century) writers as Kant (1964) and Herbart (1965) see the educational relationship between the adult and the child undergoing education to be one whose primary aim is the adulthood of the child. The influence adults exert on children will bring them to the point where they can take up for themselves what is called a dignified life-project. Adults, supposedly being a representation, though certainly not the ultimate embodiment, of what is objectively good, are in a position to educate, since they themselves have already achieved adulthood. Responsibility for realizing one's life-project is dictated by reason. Adulthood shows itself by being in command of oneself, able to bind oneself to a law of one's choosing, to maintain steady relationships both morally and practically, and not being reliant upon the judgements of others; to put this more positively, having personal access to objective standards of value and being able to place oneself under a higher moral authority. This will show itself in the adult's taking part in societal life in a constructive manner. Children, on the other hand, are helpless in a moral sense. They do not know what is good and therefore cannot yet take responsibility for their own actions. They cry out for guidance and only if such guidance is offered, if adults (first the parents, and subsequently the teachers) make the necessary decisions in relation to them, will they be able to reach adulthood. Central to this traditional concept of education is this intention on the part of the educator, and it is this that makes an activity educational. What the educator undertakes can only be justified as education in so far as it aims at and contributes to adulthood, and to the autonomy of the young person. Educators are, thus, responsible by proxy and the relationship they have with children is based on trust. This is no simplistic reasoning of a manipulative kind. The adult decides on behalf of the not yet rational child and in the child's best interests. By confronting the child with rationality in this way the adult seeks to awaken the child's potentialities to become a rational human being.

Such was the manner in which relations between adults and children were paradigmatically conceived in the German Enlightenment tradition from the eighteenth century until the time of World War II (Langeveld, 1946). Such a view of the justification of parental authority belonged to the conception of a just, well-ordered society which, for various reasons, has more recently lost some of its attraction. This Enlightenment tradition was itself, however, initially seen as a "modern" reaction to an even older tradition in which discipline was simply perceived as the uncritical inculcation of facts or bodies of information and in which discipline was understood as obedience to authority.

In itself, the Enlightenment tradition is, by contrast, rational, even liberal, being concerned with the initiation of the learner into forms of thought and understanding that are part of a critical cultural heritage. Here, discipline is primarily an attuning of the mind to the inherent norms of these forms of understanding. The learner is initiated into forms of thought that are public but as yet beyond the child's understanding. In their strongest formulation these norms of rationality were thought to be stable and valid for all cultures. In the German version of this tradition, the concept of education also encompasses child-rearing more broadly. In the first instance the adults concerned will be the parents but, in more explicitly Hegelian versions, reason is also embodied in social institutions, especially in the state. Such a view necessarily implies a transmission model of education and upbringing. The child may be conceived as a passive recipient of rationality and culture or as recalcitrant material to be molded or inscribed. Alternatively, he or she must, like the barbarian outside the citadel (Hirst and Peters, 1970), be lured in and skillfully initiated into the stock of worthwhile knowledge, sentiment, and inherently valuable activities and practices of civilized life.

The "Progressive" Picture

For Rousseau (1957), by contrast, and the many child-centered educators that followed him, the adult world, far from representing reason, is essentially corrupt and given over to the superficialities of worldly vanity. The topic of progressive education is extensively dealt with in chapter 16 of the present volume and here it suffices to highlight the particular features of childhood that such an approach to education and upbringing imply. On this view, the child, as a product of nature, is essentially good and will, in accordance with an empiricist theory of knowledge, learn all she or he needs to know from experience. Though the adult world is ostensibly represented by the teacher or tutor rather than the parent, his or her role is depicted essentially as that of nurturing or, as expressed in the much abused horticultural metaphor, of protecting the burgeoning plant from harm or noxious influences and permitting the development of that adult perfection supposed to be already precontained in the child, as the seed precontains the ideal pattern of the fully grown plant.

More rigorous and relatively more recent philosophers of education (R. Peters, 1969; Dearden, 1972a) have applauded the ethical concern of child-centered educators to respect the vulnerability and individuality of the child but have questioned their noninterventionist claims, pointing out that reference to natural growth and the supposed needs and interests of the child embody a number of covert value judgements. Particularly of note, in view of later developments in our picture of the child, is the recognition by these writers of the significance of the child's present and future ethical interests and the psychological distinctiveness of the child's motivational pattern and view of the world. They nevertheless maintain that, far from being generated spontaneously in the child's contact with the physical world, much of what the future adult has to learn is of a conceptual nature and therefore social, not to say traditional, in origin.

Certain later conceptions of the relationship between the child and the adult world may be seen as taking the concept of child-centered education to its logical conclusion – or *reductio ad absurdum*. Writers such as Neill (1962), Holt (1969), Duane (1971), and others, though in no sense to be regarded as philosophers, nevertheless operate with a conception of the child and his or her relationship with adults that has a semblance of internal coherence, inviting philosophical comment. For these writers, the relationship between children and the adult world of teachers and parents is an essentially romantic one of persecuted innocence in which sensitive and intelligent children are constantly thwarted by the obtuseness and neuroses of punitive adults. Taking this one step further the so-called "deschoolers" (Illich, 1971; Reimer, 1971; Goodman, 1971) take an even more naive view of children and their capabilities. Compulsory education is standardly referred to as "incarceration" and young people are supposed capable of both identifying their own educational needs and organizing their own programs to meet them. In the case of the deschoolers, however, the "oppressor" is taken to be not flawed or bloody-minded individual teachers or parents but a hypocritical "society" or exploitive capitalist system and its needs for a docile and socially differentiated workforce.

The General Change of Society

Insofar as both language and thought are social products, changing concepts of childhood and the debates to which they give rise necessarily reflect social changes that provide an essential context for the various philosophical reflections referred to in this chapter. Such changes entail new ways of conceptualizing education and child-rearing, which in turn take account of the changing experience of human life. Under these circumstances it may be asked whether children continue to have the same significance for their parents as they once did. Before dealing with that (see section on "Educational Practice Nowadays" below), something even more general needs to be said about the situation in which parents presently find themselves vis-à-vis their offspring. For instance, most societies are nowadays characterized by ethical and religious pluralism, leading to the suggestion that parents are no longer morally justified in initiating their children into a particular way of life. This may be illustrated by the different positions taken in the debate concerning religious education at school (see for instance, D. Carr, 1995, 1996; Mackenzie, 1998). Thus it is also argued that educators in general can only indicate possible positions on these matters. Well-known current works of relevance to this topic include Chilman (1988), Lamb (1982), Macklin and Rubin (1983), Sussman and Steinmetz (1987), and the titles of relevant widely circulated journals include *Family Relations, Adolescence, Journal of Youth and Adolescence, Journal of Marriage and the Family.*

Besides the more general transformation of society, a further change of note is the fact that it is nowadays more difficult than it once was for parents to live up to their children's expectations and to what is demanded of them as family members and members of the society. Few people any longer work at home and the time spent away from the home necessarily limits that which is left for their children. The same can be said of participation in community life or the time available for the pursuit of joint amusements, hobbies, or pastimes in a family context. Family members are encouraged to behave more as individuals, and families themselves tend to be seen, rather, as institutions providing opportunities for their various members. Those families that are unable to do so are regarded as deficient. That this perceived deficiency is in part a reflection of the subculture to which they belong only adds to the insecurity parents feel concerning the upbringing of their children. Partly in consequence of this, and in line with general tendencies toward greater child-centeredness, parents may leave many choices and decisions to their children, finding it easier not to become involved themselves. There is also an increasing tension between what children directly desire and think to be important and what can be afforded by the family as a whole, to say nothing of the parents' own priorities and preferences as reflected in the time parents want to invest in family life and that which children wish to give to it. Equally, children can no longer expect their parents to be on hand whenever they think they need or want them. Furthermore, society's demand for caring conflicts with its insistence on the child's being treated as an individual. Given the low societal rating of caring practices, this may lead to a dissolving or diminution of this dimension of family life.

There may be differences in values between individual parents and between values held within the family and those held in society at large. Furthermore, due to the process of individualization currently taking place in society, the control of parents over their children is continuously slackened and yet they are expected to ensure that the latter become "good citizens." Such conflicts may generate a partial retreat or even a total withdrawal from responsibility on the part of parents, possibly leading to an attitude of "It's your life. Do as you wish." When others insist on putting values explicitly on the school curriculum, thus urging schools to take on some of the functions of "the home," parents may feel paralyzed and no longer able to decide. "Experts" may be consulted and even courses in parenting established. Their apparent lack of expertise may leave some parents feeling disempowered, yet the expertise that is sought may not bring results. At issue is whether the current problems of family life are to be conceived of as resulting from parental lack of expertise or as the predictable result of living together in a changing society in which the role of parents is being transformed.

Interest in issues of child labor and child abuse, not to mention incest, have put the way families operate in a different perspective. The context of trust in which the proclaimed common goal was "happiness and fulfillment for all family members" has come under attack and has put the language of children's rights (see below) on the social and political agenda. And the desire of children and young people to live more independently of others and pursue the kind of life they want to pursue has been encouraged by changes of an economic kind. The more children are financially independent of their parents, the less they are obliged to accept their ways and values. Children are not, of course, financially independent even in Western countries. The majority do not have an income sufficient to allow them to support themselves, and they would scarcely be able to manage such an income if they did. However, pocket money, which children may (within limits) spend as they choose, is nowadays more or less established as an institution, and many young people are able to earn money from part-time jobs in a way that was once less easy. More importantly, society now provides them with a number of facilities and opportunities which used to be at the discretion of their parents. The overall social climate has changed so that parents find themselves under pressure to provide the means for their children to behave in a more independent way. As is well known, many children may possess their own rooms, radio and TV sets, CD players, computers, individual bank or savings accounts, phones, and so on. To lead one's life independently as early as possible has almost become an educational aim and as such is consistent with the prevailing societal climate. Even if these privileges are limited to middle-class children, the background assumptions are there as an ideal or norm for all children in the Western world.

Childhood and Modern Marriage

A number of rather different issues in relation to children are raised by changing attitudes to divorce and the stability of marriage, and the supposed effects of such changes upon the development and upbringing of children. Little need be said of statistics quoted by the defenders of traditional social and family patterns to demonstrate the better health, educational development, and social integration of children growing up in traditional households in which their natural parents are, and remain permanently, married to each other. Such statistics are invariably and perhaps necessarily flawed by their failure to compare like with like. Figures for children from nonmarital, divorcing, or single-parent families are typically compared with undifferentiated statistics relating to all children from traditional families (including those from happy, stable, successful families) rather than solely with those for children from unhappy and unsuccessful families in which divorce is nevertheless avoided or prevented. Few writers attempt to disentangle the supposed "harm" that is done to children during the period in which the traditional family structure is maintained (that is, when mutually estranged and hostile parents remain "together") and that which results from the event and consequences of the divorce itself. The fact that such distinctions are difficult, not to say impossible, to make in practice provides an excellent example of the way in which the conclusions of empirical research may sometimes simply reflect the conditions under which such research must necessarily be carried out.

The moral and developmental consequences supposedly threatening the children of divorced or unmarried parents are less frequently predicted for those of war widows or those whose fathers or mothers are obliged to be away from home as part of a mobile or flexible labor force. We tremble for the fate of children brought up by lesbian couples or homosexual men while continuing to admire or envy the idyllic childhood of those brought up by, or at least spending much time in the company of, adults not necessarily forming regular couples of opposite sexes, as depicted in the children's fiction of an earlier generation (Montgomery, 1984; Ransome, 1962; Spyri, 1953). To suppose that healthy child development requires the presence of role models of both sexes implies that traditional gender roles, the relationship between them, and the traditional relationship between children and parents of each gender, will remain appropriate to the future, or indeed to the present. It suggests that family relationships as we currently conceive them are a necessary and permanent feature of a flourishing childhood rather than a historical phenomenon reflecting a particular division of labor in an age when physical robustness or protective aggression were required of men, and women might be more or less permanently incapacitated by serial child-bearing. In such times the bond between child and blood-father may have served as the justification for the accumulation of property and status ("for the sake of the children") and the means of its transmission. The child, especially the male child, was the vehicle of the family fortune "cascading down the generations." In an age of individual educational and social mobility such a conception has become increasingly irrelevant, if not socially dysfunctional.

Childrens's Rights

The declining authority of custom, tradition, and religion has had a number of other significant effects upon the way we view children and the relationship in which they stand to parents and the adult world in general. In particular such developments have led many to regard rights rather than some settled conception of the good as the primary guiding concept in a liberal society. The question "What should be done?" or "How should children be taught to live?" has been replaced by "Whose interests are to be considered?" and ultimately "Who is entitled to decide?" The period immediately following the university disturbances of 1968 was marked by a surge of interest in the rights of children. Initially this interest was expressed in terms of the supposed civil and political rights of children: rights to freedom of speech and association; rights to publish comment and opinion; rights of freedom in matters of personal appearance and access to knowledge; the right to make a democratic input into the management of their schools; to use alcohol, tobacco, or other drugs on the same basis as adults, and to engage in responsible sexual activity (Wringe, 1981). It is perhaps heartening that the results of some of these agitations have to some extent been taken on board by the adult world, even though they are now rarely expressed in terms of rights. Lists of "school rules" for instance, now characteristically draw attention to the importance of mutual respect for each others' work and aspirations, not only between student and student but also, reciprocally, between students and teachers. The habit of "consulting" students on various matters is nowadays an established part of the image of good practice in the field of student management.

At a rather more serious philosophical level, a number of other important issues, some of them already present in the work of the child-centered educators, have also come to be expressed in terms of children's rights of various categories and find expression in the 1989 Convention on Children's Rights (Freeman and Veerman, 1992).

We may, perhaps, be somewhat dismissive of the more strident claims to the rights of freedom and political participation voiced by or on behalf of children in the 1970s, given that a certain measure of rationality would seem the logical prerequisite of their exercise. This hesitation, however, implies a possible entitlement on the part of children to receive the kind of upbringing and education that will not compromise their right to an "open future" in favor of the local or parental religion or value system (Feinberg, 1980; O'Neill and Ruddick, 1979). On the contrary, it may seem to suggest a view of education and upbringing that positively reinforces the development of that autonomy and enables children eventually to choose their own conception of the worthwhile life. Children's rights of protection from interference and harm (passive rights of freedom) have also provided the framework for much writing about the damage done to children through cruelty, exploitation, or abuse, sexual or otherwise (McGillivray, 1992; Kent, 1992). With regard to rights of this kind, at least, the objection that children have no rights because they are less than rational or because they have done nothing to earn any rights, cannot be made. Teachers, for their part, are nowadays obliged to treat students as persons possessing their own dignity, who must be managed by the exercise of classroom skills rather than dominated by the force of authority. Possibly, however, the most widely discussed category of children's rights has been that of so-called welfare rights, that is, rights justified by manifest need. These are not only rights against neglect arising from the need to receive material support for a safe, healthy, and tolerable childhood, but also include the right to firm guidance before attaining the age of maturity in order that children should not unwittingly damage their own safety or life chances. An important part of this right is the right to education including, possibly, the right to compulsory education (Haydon, 1977).

It is sometimes suggested (e.g., Kleinig, 1976) that talk of rights in the context of children's upbringing and particularly in the context of family life where love, affection, and freely given mutual respect should reign, is inappropriate. No doubt this is true. If children constantly strutted around demanding their rights whenever parents displeased them, and parents were inclined to reply in kind, life would be intolerable for all concerned. It is, however, equally true that situations in which adults (colleagues, friends, neighbors) make frequent reference to their rights in their dealings with each other are also disagreeable. It is the mark of courteous and civilized relations that rights are not continuously referred to but are understood and respected all the same. The notion that we may simply flout the important rights of those who are supposed to be united with us by bonds of dependence and affection would be monstrous.

Parents' Rights and the Nature of Child-rearing

Rights in relation to education may be claimed not only on behalf of children but also for parents. Claims to rights on behalf of parents have been of two kinds: claims of parents against the wider community, usually represented by the state, and claims against children themselves, that is, the claims of parents to limit children's freedom, require certain behaviors of them, and bring them up in certain ways of the parents' choosing. Given the close historical links in many countries between education and religion, liberal democracies traditionally respect the right of parents to choose their children's schools though some (France, USA) insist that state-provided education should be secular. The 1948 Universal Declaration of Human Rights is somewhat ambivalent on this issue. Article 26/2 asserts that "parents have a prior right to choose the kind of education that shall be given to their children" but also insists that "Education shall be directed to the full development of the human personality and to the strengthening of respect for human rights and fundamental freedoms." Education, the declaration adds, "shall promote understanding, tolerance and friendship among all nations, racial or religious groups, and shall further the activities of the United Nations for the maintenance of peace," suggesting a right/duty on the part of the state, or even the world community, to intervene on certain occasions in the interests of other, public ideals as well as in the interests of the child. The article also suggests that the wider adult world may also intervene to protect the child from indoctrination or an education which in other ways falls short of that to which a future citizen is felt to be entitled. The notion of children as choosers or potential choosers, subject only to the provisional authority of parents and other adults in a pluralist world of uncertain and changing values, places emphasis on significant differences between the concepts of socialization – induction into the beliefs, values, and practices of existing society – and education, which involves the development of both critical insights and qualities of self-assurance and self-confidence essential to the development of personal autonomy.

Such considerations might be thought to limit the right of parents to choose the nature of their children's education, whether in a particular school or delivered (to quote the British 1944 Education Act) "otherwise." This right has nevertheless played an important part in the defense of private schools and also educational selection within the state system (Cohen, 1981). Thus, many parents in the UK have claimed the right to choose grammar, rather than comprehensive, schools for their own children, thereby necessarily choosing secondary modern schools for the children of others in the process. The right of parents to choose their children's schools also formed an important element in British Conservative Party rhetoric during the 1980s and 1990s in favor of replacing fixed school catchment areas by an "educational market" in which educational standards are supposedly raised by obliging schools to compete for students or face closure.

Once again, however, we must exercise some caution in discussing this issue in terms of rights, a tendency that has been vehemently criticized by Mary Midgley (1991), among others. No conceptual scheme, Midgley claims, ought to have automatic priority in the discussion of moral issues, but there is a special objection to talk of rights, which is the most competitive and litigious of moral concepts. Like the legal model it dictates a zero-sum solution where there are winners and losers but no room for the careful reflection so necessary when we are confronted with moral dilemmas. She refers to the reason why parents are taken to be normally the least bad available rearers for their children, not in terms of a belief in a particular right, but according to the widespread experience that other people are, almost always, much less willing even to try to do the job properly than parents. She also draws attention to the fact that the experience of pregnancy and childbirth normally produces a deep emotional bonding with the coming child and that culture usually does not oppose this bonding but backs it by social approval. She points to the fact that this deep emotional investment makes separation so painful and is therefore willing to speak of innate emotional tendencies. All of this, however, does not confer on parents any unconditional "right to rear." There is a nexus of sometimes conflicting claims that has to be considered and that casts serious doubts upon a legalistic view of the aims of life, that is, where rights are explicitly placed at the center of morality and where all other human values are ignored.

Educational Practice Nowadays: A Tentative Interpretation

There is no point in romanticizing education as it was in the good old days nor in trying to restore the past. Though the feeling of belonging to a family or to a community was probably much stronger in the past than it is now, there were also other sides to this life, such as the fact that members were often prevented from exploring a wider range of possibilities in life (see Macmillan, 1994). Nor does one have to go back to medieval times to be appalled by the exploitative relationships that have often existed between adults and children. Our comments on parental intentions in the matter of child-rearing in an era of postmodernity therefore relate to what may be witnessed in the contemporary Western world.

First, it is assumed that, given the means of contraception and changed laws to liberalize abortion, most children are brought into the world voluntarily and intentionally by their parents. Second, most children are brought up by at least one of their parents and the majority by both. Though many marriages nowadays end in a divorce, and granted that the number of single parents has considerably increased, the majority of children nevertheless have a relationship with both of their natural parents. Consequently, something like an "educational practice" is still very likely to occur in the context of the family. How can such a practice be characterized?

Normally, the bringing of a child into the world may be expected to indicate a willingness on the part of both parents to enter into a relationship with that child when it arrives. It goes without saying that for the parents this period in their lives will be one of deliberation and planning, for it is in the nature of human beings that what they do is a manifestation of their will and intentions rather than simply the result of something that happens to them. Deciding to have children brings with it a number of duties, such as bearing the cost, looking after them, living together with them at least until a certain age, sharing a number of material goods, being there when needed, being prepared to listen: in short, being prepared to care for them. That much seems uncontroversial but problems arise when decisions have to be made concerning, for instance, the amount of time or resources to be devoted to the children.

As is so often the case, it is easier to indicate what is not acceptable than to develop a positive account of what should be done. As studies concerning the right to state intervention show, it is far from clear what is in the child's best interests (see, for instance, De Ruyter, 1993). In cases of fostering and the placing of children in care, or where the courts have to make decisions because divorced parents cannot come to an agreement, and also in educational matters, a number of options may have to be considered, both because a number of different means can often be taken to achieve a particular end and because there may be a wide divergence of opinion regarding the ends to be achieved in education and child-rearing. Such considerations make abundantly clear the unavoidable social embeddedness of education in general.

That a number of options are open does not imply that anything goes. Because human beings are as they are, human flourishing implies certain things. Though the end does not determine exhaustively what one has to do, there is a necessary relationship between the two. In this sense morality is necessarily instrumental to human needs without ever being reducible to them. This Aristotelian thought is relevant to the determination of the aims of education. Though individual and cultural plasticity is considerable, not everything can be brought into accord with our "nature." But we can in this modern age reject our culture in ways that were impossible before. What is called pathological or deviant behavior is, however, culturally determined and, whether one likes it or not, the judgement of others may play an important role in our personal well-being. Here again the necessarily social embeddedness of human life is evident.

In terms of parental practice this may seem to point to a necessary limitation in the structure of the family. The acceptance of pluralism at the level of society cannot be simply duplicated at the family level. While it is possible to accept that different conceptions of the good life exist, for the individual who leads a particular life, this is a merely cognitive acceptance. As that person decides to live with someone else as husband and wife, divergence of their beliefs is only to a certain extent possible. To care for one's children means, among other things, to care for what they care for, and this will set limits to what is acceptable. It is difficult to love what is radically opposed to what one believes in, but it is hardly possible to live with what one hates. We stressed the limitation that is brought with this living close to each other (as opposed to living together but apart). It is possible that this will cause a problem for the child, depending upon the kind of basic beliefs the parents hold and the extent to which they regard them as indisputable. But that may be thought a fair price to be paid for a life in which not everything is the same, a practice in which not all is indifferent, and in which a child's existence is embedded.

Some means–end reasoning, and some manipulation, may be part of the context of giving meaning to life. Children cannot be taught everything rationally. Parents have a duty to prevent their children from destroying their lives or their future as long as society places children in their charge. Parental apathy must surely sometimes be blamed when children fail to develop a sense of what is morally acceptable. To remain indifferent to everything children do is, in an important sense, to neglect them. Although it may be difficult to determine in abstract terms what is "in" and what is "out" in particular cases, this does not usually seem to present grave problems. Though society may sometimes need to bring either parents or children to reason, differences between them in matters of great importance do not arise that often, or may frequently turn out to be of less dramatic significance than at first appears. We must, however, sometimes also expect that, in deciding what belongs to the good life, certain contradictions may ultimately remain, tragically, irreconcilable. Such is unavoidably the nature of human life.

Given the lack of social consensus concerning what is valuable, it is important for parents to make clear what is important and valuable for them in their way of life, and why. For even where values ultimately turn out to be misguided and are later abandoned, the process of criticism and moral development cannot begin unless some concept of the good, the right, and the valuable has first been experienced. The justification for the initiation into particular values thus depends upon what parents have found valuable themselves. Parents are necessarily – and perhaps again tragically – limited by who they are themselves in their offerings to their children. To ask for a justification beyond this point is to enter a circular debate. It goes without saying, however, that together with making explicit their adherence to particular beliefs, parents must be careful to indicate also that other alternatives are possible, but that these do not appeal to *them*. Making explicit what one stands for will be *the* response to keeping the process of valuing ongoing. Extreme cases aside, constant intervention to "improve" family life is difficult to justify. Such monitoring of human relationships not only carries with it the danger of suffocating all spontaneity and truth to oneself, but it does not seem to be either necessary or, in many cases, possible given the lack of social consensus referred to earlier. Though things might be different in a particular family, changing them may not necessarily be for the better, nor may the present situation be seriously harmful for children in general.

Education and upbringing are essentially embedded both within the fabric of every-day family life and in the life and practices of the wider community of which the family forms a part. This will be particularly so where the family enjoys religious affiliation with its own assumptions and values in relation to family life and the rearing of children.

The educational practice of parents could be described as a relationship that people have sought themselves, in which they are prepared to invest much of their time, resources, and themselves, and that makes them proud of "what they have made" of their children and feel deep sorrow if their children cannot lead satis-factory lives. The relationship they have themselves engaged in is in some sense also in fact "for the rest of their natural life." How can they not care about what their children care for and the values they live by without their own lives being fraudu-lent? The tension this creates between their own autonomy and the envisaged autonomy for their children makes it a difficult, but also a particularly worthwhile, human experience. This may not have altered over time, but the certainty parents once thought they possessed has had to be reconciled with the ultimately foundationless nature of our most fundamental beliefs. Economic necessity has also been lessened (there were no alternatives for children in the past) and the belief that children are persons and not merely *potentially* persons has been widely accepted. The idea among parents that one was always right, combined with being in author-ity almost exclusively based on physical and economic power, has generally been replaced by a sense of reasonable but by no means mindless doubt.

Though liberals may sometimes question the right of parents to impose their way of life on children in this manner, it is a central tenet of the liberal outlook both that many versions of the good life are possible and that among such versions there is no definite criterion of choice. At very least, there must be a presumption that many chosen ways of life (secular or religious) are of sufficient moral value for it to be permissible for children to be brought up according to their values, customs, and traditions. Even in these postfoundational times, however, this assumption may be defeasible in relation to the child-rearing practices of some groups and it may sometimes be thought reasonable for a humane, caring state to intervene where such practices appear demonstrably inhumane, oppressive, or corrupting. It is sometimes thought a difficulty for the liberal point of view that the liberal is obliged to hold that such upbringing must be compatible with the child's eventually becoming capable of autonomous choice (Hobson, 1984; McLaughlin, 1984). On the face of it, a fundamentalist might reasonably retort "Never mind their autonomy. Their salvation is more important. The weasel words of the liberal are the seductions of the devil." It is disingenuous of liberals to deny that there is something of a problem here, obliging them to fall back on their own fundamental assumption that we enter the world as separate and equal beings and that the right to choose a way of life that is assumed by the parent cannot ultimately be denied the child, either by physical coercion or by indoctrination or the denial of access to education and wider know-ledge. This is the burden of the oft-quoted American case of *Wisconsin v. Yoder*. In support of their position liberals may also point out that for many faiths it is important that the believer should not only follow the religious precepts but should choose to do so voluntarily. They may also add with Mill (1910) that if a way of life is truly good, any additional knowledge, speculation, or enquiry is bound to strengthen rather than undermine it.

In the modern world in which the life of children will rarely resemble what that of their parents has been, it becomes increasingly difficult for parents to envisage a precise future for their offspring. Nor is it any longer appropriate to regard their parental role as one in which they are obliged always to be right, as well as possessing absolute power and authority, though they may be as aware as ever that what they do for their children will make a significant difference to their lives.

Lyotard and the "Inhumanity" of the Child: Taking a Radical Inspiration for Philosophy of Education

Our tracing of the development of the concept of the child and the child's relationship with the adult world began with the rationalist view of the child as an untutored supplicant to the status of adulthood, to be awarded on the achievement of reason, as represented by the adult point of view. Subsequently, we have viewed children as active agents in pursuit of their own learning, as independent beings in possession of rights which make them in a certain sense the moral equals of adults, and as the object of the rights of others. These discussions have largely taken place within the traditional frameworks of rationalist and empiricist philosophies in which the child is perceived in relation to the adult world and in adult terms. Recently, however, a number of writers have reasserted the irremediable otherness of childhood, not this time as an unproblematic state of inferiority or helplessness to be overcome but, if not as a Wordsworthian state of moral superiority to be revered, then at least as one of inaccessibility, impenetrability, and incommensurability with the adult world.

Michael Peters (2000) draws our attention to Cavell's (1995) reading of certain well-known passages in Wittgenstein's *Investigations* in which Cavell describes the training of children as a process of stupefying them into the state of Wittgenstein's adult builders who are forced to work with a highly restricted range of language. The voice of the child, as yet unacquainted with language and custom, is, Cavell argues, one of the "primordial" voices in the *Investigations*, like the voice of madness, constantly bringing our assumptions about ordinary adult language and convention into question. Hart (1993), writing from a slightly different perspective, criticizes adult attempts to "understand" childhood by the stultifying methods of scientific child study, taking up Wilfred Owen's remark that children are not meant to be studied but enjoyed.

Other authors have also developed the theme of the irreducibility of childhood. From the parents' certainty in the "traditional" picture, through a new kind of certainty within the Wittgensteinian framework, we move thus to the challenge that the child confronts us with. The reinterpretation of childhood Lyotard offers may interfere with our "normal" practice. At the same time, however, it creates a highly relevant alternative stance. He argues that against the humanity of what he refers to as "the system," there is only one possible source of resistance: namely, the inhumanity of the child "who lives permanently in the human being" (Lyotard, 1988b, pp. 9–10). The inhumanity of the system that "perpetuates itself in the name of development" is responsible for our forgetting the inhumanity of childhood (ibid.). Hope, utopia, criticism, and change remain possible precisely because the inhumanity of the child, properly understood, never completely adapts itself to the human. Childhood refers neither to a particular age nor to a transient stage of development. Rather it points to a never-ending indeterminacy, unmanageability, or wildness, a transconceptual silence that Lyotard interprets. Childhood or *infantia* (literally, being incapable of speech) is the generic term for all that does not let itself be incorporated or regulated: the noneffective, the not-being-able-to, the nonrepresentable affect, the receptiveness or experience without words. It cannot be understood or learned but is, according to Lyotard, a source of resistance and sensitivity. Childhood prompts us "not to forget in order to resist and possibly not to be unjust" (Lyotard, 1988b, p. 16). Guilt is the hopeful indeterminacy out of which the child continues to be born: this resistance announces and promises the possible. But it is not the indeterminacy of ideas on which one relies in judging; it is the material indeterminacy of the event.

To clarify this further Lyotard makes an important distinction between the *quod*, the meaning of something as event (Lyotard refers in this context to the uttering of a phrase as an event), and the *quid*, the meaning of something as such (the concept). The *quod* is the event before it is given particular "meaning," before it is, as it were, labeled or named by a particular concept. The question that demands a filling-in of the "what" (the *quid*) makes us forget about the question mark: "the 'that something arrives' is always guarded from what comes in, is always incorporated in a conceptual frame and outlook which is unavoidably biased" (Lyotard, 1988a, p. 43). The *quod* has a meaning (significance) that does not dissolve in a particular concept. The event has no need for words, for meaning, for language, in order to happen.

The unrepresentability that is implied by this indeterminacy implies a transcendence. But to realize transcendence of this kind is to neuter; it must instead be allowed to be. What must be sustained is a sensitivity to this indeterminacy. For Lyotard it is no less than this that characterizes the educated human being: the person inhabited by a discomfort, by disquietude, restlessness that makes her or him think. The educated person is a distressed human being; the agony of the event marks genuine thinking, a mode of being that is not nothing, but not something either. Childhood introduces us into a time in which the future is not the consequence of a past and where what comes into the world cannot be inferred from what is already there. To be able to respond to such a future requires the capacity radically to expose oneself to question. It requires something different from a permanent movement of renewal, in which case it is immediately put to use and reinforces rather than interrupts continuity. Childhood stands not for what is possible, but for what is impossible. It cannot be realized, but its truth can manifest itself. Confrontation with its truth, sensitivity to its truth, do not teach us: they change us.

Lyotard shows us the way to a philosophy of education that starts from what may be called the reality of the child, a reality that is strange insofar as it cannot be represented or laid down, neither fact nor datum. Generally educational theory has nothing to say about this reality of the child. It is ignorant of the reality of what passes between this child and me, "eye to eye," which makes crying and laughing possible and remains invisible to objective thinking (cf. Desmond, 1995). The reality of the child cannot become a part of the world of means and ends, of representations, of what is replaceable and repeatable. It effaces those categories of cause and effect, necessity and contingency, irreversibility and publicity, that are characteristic of the theory of education and of acting and thinking understood in terms of representations.

Educational theory cannot forget the reality of "facts." The reality of the child escapes the language of theory. Of course, there is child psychology (studying children's needs and children's thinking); of course, there is sociology (studying children's loneliness or the violence they are subjected to); of course, educational theory concerns itself with matters of practical policy for the educators, teachers, therapists, psychologists, counselors, and inspectors who evaluate and intervene, this goes without saying. Childhood is something incorporated into our practices and institutions. It is explained, understood, and given a place. We know childhood only too well (cf. Larrosa, 1998). But for Lyotard there is more, something that surpasses each attempt to give it place. It upsets the certainty of our knowledge and questions the power and the capability of our practices. And this childhood has no place in our language. Our language cannot grasp the infant any more than the infant can speak our language. This lack is not a deficiency of knowledge. It is not about what we do not yet know or cannot manipulate or understand. It is not only a question of time, of more research, more measures, more institutions. The reality of the child is not an object of knowledge or of understanding, but what escapes all objectification; not the anchorage of our power to govern, but that which marks its impotence. The reality of the child is its absolute heterogeneity toward our world of representations (knowledge) and power (what we are capable of), an enigmatic reality that escapes us, manifesting itself as affect, disquietude, emptiness, yet laying its claims on us. Though childhood never is what we know, it is nevertheless the bearer of a truth to which we have to listen. And we should not forget that the reality of the child can and will only be spoken of on the basis of what moves us. Thus speaking of childhood as an event may be a task for philosophy of education, counteracting that compulsion to classify, measure, categorize, and pigeonhole childhood wherever education is institutionalized.

Recommendations for Further Reading

Aries, P. (1973) *Centuries of Childhood*, Penguin.

Chilman, C. S. (1988) *Variant Family Forms*, Sage.

Freeman, M. and Veerman, P. (1992) *The Ideologies of Children's Rights*, Martinus Nijhoff.

Lyotard, J-F. (1991) *The Inhuman: Reflections on Time*, trans. R. Bennington and R. Bowlby, Polity Press.

Chapter 18

Autonomy and Authenticity in Education

Michael Bonnett and Stefaan Cuypers

Rationalist and Existentialist
Views of Autonomy and Authenticity

The issues of autonomy and authenticity in education in large part can be seen as a development of a more general concern about the nature of freedom and its relationship to education. This latter has been expressed in a variety of ways. The notion that education should itself be liberating has a provenance that stretches back at least to Plato in *The Republic*, and the idea that freedom should not simply be a product of education but part of the *process* is a legacy of thinkers in the child-centered and humanist traditions of education such as Rousseau, Dewey, Rogers, and Illich. Autonomy and authenticity both focus on the nature of individual freedom, but offer different interpretations of this and suggest rather different sets of implications for education. We will begin by looking at the idea of autonomy.

The Greek etymon of autonomy as "self-rule" provides a useful preliminary definition, and while it was originally applied to emerging independent city states, the notion of autonomous *individuals* also gained currency and the idea of the independent, free-thinking, individual became, for some, a human excellence. In the educational context, this was the sense of freedom celebrated in the early education of Rousseau's *Émile* and in Neill's *Summerhill*, both arguing that the learner's own thinking has to be respected, that students must always see the point of what they are learning and be free to pursue their own conceptions of this in their own ways. Thus students would develop a certain self-reliance in their judgements and become resistant to unthinking acquiescence in the expectations of others and the demands of the social *status quo*. Rousseau, in particular, was keen for Émile to learn through first-hand experience, active problem solving, and the consequences of his own actions so as to develop a lively critical faculty, free of prejudice and obfuscating abstractions. Something of this tradition entered contemporary analytic philosophy of education with, for example, Robert Dearden who elaborated the concept of personal autonomy in the following terms:

A person is autonomous, then, to the degree that what he thinks and does in important areas of his life cannot be explained without reference to his own activity of mind. That is to say, the explanation of why he thinks and acts as he does in these areas must include a reference to his own choices, deliberations, decisions, reflections, judgements, plannings or reasonings. (Dearden, 1972b, p. 453)

Taking his cue from Kant, who regarded people as morally autonomous if in their actions they bound themselves by laws legislated by their own reason as opposed to being governed by their inclinations, Dearden saw the activities of mind to which he refers as either being an expression of, or needing to be based upon, the independent criteria for judgement provided by the public forms of reason. Only then can they be free from various internal sources of heteronomy such as obsessions, addictions, and the power of our wishes and purposes to distort our perceptions of truth and appropriateness. In this way freedom is conceived not simply, or even primarily, as a set of objective conditions such as noninterference with one's actions, but as a frame of mind (see also R. Peters, 1973a). Educational philosophers in this "rationalist" tradition (which would include Richard Peters, Paul Hirst, Israel Scheffler, and Charles Bailey) have tended to see autonomy as making *rationally informed* choices, and to maintain that its development therefore requires a broad compulsory curriculum that would initiate the student into the relevant forms of rationality and provide the necessary knowledge base.

A central feature of this view is that it seems either to take itself as having explained the idea of "own" that it acknowledges to be part of the formulation of autonomy, or it regards the idea as unproblematic. Seemingly, provided a thought occurs "inside one's head," as it were, and has been assessed according to rational criteria, it is one's own. The meaning and significance of this idea of "ownership" of one's beliefs, thoughts, and choices is one of the key points of divergence between advocates of rational autonomy and advocates of authenticity. The rationalist view is well illustrated by Richard Peters (1973a), who recognizes authenticity as one of two basic conditions implicit in autonomy, the other being rational reflection. But an asymmetry in their relative importance rapidly becomes apparent as he goes on to equate authenticity with the populist notion of "doing one's own thing" and claims that no value attaches to "naked mineness." Indeed, following his approval of G. H. Mead's notion of the reasonable person as one who adopts the view of the "generalized other," he suggests that ". . . in estimating anything rationally identity is as irrelevant as time and place" (Peters, 1974, p. 428). And while the rationally derived moral principle of respect for persons demands that an individual's point of view should not be disregarded ". . . this does not mean that there is any value necessarily in the *content* of his wishes, or point of view" (ibid.). The value of authenticity comes to lie solely in the fact that mere unthinking conformity to standards of rationality shows insufficient care for them as such. It is clear that for Peters authenticity is completely subordinated as functionary to the appreciation of rational standards (Bonnett, 1986).

Concerns about the facileness of this account are raised by a consideration of what we might loosely term an "existentialist" version of autonomy in which the salience of authenticity is more fully acknowledged and its meaning is more fully explored.

The issue of human freedom is a theme that runs through much existentialism. In particular, Heidegger (1962) and Sartre ([1943] 1957), from their different perspectives, have been concerned about ways in which, in their view, we hide the true nature and extent of our freedom from ourselves for much of the time. For the existentialist we are *always* free – not in the sense of having full choice over the factors that affect our lives, but in the sense of always having a choice as to how we will respond to the situations in which we find ourselves. As individuals, in many ways we are "thrown" into life, but we must decide – and take responsibility for – the commitments and projects that we give ourselves. To live in this way is to be authentic – to be true to ourselves. However, taking this degree of responsibility for our own lives can be a burden; it can be isolating, at times awesome. The angst that results can rapidly become intolerable, especially when it is acknowledged that many life decisions are not susceptible of obviously, or indisputably, correct answers. For example, how we should live our lives – what purposes to pursue, what relationships to cherish – in the knowledge of our own individual mortality is less than self-evident and almost certainly not generalizable from one person to another. And on the existentialist account moral principles or religious positions are not *of themselves* binding; ultimately they have to be chosen and responsibility has to be accepted for such choices and their consequences.

Thus, it is suggested, for much of the time we endeavor to evade our responsibility – to live inauthentically – by deceiving ourselves about the extent of our own freedom. For example, we allow external influences such as others' expectations, fashion, stereotypes, what we take to be fate or Divine Will, to determine our choices. We can even hide behind what we conveniently assume to be immutable aspects of our own personality – "I just *am* lazy, temperamental, self-centered, ..." Equally, we can remain too busy with everyday practical matters and absorbed in the all-pervasive hearsay and the taken for granted of "common sense" to allow ourselves to engage with the real decisions that confront us. For the likes of Heidegger and Sartre these are all ways in which the truth of our freedom becomes tranquilized.

Autonomy, Authenticity, and Volitional Necessity

Closely related to Heidegger's and Sartre's views of authenticity is Harry Frankfurt's conceptual analysis of caring about, or loving, certain things such as personal ideals and one's own life (Frankfurt, 1988, 1999; see also Cuypers, 1992, forthcoming, chapters 4 and 5). Apart from the superficial similarity between the verbal meaning of the English "care" and the German "*sorge,*" Frankfurt's analytical care anthropology shows a striking parallel with Heidegger's Continental analysis of human consciousness (*Dasein*). It is important, however, to distinguish clearly Frankfurt's construal of the concept of caring from its construal in feminist educational theory or care ethics such as that of Noddings (1984). Whereas many educationalists and social scientists give an account of "caring *for*" other particular people, Frankfurt gives a general account of "caring *about*" what is important to *us*, and often *only* to us. His concept of care is not so much ethical as it is anthropological and metaphysical.

Frankfurt's care anthropology first and foremost has its place within the cluster of analytical approaches to "the problem of the meaning of life" (Nozick, 1981; Nagel, 1986; Singer, 1997). In his reflections on caring Frankfurt tries to formulate the fundamental structural conditions of the fact that we are creatures to whom things matter. His view on existential meaning or value is interesting here because it is presented in the context of a complex theory of the will and a hybrid theory of personal autonomy. In particular he introduces the seminal concept of "unthinkability" into the account of autonomy.

> Unthinkability is a mode of necessity with which the will sometimes binds itself and limits choice. This limitation may be an affirmation and revelation of fundamental sanity. . . . The will of a rational [sane] agent need not be . . . empty or devoid of substantial character. It is not necessarily altogether formal and contentless, having no inherent proclivities of its own. . . . it is precisely in the particular content or specific character of his will . . . that the rationality [sanity] of a person may in part reside. (Frankfurt, 1988, pp. 189–90)

The will, as defined here, is neither a neutral place of transient appetites nor a formal executive active power under the command of reason. Accordingly, the will is a faculty with a nature of its own, independent from appetite and reason. In other words, on this conception, the will has a *substance* of its own and this lies at the kernel of Frankfurt's care anthropology. The substantial will of a person, with its inherent proclivities and specific character of its own, is constituted by that person *caring about* or *loving something*. According to Frankfurt, caring about and loving something exhibit a special kind of necessity, what he calls *volitional necessity*, in virtue of which caring and loving are not altogether under the person's voluntary control. Unthinkability, the counterpart of volitional necessity, is similarly a mode of necessity, which constrains or limits the dynamism and organization of the will. Although such necessities of the will are commonly regarded as incompatible with free will, Frankfurt argues, unusually and paradoxically at first glance, that they are *required* for true autonomy or authenticity. In addition, he claims that volitional necessities are also required for the constitution and preservation of the self's mental health. In order to keep its fundamental sanity or "rationality," the self's volitional economy needs to be bounded by necessity. Obviously, Frankfurt has not in mind here the Humean means–end conception of rationality, and certainly not the Kantian conception of practical rationality. In his care anthropology Frankfurt's leading idea is that the most genuine freedom and the preservation of the self are not only compatible with being necessitated, but that they positively require necessity. This clearly goes against the grain of much contemporary standard thinking on autonomy (such as the rationalist position previously discussed), and also, to some extent, on authenticity and self-survival (see Mele, 1995).

But if his theory of the will is accepted, at least two conceptions of autonomy are revealed (Cuypers, 2000): voluntaristic and nonvoluntaristic. And these can be interpreted as an interesting version of the distinction between autonomy and authenticity. On the one hand, autonomy can be thought of as constituted by "choosing" or "decision making." Autonomy depends upon the active will; autonomous choices and decisions stand wholly under a person's voluntary control. This *voluntaristic* conception of "being true to oneself" aligns with the standard definition of autonomy: "An autonomous agent is, by definition, governed by himself alone. He acts entirely under his own control" (Frankfurt, 1999, p. 132). On the other hand, authenticity can be thought of as constituted by "caring" or "loving" and is constrained by "volitional necessity." On this view authenticity depends upon the substantial will and, due to the necessities of this will, to a considerable extent lies beyond a person's immediate voluntary control. This *nonvoluntaristic* conception is nonstandard: "A person acts autonomously [authentically] only when his volitions derive from the essential character of his will" (ibid.). And some of these volitions are not under a person's immediate voluntary control, because they are constrained by volitional necessity. In view of the fact that for Frankfurt a person, essentially, is a volitional entity, this source of authenticity is thus the person's *"real or authentic self"*:

> The essence of a person . . . is a matter of the contingent volitional necessities by which the will of the person is as a matter of fact constrained . . . They are substantive rather than merely formal. They pertain to the purposes, the preferences, and the other characteristics that the individual cannot help having and that effectively determine the activities of his will. (Frankfurt, 1999, p. 138)

Such a notion of authenticity resonates well with some work in the philosophy of education (Cooper, 1983; Bonnett, 1978, 1986, 1994) which argues for a distinction between autonomy and authenticity that reflects the more substantial, self-referential nature of authenticity – for example, the notion of authenticity as deriving from a "constituting self" of substantial concerns whose interplay forms an evolving genealogy of outlook (Bonnett, 1978). However, there undoubtedly remains a tension between this view, which emphasizes the role of personal responsibility for the expression of such concerns in confirming true "ownership" of them, and the seemingly very high degree of passivity inherent in Frankfurt's view of authenticity.

Authenticity, Existential Meaning, and Personal Identity

These central themes can be developed in important ways from the educational point of view. In particular, the connections that are claimed between authenticity and (1) meaning and (2) the notion of personal identity suggest approaches to education that are in contrast to those implied by rationalist interpretations of autonomy. We will consider each of these connections in turn.

The connection between authenticity and meaning arises as follows. Things matter to us in relation to our authentic concerns, that is, those concerns *for the expression of which we are willing to accept personal responsibility, and that constitute our sense of our own existence* (Bonnett, 1994, chapters 9 and 10). It is only by expressing them and feeling the world's response, either actually or through acts of imagination, that we discover what our thoughts really mean and what the world means to us. In this way we can come to understand our feelings and beliefs, and the things we have learned, in terms of our sense of our own existence. Interpreting Nietzsche, Cooper (1983, pp. 82–5) develops this point well in arguing that personal meaning can be seen as a function of *valuing* – deciding how what we have learned should affect our thoughts and our actions – and that therefore philosophy, properly conceived as the enterprise of thinking through what and how we should value, belongs at the center of education for life. And *contra* the rationalist model, ". . . appreciation of the impact of certain information on our conception of ourselves and on our understanding of the 'human condition' may require very little by way of initiation into the disciplines which provide the information" (ibid., p. 54). Authentic concerns, then, are our bridge to a personally meaningful world and the kind of meanings we can experience are conditioned by the quality of the life we are leading – the authentic quality of our consciousness. The orientation that this view gives to teaching and learning will be developed after we have said a little more about the connection between authenticity and personal identity.

Clearly, on the above view, our authentic concerns give each of us our unique stance on the world and in this sense constitute to a very significant degree who we are as individuals. Their expression is the basis of true self-expression and their origins, harmonies, and tensions the proper subject of self-knowledge. We become the authors of our own lives – truly free – by acknowledging such concerns and accepting responsibility for their expression, and respect for us as individuals consists precisely in respect for this – irrespective of whether the concerns we express are adjudged rational by other people's standards. This leads to an issue that is at the heart of the debate between advocates of authenticity and advocates of rational autonomy.

Which Rationality? Which Orthodoxy?

One of the most significant consequences of drawing the distinction between autonomy and authenticity in the way that has been attempted here is to throw up an issue of rationality itself: what are the standards around which it is to be articulated? For example, are they to be the objective publicly shared standards of, in the educational context, say, the traditional disciplines of thought and knowledge, or are they to be the personal standards of individual thinkers rooted in their own lived experience of particular situations – their own immediate sense of being in the world? On the views expressed in this account, it is not that autonomy requires rationality and authenticity does not. There can be no choice that does not involve the operation of rationality at some level. The issue is: rationality of what *sort*?

Equally, it is not being claimed that in general terms there is a necessary conflict between "public" and "personal" rationality, nor is it being denied that the latter is necessarily permeated to a very significant degree by the former. An individual's framework of understanding is always hugely conditioned by a shared social environment and, in this sense, by elements of public rationality. Indeed, it is only within certain social environments that the notion of the individual and of authenticity are developed to any high degree. Further, as Charles Taylor (1991, chapter 6) points out, the "horizons of significance" that our culture provides are essential references for our sense of ourselves, the choices that lie before us and the demands and tensions with which we have to contend. A notion of self-determining freedom that denies the significance of such "external" normative considerations trivializes our predicament by yielding ". . . a flattened world in which there aren't very meaningful choices because there aren't any crucial issues" (ibid., p. 68). We will return to Taylor's essentially communitarian perspective presently, but at this point, in the light of such a claim, it might at least be said that it is an important goal of education to facilitate such permeation of the personal by the public in order to enhance the dimension of intersubjective agreement in which the demands of shared norms can be felt, experience can be checked, and certain kinds of arbitrariness can be combated – provided, that is, that such norms and standards are presented in a way that refines and maybe changes, but does not simply overwhelm or displace without engagement, the learner's own view.

But there are problematic cases where the requirements of public rationality may require a different interpretation of experience or a different choice to that which arises out of the subject's own sense of his or her own existence. For example, it may be that "from the outside" public standards of rationality make a claim to have had an experience in which one literally heard "the word of God" to be highly implausible. It may provide a range of far more likely explanations. Yet it is far from clear that the subject of this experience should be persuaded by these explanations, for that person may feel that they fail to comprehend the particular character of his or her experience – which may itself be beyond articulation. Here, authenticity requires that subjects remain true to their sense of their own experience and the choices they may make as a result. This may sound to be an extreme case, but it is not hard to envisage more ordinary – but no less acute – examples in an educational situation where a broad compulsory curriculum (of the sort required for rational autonomy) is operative. For example, there may be instances where learners are simply encouraged to give up their own interpretation of material – the product of their own rationality – and to substitute the products of the rationality of others deemed more knowledgeable. Indeed, there may be situations where the effort of producing their own views is rendered entirely otiose because the whole culture of the classroom is orientated around learning an endless procession of prespecified material (both in terms of content and "rational" canons for evaluating it) "delivered" by the teacher.

Closely related to this reservation about a heavy emphasis on public rationality in the educational context is the danger of intimidation by the power of orthodoxy: the notion that learners may feel disabled in their personal engagement – forming, however embryonically and tentatively, their own responses, opinions, criticisms, and extrapolations – by the so-called rules and the accumulated weight of thought and knowledge that experts within a domain have produced (see, for example, Elliott, 1975; Cooper, 1983, p. 62). They can easily receive the impression that there is such a large body of previously established "essential" knowledge which is a prerequisite to them forming any worthwhile opinion of their own, that they simply give up on such an aspiration. Maybe there always exists a certain tension between education as the conservation of tradition (Oakeshott, 1972; Haldane, 1995) and the authentic creativity of young people in the educational process, but to allow the one simply to substitute for the other is to condone an absence of genuine engagement.

Interestingly, a somewhat parallel consideration to this can occur within the field of philosophy of education itself. The current burgeoning of a certain "scholarly" motive which places emphasis on the history of the social construction and development of a concept – how, for example, it has been interpreted by a spectrum of "great" thinkers and what its social effects have been (which in turn requires knowledge of a mass of secondary literature) – while no doubt of interest in itself, holds the danger of frustrating personal engagement with current issues by delaying any direct attack on them indefinitely. The issue in this context is not one of the precise significance of such contributions (though this clearly *is* an issue), but the extent of the distance they put between the thinker and his or her thought.

Such reservations can be seen to relate to the potentially severe criticism that rationality is *itself* somehow inauthentic or inimical to authenticity. D. H. Lawrence is well known for his fear that the "dummy standards" of rationality – "living from the head" through ideas and conceptions – would mechanize and empty thought, removing us from the realm of more direct experience and spontaneity that vitalizes life and is a truer expression of ourselves (see, for example, *Education of the People*, 1936 and the polemical *Benjamin Franklin*, 1923). In contrast to a "Platonic" intuition about the inferiority of the unexamined life, here we have a strong "Nietzschean" intuition about the corrosiveness of the examined life. Broadly speaking, the first intuition is more akin to the tradition of the Enlightenment, whereas the second is more in the tradition of Romanticism – the one is reminiscent of Descartes and Hume, the other of Rousseau and Herder. Nietzsche himself was scathing of rationality as the vehicle for illuminating and ordering life. In *Twilight of the Idols* ([1889] 1991) he accuses Socrates of making a tyrant of reason, which reflected the destroyed trust in the vital instinctive life. Criticizing Socrates' elevation of dialectics and his "phoney" equation of "reason = virtue = happiness," Nietzsche writes:

> With Socrates Greek taste undergoes a change in favour of dialectics: what is really happening when this happens? It is above all the defeat of a *nobler* taste . . . Before Socrates, the dialectical manner was repudiated in good society: it was regarded as a form of bad manners, one was compromised by it . . . all such presentation of one's reasons was regarded with mistrust. Honest things, like honest men, do not carry their reasons exposed in this fashion. It is indecent to display all one's goods. What has first to have itself proved is of little value. (Ibid., p. 41)

Autonomy, Authenticity, and Community

The ideal of autonomy has played a pivotal role in the defense of liberal education: it is one of the most important educational ideals. Autonomy is even the most important aim of liberal education (Dearden, 1975; see also Telfer, 1975; Ackerman,

1980; Callan, 1994). This close relationship between autonomy and education is, however, contested in contemporary political philosophy (Mulhall and Swift, 1996, pt. 1) and philosophy of education (e.g., Jonathan, 1997a). Mainly under the influence of feminism (cf. Friedman, 2000) and communitarianism (e.g., Sandel, 1982), critics have launched a staunch attack on autonomy, self-control, and strength of will as educational ideals and, in place of these, they have tried to establish commitment, love, and care as the primary educational values. Against the ideas of liberal rationalism, "postanalytical" philosophers such as Alasdair McIntyre, Charles Taylor, and Richard Rorty have engaged in critiques of conceptions of rational decision making and free choice deriving from the philosophical Enlightenment. Here we will return to Taylor's mainly communitarian approach to the issues and their implications for the distinction between autonomy and authenticity (Taylor, [1977] 1985a, 1989, 1991; see also Cuypers, 1995, forthcoming, ch. 6).

For Taylor, the liberal, individualistic, and even narcissistic conception of personal autonomy as based upon radically free self-determination is only a debased and travestied expression of a more adequate conception of being true to oneself. And this more moral and ideal conception of having one's own original way, for which he uses the phrase "the ideal of *authenticity*," incorporates a communitarian view on the constitution of a person's valuation system. Taylor's general argument takes as its premise *our shared human condition*. One general feature of our shared human condition which Taylor brings to our attention is that the definition of our identity essentially depends upon the *recognition* we get from – what George Herbert Mead called – "significant others." The existential identity of a person and his or her self-esteem are not built in a monological, but in a dialogical, way. Through the medium of languages of expression, the exchange between the self and the other constitutes the narrative identity of the self. In its autobiographical self-definition the self appraises itself in terms of "strong evaluations" such as being courageous or cowardly, reacting appropriately or inappropriately, being sincere or deceptive, and these ascriptions require the recognition of other people. Without such evaluative attitudes of other people we could not keep our mental sanity and an appropriate sense of our identity, and we should be completely in the dark about our true or real personal worth. Thus, it is argued, a person's identity and self-esteem crucially depend upon other people's evaluative attitudes.

But, of course, in their measured evaluation of a person's character, other people do not simply express their own idiosyncratic values, but also the valuation framework of the community at large. In our self-definition and self-evaluation we have to take as a background a sense of what is significant independently of our autonomous will. As previously mentioned, our identity and personal worth only take on importance against a background of intelligibility, or what Taylor (after Heidegger) calls a "horizon of significance." For Taylor, a horizon of significance is a valuation system of a historically grown community. It consists of the authoritative principles, rules, values, and norms that are expressive of the normative and socially prevalent conception of the good life. The authority of other people's evaluative attitudes is derivative upon the authority of the community's horizon of significance, and this highest court of appeal has an originary or special normative status because it *transcends* people's evaluation of themselves as well as other people's evaluation of them.

Horizons of significance not only transcend the self but also the other; they are constituted by the inherited traditions and customs of valuing to which both the person who asks for recognition and the other people who give or deny it are subordinated. Knowledge of the self is therefore constituted against an inherited background of intelligibility by an "*ongoing conversation*" between the self and the other.

Although social dependence and conformism are usually regarded as incompatible with being true to oneself, this particular dependence on, and conformism with, other people's opinions and social frameworks are not so much impediments as they are constitutive contributions to living authentically. Taylor's chiefly communitarian approach leads up to the following overall definition of authenticity:

> Briefly, we can say that authenticity [on the one hand] (A) involves (i) creation and construction as well as discovery, (ii) originality, and frequently (iii) opposition to the rules of society and even potentially to what we recognise as morality. But it is also true, as we saw, that it [on the other hand] (B) requires (i) openness to horizons of significance . . . and (ii) a self-definition in dialogue. That these demands may be in tension has to be allowed. But what must be wrong is a simple privileging of one over the other, of [the active dimension] (A), say, at the expense of [the passive dimension] (B), or vice versa. (Taylor, 1991, p. 66)

From this perspective, what appears wrong with much contemporary educational practice and pedagogical theory in the liberalist tradition, is indeed that they stress the *active* dimension (A), while underplaying the passive dimension (B). Not only proponents of liberal education, but also defenders of reform pedagogics such as child-centered educationalists (e.g., Neill, 1960) and deschoolers (e.g., Illich, 1971) start from what they take to be the self-evident principle that children and students are either actual or potential autonomous beings in the *radical* sense. These educational practitioners and theorists certainly do not deny the temporal and factual dependence of autonomy on the impact of other people's attitudes and the larger communal context. But they nevertheless presume that individual children or students remain *in principle* the independent creators of their volitional character as well as their values. However, if Taylor's communitarian claims are plausible, then this exclusive emphasis on the self-determining freedom of youngsters – the exaltation of the active over the passive dimension – is unwarranted and even self-defeating. Any conception of being true to oneself that staves off horizons of significance and dialogical relationships becomes fundamentally distorted or corrupt.

On this view then, the ideal in educational practice and the starting point of pedagogical theory cannot be personal autonomy of the radical self-determining type, but *must* be authenticity in the above-defined sense. The fundamental educational ideal in the motivational or volitional field is thus not so much autonomy as it is authenticity. (For further discussion, see Morgan, 1996.) Of course, those in sympathy with Taylor's broadly communitarian approach to authenticity should guard against the opposite failure, namely the privileging of the *passive* dimension at the expense of the active dimension. Especially feminists and communitarians are prone to this opposite exaggeration. In view of Taylor's analysis, they might better opt for a more *moderate* communitarian approach that acknowledges, first, that the concept of being true to oneself comprises both autonomy as (more) active self-determination by free choice or rational decision and authenticity as (more) passive social dependence and conformism and, second, that autonomy asymmetrically depends upon authenticity (see also Cuypers, 2000). At least two consequences for feminist and communitarian philosophies of education then follow.

First, feminist and communitarian critiques of autonomy as an educational ideal are not so much directed at being true to oneself as such, as they are opposed to a specific construal of this, namely, as based upon radical free choice or rational decision. It has to be admitted that these critiques of autonomy as an educational ideal are often justified in the light of the fact that in liberal education having one's own original way is too readily *reduced* to autonomous free choice or rational decision to the neglect of those aspects of authenticity that involve social dependence and conformism. To be sure, if the asymmetrical dependence of autonomy on authenticity is true, then such a reduction is radically misguided because active autonomy cannot stand on its own. Yet feminists and communitarians must be careful not to throw the baby away with the bath water. They can perfectly well also subscribe to active autonomy as *one* important educational ideal, provided that being true to oneself consists of both autonomy as self-determination *and* authenticity as involving social dependence, and that the dependence of the former on the latter is recognized. The basic conception of being true to oneself – authenticity – remains wide enough to include such crucial elements as emotional attachment in caring and belonging to a community.

Second, and connectedly, the liberal values of self-control and strength of will are perfectly compatible with the feminist and communitarian values of care and commitment, as long as the former are viewed as a function of the latter in the sense that, for example, people can only find the will-power to make certain substantial choices and decisions if they are guided by their own fundamental concerns and devotions. Not only can we have these two sets of values, in the process of education, we should have both. (For further discussion, see Aviram, 1995.) But the *way* in which we have them is all-important. In the light of the dependence of autonomy on authenticity, the values of care and commitment are primary: liberal values are in this way derivative upon feminist and communitarian values. And although feminists and communitarians are for the most part right in seeking recognition of an important passive dimension, they must not forget to respect *the fundamental tension* in the ideal of authenticity between being active and being passive, for such a tension belongs to the very nature of the self.

Authenticity, Responsibility, and Education

So much for criticisms of rationality and rational autonomy inspired by a concern for authenticity in its various interpretations. We will now turn to a potentially severe criticism of authenticity itself in the educational context: the charge of self-centeredness. Not withstanding all that has been said about a necessary communal reference in significant choice, might not an emphasis on personal authenticity lead to a rabid preoccupation with one's own fulfillment and one's own limited perspective on the world? Is not being authentic perfectly consistent with being *immoral, socially insular, and relatively ignorant*? Hardly promising qualities in an educational context.

Clearly there is some truth in this criticism, although previous discussion has shown that there are important senses in which authenticity is *de*centering in that it requires a relationship with the world in which one is at least *acknowledging* the consequences of one's thoughts and actions and one has an awareness of their human significance. But the criticism needs to be qualified in two further senses: (1) in terms of an *internal relationship* between authenticity and certain educational aims to which the criticism attempts to oppose it; and (2) with regard to the potential of a developed sense of authenticity to invite a radically less instrumental attitude toward the world than that implicit in much modern rationality.

It is clearly implausible to suggest that authenticity should be the *only* aim of education, or even the *central* aim. This contrasts with rational autonomy, which is often set up as operating with a view of rationality that aspires to *incorporate* a wide range of other educational aims such as breadth of knowledge and understanding, and moral, social, and personal development, by conceiving them as either forms of rationality or as highly rational enterprises (e.g., morality deriving from the rational principle of respect for persons, emotions conceived as forms of cognition – Hirst and Peters, 1970). Yet, in the light of previous discussion, it can be argued that a regard for student authenticity remains a very central consideration if some of these other aims are to have educational value.

For example, in the educational context, there seems little value in breadth of knowledge that has no personal significance for the knower. Being moral is more than simply a matter of acquiescing in a certain social code: it involves a personal commitment to a particular way of life. Significant interpersonal relationships require a developed sense of ownership and responsibility for one's own life and its consequences upon others, as a prerequisite both for showing consideration to others and for *understanding* them – knowing from the inside what it is to be responsible and thus to participate in the human condition. Finally, the issue of a seeming tension between the emphasis placed on the individual by authenticity and the greater "needs of society" has to be qualified in a society that aspires to be democratic. Democratic procedures only have moral worth if they can presuppose authentic individuals who will operate them. If, say, public opinion was solely the product of media manipulation or the party machine, democracy would be a sham. Thus, in a democracy, education for citizenship will require the development of authentic individuals. In each case then, authenticity can be seen to be a necessary though not sufficient condition for the achievement of these further aims. Without it they become otiose.

Let us now develop the claim that authenticity has the potential to reconfigure an increasingly dominant instrumental attitude toward the world. It has been argued that central to the notion of authenticity is the notion of responsibility. As well as bringing authenticity into relation with the educational aims mentioned above, a developed sense of responsibility has the potential to lead it into a certain relationship with things themselves, which represents a significant reorientation of the subject–object relationship.

Consider the characterization of objectivity (the opposite of self-centeredness) provided by the rationalist perspective. Rational thinking relates us to the world and achieves its rigor by the application of public rule-governed procedures to experience in terms of which it is thus organized and validated. In this way objectivity essentially becomes a function of agreed conventions, a function of the shared criteria for deciding how things are to be classified and what is to count as true. Now from some perspectives this is itself a very self-centered – now in the sense of *anthropocentric* – version of objectivity. What shows up in this framework of objectivity is heavily conditioned by the largely instrumental purposes that underlie the standards (conventions, criteria, etc.) applied. For example, much of modern science (for many, a paradigm of the rational enterprise) – and notwithstanding its self-image of impartiality – is motivated by the desire to categorize, generalize, explain, predict, control, and increasingly to exploit, nature. In this sense, it is far from impartial and can be seen to underwrite a pervasive calculative stance toward the world whose cumulative effects on the environment are becoming only too apparent. In marked contrast to this, Martin Heidegger has frequently averred a kind of thinking that is "commissioned by things themselves." (Though see Adorno's 1986 trenchant criticisms of potential excesses in using such notions.) It will be argued that, through a heightened sense of "negation" that it invites, authenticity suggests the possibility of a less aggressively anthropocentric interpretation of "objectivity" that privileges genuine openness to *things* – as against the perception of *objects* which are heavily defined by imposed categories.

The central point here is that to see something in one way – to reveal it in a certain way on a particular occasion – is always at the expense of other ways of revealing it. There are always sides of the thing to which we will not be attending or are out of view. There are aspects that will always remain unknown or beyond our grasp, but that are not any less part of the thing itself – for example, and above all, its simple capacity to stand there, to exist. Thus openness to the thing itself, in its fullness, involves an apprehension of "denial" – a sense of the ambience of what is incipiently present but not revealed as such in our current awareness of it. Only in this way can things have restored to them their inherent "otherness" which is essential to their own integrity. In this sense, even the most familiar of things has its mysterious aspect. This is precisely what gets left behind when we think of things too readily through predetermined categories that are applied to them. Here, the instrumental approach tries to gain, as it were, a unilaterally anthropocentric control over things through the power structures of human categorical schemes.

Now such awareness of "negation" is precisely what lies at the heart of personal responsibility: an awareness of what one has denied in what one has achieved. It is only in the consciousness of the "negation" involved in all choice that responsibility arises and a sense of guilt can be possible. In this sense, then, it is the same heightened sense of finitude that comes into play in revealing the individuality and the particularity of things themselves, as is being engendered in the self-expression of individuals who are striving to live authentically in the existentialist sense – that is, responsibly and, for example, in an awareness of their own mortality. Awareness of "negation" is not awareness of nothing, but a remembrance of what is being forgotten when we sum things up in categories and attempt to order our lives and the world in terms of them. It therefore represents a fuller and less prejudiced sense of "the other," that is, "objectivity," than that vaunted by rationalism, and thereby a more authentic apprehension of the world – an apprehension in which mutuality and respect displace the disengaged rational scrutiny that has come to characterize "good" thinking.

Along with the other issues raised by the distinction between rational autonomy and authenticity, this retrieval of a more genuinely receptive-responsive relationship with things has large implications for what we are to understand by quality in learning, teaching, and the teacher–student relationship in an educational context. We now turn to these matters.

The key consideration in education for authentic development is to provide a context in which students are encouraged to engage with material in ways that both respect their own motivations and the integrity of the material with which they are engaging. Facilitating authentic learning requires the teacher to empathize with the learners – to develop a feel for the quality of their current engagement by "listening" for what is incipient in it: the issues and possibilities that their current thinking inherently holds within itself, and to challenge them to acknowledge and pursue them. To do this the teacher must also attend to what things themselves (including the traditions of thought in which they are embedded) have to contribute, so that she or he can provide invitations for the refinement and deepening of the learner's thinking. Thus the teacher is concerned to focus neither on the learner in isolation, nor on some prespecified piece of knowledge, but on the *engagement* of the learners with whatever seriously occupies them. The teacher's task is to help the learners to identify and to develop their own sense of what *calls to be thought* in this situation and to give the space for this to occur (see Bonnett, 1994, ch. 14).

Thus teaching has to be both accepting and demanding of the student, and the content of the curriculum has to arise freely from this interplay. It cannot be prespecified in detail by those external to the learning situation, nor can the learning situation itself be structured according to a set of purely external norms. This approach is clearly different to that required by advocates of rational autonomy. Here learning is to occur within a prespecified curriculum whose objectives and content will be derived from the content and structure of the rational disciplines – for example, any "essential knowledge," key concepts, procedures, and criteria for making judgements. While it would be misleading to suggest that any *one* methodology derives from this position, it would clearly lead to an approach that involved a substantial amount of "prefigured" instruction orientated around the demands of whatever the public standards for rational thinking were considered to be. In a broader calculative political context, it is also likely to involve a focus on objectives that are publicly demonstrable and measurable. This again contrasts with the less tangible qualities of personal engagement that are the concern of authenticity in education.

Properly conceived, student authenticity must remain a central concern of education because of its internal relationship with personal significance in learning, moral education, interpersonal understanding, and education for democratic citizenship. It is also, of course, integral to what it is to be a full human being – constituting as it does much of what is meant by human integrity and dignity (Bonnett, 1978). While it is not perhaps best thought of straightforwardly as an educational aim or objective – in the way that, say, numeracy may be – because while it is something to be achieved, it is also something to be maintained and respected in the process of education, it is nonetheless a fundamental consideration that sets the contours of much that could truly count as educational activity. Its importance is only under-lined by the many counterpressures in a mass consumerist society that either seek to suppress it or to trivialize it by modulating the expression of individuals in politically and economically convenient ways. Furthermore, in certain developments of the idea, authenticity, through intimating the possibility of a more genuinely open relationship with things, may have a central orientating role in addressing the bur-geoning environmental problems that confront the human race.

Recommendations for Futher Reading

Bonnett, Michael (1994) *Children's Thinking*, Cassell.
Cooper, David (1983) *Authenticity and Learning*, Routledge & Kegan Paul.
Frankfurt, Harry, G. (1999) *Necessity, Volition, and Love*, Cambridge University Press.
Taylor, Charles (1991) *The Ethics of Authenticity*, Harvard University Press.

Chapter 19

Changing Notions of the Moral and of Moral Education

Nel Noddings and Michael Slote

It is obvious to even the casual observer of contemporary life that everyday notions of the moral have changed greatly in the last century. Behaviors that were regarded as morally reprehensible by the Victorians scarcely raise an eyebrow today and some are even widely accepted. Although some observers deplore the changes in moral attitudes toward, for example, sex and church attendance, many others welcome these changes, and most of us understand that – like it or not – moral notions and customs continue to change.

Notions of the moral also change in moral philosophy and, together, changes in moral customs and in moral philosophy have influenced changes in moral education. Here we discuss briefly some of the trends in contemporary moral philosophy including related work in political philosophy, and then we look at what is happening in moral education.

Our discussion centers on two interesting challenges to Kantian ethics and the liberalism founded on Kantianism. One important challenge comes from a revival of virtue ethics; another comes from feminist ethics of caring. Both are having an influence on contemporary moral education. We discuss not only the similarities between the two approaches with respect to their critiques of Kantianism but also differences which, in turn, give rise to different, if sympathetic, views of moral education.

Moral Philosophy

Kantian ethics (Kant, [1785] 1983), as exemplified in the work of John Rawls (1971, 1993) and his students, has until recently been the dominant trend in academic moral and political philosophy. And Lawrence Kohlberg's influential theory of the stages of moral development takes a rather Kantian/Rawlsian perspective in describing the developmental psychology of individuals, thereby providing a practical basis for moral education in the family and in schools. But lately there have been major philosophical challenges to Kantian ethics, and some of the most important challenges to Kohlberg's views within the field of moral education reflect, or at least correspond to, new ideas in the philosophy of morality.

Kantianism treats certain very general moral principles as the basis of living morally (and fulfilling one's moral duties), and it regards those principles as derivable from (the practical side of) pure reason and as exerting a more or less conscious influence on morally decent individuals in all the circumstances of their lives. Kant argued that someone who acts immorally can be convicted of a kind of practical inconsistency (like someone who says that he wants to get to the office, but refuses to get up in the morning); in addition, morality is conceived as respect for the idea of universal law or lawfulness, and an immoralist is thus seen as someone who takes in some sense a blinkered view of human action and interaction. Finally, Kantian ethics stresses the autonomy and dignity of every person, and one side of Kant's doctrine focuses on a general duty of respect for such dignity and autonomy.

By contrast, Rawls makes use of the idea of a social contract, rather than relying on pure reason, to ground our political morality. But the contractual situation he envisages contains features of rationality, autonomy, and universality that are at the very least analogous to the Kantian understanding of these notions; and an analogue of Kantian respect for human dignity is similarly embodied in the political principles he thinks would be subscribed to in a just social contract. Also in parallel with Kant, Rawls holds that the moral life of a society is governed by explicit appeal to, and use of, certain justified general principles.

In recent years, this general Kantian paradigm of morality (and of moral education) has come under fire in different of its aspects and in a number of different ways. Prominent among these attacks has been the one called "communitarianism" that has directed its objections to the philosophical liberalism so closely associated with Kantianism. Alasdair MacIntyre (1981), Michael Sandel (1982), Charles Taylor (1989), and Michael Walzer (1983) have all raised questions about the liberal/Kantian emphasis on the autonomous individual, individual rights, and universal principles. They point to the moral centrality of communities, social contexts, webs of interlocution, and different ways of life. In contrast, Kantianism has its sources (at least some of them) in the Enlightenment belief in the universal power of individual human reason, in the possibility of coming up with rational social rules and institutions that need take no sustenance or brook any interference from the religious, cultural, and ethnic differences that have historically divided one community from another.

But communitarians would want to question the moral powers and potential of individual cognition and reason; they hold, contrary to Kant, that it is only in relation to community values, traditions, and *good habits* acquired in their context that we can become morally virtuous. Since communities obviously differ in their traditions and values, the communitarian typically holds, therefore, that there can be no universal enlightened morality grounded in an appeal to forms of reason or rationality that are the same for everyone everywhere. Both MacIntyre and Sandel criticize Rawls's social contract for making all distinctive community values irrelevant to the understanding of justice, and both think that being virtuous or a good citizen cannot be the product of unaided individual human reason. Rather, we can function as moral individuals only within a community or within traditions or practices that are in some sense givens.

A complaint raised by communitarians and also by virtue ethicists and care theorists (whose work we will discuss next) is that the universalizability demanded by Kant and philosophical liberalism has narrowed the domain of moral discussion in an undesirable way. In this, they are joined by some postmodern philosophers who also contend that the restriction of what counts as a moral question to those issues to which we must all respond in the same (logically determined) manner diminishes the field. Philosophical analysis of obligation, they argue, has turned us away from living others and their needs and toward the laws laid down by reason (Caputo, 1993). It has also discouraged us from asking (philosophically) the great existential questions treated by the Greeks: What sort of person should I be? What life is worth living? Where do I fit in my community and in the universe?

Virtue ethicists (including some communitarians) have urged a return to these questions and, thus, to a moral domain that recognizes both a moral obligation to develop one's character and personal potential and also a much messier, richer, and more variable field of obligation to others. During the past 15 or so years, there has been a strong revival of ancient approaches to ethics and, in particular, of the focus on virtuous character and virtuous motives and desires that for Plato, Aristotle, and almost all of the nonskeptical moralists of the ancient world are central to the ideal human life (Slote, 1992).

Recent virtue ethics has sought to question various Kantian (and utilitarian) views about the moral life, and to cast doubt on the Kantian assumption that the highest morality and human excellence require a conscious and conscientious attention and obedience to universal moral principles. Many contemporary virtue ethicists think, rather, that the highest excellence or virtue shows itself in certain habits of perception, desire, and choice. Truly benevolent or kind persons, according to this view, think about how they can help a sick neighbor or someone whose need for help they are sensitive enough to perceive, and act accordingly. The virtue of kindness then shows itself through habits like these, rather than through self-conscious concern to do one's duty or the thought that it would be wrong not to help the person in need.

Actually, however, most of those who have recently sought to develop a virtues approach to ethics would grant that there are other virtues where conscientiousness *is* appropriate, part of a relevant moral ideal. Even if the kind person doesn't think about whether what she or he is doing is kind, the just person precisely *does* worry about whether what she or he is doing is just (Williams, 1985, p. 10); and *such* virtue therefore is self-conscious and conscientious in the manner defended by Kant. There is an element of duty or conscientiousness in care theory also: that is, care theorists recognize that there are times when the spontaneous inclination to care fails, and then we must call on an ethical ideal of ourselves as carers (Noddings, 1984). In addition, even Aristotle, the ancient thinker who has exerted the greatest influence on the recent revival of virtue ethics, frequently says that the virtuous person characteristically acts "for the sake of the noble" (Korsgaard, 1998). This clearly moves in the direction of Kant's emphasis on self-conscious, conscientious morality, although Aristotelian "conscientiousness" is still with respect to nobility, not moral duty, and it relates to what, without appeal to general principles, is seen to be called for in one or another particular practical situation. Still, most contemporary virtue ethicists are convinced by examples offered by Williams (1976, 1985),

Stocker (1996), Blum (1994), Foot (1978), and others that Kant (or Rawls) puts far too great and universal an emphasis on self-conscious morality, and it is interesting here to compare what they say with the ethics of care.

Virtue ethicists typically believe that both kindness (or care or benevolence) and justice are virtues, but the ethics of caring sometimes explicitly opposes itself to the ethics of justice that it thinks of as dominating modern moral philosophy. So a morality of caring (to which we will turn next) may lack the reasons most virtue ethicists have for allowing conscientiousness a role in certain important areas of moral thought and action – reasons stemming from the belief that justice is an important virtue that is independent of person-focused virtues like caring/kindness/ benevolence. To that extent, virtue ethics occupies a middle ground between Kantian ethics and the morality of caring, in regard to the issue of proper moral self-consciousness and conscientiousness.

A third challenge to Kantian ethics is that launched by Carol Gilligan (1982) and Nel Noddings (1984). Gilligan argues that the appeal to universal principles of rights, contractual reciprocity, or justice is more typical of males than of females; girls and women are more likely to conceive moral issues in terms of concern for people's well-being, in terms of caring. Noddings argues that the care orientation arises naturally and frequently out of the experience traditionally associated with women, whereas the justice orientation arises from experience more typically iden-tified with men. The emphasis on rights in the latter treats people as separate from one another, because rights are typically rights against interference by others; but women think more in terms of their connection to, their responsibility for, others. Even if the distinction between these two ways of thinking does not correlate with gender as well as Gilligan and Noddings have held, their work and that of other care theorists have made it increasingly difficult to accept the Kohlbergian view (to be discussed in the next section) that direct caring concern for other people is morally less advanced than conscientious concern for principles of justice and human rights.

We should mention also that Gilligan's work has had a dramatic influence on feminist perspectives in almost every discipline and profession. Women's emphasis on relation, for example, has been used by feminist legal thinkers to challenge the "reasonable person" doctrine. In theology, it has raised questions about the nature of both God and humankind in traditional stories such as those of Abraham and Moses. Care theorists are cited regularly in nursing theory and in nursing ethics and, indeed, in all of the helping professions.

We mentioned above that the "masculine" appeal to human rights tends to emphasize the separateness of individuals, but the assumption that we should explic-itly appeal to moral principles also puts separateness ahead of connection, because someone who relates to another person by first consulting a principle seems intuit-ively less connected to that other than one who acts out of immediate concern for his or her welfare – or out of love or feelings of friendship. Thus consider Bernard Williams's (1976) famous example of the man who, faced with a choice between saving his drowning wife and saving a stranger, decides that one is morally permitted (or obligated) to save one's wife in such circumstances, and who then saves his wife. Such a person, says Williams, has "one thought too many," and surely we would agree that in this situation the interposition of (or conscientious attention to) a presumably valid moral principle between a man and his actions on behalf of his spouse is unnatural and unattractive, because it shows less connection to, less feeling for, his spouse than his spouse (or any spouse) would hope for.

Care theorists point out that, in cases like these, weighing one's decision according to either Kantian or utilitarian principles would tend to undermine the webs of care on which we all depend. Such an approach carried out consistently might destroy the very quality of life at which systems of morality aim. On this, care theorists, virtue ethicists, and communitarians seem to be in agreement. Reasonable people rightly expect more goods and goods of a different kind from those closely related to them than from strangers. Far from increasing the moral credit due to agents who use moral logic dispassionately, we feel – perhaps uneasily – that something is morally (or at least humanly) lacking in such thinking.

In contrast, Kant explicitly and clearly holds that being guided by valid moral principles is a necessary condition of an act's having moral worth and that such reference never detracts from the worth of an action. So, as Slote (2001) argues, the Kantian emphasis on principles that derive from human autonomy and on acting by reference to and out of respect for such principles puts a double emphasis on separateness.

By contrast an ethic of caring doubly emphasizes connection. It regards our obligations not as voluntarily contracted for (à la Rawls) or as a function of our individual autonomy, but rather as deriving from our situation vis-à-vis others, from facts about how we are connected to others, and about our ability to help or hurt them – facts that are at least partly independent of our own choice. But care theory also stresses the moral importance of focusing on (responding as positively as possible to) people without the mediation of moral principles (or of concern for the moral status of one's actions), and it does this in part because it views such mediation as interfering with or detracting from caring connection with other people.

There is one Kantian-like element in care ethics (mentioned briefly above) as described by Noddings. When the spontaneous inclination to respond in a caring way fails to arise, moral agents must refer to their own ideal of caring to motivate an appropriate response; that is, as carers we construct a "caring self" that can be conscientiously consulted to guide our response in the absence of natural caring. We "pull ourselves together" and respond "as if" the usual caring inclination were present. As Noddings has pointed out, there is some danger in these cases that the cared-for will perceive our efforts as less than genuine – that we, like the husband in Williams's case, might have "one thought too many." But where such a thought is necessary to an individual's moral response, it is morally better for the individual to have it than not to have it. Slote (2001) holds that in many cases where caring flags (e.g., when one is annoyed with a loved one or simply tired), what helps us to pull ourselves together and act caringly may be a situationally induced recognition of the "bad things that will happen," say, to our spouse if we don't act in a helpful way, rather than any sort of consultation with an ideal or rule about caring. Noddings and Slote agree that turning to a principle when natural (spontaneous) caring is already operating (or could be operating) is indeed having one thought too many. And while it remains unclear just how much conscientiousness an ethic of caring needs to appeal to, it is clear that care theory, contrary to Kant, elevates the spontaneous (or natural) act of care over any conscientious appeal to caring as an ideal.

The emphasis on natural caring also suggests a further connection between care and virtue ethics. Noddings regards the status of natural caring as a virtue to be derived from the value and desirability of the caring relationships that such virtue helps to constitute or maintain. But to ground morality in certain intimate relationships goes against the spirit of both Kantian and utilitarian ethics and harks back to (at least reminds one of) the special importance Aristotle places on friendship, and this makes Noddings's approach seem virtue-ethical, or close to virtue-ethical.

But, in addition, Slote argues that there is some reason to question whether the value of caring relationships is prior to the virtue (status) of caring for others. After all, we intuitively think that caring is a virtue in a way that being cared for is not, yet both caring and being cared for are constitutive of certain desirable relationships (say, between parent and child). So it is possible to hold, and there may be advantages to holding, that caring (or kindness or benevolence) is in itself a virtue, a morally good trait or motive. Rather than having to trace its moral admirability to the goodness of certain relationships, one might hold that the fundamental moral admirability of caring – as opposed to hostility and indifference – is part of why relationships of love and friendship are so important to our lives, but relationships in which people merely use each other, or work against each others' interests, as such add no value to human lives.

This is an area of mild (and productive) difference between the two of us. Noddings acknowledges two concepts of caring: one based on virtue and one based on relation. We do, of course, use "caring" in the virtue sense: he is a caring teacher; she is a caring friend; nurses are more caring than doctors. Moreover, the virtue sense is acknowledged in the discussion of ethical caring; in drawing on the ethical ideal that one has constructed in actual caring encounters, one is at least in part exercising a virtue.

But the relational sense has been central to feminist thought. Caring, from this perspective, is an attribute of certain relations, and both parties make substantial contributions. The carer attends – receives what-is-there in the cared-for – and responds to the needs expressed. The person cared for (the "cared-for" as the second member in a caring relation or encounter), in turn, acknowledges the efforts of the carer. This acknowledgement need not be an overt expression of gratitude. In an infant, it might consist of smiles and wriggles; in a student, it might be confident pursuit of a project; in a patient, it might be a hand pressed in gratitude for the relief of pain. The acknowledgement, even when it is not expressed explicitly, says plainly, "I am cared for." Only then do we have a caring relation.

Why is this important? First, it recognizes moral interdependence – that how good I can be depends at least in part on how you treat me. What we often take to be virtue on our own part is often more properly shared with the contribution made by a congenial, sensitive, responsive partner (or cared-for). Second, it helps us to avoid a form of self-righteousness described so well in the novels of Charles Dickens and in autobiographical and semiautobiographical works such as the essays of George Orwell (1956) and Samuel Butler's *The Way of All Flesh* (1944). In these works, we meet truly dreadful people (Mrs. Jellyby and Mrs. Pardiggle, Bingo and Sim, and

Theobald Pontifex) who could credit themselves with caring – apparently good intentions, self-sacrifice, concentration on the cared-for, and the like. But the relationships established were not caring relations.

When a relation is not one of caring because the cared-for insists, "You just don't care!" or as we hear frequently in schools, "Nobody cares!" it is not necessarily the case that a carer has failed in the virtue sense, although that was certainly the case in the accounts mentioned above. The cared-for may be obtuse or especially difficult. More likely (and this is often the case in schools), there is something wrong with the setting in which the relation is located. When teachers protest that they care and show strong signs of doing so (in the virtue sense) and students still claim, "Nobody cares!" we have a compelling reason to examine the situation in which caring is supposed to flourish. Perhaps care and virtue ethicists do not disagree strongly on this, but virtue ethicists might try to remedy the situation by using even stronger virtues, whereas care theorists would concentrate on the situation and try to make it more supportive of caring.

Virtue ethicists would surely condemn the pseudocaring described by Dickens, Orwell, and Butler, but their attention is on the agent, not the relation. As Slote (2001) puts it, if we think of caring about/for others, kindness and benevolence as basic virtues, then an ethic of care will be a pure virtue ethics. For the purest virtue ethics treats the rightness and wrongness of actions as a function of what they show about the virtuous or vicious character or motives, the inner life, of the agent, the person who acts. And in explicitly defending an ethics of caring, we certainly imply and can explicitly say that acting morally or immorally is a matter of whether our actions reflect a virtuous caring attitude toward others (or even ourselves). And this is certainly to be very virtue-ethical in one's approach.

To be sure (following Slote), taking the ethic of caring in this pure virtue-ethical direction implies that caring actions lose none of their moral value if, through bad luck and in a way that the agent couldn't possibly have anticipated, an attempt to help or care for another fails of its purpose (or is never acknowledged by the person one is trying to help). But this implication is controversial. Noddings agrees that agents may indeed sometimes deserve credit for caring even if their efforts miscarry, but sometimes not. It is notoriously difficult to ascertain someone's intentions. But even when the agent deserves moral credit for trying, that does not make the relation one of caring, and giving and withholding moral credit is not the aim of an ethic of care. The point is to find ways in which to establish, maintain, and enhance relations of care.

All moralities of caring emphasize feeling and desire (the desire to be cared for and the consequent desire to care) over pure reason, and to that extent their historical roots lie partly in the moral sentimentalism of the eighteenth century British philosophers David Hume, Francis Hutcheson, and Adam Smith. In its most characteristic form, such sentimentalism downplays the role of (practical) reason in the moral life and questions in particular the Kantian view that our moral obligations are grounded in or justified in terms of pure reason. Hutcheson especially treated sentiments/motives/virtues like benevolence and sympathy as the basis for morality. But the benevolence Hutcheson treated as fundamental to morality was a universal or impartial benevolence that shows equally strong concern for the welfare of all human beings (this is reminiscent of and indeed traceable to the Christian ideal of universal love or *agape*); and this impartialism contrasts with the partiality or particularism of the ethics of care, with its primary focus on the caring that arises in direct encounter. This focus can be traced to women's interests in what might be called the original condition, infancy and home (Noddings, 2001a), and, in philosophy, to those Continental philosophies that emphasize encounter and the face-to-face. Care theorists, however, agree with Hume ([1751] 1983) that moral motivation is rooted in feeling, not in reason.

Still, Hutcheson's and Hume's moral sentimentalism are sometimes regarded as forms of virtue ethics precisely because of the emphasis they place on inner attitudes and motives in understanding right and wrong action. But Hume also put great emphasis on the so-called social virtues, and this point is especially congenial to care theory. People who regularly demonstrate these virtues – congeniality, civility, responsiveness – contribute to a climate that helps caring relations to flourish. "Wit and humour excite love and affection," said Hume ([1777] 1983, p. 101). Again, following Hume, care theorists have difficulty separating moral, intellectual, and social virtues.

The emphasis on a full array of virtues is characteristic, of course, of virtue ethics, but the contrast with Platonic and Aristotelian virtue ethics is especially striking, because both Plato and Aristotle thought the moral life was based in the exercise of reason and because neither of them gives a philosophical defense of general or universal concern for other human beings of the sort that, for Hutcheson at least, is basic to moral goodness. But what about the ethic of caring? Does it preclude a general concern for other human beings?

Not necessarily. Those who have defended an ethic of care sometimes want to leave room for an ethics of justice operating beyond the sphere of intimate personal relationships in the larger arena of national and international public and political life. Other defenders of a care ethic think that caring can do the work of justice in the larger spheres of public life. Sara Ruddick (1989), for example, holds that maternal thinking can and should have its analogues in general society and in the relations between a state or government and its citizens. Virginia Held (1993), Michael Slote (1998), and others (see Haber and Halfon, 1998) have maintained that there is a kind of moral caring that goes well beyond the narrowly personal to the political and the public. Noddings (1998a, 2001a) agrees with this and identifies "caring about" as the foundation for a sense of justice. So a care ethic can say that we all ought to be concerned with, care about, the fate of distant people we don't know, even if (contrary to Hutchesonian impartialism) we ought to care more or differently for those near and dear to us. But even some contemporary Aristotelians wish to extend the scope of Aristotelian justice and defend virtues like kindness that Aristotle hardly talks about, so as to take in a broader humane concern than one finds in either Aristotle or Plato (though one can indeed find such concern in the rationalistic ethics of ancient Stoicism).

Communitarianism shares some important features with, but also significantly differs from, the ethics of caring. Both are skeptical about grounding a universal morality in reason, to be sure. But care theory's focus on caring relations and encounters potentially allows a universal morality to be based on sentiment. Nothing in the ethics of caring precludes using such an ethics as a universal standard for individual behavior or social norms (though one that, like utilitarianism, would accommodate differences in the factual situations and responses of different individuals and societies). Care theory identifies a natural (empirical) universal in the desire to be cared for (that is, to receive some form of positive response) and a moral universal in the desire to respond with caring. But the communitarian emphasis on different traditions seems to exclude any form of ethical universalism (and to celebrate the exclusion), and one important difference between caring and communitarianism, therefore, lies in the way the former, but seemingly not the latter, allows for moral criticism from within a given society. Where women or a minority group lack some of the advantages of a hegemonic group in a given society, that situation can potentially come under moral criticism in relation to the ideal of caring and (carefully defined) a caring society. But (except when community values can be shown to be internally inconsistent) it is at best unclear how a hegemonic situation can right itself through the critical moral resources available to a communitarian. (But see Nussbaum, 1988.) And so caring might be better able to accommodate diversity than a communitarianism that treats social morality as necessarily dependent on (and relative to) a unified, historically given set of values, practices, and traditions.

However, both the communitarian and the care ethicist differ from contract theorists in the way they regard our obligations to others as depending on connections to others that are not of our own choosing. And at least some communitarians, like MacIntyre, regard themselves as virtue ethicists and see tradition and community as making possible a moral life that is best or primarily conceived as involving the possession and demonstration of certain virtues. Indeed, as we will see, the long-standing tradition of character education takes its inspiration nowadays as much from communitarian critiques of liberal democracy as from the revival of virtue ethics within philosophy.

Moral Education

There seem to be three main philosophical theories of morality (or four, if we separate virtue ethics and communitarianism) that could potentially influence current understanding of moral education. Virtue ethics and mainstream communitarianism would naturally encourage a form of moral education in which schools and parents would seek to inculcate good character in the form of specific (labeled) habitual virtues. Kantian/Rawlsian rationalism/liberalism would seemingly encourage moral education to take the form of developing certain capacities for moral reasoning and certain very general principles that can be applied to different moral dilemmas or decisions. Finally, an ethic of care would most naturally see moral education as a matter of children's coming to an intelligent emotional understanding of the good or harmful effects of their actions on the lives of other people as well as a deepening understanding of defensible ways to live their own lives. Care involves caring for oneself as well as others.

The history of moral education – not only in Western cultures but in most Eastern ones as well – has been dominated by character education. Restricting our discussion to Western societies, we see that both Greek and Judaic legacies have promoted character education. From Aristotle's insistence that children must practice desirable virtues (well before they can reason adequately about them) to the biblical injunction to "train up a child in the way he should go," character education has been the model used in both homes and religious institutions. Indeed, until recently it has been the main approach to moral education in the school also.

In reasonably stable, homogeneous communities or in those with well-defined social and occupational hierarchies, it was not difficult to identify the virtues to be inculcated. In an early twentieth century publication in the USA (White, 1909), for example, educators listed 32 virtues that were to be taught directly, grade by grade. One, "amiability," is what Hume would have called a social virtue; another, "imagination," might be classed as an intellectual virtue. All of the others are properly considered moral virtues. Today we might omit some – "ambition," for one – and members of various groups would certainly define most of them differently. "Justice," for example, is described as "the application of Truth and Obedience to affairs." How many different definitions of justice might we hear today?

The decline of character education in the USA can be traced in part to empirical studies that seemed to show that it was not working well. But the diversity of American society also puts stumbling blocks in the way of character education. There are problems about whose values and whose traditions should form the basis for public moral education, and these very problems have encouraged the development of other models, including the Kohlbergian model of moral growth, with its stress on general patterns of cognitive or rational development and its freedom from reliance on particular community values.

Kohlberg's approach to moral development basically conforms to the Kantian paradigm. His model shows its Kantian and Enlightenment roots in the way it focuses on individual cognitive growth and sees moral differences as relating chiefly to how individuals *reason* about (hypothetical or actual) moral issues. The highest of Kohlberg's stages of development is one in which the individual is governed by explicit general principles of rights, reciprocity, or justice. Following Piaget, Kohlberg views his stage sequence as embodying increasing individual cognitive development, and this fits well with the Kantian idea that morality is a matter of autonomously expressing one's rationality. Indeed, both Piaget and Kohlberg see the rationality of higher stages of moral development as involving greater consistency and universality of judgement, characteristics that earlier in Kant were also regarded as essential to moral rationality. Moreover, in regarding the highest principles of morality as appealing to notions like reciprocity, universal justice, and human rights, Kohlberg essentially opposes (or relegates to a lower stage of moral development) the kind of outright concern with human welfare to be found in utilitarianism and earlier in eighteenth century moral sentimentalism, and Kant too regarded sentimentalism as giving inadequate recognition to human moral dignity.

In presenting his philosophy of moral development, Kohlberg (1981) explicitly dismisses character education – the "bag of virtues" approach. More broadly, he criticizes "cultural transmission" as it has been described from Aristotle to R. S.

Peters (1973b), pointing out (as we have above) that such an approach assumes a consensus that rarely exists or is forced on everyone by authority. He also rejects values clarification on the grounds that not enough attention is given to the intrinsic worth of the values students espouse. The Kohlbergian model aims at a liberal-democratic ideal of justice.

There is little doubt about the Kantian roots of Kohlberg's theory, but philosophical confusion arises early on when Kohlberg says that he will draw on Socrates, Kant, and Dewey. He attempts to reconcile Socrates and Kant by addressing Socrates' question whether virtue can be taught. Using Socrates' legitimate doubts on this to support his rejection of character education, he also rejects Plato's two-phase system of indoctrination followed by reasoned dialogue. Kohlberg opts for age-appropriate reason throughout. But he seems to stay with Socrates on the centrality of knowledge and reason in morality: to know the good is to do the good. This position and the obvious question that it invites – "What is the relation between moral reasoning and moral behavior?" – is one that Kohlberg never answered adequately. His continued emphasis on reasoning has been judged by today's advocates of character education as a flaw. That is, character educators accuse Kohlbergians of concentrating exclusively on moral process to the neglect of moral content. This objection is reminiscent of one directed at liberalism (as a political philosophy) by communitarians.

Philosophically, it is harder to understand Kohlberg's coupling of Kant and Dewey. In his practical work with "just community schools," there is a strong Deweyan influence. But what can we say about the Kantian emphasis on autonomy and universalizability? Dewey disagreed explicitly with the Kantian approach to morality, criticizing its separation of moral reasoning from empirical life, its noncontextual emphasis on duty, its absolutism, its insistence on obedience in the realm of practice and its denigration of experience. In a passage that might give comfort to character educators, Dewey complains that Kant's conception of duty (empty and formal) "tells men that to do their duty is their supreme law of action, but is silent as to what men's duties specifically are" ([1915] 1985, p. 163). However, Dewey ([1897] 1972) is also critical of character education and for reasons very like those offered by care theorists (Noddings, 1998b). The education of character must take place through intelligent and caring interaction between adults and children; it must focus on practice. Second, it must include the encouragement of social, intellectual, and emotional virtues, not just the traditional moral virtues. On both of these points, Dewey, care theorists, and virtue ethicists seem to be in agreement.

Kohlberg also draws heavily, and more understandably, on Jean Piaget ([1932] 1948). Using Piaget's notions of development and stage theory, he builds an impressive theory of stages of moral development. Here, again, we wonder about the connection to Dewey. Dewey did speak of "development" and "growth," but he would almost certainly have rejected stage theories as too rigid, noncontextual, and hard to demonstrate empirically. Although the Piagetian emphasis on development through experience is certainly compatible with Deweyan philosophy, the fixed ends or terminations of various stages are not. Piaget (1971), identifying himself as very close to the spirit of Kantianism, nevertheless rejects Kant's reliance on the priority of logic over experience. This move would place Dewey very close to Piaget, but

Dewey would, in turn, find Piaget's scheme unnecessarily abstract and too fixed in its elaboration of stages. Kant prespecifies the starting point, but Piaget and Kohlberg prespecify the ends. Dewey rejects both.

Just as character education declined for a variety of reasons, Kohlbergian moral education has been attacked from several directions. There are philosophical inconsistencies as described above. But a more powerful attack came from feminism in the work of Carol Gilligan (1982). Kohlberg's use of an all-male sample invited the criticism that his model might not apply to females and, indeed, it seemed to be the case that the average woman was "stuck" at Stage 3, whereas the average man attained Stage 4. Gilligan suggested that an alternative scheme might reveal a powerful model of development emerging from Stage 3 – one concentrating on increased competence in establishing and maintaining relationships. Gilligan's own research, documenting the existence of a "different moral voice," could be (and has been) interpreted in two ways. First, the different voice has often been called "woman's" voice but, second, it is sometimes said to be simply a "different" moral voice that happened to be discovered in interviews with women. The first interpretation endorses a specific gender difference in moral orientation; the second suggests that the care approach can be found in both females and males. Although Gilligan has at one time or another endorsed both of these views, it seems reasonable (and more useful) to emphasize the second but to recognize that the care orientation captured in the different voice is more likely to arise out of women's traditional experience than out of men's. The emphasis on experience avoids essentialism. That said, if we value the care orientation, we should recommend that boys receive a social education more nearly like that traditionally offered to girls.

It is noteworthy that Gilligan did not challenge either stage theory or moral developmentalism. From a philosophical perspective, either or both could be challenged. One could remain a developmentalist and yet reject the notion of invariant stages, or one could argue that what develops is a capacity for reasoning (as described by Piaget) that is only peripherally related to morality. In the latter case, one would reject *moral* developmentalism but not developmentalism as it applies to intellectual growth. There is some reason to consider this alternative. As some psychologists have argued, the apparent fact that only the most highly educated people reach Kohlberg's highest stages implies that the phenomena are not developmental: that is, they do not emerge under the merely adequate stimulation usually productive of developmental growth but only from the cultivation characteristic of higher education. If such a finding holds up in further empirical testing, it would cast grave doubt on Kohlberg's claims that his stages are universal. Kohlberg's followers would then have to admit (as Rawls has recently done with his description of liberalism) that the Kohlbergian model contains a substantial layer of specifically Western moral and political content.

It is not clear, however, that the philosophical and psychological attacks mentioned here have been decisive in reducing the influence of cognitive developmentalism in schools. A greater effect has grown out of a widespread public belief that the morals of young people are deteriorating. School violence, drug use, declining test scores, sexual harassment of peers, bad language, and questionable patterns of dress have all contributed to the charge that morals among the young have degenerated. Underlying this general charge is the question Kohlberg had such difficulty answering: "What is the relation between moral reasoning and moral behavior?" If teaching children to reason more effectively does not result in improved moral behavior, why engage in such instruction?

The charge that the morals of the young are seriously impaired can itself be challenged. There is no clear evidence that this is true, and such charges have been made continually since the days of Socrates. Killings in US schools have increased, but the increase might convincingly be traced to the easy accessibility of guns. All of the other complaints are at least questionable. It is not clear, for example, given great changes in the population of teenagers who remain in school, that test scores have actually declined (Berliner and Biddle, 1996). Nor is it clear that drug use or sexual harassment can be reliably traced to school practices or failures. It seems far more likely that larger social factors such as changes in the popular media are at least partly at fault. Nevertheless, the Kohlbergian model has come under the very complaint directed at character education in the 1920s and 1930s: it does not work.

Character education is now back in favor, and some advocates have challenged the studies by Hartshorne and May (1928–30) that originally called traditional practices into question. Character education has much to commend it from the perspective of virtue ethics. In particular, it opens opportunities to expand the moral domain once again – that is, to consider the obligations agents have to themselves as well as to others. It holds at least the possibility of extending moral discussion into the great existential questions mentioned earlier. But it also contains the seeds of dissension – the unfortunate tendency to view outsiders as bad, their habits as morally reprehensible, their beliefs as questionable (Noddings, 1997). Clearly, character education does not necessarily imply such results, but the historical record counsels caution. Moreover, in those programs operating today, there seems to be little attention to existential questions. Most instruction concentrates on the inculcation of specific moral virtues.

Not all character educators neglect the role of reason, and some even speak favorably of the Kohlberg model but see it as lacking in moral content (see Lickona, 1991). However, sometimes these same writers rely heavily on harrowing anecdotes and questionable figures (e.g., the number of Satanic cults in America) to arouse readers' concern. This practice raises further questions for moral educators who would concentrate on moral reasoning and critical thinking. They want to ask: "Are these figures accurate? Are the reports true? How widespread are the reported abuses? How much has the moral picture changed in two decades? Should critical thinking be part of moral education?"

Care theorists share the concern of character educators about the Kohlbergian emphasis on reasoning, but they share with Kohlbergians the concern over a perceived lack of careful reasoning in some character education programs. Although both character educators and care theorists use reason, of course, neither see it as the source of morality or its main component. However, character educators might object that care theory, too, lacks "moral content." Care theorists want children to learn how to care, but they do not usually specify a list of virtues. Instead, they concentrate on how children are treated and on the practice provided – what is modeled, discussed, and confirmed in daily interaction.

The use of models and modeling in moral education raises interesting questions. In closing, we suggest that this is an area that might profit from further philosophical work. Every known form of moral education makes some use of models or exemplars. Certainly it seems reasonable to recommend that teachers should "practice what they preach." But how effective is modeling and, when it is effective, what makes it so? Modeling mathematical thinking – still often recommended by mathematics educators – has no reliable, demonstrable effects on the thinking of students. Some students may learn a great deal from teachers who model such thinking, but it is not clear that modeling itself has the most powerful effect. Practice seems more important. But would students come to practice mathematical thinking (or any desirable trait) if they had no models? And, on the opposite side, why are so many students resistant to even very powerful forms of modeling?

Character educators make heavy use of exemplars, but the stress is not as much on the modeling done by teachers as on real or fictional characters depicted in stories. Some programs are careful to choose not only outstanding moral exemplars but also stories high in literary value. Such stories serve several purposes: they provide moral exemplars, they contribute to cultural literacy, and they encourage an appreciation of literature. However, the stories are often about heroes, and a question arises about the general efficacy of hero-models. After all, by definition, a heroic act is one out of the ordinary – one we do not expect of everyone. Such stories may provide inspiration, but it is unclear whether they contribute very much to real moral growth.

In cognitive-developmental programs, it is usually problems (not characters) that are exemplified. Again, there is little hard evidence on the effectiveness of these programs, but we do hear a common complaint from students: the "stories" are boring. Sometimes, too, students want to know more about the characters and settings, and they become frustrated when they are asked to engage in moral analysis with so little knowledge of the characters and their lives. This sort of reaction (one common in females) has sometimes been used as evidence that women "just don't understand" the nature of moral dilemmas. On a more positive note, these requests for more information have been used to challenge the reasonableness of treating moral problems like geometry problems.

Care theorists use stories often, but their objective is to share and to invite discussion, usually not to exemplify any one virtue. Further, because care theorists and some virtue ethicists put great emphasis on social, emotional, and intellectual virtues, they are likely to choose literature that qualifies as great literature insofar as it speaks to the human condition. Such literature does not merely illustrate a virtue.

A caring teacher models care, of course, but it is not the modeling that is thought to have greatest effect. Rather, it is the effects on students of being cared for. The idea is that children who are cared for, who share with adults stories of humor, adventure, and tragedy, will grow up ready to care; that is, they will be prepared for the practice in caring that all educators should provide. Further, care theorists are interested in social and intellectual virtues that contribute to helping people, avoiding harm, and building friendly relations.

The psychologist Martin Hoffman (1984, 2000) has also made some interesting suggestions about ways in which the idea of caring might be implemented through moral education. He describes a process he calls "induction" or "inductive discipline" in which parents and teachers, drawing upon the naturally developing sympathy and empathy of children, make children aware of the bad (and good) effects of their actions on others and thereby lead them to be more considerate or caring in their actions. Induction involves getting children into the habit of thinking about the effects of what they are thinking of doing, and to a substantial extent it can occur without explicit reference to moral strictures or ideals. But Hoffman also thinks stories (and films and television) can help make children more aware of the needs of others and the potential effects of their own and others' actions (and inactions), and he has a number of suggestions along these lines that seem very compatible with an ethic of caring.

Care theorists and character educators (and virtue ethicists) agree that the way to a better world is more likely to depend on better people than on better principles, but care theorists rely more heavily on establishing conditions likely to encourage goodness than on the direct teaching of virtues (Noddings, 2001b). Both groups encourage the development of a wide range of virtues, not just the virtues tradition-ally labeled "moral." For care theorists, this emphasis grows from the centrality of the caring relation. One who is a delight as a cared-for contributes to the caring relation and, thus, to moral life, whether or not we give such contributions formal moral credit. For virtue ethicists (Slote, 2001), a wide range of virtues is essential to avoid the asymmetry of Kantian ethics (its concentration on our moral obligations to others).

In conclusion, we note that character education is far more widely encouraged and actually put into some form of practice than moral education based on car-ing. The challenge for philosophers is to help character educators understand the philosophical arguments underlying character education. Such understanding might eliminate some of the superficiality and inconsistency associated with character edu-cation today.

Recommendations for Further Reading

Hoffman, M. (2000) *Empathy and Moral Development: Implications for Caring and Justice*, Cambridge University Press.

Noddings, N. (2001) *A Sympathetic Alternative to Character Education*, Teachers College Press.

Rawls, R. (1971) *A Theory of Justice*, Harvard University Press.

Slote, M. (2001) *Morals from Motives*, Oxford University Press.

Chapter 20

Education in Religion and Spirituality

Hanan Alexander and Terence H. McLaughlin

Three apparent tensions complicate attempts to achieve a coherent and justifiable account of education in religion and in spirituality. First, many conceptions of education emphasize knowledge and critical rationality which, while not wholly incompatible with religion and spirituality, are in tension with a number of features in these domains. These features include an embrace of faith, trust, and receptivity, often in the face of uncertainty; an emphasis on the complex and often opaque meanings embodied in rituals and practices; a longing for personal engagement, experience, and transformation; an acceptance of dogma and religious authority; and a recognition of the limits, scope, and clarity of rationality and justification.

Second, education regularly embodies a commitment to some notion of personal liberation and flourishing. According to many analytic philosophers of education, liberation and flourishing is best seen in terms of the development of rational autonomy, while in much postmodern and neo-Marxist thought it is seen as involving personal or collective empowerment in relation to prevailing oppressions of various kinds. To the extent that religion and spirituality are in tension with critical rationality, however, they may undermine the achievement of rational autonomy, and many religious and spiritual practices stand accused of complicity in oppression against women, people of color, and other alienated or underprivileged groups. The distinctive visions of liberation and flourishing embodied in religious and spiritual traditions may be seen as widely contested and as in conflict with educational values in other ways.

Third, education is often linked to the values, principles, and practices of liberal democratic societies, including such notions as pluralism, multiculturalism, tolerance, and mutual respect and understanding. Common educational influence in such a society must strive to be appropriate for, and acceptable to, a large majority of its citizens. Education in religion and spirituality, however, is often seen as addressing beliefs and practices that are not held in common by the wider public and that are significantly controversial. Further, liberal democratic societies derive their right to rule from the consent of the governed and locate moral authority and responsibility in the reflective decisions of individual persons. Many religious and spiritual traditions, on the other hand, justify political and moral decisions with reference to higher authorities such as sacred texts, religious authorities, and divine revelation. In the light of the intricate relationship between the religious and the civic in liberal democratic societies (cf. Audi 2000; Rosenblum, 2000) complex tensions can arise between education for democratic citizenship and education in religion and spirituality.

In additional to their theoretical significance, these tensions raise important practical concerns. These concerns are manifested in long-running, continuing, and deep-seated disputes about educational policy and practice relating to such matters as the place of religion and spirituality in common schooling and the extent to which separate religious schools should be tolerated, encouraged, or supported by the state. The matters at stake extend to the nature and justification of parental rights and of public educational influence.

Those who view these tensions as unresolvable offer little hope for addressing these practical concerns. However, the tensions may be eased, if not completely resolved, by an exploration of the complex philosophical issues involved. This chapter attempts such an exploration. The chapter has three sections, dealing with religion, spirituality, and education respectively.

Religion

Our task here is not to engage in an extended account of the nature of religion, but rather to make three basic points about the domain that is significant for our overall discussion.

First, given the diversity of the faiths, traditions, and communities of practice found under the heading of religion, it is appropriate to speak of religions in the plural, not religion in the singular (Wach, 1958; Eliade, 1959).

Second, one can sketch the contours of what might count as a religious tradition, faith, community, or category by adumbrating four overlapping concerns with which religious communities grapple in varied ways: the theological, the epistemological, the ethical, and the collective. It is important to note that these are "overlapping concerns" and not necessary conditions for the ascription of the term "religious."

Theological concerns are related to "ultimate" commitments and highest ideals addressing such fundamental existential questions as the purposes of existence; appropriate responses to suffering, tragedy, and death; and the celebration of life, love, and beauty (Tillich, 1957). The way in which these ideals are embodied in different traditions varies, as does the account given of the nature of the reality to which they are seen as related. Some traditions invoke divine concepts, images, and realities (gods, goddesses, God) while others refer to elevated states of being, such as the Buddhist notion of nirvana or the Hindu conception of reincarnation. These realities, and the ideals to which they are related, are often seen as the highest good in that they define or exemplify the good life and motivate intelligent deliberation, dialogue, striving, devotion, and worship (Otto, 1950).

Epistemological concerns relate to the ways in which religious communities claim to acquire understanding and knowledge about such ultimate or transcendent realities, ideals, and commitments. Prominent among the many approaches to the achievement of religious understanding and knowledge are the appeal to rational argument (as in the various classical "proofs" for the existence of God), to religious experience (including mystical experience), and to the authority of sacred texts, rituals, and traditions (Peterson et al., 1991).

Ethical concerns arise because religious people see their theological commitments as having implications for how a worthwhile life in the fullest sense is to be conceived and pursued (Alexander, 2001). Finally, collective concerns come into focus because religious meaning and practice is largely possible in virtue of the existence of communities of discourse and life where people share common assumptions, concepts, and practices. Religious people wish to transmit their faith to future generations over time and, in particular, to their own children (Bellah et al., 1985).

Third, it is useful to draw attention to differing reactions of religions to the two great European revolutions: the Enlightenment and the Emancipation. The seventeenth century European Enlightenment was an intellectual revolution that produced a new type of rationalism more skeptical and empirical than its medieval Aristotelian predecessors. This revolution placed individual experiences and perceptions, rather than axiomatic or authoritative assumptions, at the heart of reasoning. It resulted in the growth of science and technology and posed significant challenges to prevailing religious doctrines and practices in the West. The eighteenth and nineteenth century Emancipation was a political and economic revolution that grew from Enlightenment discoveries and sensibilities. This revolution produced the modern nation-state that enfranchised citizens on the basis of individual rather than collective identity, and replaced sovereigns whose authority derived from tradition, wealth, or God with governments who claimed legitimacy drawn from the people. It too had a powerful impact on religions, as did urbanization, industrialization, and other processes of secularization.

Clearly, religions in many, perhaps even most, parts of the world have not been affected by the Enlightenment and the Emancipation. The sorts of religious sensibility that prevail in the absence of these two revolutions include naive faith (an unquestioning acceptance of traditions received from, and supported by, family, friends, and community); mystical faith (a drive or urge to confront, see, experience, or cleave to transcendent reality and ultimate truth); and scholasticism (a synthesis between Aristotelian rationalism and revealed Scripture). Among those mostly Western societies that have experienced these revolutions, however, we can identify three kinds of response that religions have made: liberalism (the attempt to adapt received religion to the various challenges posed by the revolutions); fundamentalism or ultraorthodoxy (a literal and uncompromising appeal to the authoritativeness of a sacred text or texts and an insistence upon the limitations of the scope and validity of critical reason); and traditionalism or neoorthodoxy (a "middle way" between the two other responses) (Alexander, 2001, pp. 139–56).

The domain of religion is related to, though is not straightforwardly identifiable with, the domain of the spiritual, and it is to this second domain that we now turn.

Spirituality

Spirituality is difficult to define. For our purposes, it is useful to distinguish between religiously "tethered" and "untethered" conceptions of spirituality, based on whether or not they are linked to, or housed within, the tradition of a religious faith (cf. Nash, 1999; Alexander, 2001, pp. ix–xvii).

Religiously "tethered" spirituality takes its shape and structure from various aspects of the religion with which it is associated and that make it possible for us to identify criteria for "spiritual development," such as those outlined by Ignatius of Loyola or Nahman of Bratzlav. The spirituality of religious people consists in part in their discovery of meaning and purpose in the theological aspects of religion, through devotion to God or gods, or through the achievement of a favored state of contemplation or consciousness. The epistemological concerns of religion underpin forms of spirituality related to the search to know God through prayer, sacred study, or participation in ritual and ceremony. The ethical concerns of religion generate spiritual resources for the pursuit of, say, prophetic justice or good works, as part of a distinctive, religiously inspired, vision of the good life. The collective aspect of religion is related to aspects of spirituality arising from the experience of participation in a faith community of belonging, shared memory, discourse, and practice.

Spirituality, however, cannot be confined to the religious domain. Religiously "untethered" spirituality involves beliefs and practices that are disconnected from, and may even be discomfiting to, religions. In some conceptions, spirituality is seen as having a greater value than institutionalized religion and as serving as a touchstone in terms of which religions can be assessed. Religiously untethered spirituality takes many forms, some of which lack a definite shape and structure. This poses difficulties to those who seek specific criteria for spiritual development in relation to them.

The contrast between religiously "tethered" and "untethered" conceptions of spirituality can be illustrated by reference to five interrelated strands that often characterize the spiritual domain, although they are not necessary conditions of a phenomenon or a person being described as "spiritual."

The first strand involves an emphasis on a search for meaning. This search typically takes the form of a personal quest for value and significance in life, which is related to personal identity and to the forging of personal commitments and life plans. In the context of religion, such a quest is conducted from a particular framework of belief, practice, and value and is aimed at the search for "purpose" and "truth" conceived in rather specific ways (as in the search for what is "ultimate" or "sacred"). The religiously untethered spiritual search can proceed from little more than an apprehension that there is something more to life than is apparent on its surface, and can be radically unstructured and open-ended.

A second strand involves the cultivation of "inner space." Here notions such as awareness, centeredness, and stillness are prominent. In religious contexts, this cultivation is conducted in the light of specific beliefs and ideals expressed, for example, in forms of prayer, meditation, and ritual as part of an ordered pursuit of an articulated notion of "spiritual development." In religiously untethered conceptions of spirituality, such a cultivation may be seen in much less specific and more diffuse ways, including under a merely therapeutic aspect.

A third strand refers to the manifestations of spirituality in life. These relate to the basic orientations, motivations, and dispositions of individuals with respect to themselves, others, the world, and to life. They include widely recognized personal qualities such as self-possession, self-control, self-knowledge, humility, calmness, serenity, openness, trust, hope, gratitude, love, generosity, self-transcendence, and wisdom. Often such "manifestations" may be accompanied by, or involve, "vitality" and "dynamism," which are particularly related to the notion of "spirit." In the case of "religiously tethered" conceptions of spirituality, these "manifestations" are related to, and articulated in terms of, the vision of the person, the "good life," and "spiritual development" that the religion in question embodies. This vision will typically include an account of how the various personal qualities should be properly balanced and prioritized in relation to each other to create the overall "shape" of a human life. In the case of religiously untethered spirituality, such manifestations may be seen in a more piecemeal way, and may be disconnected from a wider, determinate, view of their meaning, significance, and structural relationship to each other.

A fourth strand stresses the notion of distinctive responses to aspects of the natural and human world. Prominent among such wide-ranging responses are awe, wonder, and reverence. In religious spiritualities these phenomena are informed by religious faith. In untethered conceptions of spirituality responses of this kind are more open.

A fifth strand of the spiritual domain is collective or communal. Forms of spirituality, whether "religiously tethered" or "religiously untethered," often have a collective or communal dimension relating to the significance of shared memory and meaning, a sense of belonging, and a commitment to common behaviors. These communities of whatever form vary in many respects (for example, the extent to which they are open to outsiders).

The complexities involved in the notion of spirituality are readily apparent. The domain involves a wide range of categories of human quality, achievement, and reaction, and a wide range of presuppositions and commitments with respect to underlying matters such as the nature of reality and of the good life. In the case of "religiously tethered" forms of spirituality, such presuppositions and commitments are often more readily identified than in "religiously untethered" forms, where they may be underarticulated.

It is, of course, important to insist that the distinction between "religiously tethered" and "religiously untethered" conceptions of spirituality needs to be handled with considerable caution. The domain of religion is not itself one with clear features and boundaries, and the phenomenology of spirituality does not correspond to any rigid distinction of the sort that has been drawn. Nevertheless, despite its imprecision, the distinction may serve a useful purpose for the present discussion (for general discussions of the spiritual domain see, for example, Hadot, 1995; Haldane, 2000; Hick, 1999; McGhee, 2000).

Having outlined central features of the domains of religion and spirituality we turn now to the complex educational questions that arise in relation to the domains.

Education

In elaborating the central philosophical issues that arise in relation to education in religion and spirituality, we shall focus attention upon education for children and young people (hereinafter "students") up to the age of 18 and shall not address matters relating to religion and spirituality in higher education. In the context of this focus it is useful to draw a distinction between two broad conceptions of education in religion and spirituality, which we shall label "education in religion and spirituality from the outside" and "education in religion and spirituality from the inside" respectively.[1]

"Education in religion and spirituality from the outside" refers to forms of education in these domains in which no one religious or spiritual tradition is given normative status. Issues of meaning, truth, and value relating to the religious and spiritual domains are seen primarily as matters for exploration, discussion, and critical assessment. Religious and spiritual belief, commitment, and practice on the part of individuals are neither presuppositions of, nor aims of, the enterprise. For these reasons, education of this kind can be described as "from the outside" of particular religious and spiritual traditions. It is important to insist, however, that education of this form cannot remain "on the outside" in the sense that no attempt is made to understand the religious and spiritual domains from the insider's point of view. Such attempts are necessary if religious and spiritual traditions and ideas are to be properly illuminated for the purposes of understanding and assessment. Forms of "education in religion and spirituality from the outside" are typically offered in the common schools of liberal democratic societies, and are seen as appropriate for the large majority of the citizens of such societies regardless of their religious or spiritual persuasions.

The term "education in religion and spirituality from the inside" refers to the forms of education and spirituality that are seen as appropriate for those *within* a particular religious and spiritual tradition, or those who are being initiated into such a tradition. These forms of education are typically offered in separate religious schools, whether full-time or supplementary, and in other educative contexts within religious communities, such as youth groups, summer camps, and educational tours. Central to these forms of education in religion and spirituality is the attempt to *form* and *nourish* a commitment to the particular beliefs, values, and practices of a specific religious and spiritual tradition. The mandate for these forms of education in pluralist liberal democratic societies is seen as arising from the exercise of the rights of parents and religious communities in relation to the formation of their children and young people and an acknowledgement of the demands of legitimate plurality in educational arrangements.

Any liberal democratic society, we argue, needs to acknowledge the importance of both forms of education in religion and spirituality. These forms represent different aspects of the tensions that are inherent in the values, interests, and needs of such societies. One way of representing these tensions is in terms of the contrasting demands of "openness" and "rootedness." On the side of "openness," liberal democratic societies should be committed, within familiar limits, to a robust pluralism that accommodates a diversity of religious and spiritual belief, commitment, and activity and ensures the development for individuals of the tools of self-definition. Such societies are rightly wary of the employment of state power in the promotion or valorization of particular religious or spiritual beliefs, values, and practices since these are significantly controversial. From this perspective, both democracy and religion suffer when state power is employed in matters of conscience. This view is seen in its clearest form in the constitution of the United States, which protects the free expression of religion and precludes the establishment of a state religion, thereby guaranteeing not only freedom of, but freedom from, religion. In liberal democratic societies, such as England and Wales, where there is an established church, a rather different cultural milieu prevails, but one that is still alert to the dangers of employing state power in matters of religious and moral conviction. On the side of "rootedness," however, liberal democratic societies also have an interest in the flourishing, again within familiar limits, of forms of religious and spiritual belief, commitment, and activity that constitute not only important contexts for the formation of persons and of democratic character, but also resources for the shaping of lives (Tocqueville, 1961; Bellah et al., 1985).

Education in religion and spirituality "from the outside" is related especially to the demands of "openness," and education in religion and spirituality "from the inside" to the corresponding demands of "rootedness." Care is needed, however, in interpreting the implications of these forms of education for schooling arrangements in particular societies. Such institutional arrangements and provisions are influenced and determined by many factors (especially social and political ones) and philosophical considerations have only a contributory role to play in policy making. It seems clear, however, that any liberal democratic society should make provision for forms of education in religion and spirituality of both kinds, although precisely how this is to be achieved in any context involves complex contextually significant matters.[2]

Education in religion and spirituality "from the outside" is needed because, in its absence, students from nonreligious backgrounds will lack the opportunity of exposure to the religious and spiritual domains, thereby inhibiting the range of perspectives in the light of which they may shape their lives. In addition, students may be left vulnerable to unthinking prejudices of various kinds about religious and spiritual matters and to the widely recognized dangers of religious or spiritual cults and movements (Alexander, 1981). Further, students may be left underassisted in the development of aspects of "civic virtue" in relation to religious and spiritual matters, where these require the achievement of appropriate forms of understanding, respect, and tolerance. These considerations suggest that there is something deeply problematic about the exclusion from common schools of the study of religious and spiritual matters, as happens in the United States. Despite its justification in terms of neutrality, such a policy tends to lead *de facto* to a lack of understanding and sympathy for religion and spirituality, and even to suspicion of these domains. This outcome is apparent in Israel, where students who attend common schools receive little if any education in religion and spirituality. The demands of "openness" do not, however, only apply to "education in religion and spirituality from the outside." They suggest that there should be an element of "openness" in all forms of education of religion and spirituality, including those offered "from the inside." Liberal democratic societies cannot be indifferent to forms of uncritical indoctrination or formation in religious and spiritual matters, even if they are at a loss to know how best to respond to them.

Education in religion and spirituality "from the inside" is needed if some students are to be given the opportunity for a detailed understanding of a particular religious and spiritual tradition and for the educative development of their "rootedness" in such a tradition. The considerations indicated above indicate that such a form of education in religion and spirituality cannot be provided in the common school in any straightforward way. As mentioned earlier, the most obvious context for this form of education is the separate religious school in relation to which parents can exercise rights of choice. As is well known, the extent to which such schools receive public financial support and subsidy varies across liberal democratic societies, and is a focus for much debate. In the light of the demands of "rootedness," liberal democratic societies should be concerned about any serious inaccessibility for voluntary choice of forms of education in religion and spirituality "from the inside." Although the concern has been noted that these forms of education should adequately embody considerations relating to the demands of "openness," it should be noted that the corresponding demands of "rootedness" bear upon forms of education in religion and spirituality "from the outside." Such forms must strive to illuminate the "internal" perspective in ways indicated earlier.

The contrasting demands of "openness" and "rootedness" inherent in the theory and practice of liberal democratic societies therefore require careful balances to be struck in educational policy and practice between the corresponding demands of education in religion and spirituality "from the outside" and "from the inside." Both forms of education and spirituality are not unproblematic, however, and we now turn to an exploration of philosophical complexities arising in relation to each form.

Education in religion and spirituality "from the outside"

Lying behind the conception of education in religion and spirituality "from the outside" is the existence of deep-seated, well-founded, and perhaps ineradicable value disagreements of the sort that are given philosophical expression by John Rawls via his notion of "the burdens of judgement" – the sources of ineliminable rational disagreement between well-intentioned and well-informed persons (Rawls, 1993, pp. 54–8). These disagreements and differences, which are prominent in liberal democratic societies, are "significantly controversial." They generate concern about how educational influence aimed at all members of society regardless of their various differences can be justified. Values such as respect, toleration, and mutual recognition must be taken into account when considering the introduction of matters that are "significantly controversial" into the curriculum of the common school.

A basis for common educational influence in the face of legitimate diversity can be found in the common values, principles, and commitments that are presupposed in, and necessary to, the very notion of a pluralist liberal democratic society itself. These values, principles, and commitments include the rational autonomy of the individual and the demands of democratic citizenship, which serve as important general educational aims. Other ingredients that play a role in the articulation of common educational influence include the distinction between public and nonpublic considerations and domains and between thin and thick conceptions of the good, together with the importance of developing public or civic reason. (On the general conception of education associated with liberal democratic societies see, for example, Callan, 1997; Gutmann, 1987; Levinson, 1999; Macedo, 2000; J. White, 1990; P. White, 1996). There is a strong presumptive link between this conception of educational influence and the common school: a school that is open to, and intended for, all students in a liberal democratic society regardless of religious, ethnic, class, or cultural background. (On the concept of the common school see, for example, Callan, 1997, especially chapter 7, 2000; Feinberg, 1998; McLaughlin, 1995a; Salomone, 2000.)

In this context, religious and spiritual beliefs, values, and practices are seen as "significantly controversial" and therefore as matters for the reflective evaluation, decision, and response of individuals and families. They cannot be imposed on all citizens and their children through the use of political power, or common schooling, which assumes the truth of a particular religious or spiritual tradition and seeks to shape students as members of such a tradition. Liberal democratic conceptions of the educative role of the common school are therefore in significant contrast with that prevalent in "theocratic" societies, such as Saudi Arabia.

The inclusion of education in religion and spirituality "from the inside" in the curriculum of common schools in pluralistic, liberal democracies is, therefore, highly problematic. It cannot be part of the required curriculum of the common school over which students and families have no choice. In the United States of America it is excluded from such schools because the state is precluded by the Constitution from endorsing any particular religious or spiritual tradition. In other liberal democratic contexts, "education in religion and spirituality from the inside" is only offered in common schools as a voluntary option within the common school curriculum (say, as an alternative to a study of "ethics") or as a voluntary supplementary subject. In these cases, visiting religious leaders may assume responsibility for this work.

We need to be careful, therefore, when speaking of the need to "educate the whole child" in the common school. To the extent that this holistic ambition entails the cultivation of particular religious or spiritual perspectives and qualities of personhood, it may not be justifiable within the setting of the common school, given the demand for educational forbearance from influence on matters on which there is no public agreement (McLaughlin, 1996a). The mandate possessed by common schools emphasizes the importance of influence that is broadly acceptable to a wide public and is compatible with the sorts of liberal democratic principles that have been indicated.

"Education in religion and spirituality from the outside" is based, however, on the judgement that it is possible in religious and spiritual matters to achieve an educational approach to these domains that is defensible in terms of the principles governing common educational influence. Such an approach in relation to religion has been adopted in common schools for many years in England and Wales (where "religious education" is a compulsory subject) and elsewhere (see, for example, Hobson and Edwards, 1999; Hull, 1984; Astley, 1994). Even in the USA there have been increasing calls for the introduction of the study of religion in public schools, since the establishment clause of the first amendment to the constitution does not prevent education *about* religion in this context (See, for example, Noddings, 1993; Spinner-Halev, 2000). Arguments in favor of such developments are often complicated by popular problematic claims that religion and spirituality are needed in schools to provide a firm basis for moral education, and, in particular, for the development of character.

"Education in religion and spirituality from the outside" seeks to engage students in an open exploration of the domains of religion and spirituality with the aim of achieving appropriate forms of understanding and critical response. "Open" here refers to the range of traditions and perspectives considered, the attitude that is invited toward them, and the forms of autonomous judgement and response sought on the part of students. This stance is not incompatible with students embracing, or coming to embrace, a particular religious or spiritual commitment, but neither does it suggest that students should be required to do so. In exploring a broad range of features of the religious and spiritual domains, it is recognized that attempts need to be made to ensure (at least to some extent) an "internal" perspective for students on these features through strategies such as sympathetic imaginative engagement and (forms of) participation.

While the presence of religion in common schools has been the subject of discussion and debate for many years, the claim that such schools should be concerned with spirituality is relatively recent. In England and Wales, all publicly supported schools have an obligation to promote the spiritual development of their students (Erricker, 2000), and a similar concern with spirituality is evident in public schools in the USA. Exactly how it is envisaged that spirituality should be dealt with in such schools is often not clear, except that a separate subject does not seem to be envisaged. This upsurge of interest in spirituality in common schools is due to a number of factors, some of which resonate with factors mentioned earlier concerning the contemporary interest in spirituality in general (Alexander, 2001). Many contemporary schools have become obsessed with academic success and narrowly defined goals. In this context, spirituality serves as a marker for a more humane education and for a concern with the personal and all-round development and enrichment of students. Spirituality can also be seen as an antidote to anomie among young people and an aid in the search for meaning and rootedness in modern life and the forging of a concrete life path rooted in visions of the good person and the good society that can enhance opportunities to flourish. Many of these factors can be summed up in the perception that "something is missing" in education that spirituality can provide.

However, the project of common spiritual education seems to be caught between the horns of a dilemma. On the one hand, any attempt to involve students in any specific spiritual traditions that are "religiously tethered" seems to fall foul of an insistence that common schools should avoid exerting "significantly controversial" educational influence. Such forms of spirituality must therefore be treated in an appropriately critical manner – which requires approaching them "from the outside." From such a perspective, there are concerns that the introduction of "religiously tethered" spirituality into common schools may be a disguised way of smuggling religion into this context (Beck, 1999). On the other hand, an emphasis on "religiously untethered" forms of spirituality may buy an escape from strictures relating to the importance of avoiding "significantly controversial" influence at the cost of blandness and obscurity derived from an insufficiently clearly defined notion of spirituality. David Carr notes how notions of spirituality in an educational context often amount to little more than "a hotchpotch of only vaguely connected items of cognition, intuition and feeling between which it is well nigh impossible to discern any coherent conceptual connections" (Carr, 1995, p. 84). In this situation, it is widely argued that categories such as "personal development" or "self-knowledge" would be more appropriate for capturing the educational objectives being sought. In any event, it seems that any treatment of spirituality in the common school must be "from the outside." (On the notion of education in spirituality see, for example, Best, 1996; Blake, 1996b; D. Carr 1995, 1996; Copley, 2000; Erricker, 2000; Hull, 1996; Thatcher, 1999; Wright, 2000.)

"Education in religion and spirituality from the outside" is, however, open to a range of difficulties and objections. In practical terms, most common schools can devote only a relatively small proportion of their resources (including staffing and curriculum time) to this aspect of their educational provision, and this limits what such a complex and ambitious program of education can achieve. In addition, the overwhelmingly *de facto* secular nature of the ethos of many common schools, together with similar conditions in the broader society as a whole, constitute obstacles to the sort of educational influence in religion and spirituality that is being aimed at.

A number of difficulties and objections relating to "education in religion and spirituality from the outside" do, however, have a philosophical flavor to them. Four are considered here.

The first difficulty relates to the salience given to critical thinking and rational autonomy in education in religion and spirituality "from the outside." This emphasis invites a number of lines of query and criticism. Radical critiques argue that critical rationality and its associated ideals constitute merely an alternative ideological position on a par with religious and spiritual traditions. Critical rationality too must therefore be seen as "significantly controversial": it cannot serve as an "Archimedean point" from which other traditions can be understood, evaluated, and judged (Apple, 1990; Aronowitz and Giroux, 1991). On such views we are therefore faced merely with choices between ideologies, and the criteria on which such choices should be made are not based on "rationality" but on, say, what will serve the power interests of those being schooled (McLaren, 1989). This kind of critique is confronted by arguments relating to the various contradictions inherent in strong relativism (Siegel, 1988) and to the presence of some conception of rationality in the very idea of "goodness" that allows us to claim that one form of life is better than another, according to some account of the good (Alexander, 1997a, 2001, pp. 156–70). The liberal educational tradition requires the vindication of the validity of the ideals of critical thinking and rational autonomy, although there are disputes about the extent of criticism of, say, religious perspectives that liberal educational ideals require (Galston, 1989), and about the precise way in which the ideals should be formulated. Care is needed to ensure that the notions of critical rationality and rational autonomy are not characterized in a way that is unduly inhospitable to religious and spiritual perspectives.

A second difficulty, as the name of this form of education indicates, concerns the ability of education in religion and spirituality "from the outside" to achieve appropriate forms of understanding on the part of students. There are a number of philosophically significant aspects to this difficulty. One aspect concerns the connection between the relevant forms of understanding and religious and spiritual practice. To what extent can religious and spiritual understanding be achieved independent of such practice, and, more specifically, independent of participation in particular religious and spiritual traditions and forms of life? The significance of involvement in, and engagement with, a specific religious and spiritual tradition for understanding is considerable. The perception of superficiality involved in any attempt to exhibit, however sympathetically and imaginatively, a range of religious and spiritual perspectives and traditions "from the outside" for consideration has significant philosophical support. The limitations of any generic or general understanding of the religious and spiritual domains are widely felt. (On the illumination of these difficulties from a broadly Wittgensteinian perspective and their educational implications see, for example, McLaughlin, 1995b. On the Wittgensteinian perspective on religion in general see, for example, Kerr, 1998; D. Z. Phillips 1993, 1997.)

A third, related, difficulty relates to the possibility that, despite its aspirations to the contrary, this form of education may give an unbalanced and unfair characterization of the religious and spiritual domains to students in virtue of a distortive mishandling by teachers of underlying philosophical questions relevant to the domains. The dangers of invoking an inappropriate conception of critical rationality and rational autonomy have already been mentioned. Among the other dangers that arise from a careless, let alone partisan, mishandling of underlying philosophical questions is the possibility that students may be given the impression that relativism in its various forms is an appropriate (or inevitable) perspective to take toward the possibility and nature of "truth" in the religious and spiritual domains (cf. Carr, 1994; Kerr, 1998), that differing religions should be seen as apt for choice by individuals simply on criteria relating to individual appeal, that spirituality should be seen under a therapeutic aspect, that religion should be seen in reductionist or functionalist terms, and so forth. (On the range of philosophical issues that require careful handling here see, for example, Hobson and Edwards, 1999, chapters 2, 3.)

A fourth difficulty relates to the broader context of the common school and the extent to which it can be seen to be fair with respect to the value influence that it exerts. No common school is, or could aspire to be, value-neutral. Education is, after all, inherently saturated with value. The aspiration of the common school is better described as seeking to achieve fairness in the handling of significant value diversity.

Disputes about the fairness of common schools in this matter often involve heated disputes and deep-seated emotions. This aspect of the work of the common school is a complex and challenging one, and it gives rise to various demands on such schools relating to the illumination of value texture and complexity. For example, the common school must not give the impression that "public" or "civic" norms constitute the sole basis on which value judgements should be made. Whether a given perspective or action should be tolerated or accepted from a "public" or "civic" point of view does not *ipso facto* make it fully acceptable from all points of view. Common schooling should seek to achieve a form of "moral bilingualism" on the part of students (McLaughlin, 1995a, pp. 248–50) and this involves ensuring that moral and value questions are fully illuminated by a full range of relevant considerations. Therefore, while religious and spiritual perspectives should not be seen as settling discussions of matters of a moral, social, and political kind that are discussed in the common school, such perspectives should not be excluded or marginalized from such discussions either. (On the general matters at stake here see, for example McLaughlin, 1995a. For a discussion of the points in relation to the example of sex education see McLaughlin, 1998.) The question of the extent of the demands that can be legitimately made on the common school for the accommodation of religious perspectives is an interesting one, and is illuminated by the US court case *Mozert v. Hawkins County Board of Education*, where parents objected to a reading program on the grounds that their children were thereby exposed to views that they found religiously offensive. At the heart of this debate are the questions of whether respectful exposure to diversity can interfere with the free exercise of religious beliefs and whether common schools can insist upon exposure to diversity as a basic principle of their educational mandate. In this case, the parents were content with their children remaining in the common school, but sought exemption from a particular program. The case therefore contrasts with the case of *Wisconsin v. Yoder*, where Amish parents sought exemption for their children from public education after the age at which they gained basic skills. However, both cases are concerned with the extent to which the religious sensibilities of parents can be accommodated within the principles and demands of common schooling. The complexity and controversiality of the court decisions in these cases, and the reasoning behind them, bring into focus the difficulty of reaching a clear judgement about the matters at stake. (For a discussion of these cases, see, for example, Macedo, 2000, chapter 6. On the educational rights and duties of parents see, for example, McLaughlin, 1984, 1990, 1994.)

The requirements on the part of the common school arising from these difficulties are extensive and demanding. They give rise to continuing doubts about whether the ambition of the common school to achieve its aims with respect to value influence can in fact be achieved, and whether unduly secular influence can be avoided. (On such doubts see, for example, Sandsmark, 2000; cf. Haydon, 1997, chapter 10.)

One reaction to these difficulties is to claim that the common school should base its influence not on an attempt to meet impossible demands relating to the illumination of value texture and complexity but on a set of "default" norms arising from the dominant norms (including religious norms) prevalent in a society (see McLaughlin, 1995a, pp. 245–8; Haldane, 1986).

Notwithstanding the difficulties, however, it might be felt that the project of education in religion and spirituality "from the outside" represents the best that can be attempted in the context of the common school. Its difficulties and shortcomings lead at least some parents and others, however, to seek an alternative form of education in religion and spirituality that proceeds from a rather different basis and set of assumptions and that has rather different aims. It is to this second form of education in religion and spirituality that we now turn.

Education in religion and spirituality "from the inside"

Education in religion and spirituality from the inside is conducted within a specific or distinctive religious or spiritual tradition and is aimed at, and to some extent presupposes, religious and spiritual belief, faith, and practice on the part of students, as well as understanding. It is therefore supportive of tradition in ways that education in religion and spirituality "from the outside" cannot be. Education in religion and spirituality in this sense provides an appropriate option for parents who actively seek it, and is best located in separate full-time or part-time religious schools or in other contexts within religious communities, where a distinctive conception of education can be realized not only through the curriculum but also through the ethos of the school and processes such as teacher exemplification (McLaughlin, 1996b; Scheffler, 1995). It is the voluntary nature of this form of education that eases the requirements for forbearance from educational influence found in relation to education in religion and spirituality "from the outside" offered in common schools.

This form of education can be easily confused with uncritical confessionalism in education, which often tends toward indoctrination of one sort or another. Uncritical confessionalism is particularly associated with forms of religion identified earlier that have either not been exposed to the Enlightenment or the Emancipation or have reacted to them in terms of fundamentalism or ultraorthodoxy. We shall discuss uncritical "confessionalism" in more detail shortly. However, our interest at the outset here is in identifying a form of education in religion and spirituality that is recognizably educational, not indoctrinatory, in that it is both supportive of religious and spiritual traditions by aiming at religious belief, faith, and practice on the part of students and also at the same time aiming at the development of a form of rational autonomy and democratic citizenship.

The form of education in religion and spirituality "from the inside" that we wish to describe here, therefore, is first and foremost a form of *education*. It is particularly harmonious with religious and spiritual traditions that have embraced the challenges of the Enlightenment and the Emancipation described earlier and that are in dialogue with the values, principles, and practices of liberal democratic societies. In these forms of education in religion and spirituality, a particular religious and spiritual tradition is seen as a legitimate starting point for a person's growth and development via recognizably educational processes into autonomy and democratic citizenship (Alexander, 1995, 1997b, 2000, 2001, pp. 198–203; McLaughlin, 1992b; Scheffler, 1995; Thiessen, 1993). Here, exposure to, and involvement in, a substantial religious and spiritual tradition is seen as laying the foundations for a kind of "openness with roots." Students are exposed to, and involved in, a form of education articulated by a particular conception of the good, but they are encouraged to put their formation into critical perspective and to make any acceptance of it on their part authentic. Concerns may be raised about the coherence of this form of education: is it aiming at critical understanding or faith? Such concerns are eased by recognition of the point that in such conceptions of education what is being aimed at is critical, authentic faith, not mere lip service. Since the basic norms and principles of a liberal democratic society often find their roots in agreements among the variety of religious and spiritual traditions that comprise the variety of visions of the good within such societies, it can be argued that the existence of a robust common culture within such societies depends significantly on forms of education that sustain religious and spiritual perspectives and commitments. Contemporary Catholic schools in the United States, for example, have been shown to be more effective in preparing their students for democratic citizenship than their public school counterparts (Bryk et al., 1993).

One of the major benefits of this form of education from some points of view is that it can ease the four forms of difficulty noted earlier in relation to education in religion and spirituality "from the outside." First, by offering a form of education linked to religious and spiritual practice within a specific tradition, inappropriate conceptions of critical thinking and rational autonomy are less likely to be invoked. Second, such an educational approach is more readily able to satisfy the demands of involvement and engagement for the achievement of significant understanding. In the case of spirituality, for example, it is possible to form a clear sense of how "development" can be understood and aimed at. Third, engagement with a particular religious and spiritual tradition can offer a sustained and coherent exposure to the underlying philosophical assumptions of at least one tradition, and students may thereby be better placed to make judgements about the nature of the kinds of philosophical assumptions relevant to the religious and spiritual domains as a whole than those who have experienced a form of education in which underlying philosophical assumptions are mishandled in the way referred to earlier. Finally, the "separate" religious school offers a sustained exposure to a particular view of life and perspective on value. This may offer a more coherent and consistent form of influence than that resulting from the efforts on the part of the common school to satisfy the demands upon it outlined earlier relating to the illumination of value texture and complexity.

Forms of education in religion and spirituality "from the inside" presuppose the justification of a range of parental and other rights that underpin the mandate for educational influence of this kind. The extent to which a liberal democratic state should support such forms of education (for example, by providing financial support for religious schools) is one of a number of issues that requires detailed attention in a fuller account.

The major concern about this form of education in religion and spirituality is that it may fail to be properly educational. If, as we claim, this form of education can be distinguished from uncritical "confessionalism" in virtue of its embodying a concern with critical reason and rational autonomy, how can this embodiment be reconciled with a focus upon one among a range of religious and spiritual traditions and the aim of bringing about belief, faith, and practice, and not merely understanding, on the part of students? Some thinkers have drawn a negative conclusion about this matter and have inferred that such forms of education are inherently indoctrinatory (Flew, 1968; Dwyer, 1998). Others have argued that while activities such as those involved in education in religion and spirituality from the inside may be justifiable in certain contexts, they should be sharply marked off from "education" (say by use of the term "catechesis") for the reason that properly educational influence should be epistemologically well grounded (Hirst, 1981, 1985).

Progress in discussion of questions such as these is inhibited by the contestability of the concepts of "education," "critical reason," and "rational autonomy." This makes it very difficult to distinguish education in religion and spirituality from the inside from uncritical confessionalism in any very sharp way. With regard to critical reason, for example, reasoning of some kind is a part of any coherent and flourishing tradition and it is difficult to specify the precise features that reason should possess if it is to be appropriately critical. The difficulties that attend any attempt to specify these features in terms of the extent to which basic assumptions or conceptualizations are held up to critical scrutiny are well known and are intensified by appropriate caution about whether complex notions of criticism embodied within religious traditions have been properly understood. For example, Islamic conceptualizations of education require careful and nuanced interpretation and should not be too quickly dismissed (Halstead, 1995b; Ashraf and Hirst, 1994). Liberal democratic assumptions and values need themselves to be problematized.

One strategy in discussions of these matters is to make a distinction between forms of reasoning in religious and spiritual matters that are markedly "internal" to a particular form of life, and those that possess "external" elements. Many vibrant fundamentalist or ultraorthodox communities, for example, engage in argumentation and justification that is internal to their religious tradition in that they are based on forms of reasoning associated with the interpretation of sacred texts. Such communities and traditions may be markedly resistant to forms of reasoning that expose their beliefs and commitments to critique from other perspectives and enable their adherents to engage in a significant way in debates in the public domain on the basis of their faith position. Without entering into an extensive discussion of the philosophical complexities that arise in attempting to distinguish between "internal" and "external" forms of reasoning, it can be noted that liberal democratic societies require their citizens to engage in public or civic forms of reasoning as well as those that are internal to their own substantial vision of the good. The assassination of Israeli Prime Minister Yitzak Rabin by a graduate of strongly nationalistic, religious schooling in Israel, for example, raises serious concerns within liberal democracies about forms of nationalist or religious instruction that avoid or even undermine such forms of public or civic reasoning.

Liberal democratic societies are therefore justifiably concerned when education in religion and spirituality "from the inside" becomes unduly narrow. Although the common ground norms of pluralistic democracies may in some important senses depend upon citizens with robust commitments to thick visions of the good, to the extent that those citizens are ignorant or intolerant of those adhering to competing traditions, or of the demands of civic virtue, the delicate and integrative fabric of that commonality may be threatened, and as a consequence also the very viability of the pluralistic society. Hence education in religion and spirituality "from the inside" in liberal democratic societies ought to include significant exposure to other visions of the good embraced and protected by democracy, as well as seeking to encourage forms of civic virtue including appropriate forms of tolerance (on these matters see, for example, Bishops' Conference of England and Wales, 1997; Bryk et al., 1993).

The steps that liberal democratic societies can legitimately and effectively take to ensure that these civic imperatives are secured in separate religious schools give rise to complex issues, including the nature and role of regulation requirements that might be imposed on such schools, the extent to which "uncritical confessionalism" in religious matters may be compatible with satisfaction of the civic imperatives, and the significance of "second best" practical compromises. One ingredient in an appropriate response to these matters is a disinclination to ascribe "uncritical confessionalism" to concepts of education and to schooling arrangements in too uncritical a way (McLaughlin, 1992b, pp. 125–8). While we have argued that education in religion in spirituality in its different forms is compatible with, and necessary for, the values, principles, and practices of liberal democratic societies, the complexities that have been identified throughout the discussion indicate the need for sensitivity in the making of such ascriptions, as in other matters.

Notes

1   It is not easy to find the best vocabulary for capturing the distinction that we propose between (1) "education in religion and spirituality from the outside" and (2) "education in religion and spirituality from the inside." One possibility is to label (1) as "common and open education in religion and spirituality" and contrast it with (2), labeled as "distinctive and tradition-supporting education in religion and spirituality." Another possibility is to label (1) as "educating about" religion and spirituality and (2) as "educating within" these domains. A further possibility is to label (1) as "educating for understanding" and (2) as "education for faith commitment" in religion and spirituality. The difficulty with these contrasting labels, however, is that they give the impression that the features in terms of which each form of education is distinguished are unique to that form. Thus the impression may be given that stark choices exist in education in religion and spirituality between openness and tradition-supportiveness, between "educating about" and "educating within," and between educating for understanding and educating for commitment. In fact the distinction we are seeking to capture involves a more complex mixture of contrasting elements. For example, since forms of education of the sort indicated in (1) must "transcend the (merely) informative" if they are to be genuinely educative, they must go beyond educating *about* to educating (in some sense) *within*. Further, such forms of education should not confine their attention solely to matters of *understanding* since matters of *belief and commitment* are part of what needs to be understood. Conversely, forms of education of the sort indicated in (2) often engage in educating *about* as well as educating *within*, as in, for example, attempts to situate their own tradition in comparative perspective, which is arguably highly desirable in a liberal democratic society. Nor can attempts on the part of such forms of education to educate for *belief and commitment* be separated from educating for *understanding*.

2   In most liberal democratic contexts, debate is centered upon the extent to which the state should support separate religious schools. In Israel, however, the only form of education in religion and spirituality that is given state support is of an Orthodox kind.

Recommendations for Further Reading

Alexander, H. A. (2001) *Reclaiming Goodness: Education and the Spiritual Quest*, University of Notre Dame Press.

Dwyer, J. G. (1998) *Religious Schools v Children's Rights*, Cornell University Press.

Hobson, P. R. and Edwards, J. S. (1999) *Religious Education in a Pluralist Society. The Key Philosophical Issues*, Woburn Press.

Nash, R. (1999) *Faith, Hype and Clarity: Teaching about Religion in American Schools and Colleges*, Teachers College Press.

References

Abu-Lughod, J. (1981) *Before European Hegemony: The World System AD 1250–1350* (Oxford: Oxford University Press).

Ackerman, B. (1980) *Social Justice and the Liberal State* (New Haven, CT: Yale University Press).

Adams, J. (1933) *Modern Developments in Educational Practice* (London: University of London Press).

Adorno, T. (1966) *Negative Dialektik* (Frankfurt am Main: Suhrkamp).

Adorno, T. (1971a) Erziehung nach Auschwitz, in: T. Adorno *Erziehung zur Mündigkeit* (Frankfurt am Main: Suhrkamp).

Adorno, T. (1971b) *Erziehung zur Mündigkeit* (Frankfurt am Main: Suhrkamp).

Adorno, T. (1972) Theorie der Halbbildung, in: R. Tiedemann (ed.) *Gesammelte Schriften*, vol. VIII (Frankfurt am Main: Suhrkamp).

Adorno, T. (1986) *The Jargon of Authenticity* (London: Routledge & Kegan Paul).

Adorno, T., Frenkel-Brunswik, E., Jahoda, M., and Sanford, P. (eds.) (1950) *The Authoritarian Personality* (New York: Norton).

Ainley, P. (1993) *Class and Skill* (London: Cassell).

Albrecht, C., Behrmann, G., and Bock, M. (1999) *Die Intellektuelle Gründung der Bundesrepublik. Eine Wirkungsgeschichte der Frankfurterschule* (Frankfurt am Main and New York: Campus).

Alexander, H. A. (1981) Schools without faith, *Religious Education*, 77, pp. 307–21.

Alexander, H. A. (1995) On the possibility of teaching theology, *Panorama: International Journal of Religious Education and Values*, 7, pp. 83–93.

Alexander, H. A. (1997a) Rationality and redemption: Ideology, indoctrination, and learning communities, in *Philosophy of Education Yearbook 1996* (Urbana, IL: Philosophy of Education Society).

Alexander, H. A. (1997b) Jewish education and the search of authenticity: A study in Jewish identity, in: D. Zisenwein and D. Schers (eds.) *Making a Difference: Jewish Identity and Education* (Tel Aviv: Tel Aviv University, Kelman Center for Jewish Education).

Alexander, H. A. (2000) Literacy, education, and the good life, in: D. Zisenwein and D. Schers (eds.) *Identity, Language, and Culture: Studies in Jewish Culture, Identity, and Community* (Tel Aviv: Tel Aviv University, Kelman Center for Jewish Education).

Alexander, H. A. (2001) *Reclaiming Goodness: Education and the Spiritual Quest* (Notre Dame, IN: University of Notre Dame Press).

Alibhai-Brown, Y. (1995) *No Place Like Home: An Autobiography* (London: Virago).

Allott, K. (ed.) (1968) *The Penguin Book of Contemporary Verse* (London: Penguin Books).

Apple, M. (1990) *Ideology and Curriculum* (New York: Routledge).

Arcilla, R. V. (1992) Tragic absolutism in education, *Educational Theory*, 42, pp. 473–81.

Arendt, H. (1958) *The Human Condition* (Chicago: University of Chicago Press).

Arendt, H. ([1961] 1993) *Between Past and Future* (Harmondsworth, UK: Penguin Books).

Arendt, H. (1968) *The Origins of Totalitarianism* (New York and London: Harvester and Harcourt Brace).

Arguelles, A. and Gonczi, A. (eds.) (2000) *Competency Based Education and Training: A World Perspective* (Balderas, Mexico: Conalep/Noriega).

Aries, P. (1973) *Centuries of Childhood* (Harmondsworth, UK: Penguin Books).

Arnold, M. (1932) *Culture and Anarchy* (London: Cambridge University Press).

Arnot, M. (1997) "Gendered citizenry": New feminist perspectives on education and citizenship, *British Educational Research Journal*, 23, pp. 275–95.

Arnot, M. and Dillabough, J.-A. (eds.) (2000) *Challenging Democracy: International Perpectives on Gender, Education and Citizenship* (New York: Routledge).

Aronowitz, S. and Giroux, H. (1991) *Postmodern Education: Politics, Culture and Social Criticism* (Minneapolis and London: University of Minnesota Press).

Arthurs, J. and Grimshaw, J. (eds.) (1998) *Women's Bodies: Representation, Discipline and Transgression* (London: Cassell).

Ashby, E. (1946) Universities in Australia, in: E. Ashby (ed.) *Challenge to Education* (Sydney and London: Angus and Robertson).

Ashby, E. (1966) *Technology and the Academics* (London: Macmillan).

Ashraf, S. A. (1986) Foreword, in: J. M. Halstead *The Case for Muslim Voluntary-Aided Schools: Some Philosophical Reflections* (Cambridge, UK: Islamic Academy).

Ashraf, S. A. and Hirst, P. H. (eds.) (1994) *Religion and Education. Islamic and Christian Approaches* (Cambridge, UK: The Islamic Academy).

Assiter, A. (1996) *Enlightened Women: Modern Feminism in a Postmodern Age* (London: Routledge).

Astley, J. (1994) *The Philosophy of Christian Religious Education* (Birmingham, AL: Religious Education Press).

Audi, R. (1989) *Practical Reasoning* (London and New York: Routledge).

Audi, R. (1993) *The Structure of Justification* (Cambridge, UK: Cambridge University Press).

Audi, R. (2000) *Religious Commitment and Secular Reason* (Cambridge, UK: Cambridge University Press).

Aviram, A. (1995) Autonomy and commitment: Compatible ideals, *Journal of Philosophy of Education*, 29, pp. 61–73.

Avis, J., Bloomer, M., Esland, G., Gleeson, D., and Hodkinson, P. (1996) *Knowledge and Nationhood: Education, Politics and Work* (London: Cassell).

Ayim, M. (1987) Warning: Philosophical discussion, violence at work, in: *Women and Philosophy, Resources for Feminist Research*, Ontario Institute for Studies in Education, September, pp. 23–5.

Bailey, C. H. (1984) *Beyond the Present and the Particular: A Theory of Liberal Education* (London: Routledge & Kegan Paul).

Bailin, S. (1987) Critical and creative thinking, *Informal Logic*, 9, pp. 23–30.

Bailin, S. (1990) Argument criticism as creative, in: R. Trapp and J. Schuetz (eds.) *Perspectives on Argumentation: Essays in Honor of Wayne Brockriede* (Prospect Heights, IL: Waveland Press), pp. 232–40.

Bailin, S. ([1988] 1992a) *Achieving Extraordinary Ends: An Essay on Creativity* (Norwood, NJ, Ablex).

Bailin, S. (1992b) Culture, democracy and the university, *Interchange*, 23, pp. 63–9.

Bailin, S. (1995) Is critical thinking biased? Clarifications and implications, *Educational Theory*, 45, pp. 191–7.

Bailin, S. (1998) Education, knowledge and critical thinking, in: D. Carr (ed.) *Education, Knowledge and Truth: Beyond the Postmodern Impasse* (London: Routledge), pp. 204–20.

Bailin, S., Case, R., Coombs, J. R., and Daniels, L. B. (1999) Conceptualizing critical thinking, *Journal of Curriculum Studies*, 31, pp. 285–302.

Ball, S. (1990) (ed.) *Foucault and Education: Disciplines and Knowledge* (London: Routledge).

Ball, S. (1994) *Education Reform: A Critical and Post-Structural Approach* (Buckingham, UK and Philadelphia: Open University Press).

Banks, J. A. and McGee-Banks, C. A. (eds.) (1999) *Multicultural Education: Issues and Perspectives* (New York: Wiley).

Barnes, J. (ed.) (1984) *The Complete Works of Aristotle* (Princeton, NJ: Princeton University Press).

Barnett, C. (1986) *The Audit of War* (London: Macmillan).

Barnett, R. (1990) *The Idea of Higher Education* (Buckingham, UK: The Society for Research into Higher Education and Open University Press).

Barnett, R. (2000) *Realizing the University in an Age of Supercomplexity* (Buckingham, UK: Open University Press).

Bar On, B.-A. and Ferguson, A. (eds.) (1998) *Daring to Be Good: Essays in Feminist Ethico-Politics* (New York: Routledge).

Barr, J. (1999) *Liberating Knowledge: Research, Feminism and Adult Education* (Leicester, UK: National Institute for Adult Continuing Education).

Barrow, R. (1987) Skills talk, *Journal of Philosophy of Education*, 21.2, pp. 87–201.

Bassey, M. (2001) A solution to the problem of generalisation in educational research: Fuzzy prediction, *Oxford Educational Review*, 27.1, pp. 5–22.

Battersby, C. (1998) *The Phenomenal Woman: Feminist Metaphysics and the Patterns of Identity* (Cambridge, UK: Polity Press).

Bayer, L. E. and Liston, D. P. (1992) Discourse or moral action? A critique of postmodernism, *Educational Theory*, 42, pp. 371–93.

Bearn, G. (2000) The University of Beauty, in: P. Dhillon and P. Standish (eds.) *Lyotard: Just Education* (London: Routledge), pp. 230–58.

Beck, J. (1999) "Spiritual and moral development" and religious education, in: A. Thatcher (ed.) *Spirituality and the Curriculum* (London: Cassell).

Beck, U. (1992) *The Risk Society* (London: Sage Publications).

Beckett, D. (1996) Critical judgment and professional practice, *Educational Theory*, 46, pp. 135–49.

Bell, D. (1993) *Communitarianism and its Critics* (Oxford: Oxford University Press).

Bellah, R. N., Madsen, R., Sullivan, W. M., Swidler, A., and Tipton, S. M. (1985) *Habits of the Heart. Individualism and Commitment in American Life* (Berkeley: University of California Press).

Belser, H. (ed.) (1972) *Kinder, Schule, Elternhaus: eine Untersuchung über das englische Primarschulwesen (Plowden-Report)* (Abridged edition in German). (Frankfurt, Berlin, München: Diesterweg).

Benhabib, S. (1992) *Situating the Self: Gender, Community and Postmodernism in Contemporary Ethics* (Cambridge, UK: Polity Press).

Benhabib, S. (ed.) (1996a) *Democracy and Difference: Contesting the Boundaries of the Political* (Princeton, NJ: Princeton University Press).

Benhabib, S. (1996b) Toward a deliberative model of democratic legitimacy, in: S. Benhabib (ed.) *Democracy and Difference: Contesting the Boundaries of the Political* (Princeton, NJ: Princeton University Press).

Benjamin, H. ([1939] 1975) The saber-tooth curriculum, in: M. Golby, J. Greenwald, and R. West (eds.) *Curriculum Design* (London: Croom Helm/Open University Press).

Benner, D. (1998) Die Permanenz der Reformpädagogik, in: T. Rülcker and J. Oelkers (eds.) *Politische Reformpädagogik* (Bern, Switzerland: Peter Lang).

Benner, D. and Kemper, H. (1993) *Zur Theorie und Geschichte der Reformpädagogik 1–2.* (Hagen, Germany: Fernuniversität).

Berlin, I. (1969) *Four Essays on Liberty* (Oxford and New York: Oxford University Press).

Berliner, D. and Biddle, B. (1996) *The Manufactured Crisis: Myths, Fraud and the Attack on America's Public Schools* (New York: Perseus Books).

Bernauer J. and Rasmussen D. (eds.) (1988) *The Final Foucault* (Cambridge, MA: MIT Press).

Bernstein, R. (1992) *The New Constellation* (Cambridge, MA: MIT Press).

Bertens, H. (1995) *The Idea of the Postmodern. A History* (London and New York: Routledge).

Best, R. (ed.) (1996) *Education, Spirituality and the Whole Child* (London: Cassell).

Best, S. and Kellner, D. (1991) *Postmodern Theory: Critical Interrogations* (London: Macmillan).

Biesta, G. J. J. and Miedema, S. (1999) Dewey in Europe. Ambivalences and contradictions in the turn-of-the-century educational reform, in: J. Oelkers and F. Osterwalder (eds.) *Die neue Erziehung. Beiträge zur Internationalität der Reformpädagogik* (Bern: Per Lang), pp. 99–124.

Bishops' Conference of England and Wales (1997) *Catholic Schools and Other Faiths* (London: Bishops' Conference of England and Wales).

Blacker, D. (1993) Allowing educational technologies to reveal: A Deweyan perspective, *Educational Theory*, Spring, pp. 181–94.

Blacker, D. (1995) Philosophy of technology and education: An invitation to inquiry, in: M. S. Katz (ed.) *Philosophy of Education 1994* (Urbana, IL: Philosophy of Education Society), pp. 320–8.

Blake, N. P. (1992) Modernity and the problem of cultural pluralism, *Journal of Philosophy of Education*, 26, pp. 3–50.

Blake, N. P. (1995a) Truth, identity and community in the university, *Curriculum Studies*, October, pp. 263–81.

Blake, N. P. (1995b) Ideal speech conditions, modern discourse and education, *Journal of Philosophy of Education*, 29, pp. 355–68.

Blake, N. P. (1996a) The democracy we need: Situation, post-foundationalism and enlightenment, *Journal of Philosophy of Education*, 30, pp. 215–38.

Blake, N. (1996b) Against spiritual education, *Oxford Review of Education*, 22, pp. 443–56.

Blake, N., Smeyers, P., Smith, R., and Standish, P. (1998) *Thinking Again: Education after Postmodernism* (Westport, CT and London: Bergin & Garvey).

Blake, N., Smeyers, P., Smith, R., and Standish, P. (2000) *Education in an Age of Nihilism* (London: RouledgeFalmer).

Blake, N., Smith, R., and Standish, P. (1998) What we teach and what students learn, in: *The Universities We Need: Higher Education After Dearing* (London: Kogan Page), pp. 27–48.

Blake, N. and Standish, P. (eds.) (2000) *Enquiries at the Interface: Philosophical Problems of On-line Education* (Oxford: Blackwell); also in *Journal of Philosophy of Education*, 34 (special issue).

Bloom, A. (1987) *The Closing of the American Mind: How Higher Education Has Failed Democracy and Impoverished the Souls of Today's Students* (New York: Simon and Schuster; London: Penguin Books).

Bloom, B. S. (1956) *Taxonomy of Educational Objectives, Part I, Cognitive Domain* (New York: Longmans Green).

Bloom, H., De Man, P., Derrida, J., Hartman, G., and Miller, J. H. (eds.) (1979) *Deconstruction and Criticism* (New York: Seabury).

Bloomer, M. (1997) *Curriculum Making in Post-16 Education* (London: Routledge).

Blum, L. (1993) Vocation, friendship, and community: Limitations of the personal–impersonal framework, in: O. Flanagan and A. O. Rorty (eds.) *Identity, Character and Morality: Essays in Moral Psychology* (Cambridge, MA: MIT Press).

Blum, L. A. (1994) *Moral Perception and Particularity* (Cambridge, UK: Cambridge University Press).

Blunkett, D. (1998) Opportunities to live and learn, *Times Higher Education Supplement*, February 27, p. 18.

Bohman, J. (1997) The public spheres of the world citizen, in: J. Bohman and M. Lütz-Bachman (eds.) *Perpetual Peace: Essays on Kant's Cosmopolitan Ideal* (Cambridge, MA: MIT Press).

Bohman, J. (1998) The globalisation of the public sphere: Cosmopolitan publicity and the problem of cultural pluralism, *Philosophy and Social Criticism*, 24, pp. 199–216.

Bohnsack, F. (1976) *Erziehung zur Demokratie. John Deweys Pädagogik und ihre Bedeutung für die Reform unserer Schule* (Ravensburg, Germany: Otto Maier Verlag).

Boisvert, R. D. (1999) The nemesis of necessity: Tragedy's challenge to Deweyan pragmatism, in: C. Haskins and D. I. Seiple (eds.) *Dewey Reconfigured. Essays on Deweyan Pragmatism* (Albany: State University of New York Press).

Bonnett, M. (1978) Authenticity and education, *Journal of Philosophy of Education*, 12, pp. 51–61.

Bonnett, M. (1986) Public standards and personal significance, in: D. E. Cooper (ed.) *Education, Values and Mind* (London: Routledge & Kegan Paul).

Bonnett, M. (1994) *Children's Thinking* (London: Cassell).

Bono, P. and Kemp, S. (1991) *Italian Feminist Thought* (Oxford: Blackwell).

Bordo, S. (1987) *The Flight to Objectivity* (Albany, NY: State University of New York).

Bordo, S. (1993) *Unbearable Weight: Feminism, Western Culture, and the Body* (Berkeley: University of California Press).

Borgmann, A. (1984) *Technology and the Character of Contemporary Life* (Chicago: University of Chicago Press).

Bowers, C. A. (1982) The reproduction of technological consciousness: Locating the ideological foundations of a radical pedagogy, *Teachers College Record*, 83.4, pp. 529–57.

Bowers, C. A. (1988) *The Cultural Dimensions of Educational Computing: Understanding the Non-Neutrality of Technology* (New York: Teachers College Press).

Bowles, S. and Gintis, H. (1976) *Schooling in Capitalist America* (New York: Basic Books).

Braidotti, R. (1994) *Nomadic Subjects: Embodiment and Sexual Difference* (New York: Columbia University Press).

Braudel, F. (1981) *The Structures of Everyday Life: The Limits of the Possible* (trans. S. Reynolds) (New York: Harper & Row).

Brehony, K. J. (1997) An "Undeniable" and "disastrous" influence? Dewey and English education (1895–1939), *Oxford Review of Education*, 23.4, pp. 427–45.

Brent, A. (1978) *Philosophical Foundations for the Curriculum* (London: Allen & Unwin).

Bricker, D. C. (1988) *Classroom Life as Civic Education* (New York: Teachers College Press).

Bridges, D. (1994) Parents: Customers or partners? in: D. Bridges and T. McLaughlin (eds.) *Education and the Market Place* (London: Falmer Press).

Bridges, D. and Husbands, C. (eds.) (1996) *Consorting and Collaborating in the Education Market Place* (London: Falmer Press).

Bridges, D. and Mclaughlin, T. H. (eds.) (1994) *Education and the Market Place* (London: Falmer).

Bridges, T. (1991) Modern political theory and the multivocity of postmodern critical discourses, *Inquiry: Critical Thinking Across the Disciplines*, 8, pp. 3–7.

Brine, J. (1999) *underEducating Women: Globalizing Inequality* (Buckingham, UK: Open University Press).

Bronfenbrenner, U. (1970) *Two Worlds of Childhood, USA and USSR* (New York: Russell Sage).

Brontë, A. (1994) *Agnes Grey* (Ware, UK: Wordsworth).

Bryk, A. S., Lee, V. E., and Holland, P. B. (1993) *Catholic Schools and the Common Good* (Cambridge, MA: Harvard University Press).

Bubner, R. (1981) *Modern German Philosophy* (Cambridge, UK: Cambridge University Press).

Bukatman, S. (1993) *Terminal Identity: The Virtual Subject in Postmodern Science Fiction* (Durham, NC: Duke University Press).

Bullivant, B. (1986) Towards radical multiculturalism: Resolving tensions in curriculum and educational planning, in: S. Modgil, G. Verma, K. Mallick, and C. Modgil (eds.) *Multicultural Education: The Interminable Debate* (London: Falmer Press).

Burbules, N. C. (1990) The tragic sense of education, *Teachers College Record*, 91, pp. 467–79.

Burbules, N. C. (1995) Reasonable doubt: Toward a postmodern defense of reason as an educational aim, in: W. Kohli (ed.) *Critical Conversations in Philosophy of Education* (New York: Routledge), pp. 82–102.

Burbules, N. C. (1997) Rhetorics of the Web: Hyperreading and critical literacy, in: I. Snyder *Page to Screen: Taking Literacy into the Electronic Era* (Sydney, NSW: Allen and Unwin), pp. 102–22.

Butler, J. (1990) *Gender Trouble: Feminism and the Subversion of Identity* (New York: Routledge).

Butler, J. (1993) *Bodies that Matter* (New York: Routledge).

Butler, J. (1997) *The Psychic Life of Power: Theories in Subjection* (New York: Routledge).

Butler, S. (1994) *The Way of all Flesh* (Garden City, NY: Doubleday).

Byatt, A. S. (1995) *Sugar and Other Stories* (London: Vintage).

Callan, E. (1994) Autonomy and alienation, *Journal of Philosophy of Education*, 28, pp. 35–53.

Callan, E. (1997) *Creating Citizens: Political Education and Liberal Democracy* (Oxford: Clarendon Press).

Callan, E. (2000) Discrimination and religious schooling, in: W. Kymlicka and W. Norman (eds.) *Citizenship in Diverse Societies* (Oxford: Oxford University Press).

Caputo, J. D. (1993) *Against Ethics* (Bloomington: Indiana University Press).

Carr, D. (1994) Knowledge and truth in religious education, *Journal of Philosophy of Education*, 28, pp. 221–38.

Carr, D. (1995) Towards a distinctive conception of spiritual education, *Oxford Review of Education*, 21, pp. 83–98.

Carr, D. (1996) Rival conceptions of spiritual education, *Journal of Philosophy of Education*, 30, pp. 159–78.

Carr, D. (1998) *Education, Knowledge and Truth: Beyond the Postmodern Impasse* (London and New York: Routledge).

Carr, D. (2000) *Professionalism and Ethics in Teaching* (London: Routledge).

Carr, W. (1995) *For Education: Towards Critical Educational Enquiry* (Buckingham, UK and Philadelphia: Open University Press).

Carr, W. (1997) Professing education in a post-modern age, *Journal of Philosophy of Education*, 31, pp. 309–27.

Carr, W. and Hartnett, A. (1996) *Education and the Struggle for Democracy* (Buckingham, UK: Open University Press).

Carr, W. with Kemmis, S. (1986) *Becoming Critical: Education, Knowledge and Action Research* (Brighton, UK: Falmer Press).

Castells, M., Flecha, R., Freire, P., Giroux, H. A., Macedo, D., and Willis, P. (1999) *Critical Education in the New Information Age* (Lanham, MD: Rowman and Littlefield).

Cavarero, A. (1995) *In Spite of Plato: A Feminist Rewriting of Ancient Philosophy* (Cambridge, UK: Polity Press).

Cavell, S. (1972) *The Senses of Walden* (New York: Viking Press).

Cavell, S. (1995) Notes and afterthoughts on the opening of *Wittgenstein's Investigations*, in: S. Cavell, *Philosophical Passages: Wittgenstein, Emerson, Austin, Emerson* (Oxford: Blackwell).

Central Advisory Council for Education (1967) *Children and Their Primary Schools* (The Plowden Report) (London: HMSO).

Chilman, C. S. (1988) *Variant Family Forms* (London: Sage).

Chubb, J. and Moe, T. (1990) *Politics, Markets and America's Schools* (Washington, DC: The Brookings Institution).

Chubb, J. and Moe, T. (1992) *A Lesson in School Reform from Great Britain* (Washington, DC: The Brookings Institution).

Clark, B. R. (1998) *Creating Entrepreneurial Universities* (Oxford: Pergamon).

Coffey, D. (1992) *Schools and Work: Developments in Vocational Education* (London: Cassell).

Cohen, B. (1981) *Education and the Individual* (London: Allen & Unwin).

Cohen, G. A. (1994) Back to socialist basics, *New Left Review*, 207, September/October, pp. 3–16.

Conlon, T. (1997) The internet is not a panacea, *Scottish Educational Review*, 29, pp. 30–8.

Coons, J. E. and Sugarman, S. D. (1978) *Education by Choice: The Case for Family Control* (Berkeley: University of California Press).

Cooper, D. E. (1980) *Illusions of Equality* (London: Routledge & Kegan Paul).

Cooper, D. E. (1983) *Authenticity and Learning* (London: Routledge & Kegan Paul).

Copley, T. (2000) *Spiritual Development in the State School* (Exeter, UK: University of Exeter Press).

Cousinet, R. (1950) *L'Education Nouvelle*. (Neuchâtel, Switzerland: Delachaux et Niestlé).

Cox, C., Douglas-Hume, J., Marks, J., Norcross, L., and Scruton, R. (1986) *Whose Schools? A Radical Manifesto* (London: The Hillgate Group).

Cranston, M. (1967) Human rights, real and supposed, in: D. D. Raphael (ed.) *Political Theory and the Rights of Man* (London: Macmillan).

CSUP (Committee of Scottish University Principals) (1992) *Teaching and Learning in an Expanding Higher Education System* (the MacFarlane Report) (Lasswade, Scotland: Polton House Press).

Cuypers, S. E. (1992) Is personal autonomy the first principle of education? *Journal of Philosophy of Education*, 26, pp. 5–17.

Cuypers, S. E. (1995) What Wittgenstein would have said about personal autonomy, *Studies in Philosophy and Education*, 14, pp. 251–65.

Cuypers, S. E. (2000) Autonomy beyond voluntarism: In defence of hierarchy, *Canadian Journal of Philosophy*, 30, pp. 225–56.

Cuypers, S. E. (forthcoming) *Self-Identity and Personal Autonomy. An Analytic Anthropology* (Aldershot, UK: Ashgate).

Daniel, D. (1987) *The Intentional Stance* (Cambridge, MA: MIT Press).

Darling, J. (1994) *Child-Centred Education and its Critics* (London: Paul Chapman Publishing).

Darling, J. and Nisbet, J. (2000) Dewey in Britain, *Studies in Philosophy and Education*, 19.1–2, pp. 39–52.

Davidson, D. (1985) Rational animals, in: E. LePore and B. McLaughlin (eds.) *Actions and Events* (Oxford: Blackwell).

Davies, B. (1989) *Frogs and Snails and Feminist Tales* (Sydney, NSW: Allen & Unwin).

Davies, B. (1993) *Shards of Glass: Children Reading and Writing Beyond Gendered Identities* (Sydney, NSW: Hampton Press).

Davis, A. (1998) *The Limits of Educational Assessment* (Oxford: Blackwell).

Day, J. (1999) The primacy of relationship: A meditation on education, faith and the dialogical self, in: J. C. Conroy (ed.) *Catholic Education: Inside Out, Outside In* (Dublin: Veritas).

de Alba, A. (1995) *Postmodernidad y Educación* (Mexico, Grupo Editorial).

Dearden, R. F. (1968) *The Philosophy of Primary Education* (London: Routledge & Kegan Paul).

Dearden, R. F. (1972a) Education as a process of growth, in: R. Dearden, P. Hirst, & R. S. Peters (eds.) *Education and the Development of Reason* (London: Routledge & Kegan Paul).

Dearden, R. F. (1972b) Autonomy and education, in: R. Dearden, P. Hirst, and R. S. Peters (eds.) *Education and the Development of Reason* (London: Routledge & Kegan Paul).

Dearden, R. F. (1975) Autonomy as an educational ideal *I*, in: S. C. Brown (ed.) *Philosophers Discuss Education* (London: Macmillan).

Dearden, R. F. (1982) Philosophy of education, 1952–82, *British Journal of Educational Studies*, 30, pp. 57–71.

De Beauvoir, S. ([1949] 1972) *The Second Sex* (Harmondsworth, UK: Penguin).

de Bono, E. (1970) *Lateral Thinking* (London: Ward Lock Educational).

de Bono, E. (1976) *Practical Thinking* (Harmondsworth, UK: Penguin Books).

Delanty, G. (1997) Models of citizenship: Defining European identity and citizenship, *Citizenship Studies*, 1, pp. 285–303.

Deleuze, G. (1983) *Nietzsche and Philosophy* (trans. H. Tomlinson) (New York: Columbia University Press).

Dennett, D. C. (1987) *The Intentional Stance* (Cambridge, MA: MIT Press).

Department of Education and Science (DES) (1991) The Parents' Charter (London: Department of Education and Science).

Derrida, J. (1981) *Positions* (trans. A. Bass) (Chicago: University of Chicago Press).

Derrida, J. (1992) Mochlos: Or, the conflict of the faculties, in: R. Rand (ed.) *Logomachia: The Conflict of the Faculties*. (Lincoln, NE: University of Nebraska Press).

Derrida, J. (1997) *Politics of Friendship* (trans. G. Collins) (London: Verso Books).

Derrida, J. (n.d.) The Future of the Profession or The Unconditional University (Thanks to the "Humanities",What *Could Take Place* Tomorrow) (trans. P. Kamuf).

De Ruyter, D. (1993) Met recht ingrijpend. Een pedagogisch criterium voor het opleggen van hulp [The right to interfere. An educational criterion for the enforcement of guidance] (Unpublished doctoral dissertation: Vrije Universiteit, Amsterdam).

Desmond, W. (1995) *Perplexity and Ultimacy. Metaphysical Thought From the Middle* (Albany: State University of New York Press).

Dewey, J. (1927) *The Public and Its Problems* (Chicago: Sage).

Dewey, J. (1938) *Logic: The Theory of Inquiry.*

Dewey, J. ([1916] 1966) *Democracy and Education* (New York: Free Press/Macmillan).

Dewey, J. ([1891] 1969) Outlines of a critical theory of ethics, in: J. A. Boydston (ed.) *John Dewey: The Early* Works, vol. 3 (Carbondale: Southern Illinois University Press).

Dewey, J. ([1897] 1972) Ethical principles underlying education, in: J. A. Boydston (ed.) *John Dewey: The Early Works, 1882–1898*, vol. 5 (Carbondale: Southern Illinois University Press).

Dewey, J. ([1916] 1980) Democracy and education, in: J. A. Boydston (ed.) *John Dewey: The Middle* Works, vol. 9 (Carbondale: Southern Illinois University Press).

Dewey, J. ([1925] 1981) Experience and nature, in: J. A. Boydston (ed.) *John Dewey: The Later Works*, vol. 1 (Carbondale: Southern Illinois University Press).

Dewey, J. ([1922] 1983a) Individuality, equality and superiority, in: J. A. Boydston (ed.) *John Dewey: The Middle Works*, vol. 13 (Carbondale: Southern Illinois University Press).

Dewey, J. ([1922] 1983b) Human nature and conduct, in: J. A. Boydston (ed.) *John Dewey: The Middle Works*, vol. 14 (Carbondale: Southern Illinois University Press).

Dewey, J. ([1925] 1984) The development of American pragmatism, in: J. A. Boydston (ed.) *John Dewey: The Later Works*, vol. 2 (Carbondale: Southern Illinois University Press).

Dewey, J. ([1927] 1984) The public and its problems, in: J. A. Boydston (ed.) *John Dewey: The Later Works*, vol. 2 (Carbondale: Southern Illinois University Press).

Dewey, J. ([1930] 1984) From absolutism to experimentalism, in: J. A. Boydston (ed.) *John Dewey: The Later Works*, vol. 5 (Carbondale: Southern Illinois University Press).

Dewey, J. ([1915] 1985) German philosophy and politics, in: J. A. Boydston (ed.) *John Dewey: The Middle Works*, vol. 8 (Carbondale: Southern Illinois University Press).

Dewey, J. ([1932] 1985) Ethics, in: J. A. Boydston (ed.) *John Dewey: The Later Works*, vol. 7 (Carbondale: Southern Illinois University Press).

DfEE (1997) *Design of the New Deal for 18–14 Year Olds* (London: Department for Education and Employment).

DfEE (1998) *The Learning Age: A Renaissance for a New Britain* (London: Department for Education and Employment).

Dhillon, P. A. (1994) *Multiple Identities: A Phenomenology of Multicultural Communication* (Frankfurt: Peter Lang).

Dhillon, P. A. (1996) Where do the birds go after the last sky? in: T. S. Popkewitz and L. Fendler (eds.) *Critical Theories in Education: Changing Terrains of Knowledge and Politics* (New York: Routledge).

Dhillon, P. A. (2001) The longest way home: Language, philosophy and creativity in diaspora, in: B. Kachru and C. Nelson (eds.) *Language and Identity in Diaspora Communities* (Urbana-Champaign: University of Illinois Press).

Dhillon, P. and Standish, P. (eds.) (2000) *Lyotard: Just Education* (London: Routledge).

Dickenson, D. (1997) *Property, Women and Politics: Subjects or Objects?* (Cambridge, UK: Polity Press).

Diprose, R. (1994) *The Bodies of Women: Ethics, Embodiment and Sexual Difference* (New York: Routledge).

Docherty, J. (1993) (ed.) *Postmodernism: A Reader* (New York: Harvester Wheatsheaf).

Doll, W. (1993) *A Post-Modern Perspective on Curriculum* (New York: Teachers College Press).

Doyle, R. (1996) *The Woman Who Walked Into Doors* (London: Jonathan Cape).

Dryzek, J. (1999) Transnational democracy, *Journal of Political Philosophy*, 7, pp. 30–51.

Duane, M. (1971) Freedom and the state system of education, in: P. Adams, A. S. Neill, and R. Ollendorff (eds.) *Children's Rights* (London: Elek Books).

Dubiel, H. (1978) *Wissenschaftsorganisation und Politische Erfahrung. Studien zur Frühen Kritischen Theorie* (Frankfurt am Main: Suhrkamp).

Dunne, J. (1997) *Back to the Rough Ground: Practical Judgment and the Lure of Technique* (Notre Dame, IN: University of Notre Dame Press).

Dunne, J. (1995) What's the good of education?, in: P. Hogan (ed.) *Partnership and the Benefits of Learning: A Symposium on Educational Policy* (Maynooth: Educational Studies Association of Ireland).

Dunne, J. (1999a) Professional judgment and the predicaments of practice, *European Journal of Marketing* (special issue on pedagogy), 33, pp. 707–19.

Dunne, J. (1999b) Phronesis, virtue and learning, in: D. Carr and J. Steutel (eds.) *Virtue Theory and Moral Education* (London: Routledge).

Dwyer, J. G. (1998) *Religious Schools v Children's Rights* (Ithaca, NY: Cornell University Press).

Edel, A. (1972) Analytic philosophy of education at the cross-roads. *Educational Theory*, 22, pp. 131–52.

Edgerton, S. H. (1997) *Translating the Curriculum: Multiculturalism Into Cultural Studies* (New York: Routledge).

Educa (2000) New Deal, *Educa*, 205, September, pp. 5–6.

Eliade, M. (1959) *The Sacred and the Profane. The Significance of Religious Myth, Symbolism and Ritual Within Life and Culture* (New York: Harcourt, Brace and World).

Eliot, G. (1970) *Daniel Deronda* (London: Panther).

Eliot, G. (1976) *Scenes of Clerical Life* (London and New York: Dent and Dutton).

Elliott, J. (1991) *Action Research for Educational Change* (Milton Keynes, UK: Open University Press).

Elliott, R. K. (1975) Education and human being, in: S. C. Brown (ed.) *Philosophers Discuss Education* (London: Macmillan).

Ellul, J. (1964) *The Technological Society* (trans. J. Wilkinson) (New York: Vintage Books).

Elshtain, J. B. (1981) *Public Man, Private Woman: Women in Social and Political Thought* (Princeton, NJ: Princeton University Press).

Ennis, R. H. (1961) Learning one's responses and only one's responses, *Studies in Philosophy of Education*, 1. 4–5, pp. 202–11.

Ennis, R. H. (1962) A concept of critical thinking, *Harvard Educational Review*, 32, pp. 81–111.

Ennis, R. H. (1987) A taxonomy of critical thinking dispositions and abilities, in: J. Boykoff-Baron and R. J. Sternberg (eds.) *Teaching Thinking Skills: Theory and Practice* (New York: W. H. Freeman), pp. 9–26.

Ennis, R. H. (1996) *Critical Thinking* (Upper Saddle River, NJ: Prentice-Hall).

Enslin, P. (1999) The place of national identity in the aims of education, in: R. Marples (ed.) *The Aims of Education* (London: Routledge).

Enslin, P., Pendlebury, S., and Tjiattas, M. (2001) Deliberative democracy, diversity and the challenges of citizenship education, *Journal of Philosophy of Education*, 35, pp. 115–30.

Eraut, M. (1985) Knowledge creation and knowledge use in professional contexts, *Studies in Higher Education*, 10, pp. 117–33.

Eraut, M. (1994) *Developing Professional Knowledge and Expertise* (London: The Falmer Press).

Erricker, C. (2000) A critical review of spiritual education, in: C. Erricker and J. Erricker (eds.) *Reconstructing Religious, Spiritual and Moral Education* (London: RoutledgeFalmer).

Esland, G. (ed.) (1990) *Education, Training and Employment* (Wokingham, UK: Addison-Wesley/Open University Press).

Faubion, J. (1998) (ed.) *Michel Foucault: Aesthetics, Method and Epistemology* (London: Allen Lane, The Penguin Press).

Feenberg, A. (1991) *A Critical Theory of Technology* (New York: Oxford University Press).

Feinberg, J. (1980) The child's right to an open future, in: W. Aiken and H. Lafollette (eds.) *Whose Child?* (Totowa, NJ: Littlefield Adams).

Feinberg, W. (1998) *Common Schools/Uncommon Identities. National Unity and Cultural Difference* (New Haven, CT and London: Yale University Press).

Fenstermacher, G. (1986) Philosophy of research on teaching, in: M. C. Wittrock (ed.) *Handbook of Research on Teaching*, 3rd edn. (New York: Macmillan).

Fenstermacher, G. (1987) Prologue to my critics, *Educational Theory*, 37, pp. 357–60.

Fenstermacher, G. and Richardson, V. (1993) The elicitation and reconstruction of practical arguments in teaching, *Journal of Curriculum Studies*, 25, pp. 101–14.

Ferry, L. and Renaut, A. (1990) *French Philosophy of the Sixties. An Essay on Antihumanism* (trans. M. Cattani) (Amherst: The University of Massachusetts Press).

Fielding, M. (1996) Beyond collaboration: On the importance of community, in: D. Bridges and C. Husbands (eds.) *Consorting and Collaborating in the Educational Market Place* (London: Falmer Press).

Fiske, J. (1996) Postmodernism and television, in: J. Curran and M. Gurevitch (eds.) *Mass Media and Society* (London: Arnold).

Flew, A. (1968) Against indoctrination, in: A. J. Ayer (ed.) *The Humanist Outlook* (London: Pemberton).

Flew, A. (1991) Education services: independent competition or maintained monopoly? in: D. G. Green (ed.) *Empowering Parents* (London: Inner London Education Authority, Health and Welfare Unit).

Flude, M. and Sieminski, S. (eds.) (1999) *Education, Training and the Future of Work II: Developments in Vocational Education and Training* (London: Routledge/Open University Press).

Foot, P. (1978) *Virtues and Vices* (Berkeley: University of California Press).

Foucault, M. (1972) *The Archaeology of Knowledge* and *The Discourse on Language* (trans. A. M. Sheridan Smith) (New York: Pantheon Books).

Foucault, M. (1977) Nietzsche, genealogy, history, in: D. F. Bouchard and S. Simon (eds.) *Language, Counter-Memory, Practice: Selected Essays and Interviews* (Ithaca, NY: Cornell University Press).

Foucault, M. (1984) What is enlightenment? in: P. Rabinow (ed.) *The Foucault Reader* (London: Pantheon Books).

Foucault, M. (1991a) *Discipline and Punish, The Birth of the Prison* (Harmondsworth, UK: Penguin Books).

Foucault, M. (1991b) *The Foucault Effect: Studies in Governmentality* (with two lectures by and an interview with Michel Foucault), in: G. Burchell, C. Gordon, and P. Miller (eds.) (London: Harvester Wheatsheaf).

Frank, M. (1988) *What is Neo-Structuralism?* (trans. S. Wilke and R. Gray; foreword by M. Schwab) (Minneapolis: University of Minnesota Press).

Frankfurt, H. G. (1988) *The Importance of What We Care About* (Cambridge, UK: Cambridge University Press).

Frankfurt, H. G. (1999) *Necessity, Volition, and Love* (Cambridge, UK: Cambridge University Press).

Fraser, N. (1997) *Justice Interruptus: Critical Reflections on the "Postsocialist" Condition* (London: Routledge).

Fraser, R. (1972) *In Hiding: The Life of Manuel Cortez* (Harmondsworth, UK: Penguin Books).

Frazer, E. (1999) Introduction: The idea of political education, *Oxford Review of Education*, 25, pp. 5–22.

Freeman, A. (1999) Light without heat, *Lehigh Review*, 7.

Freeman, M. and Veerman, P. (1992) *The Ideologies of Children's Rights* (Dordrecht, Netherlands: Martinus Nijhoff).

Freire, P. (1973) *Pedagogy of the Oppressed* (New York: Seabury Press).

Friedman, G. (1981) *The Political Philosophy of the Frankfurt School* (Ithaca, NY: Cornell University Press).

Friedman, M. (2000) Feminism in ethics: conceptions of autonomy, in: M. Fricker and J. Hornsby (eds.) *The Cambridge Companion to Feminism in Philosophy* (Cambridge, UK: Cambridge University Press).

Fuller, T. (1989) (ed.) *The Voice of Liberal Learning: Michael Oakeshott on Education* (New Haven, CT and London: Yale University Press).

Gadamer, H.-G. (1975) *Truth and Method* (ed. G. Barden and J. Cumming) (London: Sheed & Ward).

Gadamer, H.-G. (1977) *Philosophical Hermeneutics* (trans. D. E. Linge) (Berkeley: University of California Press).

Gaden, G. (1983) The case for specialisation, *Irish Educational Studies*, 3, pp. 47–60.

Gaden, G. (1990) Rehabilitating responsibility, *Journal of Philosophy of Education*, 24, pp. 27–38.

Gadet, F. (1989) *Saussure and Contemporary Culture* (trans. G. Elliot) (London: Hutchinson).

Gale, R. (1999) *The Divided Self of William James* (Cambridge, UK: Cambridge University Press).

Galston, W. (1989) Civic education in the liberal state, in: N. L. Rosenblum (ed.) *Liberalism and the Moral Life* (Cambridge MA: Harvard University Press).

Gardner, P. and S. Johnson (1996) Thinking critically about critical thinking: An unskilled inquiry into Quinn and McPeck, *Journal of Philosophy of Education*, 30, pp. 441–56.

Garrison, J. W. and A. Phelan (1989) Toward a feminist poetic of critical thinking, in: R. Page (ed.) *Philosophy of Education 1989* (Normal, IL, Philosophy of Education Society), pp. 304–414.

Garry, A. and Pearsall, M. (eds.) (1996) *Women, Knowledge, and Reality: Explorations in Feminist Philosophy*, 2nd edn. (London: Routledge).

Gatens, M. (1996) *Imaginary Bodies: Ethics, Power and Corporeality* (London: Routledge).

Gee, J. P, Hull, G., and Lankshear, C. (1996) *The New Work Order. Behind the Language of the New Capitalism* (St. Leonards, UK: Allen & Unwin).

Gibbons, M., Limoges, C., Nowotny, H., Schwartzman, S., Scott, P., and Trow, M. (1994) *The New Production of Knowledge: The Dynamics of Science and Research in Contemporary Societies* (London: Sage).

Giddens, A. (1991) *Modernity and Self-Identity: Self and Society in the Late Modern Age* (Cambridge: Polity Press).

Giddens, A. (1998) *The Third Way: The Renewal of Social Democracy* (Cambridge: Polity Press).

Giesecke, H. (1987) *Das Ende der Erziehung: neue Chancen für Familie und Schule* (Stuttgart: Klett-Cotta).

Gilbert, R. (1992) Citizenship, education and postmodernity, *British Journal of Sociology of Education*, 13, pp. 51–68.

Gilligan, C. J. (1982) *In a Different Voice* (Cambridge, MA: Harvard University Press).

Gilroy, P. (1993) Reflections on Schön: An epistemological critique and a practical alternative, in: P. Gilroy and M. Smith (eds.) *International Analyses of Teacher Education: Festschrift for Edgar Stones* (Oxford: Carfax Publishing).

Giroux, H. (1983a) *Critical Theory and Educational Practice* (Geelong, Victoria: Deakin).

Giroux, H. (1983b) *Theory and Resistance in Education. A Pedagogy for the Opposition* (London: Heinemann).

Giroux, H. (1989) *Schooling for Democracy. Critical Pedagogy in the Modern Age* (London: New York: Routledge).

Giroux, H. (1997) *Pedagogy and the Politics of Hope: Theory, Culture and Schooling* (Boulder, CO: Westview Press).

Giroux, H., Lankshear, C., McLaren, P., and Peters, M. (1996) *Counternarratives: Cultural Studies and Critical Pedagogies in Postmodern Spaces* (London and New York: Routledge).

Giroux, H. and McLaren, P. (ed.) (1989) *Critical Pedagogy, the State, and Cultural Struggle* (Albany, NY: State University of New York Press).

Gleeson, D. (1996) Continuity and change in post-compulsory education and training, in: R. Halsall and M. Cockett (eds.) *Education and Training 14–19: Chaos or Coherence?* (London: David Fulton).

Gokulsing, K. and DaCosta, C. (eds.) (1997) *Usable Knowledges as the Goal of University Education* (Lampeter, UK: Edwin Mellen Press).

Goodman, P. (1971) *Compulsory Miseducation* (Harmondsworth, UK: Penguin Books).

Gordon, P. and White, J. (1979) *Philosophers as Educational Reformers* (London: Routledge & Kegan Paul).

Grace, G. R. (1988) *Education: Commodity or Public Good? Inaugural Lecture in Education* (Wellington, NZ: Victoria University Press).

Grace, G. R. (1989) Education: Commodity or public good? *British Journal of Educational Studies*, 37, pp. 207–21.

Grace, G. R. (1994) Education is a public good, in: D. Bridges and T. McLaughlin (eds.) *Education and the Market Place* (London: Falmer Press).

Gramsci, A. (1980) *The Modern Prince and Other Writings* (New York: International Publishers).

Greco, J. (1999) Introduction, in: J. Greco and E. Sosa (eds.) *The Blackwell Guide to Epistemology* (Blackwell: Oxford).

Green, A. (1994) Postmodernism and state education, *Journal of Education Policy*, 9, pp. 67–83.

Green, A. (1997) Core skills, general education and unification in post-16 education, in: A. Hodgson and K. Spours (eds.) *Dearing and Beyond: 14–19 Qualifications, Frameworks and Systems* (London: Kogan Page).

Green, D. G. (ed.) (1991) *Empowering the Parents: How to Break the Schools' Monopoly* (Choice in Welfare no. 9) (London: The Institute of Economic Affairs, Health and Welfare Unit).

Green, J. A. (ed.) (1912) *Pestalozzi's Educational Writings* (London: Edward Arnold).

Greene, M. (1988) *The Dialectic of Freedom* (New York: Teachers College Press).

Greene, M. (1995) *Releasing the Imagination: Essays on Education, the Arts and Social Change* (San Francisco: Jossey Bass).

Greene, M. (2000) Lived spaces, shared spaces, public spaces, in: M. Fine and L. Weiss (eds.) *Construction Sites* (New York: Teachers College Press).

Griffiths, M. (1995) *Feminisms and the Self: The Web of Identity* (London: Routledge).

Griffiths, M. (1998) *Educational Research for Social Justice: Getting off the Fence* (Buckingham, UK and Philadelphia: Open University Press).

Griffiths, M. (2000) Collaboration and partnership in question: Knowledge, politics and practice, *Journal of Education Policy*, 15, pp. 383–95.

Griffiths, M. and Davies, C. (1995) *In Fairness to Children: Working for Social Justice in the Primary School* (London: David Fulton).

Griffiths, M. and Whitford, M. (eds.) (1988) *Feminist Perspectives in Philosophy* (Bloomington: Macmillan and Indiana University Press).

Gross, B. and Gross, R. (1977) *The Childrens Rights Movement: Overcoming the Oppression of Young People* (New York: Doubleday).

Grosz, E. (1994) *Volatile Bodies: Towards a Corporeal Feminism* (Bloomington: Indiana University Press).

Gunew, S. (ed.) (1990) *Feminist Knowledge: Critique and Construct* (London: Routledge).

Gur Ze'ev, I. (1998) Toward a nonrepressive critical pedagogy, *Educational Theory*, 48, pp. 463–87.

Gur-Ze'ev, I. (1999) Cyberfeminism and education in the era of the exile of spirit, *Educational Theory*, 49.4, pp. 437–56.

Gustavsson, B. (1996) *Bildning i vår tid. Om bildningens möjligheter och villkor i det moderne samhället.* (Stockholm: Wahlström & Widstrand).

Gutmann, A. (1987) *Democratic Education* (Princeton, NJ: Princeton University Press).

Gutmann, A. (1995) Civic education and social diversity, *Ethics*, 105, pp. 516–34.

Gutmann, A. and Thompson, D. (eds.) (1996) *Democracy and Disagreement* (Cambridge, MA: Belknap Press).

Haber, J. G. and Halfon, M. S. (eds.) (1998) *Norms and Values: Essays on the Work of Virginia Held* (Lanham, MD: Rowman & Littlefield).

Habermas, J. (1968) *Erkenntnis und Interesse* (Frankfurt am Main: Suhrkamp).

Habermas, J. (1969) *Protestbewegung und Hochschulreform* (Frankfurt am Main: Suhrkamp).

Habermas, J. (1970a) *Toward a Rational Society* (Boston: Beacon Press).

Habermas, J. (1970b) Toward a theory of communicative competence, in: H. Dreitzel (ed.) *Patterns of Communicative Behaviour* (New York: Macmillan).

Habermas, J. (1971a) Vorbereitende Bemerkungen zu einer Theorie der kommunikativen Kompetenz, in: *Theorie der Gesellschaft oder Sozialtechnologie* (Frankfurt am Main: Suhrkamp).

Habermas, J. (1971b) *Knowledge and Human Interests* (trans. J. Shapiro) (Boston: Beacon Press).

Habermas, J. (1971c) Science and technology as ideology, in: *Towards a Rational Society* (London: Heinemann).

Habermas, J. (1981a) *Theorie des Kommunikativen Handelns*, 2 vols. (Frankfurt am Main: Suhrkamp).

Habermas, J. (1981b) *The Theory of Communicative Action*, vol. 1 (trans. T. McCarthy) (Boston: Beacon Press).

Habermas, J. (1981c) Modernity versus postmodernity, *New German Critique*, 22, pp. 3–22.

Habermas, J. (1987a) *The Philosophical Discourse of Modernity* (trans. F. Lawrence) (Cambridge, MA: MIT Press).

Habermas, J. (1987b) *Towards a Rational Society* (Cambridge, UK: Polity Press).

Habermas, J. (1990a) Philosophy as stand-in and interpreter, in: J. Habermas *Moral Consciousness and Communicative Action* (Cambridge, UK: Polity Press).

Habermas, J. (1990b) *The Philosophical Discourse of Modernity* (Oxford: Polity Press).

Habermas, J. (1990c) Remarks on the discussion, *Theory, Culture and Society*, 7, pp. 127–32.

Habermas, J. (1992) Citizenship and national identity: Some reflections on the future of Europe, *Praxis International*, 12, pp. 1–19.

Habermas, J. (1996) Citizenship and national identity, in: *Between Facts and Norms: Contributions to a Discourse Theory of Law and Democracy* (Cambridge, UK: Polity Press).

Habermas, J. (1998) *Between Facts and Norms* (Cambridge, UK: Polity Press).

Hadot, P. (1995) *Philosophy as a Way of Life. Spiritual Exercises from Socrates to Foucault* (trans. M. Chase, ed. with an introduction by A. I. Davidson) (Oxford: Blackwell).

Hager, P. (1990) Vocational education/general education – a false dichotomy?, *Studies in Continuing Education*, 12, pp. 13–23.

Hager, P. (1996) Professional practice in education: research and issues, *Australian Journal of Education*, 40, pp. 235–47.

Hager, P. (1998) On-the-job and off-the-job assessment: Choosing a balance, *Australian and New Zealand Journal of Vocational Education Research*, 6, pp. 87–103.

Hager, P. (1999) Review of J. White (1997) *Education and the End of Work: A New Philosophy of Work and Learning*, *Journal of Education and Work*, 12, pp. 95–100.

Hager, P. and Beckett, D. (1995) Philosophical underpinnings of the integrated conception of competence, *Educational Philosophy and Theory*, 27, pp. 1–24.

Haldane, J. (1986) Religious education in a pluralist society: A philosophical examination, *British Journal of Educational Studies* 34, pp. 161–81.

Haldane, J. (1995) Education: Conserving tradition, in: B. Almond (ed.) *Introducing Applied Ethics* (Oxford: Blackwell).

Haldane, J. (2000) On the very idea of spiritual values, in: A. O'Hear (ed.) *Philosophy, the Good and the Beautiful* (Cambridge, UK: Cambridge University Press).

Halpin, D. (1997) *Utopian Ideals, Democracy and the Politics of Education* (London: University of London, Goldsmiths College).

Halsall, R. and Cockett, M. (eds.) (1996) *Education and Training 14–19: Chaos or Coherence?* (London: David Fulton).

Halsey, A. H. (1992) *Decline of Donnish Dominion* (Oxford: Oxford University Press).

Halstead, J. M. (1995a) Voluntary apartheid? Problems of schooling for religious and other minorities in democratic societies, *Journal of Philosophy of Education*, 29, pp. 257–72.

Halstead, J. M. (1995b) Towards a unified view of Islamic education, *Islam and Christian–Muslim Relations*, 6, pp. 25–44.

Halstead, J. M. (1996) Liberal values and liberal education, in: J. M. Halstead and M. J. Taylor (eds.) *Values in Education and Education in Values* (London: Falmer Press).

Hand, S. (1989) *The Levinas Reader* (Oxford: Blackwell).

Haraway, D. (1985) A manifesto for cyborgs: Science, technology, and socialist feminism in the 1980s, in: L. J. Nicholson (ed.) *Feminism/Postmodernism* (London: Routledge).

Haraway, D. J. (1991) *Simians, Cyborgs, and Women: The Reinvention of Nature* (London: Free Association Books).

Haraway, D. J. (1996) Modest_Witness@Second_Millennium.FemaleMan©*Meets_Oncomouse*^TM: *Feminism and Technoscience* (London: Routledge).

Harding, S. (1991) *Whose Science? Whose Knowledge? Thinking from Women's Lives* (Milton Keynes, UK: Open University Press).

Harding, S. and Hintikka, M. B. (eds.) (1983) *Discovering Reality* (Dordrecht, Netherlands and London: D. Reidel).

Hare, W. (1979) *Open-Mindedness and Education* (Kingston, ONT: McGill-Queen's University Press).

Hare, W. (1985) *In Defense of Open-Mindedness* (Kingston, ONT: McGill-Queen's University Press).

Hare, W. (1995) Content and criticism: The aims of schooling, *Journal of Philosophy of Education*, 29, pp. 47–60.

Harland, R. (1987) *Superstructuralism: The Philosophy of Structuralism and Post-Structuralism* (London and New York: Methuen).

Harland, R. (1993) *Beyond Superstructuralism: The Syntagmatic Side of Language* (London: Routledge).

Harman, G. and Thompson, J. J. (1996) *Moral Relativism and Moral Objectivity* (Oxford: Blackwell).

Hart, W. (1993) Children are not meant to be studied, *Journal of Philosophy of Education*, 27, pp. 17–26.

Hartshorne, H. and May, M. (1928–1930) *Studies in the Nature of Character, vol. 1: Studies in Deceit; vol. 2: Studies in Self-control; vol. 3: Studies in the Organization of Character* (New York: Macmillan).

Harty, S. (1994) Pied Piper revisited, in: D. Bridges and T. McLaughlin (eds.) *Education and the Market Place* (London: Falmer Press).

Hassan, I. (1993) Toward a concept of postmodernism, in: J. Docherty (ed.) *Postmodernism: A Reader* (New York: Harvester, Wheatsheaf).

Hawkins, E. (1999) *Listening to Lorca: A Journey Into Language* (London: Centre for Information on Language Teaching and Research).

Haydon, G. (1977) The "right to education and compulsory schooling," *Educational Philosophy and Theory*, 9, pp. 1–15.

Haydon, G. (1997) *Teaching About Values. A New Approach* (London: Cassell).

Heidegger, M. (1962) *Being and Time* (trans. J. Macquarrie and E. Robinson) (New York: Harper & Row).

Heidegger, M. (1991) *Nietzsche*, 2 vols. (trans. D. Krell) (San Francisco: Harper).

Held, D. (1980) *Introduction to Critical Theory. Horkheimer to Habermas* (Berkeley: University of California Press).

Held, V. (1993) *Feminist Morality* (Chicago: University of Chicago Press).

Herbart, J. F. (1806) *The Science of Education* (trans. H. M. and E. Felkin) (London: Swan Sonnenschein).

Herbart, J. F. (1965) *Pädagogische Schriften*, vol. 2 (Düsseldorf, Germany: Kupper).

Herrmann, U., Kaufmann, H. B., Flitner, W., and Bollnow, O. F. (1987) *Kontinuität und Traditionsbrücke in der Pädagogik*. (Münster: Comenius).

Hick, J. (1999) *The Fifth Dimension. An Exploration of the Spiritual Realm* (Oxford: Oneworld Publications).

Hickman, L. A. (1990) *John Dewey's Pragmatic Technology* (Bloomington and Indianapolis: Indiana University Press).

Hillman, J. (1997) *University for Industry: Creating a National Learning Network* (London: Institute for Public Policy Research).

Hirsch, E. D. (1988) *Cultural Literacy: What Every American Needs to Know* (New York: Vintage Books).

Hirst, P. H. (1974a) Realms of meaning and forms of knowledge, in: P. H. Hirst *Knowledge and the Curriculum: A Collection of Philosophical Papers* (London: Routledge & Kegan Paul).

Hirst, P. H. (1974b) *Knowledge and the Curriculum: A Collection of Philosophical Papers* (London: Routledge & Kegan Paul).

Hirst, P. H. (1981) Education, catechesis and the church school, *British Journal of Religious Education*, Spring, pp. 85–93, 101.

Hirst, P. H. (1985) Education and diversity of belief, in: M. C. Felderhof (ed.) *Religious Education in a Pluralistic Society* (London: Hodder & Stoughton).

Hirst, P. and Peters, R. (1970) *The Logic of Education* (London: Routledge & Kegan Paul).

Hobson, P. (1984) Some reflections on parents' rights in the upbringing of their children, *Journal of Philosophy of Education*, 18, pp. 63–74.

Hobson, P. R. and Edwards, J. S. (1999) *Religious Education in a Pluralist Society. The Key Philosophical Issues* (London: Woburn Press).

Hodgson, A. and Spours, K. (eds.) (1997) *Dearing and Beyond: 14–19 Qualifications, Frameworks and Systems* (London: Kogan Page).

Hoffmann, D. (1978) *Kritische Erziehungswissenschaft* (Stuttgart and Berlin: Kohlhammer).

Hoffman, M. (1984) Empathy, its limits, and its role in a comprehensive moral theory, in: W. Kurtines and J. Gewirtz (eds.) *Morality, Moral Behavior, and Moral Development* (New York: Wiley).

Hoffman, M. (2000) *Empathy and Moral Development: Implications for Caring and Justice* (New York: Cambridge University Press).

Hogan, P. (1995) *The Custody and Courtship of Experience: Western Education in Philosophical Perspective* (Dublin: The Colomba Press).

Hollinger, R. (ed.) (1985) *Hermeneutics and Praxis* (Notre Dame, IN: Notre Dame University Press).

Holmes, S. (1995) *Passions and Constraint: On the Theory of Liberal Democracy* (Chicago: University of Chicago Press).

Holt, J. (1969) *How Children Fail* (Harmondsworth, UK: Penguin Books).

Holub, R. (1991) *Jürgen Habermas: Critic in the Public Sphere* (London: Routledge).

Honneth, A. and Bonss, W. (1982) *Materialen zur Kritischen Theorie* (Frankfurt am Main: Suhrkamp).

Hook, S. (1974) *Pragmatism and the Tragic Sense of Life* (New York: Basic Books).

Horkheimer, M. (1972) *Gesellschaft im Übergang. Aufsätze, Reden und Vorträge 1942–1970* (ed. W. Brede) (Frankfurt am Main: Fischer).

Horkheimer, M. (1974) *Eclipse of Reason* (New York: Continuum).

Horkheimer, M. (1976) *Zur Kritik der Instrumentellen Vernunft* (Frankfurt am Main: Fischer).

Horkheimer, M. (1977) Traditionelle und kritische Theorie, in: A. Schmidt (ed.) *Kritische Theorie* (Frankfurt am Main: Fischer).

Horkheimer, M., Fromm, E., and Marcuse, H. ([1936] 1987) *Studien über Autorität und Familie: Forschungsberichte aus dem Institut für Sozialforschung* (Lüneburg, Germany: zu Klampen).

Horkheimer, M. and Adorno, T. (1947) *Dialektik der Aufklärung* (Frankfurt am Main: Fischer).

Horkheimer, M. and Adorno, T. (1991) *Dialectic of Enlightenment* (New York: Continuum).

Hoy D. Couzens (1986) (ed.) *Foucault: A Critical Reader* (Oxford: Basil Blackwell).

Hughes, J. (1988) The philosopher's child, in: M. Griffiths and M. Whitford (eds.) *Feminist Perspectives in Philosophy* (Bloomington: Macmillan and Indiana University Press).

Hull, J. (1984) *Studies in Religion and Education* (London: Falmer Press).

Hull, J. (1996) The ambiguity of spiritual values, in: J. M. Halstead and M. J. Taylor (eds.) *Values in Education and Education in Values* (London: Falmer Press).

Hume, D. ([1751] 1983) *An Enquiry Concerning the Principles of Morals* (Indianapolis, IN: Hackett).

Hunter, I. (1996) Assembling the school, in: A. Barry, T. Osborne, and N. Rose (eds.) *Foucault and Political Reason. Liberalism, Neo-liberalism and Rationalities of Government* (London: UCL), pp. 143–66.

Hutchings, K. (1996) *Kant, Critique and Politics* (New York: Routledge).

Hyland, T. (1994) *Competence, Education and NVQs: Dissenting Perspectives* (London: Cassell).

Hyland, T. (1999) *Vocational Studies, Lifelong Learning and Social Values* (Aldershot, UK: Ashgate).

Hyland, T. (2000a) Vocational education and training under the New Deal: Towards a social theory of lifelong learning, *Journal of Vocational Education and Training*, 52, pp. 395–411.

Hyland, T. (2000b) Values and studentship in post-compulsory education and training, in: M. Leicester, C. Modgil, and S. Modgil (eds.) *Education, Culture and Values IV-Moral Pluralism* (London: Falmer).

Ihde, D. (1990) *Technology and the Lifeworld: From Garden to Earth* (Bloomington: Indiana University Press).

Illich, I. (1971) *Deschooling Society* (London: Calder Boyars).

Irigaray, L. (1985a) *This Sex Which is Not One* (Ithaca, NY: Cornell University Press).

Irigaray, L. (1985b) *Speculum of the Other Woman* (Ithaca, NY: Cornell University Press).

Jagger, A. (1983) *Feminist Politics and Human Nature* (Brighton, UK: Harvester).

James, W. ([1890] 1950) *The Principles of* Psychology, vols 1 and 2 (New York: Dover Publications).

James, W. ([1899] 1958) *Talks To Teachers on Psychology* (New York: W. W. Norton).

James, W. (1985) *The Varieties of Religious Experience* (New York: Penguin Books).

James, W. (1992) Talks to teachers on psychology, in: *James: Writings 1878–1899* (New York: The Library of America).

Jaspers, K. ([1946] 1965) *The Idea of the University* (London: Peter Owen).

Jay, M. (1973) *The Dialectical Imagination* (Boston: Little, Brown).

Jencks, C. (1996) *What is Post-Modernism?* 4th rev. edn. (London: Academy Editions).

Joas, H. (ed.) (2000) *Philosophie der Demokratie. Beiträge zum Werk von John Dewey* (Frankfurt: Suhrkamp).

Johnson, R. H. and Blair, J. A. (1994) Informal logic: Past and present, in: R. H. Johnson and J. A. Blair (eds.) *New Essays in Informal Logic* (Windsor, UK: Informal Logic), pp. 1–20.

Johnson, S. and Gardner, P. (1999) Some Achilles' heels of thinking skills: A response to Higgins and Baumfield, *Journal of Philosophy of Education*, 33, pp. 435–49.

Jonathan, R. (1983) The manpower service model of education, *Cambridge Journal of Education*, 13, 2.

Jonathan, R. (1989) Choice and control in education: Parental rights, individual liberties and social justice, *British Journal of Educational Studies*, 37, pp. 321–38.

Jonathan, R. (1990) State education service or prisoner's dilemma: The "hidden hand" as a source of education policy, *British Journal of Education Studies*, 38, p. 116–32.

Jonathan, R. (1993) Parental rights in schooling, in: P. Munn (ed.) *Parents and Schools: Customers, Managers or Partners?* (London: Routledge).

Jonathan, R. (1997a) Illusory freedoms: Liberalism, education and the market, *Journal of Philosophy of Education*, 31, pp. 1–220.

Jonathan, R. (1997b) *Illusory Freedoms: Liberalism, Education and the Market* (Oxford: Blackwell).

Jonathan, R. (2000) Cultural diversity and public education: Reasonable negotiation and hard cases. *Journal of Philosophy of Education*, 34, 2, pp. 377–93.

Joncich, G. (1968) *The Sane Positivist* (Middleton, CT: Wesleyan University Press).

Jones, A. R. (ed.) (1990) *Wordsworth: The 1807 Poems* (Basingstoke and London: Macmillan).

Jones, K. (1990) Citizenship in a women-friendly polity, *Signs*, 15, pp. 781–812.

Judd, C. H. (1936) *Education as Cultivation of the Higher Mental Processes* (New York: Macmillan).

Kaminsky, James S. (1993) *A New History of Educational Philosophy* (Westport, CN: Greenwood Press).

Kane, P. (2000) Play for today, in: *The Observer Magazine*, 22 October.

Kant, I. (1964) *Werke Bd. VI. Schriften zur Anthropologie, Geschichtsphilosophie, Politik und Pädagogik* (Frankfurt am Main: Suhrkamp).

Kant, I. ([1785] 1983) *Ethical Philosophy: The Metaphysics of Morals* (trans. J. W. Ellington) (Indianapolis, IN: Hackett).

Kearney, R. (1988) *The Wake of Imagination* (London: Huchinson).

Keller, E. Fox (1985) *Reflections on Gender and Science* (New Haven, CT: Yale University Press).

Kellner, D. and Best, S. (1991) *Postmodern Theory: Critical Interrogations* (London: Macmillan).

Kent, G. (1992) Little foreign bodies: International dimensions of child prostitution, in: M. Freeman and P. Veerman (eds.) *The Ideologies of Children's Rights* (Dordrecht, Netherlands: Martinus Nijhoff).

Kenway, J. and Nixon, H. (1999) Cyberfeminisms, cyberliteracies, and educational cyberspheres, *Educational Theory*, 49.4, pp. 457–74.

Kerr, C. (1972) *The Uses of the University* (Cambridge, MA: Harvard University Press).

Kerr, F. (1998) Truth in religion: Wittgensteinian considerations, in: D. Carr (ed.) *Education, Knowledge and Truth. Beyond the Postmodern Impasse* (London: Routledge).

Kilpatrick, W. H. ([1918] 1961) In retrospect at ninety, *Studies in Philosophy and Education*, 1.4–5, pp. 146–52.

Kincheloe, J. L. and Steinberg, S. R. (1997) *Changing Multiculturalism* (Buckingham: Open University Press).

King, A. (1984) *The Bungalow: The Production of a Global Culture* (London: Routledge & Kegan Paul).

Kirp, D. L. (1979) *Doing Good by Doing Little: Race and Schooling in Britain* (Berkeley: University of California Press).

Kiziltan, M. U., Bain, W. J. and Canizares, A. M. (1990) Postmodern conditions: Rethinking public education, *Educational Theory*, 40, pp. 351–69.

Klafki, W. (1976) *Aspekte kritisch-konstruktiver Erziehungswissenschaft* (Weinheim, Germany: Beltz).

Kleinespel, K. and Tillmann, K.-J. (1998) Reformpädagogische Argumente in der bildungspolitischen Debatte – zwei Fallstudien, in: T. Rülcker and J. Oelkers (eds.) *Politische Reformpädagogik* (Bern: Peter Lang), pp. 715–41.

Kleinig, J. (1976) Mill, children and rights. *Educational Philosophy and Theory*, 8, pp. 1–15.

Kohlberg, L. (1981) *The Philosophy of Moral Development*, vol. 1 (San Francisco: Harper & Row).

Korsgaard, C. (1998) From duty and for the sake of the noble: Kant and Aristotle on morally good action, in: S. Engstrom and J. Whiting (eds.) *Aristotle, Kant, and the Stoics: Rethinking Happiness and Duty* (Cambridge, UK: Cambridge University Press).

Korthals, M. (1981) *Inleiding*, in: M. Horkheimer and H. Marcuse *Filosofie en Kritische Theorie* (Meppel, Netherlands: Boom), pp. 7–61.

Kourany, J. A. (1998) *Philosophy in a Feminist Voice: Critiques and Reconstructions* (Princeton, NJ: Princeton University Press).

Kuhn, T. (1962) *The Structure of Scientific Revolutions* (Chicago: University of Chicago Press).

Kumar, R. (1993) *The History of Doing: An Illustrated Account of Movements for Women's Rights and Feminism in India 1800–1990* (London: Verso and New Delhi: Kali for Women).

Kymlicka, W. (1989) *Liberalism, Community and Culture* (Oxford: Oxford University Press).

Kymlicka, W. (1995) *Multicultural Citizenship* (Oxford: Clarendon Press).

Kymlicka, W. (1996) Three forms of group-differentiated citizenship in Canada, in: S. Benhabib (ed.) *Democracy and Difference* (Princeton, NJ: Princeton University Press).

Kymlicka, W. (1999) Education for citizenship, in: J. M. Halstead and T. McLaughlin (eds.) *Education in Morality* (London: Routledge).

Kymlicka, W. and Norman, W. (1994) Return of the citizen: A survey of recent work on citizenship theory, *Ethics*, 104, pp. 352–81.

Lakoff, G. and Johnson, M. (1980) *Metaphors We Live By* (Chicago: University of Chicago Press).

Lamb, M. E. (ed.) (1982) *Nontraditional Families. Parenting and Child Development* (London: Erlbaum).

Langeveld, M. (1946) *Beknopte Theoretische Pedagogiek* [Concise Philosophy of Education] (Groningen, Netherlands: Wolters-Noordhoff).

Lankshear, C., Knobel, M. and Peters, M. (2000) Information, knowledge and learning: Some issues facing epistemology and education in a digital age, in: N. Blake and P. Standish (eds.) *Enquiries at the Interface: Philosophical problems of on-line education, Journal of Philosophy of Education*, 34 (special issue), pp. 17–40.

Lankshear, C. and McLaren, P. (eds.) (1993) *Critical Literacy: Politics, Praxis and the Postmodern* (Albany, NY: State University of New York Press).

Larrosa, J. (1998) *Apprendre et Être. Langage, Littérature et Expérience de Formation* (Paris: ESF).

Lash, N. (1988) *Easter in Ordinary: Reflections in Human Experience and the Knowledge of God* (Notre Dame, IN: University of Notre Dame Press).

Lather, P. (1991) *Getting Smart: Feminist Research and Pedagogy With/In the Postmodern* (London: Routledge).

Lave, J. and Wenger, E. (1991) *Situated Learning: Legitimate Peripheral Participation* (Cambridge, UK: Cambridge University Press).

Lawrence, D. H. ([1923] 1973) Benjamin Franklin, in: J. Williams and R. Williams (eds.) *D. H. Lawrence on Education* (Harmondsworth, UK: Penguin Books).

Lawrence, D. H. ([1936] 1973) Education of the people, in: J. Williams and R. Williams (eds.) *D. H. Lawrence on Education* (Harmondsworth, UK: Penguin Books).

Leavis, F. R. (1943) *Education and the University* (Cambridge, Cambridge University Press).

Le Doeuff, M. (1991) *Hipparchia's Choice: An Essay concerning Women, Philosophy, Etc.* (trans. T. Selous) (Oxford: Blackwell).

Lee, D., Marsden, D., Rickman, P. and Dunscombe, J. (1990) *Scheming for Work: A Study of the YTS in the Enterprise Culture* (Milton Keynes, UK: Open University Press).

Lennon, K. and Whitford, M. (eds.) (1994) *Knowing the Difference: Feminist Perspectives in Epistemology* (London: Routledge).

Levinas, E. (1987) *Time and the Other* (Pittsburgh, PA: Duquesne University Press).

Levinson, M. (1999) *The Demands of Liberal Education* (Oxford: Oxford University Press).

Lewis, T. (1991) Difficulties attending the new vocationalism in the USA, *Journal of Philosophy of Education*, 25, pp. 95–108.

Lewis, T. (1997) Towards a liberal vocational education, *Journal of Philosophy of Education*, 31.3, pp. 477–89.

Lickona, T. (1991) *Educating for Character: How Our Schools Can Teach Respect and Responsibility* (New York: Bantam Books).

Lifton, R. J. (1993) *The Protean Self: Human Resilience in an Age of Fragmentation* (Ithaca, NY: Cornell University Press).

Lilley, I. M. (1967) *Friedrich Froebel: A Selection from his Writings* (Cambridge, UK: Cambridge University Press).

Lipman, M. (1991) *Thinking in Education* (Cambridge, UK: Cambridge University Press).

Lloyd, G. ([1984] 1993) *The Man of Reason: "Male" and "Female" in Western Philosophy*, 2nd edn. (London: Routledge).

Løvlie, L. (1997) On the uses of example in moral education, *Journal of Philosophy of Education*, 33, p. 3.

Luhmann, N. and Schorr, K. E. (eds.) (1982) *Zwischen Technologie und Selbstreferenz: Fragen an die Pädagogik.* (Frankfurt: Suhrkamp).

Lukasiewicz, J. (1994) *The Ignorance Explosion* (Ottawa, ONT: Carleton University Press).

Lum, G. (1999) Where's the competence in competence-based education and training? *Journal of Philosophy of Education*, 33, pp. 403–18.

Lustgarten, L. S. (1983) Liberty in a culturally plural society, in: A. Phillips Griffiths (ed.) *Of Liberty* (Cambridge, UK: Cambridge University Press).

Lyotard, J.-F. (1984) *The Postmodern Condition: A Report on Knowledge* (trans. G. Bennington and B. Massumi; foreword by F. Jameson) (Minneapolis: University of Minnesota Press and Manchester, UK: University of Manchester Press).

Lyotard, J.-F. (1985) *The Postmodern Condition: A Report on Knowledge* (Minneapolis: University of Minnesota Press).

Lyotard, J.-F. (1988a) *L'inhumain: Causeries sur le temps* (Paris: Galilée).

Lyotard, J.-F. (1988b) *The Differend: Phrases in Dispute* (trans. G. Van Den Abbeele) (Minneapolis: University of Minnesota Press).

Lyotard, J.-F. (1992) *The Postmodern Explained to Children: Correspondence 1982–1985* (Sydney, NSW: Power Publications).

Lyotard, J.-F. (1993a) *Libidinal Economy* (trans. I. Grant) (Bloomington, Indiana University Press).

Lyotard, J.-F. (1993b) *Political Writings* (trans. B. Readings and K. P. Geiman) (Minneapolis: University of Minnesota).

Lyotard, J.-F. (1994) *Lessons on the Analytic of the Sublime* (trans. E. Rottenberg) (Stanford, CA: Stanford University Press).

Lyotard, J.-F. (1998) A propos du différend. Entretien avec Jean-François Lyotard. *Les Cahiers de Philosophie*, 5, pp. 35–62.

MacDowell, J. (1996) Deliberation and moral development in Aristotle's ethics, in: S. Engstrom and J. Whiting (eds.) *Aristotle, Kant and the Stoics* (Cambridge, UK: Cambridge University Press).

Macedo, S. (1990) *Liberal Virtue: Citizenship, Virtue and Community in Liberal Constitutionalism* (Oxford: Clarendon).

Macedo, S. (ed.) (1999) *Deliberative Politics* (Oxford: Oxford University Press).

Macedo, S. (2000) *Diversity and Distrust: Civic Education in a Multicultural Democracy* (Cambridge, MA: Harvard University Press).

MacIntyre, A. (1977) Epistemological crises, dramatic narrative, and the philosophy of science. *The Monist*, 60, pp. 453–72.

MacIntyre, A. (1981) *After Virtue: A Study in Moral Theory* (Notre Dame, IN: University of Notre Dame Press).

Mackenzie, P. J. (1998) David Carr on religious knowledge and spiritual education. *Journal of Philosophy of Education*, 32, pp. 409–27.

Macklin, E. D. and Rubin, R. (eds.) (1983) *Contemporary Families and Alternative Lifestyles. Handbook on Research and Theory* (London: Sage).

Maclure, S. (1991) *Missing Links: The Challenge to Further Education* (London: Policy Studies Institute).

Macmillan, C. J. B. (1994) Is community necessary? Quasi-philosophical ruminations, *Studies in Philosophy and Education*, 15, pp. 77–8.

Malkin, J. and Wildavsky, A. (1991) Why the traditional distinction between public and private goods should be abandoned, *Journal of Theoretical Politics*, 3, pp. 355–78.

Mani, L. (1998) *Contentious Traditions: The Debate on Sati in Colonial India* (Berkeley: University of California Press).

Marcuse, H. (1964) *One-Dimensional Man: Studies in the Ideology of Advanced Industrial Society* (Boston: Beacon Press).

Marcuse, H. (1972) Philosophy and critical theory, in: M. Marcuse and J. J. Shapiro (eds.) *Negations: Essays in Critical Theory* (Harmondsworth, UK: Penguin Books).

Marshall, J. (1996) *Michel Foucault: Personal Autonomy and Education* (Dordrecht, Netherlands: Kluwer).

Marshall, T. H. (1950) *Citizenship and Social Class and Other Essays* (Cambridge, UK: Cambridge University Press).

Martin, J. R. (1985) *Reclaiming a Conversation: The Ideal of the Educated Woman* (New Haven, CT: Yale University Press).

Martin, J. R. (1992) Critical thinking for a humane world, in: S. P. Norris (ed.) *The Generalizability of Critical Thinking* (New York: Teachers College Press), pp. 163–80.

Martin, J. R. (1994) *Changing the Educational Landscape: Philosophy, Women and Curriculum* (London: Routledge).

Maskell, D. (1999) Education, education, education: Or, what has Jane Austen to teach Tony Blunkett? *Journal of Philosophy of Education*, 33.2, pp. 157–76.

Masschelein, J. (1991a) *Kommunikatives Handeln und Pädagogisches Handeln* (Leuven, Belgium: Leuven University Press and Weinheim, Germany: Deutscher Studien Verlag).

Masschelein, J. (1991b) The relevance of Habermas' communicative turn. Some reflections on education as communicative action. *Studies in Philosophy and Education*, 11, pp. 95–111.

Masschelein, J. (1997) In defence of education as problematisation: Some preliminary remarks on a strategy of disarmament, in: D. Wildemeersch, M. Finger, and T. Jansen (eds.) *Adult Education and Social Responsibility. Reconciling the Irreconcilable* (Frankfurt and Bern: Peter Lang).

Masschelein, J. (1998) How to imagine something exterior to the system: Critical education as problematization. *Educational Theory*, 48, pp. 521–30.

Masschelein, J. and Smeyers, P. (2000) *L'enfance*, education, and the politics of meaning, in: P. A. Dhillon and P. Standish (eds.) *Lyotard. Just Education* (London: Routledge).

Matthews, J. (ed.) (1998) *Jane Gallop Seminar Papers* (Canberra, ACT: Humanities Research Centre, Monography Series 7, ANU).

May, S. (1999) Critical multiculturalism and cultural difference: Avoiding essentialism, in: S. May (ed.) *Critical Multiculturalism: Rethinking Multicultural and Antiracist Education* (London: Falmer Press).

McClintock, R. O. (1988) Introduction: Marking the second frontier, in: R. O. McClintock (ed.) *Computing and Education: The Second Frontier* (New York: Teachers College Press).

McCormick, R. and Paechter, C. (eds.) (1999) *Learning and Knowledge* (London: Paul Chapman).

McGhee, M. (2000) *Transformations of Mind. Philosophy as Spiritual Practice* (Cambridge, UK: Cambridge University Press).

McGillivray, A. (1992) Reconstructing child abuse: Western definition and non-western experience, in: M. Freeman and P. Veerman (eds.) *The Ideologies of Children's Rights* (Dordrecht, Netherlands: Martinus Nijhoff).

McLaren, P. (1989) *Life in Schools. An Introduction to Critical Pedagogy in the Foundations of Education* (New York: Longman).

McLaren, P. (ed.) (1995) *Postmodernism, Postcolonialism and Pedagogy* (Albert Park, Victoria: James Nicholas).

McLaren, P. (1999) *Schooling as Ritual Performance: Towards a Political Economy of Educational Symbols and Gestures* (Lanham, MD: Rowman & Littlefield).

McLaren, P. (2000) *Che Guevara, Paulo Freire, and the Pedagogy of Revolution* (New York and Oxford: Rowman & Littlefield).

McLaughlin, T. H. (1984) Parental rights and the religious upbringing of children, *Journal of Philosophy of Education*, 18, pp. 75–83.

McLaughlin, T. H. (1990) Peter Gardner on religious upbringing and the liberal ideal of religious autonomy, *Journal of Philosophy of Education*, 24, pp. 107–25.

McLaughlin, T. H. (1992a) Citizenship, diversity and education: A philosophical perspective, *Journal of Moral Education*, 21, pp. 235–50.

McLaughlin, T. H. (1992b) The ethics of separate schools, in: M. Leicester and M. Taylor (eds.) *Ethics, Ethnicity and Education* (London: Kogan Page).

McLaughlin, T. H. (1994) The scope of parents' educational rights, in: J. M. Halstead (ed.) *Parental Choice and Education. Principles, Policy and Practice* (London: Kogan Page).

McLaughlin, T. H. (1995a) Liberalism, education and the common school, *Journal of Philosophy of Education*, 29, pp. 239–55.

McLaughlin, T. H. (1995b) Wittgenstein, education and religion, in: P. Smeyers and J. D. Marshall (eds.) *Philosophy and Education: Accepting Wittgenstein's Challenge* (Dordrecht, Netherlands: Kluwer).

McLaughlin, T. H. (1996a) Education of the whole child? in: R. Best (ed.) *Education, Spirituality and the Whole Child* (London: Cassell).

McLaughlin, T. H. (1996b) The distinctiveness of Catholic education, in: T. H. McLaughlin, J. O'Keefe and B. O'Keeffe (eds.) *The Contemporary Catholic School: Context, Identity and Diversity* (London: Falmer).

McLaughlin, T. H. (1998) Sex education, moral controversy and the common school, *Muslim Education Quarterly*, 15.3, pp. 28–52.

McPeck, J. E. (1981) *Critical Thinking and Education* (New York: St. Martin's Press).

McPeck, J. E. (1990) *Teaching Critical Thinking* (New York: Routledge).

McWilliam, E. and Taylor, P. (eds.) (1998) *Pedagogy, Technology and the Body* (New York: Peter Lang).

Mele, A. R. (1995) *Autonomous Agents. From Self-Control to Autonomy* (New York: Oxford University Press).

Mernissi, F. (1987) *Beyond the Veil: Male-Female Dynamics in Modern Muslim Society* (Bloomington: Indiana University Press).

Merquior, J. G. (1985) *Foucault* (London: Fontana Press and Collins).

Middleton, S. (1998) *Disciplining Sexuality: Foucault, Life Histories and Education* (New York: Teachers College Press).

Midgley, M. (1989) *Wisdom, Information, and Wonder: What is Knowledge For?* (London: Routledge).

Midgley, M. (1991) *Can We Make Moral Judgments?* (New York, St. Martin's Press).

Milan Women's Bookstore Collective (1990) *Sexual Difference: A Theory of Social-Symbolic Practice* (Bloomington: Indiana University Press).

Miliband, D. (1991) *Markets, Politics and Education* (Education and Training Paper 3) (London: Institute for Public Policy Research).

Mill, J. S. ([1867] 1979) Inaugural address at the University of St Andrews, in: F. W. Garforth *John Stuart Mill's Theory of Education* (Oxford: Martin Robertson).

Mill, J. S. (1910) On liberty, in: J. S. Mill, *Utilitarianism, Liberty, Representative Government* (London: Dent).

Miller, D. (1989) In what sense must socialism be communitarian? in: E. F. Paul, F. D. Miller Jr, J. Paul, and D. Greenberg (eds.) *Socialism* (Oxford: Blackwell).

Miller, D. (1992) Community and citizenship, in: S. Avinieri and A. De-Shalit (eds.) *Communitarianism and Individualism* (Oxford: Oxford University Press).

Minogue, K. (1973) *The Concept of a University* (London: Weidenfeld & Nicolson).

Missimer, C. (1990) Perhaps by skill alone, *Informal Logic*, 12, pp. 145–53.

Moberly, W. (1949) *The Crisis in the University* (London: SCM Press).

Mollenhauer, K. (1972) *Theorien zum Erziehungsprozess* (München: Juventa).

Montgomery, L. M. (1994) *Anne of Green Gables* (London: Puffin).

Moody-Adams, M. (1997) *Fieldwork in Familiar Places: Morality, Culture, and Philosophy* (Cambridge, MA: Harvard University Press).

Morgan, J. (1996) A defence of autonomy as an educational ideal, *Journal of Philosophy of Education*, 30, pp. 239–52.

Morris, G. (1994) Local education authorities and the market place, in: D. Bridges and T. McLaughlin (eds.) *Education and the Market Place* (London: Falmer Press).

Mourad, R. (1997) *Postmodern Philosophical Critique and the Pursuit of Knowledge in Higher Education* (Westport, CT and London: Bergin & Garvey).

Mulhall, S. and Swift, A. (1996) *Liberals and Communitarians*, 2nd edn. (Oxford: Blackwell).

Murdoch, I. (1992) *Metaphysics as a Guide to Morals* (London: Chatto & Windus).

Murphy, J. P. (1990) *Pragmatism. From Peirce to Davidson* (Boulder, CO: Westview Press).

Murungi, K. (1994) Get away from my genitals! A commentary on Warrior Marks, *Interstices*, 2.11, p. 13.

Nagel, T. (1986) *The View from Nowhere* (Oxford: Oxford University Press).

Naismith, D. (1994) In defence of the educational voucher, in: D. Bridges and T. McLaughlin (eds.) *Education and the Market Place* (London: Falmer).

Narayan, U. (1997) *Dislocating Cultures: Identities, Traditions, and Third World Feminisms* (London: Routledge).

Nash, P. (1966) *Authority and Freedom in Education* (New York: Wiley).

Nash, R. (1999) *Faith, Hype, and Clarity: Teaching about Religion in American Schools and Colleges* (New York: Teachers College Press).

Neill, A. S. (1928) Summerhill, *The New Era*, 9.34, pp. 70–2.

Neill, A. S. (1960) *Summerhill* (New York: Hart).

Neill, A. S. (1962) *Summerhill. A Radical Approach to Education* (London: Gollancz).

Neiman, A. (2000) Self examination, spirituality, and philosophical education, *Journal of Philosophy of Education*, 34.4, pp. 571–90.

Newman, J. H. ([1853] 1976) *The Idea of a University* (ed. I. T. Ker) (Oxford: Oxford University Press).

New Zealand Treasury (1987) *Government Management: Brief to the Incoming Government*, vol. 2 (Wellington: Education Issues, Government Printer).

Nicholls, D. (1974) *Three Varieties of Pluralism* (London: Macmillan).

Nicholls, D. (1975) *The Pluralist State* (London: Macmillan).

Nicholson, L. (ed.) (1990) *Feminism/Postmodernism* (New York: Routledge).

Nietzsche, F. ([1889] 1981) *Twilight of the Idols* (trans. R. J. Hollingdale) (Harmondsworth, UK: Penguin Books).

Nietzsche, F. (1967) *On the Genealogy of Morals* (trans. W. Kaufmann and R. J. Hollingdale) (New York: Vintage Books).

Nietzsche, F. (2000) *The Birth of Tragedy* (trans. and with an introduction by D. Smith) (Oxford: Oxford University Press).

Noddings, N. (1984) *Caring: A Feminine Approach to Ethics and Moral Education* (Berkeley: University of California Press).

Noddings, N. (1986) Fidelity in teaching, teacher education and research for teaching, *Harvard Educational Review*, 56, pp. 496–510.

Noddings, N. (1993) *Educating for Intelligent Belief or Unbelief* (New York and London: Teachers College Press).

Noddings, N. (1995) *Philosophy of Education* (Boulder, CO: Westview Press).

Noddings, N. (1997) Character education and community, in: A. Molnar (ed.) *The Construction of Children's Character* (Chicago: National Society for the Study of Education).

Noddings, N. (1998a) Feminist morality and social policy, in: J. G. Haber and M. S. Halfon (eds.) *Norms and Values* (Lanham, MD: Rowman and Littlefield).

Noddings, N. (1998b) Thoughts on John Dewey's "Ethical principles underlying education." *The Elementary School Journal*, 98, pp. 479–88.

Noddings, N. (2001a) *Starting at Home: Care Theory and Social Policy* (Berkeley: University of California Press).

Noddings, N. (2001b) *A Sympathetic Alternative to Character Education* (New York: Teachers College Press).

Nohl, H. (1970) *Die pädagogische Bewegung in Deutschland und ihre Theorie* (Frankfurt: Verlag G. Schulte-Bulmke).

Nordenbo, S. E. (1984) *Bidrag til den danske pædagogiks historie* (Copenhagen: Museum Tusculanum).

Nordenbo, S. E. (1986) Justification of paternalism in education, *Scandinavian Journal of Educational Research*, 30, pp. 121–39.

Norris, S. P. (ed.) (1992) *The Generalizability of Critical Thinking* (New York: Teachers College Press).

Nozick, R. (1974) *Anarchy, State and Utopia* (Oxford: Blackwell).

Nozick, R. (1981) *Philosophical Explanations* (Cambridge, MA: The Belknap Press of Harvard University Press).

Nunn, P. (1945) *Education: Its Data and First Principles*, 3rd edn. (London: Arnold).

Nussbaum, M. (1985) The discernment of perception: An Aristotelian conception of private and public rationality, in: J. Cleary (ed.) *Proceedings of the Boston Area Colloquium in Ancient Philosophy*, vol. 1.

Nussbaum, M. (1986) *The Fragility of Goodness: Luck and Ethics in Greek Tragedy and Philosophy* (Cambridge, UK: Cambridge University Press).

Nussbaum, M. (1988) Non-relative virtues: An Aristotelian approach, *Midwest Studies in Philosophy*, 13, pp. 32–53.

Nussbaum, M. (1990) *Love's Knowledge: Essays in Philosophy and Literature* (Oxford: Oxford University Press).

Nussbaum, M. (1996) *For Love of Country* (Boston: Beacon Press).

Nussbaum, M. (1997) *Cultivating Humanity: A Classical Defense of Reform in Liberal Education* (Cambridge, MA: Harvard University Press).

Nussbaum, M. (2000) *Women in Development* (Cambridge, UK: Cambridge University Press).

Nye, A. (1990) *Words of Power: A Feminist Reading of the History of Logic* (New York: Routledge).

Oakeshott, M. (1972) Education: The engagement and its frustration, in: R. Dearden, P. Hirst, and R. Peters (eds.) *Education and the Development of Reason* (London: Routledge & Kegan Paul).

Oakeshott, M. (1981) *Rationalism in Politics and Other Essays* (London: Methuen).

Obeyesekere, G. (1992) *The Apotheosis of Captain Cook: European Mythmaking in the Pacific* (Princeton, NJ: Princeton University Press).

Oelkers, J. (1989) *Reformpädagogik. Eine kritische Dogmengeschichte* (Weinheim and München: Juventa).

Okin, S. M. (1979) *Women in Western Political Thought* (Princeton, NJ: Princeton University Press).

Okin, S. M. (1989) *Justice, Gender, and the Family* (New York: Basic Books).

Okin, S. M. (1992) Women, equality and citizenship, *Queen's Quarterly*, 99, pp. 56–71.

Okin, S. M. (1995) Women and the complex inequality of gender, in: D. Miller and M. Walzer (eds.) *Pluralism, Justice, and Equality* (Oxford: Oxford University Press).

Okin, S. M. (1999) Is multiculturalism bad for women? in: J. Cohen and M. Howard (eds.) *Is Multiculturalism Bad for Women?* (Princeton, NJ: Princeton University Press).

Oldfield, A. (1990) *Citizenship and Community: Civic Republicanism and the Modern World* (London: Routledge).

O'Neill, O. and Ruddick, W. (eds.) (1979) *Having Children: Philosophical and Legal Reflections on Parenthood* (New York: Oxford University Press).

Orr, D. (1989) Just the facts ma'am: Informal logic, gender and pedagogy, *Informal Logic*, 11, pp. 1–10.

Ortega y Gasset, J. (1946) *Mission of the University* (London: Kegan Paul).

Orwell, G. (1956) *The Orwell Reader* (New York: Harcourt, Brace).

Oser, F. (1986) *Transformation und Entwicklung: Grundlagen der Moralerziehung* (Frankfurt: Suhrkamp).

Otto, R. (1950) *The Idea of the Holy* (Oxford: Oxford University Press).

Papert, S. (1980) *Mindstorms: Children, Computers and Powerful Ideas* (New York: Basic Books).

Parekh, B. (1986) The concept of multicultural education, in: S. Modgil, G. Verma, K. Mallick, and C. Modgil (eds.) *Multicultural Education: The Interminable Debate* (London: Falmer).

Parekh, B. (1999) The logic of intercultural evaluation, in: J. Horton and S. Mendus (eds.) *Toleration, Identity and Difference* (London: Macmillan).

Parekh, B. (2000) *Rethinking Multiculturalism: Cultural Diversity and Political Theory* (London: Palgrave).

Parker, S. (1997) *Reflective Teaching in the Postmodern World: A Manifesto for Education in Postmodernity* (Buckingham, UK and Philadelphia: Open University Press).

Parry, G. and Moyser, G. (1994) More participation, more democracy? in: D. Beetham (ed.) *Defining and Measuring Democracy* (London: Sage).

Pateman, C. (1988) *The Sexual Contract* (Cambridge, UK: Polity Press).

Pateman, C. (1989) *The Disorder of Women* (Cambridge, UK: Polity Press).

Pateman, C. and Grosz, E. (eds.) (1986) *Feminist Challenges: Social and Political Theory* (London and Sydney: Allen and Unwin).

Patten, P. (1989) Taylor and Foucault on power and freedom, *Political Studies*, 37, pp. 260–76.

Paul, R. (1990) *Critical Thinking: What Every Person Needs to Survive in a Rapidly Changing World* (Rohnert Park, CA: Center for Critical Thinking and Moral Critique).

Pearson, A. T. ([1980] 1984) Competence: A normative analysis, in: E. C. Short (ed.) *Competence: Inquiries Into its Meaning and Acquisition in Educational Settings* (Lanham, MD: University Press of America).

Pedretti, C. (1980) *Leonardo da Vinci Nature Studies from the Royal Library at Windsor Castle* (London: Phaidon).

Peirce, C. S. ([1868] 1992) Some consequences of four incapacitates, in: N. Houser and C. Kloesel (eds.) *The Essential Peirce*, vol. 1 (Bloomington: Indiana University Press).

Peirce, C. S. ([1878] 1992) How to make our ideas clear, in: N. Houser and C. Kloesel (eds.) *The Essential Peirce*, vol. 1 (Bloomington: Indiana University Press).

Peirce, C. S. ([1887] 1992) The fixation of belief, in: N. Houser and C. Kloesel (eds.) *The Essential Peirce*, vol. 1 (Bloomington: Indiana University Press).

Peirce, C. S. ([1887–8] 1992) A guess at the riddle, in: N. Houser and C. Kloesel (eds.) *The Essential Peirce*, vol. 1 (Bloomington: Indiana University Press).

Peirce, C. S. ([1905] 1998) Pragmatism, in: N. Houser and C. Kloesel (eds.) *The Essential Peirce*, vol. 2 (Bloomington: Indiana University Press).

Pelikan, J. (1992) *The Idea of the University: A Reexamination* (New Haven, CT and London: Yale University Press).

Pendlebury, S. (1990a) Practical reasoning and situational appreciation in teaching, *Educational Theory*, 40, pp. 171–9.

Pendlebury, S. (1990b) Liberty, community and the practice of teaching, *Studies in Philosophy and Education*, 10, pp. 263–79.

Pendlebury, S. (1993) Practical arguments, rationalization and imagination in teachers' practical reasoning, *Journal of Curriculum Studies*, 25, pp. 145–51.

Pensky, M. (ed.) (1994) *The Past as Future: Jürgen Habermas, interviewed by Michael Haller* (trans. and ed. M. Pensky; foreword by P. Hohendahl) (Cambridge, UK: Polity Press).

Perelman, L. J. (1992) *School's Out: Hyperlearning, the New Technology, and the End of Education* (New York: William Morrow).

Peters, M. A. (1994) Habermas, poststructuralism and the question of postmodernity: The defiant periphery, *Social Analysis*, 36, September, pp. 1–18. Reprinted as: Habermas, poststructuralism and the question of postmodernity, in: M. A. Peters, J. D. Marshall, W. Hope, and S. Webster (eds.) (1996) *Critical Theory, Poststructuralism and the Social Context* (Palmerston North, NZ: Dunmore Press).

Peters, M. A. (ed.) (1995) *Education and the Postmodern Condition* (Westport, CT and London: Bergin & Garvey).

Peters, M. A. (1996) *Poststructuralism, Politics and Education* (Westport, CT and London: Bergin & Garvey).

Peters, M. A. (1997) Poststructuralism and the French reception of Nietzsche, *Political Theory Newsletter*, 8, pp. 39–55.

Peters, M. A. (1998a) Introduction: Naming the multiple: Poststructuralism and education, in: M. A. Peters (ed.) *Naming the Multiple: Poststructuralism and Education* (Westport, CT and London: Bergin & Garvey).

Peters, M. A. (ed.) (1998b) *Naming the Multiple: Poststructuralism and Education* (Westport, CT and London: Bergin & Garvey).

Peters, M. A. (ed.) (1999) *After the Disciplines? The Emergence of Cultural Studies* (Westport, CT and London: Bergin & Garvey).

Peters, M. A. (2000) Deranging the *Investigations*: Cavell on the figure of the child, *Educational Philosophy and Theory*, 21, pp. 88–96.

Peters, M. A. and Ghiraldelli, P. Jr. (eds.) (2001) *Richard Rorty: Philosophy, Education, and Politics* (Boulder, CO: Rowman & Littlefield).

Peters, M. A., Hope, W., Marshall, J., and Webster, S. (eds.) (1996) *Critical Theory, Poststructralism and the Social Context* (Palmerston North, NZ: The Dunmore Press).

Peters, M. A. and Lankshear, C. (1996) Postmodern counternarratives, in: H. Giroux, C. Lankshear, P. McLaren, and M. Peters (eds.) *Counternarratives: Cultural Studies and Critical Pedagogies in Postmodern Spaces* (New York and London: Routledge).

Peters, M. A. and Marshall, J. D. (1996) *Individualism and Community: Education and Social Policy in the Postmodern Condition* (London: Falmer).

Peters, M. A. and Marshall, J. D. (1999) *Wittgenstein: Philosophy, Postmodernism, Pedagogy* (Westport, CT and London: Bergin & Garvey).

Peters, M. A., Marshall, J. D., and Smeyers, P. (eds.) (2000) *Nietzsche's Legacy for Education: Past and Present Values* (Westport, CT and London: Bergin & Garvey).

Peters, R. S. (1966) *Ethics and Education* (London: Allen & Unwin).

Peters, R. S. (1969) *Perspectives on Plowden* (London: Routledge & Kegan Paul).

Peters, R. S. (1973a) Freedom and the development of the free man, in: J. F. Doyle (ed.) *Educational Judgements* (London: Routledge & Kegan Paul).

Peters, R. S. (ed.) (1973b) *The Philosophy of Education* (Oxford: Oxford University Press).

Peters, R. S. (1974) Subjectivity and standards, in: *Psychology and Ethical Development* (London: Allen & Unwin).

Peters, R. S. (1975) The justification of education, in: R. S. Peters (ed.) *Philosophy of Education* (Oxford: Oxford University Press).

Peters, R. S. (1978) Ambiguities in liberal education and the problem of its content, in: K. A. Strike and K. Egan (eds.) *Ethics and Educational Policy* (London: Routledge & Kegan Paul).

Peterson, M., Hasker, H., Reichenbach, B., and Basinger, D. (1991) *Reason and Religious Belief: An Introduction to the Philosophy of Religion* (Oxford: Oxford University Press).

Peukert, H. (1983) Kritische Theorie und Pädagogik. *Zeitschrift für Pädagogik*, 30, pp. 195–217.

Phillips, A. (1991) *Engendering Democracy* (Cambridge, UK: Polity Press).

Phillips, A. (1993) *Democracy and Difference* (Cambridge, UK: Polity Press).

Phillips, A. (1996) Dealing with difference: A politics of ideas, or a politics of presence?, in: S. Benhabib (ed.) *Democracy and Difference* (Princeton, NJ: Princeton University Press).

Phillips, D. Z. (1993) *Wittgenstein and Religion* (London: Macmillan).

Phillips, D. Z. (ed.) (1997) *Rush Rhees on Religion and Philosophy* (Cambridge, UK: Cambridge University Press).

Piaget, J. ([1932] 1948) *The Moral Judgment of the Child* (New York: Free Press).

Piaget, J. (1971) *Insights and Illusions of Philosophy* (New York: World).

Plant, S. (1997) *Zeros + Ones* (London: Fourth Estate).

Plato (1937) *The Dialogues of Plato*, 2 vols (trans. B. Jowett) (New York: Random House).

Plato (1979) *The Symposium* (trans. W. Hamilton) (London: Penguin Books).

Pleines, J. E. (ed.) (1987) *Das Problem des Allgemeinen in der Bildungstheorie.* (Wurzburg, Germany: Königshausen und Neumann).

Poirier, R. (1987) Writing off the self, in: R. Poirier (ed.) *The Renewal of Literature* (New York: Random House).

Poirier, R. (1992) *Poetry and Pragmatism* (Cambridge, MA: Harvard University Press).

Polanyi, M. (1964) *Personal Knowledge: Towards a Post-Critical Philosophy* (New York: Harper).

Popkewitz, T. S. and Fendler, L. (eds.) (1999) *Critical Theories in Education* (New York and London: Routledge).

Poster, M. (1989) *Critical Theory and Poststructuralism: In Search of a Context* (Ithaca, NY: Cornell University Press).

Power, M. (1999) *The Audit Society* (Oxford: Oxford University Press).

Pring, R. (1995) *Closing the Gap: Liberal Education and Vocational Preparation* (London: Hodder & Stoughton).

Pring, R. (2000) *Philosophy of Educational Research* (London: Continuum).

Quinn, J. (1997) *My Education* (Dublin: Town and Country House).

Radice, B. (ed.) (1974) *The Letters of Abelard and Heloise* (trans. with Introduction by B. Radice) (London: Penguin).

Raggatt, P. and Williams, S. (1999) *Government, Markets and Vocational Qualifications: An Anatomy of Policy* (London: Falmer).

Rand, R. (ed.) (1992) *Logomachia: The Conflict of the Faculties* (Lincoln, NE and London: University of Nebraska Press).

Ransome, A. (1962) *Swallows and Amazons* (Harmondsworth, UK: Penguin Books).

Rawls, J. (1971) *A Theory of Justice* (Cambridge, MA: Harvard University Press).

Rawls, J. (1993) *Political Liberalism* (New York: Columbia University Press).

Raz, M. (1986) *The Morality of Freedom* (Oxford: Oxford University Press).

Readings, B. (1996) *The University in Ruins* (Cambridge, MA: Harvard University Press).

Reeves, M. (1988) *The Crisis in Higher Education: Competence, Delight and the Common Good* (Milton Keynes, UK: Open University Press).

Reimer, E. (1971) *School is Dead* (Harmondsworth, UK: Penguin Books).

Robertson, E. (1995) Reconceiving reason, in: W. Kohli (ed.) *Critical Conversations in Philosophy of Education* (New York: Routledge), pp. 116–26.

Robertson, E. (1999) The value of reason: Why not a sardine can opener?, in: R. Curren (ed.) *Philosophy of Education 1999* (Urbana, IL: Philosophy of Education Society), pp. 1–14.

Rorty, A. (1985) Postmodernist bourgeois liberalism, in: R. Hollinger (ed.) *Hermeneutics and Praxis* (Notre Dame, IN: Notre Dame University Press).

Rorty, A. (1988) *Mind in Action: Essays in the Philosophy of Mind* (Boston: Beacon Press).

Rorty, A. (1998) *Philosophers of Education: Historical Perspectives* (London: Routledge).

Rorty, R. (1980) *Philosophy and the Mirror of Nature* (Oxford: Basil Blackwell).

Rorty, R. (1982) *Consequences of Pragmatism* (Minneapolis: University of Minnesota Press).

Rorty, R. (1986) Foucault and epistemology, in: D. Couzens-Hoy (ed.) *Foucault: A Critical Reader* (Oxford: Basil Blackwell).

Rorty, R. (1989) *Contingency, Irony, and Solidarity* (Cambridge, UK: Cambridge University Press).

Rorty, R. (1990a) The dangers of over-philosophication: Reply to Arcilla and Nicholson, *Educational Theory*, 40, pp. 41–4.

Rorty, R. (1990b) Education without dogma, *Dialogue*, 2, pp. 44–7.

Rorty, R. (1992) Trotsky and the wild orchids, *Common Knowledge*, 1, pp. 140–53.

Rorty, R. (1999) *Philosophy and Social Hope* (Harmondsworth, UK: Penguin Books).

Rosen, M. (1997) *On Voluntary Servitude* (Cambridge, UK: Polity).

Rosenau, J. (1998) Governance and democracy in a globalizing world, in: D. Archibugi, D. Held, and M. Köhler (eds.) *Re-imagining Political Community: Studies in Cosmopolitan Democracy* (Cambridge, UK: Polity Press).

Rosenblum, N. L. (ed.) (2000) *Obligations of Citizenship and Demands of Faith. Religious Accommodation in Pluralist Democracies* (Princeton, NJ: Princeton University Press).

Rothblatt, S. ([1988] 1997a) The idea of the idea of a university and its antithesis, in: *The Modern University and its Discontents* (Cambridge, UK: Cambridge University Press).

Rothblatt, S. (1997b) *The Modern University and its Discontents* (Cambridge, UK: Cambridge University Press).

Rousseau, J. J. ([1762] 1957) *Émile ou de l'Éducation* (Paris: Garnier).

Ruddick, S. (1989) *Maternal Thinking: Towards a Politics of Peace* (Boston: Beacon Press).

Sagzebski, L. T. (1996) *Virtues of the Mind. An Inquiry into the Nature of Virtue and the Ethical Foundations of Knowledge* (Cambridge, UK: Cambridge University Press).

Salomone, R. C. (2000) *Visions of Schooling. Conscience, Community and Common Education* (New Haven, CT: Yale University Press).

Sandel, M. (1982) *Liberalism and the Limits of Justice* (Cambridge, UK: Cambridge University Press).

Sandel, M. (1996) *Democracy's Discontent: America in Search of a Public Philosophy* (Cambridge, MA: Harvard University Press).

Sandsmark, S. (2000) *Is World-View Neutral Education Possible and Desirable? A Christian Response to Liberal Arguments* (Carlisle, UK: Paternoster Press and the Stapleford Centre).

Sartre, J.-P. ([1943] 1957) *Being and Nothingness* (trans. H. Barnes) (London: Methuen).

Saussure, F. (1959) *Course in General Linguistics*, in: C. Bally and A. Sechehaye (eds.) (New York: The Philosophical Library).

SCANS (1991) *US Department of Labor, Secretary's Commission on Achieving Necessary Skills: What Work Requires of Schools* (Washington, DC: US Department of Labor).

Scheffler, I. (1960) *The Language of Education.* (Springfield, IL: Thomas).

Scheffler, I. (1965) *Conditions of Knowledge: An Introduction to Epistemology and Education* (Chicago: Scott Foresman).

Scheffler, I. ([1967] 1982) *Science and Subjectivity*, 2nd edn. (Indianapolis: Hackett).

Scheffler, I. ([1973] 1989) *Reason and Teaching* (Indianapolis: Hackett).

Scheffler, I. (1991) *In Praise of the Cognitive Emotions* (New York: Routledge).

Scheffler, I. (1995) *Teachers of My Youth. An American Jewish Experience* (Dordrecht, Netherlands: Kluwer).

Scheibe, W. ([1969] 1994) *Die Reformpädagogische Bewegung* (Weinheim, Germany and Basel, Switzerland: Beltz Taschenbuch).

Scheman, N. (1993) *Engenderings: Constructions of Knowledge, Authority and Privilege* (New York and London: Routledge).

Schofield, H. (1972) *The Philosophy of Education – An Introduction* (London: Allen & Unwin).

Schön, D. A. (1983) *The Reflective Practitioner* (New York: Basic Books).

Schön, D. A. (1987) *Educating the Reflective Practitioner* (San Francisco: Jossey Bass).

Scott, P. (1995) *The Meanings of Mass Higher Education* (Buckingham, UK: Open University Press).

Scottish Education Department (SED) (1965) *Primary Education in Scotland (the Primary Memorandum)* (Edinburgh, HMSO).

Searle, J. (1969) *Speech Acts* (London: Cambridge University Press).

Searle, J. (1992) *The Rediscovery of the Mind* (Cambridge, MA: MIT Press).

Searle, J. (1995) *The Construction of Social Reality* (London: Penguin).

Seigfried, C. H. (1996) *Pragmatism and Feminism: Reweaving The Social Fabric* (Chicago: University of Chicago Press).

Seldon, A. (1986) *The Riddle of the Voucher: An Inquiry Into the Obstacles to Introducing Choice and Competition in State Schools* (London: Institute of Economic Affairs).

Seller, A. (1996) Hannah Arendt's politics of difference, in: M. Griffiths and M. Whitford (eds.) *Women Review Philosophy* (Nottingham, UK: Nottingham University Press).

Sergiovanni, T. J. (1994) *Building Community in Schools* (San Francisco: Jossey Bass).

Shanley, M. L. and Pateman, C. (eds.) (1991) *Feminist Interpretations and Political Theory* (Cambridge, UK: Polity Press).

Sherman, N. (1989) *The Fabric of Character: Aristotle's Theory of Virtue* (Oxford: Clarendon Press).

Shklar, J. (1995) *American Citizenship: The Quest for Inclusion* (Cambridge, MA: Harvard University Press).

Shohat, E. (ed.) (1998) *Talking Visions: Multicultural Feminism in a Transnational Age* (Cambridge, MA: The MIT Press).

Shohat, E. and Stam, R. (1994) *Unthinking Eurocentricism: Multiculturalism and the Media* (London and New York: Routledge).

Siegel, H. (1988) *Educating Reason: Rationality, Critical Thinking and Education* (New York: Routledge).

Siegel, H. (1993) Not by skill alone: The centrality of character to critical thinking, *Informal Logic*, 15, pp. 163–77.

Siegel, H. (1995) "Radical" pedagogy requires "conservative" epistemology, *Journal of Philosophy of Education*, 29, pp. 33–46.

Siegel, H. (1997) *Rationality Redeemed? Further Dialogues on an Educational Ideal* (New York: Routledge).

Siegel, H. (1998) Knowledge, truth and education, in: D. Carr (ed.) *Education, Knowledge and Truth: Beyond the Postmodern Impasse* (London: Routledge), pp. 19–36.

Siegel, H. (1999) What (good) are thinking dispositions?, *Educational Theory*, 49, pp. 207–21.

Siltanen, J. and Stanworth, M. (1984) The politics of private woman and public man, in: J. Siltanen and M. Stanworth (eds.) *Women and the Public Sphere* (London: Hutchinson).

Silver, H. and Brennan, J. (1988) *A Liberal Vocationalism* (London: Methuen).

Simon, L. (1999) *Genuine Reality: A Life of William James* (Chicago: University of Chicago Press).

Singer, P. (1997) *How Are We to Live? Ethics in an Age of Self-Interest* (Oxford: Oxford University Press).

Skilbeck, M., Connell, H., Lowe, N., and Tait, K. (1994) *The Vocational Quest: New Directions in Education and Training* (London: Routledge).

Skinner, Q. (1992) On justice, the common good and the priority of liberty, in: C. Mouffe (ed.) *Dimensions of Radical Democracy: Pluralism, Citizenship and Community* (London: Verso).

Slater, D. (1995) Photography and modern vision, in: C. Jenks (ed.) *Visual Culture* (London and New York: Routledge).

Slaughter, S. and Leslie, L. (1997) *Academic Capitalism: Politics, Policies, and the Entrepreneurial University* (Baltimore, MD: Johns Hopkins University).

Slote, M. (1992) *From Morality to Virtue* (Oxford: Oxford University Press).

Slote, M. (1998) Caring in the balance, in: J. G. Haber and M. S. Halfon (eds.) *Norms and Values* (Lanham, MD: Rowman & Littlefield).

Slote, M. (2001) *Morals from Motives* (Oxford: Oxford University Press).

Smith, A. (1986) *The Ethnic Origins of Nations* (Oxford: Blackwell).

Smith, R. (1987) Skills: The middle way, *Journal of Philosophy of Education*, 21.2, pp. 197–201.

Smith, R. (1999) Paths of judgment: The revival of practical wisdom, *Educational Philosophy and Theory*, 31, pp. 327–40.

Sockett, H. (1976) *Designing the Curriculum* (London: Open Books).

Sockett, H. (1987) Has Shulman got the strategy right? *Harvard Educational Review*, 57, pp. 208–19.

Spinner-Halev, J. (2000) Extending diversity: Religion in public and private education, in: W. Kymlicka and W. Norman (eds.) *Citizenship in Diverse Societies* (Oxford: Oxford University Press).

Spyri, J. (1953) *Heidi* (London: Blackie).

Standish, P. (1995) Postmodernism and the education of the whole person, *Journal of Philosophy of Education*, 29, pp. 121–35.

Standish, P. (2000) Only connect: Computer literacy from Heidegger to cyberfeminism, *Educational Theory*, 49:3, pp. 417–35.

Stanley, L. (1997) *Knowing Feminisms: On Academic Borders, Territories and Tribes* (London: Sage).

Steedman, C. (1986) *Landscape for a Good Woman: A Story of Two Lives* (London: Virago).

Stehr, N. (1994) *Knowledge Societies* (London: Sage).

Stich, S. (1996) *Deconstructing the Mind* (New York: Oxford University Press).

Stocker, M. (1996) *Valuing Emotions* (Cambridge, UK: Cambridge University Press).

Strike, K. (1994) On the construction of public speech, *Educational Theory*, 44, pp. 1–26.

Strike, K. (1996) *Democracy's Discontent* (Cambridge, MA: Harvard University Press).

Stronach, I. (1990) Education, vocationalism and economic recovery: The case against witchcraft, in: G. Esland (ed.) *Education, Training and Employment* (Wokingham, UK: Addison-Wesley/Open University Press).

Sturrock, J. (1986) *Structuralism* (London: Paladin).

Sünker, H. and Krüger, H. H. (eds.) (1999) *Kritische Erziehungswissenschaft am Neubeginn?* (Frankfurt am Main: Suhrkamp).

Sussman, M. B. and Steinmetz, S. K. (eds.) (1987) *Handbook of Marriage and the Family* (New York: Plenum).

Swartz, R. J. and Perkins D. N. (1989) *Teaching Thinking: Issues and Approaches* (Pacific Grove, CA: Midwest Publications).

Symes, C. and McIntyre, J. (eds.) (2000) *Working Knowledge: The New Vocationalism and Higher Education* (Buckingham, UK: SRHE/Open University Press).

Tamir, Y. (1993) *Liberal Nationalism* (Princeton, NJ: Princeton University Press).

Tamir, Y. (1995) *Democratic Education in a Multicultural State* (Oxford: Blackwell).

Taylor, C. (1975) *Hegel* (Cambridge, UK: Cambridge University Press).

Taylor, C. ([1977] 1985a) What is human agency? in: C. Taylor *Human Agency and Language, Philosophical Papers 1* (Cambridge, UK: Cambridge Universtity Press).

Taylor, C. (1985b) Foucault on freedom and truth, in: *Philosophy and the Human Sciences, Philosophical Papers 2* (Cambridge, UK: Cambridge University Press).

Taylor, C. (1989) *Sources of the Self: The Making of the Modern Identity* (Cambridge, MA: Harvard University Press).

Taylor, C. (1991) *The Ethics of Authenticity* (Cambridge, MA: Harvard University Press).

Taylor, C. (1992) *Multiculturalism and "The Politics of Recognition"* (ed. A. Gutmann) (Princeton, NJ: Princeton University Press).

Taylor, C. (1995a) Overcoming epistemology, in: C. Taylor *Philosophical Arguments* (Cambridge, MA: Harvard University Press).

Taylor, C. (1995b) Explanation and practical reason, in: C. Taylor *Philosophical Arguments* (Cambridge, MA: Harvard University Press).

Telfer, E. (1975) Autonomy as an educational ideal *II*, in: S. C. Brown (ed.) *Philosophers Discuss Education* (London: Macmillan).

Tenorth, H.-E. (1994) Nachwort, in: W. Scheibe (ed.) *Die reformpädagogische Bewegung* (Weinheim and Basel: Beltz Taschenbuch), pp. 438–49.

Thatcher, A. (ed.) (1999) *Spirituality and the Curriculum* (London: Cassell).

Thayer-Bacon, B. (1992) Is modern critical thinking sexist? *Inquiry: Critical Thinking Across the Disciplines*, 10, pp. 3–7.

Thayer-Bacon, B. (1993) Caring and its relationship to critical thinking, *Educational Theory*, 43, pp. 323–40.

Thiessen, E. J. (1993) *Teaching for Commitment. Liberal Education, Indoctrination and Christian Nurture* (Montreal: McGill-Queen's University Press).

Thompson, D. (1999) Democratic theory and global society, *Journal of Political Philosophy*, 7, pp. 111–25.

Thomson, J. A. C. (trans.) (1976) *Aristotle: Ethics* (Harmondsworth, UK: Penguin).

Tillich, P. (1957) *Dynamics of Faith* (New York: Harper).

Tillmann, K.-J. (ed.) (1987) *Schultheorien.* (Hamburg: Bergmann-Hellig).

Tocqueville, A. de (1961) *Democracy in America* (New York: Schocken Books).

Tooley, J. (1992a) The prisoner's dilemma and educational provision: A reply to Ruth Jonathan, *British Journal of Educational Studies*, 40, pp. 118–33.

Tooley, J. (1992b) The "Pink Tank" on the educational reform act, *British Journal of Educational Studies*, 40, pp. 335–49.

Tooley, J. (1993a) *A Market-led Alternative for the Curriculum: Breaking the Code* (London: Tufnell Press).

Tooley, J. (1993b) Education and "public goods": Markets versus the state. Paper presented to the annual conference of the Philosophy of Education Society of Great Britain, New College, Oxford.

Tooley, J. (1994) In defence of markets in educational provision, in: D. Bridges and T. McLaughlin (eds.) *Education and the Market Place* (London: Falmer Press).

Tooley, J. (2000) *Reclaiming Education* (London: Cassell).

Turkle, S. (1996) *Life on the Screen: Identity in the Age of the Internet* (London: Weidenfeld & Nicolson).

Usher, R. and Edwards, R. (1994) *Postmodernism and Education* (London: Routledge).

Vaage, S. (2000) Innleiing, in: S. Vaage (ed.) *Learning by Dewey. Barnet, Skolen og den Nye Pædagogik.* (Oslo: Gyldendal Uddannelse).

van Eemeren, F. H. et al. (1996) *Fundamentals of Argumentation Theory: A Handbook of Historical Backgrounds and Contemporary Developments* (Mahwah, NJ: Erlbaum).

van Gunsteren, H. (1978) Notes towards a theory of citizenship, in: F. Dallmayr (ed.) *From Contract to Community* (New York: Marcel Decker).

Vogt, W. P. (1997) *Tolerance and Education: Learning to Live With Diversity and Difference* (Thousand Oaks, CA: Sage).

Wach, J. (1958) *The Comparative Study of Religions* (New York: Columbia University Press).

Wacjman, J. (1988) *Feminism Confronts Technology* (University Park: Pennsylvania State University Press).

Waldron, J. (1995) Rights, in: R. E. Goodin and P. Pettit (eds.) *A Companion to Contemporary Political Philosophy* (Oxford: Blackwell).

Walker, L. (1998) Home and away: The feminist remapping of public and private space in Victorian London: in: R. Ainley (ed.) *New Frontiers of Space, Bodies and Gender* (New York: Routledge).

Walkerdine, V. (ed.) (1989) *Counting Girls Out* (London: Virago Press).

Walkerdine, V. (1990) *Schoolgirl Fictions* (London: Verso).

Walsh, P. D. (1978) Upgrading practical subjects, *Journal of Further and Higher Education*, 2.3, pp. 58–71.

Walzer, M. (1983) *Spheres of Justice: A Defense of Pluralism and Equality* (New York: Basic Books).

Walzer, M. (1986) The politics of Michel Foucault, in: D. Couzens-Hoy (ed.) *Foucault: A Critical Reader* (Oxford: Basil Blackwell).

Warren, M. (1996) Deliberative democracy and authority, *American Political Science Review*, 90, pp. 46–60.

Wellbery, D. (1985) Postmodernism in Europe: On recent German writing, in: S. Trachtenberg (ed.) *The Postmodern Moment* (London: Greenwood Press).

Wellman, D. T. (1977) *Portraits of White Racism* (Cambridge, UK: Cambridge University Press).

Wenger, E. (1998) *Communities of Practice: Learning, Meaning and Identity* (Cambridge, UK: Cambridge University Press).

Wertsch, J. (1985) *Vygotsky and the Social Formation of Mind* (Cambridge, MA: Harvard University Press).

West, C. (1989) *The American Evasion of Philosophy* (Madison: University of Wisconsin Press).

West, C. (1993) The new cultural politics of difference, in: C. West (ed.) *Keeping Faith: Philosophy and Race in America* (New York and London: Routledge).

Wharton, E. (1995) *Madame de Treymes* (London: Penguin Books).

White, J. (1973) *Towards a Compulsory Curriculum* (London: Routledge & Kegan Paul).

White, J. (1990) *Education and the Good Life. Beyond the National Curriculum* (London: Kogan Page).

White, J. (1996) Education and nationality, *Journal of Philosophy of Education*, 30, pp. 327–43.

White, J. (1997) *Education and the End of Work: A New Philosophy of Work and Learning* (London: Cassell).

White, J. T. (1909) *Character Lessons in American Biography* (New York: Character Development League).

White, P. (1996) *Civic Virtues and Public Schooling: Educating Citizens for a Democratic Society* (New York: Teachers College Press).

White, S. (1988) *The Recent Work of Jürgen Habermas: Reason, Justice and Modernity* (Cambridge, UK: Cambridge University Press).

Whitehead, A. N. (1950) *The Aims of Education and Other Essays* (London: Ernest Benn).

Whiteside, T., Sutton, A., and Everton, T. (eds.) (1992) *16–19 Changes in Education and Training* (London: David Fulton).

Whitford, M. (1991) *Luce Irigaray: Philosophy in the Feminine* (London: Routledge).

Wiener, M. (1981) *English Culture and the Decline of the Industrial Spirit, 1850–1980* (Cambridge, UK: Cambridge University Press).

Wiggershaus, R. (1995) *The Frankfurt School: Its History, Theories and Political Significance* (Cambridge, UK: Polity Press).

Wiggins, D. (1980) Deliberation and practical reason, in: A. O. Rorty (ed.) *Essays on Aristotle's Ethics* (Berkeley: University of California Press).

Wilds, E. H. and Lottich, K. V. (1970) *The Foundations of Modern Education* (New York: Holt, Rinehart & Winston).

Williams, B. (1976) Persons, character, and morality, in: A. M. Rorty (ed.) *The Identities of Persons* (Berkeley: University of California Press).

Williams, B. (1981) The truth in relativism, in: B. Williams *Moral Luck* (Cambridge, UK: Cambridge University Press).

Williams, B. (1985) *Ethics and the Limits of Philosophy* (Cambridge, MA: Harvard University Press).

Williams, K. (1996) The discipline of inclination: Michael Oakeshott's treatment of the issue of compulsion in the teacher-pupil relationship, *Westminster Studies in Education*, 19, pp. 15–23.

Williams, K. (1998) Assessment and the challenge of scepticism, in: D. Carr (ed.) *Education, Knowledge and Truth: Beyond the Postmodern Impasse* (London and New York: Routledge).

Williams, M. (1994) The significance of learning in Wittgenstein's later philosophy, *Canadian Journal of Philosophy*, 24, pp. 173–203.

Williams, P. (1993) *The Alchemy of Race and Rights* (London: Virago).

Williams, R. (1977) *Marxism and Literature* (Oxford: Oxford University Press).

Williams, R. (1981) *Culture* (London: Fontana).

Wilson, A. (1992) New maps of old terrain, *Times Higher Education Supplement*, May 1, pp. 17–20.

Winch, C. (1995) Education needs training, *Oxford Review of Education*, 21, pp. 315–25.

Winch, C. (1996) *Quality and Education* (Oxford: Blackwell).

Winch, C. (1998) *The Philosophy of Human Learning* (London and New York: Routledge).

Winch, P. (1958) *The Idea of a Social Science and its Relation to Philosophy* (London: Routledge & Kegan Paul).

Wittgenstein, L. (1953) *Philosophical Investigations* (Oxford: Blackwell).

Wittgenstein, L. (1979) *Remarks on Frazer's* Golden Bough (ed. R. Rhees, trans. A. C. Miles) (Doncaster, UK: Brynhill Press).

Wlodkowski, R. J. and Ginsberg, M. B. (1995) *Diversity and Motivation: Culturally Responsive Teaching* (San Francisco: Jossey-Bass).

Wolf, A. (1989) Can competence and knowledge mix? in: J. W. Burke (ed.) *Competency Based Education and Training* (London: Falmer).

Woolf, V. ([1938] 1977) *Three Guineas* (Harmondsworth, UK: Penguin Books).

Wright, A. (2000) *Spirituality and Education* (London: RoutledgeFalmer).

Wringe, C. (1981) *Children's Rights.* (London: Routledge & Kegan Paul).

Young, I. M. (1990a) *Justice and the Politics of Difference* (Princeton, NJ: Princeton University Press).

Young, I. M. (1990b) *Throwing like a Girl* (Bloomington: Indiana University Press).

Young, I. M. (1996) Communication and the other: Beyond deliberative democracy, in: S. Benhabib (ed.) *Democracy and Difference: Contesting the Boundaries of the Political* (Princeton, NJ: Princeton University Press).

Young, I. (1997) Difference as a resource for democratic communication, in: J. Bohman and W. Rehg (eds.) *Democracy: Essays on Reason and Politics* (Cambridge, MA: MIT Press).

Young, I. M. (2000) *Inclusion and Democracy* (Oxford: Oxford University Press).

Young-Bruehl, E. (1982) *Hannah Arendt: For Love of the World* (New Haven, CT: Yale University Press).

Zagzebski, L. T. (1996) *The Dilemma of Freedom and Foreknowledge* (Oxford: Oxford University Press).

Zembylas, M. (2000) Something "paralogical" under the sun: Lyotard's *Postmodern Condition* and science education, *Educational Philosophy and Theory*, 32, pp. 159–84.

Index